Place Names
of Canada

Alan Rayburn

OXFORD
UNIVERSITY PRESS

OXFORD

UNIVERSITY PRESS

70 Wynford Drive, Don Mills, Ontario M3C 1J9
www.oupcanada.com

Oxford University Press is a department of the University of Oxford.
It furthers the University's objective of excellence in research, scholarship, and education by publishing worldwide in

Oxford   New York
Auckland   Cape Town   Dar es Salaam   Hong Kong   Karachi   Kuala Lumpur   Madrid   Melbourne   Mexico City   Nairobi
New Delhi   Shanghai   Taipei   Toronto

With offices in
Argentina   Austria   Brazil   Chile   Czech Republic   France   Greece   Guatemala   Hungary   Italy   Japan   Poland   Portugal   Singapore
South Korea   Switzerland   Thailand   Turkey   Ukraine   Vietnam

Oxford is a trade mark of Oxford University Press in the UK and in certain other countries

Published in Canada by Oxford University Press

Library and Archives Canada Cataloguing in Publication

Rayburn, Alan
Place names of Canada / Alan Rayburn.

ISBN 978-0-19-543153-7

1. Names, Geographical—Canada. 2. Canada—History, Local.
I. Title.

FC36.R39 2009   917.1'0014   C2009-905113-3

Cover image: "Lupines and Shore", Grand Manan, New Brunswick, (Marilyn Trenchard Photography)

Oxford University Press is committed to our environment.
This book is printed on Forest Stewardship Council certified paper which contains 100% post-consumer waste.
Printed and bound in Canada.

1 2 3 4 -- 13 12 11 10

The production of the title *Rayburn-Place Names of Canada* on Rolland Enviro 100 Print paper
instead of virgin fibres paper reduces your ecological footprint by :

Tree(s) : 27
solid waste : 781 kg
Water : 73,885 L

Suspended particles in the water : 4.9 kg
Air emissions : 1,715 kg
Natural gas : 112 m3

Printed by Transcontinental. Text pages on Rolland Enviro 100, containing 100% post-consumer recycled fibers,
Eco-Logo certified, processed without chlorinate, FSC Recycled and manufactured using biogaz energy.

FSC
Mixed Sources
Product group from well-managed
forests, controlled sources and
recycled wood or fibre

Cert no. SW-COC-000952
www.fsc.org
© 1996 Forest Stewardship Council

Contents

Acknowledgements

The idea of producing a second edition of the *Dictionary of Canadian Place Names* was first proposed to me in the spring of 2008 by Matt Adamson, director of the trade sales group at Oxford University Press Canada. The book was edited by Jennie Rubio, Sabrina Stuart, and Katie Scott. They offered a range of helpful suggestions.

A special debt of gratitude is extended to Helen Kerfoot, who succeeded me as the executive secretary of the Canadian Permanent Committee on Geographical Names in 1988. In March 2000 the committee became the Geographical Names Board of Canada (GNBC). Jocelyne Revie is the GNBC secretariat manager and her staff includes Heather Ross and Jackie St-Clair. My wife Mary arranged the Index for the 208 place names.

I am especially indebted to the suggestions and corrections provided by many individuals in the provincial and territorial offices who are responsible for mapping and naming, and sending them to the Geographical Names Board's staff in Ottawa. In Ontario Jeffrey Ball performed many changes of place names between 1997 and 2001 and the new director, Brian Maloney, thereafter; Marcel Fourcaudot provided information for the Commission de toponymie du Québec; David Link, director of Alberta's geographic names in the Historic Resources Management Branch; Janet Mason, British Columbia's geographical names officer in the Ministry of Environment, Lands and Parks; Des Kappel, Manitoba's provincial toponymist in the Department of Natural Resources; Danny Gray, Nova Scotia's geographical names research officer in the Department of Natural Resources; Nathan Friesen, the secretary of the Saskatchewan Geographic Names; Gilles Bourque, manager of New Brunswick's toponymy department; Randy Hawkins, administrative officer of the Newfoundland and Labrador Geographical Names Board; Jeff Hunston, manager of the Yukon Geographical Names Program in the Department of Tourism; Tom Andrews, territorial archaeologist for the Northwest Territories; and Judah Sarpinak in charge of the toponymy for the government of Nunavut. I thank all of these individuals for their efforts to provide me with thorough, accurate, and up-to-date information.

This book is dedicated to the Geographical Names Board of Canada, whose antecedent, the Geographic Board of Canada, was founded on 18 December 1897. It commemorates the initiative of the pioneers who perceived the need to standardize and record Canada's toponymic heritage. And it honours the scholars, scientists, and other researchers who have recognized, over the past 110 years, the significance of place names to the culture and character of each province and territory as well as the country as a whole.

Preface

Place names are a significant reflection of a nation's cultural and linguistic heritage. They are ever-present on road signs and maps, in correspondence, magazines, and newspapers, and in all kinds of official and unofficial records and documents.

The Canadian Geographical Names Database, maintained by Natural Resources Canada in Ottawa for the Geographical Names Board, comprises some 450,000 official place names, from Cape Spear in the east to Demarcation Point in the west, and from Middle Island in the south to Cape Columbia in the north. Each name has specific detail as to its location and jurisdiction, and a brief account of origins and meanings is available for about 25 percent of them. These data are supplemented by a vast collection of paper records in files and cards managed by the Board's secretariat. In addition, each province and territory, which has authority over place names within its jurisdiction and joint authority over names within federal crown lands, has developed its own computerized and paper records on the locations, origins, and meanings of its toponyms.

Considering the richness and variety of Canada's toponymic tapestry, there have been very few place-name books written about the country as a whole. The first was George Armstrong's *The Origin and Meaning of Place Names in Canada*, published by Macmillan of Canada in 1930. Most of his choices were drawn from Ontario, with a very small number selected from the other provinces and territories. In 1972 Macmillan republished the book without correcting its errors and misinterpretations. Names given after 1930 by the numerous expeditions to the North and to the Cordillera in Alberta, British Columbia, and Yukon were ignored, and no information from Canada's newest province, Newfoundland, was provided.

In the mid-1970s Macmillan invited William B. Hamilton, then a professor of education at the University of Western Ontario, to revise the Armstrong volume, but he instead recommended a completely new book. In January 1978 *The Macmillan Book of Canadian Place Names* was published to much acclaim. It provided brief details on the background and significance of more than 2500 place names, and listed an extensive bibliography of toponymic sources. Five years later a second edition was published.

A third book that deals with Canadian place names is not well known in Canada, even among place-name researchers. It is the *Illustrated Dictionary of Place Names: United States and Canada*, edited by Kelsie B. Harder of the State University College in Potsdam, New York.[1] The Canadian names were compiled by Robert O'Brien of Morningside Editorial Associates. Although only five of the book's 100 references refer directly to Canadian toponymic sources, there are interesting, albeit brief, details on Canadian places that could only have come from a large number of published Canadian sources. Errors in spelling (e.g., St. Catherines for St. Catharines, Louisville for Louiseville), spurious origins and meanings

---

[1] It was first published by Van Nostrand Reinhold in the city of New York in 1976, and reprinted in 1985 by Facts on File Publications of the city of New York and Oxford, England.

(e.g., Milton, Moncton, Peterborough, Taber), and curious omissions of cities (e.g., Corner Brook, Red Deer, Woodstock) render the book a questionable source for reliable information on Canada's names. A good feature of the book, however, is the straightforward alphabetical arrangement of both countries together, even listing Mac- and Mc- names in their appropriate alphabetical order, rather than bundling them together.

There is a youthful vigour in Canada's toponymic character, although documentary evidence for some of its place names may be traced back over 500 years. Change has been a constant, with hundreds of new names and redesignations having taken place since 1990. The cities of Halifax and Dartmouth in Nova Scotia, for example, are now in the regional municipality of Halifax. The city of Miramichi in New Brunswick embraces the former towns of Chatham and Newcastle as well as some adjacent villages. In Prince Edward Island the town of Stratford comprises four former municipal communities. In Quebec the Communauté-Urbaine-de-l'Outaouais became the city of Gatineau, while the outlying municipalities were kept together as Les Collines-de-l'Outaouais. Fort McMurray in Alberta is no longer a city, having become an urban service centre in the regional municipality of Wood Buffalo. The city of Abbotsford in British Columbia swallowed the district municipality of Matsqui. The Ontario municipality of Clarington, with over 50,000 people, emerged from the redesignation of the town of Newcastle. And finally, the municipal township of Flos, whose name recalled one of the three pet dogs (the others, Tay and Tiny) of Lady Sarah Maitland, has now disappeared into the blandly named municipal township of Springwater.

Change will continue to mark Canada's municipal structures. At the end of 1996 the Ontario government peremptorily announced that as of 1 January 1998 the city of Toronto would be enlarged to take over the municipality of Metropolitan Toronto, the cities of Etobicoke, North York, Scarborough, and York, and the borough of East York, to form the new city of about 2,300,000 people. There may be other dramatic changes in Ontario's administrative structure in the next few years, resulting in its 815 municipalities being trimmed to 450 or less.

On 1 April 1999 the misnamed Northwest Territories (a single territory since 1905) was divided in two. The territory of Nunavut extends from the border of Manitoba to Cape Columbia at the north end of Ellesmere Island, and has a larger land area than any of Canada's provinces. The rest of the Northwest Territories, based on the Mackenzie River valley, has kept the original name.

Alan Rayburn
Ottawa, Ontario
7 April 2009

Introduction

There are approximately 450,000 official geographical names in Canada. The *Dictionary of Canadian Place Names* (1999) contained 5075 entries, as well as 1150 additional 'associative' names, for a total of 6225 names. This new edition of *Place Names of Canada* contains 5675 names (names within cities and towns have been dropped). Even so, that total is more than twice as many as in any previous books written on Canada's toponymy. Associative names—such as Niagara Escarpment, found within the entry for Niagara— are displayed in bold type. It is worth noting that if all associative names listed in the most recent volumes of the *Gazetteer of Canada* and the *Répertoire toponymique du Québec* (such as Niagara Gorge or Nepisiguit Falls) had been included, the total number of names in this book could easily have surpassed 12,000.

Precedence is given to incorporated cities, towns, villages, and similar urban centres designated by other municipal terms with populations of 150 or more. Added to these are unincorporated places with at least 150 people, and well-known urban neighbourhoods. Also included are regional, district, and county municipalities. All incorporated rural municipalities in Ontario and Quebec with populations over 1500 are included, as well as many with smaller populations. The names of Canada's national parks and many of the provincial parks are also noted.

All lakes and islands with an area of 350 square kilometres, and many even smaller, are included. Similarly, rivers with lengths of 75 kilometres, as well as some well-known rivers shorter than 75 kilometres, are listed. The names of falls with heights of 200 metres or more, and several with lesser heights, are noted. All mountains with elevations of 2900 metres or more, and some other well-known mountains and peaks with lower elevations, are listed. The better-known names of capes, points, straits, channels, and bays are also included.

In most instances the year of populated centres being named is related to either the opening of postal service or the creation of a railway stop, although many originated before either of these important services were established. For each municipality the incorporation year of its current status (i.e., city, town, etc.) is provided in brackets. Terms such as town and village are used only for municipalities incorporated as such; this avoids the common mispractice of applying such terms to any grouping of people.

For each populated place and physical feature named after an individual, the person's years of birth and death are given, when readily available. Such dates serve two useful purposes: first, to differentiate between two persons with identical names (there are, for example, two mountains in Canada named after Sir James Outram, but one Sir James is the grandson of the other); and second, to guide readers toward biographical resources to learn more about the careers of the persons honoured.

Italics identify precise forms of previous names shown on early maps and in documents, such as *cap de lorraine* for Cape St. Lawrence, at the northwestern end of Cape Breton Island. They are also used for non-English words (*alameda*), for the names of ships (HMS *Ajax*), and for former names of places, such as *Bytown*, which preceded Ottawa. As well, historical Aboriginal names of places and Aboriginal words from which official names have been derived are shown in italics. Efforts have been made to ensure the appropriate Aboriginal language (e.g., Cree, Gwitch'in, Inuvialuktun, Mi'kmaq, Ojibwa) is used to identify the sources of names, rather than using the general word 'Indian', which is about as useful as describing Paris as 'a name of European origin'.

The names of physical features whose generic terminology precedes the specific (e.g., Mount Assiniboine, Point Pelee, Île d'Orléans) are alphabetized under the specific words, that is, Assiniboine, Pelee, and Orléans. At least one good toponymic reference, William B. Hamilton's *Place Names of Atlantic Canada* (1996), lists such names under the generic—in other words, without cross-references, so that Bay d'Espoir, Cape Race, and Mount Caubvick are listed under the letters B, C, and M respectively.

Sources for Toponymic Information

General. To compile the entries in this book several sources—mainly toponymic, but also biographical, historical, and geographical—have been consulted. The voluminous files and card records of the Canadian Permanent Committee on Geographical Names (in 2000 this became the Geographical Names Board of Canada) dating from the 1890s are the basis for much of the information provided. Especially important are the 2850 letters received from postmasters by geographer James White in the period 1905–9, which few writers of other books on Canadian toponymy have consulted. The 13 volumes of the *Dictionary of Canadian Biography* were essential in resolving several points about the careers of noted individuals involved in the development of Canada before 1911. I also relied extensively on William F. Ganong's *Crucial Maps in the Early Cartography and Place-Nomenclature of the Atlantic Coast of Canada* (1964), John Robert Colombo's *Canadian Literary Landmarks* (1984), and Alan Cooke and Clive Holland's *The Exploration of Northern Canada* (1978).

Alberta. No province has had more toponymic studies published about its places than Alberta. The first, *Place-Names of Alberta* (1928), was written by Robert Douglas, who was then the secretary of the Geographic Board of Canada. It was the basis of most of the information compiled in *2000 Place Names of Alberta* (1972) by Eric and Patricia Holmgren, which they supplemented in a subsequent volume before publishing *Over 2000 Place Names of Alberta* in 1976. Meanwhile in 1973 Ernest Mardon produced *Community Names of Alberta*. Between 1991 and 1996 the four volumes of *Place Names of Alberta*, compiled by three successive geographical names program coordinators of Alberta's Historic Sites Service, have resulted in a comprehensive and reliable overview of the province's toponymy. Two recent books about the names of Alberta are also worth noting: Merrily K. Aubrey's *Concise Place Names of Alberta* (University of Calgary Press, 2006) and Harry M Sanders's *The Story Behind Alberta Names: How Cities, Towns, Villages and Hamlets Got their Names* (Red Deer Press, 2007).

British Columbia. In 1906 the Geographic Board of Canada published Captain John Walbran's excellent *British Columbia Coast Names*, which remains a masterpiece for both its research and elaborate details. In 1969 Philip and Helen Akrigg published the first edition of *1001 British Columbia Place Names*, followed by revised editions in 1970 and 1973. Thirteen years later they produced their much enlarged and well-written *British Columbia Place Names*. *Place Names of the Canadian Alps*, an excellent study of the names of mountains, valleys, and populated places in the Rocky Mountains (in both British Columbia and Alberta) and the Columbia Mountains, both as far north as Prince George, was published in 1990 by climbers William L. Putnam, Glen W. Boles, and Roger W. Laurilla. Because very little information has been published on the names of peaks in the Coast Mountains northwest of Vancouver, and in the Cassiar Mountains in the northern part of the province, the files and card records of the Geographical Place Names of Canada's (GPNC) secretariat were consulted to furnish the necessary details on the names of mountains and other physical features in these areas of the province.

Manitoba. The Geographic Board of Canada published Robert Douglas's *Place-Names of Manitoba* in 1933, three years after he died. This remained the definitive work on the province's toponymy until J.B. Rudnyckyj published *Manitoba Mosaic of Place Names* (1970), which relied almost entirely on the Douglas work. Ten years later a much better study by Penny Ham, titled *Place Names of Manitoba*, was published; this study is based on the records of the provincial names office and extensive correspondence with knowledgeable individuals across the province. In 2000 Manitoba Conservation published the *Geographical Names of Manitoba*.

New Brunswick. In 1896 naturalist William F. Ganong produced a huge study on New Brunswick's place names, and supplemented it 10 years later with additions and corrections. His published toponymic works, including several on names of Aboriginal origin and unpublished notes at the New Brunswick Museum in Saint John, formed the basis of my *Geographical Names of New Brunswick* (1975).

Newfoundland and Labrador. Without the *Encyclopedia of Newfoundland* (1981–94) and William B. Hamilton's *Place Names of Atlantic Canada* (1996), it would not have been possible to give Newfoundland justice in the treatment of its geographical names. Before Newfoundland entered Confederation in 1949 no records for the province's names had been collected by the names office in Ottawa. Other than the scholarly *Place Names of the Avalon Peninsula* (1971) by Edgar R. Seary, there had been very little published toponymic material on the rest of the province before Joseph Smallwood's five-volume *Book of Newfoundland*, completed in 1975, and his five-volume *Encyclopedia of Newfoundland*, completed in 1994, were published.

Northwest Territories. In 1910 geographer James White published *Place Names: Northern Canada*, which provided brief details on the 450 years of documents naming in the North. Subsequently his fine work was added to by staff member Frank Stevenson in the 1960s and early 1970s, and supplemented since then by GPNC staff members and by Randolph Freeman in the mid-1980s, the territorial toponymist until 1999. Since 1999 Tom Andrews has been the territorial individual responsible for the geographical names and part of the Cultural Places Program, including archaeological and historic sites.

Nunavut. This territory extends from Manitoba's border to Cape Columbia at the north end of Ellesmere Island, and all of the islands in Hudson Bay, James Bay, Hudson Strait, and Ungava Bay. Nunavut's land is much larger than any of Canada's provinces. It has 1,994,000 square kilometres (770,000 square miles) and occupies one-fifth of the country.

Nova Scotia. In 1922 Thomas Brown published the slim *Nova Scotia Place Names*, which remained the only general study of the province's toponymy until 1967, when provincial archivist Bruce Fergusson published *Place Names and Places of Nova Scotia*. William B. Hamilton's *Place Names of Atlantic Canada* (1996) gives a better reflection of the toponymy of the province.

Ontario. The entries for this province are based extensively on my *Place Names of Ontario* (University of Toronto Press, 1997). That work was produced after extensive research in the records of the GPNC, some 250 local histories, Herbert F. Gardiner's superb study of Ontario's county and township names *Nothing But Names* (1899), the comprehensive review of the province's places by Nick and Helma Mika in their three-volume *Places of Ontario* (1977–83), Floreen Carter's two-volume *Place Names of Ontario* (1984), and her *Ghost and Post Offices of Ontario* (1986).

Quebec. This study has relied almost entirely on one of the best toponymic studies ever produced in the world, the well-documented and beautifully illustrated *Noms et lieux du Québec* (1994). The letters from postmasters received by geographer James White, 1905–9, were the only other significant sources used to verify the backgrounds of some of the approximate 500 Quebec place names included in the *Dictionary of Canadian Place Names* (1999). In 2006 Gilles Vigneault updated the first *Noms et lieux du Québec*.

Prince Edward Island. In 1925 Robert Douglas produced *Place-Names of Prince Edward Island*. Using this study as a base, I published *Geographical Names of Prince Edward Island* in 1973, the centennial of the province's entry into Confederation. The records of new names and name changing in Prince Edward Island have been kept up to date by the GPNC's secretariat.

Saskatchewan. In 1968 E.T. Russell, a public school principal in Saskatoon, published *What's in a Name?*, a compilation of 679 of the province's populated places. The material was essentially gathered by students, and verified through extensive correspondence with knowledgeable individuals throughout the province. A second edition was published in 1973 with 1604 names, and a third followed in 1980 with 1837 names. In 2005 Bill Barry published *Geographic Names of Saskatchewan*.

Yukon. One of the better books on Canadian toponymy is Robert Coutts's *Yukon Places and Names* (1980). Relying on the excellent records from the secretariat of the Canadian Permanent Committee on Geographical Names, he was able to supplement his research with other territorial sources. An important reference for the names of features on the Alaska border from Stewart, BC, to the Beaufort Sea has been Donald J. Orth's *Dictionary of Alaska Place Names* (1971).

Provincial and Territorial Administrative Terminology

Each of the provinces and territories has a different set of municipal and territorial designations. For example, Ontario stands apart from the rest by being the only jurisdiction with municipalities called 'separated town' and 'united counties,' and Quebec uses regional county municipality, Cree village municipality, and urban community. While all incorporated places in Canada are in fact municipalities, both Ontario and Quebec have permitted the use of 'municipality' alone for some places without qualifying it. 'Community' is generally used in this book, outside Prince Edward Island and Newfoundland, for any grouping of people, whether located within a municipality or not, and I have used it interchangeably with 'place' outside these two provinces to describe *unincorporated* centres of population. I have distinguished the *incorporated* communities in Prince Edward Island and Newfoundland as 'municipal communities'.

Alberta. All of the province's 15 cities and 112 towns have separate entries in the dictionary. The same is true for 96 of its 110 villages. The remaining 14 villages, having populations of less than 150, are excluded. The municipality of Crowsnest Pass is included, but none of the 37 municipal districts, 29 counties, and 53 summer villages are listed, because their names are relatively lesser known.

British Columbia. Described in the book are British Columbia's 43 cities, 50 district municipalities, 14 towns, 120 villages, and 1 resort municipality. Excluded are the names of the 29 regional districts and the 33 Indian government districts, although many of their names are noted under other municipal categories.

Manitoba. This province's 5 cities, 36 towns, and 38 villages are described. Its 106 rural municipalities are excluded, but the names of many of them are noted under other municipal entries.

New Brunswick. Included are New Brunswick's 7 cities, 29 towns, and 76 villages. Also listed are its 14 counties; while these are no longer organized as municipalities, their names are well known.

Newfoundland and Labrador. This province has 3 cities, 157 towns, 99 of its 131 municipal communities, and 5 of its 168 local service districts are listed. There are no villages, counties, or regional municipalities in Newfoundland and Labrador.

Northwest Territories. Incorporated municipalities in this jurisdiction include 1 city, 5 towns, 1 village, 35 hamlets, 2 settlement corporations, and 2 settlements. Twelve places identified in territorial records as communities have no legal community status, but their names are included.

Nova Scotia. Entries have been compiled for this province's 9 municipal counties, 12 municipal districts, 3 regional municipalities, 31 towns, and 22 villages. The former cities of Halifax and Dartmouth are one in the Halifax regional municipality. Sydney is in the Cape Breton regional municipality.

Nunavut. Entries include the city of Iqaluit and 25 other communities, from Sanikiluaq in James Bay, Arviat and Rankin Inlet on the west side of Hudson Bay, to Resolute on Cornwallis Island and Grise Fiord on Ellesmere Island, both in the Queen Elizabeth Islands.

Ontario. In 2001 this province had 25 counties, 11 district municipalities, 3 united counties, 45 cities, 52 municipalities, 77 towns, 4 separated towns, 3 united counties, 10 villages, and 196 townships, and all their names are included in this book. A separated town is a municipality within a county, but does not participate as part of a county's administration. This province has undergone significant municipal change since the 1990s. In all, the number of municipalities was reduced by 40 percent between 1996; there was a peak of 815 municipalities in 1996 followed by a low in 2008 of 444.

Quebec. Quebec's municipal structure is the most complex in the country. It has 3 urban communities, 96 regional county municipalities, 2 cities, 261 *villes*, 160 villages, 90 township municipalities, 8 united township municipalities, 346 parish municipalities, 564 municipalities, 14 northern villages, 8 Cree villages, and 1 Naskapi village. All their names are included except those of *villes* with less than 150 people, township and united township municipalities with less than 1000 people, and municipalities and parish municipalities with less than 1500 people. The two cities are Dorval and Côte-Saint-Luc, both on the west side of Montreal. Otherwise *ville* is used for urban centres ranging from Montreal (population 1,018,000) to L'Île-Dorval (population 6). Although *ville* normally translates as 'town', it would not be appropriate to describe Montreal, Sherbrooke, and Hull as towns, or to call Beauceville, Témiscaming, and Lennoxville cities. Therefore, the standard used in Ontario that towns must have 15,000 people to apply for city status has been used to distinguish Quebec's cities from its towns. Gaspé is the only exception: it is described in the book as a town—although it encompasses over 17,000 people, they are widely distributed over 950 square kilometres.

Prince Edward Island. Incorporated municipalities in this province include 2 cities, 7 towns, and 64 municipal communities. Incorporated villages were converted to municipal communities in 1983. The province's 3 counties have never been organized along municipal lines, but they are well-known names and are therefore included.

Saskatchewan. This province has a wide variety of incorporated municipalities. It has 12 cities, 147 towns, 324 villages, 40 resort villages, 299 rural municipalities, 166 organized hamlets, 13 northern hamlets, 13 northern villages, and 10 northern settlements. The names of all the towns and cities are included in this book, but only those 118 villages with populations exceeding 150 are listed. None of the rural municipalities and resort villages is given a separate entry, and only some of the larger organized hamlets and northern municipalities are listed separately.

Yukon. This territory has 1 city, 3 towns, 4 villages, and 3 hamlets. All are included except the hamlet of Elsa, which has a population of fewer than 10.

Selected References

Akrigg, G.P.V., and Helen B. *British Columbia Place Names*. Victoria: Sono Nis Press, 1986.

Armstrong, G.H. *The Origin and Meaning of Place Names in Canada*. Toronto: Macmillan of Canada, 1930, 1972.

Aubrey, Merrily K. *Concise Place Names of Alberta*. Calgary: University of Calgary Press, 2006.

———. *Place Names of Alberta*, Vol. 4, Northern Alberta. Calgary: University of Calgary Press, 1996.

[Barkham, Selma Huxley]. *The Basque Coast of Newfoundland*. [Plum Point, NF]: Great Northern Peninsula Development Corporation, 1989.

Barry, Bill. *People Places, the Dictionary of the Saskatchewan Place Names*. Regina, SK: Centax Books, 1998.

———. *People Places: Saskatchewan Place Names*. Regina, SK: Centax Books, 2003.

———. *Geographic Names of Saskatchewan*. Regina, SK: People Places Publishing Ltd., 2005.

———. *Ukraininian People Places*. Regina, SK: People Places Publishing Ltd., 2001.

Brown, Steven J. *East Garafraxa: A History*. Orton, ON: The Corporation of the Township of East Garafraxa, 2006.

Carter, Floreen. *Ghost & Post Offices of Ontario*. Oakville, ON: Personal Impressions Publishing, 1986.

———. *Place Names of Ontario*. 2 vols. London: Phelps Publishing Company, 1984.

Chisholm, Doug. *Their Names Live On: Remembering Saskatchewan's Fallen in World War II*. Regina: Canadian Research Center, University of Regina, 2001.

Colombo, John Robert. *Canadian Literary Landmarks*. Willowdale, ON: Hounslow Press, 1984.

Commission de toponymie du Québec. *Noms et lieux du Québec: Dictionnaire illustré*. Quebec: Les Publications du Québec, 1994.

Cooke, Alan, and Clive Holland. *The Exploration of Northern Canada, 500 to 1920*. Toronto: The Arctic History Press, 1978.

Coutts, R. *Yukon Places & Names*. Sidney, BC: Gray's Publishing Limited, 1980.

Dahms, Fred. *Wellington County*. Erin, ON: Boston Mills Press, 2008.

Dawber, Michael. *Where the Heck is Balaheck? Unusual Place-Names from Eastern Ontario*. Burnstown, ON: General Store Publishing House, 1995.

Dictionary of Canadian Biography. Vols. 1–13. Toronto: University of Toronto Press, 1967–94.

[Douglas, Robert]. *Place-Names of Manitoba.* Ottawa: Geographic Board of Canada, 1933.

———. *Geographical Names of Manitoba*. [Winnipeg]: Manitoba Conervation, 2001.

———. *Place-Names of Alberta*. Ottawa: Geographic Board of Canada, 1928.

———. *Place-Names of Prince Edward Island, with Meanings*. Ottawa: Geographic Board of Canada, 1925.

Encyclopedia of Newfoundland and Labrador. St. John's: Newfoundland Book Publishers (1967) Ltd. Joseph R. Smallwood, ed. in chief. Vol. 1 1981, Vol. 2 1984. Harry

Cuff Publications Ltd., Vol. 3 1991. Cyril R. Poole, ed. in chief. Harry Cuff Publications Ltd., Vol. 4 1993; Vol. 5 1994.

Fergusson, Charles Bruce, ed. *Place-Names and Places of Nova Scotia.* Halifax: The Public Archives of Nova Scotia, 1967.

Ganong, W.F. *Crucial Maps in the Early Cartography and Place-Nomenclature of the Atlantic Coast of Canada.* Toronto: University of Toronto Press, 1964.

————. *A Monograph of the Place-Nomenclature of the Province of New Brunswick.* Transactions of the Royal Society of Canada, Ser. 3, Sect. 2, Vol. 2, pages 216–89, 1896; Additions and Corrections, *ibid*, Ser. 3, Sect. 1, Vol. 2, pages 4–57, 1906.

————. *An Organization of the Scientific Investigation of the Indian Place-Nomenclature of the Maritime Provinces of Canada.* Transactions of the Royal Society of Canada, Ser. 3, Sect. 2, Vol. 5, pages 179–93, 1912; Ser. 3, Sect. 2, Vol. 6, pages 179–96, 1912; Ser. 3, Sect. 2, Vol. 7, pages 81–106, 1913; Ser. 3, Sect. 2, Vol. 8, pages 259–93, 1914; Ser. 3, Sect. 2, Vol. 9, pages 375–448, 1915.

Gardiner, Herbert Fairbairn. *Nothing but Names: An Inquiry into the Origin of the Names of the Counties and Townships of Ontario.* Toronto: George N. Morang, 1899.

Ham, Penny. *Place Names of Manitoba.* Saskatoon, SK: Western Producer Prairie Books, 1980.

Hamilton, William B. *Place Names of Atlantic Canada.* Toronto: University of Toronto Press, 1996.

————. *The Macmillan Book of Canadian Place Names.* Toronto: Macmillan of Canada, 1978.

Harder, Kelsie, ed. *Illustrated Dictionary of Place Names: United States and Canada.* New York: Facts on File Publications, 1985.

Harrison, Tracey. *Place Names of Alberta*, Vol. 3, Central Alberta. Calgary: University of Calgary Press, 1994.

Holm, Gerald F. and Anthony Buchner. *A Place of Honour: Manitoba's War Dead Commemorated in its Geography.* Winnipeg: Manitoba Conservation, 2003.

————. *Lieux de mémoire: Des lieux du Manitoba perpétuent des soldats morts à la guerre.* Winnipeg: Programme des noms géographiques du Manitoba, 2003.

Holmgren, Eric J. and Patricia M. Holmgren. *Over 2000 Place Names of Alberta*, 3rd ed. Saskatoon, SK: Western Producer Prairie Books, 1976.

Houghton, Margaret. *Hamilton Street and Names.* Toronto: James Lorimer & Co., Ltd., 2002.

Jackson, John N. *Names Across Niagara.* St. Catharines, ON: Vanwell Publishing Limited, 1989.

Karamitsanis, Aphrodite. *Place Names of Alberta*, Vol. 1, Mountains, Mountain Parks and Foothills. Calgary: University of Calgary Press, 1991.

————. *Place Names of Alberta*, Vol. 2, Southern Alberta. Calgary: University of Calgary Press, 1992.

Kearney, Mark and Randy Ray. *I Know that Name!* Toronto: Dundurn Press, 2002.

Lapierre, André. *Toponymie française en Ontario.* Montreal: Éditions Études Vivantes, 1981.

MacDonald, Cheryl. *Place Names of Haldimand and Norfolk.* Nanticoke, ON: Heronwood Writing Services, 1996.

Macpherson, L.B. *Nova Scotia Postal History, Vol. 1: Post Offices (1754–1981).* Halifax: Petheric Press Ltd., 1982.

Mardon, Ernest G. *Community Names of Alberta.* Lethbridge: University of Lethbridge, 1973.

McManus, George. *Post Offices of New Brunswick, 1783–1930.* Toronto: Jim A. Hennock Ltd., 1984.

Melvin, George H. *The Post Offices of British Columbia, 1858–1970.* Vernon, BC: Vernon Press, 1972.

Mika, Nick and Helma. *Community Spotlight: Leeds, Frontenac, Lennox and Addington, and Prince Edward Counties.* Belleville, ON: Mika Publishing, 1974.

———. *Places in Ontario, Their Name Origins and History.* Belleville, ON: Mika Publishing Company, 1977–83. Part 1, A-E, Part 2, F-M, Part 3, N-Z.

Murray, G. Douglas. *The Post Office on Prince Edward Island (1787–1990).* Bridgetown, NS: Mailman Publishing, 1990.

National Atlas Information Service. *Facts from Canadian Maps: a Geographical Handbook,* 2nd ed. Ottawa: Geographical Services Division, Canada Centre for Mapping, Energy, Mines and Resources Canada, 1989.

Orth, Donald J. *Dictionary of Alaska Place Names.* Geological Survey Professional Paper 567. Washington: United States Government Printing Office, 1967, with minor revisions, 1971.

Phillips, James W. *Washington State Place Names.* Seattle and London: University of Washington Press, 1971.

Putnam, William, Glenn W. Boles, and Roger W. Laurilla. *Place Names of the Canadian Alps.* Revelstoke, BC: Footprint Publishing, 1990.

Rayburn, Alan. *Geographical Names of New Brunswick.* Ottawa: Surveys and Mapping Branch, Energy, Mines and Resources Canada, 1975.

———. *Geographical Names of Prince Edward Island.* Ottawa: Surveys and Mapping Branch, Energy, Mines and Resources Canada, 1973.

———. *Naming Canada: Stories About Place Names From Canadian Geographic.* Toronto: University of Toronto Press, 1994.

———. *Naming Canada Stories About Place Names.* Revised and Expanded. Toronto: University of Toronto Press, 2001.

———. *Place Names of Ontario.* Toronto: University of Toronto Press, 1997.

Robinson, William G., ed. *Manitoba Post Offices.* Vancouver: William Topping, 1988.

———. *Saskatchewan Post Offices.* Vancouver: William Topping, 1987.

Rudnyckyj, J.B. *Manitoba Mosaic of Place Names.* Winnipeg: Canadian Institute of Onomastic Sciences, 1970.

Russell, E.T. *What's In A Name: The Story Behind Saskatchewan Place Names,* 3rd ed. Saskatoon: Western Producer Prairie Books, 1973.

Sanders, Harry M. *The Story Behind Alberta Names: How Cities, Towns, Villages and Hamlets Got Their Names.* Calgary: Red Deer Press, 2003.

Scott, David E. *Ontario Place Names: The Historical, Offbeat or Humorous Origins of Close to 1,000 Communities.* Vancouver and Toronto: Whitecap Books, 1993.

Seary, E.R. *Family Names of the Island of Newfoundland.* St. John's: Memorial University of Newfoundland, 1977.

———. *Place Names of the Avalon Peninsula of the Island of Newfoundland.* Toronto: University of Toronto Press, 1971.

Smith, Robert C. *Ontario Post Offices, Volume 1: An Alphabetical Listing.* Toronto: The Unigrade Press, 1988.

Taylor, Bruce. *Place Names of Temiskaming*. New Liskeard, ON: White Mountain Publications, 2000.

Voorhis, Ernest. *Historic Forts of the French Regime and of the English Fur Trading Companies*. Typescript. Ottawa: Department of the Interior, 1930.

Walbran, Captain John T. *British Columbia Coast Names, 1592–1906*. Vancouver: J.J. Douglas Ltd. for the Vancouver Public Library, 1971. (Originally published by the Geographic Board of Canada in 1906.)

White, James, ed. *Handbook of Indians of Canada*. Toronto: Coles Publishing Company, 1974. (Facsimile ed. of the 1913 edition by the Geographic Board of Canada.)

———. 'Place-names in Georgian Bay', *Papers and Records*. Ontario Historical Society, Vol. 11, 1913.

———. 'Place-names: Northern Canada', *Ninth Report*. Part 4. Ottawa, Geographic Board of Canada, 1910, pp. 231–455.

CANADA

Its Origin, Meaning, and Application

Explorer Jacques Cartier approached Île d'Anticosti in August 1535, and learned from his two young Aboriginal companions, who had returned from Gaspé to France with him the previous year, that the *chemin de Canada* (route to Canada) lay beyond. Cartier knew that their father, Donnaconna, was a chief of an Iroquoian-speaking tribe at Stadaconé, the present-day site of Quebec City, and found out that it was also called Canada. In the report of his voyage Cartier appended a list of words, noting that *kanata* meant 'town', interpreted as a cluster of dwellings. By the mid–1540s French maps portrayed the territory north of Île d'Anticosti as Canada, and maps in the 1550s had the name inscribed on both sides of what became known as the *grande rivière du Canada*. In 1791, Canada gained official status when the two jurisdictions of Upper Canada and Lower Canada were created, comprising the southern parts of present-day Ontario and Quebec. Together they became the Province of Canada in 1841, with the two regions being called Canada West and Canada East. When union with the Atlantic provinces was proposed in the 1860s more than 30 suggestions were made for the new country's name, including Acadia, Borealia, Cabotia, Hochelaga, Mesapelagia, Tuponia, and Transatlantica. Father of Confederation Thomas D'Arcy McGee settled the choice by remarking: 'Now I would ask any Honourable Member of the House how he would feel if he woke up some fine morning and found himself, instead of a Canadian, a Tuponian or Hochelagander?' With the implementation of the British North America Act on 1 July, Canada became the name of the new dominion.

Abbey SK Northwest of Swift Current, this village (1913) had a post office serving the area that was called *Longworth* in 1910. In 1913 the Canadian Pacific Railway named its station after Abbey in County Galway, Ireland, with the post office renamed that year.

Abbotsford BC A city (1995) southeast of Vancouver, on the south side of the Fraser River, it comprises the former district municipalities of Abbotsford and Matsqui. The original townsite was chosen in 1889 by J.C. Maclure for the Canadian Pacific Railway, and named after Harry Braithwaite Abbott (1829–1915), general superintendent of the Pacific Division of the CPR, and brother of Sir John J.C. Abbott (1821–93), prime minister of Canada, 1891–2. Its post office (first *Abbottsford*, then Abbotsford) opened in 1892, and replicated a post office named after his parents in Quebec (now Saint-Paul-d'Abbottsford), and Sir Walter Scott's mansion near Melrose, Roxburghshire, Scotland. **Abbott Peak**, northwest of the head of Duncan Lake, was also named for Harry Abbott.

Abegweit Passage NB, PE This passage, at the narrowest point of Northumberland Strait, where the Confederation Bridge crosses from the mainland, was named in 1962 after MV *Abegweit*, a ferry that was put in service to the island in 1947. The vessel's name derives from the Mi'kmaq name for Prince Edward Island, *Abahquit* ('lying parallel with the land'), often translated loosely as 'cradled by the waves'.

Abercorn QC A village (1929) in the regional county of Brome-Missisquoi and on the Vermont border south of Cowansville, it was named in 1848, possibly after James Hamilton, 1st Duke of Abercorn (1811–85), a member of the household of the Prince of Wales. His title was derived from a place west of Edinburgh, Scotland.

Aberdeen SK A town (1988) northeast of Saskatoon, it was named in 1905 by the Canadian Northern Railway after John Campbell Gordon, 1st Marquess of Aberdeen and Temair (1847–1934), governor general of Canada, 1893–8.

Aberdeen Lake NU A widening of the Thelon River, 140 km west of Baker Lake, this lake (1095 km²) was named in 1893 by Joseph Burr Tyrrell (1858–1957) after John Hamilton Gordon, 7th Earl of Aberdeen (1847–1934), governor general of Canada, 1893–9.

Abernethy SK Located southwest of Melville, this village (1904) has a post office named in 1884 by Robert Balcarres Crawford, the postmaster at Indian Head.

Abitibi QC A regional county in the area of Amos in northwestern Quebec, it was formed in 1983 from the former county of Abitibi. At the same time, the regional county of Abitibi-Ouest, in the area of La Sarre and Macamic, was created. The area of these regional counties, formerly part of the district of Ungava, became part of the province of Quebec in 1898.

Abitibi, Lake ON, QC Situated midway between James Bay and Lake Timiskaming, this lake has a name meaning 'waters of the middle' in both Cree and Algonquin. With an area of 932 km², the lake is about four-fifths in Ontario and one-fifth in Quebec. The **Abitibi River** (547 km) drains the lake into the Moose River, which flows north into James Bay.

Abraham, Plaines d' QC This famous landmark in Quebec City was named after Abraham Martin (1589–1664), an early pioneer who acquired the property in 1635 and 1645. It was the site of the historic battle in September 1759 between the British forces led by Maj. Gen. James Wolfe (1727–59) and the French forces of the Marquis de Montcalm (1712–59). Known at that time as *Hauteurs d'Abraham* and *Heights of Abraham*, it was called *Plains of Abraham* in 1759 by British Capt. John Knox. The French name was introduced by Surveyor General Joseph Bouchette (1774–1841) in 1815. The area is also known as Battlefields National Park and Parc des Champs-de-Bataille.

Abrams Village PE West of Summerside, this municipal community (1974) was named after Abraham Arsenault, the first settler in the area. Noted as early as 1829 as *Abraham's Village*, Abrams Village's post office was open from 1880 to 1918.

Abruzzi, Mount BC In the Rocky Mountains, north of Sparwood, this mountain (3267 m) on the British Columbia–Alaska border was named in 1920 after Luigi Amadeo di Savoia-Aosta, Duke of the Abruzzi (1873–1933), who became the first to climb Mount St. Elias in 1899.

Acadieville NB This community west of Richibucto had its post office named Acadie in 1879 after **Acadieville Parish** and was changed to Acadieville in 1955. The parish was named in 1876 after Acadian settlers had been given free land grants, and for the early French name for the area of the Maritime provinces. Acadie and Acadia have their roots in *Archadia*, a name given in 1524 to the present-day Atlantic seaboard from Virginia to Nova Scotia by explorer Giovanni de Verrazzano, who was exploring on behalf of the King of France.

Acme AB A village (1910) northeast of Calgary, it had a post office called *Tapscott* from 1905 to 1909, when the Canadian Pacific Railway had built as far north as that point and chose a name derived from Greek, meaning 'highest point'.

Acton ON Settled about 1820, and named *Danville*, and later *Adamsville* for early settlers, Acton was named in 1844 by postmaster Robert Swan after Acton, Northumberland, England. It was united in 1974 with the town of Georgetown and most of the township of Esquesing to form the town of Halton Hills in the regional municipality of Halton.

Acton QC A regional county south of Drummondville, it was formed in 1982 from the county of Bagot and part of the county of Shefford. Its main centre is the town of **Acton Vale**, which was established in 1861 and named after the township of **Acton**. The township, proclaimed in 1806, was named in 1795 after the town of Acton in England's Greater London, west of the London city centre.

Adamant Mountain BC In the Selkirk Mountains, north of Revelstoke, this mountain (3365 m) anchors the northwest corner of the **Adamant Range**. The mountain was named in 1909 by climber Howard Palmer (1883–1944) after its precipitous south face.

Adams Lake BC Located northeast of Kamloops, this lake is drained south by the **Adams River** into the west end of Shuswap Lake. Its name derives from Chief Sel-howt-ken of the Shuswap, who had been baptized Adam by Fr. John Nobili in 1849. It was called *Sl-hes-tal-len* by the Shuswap and identified on an 1827 map as *choo-choo-ach*.

Adamsville QC In the town of Bromont and the regional county of La Haute-Yamaska, this community was named after miller George Adams (1813–85), a native of Vermont who settled here in 1847 and became the postmaster 20 years later.

Adelaide-Metcalfe ON In 2001 Adelaide became part of the municipality of **Adelaide-Metcalfe**, Middlesex County. The township of Adelaide was named in 1830 for Amelia Adelaide Louisa Theresa Carolina (1792–1849), wife of William IV, who became King that year. *See also* Metcalfe Township.

Adelaide Peninsula NU Separating Queen Maud Gulf from Rasmussen Basin, this peninsula was named in 1839 by Hudson's Bay Company explorer Thomas Simpson (1808–40) after Queen Adelaide (1792–1849), wife of William IV.

Adjala-Tosorontio ON In 1994 Adjala became part of the municipal township of **Adjala-Tosorontio**, Simcoe County. Adjala is a name of uncertain origin, claimed to be named after a daughter of Shawnee chief Tecumseh, although he is not known to have had a daughter. With nearby townships named after noted Aboriginal chiefs, Adjala may have been named after an Ojibwa family group called *Ad-je-jawk*, noted by traveller John Tanner in 1830. *See also* Tosorontio.

Admaston-Bromley ON This municipal township in Renfrew County was named in 2000. Admaston township received its name in 1843 after a village in Staffordshire, England, near Blithfield Hall and Bagot's Bromley, the home of Sir Charles Bagot (1781–1843), governor general of Canada, 1841–3. The village is some 38 km north of Birmingham. An 1836 map identifies the township of Admaston as *Kanmore*.

Admirals Beach NL This municipal community (1968) in St. Mary's Bay, southwest of St. John's, received its name from the practice in the late 1700s and throughout the 1800s of calling the first captain of a vessel arriving in a harbour 'the admiral'.

Admiralty Inlet NU At the north end of Baffin Island, and separating Brodeur and Borden peninsulas, this 280-km inlet was named in 1820 by Lt. Sir William E. Parry (1790–1855) after the board of the British Admiralty.

Adolphustown ON A township in Lennox and Addington County, Adolphustown was named in 1784 for Prince Adolphus Frederick (1774–1850), seventh son of George III. Adolphustown post office opened in 1822.

Afton PE A municipal community (1974), it embraces the localities of Cumberland, Fairview, New Dominion, Nine Mile Creek, Rice Point, and Rocky Point. The name was chosen in 1974, probably after the Robbie Burns poem, 'Flow Gently, Sweet Afton'.

Agassiz Ice Cap NU In central Ellesmere Island, this ice cap was named *The Chinese Wall* in 1883 by Lt. James B. Lockwood, who explored the northwest coast of Kalaallit Nunaat (Greenland) the previous year. Adolphus Greely (1844–1935), who organized expeditions, 1881–4, named it *Mer de Glace Agassiz* after Swiss-American naturalist Jean Louis Rodolphe Agassiz (1807–73). It was subsequently called *Agassiz Glacier* before 1910, and amended to Agassiz Ice Cap in 1967.

Agawa Bay ON Located on the east side of Lake Superior, 95 km north of Sault Ste. Marie, this bay is the site of famous pictographs on **Agawa Rock** rediscovered in 1851 by American ethnologist Henry Rowe Schoolcraft. **Agawa Canyon** is a popular tourist destination for the changing of the leaf colours in autumn. In Ojibwa *agawa* may mean 'sheltered harbour'.

Aguanish QC A municipality (1957) in the regional county of Minganie and on the north shore of the Gulf of St. Lawrence, it was settled in the mid-1800s. It was named after the **Rivière Aguanus**, whose name in Montagnais is believed to mean 'little shelter'.

Ailsa Craig ON This village (1874) became a part of the municipality of North Middlesex, Middlesex County in 2001. Ailsa Craig was named in 1858 after David Craig, and after the rocky island of Ailsa Craig at the entrance to the Firth of Clyde in Scotland.

Ainslie, Lake NS Southeast of Inverness, this lake was named about 1820 after George Robert Ainslie (1776–1839), the last lieutenant-governor of Cape Breton Island, 1816–20.

Airdrie AB Directly north of Calgary, this city (1985) was founded by the Canadian Pacific Railway in 1889, and named by engineer William MacKenzie after Airdrie, a town in Lanarkshire, Scotland, east of Glasgow.

Air Force Island NU In Foxe Basin, and west of Baffin Island, this island (1720 km²) was discovered in 1948 by a Royal Canadian Air Force aerial survey. It was officially named the following year. It was one of the last major islands found in the Canadian North.

Ajax ON The site of an armed forces munitions factory during World War II, this town (1955) was named in 1941 after the British cruiser HMS *Ajax*. In December 1939 the cruiser forced the German battleship *Admiral Graf Spee* to scuttle itself in the mouth of the Rio de la Plata, off Montevideo, Uruguay.

Akimiski Island NU On the west side of James Bay, and opposite the mouth of Attawapiskat River, this island (3001 km²) was named *Viner's Island* in 1674 by Hudson's Bay Company governor Charles Bayley after Sir Robert Viner (Vyner), a charter member of the company and a London financier. It was identified on a 1901 geological map as Akimiski Island after the Cree word for 'land across' and officially endorsed in 1948.

Aklavik NT Located on the west bank of Peel Channel and in the Mackenzie Delta, this hamlet (1974) was named *Aklavuk* in 1910 by Col. G.L. Jennings of the Royal Canadian Mounted Police after the Inuvialuktun word for 'place where they hunt brown bears'. The present spelling was authorized in 1921. **Aklavik Channel** unites the East and West channels of the Mackenzie River. *See also* Inuvik.

Akulivik QC This village (1979) north of Povungnituk and on the shore of Hudson Bay was founded in 1922. Its name in Inuktitut means either 'middle point of a trident', or 'point between two bays'.

Akwesasne ON, QC This Indian reserve, opposite Cornwall, embraces lands not only in ON and QC, but also extends into New York. The name in Mohawk means 'place where the partridge beats its wings'.

Alameda SK A town (1907) east of Estevan, it has a post office that was named in 1883 by Christian Troyer after the city of Alameda, CA, on San Francisco Bay, adjacent to Oakland. He went there in the 1850s and moved back to Canada in 1882. In Spanish, *alameda* describes the poplar or cottonwood tree.

Alaska Highway BC, YT Beginning in Dawson Creek, BC, this highway extends for 2451 km to Fairbanks, AK, with 1965 km in Canada. It was built in 1942–3 to provide a better connection with the Soviet Union during the Second World War. First called the *Alaska Military Highway*, it became known as the *Alcan Highway* among the engineers and workers who built it. United States Congressman Anthony J. Dimond of Alaska proposed the title Alaska Highway, which was adopted by both the Canadian and American governments on 19 July 1943.

Albanel QC This municipality (1990) northwest of Lac Saint-Jean and in the regional county of Maria-Chapdelaine was named after the township of **Albanel**, created in 1883 in honour of the Jesuit missionary Charles Albanel (1616–96).

Albany River ON This river was named in 1683 by the Hudson's Bay Company for James, Duke of York and Albany (1633-1701), who became King James II in 1685. It is the largest river (982 km to the head of Cat River) entirely within the province.

Albemarle ON This township became part of the town of South Bruce Peninsula in 2001. The township was named in 1855 by William Coutts Keppel, Viscount Bury (1852–94), superintendent of Indian Affairs in Canada, after his father George Thomas Keppel, 6th Earl of Albemarle (1799–1891), a military officer and diplomat.

Albert NB This county in the southeastern part of the province was named in 1845 after Prince Albert (1819–61), who had married Queen Victoria in 1840. *See also* Riverside-Albert.

Alberta In 1882 the Marquess of Lorne (1845–1914) named the provisional district of Alberta after his wife, Princess Louise Caroline Alberta (1848–1939), daughter of Queen Victoria. The district embraced that part of the present province (1905) south of Grande Prairie and west of Medicine Hat. The province was established in 1905. **Mount Alberta** (3619 m), on the continental divide northwest of Calgary, was named in 1898 by British climber Norman Collie (1859–1942). The summer village (1920) of **Alberta Beach**, on the east side of Lac Ste. Anne, 52 km northwest of Edmonton, was named by the Canadian Northern Railway, with its post office opening in 1917. In 1999 this community became a village.

Alberta, Mount YT In the Centennial Range of the St. Elias Mountains, this mountain (3348 m) was named in 1967 after the province of Alberta, and in honour of the centennial of Confederation.

Albert, Mont QC Rising to 1151 m in the Monts Chic-Chocs and west of Gaspé, this mountain was named in 1845 by geologist Alexander Murray (1810–84) after Prince Albert (1819–61), the consort of Queen Victoria.

Alberton PE The post office in this town (1913) in the northwest part of the province was named in 1868 by Benjamin Rogers after Albert Edward, the Prince of Wales (1841–1910), who visited Charlottetown in 1860. Its post office had been called Cascumpec in 1839 after the adjacent Cascumpec Bay.

Albion ON This township was named in 1819 after an ancient poetical name of England, in allusion to the cliffs of Dover. It was united in 1974 with Caledon Township and half of Chinguacousy Township to become part of the town of Caledon in the regional municipality of Peel.

Albreda, Mount BC In the Monashee Mountains, southeast of Valemount, this mountain (3075 m) was named in 1863 by William Wentworth Fitzwilliam, Viscount Milton (1839–77) after his aunt, Lady Albreda Elizabeth Wentworth-Fitzwilliam (1907–70). The viscount accompanied Dr. Walter Cheadle (1836–1910) during an expedition through the West, 1862–3.

Aldborough ON In 1998 this township became part of the municipality of West Elgin, Elgin County. It was named in 1792 after the town of Aldeburgh, on the North Sea coast of Suffolk, England.

Aldershot NS This name was first used after 1867 for a militia-drilling site at Aylesford, taking its name from the military camp of Aldershot, southwest of London, England. In 1904 it was relocated to the north side of Kentville and developed into a suburban residential area.

Alderville ON An Aboriginal community in the township of Alnwick-Haldimand, Northumberland County, northeast of Cobourg, this place was first named Alnwick in 1841. In 1860 it was renamed after the Reverend Robert Alder (1796–1873), a noted English preacher who visited the Mississauga on the Alderville Reserve about 1839.

Aldrich, Cape NU On Ellesmere Island, east of Cape Columbia, this cape was named in 1875–6 by British explorer Sir George Nares (1716–86) for his first lieutenant, Pelham Aldrich. Nares established that the area of the two capes was the most northerly land of the Arctic Archipelago.

Alert NU The name of this weather station and military base, near the most northerly point of Canada, was proposed in 1948 by W/Cdr. G.H. Newcome to the interdepartmental meteorological committee. Established the following year, the station took its name from HMS *Alert*, the flagship of the proposed British Admiralty expedition to the North Pole in 1875–6. Led by Sir George S. Nares (1831–1915), the expedition was the first to pass by the site of Alert.

Alert Bay BC This village (1946) on Cormorant Island—the north side of Vancouver Island, where Johnstone Strait joins Queen Charlotte Strait—took its post office name from the bay in 1885. The bay was named in 1860 by Capt. George H. Richards (1819–96) after HMS *Alert*, which served on the Pacific station, 1858–61 and 1865–8.

Alexander Island NU In the Queen Elizabeth Islands and between Bathurst and Melville Islands, this island (484 km²) was named in 1962 after Harold Rupert Leofric George, 1st Earl Alexander of Tunis (1891–1969), governor general of Canada, 1946–52.

Alexandra PE Located southeast of Charlottetown, this municipal community (1972) was named about 1870 after Princess Alexandra Caroline Maria Charlotte Louise Julia (1844–1925), who married the Prince of Wales, the future Edward VII, in 1863. Its post office was open from 1884 to 1915.

Alexandra Falls NT Located 42 km upriver from the mouth of Hay River, this feature (32 m) was named in 1872 by Anglican bishop William C. Bompas (1834–1906) after the Princess of Wales, who became Queen Alexandra in 1901, when Edward VII succeeded Queen Victoria.

Alexandra, Mount AB, BC This summit (3338 m) on the continental divide, northeast of Calgary, was named in 1902 by British climber Norman Collie (1858–1942) after Queen Alexandra, consort of Edward VII.

Alexandria ON This town (1903) was called *Priest's Mill* in the early 1800s after a grist mill built by the Most Reverend Alexander McDonell (1762–1840), the first Catholic bishop of Upper Canada. He resettled many disbanded soldiers of the Scottish Glengarry Regiment in Glengarry County. In 1825 the name was changed to Alexandria in his honour.

Alfred ON In 1997 this township became part of the township of Alfred and Plantagenet, united counties of Prescott and Russell. Alfred Township was named in 1798 for Prince Alfred (1780–82), a son of George III. The village of **Alfred** (1952) was first known as *Bradyville* for hotelkeeper Thomas Brady, but became Alfred on the opening of the post office in 1842.

Algoma ON The name of this district (1859) in Northern Ontario may have been devised by American ethnologist Henry Rowe Schoolcraft (1793–1864) from the Ojibwa *ah-ga-mic* ('the other side of the water'), describing the north shore of Lake Huron in relation to Manitoulin Island.

Algonquin Provincial Park ON This park was created in 1893, and now covers an area of 7536 km². It was named after the Algonquin nation, which has occupied the Ottawa Valley since at least the early 1600s. The Mi'kmaq named the nation, interpreted as 'at the place of spearing fish from the bow of a canoe'.

Alice ON This township in Renfrew County is now part of the municipal township of Laurentian Valley. The township was named in 1855 for Princess Alice Maud Mary (1843–78), the second daughter of Queen Victoria. In 1859 Alice Township was joined to Fraser Township to become a single township municipality.

Alida SK A terminus of a Canadian Pacific Railway line, northeast of Estevan, this village (1926) has a post office that opened in 1913. It was named by CPR president Lord Thomas Shaughnessy (1850–1933) after Lady Alida (1884–1943), wife of Sir Harry Brittain. Brittain was an English author who participated in Imperial conferences.

Alix AB Northeast of Red Deer, this village (1907) has a post office that was established in 1905 and named after Alexia ('Alix') Westhead, the wife of a pioneer rancher.

Allan SK This town (1965) was founded as a Canadian Northern Railway station southwest of Saskatoon; both the post office and the station were established in 1908 and named after Sir Hugh Allan (1810–82). Sir Hugh was a director of the Grand Trunk Railway. The name also reflects the practice of the Grand Trunk of identifying its stations in alphabetical order, with Bradwell to the northwest and Zelma to the southeast. *Curzon* post office served the area from 1904 to 1909.

Allen, Mount AB, BC Near Lake Louise, this mountain (3310 m) was named in 1924 after American alpinist Samuel Evans Stokes Allen (1874–1945). Allen had named it *Mount Shappee* after the Stoney word for 'sixth', as it was the sixth of the Ten Peaks (now Wenkchemna Peaks).

Alliance AB Southeast of Camrose, this village (1918) was named in 1916 by Canadian Northern Railway land buyer Tom Edwards after his hometown of Alliance, OH, southeast of Cleveland. Its post office had been called Galahad in 1907, but this name was transferred in 1916 to the next village to the northwest.

Alliston ON An urban community in the town of New Tecumseth, Simcoe County, Alliston was founded in 1847 by William Fletcher (1765–1839), naming it after his birthplace in Allerston, Yorkshire, west of the east coast city of Scarborough, England.

Allumettes, Île aux QC In the Ottawa River, opposite Pembroke, this island was called *Isle des Algoumequins* by Samuel de Champlain (1567–1635) in 1613. In the second half of the seventeenth century, explorer Nicolas Perrot referred to it as *Isle du Borgne autrement ditte l'Isle des Allumettes*. Le Borgne was a one-eyed Aboriginal leader on the island. The name is attributed to reeds that reminded travellers of matches.

Allumette Lake, Lac des Allumettes ON, QC A 30-km-long widening of the Ottawa River, Allumette Lake extends from Chalk River to **Allumette Rapids/Rapides des Allumettes** at Morrison Island, below Pembroke. **Lower Allumette Lake** extends for 20 km from there to the rapids below the township of Westmeath. The first explorers found reeds there suitable for the making of *allumettes* ('matches').

Alma NB A village (1966), 45 km southwest of Moncton, it had a post office called *Salmon River* in 1848 that was renamed after **Alma Parish** in 1873. The parish had been named in 1855 after the victory in 1854 of British and French forces on the heights of the Alma River in the Crimea.

Alma NS The post office in this community located west of Stellarton was named in 1855 after the British-French victory over the Russians a year earlier, on the heights of the Alma River in the Crimea. Earlier it was called *Middle River* after the Middle River of Pictou.

Alma QC This city (1924) on the Saguenay River and in the regional county of Saint-Jean-Est was called after **Île d'Alma**, named about 1861 by surveyor Edmond A. Duberger after the 1854 Crimean War battle. The municipality was first created as *Saint-Joseph-d'Alma* in 1879, but the city's name was shortened to Alma in 1954.

Almonte ON This town (1880) in Lanark County, Almonte replaced Ramsay and Waterford in 1856. It was named for Juan Nepomucene Almonte (1804–69), Mexican ambassador to the United States. His name was presumably chosen because he strongly opposed the American government's aggressive trading practices, which were affecting Mexico, as well as the British provinces to the north. Before 1856 it was *Shepherd's Falls* for David Shepherd, *Shipman's Mills* for Daniel Shipman, and *Ramsayville* after Ramsay Township.

Alnwick ON In 2001 Alnwick Township and Haldimand Township became the municipal township of Alnwick-Haldimand in Northumberland County. The township was named in 1798 after a town in Northumberland, England, north of Newcastle upon Tyne.

Alsask SK This village (1947) on the Alberta border, west of Kindersley, had its station named in 1909 by the Canadian Northern Railway by joining the first syllables of Alberta and Saskatchewan. Its post office opened two years later.

Alsek River YT Rising in the Kluane Ranges of the St. Elias Mountains, this river (386 km) flows south across the Alaska border into Dry Bay, part of Yakutut Bay, an inlet of the Pacific Ocean. Although noted as R Alsehk as early as 1825 by Russian Capt. Tebenkov, other names (*Behring, Jones, Harrison*) were proposed before Alsek River was officially recognized in 1891 by the Canadian and American governments.

Altona MB This town (1956) northwest of Emerson had its Canadian Pacific Railway station named in 1894 after a suburb of Hamburg, Germany. A post office opened the following year.

Altruist Mountain BC In the Coast Mountains, northwest of Pemberton, this mountain (3124 m) was named in the 1950s by Alpine Club of Canada climbers. Because they had been lured to ascend peaks that did not lead to the top of the mountain, this 'delightfully cynical name' was proposed.

Alverstone, Mount YT In the St. Elias Mountains and on the Yukon–Alaska boundary, this mountain (4439 m) was named in 1908 by the Canadian government after Lord Richard Everard Webster Alverstone (1842–1915). A British commissioner in 1903 on the northwestern Canada–United States boundary dispute, he voted in favour of the American claims.

Alvinston ON Located in Lambton County, southeast of Sarnia, this village (1880) was named in 1854 after Alverstone on England's Isle of Wight. In 2001 this village was connected to Brooke township to become the municipal township of **Brooke-Alvinston**. *See also* Brooke.

Amabel ON This township became part of the town of South Bruce Peninsula in 2001. The township had been named in 1856 by William Coutts Keppel, Viscount Bury (1832–94), superintendent of Indian Affairs of Canada, after Henrietta Amabel Yorke. She was the sister-in-law of Sir Edmund Head (1805–68), who was then governor general of Canada.

Amadjuak Lake NU On Baffin Island and northwest of Iqaluit, this lake (3058 km²) was named Amaxdjuak in 1945 by anthropologist Franz Boas (1858–1942). The present spelling was used in 1897 by geologist Robert Bell. The name means 'great water' in Inuktitut.

Amaranth ON This township in Dufferin County was named in 1821 after the never-fading flower of the poets, as well as the common plant known as pigweed.

Ameliasburgh ON This township became part of the municipality of Prince Edward County. The township of Ameliasburgh was named in 1787 for Princess Amelia (1783–1810), fifth daughter and youngest child of George III. The community of **Ameliasburg** (without the terminal 'h'), in the township south of Belleville, was named in the 1832. The two forms of the name continue to be used.

Amery, Mount AB This mountain (3329 m) was named by Order-in-Council in 1927 after Leopold Charles Morris Stenet Amery (1873–1955), who was then secretary for the Dominions, 1925–9.

Amet Sound NS On the south side of Northumberland Strait, the name of this sound derives from a former French designation of **Amet Island**, Isle Darmet (from *ormet*, 'helmet island'). Pierre Jumeau in 1685 referred to it as *Isle porképic*, other map-makers showed it in the 1750s as *Isle Remedy*, and in 1775 map-maker Joseph Frederick Wallet DesBarres (1722–1824) called it *Frederick Bay*.

Amherst NS This town (1889) near the New Brunswick border had its first post office named *Cumberland* in 1810 after the county. It was renamed Amherst in 1841 after Amherst Township. The township was given its name after 1759 for Jeffery Amherst, 1st Baron Amherst (1717–97), who with Adm. Edward Boscawen (1711–61), had captured the French fortress of Louisbourg in 1758 and Montreal in 1760. He was the commander-in-chief of the British forces in North America, 1760–3.

Amherstburg ON This town (1878) in Essex County, south of Windsor, was the site in the late 1790s of Fort Amherstburg (later called Fort Malden). The place and fort were named for Lord Jeffery Amherst, commander-in-chief of the British forces in North America, 1760–3. In 1998 Amherstburg and the townships of Anderdon and Malden became the town of Amherstburg.

Amherst Island ON The island and township in Lennox and Addington County were both named in 1792 for Lord Jeffery Amherst, who led the British troops in the capture of Louisbourg in 1758 and of Montreal in 1760.

Amisk AB The post office in this village (1956), southwest of Wainwright, was named in 1908, just before the Canadian Pacific Railway arrived. The name derives from the Cree word for 'beaver'.

Amos QC The name of this town in the regional county of Abitibi originated in 1914 after Alice Amos, the wife of Sir Lomer Gouin (1861–1929). He was then premier of Quebec.

Amqui QC This town (1961) in the valley of the Rivière Matapédia, and in the regional county of La Matapédia, replaced *Saint-Benôit-Joseph-Labre* in 1948. Amqui post office opened in 1879, taking its name from the Rivière Humqui, derived from a Mi'kmaq word possibly meaning 'place where it plays', perhaps in reference to the turbulent waters of the rapids here. Or it may refer to joyous gatherings here by the Mi'kmaq.

Amund Ringnes Island NU One of the Sverdrup Islands and in the central part of the Queen Elizabeth Islands, this island (5255 km²) was named *Amund Ringnes's Land* in 1900 by Otto Sverdrup (1854–1930) during his 1898–1902 Norwegian Arctic expedition, after Amund Ringnes, a Norwegian patron.

Amundsen Gulf NT Separating Victoria and Banks Islands from the mainland, this extension of the Beaufort Sea was named before 1910 by the British Admiralty after Norwegian explorer Roald Amundsen (1872–1928). In 1906 he became the first person to sail a ship through the famous Northwest Passage from the Atlantic to the Pacific.

Anahim Lake BC In the Chilcotin country, between Williams Lake and Bella Coola, this lake was named after Chilcotin chief Anahim. In 1861 explorers Ranald Macdonald and John Barnston passed by *Lake Anawhim. Anaham Lake* post office opened at the south end of the lake in 1907 and was changed to Anahim Lake in 1939.

Anarchist Mountain BC East of Osoyoos, this mountain (1499 m) is adjacent to the 900-m climb of steep hairpin turns on Highway 3 from the Okanagan Valley to the Okanagan Highlands. It was named after Richard G. Sidley, who arrived in the district in 1889 and was appointed a Justice of the Peace and customs officer at Sidley, on the Washington State border, southeast of the mountain. His extreme anarchistic political views resulted in his dismissal.

Ancaster ON A town (1974) in Hamilton-Wentworth Region, Ancaster was created as a township in 1792 in Lincoln County, taking its name from Ancaster in England's Lincolnshire, south of the city of Lincoln. It had been earlier called *Wilson's Mills* after miller James Wilson, and *Rousseaux's Mills* after noted interpreter and trader Jean-Baptiste Rousseau. In 2001 Ancaster was annexed to the city of Hamilton.

Anchor Point NL On the Strait of Belle Isle, west of St. Anthony, this municipal community (1974) may have been named after an adjacent safe anchorage for travellers crossing from the southern Labrador coast.

Anderdon ON A township in Essex County, Anderdon was created in 1837. It may have been named after an Aboriginal clan called *Arendharenon* ('rock people', probably a euphemism for 'snakes') or after an officer stationed at Fort Malden. In 1998 the town of Amherstburg and the townships of Anderdon and Malden became the town of Amherstburg.

Anderson River NT Rising north of Great Bear Lake, this river (692 km) flows northwest into Wood Bay of the Beaufort Sea. It was named in 1857 by Hudson's Bay Company explorer Roderick MacFarlane (1833–1920) after HBC chief factor James Anderson (1800–67). Anderson, who was in charge of the HBC's Mackenzie district, referred to it two years earlier as *Inconnue* or *Beghulatesse*.

Andrew AB Northeast of Edmonton, this village (1930) was named in 1902, when the post office opened. It was named after pioneer settler Andrew Whitford (b.1844). Whitford, the next Canadian Pacific station to the east, and nearby Whitford Lake were also named after him.

Andromeda, Mount AB This mountain (3450 m), near the head of Athabasca River, was named in 1938 by alpinist Rex Gibson after the mythological wife of Perseus.

Angikuni Lake NU A widening of the Kazan River, and southeast of Dubawnt Lake, this lake (437 km²) was named before 1910 after the Chipewyan word for 'big'.

Anguille, Cape NL This cape is the most westerly point of Newfoundland; its name translates to 'eel' in French. The **Anguille Mountains**, rising to 526 m, extend for 50 km along the coast of St. George's Bay.

Angus ON Located in Simcoe County, west of Barrie, this community was named in 1857 by the Canadian Northern Railway for Angus Morrison (1822–82), a director of the company and a member of the Legislative Assembly, 1854–67, and of the House of Commons, 1867–74.

9

Angusville MB Northwest of Brandon, near Riding Mountain National Park, this community had a post office called *Snake Creek* in 1909, but it was renamed in 1911 after pioneer settlers John, Frank, William, Sam, and Adam Angus.

Anjou QC In 2002 Anjou became a sector of the city of Montreal, and in 2006 it became a borough in Montreal. Anjou had been a city northeast of the Montreal city centre. It had been created in 1956 from the parish of Saint-Léonard-de-Port-Maurice. Anjou was named after the ancient province in west central France.

Anmore BC The post office of this village (1987) north of Port Moody was named in 1951 after resident Ann Moore.

Annaheim SK Located northeast of Humboldt, this village (1977) had a post office named in 1904 after St. Ann's Parish, established by Fr. Dominic Holmann on 26 July 1903, the feast day of the mother of the Virgin Mary. The name literally means 'home of Ann' in German.

Annandale-Little Pond-Howe Bay PE This municipal community (1975) embraces the localities of Annandale, Howe Bay, and Little Pond. Annandale was named about 1868 by James Johnston, whose parents came from Annan, Dumfriesshire, Scotland in 1840. About 1880 the school district of Howe Bay was called after the adjacent bay, named in 1765 by Samuel Holland (1728–1801) for Sir William Howe (1729–1814), commander-in-chief of British forces in North America in 1755. The post office at Howe Bay was called Sailors Hope from 1884 to 1913. Little Pond had a post office from 1886 to 1913.

Annapolis Royal NS This town (1893) on the **Annapolis River** is located at the site where Samuel de Champlain (1567–1635) established *Port-Royal* in 1604. After its capture in 1710 by Col. Francis Nicholson, the town was renamed after Queen Anne (1665–1714). *Annapolis* post office opened in 1785 and the word 'Royal' was added to it in 1903. The Annapolis River rises south of Berwick, and flows southwest into the **Annapolis Basin**. The **Annapolis Valley** embraces the valleys of the Annapolis and Cornwallis Rivers, from Digby in the southwest to Grand Pré in the northeast.

Annieopsquotch Mountains NL These mountains in the central part of Newfoundland, between Victoria Lake on the east and Red Indian Lake on the west, rise to 687 m. In Mi'kmaq the name means 'rocky mountains'.

Anticosti, Île d' QC Quebec's largest island lies in the estuary of the St. Lawrence River. Named *isle de l'Assumption* by Jacques Cartier (1491–1557) in 1535, the island was called Anticosti by historian Marc Lescarbot (1570–1629) in 1609. The Mi'kmaq at that time called it *Natigôsteg* ('forward land')

whereas the Montagnais on the north shore still know it as *Natashquan* ('where bears are hunted').

Antigonish NS In **Antigonish County**, and at the head of **Antigonish Harbour**, this town (1889) was settled in 1784 by Col. Timothy Hierlihy and officers and men of the Nova Scotia Volunteers. The post office was called Antigonish in 1816. The name, noted in 1672 by Acadian Gov. Nicolas Denys (c.1598–1688) as *Articougnesche*, likely means 'flowing through broken marsh' from the Mi'kmaq *nalegitkoonech*. The town's site had another Mi'kmaq name that meant 'where the bears tear the branches off trees'. What remained of *Sydney County*, established in 1784 after Guysborough County was separated from it in 1836, became Antigonish County in 1863.

Appin ON In 2001 this community became part of municipality of Southwest Middlesex, Middlesex County. Southwest of London, this place was first called *Ekfrid Centre* in 1854. Seven years later Dr. D.S. McKellar named it after his birthplace in the Appin district of Scotland, near Fort William, northwest of Glasgow.

Apple Hill ON In 1998 this community located north of Cornwall became part of the township of North Glengarry, united counties of Stormont, Dundas, and Glengarry. The name was given in 1882 when the Canadian Pacific Railway was built through Sandy Kennedy's apple orchard.

Appleton ON In Lanark County, east of Carleton Place, this community was first called *Teskeyville* and *Appletree Falls* after some apple trees at the foot of the falls on the Mississippi River. It was named Appleton when the post office opened in 1857.

Aquaforte NL This municipal community (1972) is located on the east coast of the Avalon Peninsula. The name, derived from Portuguese *aguaforte* ('freshwater'), appeared as *R. da aguea* on a 1519 map and as *Agoforte* in the early 1600s. The change to Aquaforte may have been made by Sir Robert Robinson in 1669.

Arborfield SK The post office in this town (1950) northeast of Tisdale was named in 1910 by the post office department after Arbor Day, when public tree planting is undertaken in the spring. Fairfield had been requested, but was rejected because it was already in use in the province. There is also an Arborfield in Berkshire, England.

Arborg MB The post office of this village (1964), northwest of Gimli and on the Icelandic River, was called *Ardal* (Icelandic for 'river dale') in 1909. The village was renamed in 1911 after the Icelandic for 'river town'.

Arcadia NS Located east of Yarmouth, the post office in this community was first called *Upper Chebogue* in 1860 after its location on the Chebogue River. It was renamed in 1875 for the brig *Arcadia*, built here in 1817. The brig may have been named after Archadia by the explorer Giovanni de Verrazzano (1485–1528), recalling the ancient Greek *Archadia* and its classical land of rustic pleasure. Subsequently the regional name Acadia was given to the Atlantic seaboard from Virginia to Nova Scotia. From about 1628 to 1763 Acadia was defined as the territory of the Maritime provinces.

Archerwill SK When the Canadian Pacific Railway built a line north from Wadena to Tisdale in 1924, a station was established midway between the two. William Pierce, secretary-treasurer of the rural municipality of Barrier Valley, met with councillors Archie Campbell and Ervie Hanson to devise a name from the first syllables of their three given names. The post office opened in 1925, and the place became an incorporated village in 1947.

Archibald, Mount YT In the St. Elias Mountains, west of Haines Junction, this mountain (2560 m) was named in 1971 after Dr. E.S. Archibald, director of the Department of Agriculture's experimental farm service.

Arcola SK This town (1903) located northeast of Estevan had its post office named in 1889 by postmaster Peter McLellan after a place in Italy, where Napoleon had defeated the Austrians in 1800.

Arctic Bay NU Located on **Arctic Bay**, a small arm of Admiralty Inlet and on the northwestern side of Baffin Island, this hamlet (1976) was officially named in 1951. In 1926 it had been called *Tukik*.

Arctic Red River NT Rising in the Mackenzie Mountains, this river flows north to join the Mackenzie River at the charter community of Tsiigehtchic. The community was the site of the Hudson's Bay Company post of *Arctic Red River* about 1900. The river's name appeared in a 1906 report by Charles Camsell (1876-1958) and was approved in 1945. *See also* Tsiigehtchic.

Arden MB The Manitoba and North Western Railway station of this community, located east of Neepawa, was named before 1883 by Frederick W. Stobart, a Winnipeg dry goods merchant and promoter of the railway. He named it after his father's birthplace in North Yorkshire, England, northeast of Thirsk. It had earlier been called *Beautiful Plains*. The post office opened as *Arden Station* in 1884 and was changed to Arden in 1897.

Argenteuil QC The name of this regional county west of Montreal derives from a seigneury granted in 1682 to Charles-Joseph d'Ailleboust Des Muceaux (c.1623–1700) and transferred in 1697 to his son, Pierre d'Ailleboust d'Argenteuil (1659–1711). The name has its roots in the town of Argenteuil, a northwestern suburb of Paris.

Argentia NL On the east coast of Placentia Bay, this neighbourhood in the town of Placentia was first known as *Little Placentia*. In the early part of the twentieth century, the present name was proposed by Fr. St. John after the mining of silver (*argentum* in Latin) in an adjacent cliff. Although the mine failed, the name survived.

Argonaut Mountain BC Located in the Selkirk Mountains, north of Revelstoke, this mountain (2976 m) was named in 1913 by mountaineer Howard Palmer (1883–1944) after some 200 Overlanders who trekked from Eastern Canada in 1862. They had also acquired the nickname Argonauts of '62. In 1912 Palmer had proposed Dentiform Mountain, and the next year he suggested Big Tooth before the present name was adopted by the Geographic Board.

Argyle NS A municipal district in Yarmouth County, it was established in 1879. It was named after the settlement of Argyle, named in 1766 by Capt. Ranald MacKinnon, who received a grant there a year earlier. He named it after Argyllshire, Scotland. Argyle's post office opened in 1852 and a string of communities around **Argyle Sound** that received post offices included **Lower Argyle** (1865), **Central Argyle** (1878), **Argyle Sound** (1879), **Argyle Head** (1884), and **Argyle South** (1913).

Arichat NS The name of this community, located on the south side of Isle Madame, derives from the Mi'kmaq *neliksaak* (possibly 'camp ground' or 'split rocks'). Arichat was referred to as *Nerichat* and *Nerichac* on early maps. Arichat's post office was established in 1824 and that of **West Arichat** was opened in 1867.

Arkell, Mount YT Southwest of Whitehorse, this mountain (2209 m) was named around 1926 after **Arkell Creek**. The creek was named in 1890 by E.J. Glave and Jack Dalton after William J. Arkell, owner of the *Frank Leslie Illustrated News of New York*. Arkell organized the Glave-Dalton expedition to the rich goldfields on the Fortymile River in 1890 and 1891. When news of the fabulous wealth of the Yukon reached Arkell in 1897, he tried to lay claim to the whole of the Klondike area.

Arkona ON This village (1876) in Lambton County, northeast of Sarnia, was first called *Eastman's Corners* (Nial Eastman was among the community's first German settlers in the 1830s) and *Bosanquet*. In 1857 it was named Arkona after the German cape that extends into the Baltic Sea. In 2001 Arkona was taken into the municipality of Lambton Shores.

Armagh QC This village (1950) in the regional county of Bellechasse, east of Quebec City, was called after the township of **Armagh**, which was named in 1795 and proclaimed in 1799. The township's name was given after the city of Armagh, the principal centre of County Armagh, Ireland.

Armstrong BC Near the north end of the Okanagan Valley, this city (1913) was named in 1891–2 by the Shuswap and Okanagan Railway (a subsidiary of the Canadian Pacific) after financier William Charles Heaton-Armstrong (1853–1917) from London, England, who visited here in 1892.

Armstrong, Mount YT This mountain (2157 m) in the Russell Range, north of Macmillan River, was named in 1926 by Member of Parliament George Black and Gold Commissioner Percy Reid after Neville Alexander Drummond Armstrong (1874–1954), who managed the Yukon Goldfields Company in the Klondike, 1898–1903. He remained in the Yukon searching for gold until 1928, except for service overseas with the Canadian Expeditionary Forces during the First World War.

Arnaud, Rivière QC This river (150 km) in the region of Kativik in the north of Quebec flows east into Ungava Bay. It was earlier named *Rivière Payne* (the river's source was Lake Payne, named in the 1880s after meteorologist Frank F. Payne). The river was renamed in 1968 after Oblate Fr. Charles-André Arnaud (1826–1914), who had served in the 1870s at Fort Chimo (now Kuujjuaq).

Arnold's Cove NL The name of this town (1972) on Placentia Bay, and near the narrowest part of the Isthmus of Avalon, is found in population returns of 1836. The name may have been given after the forename of a fisherman.

Arnprior ON A town (1892) in Renfrew County, Arnprior was named in 1831 by brothers George and Andrew Buchanan after their birthplace in Stirlingshire, Scotland, north of Glasgow. Their cousin, Archibald McNab, opened McNab Township and persuaded them to build mills at the mouth of the Madawaska River.

Aroostook NB This village (1966) is located on the west bank of the Saint John River and at the mouth of the Aroostook River, south of Grand Falls. Its post office was first called *Arestook* in 1852 and renamed Aroostook two years later. The river, which rises in the state of Maine, was named from the Maliseet *woolahstook* ('good river for everything'), the same description they used for the Saint John River above tide. The river's name took several forms after 1699; it was spelled Arassatuk until 1832, when map-maker Joseph Bouchette (1774–1841) called it *Ristook* or *Aroostook River*. Surveyor General Thomas Baillie (1796–1863) settled on the

present form in the 1850s. In 1839 a boundary dispute called the Aroostook War broke out between New Brunswick and Maine in the river's valley, with each side calling out its troops. The route of the boundary was resolved three years later by the Webster–Ashburton Treaty.

Arrowsmith, Mount BC East of Port Alberni on Vancouver Island, this mountain (1817 m) was named about 1853 after British map-maker Aaron Arrowsmith (1750–1823) and his nephew John Arrowsmith (1790–1873), who continued the Arrowsmith reputation for excellence in cartography.

Artemesia ON This township in Grey County became part of the municipality of Grey Highlands in 2001. The township was named by Lt-Gov Peregrine Maitland (1777–1854) in 1822 after the Greek *artemisia*, a genus of plants.

Arthabaska QC A regional county in the area of Victoriaville, southeast of Quebec City, it was named in 1982 after the township of **Arthabaska**. The township was proclaimed in 1802, and was named after the Cree *ayabaskaw* ('place of bulrushes and reeds'). The former town of **Arthabaska** has been part of the city of Victoriaville since 1994.

Arthur ON This township in Wellington County was named in 1835 for Arthur Wellesley, the Duke of Wellington (1769–1852). The village (1871) of **Arthur** was named in 1847.

Arthur Wheeler, Mount YT In the St. Elias Mountains, this mountain was named in 1970 by the Alpine Club of Canada after surveyor Arthur Oliver Wheeler (1860–1945), who was the founder and first president of the club.

Artillery Lake NT Northeast of Great Slave Lake, this lake (535 km²) was named in 1834 by explorer Sir George Back (1796–1872) after the Royal Artillery. Some of Back's crew were members.

Arviat NU Located on the west coast of Hudson Bay and near the centre of Canada, this hamlet (1977) received its name in 1989, replacing *Eskimo Point*. The name means 'place of the bowhead whale' in Inuktitut. The hamlet was first settled in 1946 and *Eskimo Point* post office opened here two years later.

Arvida QC Now in the city of Saguenay, Arvida was an incorporated town from 1926 to 1975. Its name was devised from the first two letters of each name of Arthur Vining Davis. He was then the president of Alcoa, the Aluminum Company of America, whose subsidiary, the Aluminum Company of Canada, built an aluminum plant here in 1925.

Asbestos QC The name of this town (1939) in the regional county of **Asbestos**, north of Sherbrooke, first occurred in

1884, five years after prospector Evan William found asbestos here. The regional county was known as *L'Or-Blanc* from 1982 to 1990, after which it was changed to Asbestos.

Ascot QC In the regional county of Sherbrooke, east of the city of Sherbrooke, this municipality was named in 1989 after the township of **Ascot**. The township was named in 1803 after a village in England's Berkshire, west of London. The municipality of **Ascot Corner** was named in 1901.

Ashcroft BC A village (1952) on the Thompson River, west of Kamloops, it was named in 1865 after the Ashcroft Ranch, established in 1862 by brothers Clement Francis and Henry Pennant Cornwall. The ranch was named after their family home in England. The Canadian Pacific Railway laid out the present site in 1880. The post office was called *Ashcroft Station* from 1886 to 1899, when it was changed to Ashcroft.

Ashfield ON In 2001 this township and the townships of Colborne and Wawanosh became the township of **Ashfield-Colborne-Wawanosh** in Huron County. Ashfield Township was named in 1840 after Ashfield in Suffolk, England, the home of Lord Thomas John Thurlow (1838–1916). He was the son-in-law of Lord Elgin (1811–63), governor general of Canada, 1847–54.

Asperity Mountain BC In the Waddington Range of the Coast Mountains, this mountain (3716 m) was named in 1928 by Walter Alfred (Don) Munday (1890–1950). He chose the name because the mountain's sharp features established a mood of danger among climbers.

Asphodel ON This township in Peterborough County was named in 1821 by Lt-Gov Peregrine Maitland (1777–1854) after *asphodelus*, a Greek word for the lily family and the daffodil. In classical mythology, dead heroes wandered sadly in the asphodel fields.

Aspy Bay NS On the northeast side of Cape Breton Island, just south of Cape North, this community likely took its name from the Mi'kmaq *kespoogwit* ('end place'). A Basque map of the early 1600s displays *Aispe* in the area. Pierre Jumeau's map of 1685 has *B. d'Aspé*, while earlier maps locate *C. Gaspa* at Cape North. There would appear to be a connection with Gaspé in Quebec.

Asquith SK This town (1908) west of Saskatoon had its station and post office named in 1907 by the Canadian Pacific Railway after Herbert Henry Asquith, 1st Earl of Asquith (1852–1928), Liberal prime minister of Great Britain, 1908–16. The Canadian National Railways had a station called Iwona (a Polish girl's name) near the CPR station, so the CNR called it Asquith. Locally the name was *South Asquith*.

Assiginack ON A township in Manitoulin District, it was named in 1864 for Jean-Baptiste Assiginack (c.1768–1866), a chief of the Ottawa nation, and the chief interpreter for the Manitoulin Island region in the early 1800s. His son, Francis Assikinack (1824–63), was also an interpreter and teacher.

Assiniboia SK Situated southwest of Moose Jaw, this town (1913) was named in 1912 by the Canadian Pacific Railway after the district of *Assiniboia*, which was the southern part of present Saskatchewan and a part of southern Alberta between 1882 and 1905. The district was named after the Saulteaux nation's *ahsinipwan* ('Stoney Sioux'). The first post office from 1908 to 1912 in the area of Assiniboia was called Leeville after Hubbard Lee. He took his store to Assiniboia in 1912, then sold it in 1916 and moved to British Columbia. Louis Riel (1844–85) first proposed Assiniboia as the name of Canada's fifth province in 1870, but subsequently substituted Manitoba.

Assiniboine River MB, SK The principal western tributary of the Red River, it rises north of Yorkton, SK, and flows southeast, then east through Brandon, Portage la Prairie, and Winnipeg. In Ojibwa the name describes the Siouan tribe's practice of cooking their food by using heated stones. The tribe was first encountered in the area of the Lake of the Woods and Lake Winnipeg, and Pierre Gaultier de La Vérendrye (1685–1755) referred to the people as Assiniboils in 1730. In his 1738–9 journal, La Vérendrye called the river *rivière des Assibiboiles*, and its junction with the Red as la *fourche de Assiliboiles*.

Assiniboine, Mount AB, BC Southwest of Banff, this mountain was named in 1884 by geologist George M. Dawson (1849–1901) after the Assiniboine, a variant name of the Stoney tribe of the Siouan nation.

Aston-Jonction QC A village (1951) in the regional county of Nicolet-Yamaska, northwest of Victoriaville, it was named after the township of **Aston**, created in 1806, and the crossing of two rail lines. Aston derives from Ashton-under-Lyne, on the northeast side of Manchester, England.

Athabasca AB The Hudson's Bay Company post of *Athabasca Landing* was established north of Edmonton in 1877. Located on the **Athabasca River**, this community's post office opened in 1901. Incorporated as the town of *Athabasca Landing* in 1911, it became Athabasca two years later. At the beginning of the nineteenth century both geographer David Thompson (1770–1857) and fur trader Peter Fidler (1769–1822) called the river Athabasca. The name was likely adapted from the Cree *athabaska*, 'where there are reeds', describing the mouth of the river on the southwestern side of **Lake Athabasca**. Peter Pond (1740–1807) identified Lake Athabasca (7936 km², with about three-quarters in Saskatchewan) as *Great Araubaska* on a 1790 map. **Athabasca Pass** (1748 m) was discovered by David Thompson in 1810. **Mount Athabasca** (3491 m) was named in 1898 by British climber Norman Collie (1859–1942). In 1882 the district of Athabasca was created as part of the North-West Territories, but in 1902 the Geographic Board of Canada renamed the district, the town, and all names with Athabasca to *Athabaska*. In 1948 the board restored the preferred local spelling.

Athens ON In 2001 Athens joined the township of Rear of Yonge and Escott to become the municipal township of **Athens and Rear of Yonge and Escott**. Athens was a village (1888) in the united counties of Leeds and Grenville, northwest of Brockville. It was first known as *Dixon's Corners* and Bates' Mills before it was named *Farmersville* in 1836. In 1888, after a new high school joined a grammar school and a model school for teachers, merchant Arza Parish was inspired to rename the educational centre for the Greek classical city of education and learning.

Athol ON In 1998 this township became part of the municipality of Prince Edward County. It was named in 1835 after the Atholl district of Perthshire, Scotland.

Atholville NB The post office of this village (1966), on the south shore of the Restigouche River and on the west side of Campbellton, was called *Shives Athol* in 1906 after Athol House. The house was built in the early 1800s by Robert Ferguson, a native of Blair Atholl, Scotland, who settled here in 1796. Another post office called *Ferguson Manor* was opened in 1916 and was renamed Atholville in 1922.

Atikokan ON A township in Thunder Bay District, between Thunder Bay and Fort Frances, Atikokan was a divisional point of the Canadian Northern Railway in 1899, taking its name from Atikokan River, whose name means 'caribou bones' in Ojibwa. An open-pit mine began operating in 1939, and a planned community was laid out three years later.

Atikonak Lake NL The name of this lake (358 km²), south of Churchill Falls, derives from the Montagnais word for 'whitefish lake'.

Atlin BC Atlin is located on the east shore of **Atlin Lake** (589 km²), and in the northwestern part of the province. The post office in this community was named in 1899. The name of the 95-km-long lake derives from the Inland Tlingit *ahklen* or *aht'lah* ('big lake').

Atna Peak BC Located in the Coast Mountains, southeast of Kitimat, this mountain (2755 m) was named about 1907 after the Carrier word for 'strangers' or 'other people'. **Atna Lake** lies to the northeast of the peak.

Attawapiskat ON Located on the **Attawapiskat River**, northwest of Moosonee, the Hudson's Bay Company trading post *Attawapiscat House* was established in 1900. Attawapiskat post office opened in 1961. The name possibly derives from the Cree *atawao* ('he trades') and *pisket* ('divided'), suggesting a 'trading post beside a divided outlet' of the river.

Augusta ON This township in the united counties of Leeds and Grenville was named in 1787 for Princess Augusta Sophia (1768–1840), second daughter of George III.

Augusta, Mount YT On the Yukon–Alaska boundary, and in the St. Elias Mountains, this mountain (4289 m) was named in 1891 by American geologist Israel C. Russell (1852–1906) after his wife J. Augusta (Olmsted) Russell.

Augustine Cove PE Situated southeast of Borden, this community had a post office from 1854 to 1913. It was called after the adjacent cove, named in 1765 by Surveyor General Samuel Holland (1728–1801) after Lt. Col. Augustin Prévost, the father of Sir George Prévost (1767–1816). The father, a native of Switzerland, had joined the British Army and took part in the capture of Quebec in 1759, and was the governor-in-chief of British North America, 1811–15.

Aulac NB Located east of Sackville, this community's post office was first named *Westmorland Point* in 1853. It was renamed Aulac in 1919 after the **Aulac River**, which flows into the Tantramar River. As early as 1768, map-maker John Montresor (1736–88) noted *au Lac* as a populated place. Nova Scotia Surveyor General Charles Morris (1731–1802) called the river *R du Lac* in 1756. The present name was settled in 1901 by Surveyor General Thomas Loggie.

Aulavik National Park NT Located on the north side of Banks Island, this national park (12,275 km²) was established in 1992 to protect the sensitive environment in the area of Thomsen River. Its name in Inuvialuktun means 'place where people travel'.

Aulds Cove NS On the mainland side of the Canso Causeway, this community was named after Alexander Auld, who operated grist and saw mills here before 1833. There was postal service here as early as 1841, with Aulds Cove post office opening in 1877.

Aurora ON This town (1888) in York Region was named in 1854 on the suggestion of merchant and first postmaster Charles Doan. He may have been prompted to suggest the name of the Greek goddess of the dawn as a reflection of a new dawn of prosperity on that part of Yonge Street.

Ausable River ON Called by the French in the 1700s *Rivière aux Sables* ('sandy river'), this river is characterized by a long sandy beach in the area of Grand Bend, where it enters Lake Huron. Before 1892, it made a sharp bend at the village, and flowed south for 16 km to enter the lake at present Port Franks.

Austerity, Mount BC In the Selkirk Mountains, this mountain (3347 m) was named in 1911 by climber Howard Palmer (1883–1944). The west side climb was said by Palmer to be very difficult.

Austin MB The Canadian Pacific Railway station here was named in 1881 by the Marquess of Lorne (1845–1914) after Sidney Austin, a correspondent for the *London Graphic*, who followed the progress of track being laid west. Its post office opened two years later. It had been earlier called *Three Creeks*. *See also* Sidney.

Austin QC This municipality in the regional county of Memphrémagog, southwest of Magog, was named in 1938 after Loyalist Nicholas Austin, who settled here in the 1790s.

Australia Mountain YT Located southeast of Dawson, this mountain (1593 m) was named after Australian miners who prospected the nearby creeks for gold after 1891.

Auyuittuq National Park NU On the east side of Baffin Island, and north of Pangnirtung, this park reserve (21,471 km²) was established as *Baffin Island National Park* in 1972. It was renamed three years later after the Inuktitut word *auyuittuq* ('land of the big ice' or literally 'place that does not melt').

Avalanche Mountain BC In the Selkirk Mountains, this mountain (2864 m) was named in 1881 by Maj. Albert Rogers (1829–89) after his Shuswap assistants encountered a snowslide on its west side. Subsequently, the Canadian Pacific Railway built snowsheds after avalanches had disrupted traffic through Rogers Pass.

Avalanche Peak YT In the St. Elias Mountains, this peak (4212 m) was named in 1958 by George Wallerstein, who had led an expedition from southern California to the St. Elias Mountains the previous year. His party observed a huge avalanche sweep down from the peak.

Avalon Peninsula NL Joined to the main part of Newfoundland by the **Isthmus of Avalon**, this peninsula comprises four distinct peninsulas. It was named the *Province of Avalon* in 1623 by Sir George Calvert, Baron Baltimore (c.1580–1632) after the original site of Avalon, the island of the blessed in Somerset, England in the time of King Arthur. By 1813 it was known as a peninsula.

Avignon QC This regional county, extending from the mouth of the Rivière Matapédia in the west to Maria in the east was established in 1981. The name probably derives from a former post office (1886–1922) near present-day Saint-Alexis-de-Matapédia, west of the mouth of the river. The county was likely named after the famous city in the south of France.

Avondale NL Near the head of Conception Bay, this town (1974) was first known as *Salmon Cove*. It was renamed in 1906 after Avondale, County Wicklow, Ireland.

Avonlea SK This village (1912) was established in 1911 by the Canadian Northern Railway on its Moose Jaw-Radville line, southeast of Moose Jaw. It was named after a fictional village in Lucy Maud Montgomery's *Anne of Green Gables* (1908); Montgomery had relatives who had settled in the area. The post office had been called *New Warren* in 1904 after Warren, MN. It was renamed Avonlea in 1912.

Avon River ON This tributary of the North Thames River was first known as the *Little Thames River*. It was renamed about 1833 in association with the naming of Stratford.

Axel Heiberg Island NU One of the Sverdrup Islands and in the Queen Elizabeth Islands, this island (43,178 km²) was named *Heiberg Land* in 1900 by Otto Sverdrup (1854–1930), during his 1898–1902 Norwegian Arctic expedition, after Consul Axel Heiberg, a Norwegian patron.

Ayer's Cliff QC This village (1909) in the regional county of Memphrémagog and at the south end of Lac Massawippi, southeast of Magog, was named *Ayer's Flat* in 1836 after Thomas Ayer, the first settler here. Believing that 'Flat' suggested marshy and low land, it was renamed in 1904 to stimulate the sale of shoreline lots.

Aylen Lake ON Situated on the south border of Algonquin Park, this lake was known as *Little Opeongo Lake* before being renamed about 1850 for Ottawa Valley lumberman Peter Aylen (1799–1868).

Aylesford NS In the Annapolis Valley, west of Kentville, this village (1968) had its post office named in 1836 after the former *Aylesford Township*, created in 1786. The township was named after the 4th Earl of Aylesford (1751–1812), George III's lord steward of the household.

Aylmer ON A town (1887) in Elgin County, it was first known as *Hodgkinson's Corners* after long-time town clerk and postmaster Philip Hodgkinson. Some Americans from Troy, NY, wanted to call it Troy, but this connection suggested disloyalty to the Crown. It was named in 1838 for Matthew Whitworth-Aylmer, 5th Baron Aylmer (1775–1850), governor-in-chief of British North America, 1830-5. To distinguish it from Aylmer, QC, *Aylmer West* was often added to postmarks.

Aylmer QC In 2003 Aylmer became a sector of the city of Gatineau. Aylmer had been a city (1975) in the Communauté-Urbaine-de-l'Outaouais, west of Hull. It was first known in 1816 as *Symmes Landing* after Charles Symmes, a nephew of Hull founder Philemon Wright. It was renamed in 1848 after Lord Aylmer (1775–1850), governor-in-chief of British North America, 1830-5.

Aylmer Lake NT Northeast of Great Slave Lake, this lake (809 km²) was named in 1834 by explorer Sir George Back after Lord Aylmer (1775–1850), governor-in-chief of British North America, 1830–5.

Azilda ON In 2001 this community became part of the city of Greater Sudbury, Sudbury Region. This place was named *St. Azilda* in 1891 for Azilda Brisebois, the wife of Joseph Bélanger, who had settled here in the 1880s. When it was found no such saint existed, it was renamed Rayside in 1900 after the township. Residents wanted *St. Azilda* reinstated, but it was restored as simply Azilda in 1901. In 1773 Azilda was part of the town of Rayside-Balfour.

B

Babbage River YT Flowing northeast into the Beaufort Sea, southeast of Herschel Island, this river was named in 1826 by Sir John Franklin (1786–1847) after Charles Babbage (1792–1871), British mathematician and computer scientist. In 1834 Babbage conceived the principles of the modern computer.

Babine Lake BC The name of this lake (479 km²), located north of Burns Lake and near the centre of the province, means 'a large or pendulous lip' in French, which describes the distended lip of young Carrier women. Fort Babine (also called *Kilmar's Fort*) was located on the lake by the Hudson's Bay Company in 1822.

Baccaro Point NS The name of this place in the south-western part of the province may have a French origin. A 1631 map by Jean Guérard identified a bay here as B. *Careaux*, perhaps describing the right-angled bend in present Barrington Passage. Jean-Baptiste-Louis Franquelin (c.1653–1712) referred to the point as *Pte de Baccaro* in 1686. The name is less likely associated with Portuguese *baccalau* ('codfish'). The communities of **West Baccaro** and **East Baccaro** are located at the point.

Back River NU Rising northeast of Great Slave Lake, this river (974 km) flows northeast into Chantrey Inlet, an inlet of the Arctic Ocean. It was named Backs River in 1902 after Capt. Sir George Back (1796–1878), who explored the river in 1834. The name was changed to its present form by the Geographic Board in 1926. Back had called it *Thlew-ee-choh* or *Great Fish River*. Thlew-ee-choh is possibly Dogrib for 'great fish river'.

Baddeck NS The name of this village (1950) on Cape Breton Island derives from the Mi'kmaq *petecook* ('lying on the backward turn'), in reference to the entrance to the southwest flowing **Baddeck River**. Postal service at Baddeck dates from 1837, with *Bedeque* being commonly used in the early years. *See also* Bedeque.

Badger NL At the confluence of **Badger Brook** and the Exploits River, west of Grand Falls-Windsor, this town (1963) was organized as a sawmilling centre in 1908 by the Anglo-Newfoundland Development Company. The name may derive from the English fishermen looking for otters here for their skins, who also worked on the brooks flowing in to Badger Bay on the coast, north of Grand Falls-Windsor.

Badger's Quay NL This neighbourhood, in the town of New-Wes-Valley and on the northwest side of Bonavista Bay, was settled in the mid-1800s. The name was first recorded as *Badger's Key* in the 1880s in the parish records of Pool's Island. It is possible that the place took its name from a ship.

Badham, Mount YT In the St. Elias Mountains, and at the head of Donjek Glacier, this mountain (3848 m) was named in 1919 after boundary surveyor Francis Molyneaux Badham. He was killed during the First World War, while serving in the Canadian Army.

Baffin Island NU Canada's largest island (507,451 km²), and the fifth largest in the world, was named in 1819 by Sir William E. Parry (1790–1855) after William Baffin (d.1622). With Robert Bylot, Baffin explored the waters of Davis Strait and **Baffin Bay** in 1615–6. Although they carefully explored the coasts and inlets of Devon and Baffin Islands, they failed to investigate Lancaster Sound, the main eastern entrance to the Northwest Passage.

Baie-Comeau QC Located in the regional county of Manicouagan and on the north shore of the St. Lawrence River, this city had a post office named *Comeau Bay* in 1929 after noted writer Napoléon-Alexandre Comeau (1848–1923). The present form was adopted in 1936, when a pulp and paper mill was built by the *Chicago Tribune*'s Col. Robert McCormick (1880-1955), and the city was incorporated the following year.

Baie-d'Urfé QC In 2002 this town became part of Montreal. In 2006 Baie-d'Urfé was restored as a town. It is located between Sainte-Anne-de-Bellevue and Beaconsfield. It was named *Baie-d'Urfée* in 1911 (corrected 1960) after the adjacent bay of Lac Saint-Louis. The bay's name was given after pioneer missionary François-Saturnin Lascaris d'Urfé (1641–1701), who was the first resident priest here in 1686.

Baie-James QC This municipality in west central Quebec, embracing an area of 333,000 km², was named in 1972 after James Bay. The bay had been named in honour of navigator Thomas James (c.1593–1635), who explored it and Hudson Bay in 1631-2.

Baie-Saint-Paul QC Located in the regional county of Charlevoix, northeast of Quebec City, the town and parish municipality were named after the adjoining bay, whose name occurred in references before the mid-1600s. The parish was called *Saint-Pierre-et-Saint-Paul-de-la-Baie-Saint-Paul* in 1855, and was shortened to the current name in 1964. The town was incorporated in 1913, having been made a village in 1893.

Baie-Sainte-Anne NB On the south side of Miramichi Bay, the post office here was named in 1917, taking its name from the adjacent bay. Settled in the 1760s by Acadians, the bay was first identified on maps as *French Bay* and *Lower Bay du Vin*.

Baie-Trinité QC A village (1955) in the regional county of Manicouagan, northeast of the city of Baie-Comeau, it is at the mouth of the Rivière de la Trinité, noted on maps as early as 1682.

Baie Verte NB, NS At the head of **Baie Verte**, a 27-km extension of Northumberland Strait, this community was first settled in 1700 by Acadians. After their expulsion in 1755, it was resettled in 1761 by New Englanders, who retained the French name. The name was given for the green salt-water grasses at the head of the bay. French map-maker Pierre Jumeau called the bay *B. Verte ou de S. Claude* in 1685. Although English map-maker Herman Moll referred to it as *Green Bay* in 1715, English chart-maker Joseph Frederick Wallet DesBarres used *Bay Verte* in 1779, and the French form subsequently prevailed.

Baie Verte NL On the north coast of Newfoundland and at the head of **Baie Verte** ('green bay'), the names of this town (1958) and the bay relate to the period of French occupation on the French Shore both before 1763, the date of the transfer of the island to British title, and by French migratory fishermen until 1904.

Baker Brook NB The post office of this village (1967) on the Saint John River and at the mouth of Rivière Baker-Brook, 16 km southwest of Edmundston, opened as Baker's Brook in 1851. It was called Gagnon, after postmaster Jean Gagnon, from 1882 to 1893, when it was renamed Baker Brook. The river was identified in 1792 by surveyor Isaac Hedden as *Marienequactacook*, adapted from its Maliseet name, meaning 'turtle river'. Maps in the mid-1800s referred to it as *Bakers R* and *Baker's Brook* after John Baker (1796–1868), who opposed British sovereignty in the 1820s and '30s, touching off a boundary dispute between New Brunswick and Maine. The route of the boundary was settled by the Webster–Ashburton Treaty in 1842. *See also* Aroostook *and* Lac-Baker.

Baker Lake NU This hamlet (1977) on the north shore of Baker Lake was founded after the Second World War as an Inuit settlement. The lake (1783 km²) was named in 1761 by Capt. William Christopher after Sir William and Richard Baker, brothers associated with the Hudson's Bay Company.

Christopher had entered Chesterfield Inlet and explored it for 150 km in search of the Northwest Passage.

Balcarres SK This town (1951) east of Fort Qu'Appelle established its post office in 1884. It had been settled about 1880, with settlers having to haul their grain some 20 km south to Indian Head, whose postmaster was Robert Balcarres Crawford. There is a Balcarres House, south of St. Andrews, Fifeshire, Scotland.

Baleine, Grande rivière de la QC With a length of 727 km, and draining an area of 44,735 km², this river flows west into Hudson Bay. It was first called Great Whale River in 1744, with the French form *R de la Grande Baleine* occurring on a map in 1914. The present form was adopted in 1962.

Balfour, Mount AB Northwest of Banff, this mountain (3272 m) was named in 1858 by Dr. Sir James Hector (1834–1907) after Scottish botanist John Hutton Balfour (1808–84).

Balgonie SK Located 25 km east of Regina, this town (1907) was named in 1882 by the Canadian Pacific Railway after the Balgonie estate and castle in Fifeshire, Scotland. Its post office opened in 1883.

Balmertown ON In Kenora District, northeast of Red Lake, this mining centre was named in 1948 after Balmer Township, which had been named earlier for Balmer Niely, an official of McIntyre-Porcupine Gold Mines of Timmins. In 1950 the township and parts of three adjoining townships became the improvement district of *Balmertown*, which was changed to the municipal township of Golden in 1985.

Balmoral NB This village (1972) east of Campbellton was laid out in 1856 and settled after 1874 under the free grants provisions. Its post office was named in 1875 after the sovereign's residence in Perthshire, Scotland, acquired by Prince Albert (1819–1861) in 1847. **Balmoral Parish** was established in 1876.

Bancroft ON A town (1996) in Hastings County, it was first known as *York Mills* and *York River*. It was renamed in 1879 by Senator Billa Flint after his mother-in-law, Elizabeth Ann Bancroft Clement, a New Hampshire native who died in Belleville in 1851.

Banff AB This town (1992) in **Banff National Park** took its name from a nearby station on the Canadian Pacific Railway, established in 1883. It was possibly proposed by Harry Sandison (1858–1942) of Winnipeg, a member of the National Parks Board, after his birthplace of Banff, Banffshire, Scotland. The national park (6641 km²) was called the *Rocky Mountains Park Reserve* in 1887 and it was renamed after the town in 1930.

Banks Island BC On the east side of Hecate Strait, south of Prince Rupert, this island was named in 1788 by Capt. Charles Duncan after Sir Joseph Banks (1743–1820), the noted English botanist and president of the Royal Society, 1778–1820.

Banks Island NT The most westerly of the islands of the Arctic Archipelago, this island (70,028 km²) was named in 1820 by Sir William Parry after Sir Joseph Banks (1743–1820). Banks travelled to Labrador and Newfoundland in 1766. He went around the world with James Cook in 1778.

Bannockburn ON In Hastings County, north of Madoc, this place was named in 1862 to celebrate the famous fourteenth-century victory of the Scots over the English at Bannockburn, near Stirling, Scotland.

Baptiste Lake ON Located in Hastings County, northwest of Bancroft, this lake may have been named after an Ojibwa chief called St. Jean Baptiste, who was met by surveyor John Allen Snow (1824–88) at the outlet of the lake in 1854–5.

Barachois NB This community east of Shediac had its post office named in 1853. A *barachois* is a pond enclosed by a bar at sea level. The term was introduced into East-Coast geographical terminology by the Basques and the Acadians, with its original application applying to a gravel bar where fishing boats could be beached.

Barachois QC The name of this community, in the town of Percé and the regional county of Pabok, may be traced to a map of 1689 by Basque pilot Pierres Detchevery in the form of Barrachoa. The word barachois means 'lagoon', a deformation of French *barre échouée* or *barre-à-cheoir*, and an apt description of **Barachois de Malbaie** adjacent to the community.

Barbeau Peak NU The highest peak (2616 m) east of the Rocky Mountains, it was named in 1969 by the Canadian Permanent Committee on Geographical Names after Marius Barbeau (1883–1969), a folklorist and ethnologist who studied the music and traditional songs of the Québécois and Aboriginal people.

Barkers Point NB In the city of Fredericton, and on the east side of the Nashwaak River, its post office was named in 1912 after **Barkers Point**. It was an incorporated village from 1966 to 1973, when it was annexed by the city. Andrew Barker settled at the point in 1825. His father, Thomas, was a Loyalist from New York, who received a grant of 202 ha (500 a) in the area of Maugerville, downriver from Barkers Point.

Barkerville BC This restored urban site and provincial historic park in the Cariboo was the site where William 'Billy' Barker (d.1894) made a huge strike in 1862, and launched

the fabled Cariboo gold rush. After 1900 the place fell into decline, becoming a ghost town in the 1950s.

Barkley Sound BC Southwest of Port Alberni and on the west coast of Vancouver Island, this wide bay comprising many islands and channels was named by Capt. Charles William Barkley (1759–1832) while sailing up the west coast in 1787.

Barnard, Mount AB, BC Located on the continental divide, southwest of Howse Pass, this mountain (3339 m) was named in 1924, after Sir Frank Stillman Barnard (1856–1936), lieutenant-governor of British Columbia, 1914–19.

Barnes Ice Cap NU In central Baffin Island, this ice cap was named in 1950 by Patrick Baird (1912–84) of the Arctic Institute of North America after Howard Turner Barnes (1873–1950) of McGill University, a pioneer in the study of ice.

Barnston QC This township municipality (1855) in the regional county of Coaticook, southwest of the town of Coaticook was named after the township. The township was named in 1795 after a village in Sussex, England and was proclaimed in 1801.

Barons AB This village (1910) northwest of Lethbridge was first called *Blayney* in 1907 by Jack Warnock after the town of Castleblayney in County Monaghan, Ireland. Two years later Canadian Pacific Railway purchasing agent C.S. Noble named the station after an official of the CPR, either George Stephen, 1st Baron Mount Stephen, or Donald Smith, 1st Baron Strathcona and Mount Royal. When the Union Bank opened, the village was named Baron's Bank. Other businesses followed suit, and the post office and station adopted Barons.

Barraute QC Located in the regional county of Abitibi, north of Val-d'Or, the village was named in 1918 after the township, whose name had been proclaimed two years earlier. It was given after Pierre-Jean Bachoie *dit* Barraute (1723–60), an officer of the Béarn Regiment, who died during the Battle of Sainte-Foy, 1760.

Barrhead AB Located northwest of Edmonton, this town (1946) had its post office named in 1914 by the Paddle River and District Co-operative after the hometown of James McGuire. He was born in Barrhead, Renfrewshire, Scotland, a southwestern suburb of Glasgow.

Barrie ON The city (1959) of Barrie was named by surveyor William Hawkins in 1832 after Sir Robert Barrie (1774–1841), the senior naval officer in Upper and Lower Canada and commissioner of the dockyard at Kingston, 1819–34. A township in Frontenac County and an island in Manitoulin District were also named after him.

Barrington NS At the head of **Barrington Bay** and in the southwestern part of the province, this place was settled in 1761 by the families of New England fishermen from Cape Cod and Nantucket Island. Barrington Township was created in 1767, and named after William Wildman Barrington, 2nd Viscount Barrington (1717–93), British secretary of war, 1755–61 and 1765-78, and chancellor of the exchequer, 1761–2. Barrington post office opened in 1843. The community of Barrington Passage, on the passage separating Cape Sable Island from the mainland, received a post office in 1855.

Barrow Strait NU Part of Parry Channel, with Devon and Cornwallis Islands on the north, and Somerset Island on the south, this strait was named in 1819 by Sir William Parry after Sir John Barrow (1766–1848).

Barry's Bay ON The adjacent bay was probably named for lumberman William Byers (c.1810–85). In 1847 surveyor John Haslett noted Byers's hay farm nearby, but wrote Barry's Bay for the 8-km arm of Kaminiskeg Lake, and this mistake was repeated by subsequent surveyors and map-makers. The village was incorporated in 1932. In 2001, it became part of the township of Madawaska Valley.

Barss Corner NS In Lunenburg County, northwest of Bridgewater, this community was first known as *Centreville*. The site of *New Germany* post office in 1854, it was renamed Barss Corner in 1882 after an early settler.

Bartibog Bridge NB This community located at the mouth of **Bartibog River**, 13 km northeast of Chatham (a section of the city of Miramichi), had its post office named in 1878 after the bridge over the river. The river, identified on a 1785 map by its present name, may have been called after the Mi'kmaq chief Bartabogue by both the French and the English.

Bas-Caraquet NB On the shore of Chaleur Bay and east of the town of Caraquet, this village called its post office *Lower Caraquet* in 1877. It was renamed Bas-Caraquet in 1955. The village was first incorporated as Lower Caraquet in 1966, but was changed to Bas-Caraquet five years later.

Bashaw AB The post office in this town (1964) south of Camrose was named in 1910 after settler Eugene Bashaw, who owned the townsite.

Baskatong Réservoir QC Situated near the head of the Rivière Gatineau, northwest of the town of Mont-Laurier, this reservoir was created in 1926–7. It was named in 1962 after the township of Baskatong, given about 1870 after an Algonquin word for 'place where sand holds back the water'.

Bassano AB On the main line of the Canadian Pacific Railway, the station of this town (1911) was named in 1884 after the Marquis de Bassano, a native of Italy, who was a CPR shareholder.

Bass River NS On the north shore of Cobequid Bay, west of Truro, this community was founded in 1765. Located on a river known for its bass fishing, its post office opened in 1869.

Bastard ON In 1998 the municipal township of Bastard and South Burgess became part of township of Rideau Lakes, united counties of Leeds and Grenville. The township of Bastard was named in 1798 for John Pollexfen Bastard (1756–1816), a British member of Parliament. His home was at Kitley, near Plymouth, Devon. *See also* Kitley.

Batawa ON In the municipality of Quinte West, north of Trenton to Frankford and Stiarling, this place was developed in 1939 as a company village by Czech-born shoe manufacturer Thomas John Bata (1914–2008). He added the last syllable to emulate the names of Ottawa and Oshawa. The factory was closed in 1999, but is being restored by his wife, Sonja Bata.

Batchawana Bay ON The name of this bay on the east shore of Lake Superior, north of Sault Ste. Marie, possibly derives from the Ojibwa *obatchiwanang* ('where the flowing water rises to a boil through the force of its current').

Bath NB A village (1966) on the east bank of the Saint John River, north of Woodstock, it opened its post office in 1853 as *Munquart*, after the Munquart River. It was renamed Bath in 1868, possibly after the city of Bath in Somerset, England, or after Bath at the mouth of the Kennebec River in Maine.

Bath ON In Lennox and Addington County, west of Kingston, this village (1859) was named in 1819 after the famous English city on the River Avon, east of Bristol.

Bathurst NB This city (1966) in the northern part of the province was named in 1826 by Lt.-Gov. Sir Howard Douglas (1776–1861) after Henry Bathurst, 3rd Earl Bathurst (1762–1834), who was then Britain's secretary of war and for the colonies. Acadian governor Nicolas Denys (c.1598–1688) referred to it as *Nipisiguit*, after the Nepisiguit River, when he wrote *Description géographique et historique des costes de l'Amérique septentrionale* here in 1672. His son Richard Denys de Fronsac called it *St-Pierre*, when he lived here from 1671 to 1687. It was subsequently called *St. Peters* by the early English settlers.

Bathurst ON This township in Lanark County was named in 1816 for Henry, 3rd Earl Bathurst (1762–1834), then Britain's secretary of war and the colonies. He was the son-in-law of the Duke of Richmond (1764–1819), governor-in-chief of British North America, 1818–9, and a brother-in-law of Lady Sarah Maitland (1792–1873), whose husband, Sir Peregrine Maitland (1777–1854), was lieutenant-governor of Upper Canada,

1818–28. In 1998, the municipal township became part of the township of Bathurst Burgess and Sherbrooke. In 2002 the township became part the new township of Tay Valley.

Bathurst, Cape NT Northeast of Tuktoyaktuk, this cape extends into the Arctic Ocean, with Beaufort Sea on the west, and Amundsen Gulf on the east. It was likely named in 1826 by Sir John Richardson after Henry, 3rd Earl of Bathurst (1762–1834), secretary of war and for the colonies, 1812–27, and president of the council, 1828-30.

Bathurst Inlet NU A long inlet of the Arctic Ocean, southwest of the hamlet of Cambridge Bay, it was named in 1821 by Sir John Franklin (1786–1847) after Henry, 3rd Earl of Bathurst (1762–1834). The locality of **Bathurst Inlet**, on the west side of the inlet and at the mouth of the Burnside River, was the site of a Hudson's Bay Company post from 1944 to 1964, when it was moved to the present site of Umingmaktok, on the east side of the inlet. *See also* Umingmaktok.

Bathurst Island NU One of the Queen Elizabeth Islands, this island (16,042 km²) was named in 1819 by Sir William Parry (1790–1855) after Henry, 3rd Earl of Bathurst. In 1851 Capt. William Penny (1809–92) named it Queen Victoria Island, but Parry's earlier name was adopted by the Geographic Board in 1905.

Batiscan QC This municipality at the mouth of Rivière Batiscan and in the regional county of Francheville, northeast of Trois-Rivières, was named in 1986 after the parish of Saint-François-Xavier-de-Batiscan, which had been erected in 1845. Samuel de Champlain (1567–1635) mentioned the river in 1603, and referred to an Aboriginal captain called Batiscan in 1610. Among suggested meanings of the name are 'mist', 'light cloud', and 'reeds at the mouth'.

Batoche SK Located on the east bank of the South Saskatchewan River, northeast of Saskatoon, this historic locality was founded in 1871 by ferry operator François-Xavier Letendre *dit* Batoche (1841–1901). In 1885 it was Louis Riel's headquarters, and the site where Gen. Sir Frederick Middleton (d.1770) defeated the Métis leader Gabriel Dumont (1837–1906) in May of that year. Its post office opened in 1884.

Battleford SK On the south bank of the North Saskatchewan River and at the mouth of the **Battle River**, this town (1904) was chosen in 1875 as the capital of the North-West Territories, and its post office opened two years later. The North West Mounted Police built Fort Battleford here in 1876. It was eclipsed in 1905, when the Canadian Northern Railway built its line on the north side of the North Saskatchewan. The Battle River, which rises in Battle and Pigeon lakes southwest of Edmonton, recalls several battles between the Cree and the Blackfoot.

Bawlf AB The Canadian Pacific Railway station in this village (1906), southeast of Camrose, was named in 1905 after Nicholas Bawlf (1849–1914) of Winnipeg, co-founder and president of the Northern Elevator Company and the N. Bawlf Grain Company. The post office, first called *Molstad*, was renamed Bawlf in 1907.

Bay Bulls NL This town (1986) on the east coast of the Avalon Peninsula was named after the bay. The bay was identified in 1592 as *B of Bulls* by map-maker Thomas Hood. It may have been called after the bull bird (*Plautus alle alle*), a common seabird also known as the dovekie, which winters along the coasts of Newfoundland.

Bay de Verde NL This town (1950) near the north side of **Bay de Verde Peninsula**, an extension of Avalon Peninsula, may have taken its name from the Portuguese *y verde* on the La Cosa map of 1500. However, the first direct reference to it was John Guy's *Greene bay* in 1612, with variants of the present name not occurring until the late 1600s.

Bay du Vin NB At the mouth of **Bay du Vin River**, 26 km east of Chatham (a part of the city of Miramichi), this community had its post office named in 1853. The bay was originally called *Baie des Vents* after an incident about 1760, when a boat of the first French-speaking settlers was driven into the bay by a strong wind. Although Abraham Pineo Gesner (1797–1864) wrote in 1847 about 'Big Baie des Vents corrupted to big Betty Wind', a map as early as 1786 had *Baye du Vin*. A post office 22 km upriver was called Wine River from 1908 to 1951, wrongly assuming the name of Bay du Vin River was associated with wine.

Bayfield NB At the New Brunswick end of the Confederation Bridge leading to Prince Edward Island, this community's post office was named in 1866 after Admiralty surveyor Henry Wolsey Bayfield (1795–1885). He surveyed the waters of the New Brunswick coast before 1841.

Bayfield ON At the mouth of **Bayfield River**, south of Goderich, this village in Huron County was named in 1832 for Henry Wolsey Bayfield (1795–1885), who had surveyed the Great Lakes from 1816 to 1826. He recommended the place as a good site for a town. Established as a village in 1875, it became a police village in 1927, and reverted to a village in 1965. The Canada Company, which developed a large part of Southwestern Ontario, named the river in 1827. In 2001 the village became part of the municipality of Bluewater.

Bayham ON On January 1, 1998, Bayham became part of the municipality of Bayham/Port Burwell/Vienna. On January 31, 1998, it became the municipality of Bayham, Elgin County. It was named in 1810 for Charles Pratt, Earl Camden, and Viscount Bayham (1714-94).

Bay l'Argent NL The name of this town (1971), on the west side of the Burin Peninsula and near the head of Fortune Bay, derives from the French for 'bay of silver', perhaps in reference to the silvery light reflected from the surrounding cliffs.

Bay Roberts NL A town (1951) on the west side of Conception Bay, west of St. John's, it may have been named after a Jersey surname. The name appeared in its present form on several maps of the 1600s. The reference to *Bay of Robbers* in the 1681 calendar of state papers suggests its name may relate to an incident of robbery.

Bay St. Lawrence NS On Cape Breton Island and between Cape North and **Cape St. Lawrence**, this place was first settled in the 1830s. Its post office opened in 1853. In 1535 Jacques Cartier called the cape *cap de Lorraine*, which was subsequently rendered on maps as *C S Laurent*. Jacques Nicolas Bellin's 1744 map called the bay *Ance S Laurent*.

Baysville ON Located in the district municipality of Muskoka and at the southern end of the Lake of Bays, where the lake is drained by the South Branch Muskoka River, this community was named in 1874.

Baytona NL On Birchy Bay, an arm of the Bay of Exploits, this place was called *Gayside* from 1976 to 1985. It was renamed, presumably by joining 'bay' to the last two syllables of Daytona Beach in Florida. It had previously been called *Birchy Bay North*.

Beachburg ON A village (1959) in Renfrew County, southeast of Pembroke, it was named for David Beach, a United Empire Loyalist, who received a grant of 405 ha (1000 a) here in 1835. His family of five sons and four daughters ran grist- and sawmills, a tannery, a hotel, and the post office. In 1848 the post office was called *South Westmeath*, after Westmeath Township, and was changed to Beachburg 10 years later. In 2001 Beachburg became part of township of Whitewater Region.

Beachside NL On the southwestern side of Notre Dame Bay, this municipal community was incorporated in 1962 as *Wild Bight* after its location on a small bight whose waters are usually rough during the prevailing northeasterly winds. It was renamed Beachside in 1980.

Beaconsfield QC In 2002 Beaconsfield became part of the city of Montreal. Four years later it was restored as a city. Located between Baie-d'Urfé and Pointe-Claire, it was named in 1910, six years after the post office opened. The post office's name derives from an estate named in 1870 by J.H. Menzies after Benjamin Disraeli, Earl of Beaconsfield (1804–81), prime minister of Great Britain, 1868, and 1874–80.

Beardmore ON In Thunder Bay District, west of Geraldton, this municipal township (1976) was named about 1920 for Walter William Beardmore, a Toronto industrialist, who was the son-in-law of Sir William Mackenzie (1849–1923), developer of the Canadian Northern Railway. It had been created an improvement district in 1945.

Bear River NS Southeast of Digby, this community is situated on the steep banks of the **Bear River**. Its post office was established as *Bear River West* in 1870, and changed to its present name in 1901. Portrayed as *Rivière Hébert* on Marc Lescarbot's 1606 map, the river was named after either apothecary Louis Hébert, Capt. Simon Imbert-Sandrier, or both. Presumably, Imbert-Sandrier sought refuge during a storm here about 1612 in the river's mouth. Several maps in the 1700s called the river *R Imbert*.

Beatton River BC Rising in the Rocky Mountains, west of the Alaska Highway, this river flows southeast into the Peace River, southeast of Fort St. John. It was named after Frank Wark Beatton (1865–1945), who was in charge of the Hudson's Bay Company post at Fort St. John for several years.

Beauce-Sartigan QC A regional county, south of Quebec City, it was named in 1982. The original Beauce County was created in 1829, taking its name from the seigneury of Nouvelle Beauce, established in 1739. Sartigan is a variant of *Mechatigan* and *Msakkikhan*, old Abnaki forms of the Rivière Chaudière, meaning 'shaded river' or 'noisy river'.

Beauceville QC Created as a town in 1904, it is in the regional county of Robert-Cliche, north of the city of Saint-Georges. Renamed *Beauceville-Ouest* in 1930 on the incorporation of the town of *Beauceville-Est*, the two were amalgamated as the town of Beauceville in 1973.

Beaudette, Rivière ON, QC This river rises near Apple Hill in Kenyon Township, and flows east into Quebec, entering the St. Lawrence River 3 km east of the Lancaster Township boundary. The name relates to the finding in the 1600s of a wire-frame bed (baudet) in the remains of a burned shack on nearby **Pointe Beaudette**.

Beaufort Sea NT, YT North of Yukon Territory, and west of Banks and Prince Patrick Islands in the Northwest Territories, this part of the Arctic Ocean was named in 1826 by Sir John Franklin (1786–1847) after Capt. (later Adm) Sir Francis Beaufort (1774–1857), who was then the hydrographer to the British Admiralty. He designed the Beaufort scale to measure the force of wind.

Beauharnois QC A town (1863) in the regional county of Beauharnois-Salaberry, southwest of Montreal, it was created as a village in 1846, taking its name from the seigneury of

Beauharnois. The seigneury was granted in 1729 to Claude de Beauharnois de Beaumont de Villechauve (1674–1738) and to Charles de Beauharnois de La Boische, Marquis de Beauharnois (1671–1749).

Beauharnois-Salaberry QC This regional county was erected in 1982, succeeding the former county of Beauharnois, which was created in 1829. 'Salaberry' recalls the name of the largest municipality in the regional county, Salaberry-de-Valleyfield, which took its name from Charles-Michel d'Irumberry de Salaberry (1788–1829), the hero of the Battle of Châteauguay, 1813. *See also* Salaberry-de-Valleyfield *and* Valleyfield.

Beaulac QC This village in the regional county of L'Amiante, south of the city of Thetford Mines, was named in 1896 after its location on the western shore of Lac Aylmer.

Beaumont AB This town (1973) south of Edmonton, had its post office named in 1895, possibly by John Royer, because its site revealed a good view of the surrounding landscape.

Beauport QC In 2002 this city became part of Quebec City and was changed to a borough of Quebec City in 2006. Beauport traces its roots back to the municipal parish of *Notre-Dame-de-Beauport*, established in 1855; to the religious parish of Notre-Dame-de-Miséricorde-de-Beauport, created in 1694; and to the reference to *Beau port* on a 1631 map by Jean Guérard.

Beaupré QC This town in the regional county of La Côte-de-Beaupré, northeast of Quebec City, was named in 1962, having been established as the municipal parish of *Notre-Dame-de-Rosaire* in 1928. The name has its roots in the early seventeenth-century phrase 'le beau pré', agglutinated into the name **Sainte-Anne-de-Beaupré** in 1657.

Beausejour MB Northeast of Winnipeg, this town (1912) was founded in 1877 by the Canadian Pacific Railway. It may have been named by a French-speaking engineer who was relieved to encounter an elevated gravel knoll, and pronounced his campsite *beau séjour* ('a good resting place'). The post office was established in 1881.

Beauval SK Northwest of Prince Albert, this community had its post office first called *Lac la Plonge* in 1910 after a nearby lake. It was changed to Bauval in 1912, and then to Beauval in 1915. Beauval means 'beautiful valley' in French.

Beaver Brook Station NB Located 16 km north of Newcastle (part of the city of Miramichi), this community had its post office named in 1907. The brook is a tributary of Bartibog River. When Newcastle-raised Max Aitken became a peer in 1917, he intended to take the title Lord Miramichi.

Local historian Louise Manny said he might be called 'Lord Merry Mickey' and encouraged him to choose another name. Recalling a Catholic priest at Beaver Brook Station who had once loaned him a surrey for an Orange parade, he took the title Lord Beaverbrook. It also gave him the opportunity to draw attention to Canada's national animal.

Beaver Creek YT At 140°38'W, and near the Alaska border, this is the farthest west community in Canada. It was established on **Beaver Creek**, a tributary of Snag Creek, about 1955, with its post office opening in 1958. The creek was named about 1902, and was prospected between 1909 and 1914.

Beaverlodge AB On the north bank of the Beaverlodge River and west of Grande Prairie, this town (1956) was first known as *Redwillow* in 1910, since Beaverlodge had already been given to a post office 20 km to the east at Lake Saskatoon. The townsite was developed in 1928 by the Edmonton, Dunvegan, and British Columbia Railway, and Beaverlodge post office was transferred here.

Becaguimec Stream NB Rising east of Woodstock, this river flows into the Saint John River at Hartland. The name is from the Maliseet *abekaguimek*, possibly meaning 'going up to the salmon bed'.

Bécancour QC This town in the regional county of **Bécancour** was created in 1965 through the amalgamation of several neighbouring municipalities. The name evolved from the seigneury of Bécancour, established in 1684 by Pierre Robinau, 2nd Baron de Portneuf (1654–1729). The regional county was created in 1982 from the county of Nicolet. **Rivière Bécancour** rises just west of Thetford Mines, and follows a circuitous course of 125 km to empty into the St. Lawrence, 12 km downriver from the mouth of the Rivière Saint-Maurice.

Beckwith ON This township in Lanark County was named in 1816 for Sir Thomas Sydney Beckwith (1772–1831), quartermaster general of British North America, 1813–23. He was assigned responsibility for the settlement of the military townships north of the Rideau River.

Bedeque PE Located southwest of Summerside, this place takes its name from **Bedeque Bay**. Noted as early as 1806, Bedeque's post office opened in 1827, although it was referred to as late as 1880 as *Centreville*. The bay's name derives from the Mi'kmaq *petekook* ('place that lies on the backward turn'), and the bay was identified by Jacques Nicolas Bellin (1703–72) in 1744 as Bedec. In 1765 Samuel Holland (1728–1801) renamed it *Halifax Bay,* after George Montagu Dunk, Earl of Halifax (1716–71), but it did not supplant the older name. *See also* Baddeck.

Bedford NS This urban community, located in the regional municipality of Halifax since 1 April 1996, was incorporated as a town in 1980 at the head of **Bedford Basin**. *Fort Sackville* was located here in 1749, with the place becoming known as Sackville. Its post office opened as *Bedford Basin* in 1856, with the Nova Scotia Railway station being called Bedford the same year. The basin was named after John Russell, 4th Duke of Bedford (1710–71), who was the secretary of state of the southern department in England when Halifax was founded in 1749. He was also the first lord of the Admiralty, 1744–8.

Bedford ON In 1998 this township became part of the township of South Frontenac, Frontenac County. It was named in 1798 for Francis Russell, 5th Duke of Bedford (1765–1802), noted for his experiments in agriculture and sheep breeding in Bedfordshire, England.

Bedford QC This town in the regional county of Brome-Missisquoi, southeast of the town of Cowansville, was created in 1890. It was named earlier in the 1800s, possibly after Francis Russell, 5th Duke of Bedford (1765–1802), who was noted for his experiments in agriculture and sheep breeding at Woburn in Bedfordshire, England, and was a close friend of the Prince of Wales (later George IV). The name may have been given after Bedford, NH, named after the 4th Duke of Bedford (1710–71), a statesman who negotiated the end of the Seven Years' War, 1757-62.

Beebe Plain QC A village on the Vermont border and in the regional county of Memphrémagog, south of the town of Magog, it was named in 1873 after Loyalist settlers Zeeba, David, and Calvin Beebe, who came from Vermont in 1789. It is locally known as Beebe.

Beechey Island NU On the south side of Devon Island, this island was named in 1819 by Sir William Parry (1790–1855) after Lt. Frederick (later RAdm. Sir Frederick) William Beechey (1796–1856), who had served on the *Hecla* during Parry's 1819–20 expedition. **Cape Beechey**, on the south side of Melville Island, was also named for him in 1820 by Parry.

Beeton ON In the town of New Tecumseth, Simcoe County, it was first known as *Clarksville* after Robert Clark, the first settler here. It was renamed in 1876 in honour of David Alanson Jones, noted as the 'bee king' and the founder of the Ontario Beekeepers Association. It is also said to have been named after Beeton Castle in Scotland, near the birthplace of Jones's mother-in-law.

Begbie, Mount BC Located southwest of Revelstoke in the Monashee Mountains, this mountain (2732 m) was named in 1886 by Dr. Otto Klotz (1852–1923) after Sir Matthew Baillie Begbie (1819–94), chief justice of British Columbia, 1869–94. He firmly established British law during turbulent times in the colony after 1858. There are two other mountains in the province named after him, one on the Queen Charlotte Islands, southwest of Masset Inlet, the other in the Cariboo, midway between 70 Mile House and 100 Mile House.

Behchokǫ NT This community (2005) is located at the head of the North Arm of Great Slave Lake. The community had taken over the hamlet of Rae-Edzo. Rae-Edzo was divided into two distinct communities, 24 km apart. **Rae** is the site of Fort Rae, established here by the Hudson's Bay Company in 1904, having been located 8 km to the southeast in 1852 by Dr. John Rae. **Edzo** was created in 1965 as a site with better drainage, but most of the Dogrib continued to live at the older location. The name Edzo recalls a Dogrib chief who worked out a peace settlement with the Yellowknife, a Chipewyan tribe, in the early nineteenth century. *See also* Rae-Edzo.

Beiseker AB Northeast of Calgary, this village (1921) was the centre of the 101,000 ha (250,000 a) Rosebud Tract purchased by the Calgary Colonization Company from the Canadian Pacific Railway. The company was owned by two wealthy North Dakota businessmen, one of whom was Thomas Beiseker, who donated the townsite in 1910. The CPR station was named that year.

Belcarra BC This village (1979), on the east side of the mouth of Indian Arm, and northwest of Port Moody was named in the 1870s by Judge Norman Bole after the Gaelic words *bal* ('sun') and *carra* ('cliff' or 'rock'). He stated that the name meant 'fair land of the sun'.

Belcher Islands NU On the southeast side of Hudson Bay, these islands may have been named as early as 1727 by William Coats (d.1752) of the Hudson's Bay Company after James Belcher, who supplied the HBC posts from 1715 to 1724.

Belfast PE This municipal community (1972) southeast of Charlottetown was named about 1770 by Capt. James Smith of the HMS *Mermaid* after Belfast, Ireland. Its post office opened in 1832. The municipality embraces the areas of Eldon, Point Prim, Pinette, Belle River, and Wood Islands.

Belgrave ON In 2001 this community became part of the township of North Huron, Huron County. Northeast of Goderich, it was named in 1865 after Belgrave in Leicestershire, England, 4 km north of Leicester. It was first called *Haggerty's Corners* after Dan Haggerty, who managed a tavern here.

Bella Coola BC This community, situated at the head of North Bentinck Arm and at the mouth of the Bella Coola River, established its post office in 1900, having been located at the site of Hagensborg five years earlier. The name of the river, derived from the Kwakiutl description of the Bellacoola tribe of the Coast Salish, was noted in 1862 as *Bel-houla* by Cdr. Richard Mayne.

Bellechasse QC A regional county, east of Quebec City, it was created in 1982 by amalgamating the counties of Bellechasse and Dorchester. The name traces its roots to the township of Bellechasse, created in 1871; to the seigneury of Bellechasse, established in 1672; and to Isle de Bellechasse, noted by Samuel de Champlain (1567–1635) in 1632.

Belledune NB A village (1968) on the south shore of Chaleur Bay, northwest of Bathurst, it had its post office named in 1845 after **Belledune Point**. In 1739 the point was referred to as *Grand Belle doune*, suggesting the sand dune here was perceived as being especially pretty (*belle*) by the French.

Belleisle Bay NB A northeasterly extension of the Saint John River, 28 km north of Saint John, this bay was named after Alexandre Le Borgne de Belle-Isle, who lived here after 1736. His father, also Alexandre (c.1643–1693), was an acting governor of Acadia in the late 1600s.

Belle Isle, Strait of NL Separating the island of Newfoundland from Labrador, this strait was first named *Grande Baye* before Jacques Cartier's 1534 voyage, when he called it *Baye des Chasteaux* after the striking castle-like basaltic rocks on present Castle and Henley Islands. The island at its entrance was first called *I de la Fortuna* by the Portuguese about 1500, and then *Belle Isle de la Grande Baye* by pilot Jean Fontenau *dit* Alfonse in his 1544 *Cosmographie*. The strait was subsequently named after the island.

Belleoram NL This town (1946) on the west side of Fortune Bay was named after a French adventurer who spent several winters here in the late 1600s. It was occupied by English settlers after 1713 and was initially known as *Belorme's Place*.

Belle River ON In 1999 this town (1969) became part of the town of Lakeshore, Essex County. Located 23 km east of Windsor, it was settled in the early 1800s by pioneers of French extraction, with the nearby stream called *Belle Rivière*. The post office was called *Rochester*, after the township, in 1854. Twenty years later, when Belle River became a village, the postal name was changed to agree.

Belle River PE At the mouth of **Belle River**, southwest of Montague, this community had its post office named *Belle Creek* in 1867. Exactly a century later it was renamed Belle River. Military engineer Louis Franquet identified the river in 1751 as *Belle Rivière*. The adjacent **Bell Point** was settled about 1800 by a Bell family from Scotland.

Belleterre QC A town in the regional county of Témiscamingue, east of Ville-Marie, it was founded in 1942

and named after the Belleterre Gold Mines, which opened a mine here in 1935.

Belleville ON In 1998 this city (1877) and the township of Thurlow became part of the city of Belleville, Hastings County. It was called *Singleton's Creek* in the 1780s after Capt. George Singleton, who built a trading post in 1784 on the east bank of the Moira River. In 1790, a year after Singleton died, Capt. John Walden Meyers (1745–1821) built the first grist mill above the mouth of the Moira River and later built a sawmill, a distillery, a trading post, and a brick kiln. The place was informally called *Meyers' Creek* until 1816, when Lt.-Gov. Francis Gore (1769–1852) renamed the new *Singleton's Corners* post office after his wife, Annabella (Bella) Gore.

Bellevue NL Located on Tickle Harbour, near the head of Trinity Bay, this place was originally called *Tickle Harbour*. Because of rocks, tricky currents, and hazardous tides, the harbour is quite ticklish to negotiate. Since there were other places known by the name, it was changed in 1896 to promote the good view of the bay.

Bell Island NL In Conception Bay, northwest of St. John's, this island may have been named by the French after Belle Isle, off the south coast of Bretagne, France. John Guy (d.1629) referred to it in 1612 as *great Belile*, and it was called *Belle Isle* on several maps between 1669 and 1868. It became known as Bell Island only in the late 1800s. The story that it was named for its supposed inverted bell shape cannot be traced before 1819.

Belliveaus Cove NS In Digby County, southwest of Digby, this community was founded after 1755 by Charles Belliveau, who returned to Nova Scotia after the expulsion of the Acadians. *Belliveau Cove* post office opened in 1856.

Bell, Mount BC In the Coast Mountains, northwest of Mount Waddington, this mountain (3252 m) was named in 1928 by Walter Alfred (Don) Munday (1890–1950) after climber Col. Dr. F.C. Bell (1883–1971).

Bell, Mount YT West of Carcross, this mountain (1929 m) was named in 1909 by geologist Delorme Donaldson Cairnes (1879–1917) after Walter Andrew Bell (1889–1969), his field assistant. Bell became the director of the Geological Survey of Canada, 1949–53.

Bells Corners ON This urban centre in the sector of Nepean in Ottawa was named after Hugh Bell (c.1798–1872), who opened a tavern here in 1834, which he continued to run until 1863. The building is still here, with Al's Steakhouse & Seafood serving meals.

Belly River AB Rising in Montana, this river flows north
to join the Oldman River, upriver from Lethbridge. In 1858
surveyor Thomas Blakiston (1832–91) adapted the Blackfoot
mokowanis ('big bellies'), referring to the Atsina tribe, into Belly
River. He applied the name all the way to the river's junction
with the Bow River, 90 km downriver from Lethbridge.
Disgusted with having Lethbridge on a river with an embar-
rassing name, residents appealed for a new one. A solution
was reached in 1915 by making the Belly a tributary of the
Oldman.

Belmont MB The post office of this community southeast of
Brandon was first called *Craiglea* in 1884. John Bell had settled
here in 1883, and when the Canadian Northern Railway
arrived five years later, he requested its station be called
Bellsmount, which was contracted to Belmont. The post office
was changed to Belmont in 1891.

Belmont NS The post office of this community northwest
of Truro was named in 1879, possibly after Belmont, NH,
from where some of its first settlers came. It was known as
Vil Nigeganish by the Acadians in the early 1700s after the
Mi'kmaq name for the Chiganois River, *Nesakunechkik* ('eel
weirs'). The first post office in 1865 was called *Chigonaise River*.

Belmont ON In 1998 this township became part of the
township of **Havelock-Belmont-Methuen**, Peterborough
County. It was named in 1823, but the source of the name is
not known. Belmont House in Ireland's County Waterford and
Belmont Castle in Scotland's Perthshire are possible sources.

Belmont ON In 1998 this village (1961) became part of the
municipality of Central Elgin, Elgin County. Northeast of St.
Thomas, it was first called *Kettle Creek* in 1840. The first post
office opened in 1849 at *Plymouth*, 3 km north of the centre
of *Kettle Creek*. In 1854 the post office was moved to Kettle
Creek and renamed Belmont.

Beloeil QC In the regional county of La Vallée-du-Richelieu
and on the west bank of the Rivière Richelieu, east of
Montreal, this city (1914) was founded as a village in 1903. Its
origin may be traced to the religious parish of Saint-Mathieu-
de-Beloeil, established in 1772. It is believed to be named after
the beauty of the view from the summit of Mont Saint-Hilaire.

Belwood ON Located in Wellington Country, northeast of
Fergus and at the head of Lake Belwood, this community was
first called *Skenesville* after George Skene. It was later known
as Garafraxa after West Garafraxa Township, and then *Douglas*
after George Douglas Fergusson, who laid out village lots with
John Watt. In 1884 Dr. J.G. Mennie organized a court of the
Canadian Order of Foresters in *Douglas*. He called it Court
Belwood, likely after Bellwood, near Edinburgh, Scotland.

When confusion resulted in mail being sent to Douglas in the
Ottawa Valley, the place was renamed Belwood in 1885.

Bengough SK Established in 1911 by the Canadian Northern
Railway, this town (1958) is southeast of Moose Jaw. It was
named after John Wilson Bengough (1851–1923), founder of
the satirical weekly *Grip*, 1873–94, and a brilliant cartoonist
and popular lecturer. Its post office opened in 1912.

Benito MB This village (1940) is almost on the Saskatchewan
border, southwest of Swan River. The post office here was
established in 1903. It may have been named by the wife of
the first postmaster, A.C. Dykeman, after a character in a novel.

Benmiller ON In 2001 this community, located 5 km east of
Goderich, became part of the township of Ashfield-Colborne-
Wawanosh, Huron County. The name was given in 1855 after
Benjamin Miller (1801–58), an Englishman who had arrived
here in 1832 with his brothers, Daniel and Joseph.

Bennett Lake YT Extending southwest of Carcross to the
British Columbia border, this lake was named in 1883 by
American Army Lt. Frederick Schwatka (1849–92) after James
Gordon Bennett (1841–1918), editor of the *New York Herald*
and a promoter of American exploration.

Benoits Cove NL Part of the town of Humber Arm South
since 1991, this cove is located west of Corner Brook. It
was probably named after descendants of Michael Benoit
(1810–80), a native of Cape Breton Island, who settled on the
Port au Port Peninsula.

Bentinck ON In 2000 this township became part of the
township of West Grey, Grey County. It was named in 1840
for Lord William Henry Cavendish Bentinck (1774–1839),
governor general of Bengal, 1828–35.

Bentley AB Once a village (1915) and a town (2000), Bentley
became a city in 2001. Located 22 km northwest of Red Deer,
it was named in 1900 after mill worker George Bentley.

Berens River MB, ON Rising in Ontario, this river flows
west through Family Lake into Lake Winnipeg. The Cree
knew it as *Omeemee Sibi* ('pigeon river'). Pigeon River also
flows into Lake Winnipeg, 10 km to the south, from the same
source, Family Lake. The river was named after Cree chief
Joseph Berens. **Berens River** post office, at the river's mouth,
opened in 1900.

Beresford NB The post office of this town (1984) on the
northwest side of Bathurst was named in 1883. It took its
name from **Beresford Parish**, named in 1814 after William
Carr Beresford, Viscount Beresford (1768–1854). He served

with distinction during the Peninsular War in Spain, 1808–14, and was the marshal of the Portuguese Army, 1809–19.

Bernières QC This municipality in the regional county of Les Chutes-de-la-Chaudière, southwest of Quebec City, was named in 1968 after the French commune of Bernières-sur-Mer in Normandie, France. It had been established in 1912 as Saint-Nicolas-Sud.

Bernierville QC Located in the regional county of L'Érable, west of Thedford Mines, this village was named in 1898 after Julien-Melchoir Bernier (1825–87), the pastor of the religious parish of Saint-Ferdinand-d'Halifax from 1850 to 1886. The local residents prefer the name Saint-Ferdinand-d'Halifax.

Berthierville QC This town in the regional county of D'Autray, on the north side of the St. Lawrence River and opposite Sorel, was named as the village of *Berthier* in 1852 and changed to *Berthierville* in 1942. The original county of Berthier was possibly named after Isaac (Alexandre) Berthier, Sieur de Villemur (1638–1708), who had a seigneury east of Quebec City, near Montmagny.

Bertrand NB The post office of this village (1968) on the west side of the town of Caraquet was named in 1893 after a local Acadian family name.

Berwick NS This town (1923) in the Annapolis Valley, west of Kentville, was named in 1851 after Berwick, ME, on the New Hampshire border. A local resident had passed through there and was impressed with its neatness. In the early 1800s, it was called *Congdon Settlement* for pioneer settlers Benjamin and Enoch Congdon. In the 1820s it was known as *Pleasant Valley* and was later called *Davisons Corner* after William Davison, who arrived here in 1835.

Berwick ON In 1998 this community became part of the township of North Stormont, united counties of Stormont, Dundas and Glengarry. It is located 35 km northwest of Cornwall. First known as *Cockburn's Corners* after early settlers Adam and Peter Cockburn, it was later named *Finch* after the Finch Township when the post office opened in 1842. It was renamed in 1858 after the brothers' Scottish birthplace in Berwickshire. *See also* Finch.

Berwyn AB North of the Peace River, and west of Grimshaw, this village (1936) was named in 1922 after the Berwyn Hills in Denbighshire, Wales.

Bethany ON In 2001 this community southwest of the city of Peterborough became part of the city of Kawartha Lakes, Victoria County. The name was given in 1859 after Bethany (now called Al Ayzariyah) on the eastern side of Jerusalem and

on the flank of the Mount of Olives, from where Jesus made his triumphant return to Jerusalem.

Bethune SK Located 50 km northwest of Regina, this village (1912) was named in 1890 by the Qu'Appelle, Long Lake, and Saskatchewan Railway and Steamboat Company, possibly after entomologist Charles James Stewart Bethune (1838–1932). Its post office opened in 1905.

Betsiamites QC A Montagnais reserve, it is located east of the mouth of **Rivière Betsiamites** and southwest of the city of Baie-Comeau. The roots of the name have had varied spellings, beginning with *Bersiamiste* by Samuel de Champlain (1567–1635) in 1632. The post office here opened in 1863 as *Bersimis*, and was later *Moulin-Bersimis* and *Rivière Bersimis*. Although the reserve was named **Betsiamites** in 1861, Bersimis persisted until 1981, when the band persuaded postal authorities to accept its preference. The name may refer to 'place of leeches, lampreys, or eels'.

Bible Hill NS On the northeast side of Truro, this village (1953) was first settled about 1761. It owes its name to the practice of the Reverend Dr. William McCulloch—pastor of the First Presbyterian Church in Truro, 1839–85—of giving away copies of the Bible. He lived in the area of the present-day village.

Biddulph ON In 1999 Biddulph became part of the township of Lucan Biddulph, Middlesex County. It was named in 1830 for Robert Biddulph, a director of the Canada Company. This British company was organized in the 1820s to develop the Huron Tract, a large area of what is now Southwestern Ontario.

Bide Arm NL Located on the east coast of the Northern Peninsula and between Roddickton and Englee, this municipal community (1970) was founded in 1969 as a centre for resettlement.

Biencourt QC A municipality in the regional county of Témiscouata, southeast of Trois-Pistoles, it was created in 1947 and took its name from the township, which was proclaimed in 1920. It was given for Charles de Biencourt de Poutrincourt de Saint-Just (c.1591–1623), vice admiral of the seas of New France, and commander of Port-Royal in Acadia.

Bienfait SK The post office of this town (1958) east of Estevan opened in 1892, closed in 1895, and reopened in 1903, when the Canadian Pacific Railway was built to Estevan. It was named after Antoine-Charles Bienfait (1857–99), a financier with the Amsterdam financial firm of Adolphe Boissevain and Company.

Bienville, Lac QC A lake with an area of nearly 1000 km² in northern Quebec, near the head of the Grande rivière de la Baleine, it was named in 1916 after Jean-Baptiste Le Moyne de Bienville (1680–1767), who took part in the capture of English trading posts on Hudson and James bays at the end of the seventeenth century.

Biggar SK West of Saskatoon, this town (1911) was founded in 1908 by the Grand Trunk Pacific Railway and named after its general counsel, William Hodgins Biggar. Its post office opened in 1909. The town promotes itself with the slogan 'New York is Big, but this is Biggar'.

Big Presque Isle Stream NB Rising near the city of Presque Isle in Maine (where it is called Prestile Stream), this stream flows southeast to enter the Saint John River south of Florenceville. It was named after a peninsula (*presqu'île* in French) opposite the stream's mouth, not after Presque Isle Stream in Maine, which is a tributary of the Aroostook River.

Big River SK Situated northwest of Prince Albert, this town (1966) was established in 1909 by the Canadian Northern Railway. It is located at the mouth of **Big River**, which flows into a narrow, 50-km-long lake called *oklemow sipi* ('big river') by the Cree.

Big Sevogle River NB A tributary of the Northwest Miramichi River, its name derives from the Mi'kmaq *sewoku-look* ('river of many cliffs'), perhaps originally describing the Little Sevogle River. The Big Sevogle may have been *Elmunakuncheech* ('little beaver hole'), with *Elmunakun* ('beaver hole') being the Northwest Miramichi.

Big Valley AB The post office in this village (1942) south of Stettler was named in 1907 after a wide valley extending southwesterly from Ewing Lake to the Red Deer River.

Billings, Mount YT In the Logan Mountains, north of Watson Lake, this mountain (2106 m) was named in 1887 by geologist George Dawson (1849–1901) after Elkanah Billings (1820–76), paleontologist with the Geological and Natural History Survey of Canada.

Binscarth MB This village (1917), northwest of Brandon, was established as a pure-bred stock farm by the Scottish, Ontario, and Manitoba Land Company and managed by William Bain Scarth (1837–1902). The post office, called *Binscarth Farm* in 1893 and renamed Binscarth in 1891, was named after Binscarth, the location of Robert Scarth's farm on the Orkney island of Mainland.

Birch Hills SK The post office in this town (1960) southeast of Prince Albert was named in 1910. It took its name from birch trees lining the hills on both sides of the town.

Birchtown NS West of Shelburne, this place was established by African-Americans in 1783 and named after the birch trees found here. Its post office opened in 1877.

Birds Hill MB Located northeast of Winnipeg, this community has its roots in the grant of 504 ha (1245 a) of land on the east side of the Red River to James Curtis Bird (c.1773–1856). He was given the land after he retired in 1824 as the Hudson's Bay Company's chief factor at Lower Red River. Birds Hill post office was named in 1879 by Bird's son, Dr. Curtis James Bird (1838–76), who was born at the Birds Hill estate. The settlement was also known as Roseneath.

Birtle MB This town (1884) northwest of Brandon had its post office named in 1879 by contracting the name Birdtail Creek. The branches of the creek are said to resemble a bird's tail. Hudson's Bay Company maps identified *Fort Birdtail* at the junction of the creek and the Assiniboine River, a stopping place on the way to Fort Edmonton. When the settlers arrived in 1878, they wanted to call the place *St. Clair City*, but it was rejected because of similar names elsewhere in Canada.

Biscotasing ON On the shore of **Biscotasi Lake** and in Sudbury District, northwest of Sudbury, this place was established on the transcontinental Canadian Pacific Railway line in 1882. In Ojibwa, the name means 'water body with long arms'.

Bishop's Cove NL On the north side of Spaniard's Bay and south of Harbour Grace, this municipal community (1969) was first known as *Bread and Cheese Cove* after the local description of the hawthorn tree's leaves and berries. It was renamed in 1827 or 1832 by the Right Reverend John Inglis (1777–1850), who made two lengthy tours of Newfoundland when it was part of his Church of England diocese of Nova Scotia.

Bishop's Falls NL This town (1961) is on the Exploits River, northeast of Grand Falls-Windsor. It was named after the Right Reverend John Inglis (1777–1850), who made two lengthy tours of Newfoundland when it was part of his Church of England diocese of Nova Scotia. He visited the site of the falls in 1827.

Bishopton QC Situated in the regional county of Le Haut-Saint-François and northeast of Sherbrooke, this village was named in 1932. It had earlier been called *Bishop's Crossing* after the family of John Bishop, a Vermont native who had served in Benedict Arnold's regiment in 1775.

Bittern Lake AB Between Wetaskiwin and Camrose, the post office here was named in 1899 after the nearby lake, whose name derives from a genus of birds allied to the heron. The village was incorporated as *Rosenroll* in 1904 and changed to Bittern Lake seven years later.

Bizard, Île QC Located on the northwestern side of Île de Montréal, this island was named after Jacques Bizard (1642–92), who was appointed in 1678 as the governor of the island (then called *Bonaventure*). *See also* Saint-Raphaël-de-l'Île-Bizard.

Bjorkdale SK Situated southeast of Tisdale, this village (1968) was first settled by Sid Coppendale and Charlie Bjork. Its post office was named in 1911 by combining parts of their surnames.

Blackcomb Peak BC In the Coast Mountains, southeast of Whistler, this mountain (2438 m) was named by Walter Alfred (Don) and Phyllis Munday, who observed its serrated ledge of black rock in 1923.

Black Diamond AB The post office in this town (1956) southwest of Calgary was named in 1907 after Addison McPherson's Black Diamond Coal Mine. The Arnold brothers, who were to operate the post office in their general store, had wanted Arnoldville, but an elderly Aboriginal pulled Black Diamond from a hat.

Black Donald Lake ON A reservoir since 1967, it is located on the Madawaska River and on the Lanark–Renfrew boundary, upriver from Arnprior. Its name recalls early lumberman Black Donald McDonald, and the Black Donald graphite mine, now inundated. The upper part of the reservoir is called Centennial Lake.

Blackfalds AB Between Red Deer and Lacombe, this town (1980) was first known as *Waghorn* when the post office opened in 1891 and was named after the postmaster. It was renamed in 1902 by a Canadian Pacific Railway engineer after Blackfaulds, possibly an estate in Scotland.

Blackhorn Mountain BC In the Coast Mountains, northeast of Mount Waddington, this mountain (3033 m) was named in 1933 by mountaineer H.S. Hall Jr. A black rock at its summit reminded him of the horn of a saddle, which he deemed appropriate for this cattle ranching country.

Blackie AB The post office in this village (1912) southeast of Calgary was named in 1911 after Scottish novelist John Stuart Blackie (1809–95), founder of the publishing firm Blackie and Sons.

Black Lake QC A town in the regional county of L'Amiante, it was named a village in 1906 and a town two years later. The nearby lake was called Lac Noir when the developers of the asbestos mine in the 1890s translated the name for the new urban centre into English, and Lac Noir remains its name.

Black, Mount YT Northeast of Whitehorse, this mountain (2158 m) was named in 1935 by geologist Hugh S. Bostock (1901–94) after George Black (1872–1965), commissioner of the Yukon, 1912–6, and member of the House of Commons, 1921–35 and 1940–9. He was the speaker of the House of Commons, 1930–5.

Black River ON Rising 135 km east of Washago, this river flows into the Severn River downstream from the point where the West, Centre, and East branches of the Severn flow from Lake Couchiching and unite before reaching the mouth of the Black River. The clear waters of the Severn are turned much darker by the Black's waters.

Black River-Matheson ON A municipal township in Cochrane District, it was created in 1969 with the union of the municipal township of Black River and the town of Matheson. Playfair Township and the improvement district of Kingham were added four years later.

Blacks Harbour NB This village (1972) on the Bay of Fundy coast, southwest of Saint John, had its post office named in 1885. It is noted for fish processing and packing. The harbour was identified on a chart by William Fitz William Owen in 1847.

Blackville NB The post office in this village (1966) on the west bank of the Southwest Miramichi River, southwest of Newcastle (part of the city of Miramichi), was named in 1842. It was named after **Blackville Parish**, which was established in 1830 and called after William Black (1771–1866), administrator of the provincial government during the absence of Lt-Gov. Sir Howard Douglas (1776–1861). Earlier it was called *The Forks*, for its location at the mouth of the Bartholomew River.

Blaine Lake SK Founded by the Canadian Northern Railway in 1911, this town (1954) southwest of Prince Albert was called after a nearby post office. The post office was named in 1907 after a chain of alkaline lakes near Blaine Lake.

Blainville QC Situated in the regional county of Thérèse-de-Blainville, this city northwest of Montreal was named in 1968. In 1845 it had been proclaimed as the parish municipality of *Sainte-Thérèse-de-Blainville*, which acquired its name from Louis-Jean-Baptiste Céleron de Blainville (1696–1756), whose wife inherited the seigneury of Mille-Îles in 1730.

Blair ON An urban centre in the city of Cambridge, and on the west side of the Grand River, it was first known as *Shinglebridge, Durhamville,* and *New Carlisle*. It was renamed Blair in 1858 in honour of Adam Johnston Fergusson Blair (1815–67), a son of Adam Fergusson, the founder of Fergus. He added the name Blair on inheriting a Scottish estate.

He served in the Legislative Assembly of the Province of Canada, 1849–57, the Legislative Council, 1860–7, and the Senate in 1867, when he was president of the Privy Council in Sir John A. Macdonald's first cabinet. **Blair Township** in Parry Sound District was also named for him. *See also* Cambridge.

Blairmore AB This city in the municipality of Crowsnest Pass since 1979 was first named in 1898 after two Canadian Pacific Railway contractors called Blair and More (or Moore). It had been incorporated as a town in 1911.

Blakeney ON In Lanark County on the Mississippi River, this place was first called *Norway Pine Falls, Snedden's Mills*, and *Rosebank* before being named in 1874 after Dominick Edward Blake (1833–1912). Blake was premier of Ontario, 1871–2, member of the House of Commons, 1873–91, and leader of the Liberal Party of Canada, 1880–7.

Blanc-Sablon QC This municipality in the regional county of Côte-Nord-du-Golfe-Saint-Laurent, and just west of Newfoundland's Labrador border, was noted as early as 1534 in the *Relation* of Jacques Cartier, who had erected a cross at nearby Lourdes-de-Blanc-Sablon. The name means 'little white sand'. The occurrence of a cove called Blancs-Sablons, near Saint-Malo, France, from where Cartier sailed, may only be coincidental. The community of **Lourdes-de-Blanc-Sablon** was attached to the municipality when it was created in 1990.

Blandford ON · Part of the municipal township of **Blandford–Blenheim** in Oxford County since 1975, Blandford Township was named in 1798 for one of the titles of John Churchill, the Duke of Marlborough (1650–1722), who had been made the Marquess of Blandford in 1702.

Blanshard ON In 1998 this township became part of the township of Perth South, Perth County. It was named in 1830 for Richard Blanshard, a director of the Canada Company. This British company was founded in 1826 to develop the Huron Tract, a large area of Southwestern Ontario.

Blanshard, Mount BC Between Pitt and Alouette lakes, and north of Haney, this mountain (1715 m) was named in 1859 by Capt. George Richards (1820–96) after Richard Blanshard (1817–94), the first governor of Vancouver Island, 1849–51. Its two peaks are called Golden Ears, mentioned by Cdr. Richard Mayne in 1862. Golden Ears Provincial Park embraces a large area of this part of the province.

Blenheim ON In 1998 this town (1885) became part of the municipality of Chatham-Kent, Kent County. It was named in 1883 after a battle that took place in 1704, when John Churchill, the Duke of Marlborough (1650–1722), defeated the French and Bavarian forces. Blenheim had been proposed in 1849 for the post office, but an office was already called that in Oxford County. The post office was named Rondeau after nearby Rondeau Harbour until 1883, some years after the Blenheim's post office in Oxford County was closed.

Blenheim ON Part of the municipal township of **Blandford–Blenheim** in Oxford County since 1975, Blenheim Township was named in 1798 after Blenheim Palace, the home of John Churchill, the Duke of Marlborough (1650–1722) at Woodstock in England's Oxfordshire. In 1704 Churchill won a battle at Blenheim, Germany, near Augsburg.

Blind River ON At the mouth of the **Blind River**, this town (1906) in Algoma District, east of Sault Ste. Marie, was named in 1877 after the hidden outlet of the river, as perceived from a boat in the North Channel of Lake Huron.

Blockhouse NS West of Mahone Bay, this community's post office was named *Block House* in 1876 after a fortified block-house, which had been built on a hill top in 1753.

Blomidon, Cape NS The name of this eastern extremity of North Mountain, north of Wolfville, is attributed to a contraction of 'blow me down', a nautical phrase used throughout the Atlantic provinces for places susceptible to high winds. Samuel de Champlain (1567–1635) called it *Cap de Poutrincourt* after Jean de Biencourt de Poutrincourt et de Saint-Just, lieutenant-governor of Acadia, 1606–14, who had scaled its cliff. It was also known as *Cap Baptiste* and *Cape Porcupine*.

Bloomfield NL On Goose Bay, an arm of Bonavista Bay, and north of Clarenville, this place was settled after the mid-1850s. The name possibly derives from its good soils that permitted the growing of vegetables, with 60 barrels of potatoes having been produced in 1865.

Bloomfield ON In 1998 this village (1906) became part of the municipality of Prince Edward County. Located west of Picton, it was named about 1832 after the profusion of wild flowers in the vicinity.

Blue Nose Lake NT Northwest of Kugluktuk, this lake (391 km²) was named in 1953 by wildlife biologist John P. Kelsall. He chose the name because both he and his assistant, James Mitchell, were natives of Nova Scotia. He had in mind both the well-known nickname of Nova Scotians and the famous schooner *Bluenose*.

Blue River BC On the west bank of the North Thompson River, this community was named in 1917 after **Blue River**, which rises in the Cariboo Mountains. The Reverend George Monro Grant (1835–1902) explained in his *Ocean to Ocean* (1873) that the river was named after 'the deep soft blue of the distant hills, which are seen from its mouth well into the gap through which it runs'.

Blyth ON In 2002 this village (1876) east of Goderich became part of the township of North Huron, Huron County. Its post office was named Blythe in 1856 after James Blyth of England, who owned a large part of the site. The postal name was changed to Blyth in 1888.

Bobcaygeon ON In 2001 this village (1876) became part of the city of Kawartha Lakes, Victoria County. Located on the **Bobcaygeon River**, the village was named after the river in 1832. The river's name is from the Mississauga *bob-ca-je-won-unk* ('shallow rapids').

Boiestown NB In the valley of the Southwest Miramichi River, north of Fredericton, this community was named in 1842 after Thomas Boies. He came from New Hampshire in the early 1820s, and established sawmills and a grist mill at the mouth of the Taxis River.

Boisbriand QC In the regional county of Thérèse-De Blainville, this city west of the cities of Sainte-Thérèse and Blainville was named in 1974. The name recalls Michel-Sidrac Dugué de Boisbriand (1638–88), who was granted the seigneury of Mille-Îles in 1672.

Boischatel QC This municipality in the regional county of La Côte-de-Beaupré, northeast of Quebec City, was called *Saint-Jean-de-Boischatel* in 1920, and shortened to its present form in 1991. It was named for Jean-François de Beauchatel, a military officer who died in 1760.

Bois-des-Filion QC A town (1980) in the regional county of Thérèse-De Blainville, it is located east of the cities of Sainte-Thérèse and Blainville. Its post office was named *Bois-de-Filion* in 1855, and modified to its present form in 1932. The name recalls a large maple bush owned by a man called Filion.

Bois, Lac de NT This lake (469 km²), northwest of Great Bear Lake, was identified on Fr. Émile Petitot's map of 1875. He had visited the area three years earlier. The name means 'lake of the woods'.

Boissevain MB Situated directly south of Brandon, this town (1906) was first known as *Cherry Creek*. Its post office was named in 1886 after Athanase Adolphe Boissevain (1843–1921) of the Amsterdam firm Adolphe Boissevain and Company, which floated the shares of the Canadian Pacific Railway in the European financial markets.

Bolton ON An urban centre in the town of Caledon, Peel Region, it was first called *Bolton Mills* in 1824 after James and George Bolton had built mills on the Humber River. *Albion*, named after the township, was the post office from 1832 to 1892. Bolton was a village from 1873 to 1974.

Bompas, Mount YT This mountain (3056 m) in the St. Elias Mountains, west of Kluane Lake, was named in 1918 after the Right Reverend William Carpenter Bompas (1834–1906). He was the first Anglican bishop of Athabasca (1874–84), of Mackenzie River (1884–91), and of Selkirk (Yukon), 1891–1906.

Bon Accord AB North of Edmonton, this town (1964) received its name in 1896, when Alexander 'Sandy' Florence proposed Bon Accord for the name of a new school district. The name, which he had given to his farm, derives from the motto of his native Aberdeen, Scotland. The post office opened in 1901.

Bonanza Creek YT Flowing into the Klondike River, 5 km upriver from Dawson, it was known as Rabbit Creek, until the discovery of gold in its gravel beds in 1896 by George Carmack (1860–1922), Skookum Jim Mason (1855–1916), and Tagish Charlie (d.1908) touched off the great Klondike Gold Rush. The name was given by Carmack after the Spanish word for rich ore deposits.

Bonaventure QC The regional county is located southwest of Gaspé. The source of its name may be traced to the first discoveries of Jacques Cartier (1491–1557), who noted in 1534 the existence of **Île Bonaventure** at the mouth of Chaleur Bay. The island's name may have related to the excellence of the fishery around the island. The municipality of Bonaventure in the regional county was named in 1955, having been called *Saint-Bonaventure-de-Hamilton* in 1884.

Bonavista NL This town (1964) is located at **Cape Bonavista** and on the southeast side of **Bonavista Bay**. The cape may have been named about 1501 by Portuguese explorer Gaspar Corte-Real (1415–1502) after Boa Vista, one of the Cape Verde Islands off west Africa. There is also a claim that John Cabot (c.1450–98) exclaimed *'O buona vista, O happy sight'*, on reaching its shore in 1497, but the claim lacks any specific evidence. In 1534 Jacques Cartier (1491–1557) reported sighting *Cap de Bonne Vista*, suggesting it was well known to explorers and fishermen.

Bon Echo ON In 1998 this community became part of the township of North Frontenac, Frontenac County. Located 35 km north of Kaladar, it is noted for its Aboriginal pictographs on a 115-m cliff on the east shore of Upper Mazinaw Lake in **Bon Echo Provincial Park**. From the top of the cliff, the acoustics are excellent, with sounds echoing across the narrows between the Upper and Lower Mazinaw lakes. *See also* Mississippi River.

Bonfield ON This township in Nipissing District was named in 1881 after lumberman James Bonfield (1825–83), Liberal member for Renfrew South in the Ontario Legislature,

1875–83. The community of **Bonfield** was an incorporated town from 1905 to 1974.

Bonne Bay NL On the northwestern coast of Newfoundland, this bay has two arms that deeply penetrate the lofty cliffs of Gros Morne National Park. In the 1500s the Basques called it *Baya Ederra* ('beautiful bay'), which the French subsequently translated. In 1767 Capt. James Cook (1728–79) adopted the French name for his chart of the coast.

Bonnechere River ON This major tributary of the Ottawa River rises in Algonquin Park. As early as 1688 *R de la Bonnechere* occurred on maps, but its origins are obscure. With the meaning of 'good flesh', it possibly reflects the eating of a good meal by French voyageurs at the river's mouth.

Bonnechere Valley ON In 2001 this township annexed the village of Eganville and the municipal townships of Grattan, Sebastopol, and South Algona.

Bonne-Espérance QC A municipality in the regional county of La Côte-Nord-du-Golfe-Saint-Laurent, it is located west of Blanc-Sablon. It was created in 1990, with the name having been used for a post office in 1878 and for a township in 1907.

Bonnet Plume River YT Rising in the Mackenzie Mountains, this river flows northwest to join the Peel River, just south of the Arctic Circle. It was named after Gwitch'in chief Andrew Flett, nicknamed Bonnet Plume, who lived on the river with his band. He guided many lost gold-seekers during the Klondike Gold Rush, and was also an interpreter for the Hudson's Bay Company.

Bonney, Mount BC In the Selkirk Mountains, south of Rogers Pass, this mountain (3107 m) was named in 1889 by climber William S. Green after British geologist Thomas George Bonney (1833–1923), who was then president of the Alpine Club in London.

Bonnyville AB The post office of this town (1948) northeast of Edmonton was named in 1910 after Fr. F.S. Bonny, who built the first Catholic church here that year. It had been earlier called *St. Louis de Moose Lake.*

Bonshaw PE Located southwest of Charlottetown, this municipal community (1977) was named by W.W. Irving, who had come from near Bonshaw Tower, Dumfriesshire, Scotland. It was noted in a reference in 1839, with its post office opening 20 years later.

Boothia, Gulf of NU Separating Melville Peninsula on the east, and Boothia and Simpson peninsulas on the west, this large inlet of the Arctic Ocean was named in 1830 by Sir John Ross (1777–1856) after Sir Felix Booth (1775–1850), sheriff

of London, England; prominent distiller; and patron of Ross's expedition, 1829–33.

Boothia Peninsula NU The most northerly (72°N) point of mainland Canada, this peninsula (32,300 km²) was named *Boothia Felix* in 1830 by Sir John Ross (1777–1856) after Sir Felix Booth (1775–1850), patron of his expedition, 1829–33. It was renamed by the Geographic Board before 1910.

Borden ON Located in Simcoe County, west of Barrie, this place was called *Camp Borden* when a military training centre was named in 1916 after Sir Frederick William Borden (1847–1917), minister of militia and defence, 1896–1911. The camp was renamed Canadian Forces Base Borden in 1966. It occupies 7165 ha (17,704 a).

Borden SK A village (1907) northwest of Saskatoon, it was first called *Baltimore*, but it was renamed by the Canadian Northern Railway in 1905 after Sir Frederick William Borden (1847–1917), minister of militia and defence in Sir Wilfrid Laurier's cabinet, 1896–1911. Its post office was also opened in 1905.

Borden-Carleton PE A municipal community (1995) at the end of the Confederation Bridge, joining the province to the mainland at Bayfield, NB, it was created through the amalgamation of the town of Borden (1919) and the municipal community of Carleton Siding (1977). Borden was established in 1917 as the provincial terminal for ferry service to the mainland and was called after Sir Robert Borden (1854–1937), then prime minister of Canada. Its post office opened in 1918 as Port Borden. *See also* Carleton Siding.

Borden Island NU The most northerly of the Parry Islands, and in the Queen Elizabeth Islands, this island (2794 km²) was named in 1915 by Vilhjalmur Stefansson (1879–1962) after Sir Robert Borden (1854–1937), prime minister of Canada, 1911–20.

Borden Peninsula NU A broad peninsula at the north end of Baffin Island, it was named in 1913 by Alfred Tremblay, who explored the area in 1912–13. He named it after the prime minister, Sir Robert Borden.

Bosanquet ON In 2001 this town became part of the municipality of Lambton Shores, Lambton County. Northeast of Sarnia, it had been a township until 1 January 1995. The township had been named in 1830 after Charles Bosanquet, a director of the Canada Company. This British company was set up in the 1820s to develop the Huron Tract, a large area of what is now Southwestern Ontario.

Boston Bar BC This community in the Fraser Canyon, between Hope and Lytton, was named in the late 1850s by the local band of Lillooet, who described Americans panning for gold on a bar in the river 'Boston men'. The site was the scene of the Battle of Boston Bar, where the Lillooet provoked a fight with the Boston men, with seven Lillooet being killed. The post office was on the west side of the river at the site of North Bend from 1884 to 1887. It was reopened at its current site on the east side of the river in 1917.

Botha AB A village (1911) east of Stettler, it was named by the Canadian Pacific Railway in 1909 after Gen. Louis Botha (1862–1919), the first prime minister of the Union of South Africa, 1910–19. Its post office opened the following year.

Bothwell ON In 1998 this town (1886) became part of the municipality of Chatham-Kent, Kent County. It was named in 1854 by George Brown (1818–80) of Toronto's *The Globe* after Bothwell in Lanarkshire, southeast of Glasgow, Scotland.

Botwood NL At the head of the Bay of Exploits and north-east of Grand Falls–Windsor, this town (1960) was first known as *Ship Cove*. In the late 1800s it was named *Botwoodville* after the Reverend Edward Botwood (1828–1901), a Church of England archdeacon, 1894–1901. The name was subsequently shortened to Botwood.

Boucherville QC Created a village in 1857, this city (1957) became part of the city of Longueuil in 2002. Four years later, Boucherville recovered its status as a city in the regional county of Lajemmerais and on the east side of the St. Lawrence River, opposite Montreal. Pierre Boucher de Grosbois (1622–1717), the most respected Canadian of his time in his many roles of judge, writer, soldier, and governor, was granted the **Îles de Boucherville** in the St. Lawrence in 1672.

Bouchette QC Located in the regional county of La Vallée-de-la-Gatineau, south of Maniwaki, the municipality took its name from the township named in 1858 after the noted geographer and surveyor general of Lower Canada, Joseph Bouchette (1774–1841).

Bouctouche NB A town (1985) at the mouth of **Buctouche River**, it had its post office named Buctouche in 1842. It had been incorporated as the village of *Buctouche* in 1966. Persistent use of Bouctouche by its French-speaking residents resulted in its name being respelled in 1985, but leaving associated names unchanged. The river was identified on Pierre Jumeau's 1685 map as R. chibouchouch. The name may derive from the Mi'kmaq *chebuktoosk* ('big bay'), in reference to **Baie de Buctouche**, at the mouth of the river.

Boularderie Island NS Separated from Cape Breton Island by the channels of the Great Bras d'Or and the Little Bras d'Or, this island was named after Louis-Simon Le Poupet et de la Boularderie (c.1674–1738). He was the commandant of *Port d'Orléans*, at present-day Ingonish, from 1719 to 1738. In 1719 he was granted the island, then known as *Île de Verderonne*, and set out to establish an agricultural settlement here.

Bowden AB This town (1981) southwest of Red Deer had its post office named in 1892, when the Canadian Pacific Railway was built from Calgary to Edmonton. It was likely named by a CPR surveyor called Williamson after the birth name of his wife. It is also said to have been named after either Bowdon, a suburb of Manchester, England, or after Bowden near Galashiels, Roxburghshire, Scotland.

Bowen Island BC In the entrance to Howe Sound, northwest of Vancouver, this island was named in 1860 by Capt. George Richards (1820–96) after RAdm. James Bowen (1751–1835), master of HMS *Queen Charlotte*, Lord Howe's flagship during the remarkable British victory over the French on the Glorious First of June, 1794.

Bow Island AB Located 23 km east of the junction of the Bow and Oldman Rivers (where they become the South Saskatchewan River), this town (1912) was named by the Canadian Pacific Railway in 1907 after an island in the Bow River. Presumably the names Grassy Lake, south of the junction, and Bow Island were accidentally switched by the post office department in Ottawa.

Bowmanville ON The largest urban centre in the municipality of Clarington, Durham Region, it was first called *Barber's Creek* and then *Darlington Mills* and *Darlington*. It was named in 1854 after Montreal merchant, Charles Bowman, who had opened a dry goods store here 30 years earlier and donated land for a school and a church.

Bow River AB Rising in the Rocky Mountains northwest of Lake Louise, this river flows southeast through Calgary to join the Oldman River between Lethbridge and Medicine Hat, where the two become the South Saskatchewan River. It took its name from the Cree *manachaban* ('bow'), in reference to the bows they made from Douglas fir saplings along its banks. The French called it *Rivière des Arcs*, which remains in the name of Lac des Arcs, an enlargement of the Bow at Exshaw.

Bowsman MB Located north of the town of Swan River, and near the Saskatchewan border, this village (1949) received its name from **Bowsman River**. The river was named by geologist Joseph Burr Tyrrell (1858–1957) after Cree trapper and hunter Bowsman Moore, who was then living at Shoal River. First named Bowsman in 1901, the post office was called *Bowsman River* from 1908 to 1952, when Bowsman was restored.

Boyle AB A village (1953) southeast of Athabasca, it was named by the Alberta and Great Waterways Railway in 1914 after John Robert Boyle (1871–1936), then minister of education, and later a judge of the supreme court of Alberta. Its post office opened in 1916.

Bracebridge ON A town (1889) in the district municipality of Muskoka, it was named in 1864 by postal official William Dawson LeSueur (1840–1917) after Washington Irving's novel *Bracebridge Hall, or the Humorists* (1822). The town was extensively enlarged in 1971 by annexing several adjoining townships. *See also* Gravenhurst.

Brackley PE A municipal community (1983) 8 km north of Charlottetown's city centre, it had its post office named *Brackley Point Road* in 1868. It took its name from **Brackley Bay**, 13 km further north, where the legislative clerk Arthur Brackley apparently drowned in 1776. Samuel Holland (1728–1801) had called the bay *Petersham Cove* in 1765 after William Stanhope, Viscount Petersham (1719-79), but the local name supplanted it.

Bradford West Gwillimbury ON This town was created in Simcoe County in 1991. **Bradford** was named in 1840 by Joel Flesher Robinson after the city of Bradford in West Yorkshire, England, where he was born. It was an incorporated town from 1960 to 1991. **West Gwillimbury** was created as a township in 1798, and was possibly named after Lt. Col. Thomas Gwillim (d.1762), the father of Elizabeth Posthuma Gwillim Simcoe (1762–1850).

Braeside ON A village (1921) in Renfrew County, northwest of Arnprior, it was named in 1872 by W.J. McDonald, likely for Braeside in Renfrewshire, Scotland, west of Greenock.

Bralorne BC This place north of Pemberton was named in 1932 after the Bralorne Mines Limited, formed the previous year by the Bralco Development and Investment Company. It had acquired the Lorne Mine, opened here in 1897. The acronym 'Bralco' was created from British, Alberta, and Columbia.

Bramalea ON Developed in 1958 as a multi-use project, it is now a well-known area of the expanded city of Brampton in Peel Region. The name was composed from the initial letters of Brampton and Malton, plus the word 'lea' ('meadow').

Brampton ON A city (1974) in Peel Region, Brampton was laid out about 1834 by John Elliott and William Lawson, natives of Brampton, Cumberland, England, northeast of Carlisle. Its post office was called Chinguacousy after the township from 1832 to 1851, when it was renamed Brampton. *See also* Chinguacousy.

Branch NL A municipal community (1966) on the southwest side of St. Mary's Bay, it was established about 1790 as a fishing settlement. The name derives from **Branch River,** which flows into **Branch Bay**.

Brandon MB The province's second largest city, Brandon was incorporated in 1882, a year after its post office opened. The name derives from Brandon House, erected southeast on the Assiniboine River in 1793 by the Hudson's Bay Company.

Brant ON The county was named in 1852 after Joseph Brant, a.k.a. Thayendanegea, (1742–1807), the great Mohawk chief who fought on the British side during the American Revolution. **Brant Township** in Bruce County was named in 1850, also for Joseph Brant.

Brantford ON In 1784, following the American Revolution, Joseph Brant led the Six Nations confederacy to the site of this city (1877) on the Grand River. It became known as *Brant's Ford*. Its post office was named Brantford in 1825 in preference to *Biggar's Town* and *Lewisville*.

Brantville NB Located south of Tracadie, this place had its post office named in 1905 after the migration route of brant geese (*Branta bernicla*) over it in May and October.

Bras d'Or Lake NS Enclosed by Cape Breton and Boularderie Islands, this sea-level lake was likely named for the Portuguese *lavrador* ('small landholder') João Alvares Fagundes (c.1460–1525). He explored the coasts of Newfoundland and Nova Scotia about 1521. The name may have been given to reinforce Portuguese control of lands near the boundary of Spanish claims, set by the Treaty of Tordesillas in 1494. Subsequently concluding the name was French for 'arm of gold', map-makers called the water body, with many bays and channels, Bras d'Or Lake. The channels separating Boularderie Island from Cape Breton Island were designated **Great Bras d'Or** and **Little Bras d'Or.** The lake is informally called the Bras d'Or Lakes.

Bratnober, Mount YT West of Whitehorse, this mountain (1923 m) was named in 1897 by surveyor James J. McArthur (1856–1925) after Henry Bratnober, who helped him clear the Dalton Trail that year. Subsequently, Bratnober was a prospector, riverboat captain, and agent in the north for the mining interests of N.M. Rothschild and Sons.

Bray Island NU Located in Foxe Basin, west of Baffin Island, this island (689 km²) was named in 1946 by Thomas H. Manning (1911–98) after Reynold J.O. Bray, the first non-Aboriginal to explore the area.

Brazeau, Mount AB In the Rocky Mountains, west of Rocky Mountain House, this mountain (3470 m) was named in 1902 by Arthur P. Coleman (1852–1939) after Hudson's Bay Company factor Joseph Étienne Brazeau, a native of St. Louis, MO. Brazeau was in charge of the post at Rocky Mountain House, 1858–9, and at Jasper, 1861–2, and was a polyglot, speaking English, French, Spanish, Blackfoot, Cree, Crow, Saulteaux, Siouan, and Stoney.

Breadalbane PE The post office of this municipal community (1991) east of Summerside was named in 1889 after Breadalbane, Perthshire, Scotland. Both its former railway station and school names were spelled *Bradalbane*.

Bredenbury SK Located southeast of Yorktown, this town (1913) was named in 1886, when the Manitoba and North Western Railway was built from Winnipeg to Saskatoon. It was named after A.E. Breden, a railway land inspector. Postal service was established in 1890.

Brent's Cove NL On the north coast of the Newfoundland and east of Baie Verte, this municipal community (1966) was founded in the 1850s. The origin of the name is unknown. It may be a transplanted place name from the West Country of England, or a descriptive name relating to its steep cliffs or its burnt shoreline.

Breslau ON In the regional municipality of Waterloo, east of Kitchener, the post office here was named in 1856 after Breslau, then in German Silesia, but now known as Wrocław in Poland.

Breton AB Southwest of Edmonton, this village (1957) was named by the Canadian Pacific Railway in 1926 after Douglas Corey Breton (1883–1953), then a member of the provincial legislature. He migrated to Canada from South Africa in 1903 and moved to England in 1934. The post office, called Keystone in 1912, was renamed Breton in 1927.

Brew, Mount BC In the Coast Mountains, west of Whistler, this mountain (2286 m) was named in 1911 after Chartres Brew (1815–70), who was appointed the first inspector of police in British Columbia in 1858, chief gold commissioner the following year, and a member of the legislative council, 1864–8. Another **Mount Brew** (2886 m) south of Lillooet was named for him in 1950.

Bridgenorth ON In 2001 this community, located 12 km north of the city of Peterborough, became part of the township of Smith-Ennismore-Lakefield, Peterborough County. The post office here was named in 1854, when a proposal was made to build a bridge across Chemong Lake. The bridge was not opened until 1870.

Bridgetown NS The town (1897) in the Annapolis Valley was named in 1824 after a bridge constructed across the Annapolis River. This location was earlier called *Hick's Ferry*. Postal service was provided to Bridgetown in 1825.

Bridgewater NS The site of this town (1899) was first settled in the 1780s. It was named in 1837 after a bridge, which had been built over the LaHave River, 18 km above its mouth.

Brigham QC A municipality in the regional county of Brome-Missisquoi, northwest of Cowansville, it was named in 1980. Its post office opened here in 1860, and was named after brickmaker Erastus Oakley Brigham.

Bright ON Northeast of Woodstock, in Oxford County, this community has its post office named in 1863 after John Bright (1811–89), a noted British statesman and parliamentary reformer. **Bright** and **Bright Additional** townships in Algoma District were also named for him.

Brighton NL On the north coast of the Newfoundland and on the Tickle Islands and Triton Island, this municipal community (1976) was first known as *Dark Tickle*. It was renamed in the early 1900s by the Nomenclature Board, but the reason for choosing the name is not in the official records.

Brighton ON In 2001 this location in Northumberland County became the town of Brighton. It became a town in 1980, when it annexed the township of Brighton. Brighton post office was named in 1831 after the popular English seaside resort of Brighton in Sussex. **Brighton Township** was named in 1851.

Brights Grove ON This community on the shore of Lake Huron and in the city of Sarnia, 14 km northeast of the city centre, was named in 1935 after John Bright developed a summer resort among a grove of trees on his lakeshore farm.

Brigus NL A town (1964) on the western shore of Conception Bay, it was noted as *Brega* on an early map of the 1600s. It occurred on later French maps as *Brigues*, a word that suggests 'intrigue' or 'underhanded'. Its present spelling was established by an English marine pilot of 1689.

Bristol NB This village (1966) is located on the east bank of the Saint John River, north of Woodstock. The post office here was called *Shiktehawk* in 1866 after Shiketehawk Stream. It was renamed in 1878 after Bristol, Somerset, England.

Bristol QC This location in the southern part of the regional county of Pontiac was officially created in 1845 and named after the township of **Bristol**. The name can be found on a 1795 map, but was not proclaimed until 1834, and recalls the famous English seaport in Gloucestershire.

Britannia Beach BC On the east shore of Howe Sound, south of Squamish, this community was established in 1907. It took its name from the **Britannia Range** of the Coast Mountains, named in 1859 by Capt. George Richards (1820–96) after HMS *Britannia*, which served during the Battle of Trafalgar, 1805.

British Columbia The roots of the province's name may be traced to the naming of the Columbia River in 1792 by Capt. Robert Gray (c.1755-1806) after his ship *Columbia*, which had begun its journey in Boston. Subsequently, the Hudson's Bay Company named its southern district, west of the continental divide, Columbia. In 1858 Queen Victoria (1819–1901) noted Columbia on many maps of the area, but after observing it was the poetical name for the United States as well as a country in South America (actually Colombia), she proposed British Columbia in a letter to Sir Edward Bulwer-Lytton (1803–73), the colonial secretary.

British Columbia, Mount YT In the Centennial Range of the St. Elias Mountains, this mountain (3109 m) was named in 1967 in honour of the one hundredth anniversary of Confederation.

British Empire Range NU Located at the northwestern side of Ellesmere Island and between Clements Markham Inlet and Yelverton Bay, this range of mountains was named by A. Winston Moore, a member of the Oxford University Ellesmere Island expedition of 1934–5.

British Mountains YT Extending for 175 km from Mount Fitton to Mount Greenough in northern Yukon, and across the border into Alaska, this range of mountains was named *British Chain* in 1826 by Sir John Franklin (1786–1847) in honour of the people of Great Britain.

Broadback, Rivière QC Rising in west central Quebec, north of Chibougamau, this river flows west into Rupert Bay, in the southeastern part of James Bay. The origin of the name is uncertain, with its first appearances in the 1890s reports by geologist Robert Bell (1841–1917) and surveyor Henry O'Sullivan (1846–1912).

Broadview SK The post office and station of this town (1907) east of Regina were named in 1882, when the transcontinental line of the Canadian Pacific Railway was built that far. The name was given because, as far as the eye could see, there was a 'broad view' of the relatively level prairie.

Brock ON In Durham Region, north of Whitby, the present municipal township was created in 1974 by amalgamating Brock and Thorah townships, and the villages of Beaverton and Cannington. The original Brock Township was named after Maj. Gen. Sir Isaac Brock (1769–1812), who was killed at the Battle of Queenston Heights.

Brock SK East of Kindersley, this village (1910) was founded by the Canadian Northern Railway in 1909 and named after Maj. Gen. Sir Isaac Brock (1769–1812), hero of the Battle of Queenston Heights, 1812. The post office opened in 1910.

Brocket AB A community on the Peigan Indian Reserve, southwest of Fort Macleod, it was named by the Canadian Pacific Railway in 1897–8 after Brocket Hall in Hatfield, Hertfordshire, England. Brocket Hall was the residence of George Stephen, Lord Mount Stephen (1829–1921), first president of the CPR, 1880–88.

Brock Island NU Part of the Parry Islands, and in the Queen Elizabeth Islands, this island (764 km²) was named in 1916 by Vilhjalmur Stefansson (1879–1962) after Reginald Walter Brock (1874–1935). He was the director of the Geological Survey of Canada, 1907–14, and briefly deputy minister of mines in Ottawa. He was dean of applied science at the University of British Columbia, 1914–34.

Brockville ON This city (1962) in the united counties of Leeds and Grenville was first known as *Buell's Bay* after first settler William Buell (1751–1832) and later *Elizabethtown* after the township. It was renamed in 1812 for Maj. Gen. Sir Isaac Brock (1769–1812), who was killed that year at the Battle of Queenston Heights.

Brodeur Peninsula NU This 290-km peninsula at the northwest side of Baffin Island, between Prince Regent and Admiralty inlets, was named in 1907 by explorer Joseph-Elzéar Bernier (1852–1934) after Louis-Philippe Brodeur (1862–1924), who was then the minister of marine and fisheries in Ottawa.

Brome-Missisquoi QC A regional county on the Vermont border, its double name, created in 1983, has deep roots in this part of Quebec. The township of **Brome**, adjacent to **Lac Brome**, east of Cowansville, was named in 1795 after Brome Hall, the English residence of Charles, 1st Marquess Cornwallis and Viscount Brome (1738–1805), governor general of India, 1786–93. Missisquoi was created a county in 1853, taking its name from the large northeastern bay of Lake Champlain, whose name in Abnaki may mean 'place of gun flint'.

Bromley ON In 2001 this township was joined with Admaston Township to become **Admaston–Bromley Township**, Renfrew County. It was named in 1843 after Bagot's Bromley in Staffordshire, England, the estate of Sir Charles Bagot (1781–1843), governor of the Province of Canada, 1841–3.

Bromont QC Located in the regional county of La Haute-Yamaska, south of Granby, this town was named in 1964 after the township of **Brome** and nearby **Mont Brome** (553 m).

Bromptonville QC A town in the regional county of Le Haut-Saint-François, north of Sherbrooke, it was named *Brompton Falls* in 1902 and renamed Bromptonville the following year. The name derives from the township of **Brompton**, named in 1795 and proclaimed in 1801, likely named after Brompton in North Yorkshire, England.

Bronte ON At the mouth of **Bronte Creek** and in the town of Oakville, Halton Region, this urban centre was named for one of the titles of Adm. Lord Horatio Nelson (1758–1805). He received the title of Duke of Brontë in 1800 from King Ferdinand III of Naples, whom Nelson had helped restore to his throne.

Brooke ON This township in Lambton County was joined in 2001 with the village of **Alvinston** to become the township of **Brooke-Alvinston**. Brooke Township was named in 1834 after Sir James Brooke (1803–68), the rajah of Sarawak, 1838–68. Sarawak is now a state in Malaysia.

Brooke, Mount YT Located in the St. Elias Mountains, near the Alaska border, this mountain (3290 m) was named in 1918 after Pvt. William Brooke (1893–1917), who died in a German prisoner-of-war camp.

Brookfield NS South of Truro, this descriptive name was given in 1784 by William Hamilton (1758–1838), a pioneer settler from County Armagh, Ireland. Its post office opened in 1852.

Brooklyn NS East of Liverpool and at the mouth of the Mersey River, this municipal community (1995) was first called *Herring Cove*. The post office here was established in 1861. The name may derive from a small stream flowing through the community. A second **Brooklyn**, east of Windsor, has a descriptive name, which was given in the early 1800s. Because of other places called Brooklyn in the province, the post office here has been known as Newport since 1831, but it has failed to supplant Brooklyn. There is another **Brooklyn** on the northeast side of Yarmouth, and a **Brooklyn Corner**, on the west side of Kentville.

Brooks AB In 2005 this town (1911) became a city. The post office here was named in 1904 after Noel Edgall Brooks (d.1926), divisional engineer of the Canadian Pacific Railway at Calgary, 1903–13.

Brossard QC In 2002 Brossard became a sector of the city of Longueuil. Four years later Brossard recovered its status as a city. Situated in the regional county of Champlain and across the St. Lawrence from Montreal, this city was named in 1958, and enlarged in 1978. In the mid-1800s the first municipal parish was called *Brosseau* after its mayor Pierre Brosseau. Its modern founder was Georges-Henri Brossard, who was the mayor of the parish and then of the city from 1944 to 1967. In 1958 the local residents wanted to call it *Forgetville* after Mgr. Anastase Forget (1885–1955), but many, including Premier Maurice Duplessis (1890–1959), opposed a name suggesting forgetful citizens.

Brougham ON This community in the town of Pickering, Durham Region, had its post office named in 1836, probably after Henry Peter Brougham, 1st Baron Brougham and Vaux (1778–1868). He was a native of Edinburgh and lord chancellor of England, 1830–4. His father was raised at Brougham Castle, in Westmorland, England.

Brougham Township ON In 2001 this township became part of the township of Greater Madawaska, Renfrew County. It was named in 1851 after Henry Peter Brougham, 1st Baron Brougham and Vaux (1778–1868).

Broughton Island BC Between Vancouver Island and the mainland, on the north side of Queen Charlotte Strait, this island was named in 1792 by Capt. George Vancouver (1757–98) after Lt. Cmdr. (later Comm.) William Robert Broughton (1762–1821). He commanded the armed tender Chatham that year when Vancouver explored the inlets and passages of the west coast.

Broughton Island NU This hamlet (1979) on **Broughton Island** and on the northeast coast of Baffin Island, was first founded in 1956–7 as a Distant Early Warning site. The island was named in 1818 by Sir John Ross (1777–1856) after Comm. William Robert Broughton (1762–1821).

Brownsburg QC A town (1935) in the regional county of Argenteuil, west of Lachute, the post office here was named in 1854 after postmaster George Brown. A native of England, Brown settled here in 1818, and built grist and sawmills.

Bruce ON The county was named in 1849 for James Bruce, 8th Earl of Elgin (1811–63), governor of the Province of Canada, 1846–54. **Bruce Township** in the county was created in 1850. In 1999 this township became part of the municipality of Kincardine. **Bruce Peninsula** is the 90-km-long peninsula that divides Georgian Bay from the main part of Lake Huron.

Bruce Mines ON This town (1903) in Algoma District, southeast of Sault Ste. Marie, was founded in 1842; copper mines were operated here from 1847 to 1876. It was named in 1848 after James Bruce, 8th Earl of Elgin, who was then governor of the Province of Canada, and after the copper mines that operated here from 1847 to 1876.

Brudenell PE This municipal community (1973) is located north of Montague, between **Brudenell River** and Montague

River. The post office here was named in 1898. The river was named in 1765 by Samuel Holland (1728–1801) after George Brudenell, 4th Earl of Cardigan (1712–90).

Bruderheim AB A town (1980) northeast of Edmonton, the post office here was named in 1895 by Andreas Lilge and a group of Moravians, including his brothers Ludwig and William, who established a colony the year before after migrating from Volhynia, Russia. Their congregation was called Brethrens Church, with the post office name meaning 'Brethrens home'.

Brule NS A community on the south side of Amet Sound, east of Tatamagouche, it had its post office called *Point Brule* in 1859 and Brule in 1876. The name derives from the French *brûlé* ('burnt') and is said to relate to an incident when Aboriginals from Quebec encountered Mi'kmaq people at the point and set the woods on fire.

Bruno SK Located west of Humboldt, this town (1962) was named after Fr. Bruno Doerfler (1867–1919), who arranged in 1902 for the German American Land Company to buy 40,470 ha (100,000 a) in the area, with 1000 German Americans applying for homesteads before the end of the year. Postal service was set up in 1906.

Brussels ON In 2001 this village became part of the municipality of Huron East, Huron County. It was called *Ainleyville* in 1855 after developer William Ainley. The next year the post office was called *Dingle*, but Ainleyville continued in use until the village was incorporated in 1872 as Brussels after the capital of Belgium.

Bryants Cove NL Located southeast of Harbour Grace, this municipal community (1977) was settled in 1675 and was one of the first settlements in Conception Bay. The origin of the name is not available in the official records.

Bryce, Mount BC South of the Columbia Icefield, this mountain (3507 m) was named in 1899 by climber Norman Collie (1859–1942) after James Bryce, Lord Bryce (1838–1922), British ambassador to the United States, 1907–12, and an alpinist.

Bryson QC In the regional county of Pontiac, on the Ottawa River and west of Shawville, the village was named in 1873 after prominent lumberman and legislative councillor George Bryson (1813–1900).

Buchanan SK Located west of Canora, this village (1907) was established by the Canadian Northern Railway in 1904 and named after rancher Robert Buchanan (d.1919). The post office opened in 1906.

Buchans NL Midway between Corner Brook and Grand Falls-Windsor, this town (1979) was named in 1927 by developers of a copper, zinc, and lead mine after **Buchans Island**, 7 km to the southeast in Red Indian Lake. The island was called after Capt. David Buchans (c.1780–1838), a British naval officer who had served in Newfoundland. He made contact with the Beothuk at Red Indian Lake in 1811 and 1820.

Buckhorn ON At the north end of **Buckhorn Lake** in Peterborough County, north of the city of Peterborough, this community was first known as *Hall's Bridge* in 1828 after John Hall, an American who built grist and sawmills, homes for his workers, and a bridge. Having settled here permanently in the 1850s, he became the postmaster of *Hall's Bridge* in 1860. It became Buckhorn in 1941, and was called after **Buckhorn River**, **Buckhorn Falls**, and Buckhorn Lake in the late 1800s after Hall's collection of animal horns.

Buckingham QC In 2002 the town (1890) became a part of the city of Gatineau. It took its name from the township of **Buckingham**, which had been proclaimed in 1795. Although the first settlers were from England's Buckinghamshire, northwest of London, the name may have been given after George Nugent Temple Grenville, 1st Marquess of Buckingham (1753–1813), twice lord lieutenant of Ireland in the 1780s.

Buena Vista SK Situated at the south end of Last Mountain Lake, north of Regina, this village (1983) had a summer post office from 1930 to 1954. Its name reflects the beautiful view across the lake.

Bugaboos, The BC Located in the Purcell Mountains, northwest of Invermere, these peaks are a popular skiing destination. Bugaboo was noted on an 1893 map by gold commissioner A.P. Cummins. It was reported in 1906 to chief geographer James White that the name referred to the loneliness of the location.

Bulkley River BC Rising northwest of Burns Lake, this river (257 km to the head of Maxan Creek) flows west, and then north through Houston and Smithers to join the Skeena River at Hazelton. It was named about 1864–6 after Col. Charles Bulkley, chief engineer of the Western Union Extension Company, during construction of the Collins Overland Telegraph. The line only reached this part of the province; it was suspended upon learning of the successful laying of the transatlantic cable in 1866.

Bulyea, Mount AB, BC On the continental divide, northwest of Calgary, this mountain was named in 1920 after George Hedley Vicars Bulyea (1859–1926), first lieutenant-governor of Alberta, 1905–15.

Bunbury PE This community in the town of Stratford, across Charlottetown Harbour from Charlottetown was possibly named about 1798 by John Bovyer, after his ancestral home in Cheshire, England. Formerly a municipal community (1969), it became part of Stratford on 1 April 1995.

Burdett AB This hamlet (2003) located between Lethbridge and Medicine Hat was first named a village in 1913. Its station was named in 1907 by the Canadian Pacific Railway after Baroness Angela Georgina Burdett-Coutts (1814–1906), an English philanthropist and a shareholder in the North Western Coal and Navigation Company of Lethbridge. *See also* Coutts.

Burford ON This township was originally in Oxford County, but in 1853 became part of Brant County. First established in 1798, it was named for Burford, Oxfordshire, England, which is west of Oxford. The community of **Burford**, west of Brantford, was named in 1819.

Burgeo NL This town (1950) is located on the southwestern coast of Newfoundland. It took its name from the **Burgeo Islands**, which were called after an archipelago in the area of Saint-Pierre and Miquelon, named *Onze myll virgines* by Portuguese explorer João Alvares Fagundes (c.1460–1525) in 1521, and shown on a map of about 1524. That name related to the supposed slaughter by the Huns of St. Ursula and her 11,000 virgins, while returning from a pilgrimage to Rome, in either the fourth or fifth centuries. The French apparently transferred the name in the form of *Vierges* to the Burgeo Islands.

Burgess, Mount BC Located in Yoho National Park, north of Field, this mountain (2599 m) was named in 1886 by Dr. Otto Klotz (1852–1923) after Alexander Mackinnon Burgess (1850–1908), deputy minister of the interior, 1883–97. The Burgess Shale Site at the mountain has been declared a UNESCO World Heritage Site for its unique invertebrate fossil remains. Burgess was also honoured in the naming of **Mount Burgess** in the Yukon's Ogilvie Mountains in 1888 by surveyor William Ogilvie.

Burgessville ON In Norwich Township, Oxford County and south of Woodstock, this place was named in 1853 for Edward N. Burgess, who was born 5 km east of the village. A blacksmith and carriage maker, he served as postmaster of Burgessville until 1871.

Burin NL A town (1950) on the eastern side of **Burin Peninsula**, its name perhaps derives from the French *burin* ('graver' or 'chisel') and was possibly given by French fishermen. There might be a connection with the Basque word *burua* ('head'), since Basque fishermen visited the area in the early 1600s. Spanish records of the 1600s called it *Buria*.

Burk's Falls ON A village (1890) in Parry Sound District, north of Huntsville, it was named in 1879 for its first permanent settler, David Francis Burk (b.1852). He had come from Oshawa in 1876 and lived here until he died in 1901.

Burleigh ON This township was named in 1822, likely after Burghley House near Stamford, England, 45 km east of Leicester. The house was built by William Cecil, Baron Burghley (1520–98), Queen Elizabeth I's chief minister. For municipal purposes, Burleigh had been united with Anstruther Township to become *Burleigh and Anstruther Township*. In 1998 Chandos Township was connected with *Burleigh and Anstruther Township* to become *Burleigh-Anstruther-Chandos Township*. In 1999 the township became part of the township of North Kawartha, Peterborough County. The community of **Burleigh Falls**, in the township of Galway-Cavendish-Harvey, is situated where Lovesick Lake and the Trent Canal empty into Stony Lake. Its post office was named in 1864.

Burlington NL A municipal community (1953) on Green Bay, an extension of Notre Dame Bay, it was known as *North West Arm* until 1914, when it was renamed, possibly after Burlington, ON.

Burlington ON A city (1974) in Halton Region, it was first known as *Brant's Block* after a grant to Joseph Brant (c.1743-1807) for his loyalty to the British Crown. Its post office became *Wellington Square* in 1826 after the Duke of Wellington (1769–1852). In 1873 it was united with Port Nelson to become the village of Burlington, named after *Burlington Bay*. The bay was named in 1792 by Lt.-Gov. John Graves Simcoe (1752–1806) for the town of Bridlington in East Yorkshire, England, north of Kingston upon Hull. The bay was renamed Hamilton Harbour in 1919, although Burlington Bay remains in common use, as in Burlington Bay James N. Allan Skyway.

Burnaby BC On the east side of Vancouver, this city (1992) was created a district municipality in 1892. It was named after **Burnaby Lake**, in the central part of the city. The lake was called after Robert Burnaby (1828–78), the private secretary to Col. Richard Moody (1813–87), commanding officer of the Royal Engineers, 1858–9, during a survey of New Westminster in 1859.

Burns Lake BC Located at the geographical centre of British Columbia, this village (1923) is at the west end of Burns Lake. The lake, a 21-km widening of the Endako River, was named in 1866 after surveyor Michael Byrnes, who established a route through the area for the Collins Telegraph Company.

Burnstown ON In 2001 this community 10 km southeast of Renfrew became part of the township of Greater Madawaska, Renfrew County. The post office was named at a public meeting in 1853 after the great Scottish poet Robert Burns

(1759–96), when it was noted that the whole settlement was Scottish.

Burnt Islands NL This town (1977), east of Channel-Port aux Basques, was developed as a fishing community in the late 1800s. Presumably the vegetation on the islands was destroyed by a fire.

Burrard Inlet BC Separating Vancouver from the north shore, this arm of the Strait of Georgia was named in 1792 by Capt. George Vancouver (1757–98) after Sir Harry Burrard (1765–1840), who served with Vancouver in the West Indies in 1785. On marrying in 1795, he became Sir Harry Burrard-Neale. His career in the Royal Navy progressed to his appointment as an admiral in 1830.

Burritts Rapids ON Mostly situated on an island in the Rideau River northeast of Smiths Falls, this location was settled in 1793 by brothers Stephen and Daniel Burritt. A townsite was laid out in 1830, and a post office opened in 1839.

Burstall SK Located near the Alberta border, west of Swift Current, this town (1921) was founded in 1920 by the Canadian Pacific Railway. It was named after Gen. E. Henry Burstall, who was killed during the First World War while leading the 2nd Canadian Division. Postal service was established here in 1921.

Burton NB On the south bank of the Saint John River, and on the east side of the town of Oromocto, this community had its post office named *Upper Burton* in 1878. Burton post office opened in 1856, 6 km downriver at Lower Burton. **Burton Parish** was created in 1786, having been established as *Burton Township* in 1765. The township was named after Brig. Gen. Ralph Burton (d.1768), lieutenant-governor of the district of Three Rivers (Trois-Rivières), 1760–2, and of Montreal, 1763–4. He was then appointed military commander-in-chief of the Northern Department (Quebec), retiring to England in 1766.

Bury QC Situated in the regional county of Le Haut-Saint-François, east of Sherbrooke, this municipality was named in 1845 after the township of **Bury**, proclaimed in 1803. The township may have been named after the borough of Bury St. Edmunds in Suffolk, England.

Bute Inlet BC A 65-sinuous fiord extending into the Coast Mountains, northeast of Campbell River, this inlet was named in 1792 by Capt. George Vancouver (1757–98) after John Stuart, 3rd Earl of Bute (1713–92), described as the 'dearest friend' of George III. He was Britain's prime minister, 1762–3, when the Treaty of Paris was signed.

Byam Martin Island NU In the Parry Islands of the Queen Elizabeth Islands, this island (1150 km^2) was named in 1919 by Sir William E. Parry (1790–1855) after VAdm. Sir Thomas Byam Martin (1773–1854), comptroller of the British Navy. **Byam Martin Channel** separates Melville Island on the west from Alexander, Vanier, Massey, and Cameron Islands on the east. **Byam Martin Mountains** and **Cape Byam Martin**, both on Bylot Island, were named in 1818 by Sir John Ross, who served with Sir Thomas Byam Martin when the latter commanded the British fleet in the Baltic Sea in 1812.

Bylot Island NU Located on the north side of Baffin Island, this island (11,067 km^2) was likely named in 1819 by Sir William E. Parry (1795–1885) after Robert Bylot (d.1622). With William Baffin, Bylot had explored the waters of Davis Strait and Baffin Bay in 1615–6, but failed to find an eastern entrance leading to the Northwest Passage.

Byng Inlet ON A long narrow inlet in the northeastern part of Georgian Bay, it was named in the 1820s by Admiralty surveyor Henry W. Bayfield (1795–1885) after Adm. John Byng (1704–57), who had been executed for cowardice when he failed to capture Minorca in the Mediterranean Sea. The community of **Byng Inlet**, opposite Britt, was named in 1868.

C

Cabano QC This town (1962) in the regional county of Témiscouata, southeast of Rivière-du-Loup, had its post office named in 1898 after the township of **Cabano**, which was proclaimed in 1866. The name may derive from cabaneau, because of the beaver-lodge appearance of the mountains adjacent to Lac Témiscouata.

Cabonga, Réservoir QC Located in the regional county of Vallée-de-l'Or, southeast of Val-d'Or, this reservoir was created in 1928–9 from Lac Cabonga as part of a scheme to regulate the headwaters of the Ottawa and Gatineau river systems. The lake's name derives from the Algonquin *kakibonga* ('entirely blocked by sand') and was first recorded in 1864 as *Kakibonga*.

Cabot Head ON This northeast point of Bruce Peninsula was named in the 1790s by Lt.-Gov. John Graves Simcoe (1752–1806) after John Cabot (c.1461–98), who had explored North America's east coast in the 1490s.

Cabot Strait NL, NS Part of the Gulf of St. Lawrence, this strait has a width of 89 km between Cape North on Cape Breton Island, and Cape Ray on the island of Newfoundland. It was named by the British Admiralty in 1485 after John Cabot (c.1450–98), who had made a landing in the New World in 1497, but was lost at sea during a second voyage the following year.

Cabri SK A town (1917) northwest of Swift Current, Cabri opened a post office in 1912, and its station was established by the Canadian Pacific Railway the following year. The 9th Earl of Southesk, who was surveying for the Palliser Expedition, had Métis guides. They called the antelopes 'cabrees'.

Cache Bay ON On an enclosed bay of Lake Nipissing, west of North Bay, this town (1903) was established as a Canadian Pacific Railway station in 1883, and its post office was open six years later. The bay was a natural location for fur traders and voyageurs to hide (*cache*) their supplies.

Cache Creek BC This village (1967), west of Kamloops, is located at the point where Highway 97 leads north from the Trans-Canada Highway to Prince George. It was named after the nearby creek, noted as *Rivière de la Cache* in 1859, by Cdr. Richard C. Mayne (1796–1862).

Cacouna QC Located in the regional county of Rivière-du-Loup, northeast of the city of Rivière-du-Loup, this Maliseet reserve was created in 1891. In Maliseet, the name may mean 'place of the porcupine' or 'place of the turtle'.

Cadillac QC A town in the regional county of Rouyn-Noranda, northwest of Malartic, it was named in 1948 after the township of **Cadillac**, proclaimed in 1916. The name recalls Henry Preyssac de Cadillac, an officer who served with the Marquis de Montcalm in the 1750s.

Cadorna, Mount BC In the Rocky Mountains, east of Invermere, this mountain (3145 m) was named in 1918 after Gen. Luigi Cadorna (1850–1928), commander-in-chief of the Italian armies during the First World War.

Cairnes, Mount BC In the Rocky Mountains, northwest of Field, BC, this mountain (3060 m) was named by surveyor Arthur O. Wheeler (1860–1945) in 1919 after geologist Delorme Donaldson Cairnes (1879–1917). A second **Mount Cairnes** (2789 m), in the Kluane Range of the St. Elias Mountains, southeast of Kluane Lake in the Yukon, was named about 1920 after him. There is another **Mount Cairnes** in the Yukon's Ogilvie Mountains, northeast of Dawson, named in 1968 by geologist Dirk Tempelman-Kluit after the same geologist who explored and mapped the geology of the Yukon from 1905 to 1917.

Caissie Cape NB Located north of Shediac, this community was served by Cap-Caissie post office from 1930 to 1955, named after the nearby cape, **Cap de Caissie**. The cape was named after an Acadian family with Irish ancestry, with the variant forms Casey, Caissy, Kuessey and Quessy being used in land grant records. After local investigation in 1991, the province endorsed the dual forms of Caissie Cape and **Cap-des-Caissie** for the community.

Calder SK East of Yorkton, this village (1911) was established in October 1909 by the Canadian Northern Railway, and named in January 1911 after J.A. Calder, provincial minister of education. Its post office was called *Calder Station* in 1911 and was changed to Calder in 1936.

Caledon ON This town in Peel Region was created in 1974 when the townships of Caledon and Albion, the north half of Chinguacousy Township, and the villages of Bolton and Caledon East were amalgamated. **Caledon Township** was named in 1819 after a poetic description of Scotland. **Caledon Mountain** is the steep climb up the Niagara Escarpment, in the area of Highway 10. **Caledon Hills** embrace the rugged landscape between Belfountain and Caledon East. **Caledon East**, at the centre of the township of Caledon, Peel Region, was known as *Tarbox Corners*, *Munsie's Corners*, and *Paisley*, before it was named Caledon East in 1851 after its location on the eastern boundary of Caledon Township. The post office at **Caledon Village** was opened as *Charleston* in 1838, but was changed to Caledon in 1839 after the township. However, *Charleston* continued in use as the preferred local name until the end of the 1800s. The postal name was amended in 1975 to distinguish it from the town of Caledon. In its early years the place was also called *Reburn's Corners* after innkeeper Robert Reburn (c.1785–1870).

Calgary AB The city (1893) was briefly called *Fort Brisebois* when it was established by Insp. Ephrem A. Brisebois (1850–90) in 1875. However, Asst Com. A.G. Irvine of the North West Mounted Police informed Minister of Justice Edward Blake (1833–1912) of the proposal by Lt. Col. James F. Macleod (1836–94) in 1876 to name it *Fort Calgary* after the ancestral estate of his Mackenzie cousins on the west side of the Island of Mull, Scotland. Macleod's proposal was shortened to Calgary, which he stated meant 'clear running water' in Gaelic, and it was accepted. The post office here opened in 1883.

Callander ON Renowned as the nearest rail centre to the birthplace of the Dionne quintuplets in 1934, Callander is located in Parry Sound District, south of North Bay. In 1881 first settler and postmaster George Morrison named it for his native Callander in Scotland's Perthshire, northwest of Stirling.

Calmar AB Southwest of Edmonton, this town (1954) was named in 1900 by the first postmaster, C.J. Blomquist after his hometown of Kalmar, Sweden, southwest of Stockholm.

Calumet QC Situated in the regional county of Argenteuil, west of Lachute, this village was named in 1918 after Calumet post office, opened in 1887 and named after the **Rivière du Calumet**, which flows into the Ottawa River at that point. The excellent stone found here was used by the Algonquin for the production of the pipes of peace (*calumets*).

Calvert NL On the east coast of the Avalon Peninsula, this place was named in 1922 after Sir George Calvert, 1st Baron Baltimore (c.1580–1632). He established a colony at nearby Ferryland in 1621, and lived there with his family in 1628. In 1597 it was called *Caplen Bay*. This name may derive from the Portuguese *capelinas* ('capelin'), a small fish of the smelt family.

Cambray ON In 2001 Cambray and Fenelon Township became parts the city of Kawartha Lake, Victoria County. Fenelon Township was named in 1853 by postmaster Joseph Wilkinson after Cambrai in France, near the Belgian border, where the noted François de Fenélon was the archbishop, 1695–1715. *See also* Fenelon.

Cambridge ON This city was incorporated on 1 January 1974. It is in the regional municipality of Waterloo, a union of the former city of Galt, the former towns of Hespeler and Preston, and parts of adjacent townships. Galt officials suggested calling it Blair after a place on the west side of the Grand River, but the councils of Preston and Hespeler won their suggestion of Cambridge, after an early flour mill at Preston, by a narrow vote. By the narrow vote of 11,728 to 9800 (1674 ballots were spoiled), Cambridge was chosen. *See also* Blair *and* Galt.

Cambridge Bay NU This hamlet (1984) on the south coast of Victoria Island was founded in 1947 as a Loran navigational beacon, and became a Distant Early Warning site in 1955. The bay was likely named in 1851 by explorer John Rae (1813–93) after the Duke of Cambridge (1774–1850).

Cambridge-Narrows NB A village (1966) where Highway 695 crosses Washademoak Lake, 45 km east of Fredericton, this was formerly two separate communities. Cambridge post office, opened on the west side in 1860, was named after **Cambridge Parish**, itself named after Queen Victoria's uncle, Adolphus Frederick, the Duke of Cambridge (1774–1850). *Narrows* post office served the east side from 1855 to 1969.

Camden ON In 1998 this township became part of the municipality of Chatham-Kent, Kent County. Named *Camden West* in 1794 after Charles Pratt, Earl Camden and Viscount Bayham (1714–94), it was soon called simply Camden Township. Earl Camden was a British government official, including Attorney General and Chief Justice of Common Pleas.

Camden East ON In 1998 this township became part of the township of Stone Mills, Lennox, and Addington County. It was named *Camden* in 1787 after Charles Pratt, Earl Camden and Viscount Bayham (1714–94), a British government official. In 1866, it was renamed Camden East to distinguish it from Camden Township in Kent County. The community of **Camden East** was named in 1835.

Cameron Island NU In the Parry Islands of the Queen Elizabeth Islands, and between Bathurst and Melville Islands, this island (1059 km²) was named in 1952 after Maxwell George Cameron (d.1951), the chief cartographer of the surveys and mapping branch, department of mines and technical surveys.

Campbellford ON The name of this town (1906) in Northumberland County, given in 1854, recalls brothers

Lt. Col. Robert Campbell and Maj. David Campbell, who were granted 890 ha (2200 a) on the Trent River in 1831. It had been first called *Seymour West* after Seymour Township. In 1998 Campbellford was amalgamated with the township of Seymour. In 2001 Campbellford Seymour was amalgamated with the township of Percy and village of Hastings to become the municipality of Campbellford Seymour, Percy and Hastings. This became the municipality of Trent Hills in 2001.

Campbell's Bay QC The post office of this village in the regional county of Pontiac, west of Shawville, was named in 1888 after early settler Donald Campbell. The village was incorporated in 1904.

Campbell Range YT On the west side of Frances Lake, this range of mountains was named in 1887 by geologist George Dawson (1849–1901) after Robert Campbell (1808–94), a Hudson's Bay Company chief factor. He carried out extensive exploration of the Yukon between 1840 and 1852.

Campbell River BC This district municipality (1964) on the northeast side of Vancouver Island was incorporated as a village in 1947. The post office here opened in 1907, taking its name from the river that drains a series of lakes into Discovery Passage. The river may have been named in 1859 by Capt. George Richards (1820–96) after Dr. Samuel Campbell, who was the assistant surgeon on Richards's survey ship *Plumper*.

Campbellton NB This city (1958) on the south side of the Restigouche River was named in 1833 by Robert Ferguson (c.1637–1714) after Sir Archibald Campbell (1769–1843), lieutenant-governor of the province, 1831–7. In 1700 the site was called *Pointe-des-Sauvages*. It may have been the site of the Acadian settlement Petite-Rochelle, established in 1757, but destroyed by the British three years later. In the early 1800s it was variously known as *Cavenick's Point, Kavanagh's Point, Quinton's Point,* and *Martin's Point*.

Campbellton NL On the Indian Arm of the Bay of Exploits, this town (1972) was first known as *Indian Arm* after a Beothuk camp located here in the early 1800s. It was renamed in the early 1900s, possibly after John Campbell, the manager of a local sawmill.

Campbellville ON In the town of Milton, Halton Region, west of the town centre, this village was named after John Campbell (1784–1854), who settled here in 1832 and built a sawmill in 1838.

Campobello Island NB Located in Passamaquoddy Bay, and joined to Lubec, ME, by a bridge, this island was named in 1770 by its grantee William Owen (1737–78) after the governor of Nova Scotia, Lord William Campbell (c.1730–78). Impressed by its fine soil and appearance, Owen modified

Campbell's name into the Spanish and Italian forms of 'fair field'. *Campo Bello* post office was located at Welshpool from 1837 to 1924.

Camrose AB A city (1955) southeast of Edmonton, its post office was named in 1905, by selecting the name of Camrose, Pembrokeshire, Wales from the British Postal Guide.

Canal Flats BC This community is located on the Kootenay River, only 1 km from Columbia Lake, the headwaters of the Columbia River. Its post office was named in 1913. In 1889 British-Austrian capitalist William Adolph Baillie-Grohman (1851–1921) constructed a canal uniting the two river systems. The scheme essentially failed because of fears of flooding downriver on the Columbia.

Canborough ON Part of the town of Dunnville, Haldimand-Norfolk Region since 1974, this township was named in 1825 after Benjamin Canby (1767–1841) of Niagara, who had bought 7690 ha (19,000 a) of land here in 1799. Canby laid out the community of Canborough in 1800; a post office was opened in 1836.

Candiac QC A town in the regional county of Roussillon, south of Montreal, and on the south shore of the St. Lawrence, it was named in 1957 after an estate near Nîmes in Languedoc, France, birthplace of the Marquis de Montcalm (1712).

Caniapiscau QC A regional county in northeastern Quebec, its area of nearly 82,000 km² is centred on the **Rivière Caniapiscau** and the **Réservoir de Caniapiscau**. The 500-km-long river flows north to join the Rivière Koksoak, near Kuujjuaq. The reservoir was created in the 1980s as part of the vast Hydro-Quebec project in northwestern Quebec. In both the Cree and Montagnais languages, *caniapiscau* means 'rocky point'. In 1895 geologist Albert P. Low (1861–1942) had observed a prominent rock projecting above the surface of the lake, which has remained above the reservoir.

Canmore AB Located on the Bow River, west of Calgary, this town (1955) was named in 1884 by the Canadian Pacific Railway, possibly on the suggestion of Lord Strathcona (1820–1914), in honour of Malcolm III Canmore (c.1031–93), King of the Scots, 1057–93.

Canning NS Northwest of Wolfville, this village (1968) was first known as *Apple Tree Landing* and *Habitant Corner*. It was renamed about 1830 after George Canning (1770–1827), who was briefly prime minister of Great Britain in 1827, after having been the secretary of foreign affairs for five years. Postal service was established in 1846.

Canoe Lake ON This lake in Algonquin Park was named in 1853 by geologist Alexander Murray (1810–84), after his party took several days to build a canoe here. The lake became famous through the many sketches and paintings of Tom Thomson (1877–1917), who accidentally drowned here.

Canora SK This town (1910) was established by the Canadian Northern Railway in 1903–4, and its name was formed from the first two letters of each of the words of the company's name. Postal service was established in 1904.

Canso NS This town (1901), at the eastern extremity of mainland Nova Scotia, was identified as Canseau on Jean-Baptiste-Louis Franquelin's 1686 map of Acadia. Surveyor General Charles Morris (1711–81) introduced the present spelling in 1749. The name derives from the Mi'kmaq *kamsook* ('opposite the lofty cliff'), in reference to either the steep cliffs of Chedabucto Bay or the mirage of an impressive height on Isle Madame, 13 km to the north.

Canso, Strait of NS This narrow passage between the mainland and Cape Breton Island was called *Passage de Fronsac* and *Détroit de Fronsac* by the French between the 1660s and the 1750s after a title of an uncle and a son of Acadian Gov. Nicolas Denys (c.1598–1688), and also of Cardinal Richelieu. In 1715 map-maker Herman Moll (d.1732) described it as *Straits of Canceaux*, with chart-maker Joseph Frederick Wallet DesBarres (1722–1824) introducing the present name in 1776, replacing *Gut of Canso*.

Canterbury NB This village (1966) west of Fredericton was called *Howard Settlement* in the 1820s after Lt.-Gov. Sir Howard Douglas (1776–1861). Following the arrival of the St. Andrews and Quebec Railway in 1859, its post office was called *Canterbury Station*, after **Canterbury Parish**, established in 1855. The parish was named after Thomas Manners-Sutton (1814–77), lieutenant-governor of New Brunswick, 1854–61. He succeeded his father as Lord Canterbury in 1869.

Cantley QC This municipality was created in 1989 when it was severed from the city of Gatineau. The post office here was named in 1857, possibly after a place in Norfolk, England, midway between Norwich and Great Yarmouth, birthplace of an early pioneer.

Canwood SK Northwest of Prince Albert, this village (1916) was established by the Canadian Northern Railway in 1909 to exploit the timber resources of the area. Its name is a contraction of Canadian and woods. The post office here was called McQuan and McOwan in 1911, changed to *Forgaard* after Jens Forgaard (1870–1914) in 1912, and finally called Canwood in 1913.

Cap-à-l'Aigle QC The name of this village (1916) in the regional county of Charlevoix-Est, east of La Malbaie, was noted as early as 1812. It was named after the nearby **Cap à l'Aigle** ('eagle cape').

Cap-aux-Meules QC Located in the regional county of Les Îles-de-la-Madeleine, this village was named in 1950. It was named after **Île du Cap aux Meules**, noted as Île aux Meules by Joseph Bouchette (1774–1841) in 1815. Either grindstones (meules) had been quarried here, or some hills resembled haystacks (meules).

Cap-Chat QC In the regional county of Denis-Riverin, northeast of Matane, this town was incorporated in 1968. The township of **Cap-Chat** was proclaimed in 1842, taking its name from a striking rock that resembled the profile of a cat, which was noted as early as 1660 by map-maker Fr. François Du Creux (c.1596–1666).

Cap-de-la-Madeleine QC This city (1918) at the mouth of the Rivière Saint-Maurice and adjacent to Trois-Rivières, took its name from a grant to the Jesuits in 1651 by Jacques de La Ferté de La Madeleine, abbot of Sainte-Marie-Madeleine de Châteaudun, southwest of Paris, France. The religious parish of Sainte-Marie-Madeleine-du-Cap-de-la-Madeleine was established in 1651. The parish municipality was called *Sainte-Marie-Madeleine* in 1855. In 2002 the city was annexed by Trois-Rivières.

Cap-d'Espoir QC This location in the town of Percé and in the regional county of Pabok, southwest of the town centre, was named in 1935 after the cape, which was first identified on a 1685 map by Emmanuel Jumeau. Often called 'Cape Despair' in English, it was identified as that on Thomas Jefferys's 1775 map. Although *espoir* means 'hope', there is reliable linguistic evidence that it was pronounced like 'despair' in seventeenth- and eighteenth-century French.

Cap-des-Rosiers QC A community in the town of Gaspé and in the regional county of La Côte-de-Gaspé, northeast of the town centre, its harbour was visited by fishermen in the middle of the 1600s. The cape's name, which refers to wild roses, was noted by Samuel de Champlain (1567–1635) in 1632.

Cape Breton Island NS This island is named after the most southeasterly cape of the island. The cape's name, one of the oldest on the Atlantic coast, may have been given in the early 1500s after English fishermen. However, there are claims it was called after fishermen from Bretagne, France or after Capbreton in southwestern France, near ports where Basque whalers and fishermen set out to exploit the resources of the New World. The first cartographic reference to it is *c. dos bretoes* on a map produced about 1521. Before 1550 the island was commonly called *tiera de bretones* and *Terre des Bretons*. During the French regime it was called *Isle Royale*. Cape Breton was a separate crown colony from 1784 to 1820, when it became part of Nova Scotia. Cape Breton County was established in 1820 and became the regional municipality of **Cape Breton**

in 1995. **Cape Breton Highlands National Park** (951 km²) was created in 1936.

Cape Broyle NL This locality at the head of **Cape Broyle Harbour** and on the east coast of the Avalon Peninsula was named after the cape, at the southeast side of the harbour. Identified as *Cape Broile* by John Guy (d.1629) in 1612, the cape may have been named after the turbulence of the sea crashing on the rocks. It is possible that the name derives from the Portuguese *albrolho* ('pointed rock'), but there is no carto-graphic evidence for this suggestion.

Cape Croker ON On the east side of Bruce Peninsula, this community on **Cape Croker Indian Reserve** was named in the 1850s after the nearby cape. The cape was named in 1822 by Admiralty surveyor Henry W. Bayfield (1795–1885) for John Wilson Croker (1780–1853), secretary at the British Admiralty, 1809–30.

Cape Dorset NU On **Dorset Island** and on the southwest coast of Baffin Island, this hamlet (1982) was established in 1913 by the Hudson's Bay Company. The cape was named in 1631 by Luke Foxe (c.1586–1635) after Edward Sackville, 7th Earl of Dorset (1590–1652). The island was named after the cape in 1930 by naturalist J. Dewey Soper (1893–1982).

Cape Sable Island NS At the southwestern end of the province, this island takes its name from the cape identi-fied as *Cap de Sable* ('sandy cape') by Samuel de Champlain (1567–1635) in 1607. After 1761 the English adapted the name from the French *Isle du Cap de Sable*.

Cape Tormentine NB The post office in this community, which is located at the most easterly point of the province, was named in 1847 after the cape. The cape was called *Cap de Tourmentin* on Nicolas Denys's map of 1672, with the possible meaning of 'cape of storms'. Thomas Jefferys's 1755 map had *Stormy Point* and John Mitchell's 1755 map had *C. Storm*. Frederick Holland's 1791 map introduced C. Tormentine.

Caplan QC The name of this municipality-located in the regional county of Bonaventure, southeast of New Richmond-has its roots in the name **Rivière Caplan**. The river's name likely derives from the Portuguese *capelinas* ('capelin'), a small fish of the smelt family.

Cap-Pelé NB The post office in this village (1969)—21 km east of Shediac—was renamed *Cape Bald* from 1879 to 1903 and 1906 to 1947. The post office was *Cap Pelé* from 1903 to 1906, and has been Cap-Pelé from 1947. In the 1600 and 1700s the cape was variously called *C au Haran, C. Harang, C. Herring, C. Heron,* and *C. Scott*. A land petition in 1807 called it *Cap a Lee*.

Capreol ON In 2001 this town (1918) became part of the city of Greater Sudbury, Sudbury Region, north of the centre of Sudbury. It was named in 1911 after Frederick Chase Capreol (1803-86), a Toronto railway promoter in the mid-1800s.

Cap-Rouge QC In 2002 Cap-Rouge became a sector of Quebec City. Cap-Rouge was established as the parish muni-cipality of *Saint-Félix-du-Cap-Rouge* in 1872, and the town of Cap-Rouge in 1983. The cape of red schist rocks was noted as **Cap Rouge** as early as 1637. The name was deformed into Carouge from the seventeenth to the nineteenth centuries.

Cap-Saint-Ignace QC This municipality, located in the regional county of Montmagny and on the south shore of the St. Lawrence, northeast of Quebec City, was incorporated in 1981, having previously been the parish municipality of *Saint-Ignace* since 1855. The cape's name, given after Jesuit founder St. Ignatius of Loyola (c.1491–1556), was shown on Bourdon's 1641 map.

Cap-Santé QC A municipality (1979) in the regional county of Portneuf, southwest of Quebec City, its parish of La Sainte-Famille-du-Cap-Santé was founded in 1679. The cape was noted on Vincenzo Coronelli's 1689 map. The meaning of its name is uncertain.

Caradoc ON In 2001 this township became part of the township of **Strathroy-Caradoc**, Middlesex County. Caradoc was named in 1820 after a revered king of Wales, who was killed during a battle in 795 CE between the Welsh and the Saxons.

Caraquet NB A town (1961) on **Baie de Caraquet**, an extension of Chaleur Bay, it was settled about 1760 by shipwrecked sailors, and later by Acadians and French-speaking settlers from Quebec. **Rivière Caraquet**, which flows into the bay, was identified as Caraquet on Nicolas Denys's map of 1672. The name perhaps derives from the Mi'kmaq *pkalge* (possibly 'junction of two rivers'), in reference to the point where the Rivière du Nord joins the main river.

Carberry MB This town (1905) is located east of Brandon. Its Canadian Pacific Railway station was supposed to be located at De Winton in 1881, 3 km to the east. However, the next year, when the landowner proposed an excessive price for his land, the CPR moved its station to its present site. CPR director James J. Hill (1838–1916) named it after Carberry Tower in Musselburgh, Scotland, east of Edinburgh. The tower was the seat of Lord Elphinstone (1807–1860), an early director of the CPR, who accompanied Hill in 1882.

Carbon AB West of Drumheller, this village (1912) was named in 1904 by settler John M. Bogart, after the local coal mines. In 1905 it was also called *Kneehill*, after the Kneehill Coal Company, which mined the coal deposits on the banks of Kneehills Creek, a tributary of the Red Deer River.

Carbonear NL This town (1948) on **Carbonear Bay** and on the western shore of Conception Bay was first identified as *Carboneare* in the calendar of estate papers of 1674, with the present spelling occurring in 1705. John Guy (d.1629) called the bay *Carbonera Bay* in 1612, with this form persisting into the 1700s alongside *Carbonere* and *Carboniere*. The name, of either Spanish or French origin, probably relates to the production of carbon here.

Carcross YT Located where Bennett and Tagish lakes meet, this place was first known as *Caribou Crossing*. To avoid confusion with other places with similar names, the Right Reverend William Bompas (1834–1906) appealed to the Canadian government in 1901 to rename the place Carcross. The post office department complied with the request the next year, but the White Pass and Yukon Railway did not change its station name until 1916.

Cardiff ON In 2001 this township and Bicroft Township became parts of the municipality of Highlands East, Haliburton County. Cardiff was named in 1862 after the city in Wales. The community of **Cardiff** was named in 1957.

Cardigan PE North of Montague, this municipal community (1983) was incorporated as a village in 1954. Its post office opened in 1863 and was called after **Cardigan River**. The river was named in 1765 by Samuel Holland (1728–1801) after George Brudenell, 4th Earl of Cardigan (1712–90). He also named **Cardigan Bay**, into which the Montague, Brudenell, and Cardigan Rivers flow. Together they were called the *Trois Rivières* during the French regime.

Cardinal ON In 2001 Cardinal became part of the township of **Edwardsburgh/Cardinal**, united counties of Leeds and Grenville. Cardinal is on the St. Lawrence River, northeast of Brockville. The post office in the village (1878) was called *Edwardsburg* in 1837 and was changed to Cardinal in 1880. **Point Cardinal** was named by the French, possibly after Cardinal Richelieu, but a tradition claims that there was a person called Cardinal living there during the French regime.

Cardston AB Located on Lee Creek, a tributary of the St. Mary River, southwest of Lethbridge, this town (1901) was founded by Charles Ora Card (1839–1906), a son-in-law of Mormon leader Brigham Young. He had settled here in 1886, having left Utah to avoid being tried on charges of polygamy. First called *Lees Creek*, it became Cardston when a post office opened in 1892.

Cariboo BC First given to the Quesnel and Barkerville area during the gold rush of the early 1860s, the Cariboo eventually extended to a huge area from Cache Creek in the south to Prince George in the north. In adopting the word in 1861, Gov. James Douglas (1803–77) observed it should more properly be spelled *cariboeuf*. Actually its roots are the French word *caribou*, adapted from the Mi'kmaq *xalibu* ('shoveller', a reference to the way this animal shovels snow with its wide feet to access lichen). The **Cariboo Mountains**, part of the Columbia Mountains, extend from southeast of Purden Lake (east of Prince George) to Valemount and Blue River.

Caribou NS North of Pictou, this is the site of a ferry terminal connecting with Wood Islands, PE. The adjacent harbour and island were noted on an 1838 Arrowsmith map as *Carriboo Harbour* and *Carriboo Island*; these spellings persisted into the latter part of the twentieth century. In 1609 French historian Marc Lescarbot (1570–1629) used the spelling Caribou for the Mi'kmaq *xalibu* ('shoveller', a reference to the way this animal shovels snow with its wide feet to access lichen).

Carievale SK The post office in this village (1903), near the southeastern corner of the province, was named in 1891 by John Young, who had settled here in 1886. Of Scottish origin, the name is said to mean 'lovely valley'.

Carignan QC Established as a town (1965), it is located in the regional county of La Vallée-du-Richelieu, and beside the city of Chambly. In 1855, it was called the municipal parish of *Saint-Joseph-de-Chambly*, but was later renamed after the famous Carignan-Salières Regiment, which settled a large part of the province, especially the Chambly area. The name originates in the town of Carignano in Italy's province of Turino.

Carleton NB On the west side of the province and centred on the town of Woodstock, this county was named in 1831 after Thomas Carleton (1736–1817), the first lieutenant-governor of the province, 1784–1817. In 1899, naturalist William F. Ganong (1864–1941) named the highest point (820 m) in the province, **Mount Carleton**, after him.

Carleton NS Located northeast of Yarmouth, this place was first known as *Temperance*. Its post office was named in 1857 after nearby *Lake Carleton* (now Raynards Lake), called after Sir Guy Carleton, Lord Dorchester. **Carleton Village**, south of Shelburne, was named in 1900 after his brother, Thomas Carleton, the first lieutenant-governor of New Brunswick, 1784–1817.

Carleton ON The county was named in 1798 after Sir Guy Carleton, Baron Dorchester (1724–1808), governor of Quebec, 1768–78, commander-in-chief of the British forces in North America, 1782–6, and governor-in-chief of British North

America, 1786–96. In 1969 the municipalities within it, plus Cumberland Township in the united counties of Prescott and Russell, became the regional municipality of **Ottawa-Carleton**. In 2001 Ottawa-Carleton became the city of Ottawa. *See also* Cumberland, ON; Gloucester, ON; Kanata; Nepean; *and* Rockcliffe Park.

Carleton QC This town in the regional county of Avignon, southwest of Gaspé, was established in 1972 by merging the township municipalities of Carleton and *Carleton-sur-Mer*. The original township of Carleton was named in 1786 after Sir Guy Carleton, Lord Dorchester (1724–1808), governor of Quebec, 1768–78, commander-in-chief of the British forces in North America, 1782–6, and governor-in-chief of British North America, 1786–96. The mountain rising to 609 m to the rear of the town centre was first known as *Mont Tracadigache*, from the Mi'kmaq for 'many herons', with **Mont Carleton** replacing it during the early years of the twentieth century.

Carleton Place ON In Lanark County, this town (1890) was called *Morphy's Falls* in 1819 for Edmond Morphy (1794–1860), a native of County Tipperary, Ireland, and his three sons, William, John, and James. It was renamed Carlton Place in 1829 by innkeeper Alexander Morris, after a street in central Glasgow. However, postal officials spelled it Carleton Place in 1830, following the spelling of nearby Carleton County.

Carleton Siding PE This place was created as a separate municipal community in 1977, and has been in the municipal community of **Borden-Carleton** since 1995. It has been the postal designation here since 1925. Its post office was called *Carleton* in 1870, named after **Carleton Cove**. The name was given by Samuel Holland (1728–1801) in 1765 after Sir Guy Carleton (1724–1808), who subsequently became the governor-in-chief of British North America.

Carlyle SK This town (1906) was established with a post office in 1883. The name was given by John Gillander Turriff (1855–1930), a member of the House of Commons and the Senate who had operated a store here, after the Scottish writer Thomas Carlyle (1795–1881).

Carmacks YT The post office in this village, located on the west bank of the Yukon River and at the mouth of the Nordenskiold River, was named in 1908 after George Washington Carmack (1860–1922). Carmack was a native of California, who developed the coal deposits, and operated a fur trading post here after 1893. Three years later Carmack, Skookum Jim Mason (1855–1916), and Tagish Charlie (d.1908) discovered gold in the gravelly bottom of Bonanza Creek.

Carman MB Situated southwest of Winnipeg, the post office in this town (1905) was named in 1880 by Premier Rodmond Roblin (1853–1937), after the Reverend Dr. Albert Carman (1833–1917), the bishop of the Methodist Episcopal Church in Ontario until 1884, and general superintendent of the Methodist Church of Canada until 1915.

Carmangay AB The post office in this town (1911), located on the Little Bow River, northwest of Lethbridge, was named in 1907 after Charles Whitney Carman; his wife, the former Gertrude Gay; and their son, Gay. They had come from Chicago and bought 600 a (978 hec) here in 1904, and named their farm Carmangay. In 1936 the town became a village.

Carmanville NL On the north shore of Newfoundland, this town (1955) was named in 1906, after the Reverend Dr. Albert Carman (1833–1917), general superintendent of the Methodist Church of Canada. It had been earlier called *Rocky Bay*.

Carnduff SK The post office in this town (1905) in the southeastern part of the province, east of Estevan, was named in 1884 after the first postmaster, John Carnduff (1851–1929). A native of Belfast, Ireland, he settled first in Carleton Place, ON, then in southern Manitoba, and finally moved to the area of Carnduff the year the post office opened.

Carnes Peak BC Located in the Selkirk Mountains, north of Revelstoke, this mountain (3051 m) was named in 1956 by climber William Putnam (b. 1924) after prospector Henry Carnes, who had explored for gold in the creeks flowing into the Columbia in the 1860s. In 1912 alpinist Howard Palmer (1883–1944) had called it *Serenity Mountain*.

Caroline AB In 1908 the post office in this village (1951), southwest of Red Deer, was named after Caroline Langley, the daughter of postmaster Harvey Langley.

Caronport SK This village (1988) west of Moose Jaw was founded in 1946 as the site of a Briercrest Bible Institute, having been located in nearby **Caron** in 1934. It took over an abandoned airport, which had been used to train British Commonwealth airmen during the Second World War. Caronport post office opened in 1947. Caron had been named in 1883 by the Canadian Pacific Railway after Sir Joseph-Philippe-René-Adolphe Caron (1843–1908), minister of militia and defence 1880–92, who organized the forces to put down the Northwest Rebellion.

Carp ON In 2001 this community became part of the city of Ottawa. Carp was located in the township of West Carleton, and was named in 1854 after the **Carp River**, itself called after the suckers (*carpes à cochon*) found here by French voyageurs. It is commonly called 'The Carp' and 'Carp Village'.

Carrick ON In 1999 this township became part of the municipality of South Bruce, Bruce County. Carrick was named in

1850, likely after the Carrick district of Ayrshire, where Robert the Bruce, the King of Scotland, 1306–29, may have been born in 1274. He succeeded his father as the Earl of Carrick in 1292.

Carrot River SK This town (1948) northwest of Tisdale was established in 1921 as a terminus of the Canadian Northern Railway. It is located near **Carrot River**, a tributary of the Saskatchewan River, which it joins just upriver from The Pas, MB. The first Carrot River post office was situated closer to the river in 1907, but was changed the next year to *Silver Stream*. The second Carrot River post office opened in 1921 at the station, changed to *Carrot River Station* in 1931, with Carrot River being restored in 1936. The name of the river is a translation of the Cree *oskatask sipi*.

Carstairs AB This town (1966), located north of Calgary, was named in 1893 by the Calgary and Edmonton Railway Company after Carstairs, Lanarkshire, Scotland, southeast of Glasgow. Its post office opened in 1900.

Cartier ON The post office in **Cartier Township**, Sudbury District and on the Canadian Pacific Railway main line, northwest of the city of Greater Sudbury, was named in 1888. The township had been named three years earlier by surveyor H.B. Proudfoot for Sir George-Étienne Cartier (1814–73), a Father of Confederation and co-premier of the Province of Canada with Sir John A. Macdonald, 1857–62.

Cartier, Mount BC In the Selkirk Mountains, southeast of Revelstoke, this mountain (2610 m) was named in 1886 by Dr. Otto Klotz (1852–1923) after Sir George-Étienne Cartier (1814–73), a Father of Confederation.

Cartwright MB The post office in this village (1947), near the North Dakota border, southeast of Brandon, was named in 1882 after Sir Richard Cartwright (1835–1912), Canadian minister of finance, 1873–8. A native of Kingston, ON, Cartwright was a member of the House of Commons from 1867 to 1904, first as a Conservative, and then as a Liberal from 1869.

Cartwright NL On the Atlantic coast of Labrador, this municipal community (1956) was named after Capt. George Cartwright (c.1739–1819), who traded on the coast from 1770 to 1786.

Cascade Mountain AB Overlooking the town of Banff, this mountain (2998 m) was named in 1858 by Dr. Sir James Hector (1834–1907), translating an Aboriginal designation meaning 'mountain where the water falls'.

Cascumpec Bay PE South of the town of Alberton, this bay's name derives from the Mi'kmaq *kaskampek* ('bold sandy shore'), in reference to the **Cascumpec Sand Hills**, which enclose the bay. On a 1631 map by Jean Guérard the bay is called *Caisiqupet*, and in 1744 Jacques Nicolas Bellin referred to it as *Casquembec*. In 1765 Samuel Holland (1728–1801) identified it as *Holland Bay by the French Kascumpeck*. He likely intended to name it after Henry Fox, 1st Baron Holland of Foxley. The Geographic Board spelled it *Cascumpeque Bay* in 1901, but the local spelling was restored in 1966. **Cascumpec** was a postal designation in Alberton South from 1839 to 1868, and is now a locality on the southwest side of the bay.

Casselman ON In 1998 this village (1888) became part of the municipality of The Nation, united counties of Prescott and Russell. Located on the east side of the South Nation River, some 50 km east of Ottawa, the village was settled in 1843 by farmer and lumberman Martin Casselman. Casselman post office opened in 1857 on the west side of the river. The post office was moved to the east side in 1898, replacing the *South Casselman* office, opened in 1886.

Cassiar Mountains BC, YT Located mostly in the northwestern part of British Columbia, with the Coast Mountains on the west and the Rocky Mountains on the east, these mountains probably take their name from the Kaska, a First Nations people from this area. Kaska may mean 'creek' or 'small river' after the McDame Creek, where they gathered in summer to fish and trade, or 'old mocassins', a term of derision given by the neighbouring Tahltan. In 1952 the community of Cassiar was established north of Dease Lake by the Cassiar Asbestos Corporation and attained a population of over 800 by 1976. In 1992 the corporation ceased operations and all of the place's buildings were sold and moved away.

Castlegar BC This city (1974), located at the confluence of the Columbia and Kootenay Rivers, was founded in 1902 by the Canadian Pacific Railway. After constructing a station here, an observer was reminded of the Castle Garden in New York City's Battery Park, which served as the immigrant landing depot from 1859 to 1890. Following the practice of shortening the names of stations, the CPR called it Castlegar.

Castle Mountain AB Northwest of Banff, this 11-km-long mountain (2862 m) was named in 1858 by Dr. Sir James Hector, because he was reminded of a great crenellated castle in Britain. In 1946 Prime Minister Mackenzie King instructed the Geographic Board of Canada to rename it after Gen. Dwight Eisenhower, then supreme commander of the allied forces in Europe. Persistent public pressure resulted in the original name being restored in 1979, with **Eisenhower Peak** assigned to its prominent eastern elevation.

Castor AB A town (1909) east of Stettler, it was named by the Canadian Pacific Railway in 1909 after nearby **Castor Creek**, a tributary of Battle River. The French word *castor* means 'beaver'.

Catalina NL South of Bonavista, this town (1958) was probably named after *p de S Catarina*, a Portuguese name portrayed on maps of the east coast of Newfoundland in the 1500s. In 1534 Jacques Cartier spent ten days in *H Saincte Katherine*, where he prepared for further exploration. It was superseded by the Spanish name *Cataluña*.

Catalone NS Southeast of Sydney and on the west side of **Catalone Lake**, its post office opened in 1842. The lake was earlier called *Barachois de Catalogne*, after Gédéon de Catalogne (1662–1729), who commanded a company at the Fortress of Louisbourg after 1723, and undertook the growing of crops in the area of the lake and on the Mira River.

Cataract Peak AB In the Rocky Mountains, north of Lake Louise, this peak (3333 m) was named in 1908 after several waterfalls on the adjacent Pipestone River.

Cataraqui ON In 1998 this community, previously in the township of Kingston, Frontenac County, became part of the city of Kingston. It was known as *Sandville* and *Waterloo* before it was renamed Cataraqui in 1868. The **Cataraqui River** rises north of Kingston, and, from Seeleys Bay, coincides with the Rideau Canal, draining into Lake Ontario on the east side of Kingston. The **Little Cataraqui River** flows into **Cataraqui Bay**, 6 km west of the centre of Kingston. *Cataraqui* is an Iroquois word meaning 'rocks (or clay bank) rising out of the water'.

Cathedral Mountain BC In the Rocky Mountains, east of Field, this mountain (3189 m) was named in 1900 by Sir James Outram for its imposing outline.

Caubvik, Mount NL This highest point (1650 m) in the Torngat Mountains was named Mont d'Iberville in 1971 by the Commission de toponymie du Quebec. Ten years later the government of Newfoundland and Labrador named it after Caubvik, one of the Inuit who went to London with George Cartwright in 1772. Caubvik was the only Inuit traveller to survive smallpox, and she later returned to the Labrador coast. *See also* D'Iberville, Mont.

Causapscal QC Located in the regional county of La Matapédia, south of Matane, this town was named in 1965. It had previously been the village of Causapscal (1928) and the parish municipality of *Saint-Jacques-le-Majeur-de-Causapscal* (1897). The orignal township, Casupscull, was proclaimed in 1864. In Mi'kmaq, the name means 'stony and glittering bottom'.

Cavan ON In 1998 this township became part of the township of Cavan-Millbrook-North Monaghan, Peterborough County. It was named in 1816 after the north-

central county in Ireland. The post office in the community of **Cavan** was named in 1830.

Cavendish PE Northwest of Charlottetown and adjacent to Prince Edward Island National Park, this place was named about 1772 by William Winter, probably after Field Marshal Lord Frederick Cavendish (1729–1803). Its post office, opened in 1833, is now called Green Gables.

Cayley AB Between High River and Nanton, south of Calgary, this place was named in 1893 by the Canadian Pacific Railway after Hugh St. Quentin Cayley (1857–1934), then the member for Calgary in the Assembly of the North-West Territories. Cayley was an incorporated village from 1904 to 1996.

Cayuga ON The post office in this place, located in the town of Haldimand, Haldimand–Norfolk Region, was named in 1851 after **North Cayuga** and **South Cayuga** townships, themselves named in 1835 after the Cayuga nation, one of the Six Nations. There are several interpretations of Cayuga, including 'place where the canoes are drawn out', and 'advising nation'.

Cedar Lake MB This enlargement of the Saskatchewan River, east of The Pas, is located northwest of Lake Winnipeg, found at the most northerly limits of the cedar tree. Discoverer Pierre Gaultier de La Vérendrye (1685–1755) called it *Lac Bourbon* after the reigning house in France, and built *Fort Bourbon* on its shore. Alexander Henry (d.1814) the younger called it *Lac Bourbon* or *Cedar Lake* in 1808.

Centennial Range YT This range of 13 peaks in the St. Elias Mountains was named in 1967 by the Yukon Alpine Centennial Expedition in honour of the one hundredth anniversary of Canada's Confederation. The expedition's organizers named the peaks after Canada's provinces and territories, and its climbers ascended nine of them in a five-week period during that summer.

Central Butte SK Established with a post office in 1907, this town (1967) is northwest of Moose Jaw. It was named after the central opint of three buttes, the first being 27 km west near Demaine, and the third near Eyebrow, 14 km to the east.

Centralia ON In 2001 this place became part of the municipality of South Huron, Huron County. South of Exeter, this community was named *Devon* in 1852 after the many early settlers who came from Devon, England. It was changed to Centralia in 1873, probably after its location in the middle of a rich agricultural area.

Central Kings PE This municipal community (1975) in the central part of Kings County embraces the communities of Albion Cross, Bridgetown, Dundas, and Poplar Point.

Central Saanich BC This district municipality (1950) on the Saanich Peninsula, north of Victoria, takes the second part of its name from the Saanich tribe. In Straits Salish it means 'elevated', in reference to Mount Newton (307 m), the profile of which looks like a raised rump. The community of **Saanichton**, named in 1922, is in the northern part of the municipality. *See also* Saanich *and* North Saanich.

Centreville NB The post office in this village (1966), northwest of Woodstock, was named in 1862 after its location among a cluster of surrounding rural communities.

Centreville NS The post office in this community, located midway between the Cornwallis River and Minas Channel, may have been opened in 1859. A second **Centreville**, in the middle of Digby Neck, and halfway between the town of Digby and the southwest end of the neck, had a post office from about 1875 to 1970. A third **Centreville**, on Cape Sable Island, is halfway between the town of Clark's Harbour and the ferry terminal at North East Point.

Centreville-Wareham-Trinity NL This town on the northwest side of Bonavista Bay was established in 1992. **Centreville**, a neighbourhood midway between Trinity (Bonavista) and Indian Bay (Parson's Point), was created 1959-60 as a resettlement community for the families on Fair Island in the bay. It was the only completely new settlement established in the province during that period, when remote and isolated communities were encouraged to move to areas served by land-based communication and transportation links. **Wareham**, on the south side of Indian Bay, and on the northwest side of Bonavista Bay, was named in 1931 by the Firmage family, natives of Wareham, Dorset, England. The family had settled here in 1918. **Trinity**, at the head of Trinity Bay, a small bay on the northwestern side of Bonavista Bay, first appeared in the census of 1901.

Cerburus Mountain BC In the Coast Mountains, southeast of Bella Coola, this mountain (3155 m) was named in 1953 by a member of the Alpine Club of Canada because its three summits reminded him of the mythical three-headed dog guarding the gates of hell.

Cereal AB The post office in this village (1914) east of Hanna was named in 1911 on the suggestion of the Reverend R.J. McMillan, after the region's prospect of becoming the 'bread basket of the west'.

Ceylon ON In 1998 this place became part of the township of Artemesia, Grey County. First known as *Virginia, Walterville*,

and *Flesherton Station*, it was named Ceylon in 1899, when a postal inspector found a package of Ceylon tea in Tristam Chislett's store.

Ceylon SK Situated southwest of Weyburn, on the Radville-Willow Bunch line of the Canadian Northern Railway, this village and its station were established in 1911. Earlier the post office here had been called *Aldred* after pioneer settler John Aldred, but he recommended Ceylon for the station. *Ceylon Station* post office opened in 1911 and was changed to Ceylon in 1957. It may have been called after a yacht used in races by Sir Thomas Lipton (1848–1931). There is a Ceylon Street in Lipton, SK.

Chaffeys Lock ON This lock in the united counties of Leeds and Grenville and on the Rideau Canal was settled after the War of 1812 by Samuel Chaffey (d.1827), who built several mills. He died before the lock was constructed.

Chaleur Bay NB; **Baie des Chaleurs** QC This wide bay, extending from the mouth of the Restigouche River to Miscou Island, was named on 9 July 1534 by Jacques Cartier (1491–1557), who observed that the great heat (*chaleur*) reminded him of Spain.

Chalk River ON In 2000 this village (1954) northwest of Pembrooke became part of the town of Laurentian Hills, Renfrew County. The post office here was named in 1875 after the nearby river, whose name may derive from the chalk used to mark timber at its outlet in Rafting Bay.

Chambly QC This city on the Rivière Richelieu, east of Montreal, was created in 1965 when the towns of Chambly and *Fort-Chambly* were merged. In 1672 Jacques de Chambly (c.1640–87) was granted the seigneury of Chambly at the rapids on the Richelieu, where he had constructed Fort Saint-Louis in 1765, but it was subsequently named Fort Chambly.

Chambord QC This municipality (1916) is located on the south shore of Lac Saint-Jean and in the regional county of Le Domaine-du-Roy. Its post office was named in 1872 after Henri V de Bourbon, comte de Chambord (1820–83), a pretender to the French throne.

Champion AB Northwest of Lethbridge, this village (1911) was named by the Canadian Pacific Railway in 1909 after H.T. Champion of the Winnipeg banking firm of Alloway and Champion. *Cleverville* post office, opened nearby in 1907 and named after settler Martin G. Clever, was moved into Champion and renamed in 1910.

Champlain QC Established in 1983, this regional county is on the southeast side of the St. Lawrence, and now embraces the cities of Longueuil, Saint-Lambert, and Brossard, and the borough of Saint-Hubert. It was named after the founder of Quebec, Samuel de Champlain (1567–1635). Also named after him was the huge lake separating New York and Vermont, and an electoral district east of Trois-Rivières, where the municipality of **Champlain** is located at the mouth of a river also named after him.

Champlain, Mount NB Northwest of Saint John and on the perimeter of the Canadian Forces Base Gagetown, this mountain (446 m) was named in 1901 by naturalist William F. Ganong (1864–1941) after Samuel de Champlain (1567–1635). Before that it was called *Bald Mountain*, a common name in the province.

Chance Cove NL On the Isthmus of Avalon and on the southeast shore of Trinity Bay, this town (1972) is located on **Big Chance Cove** and **Little Chance Cove**. The coves may have been named because they were difficult to enter as a refuge during storms. *See also* Come-By-Chance.

Chancellor Peak BC This mountain (3280 m) in Yoho National Park, south of Field, was named in 1898 after Sir John Alexander Boyd (1837–1916), chancellor of Ontario, who arbitrated a dispute between the Canadian Pacific Railway and the Dominion of Canada over some mineral rights.

Chandler QC This town (1958) in the regional county of Pabok, southwest of Gaspé, was named a village in 1916 after Percy Milton Chandler of Philadelphia, who was the first president of the St. Lawrence Pulp and Paper Corp., which built a mill here in 1912.

Change Islands NL This town (1951) is located on a narrow tickle separating two of the **Change Islands**, which are between Fogo and New World Islands. It was established in the late 1700s as a centre of the English fishery on the Labrador coast.

Channel-Port aux Basques NL This town (1945) on the southwestern coast of Newfoundland is comprised of the former communities of Channel and Port aux Basques, as well as adjoining settlements. The original settlement of Channel was named after a narrow channel separating a small island from the peninsula on which it is located. The harbour called **Port aux Basques** was likely named by French explorers after Basque whalers, encountered here in the late 1500s. Samuel de Champlain (1567–1635) recorded it as *pot aux basque*. In the 1700s it was called *Swift Harbour* and *Swints Harbour*, with Capt. James Cook (1728–79) identifying it as *Port aux Basque* in 1764. Since 1893 it has been the main terminus linking Newfoundland with Nova Scotia.

Chantrey Inlet NU An inlet of the Arctic Ocean, and at the mouth of Back River, it was named in 1921 after the Chantrey Hills, shown on maps on the west side of the inlet. The hills were named in 1834 by Capt. Sir George Back (1796–1872) after sculptor Sir Francis Legatt Chantrey (1781–1842). However, when air photography did not reveal hills in that location in 1952, this name was rescinded.

Chapais QC This mining town northwest of Lac Saint-Jean and southwest of Chibougamau was established in 1955 and named after Senator Thomas Chapais (1858–1946), a prominent journalist, historian, and politician.

Chapeau QC The name of this village—incorporated in 1874 and located in the regional county of Pontiac, north of Pembroke, ON—is attributed to a rock shaped like a hat (*chapeau*) in the Rapides de la Culbute of the Ottawa River.

Chapel Arm NU This town (1970) is located on the Isthmus of Avalon and on Chapel Arm at the south end of Trinity Bay. The arm was possibly named after some steep hills, whose sharp elevations resembled the spires of chapels.

Chapleau ON In **Chapleau Township**, Sudbury District, this community was named in 1886 after Sir Joseph-Adolphe Chapleau (1840–98), premier of Quebec, 1879–82, secretary of state in the government of Canada, 1882–92, and lieutenant-governor of Quebec, 1892–8. The township was incorporated in 1906.

Chaplin SK Situated on the Canadian Pacific Railway, midway between Moose Jaw and Swift Current, the station of this village (1912) was named in 1883 after **Chaplin Lake**, which extends some 30 km to the south of the village. The lake had been named in 1861 by Sir John Rae (1813–93) after a hunting companion Henry Chaplin (1840–1923), later 1st Viscount Chaplin. The post office opened in 1907.

Chapman, Mount BC Located in the Selkirk Mountains, north of Revelstoke, this mountain (3075 m) was named in 1917 by climber Howard Palmer (1883–1944) after geologist Robert Hollister Chapman (1868–1920), who had accompanied Palmer in a survey of the Selkirks.

Charlemagne QC Located in the regional county of L'Assomption, northeast of Montreal, this municipality was named *Laurier* in 1907 and was changed the next year to Charlemagne, which became a town in 1969. It was given in honour of Romuald-Charlemagne Laurier (1852–1906), half-brother of Sir Wilfrid Laurier and member for L'Assomption in the House of Commons, 1900–6.

Charlesbourg QC In 2002 this city became a borough in Quebec City. It was created a village in 1914, became the municipality of *Charlesbourg-Est* in 1928, and the city of Charlesbourg in 1949. The name was mentioned in the civil registers of 1666, taking its name from the first chapel built at *Bourg-Royal*, which was dedicated to Saint Charles Borromée (1538–84). The municipal parish of *Saint-Charles-Borromée* was created in 1845 in the area of Charlesbourg.

Charleston ON Located on **Charleston Lake**, west of Brockville, this community was settled in 1836, with its post office named in 1853. It is known today as on of Canada's first vacation resorts.

Charlevoix QC A regional county northeast of Quebec City and centred on the town of Baie-Saint-Paul, it was named in 1982, succeeding the former county of Charlevoix-Ouest. The regional county of **Charlevoix-Est** was proclaimed the same year. The names originate from the noted historian Jesuit Fr. Pierre-François-Xavier de Charlevoix (1682–1761), who wrote the *Histoire et description générale de la Nouvelle-France* (1744).

Charlo NB This village (1969) southeast of Dalhousie was incorporated in 1966 as Colborne after the local territorial parish. Its post office was called *Charlo Station* in 1881 and was renamed Charlo in 1968. It took its name from the **Charlo River**, which may have been called after an early settler, such as Charles 'Charlo' Doucet, the founder of the village of Petit-Rocher, or after a trapper from Quebec.

Charlotte NB In the southwestern part of the province, this county was named in 1785 after Queen Charlotte (1744–1818), the consort of George III.

Charlottenburgh ON In 1998 this township became part of the township of South Glengarry, the united counties of Stormont, Dundas and Glengarry. Charlottenburgh Township was named in 1787 after Queen Charlotte Sophia (1744–1818), the wife of George III.

Charlottetown NL This city was first known as *Brown's Cove*. It was renamed at the end of the nineteenth century, possibly after Charlotte (Hussey) Spracklin, the first woman settler, or after Charlottetown, PE. There is a second **Charlottetown** on the coast of Labrador, north of Port Hope Simpson. First known as *Old Cove*, it was renamed about 1949 by lumberman Ben Powell after the capital of Prince Edward Island.

Charlottetown PE This city (1855) was established in **Charlottetown Royalty** in 1765 by Surveyor General Samuel Holland (1728–1801). He named both of them after Queen Charlotte Sophia (1744–1818), the consort of George III. The royalty, one of the original 70 divisions laid out by Holland, is now entirely within the city limits.

Charlton ON Located in Timiskaming District, northwest of New Liskeard, Charlton became a town in 1914; in 1996 it was Ontario's smallest town, with a population of just 275. Charlton was named in 1904 after brothers John Charlton (1829–1910), a member in the House of Commons, 1872–1904, and William Andrew Charlton (1841–1930), a member in the Ontario Legislature, 1890–1904, and a member in the House of Commons, 1911–21. In 2003 Charlton and the township of Dack became a municipality, with a population of 613.

Charlton, Mount AB On the west side of Maligne Lake and southeast of Jasper, this mountain (3217 m) was named in 1911 by Mary Schäffer, after Henry Ready Charlton (1866–1919), general advertising agent of the Grand Trunk Pacific Railway, 1898–1919.

Charny QC Located in the regional county of Les Chutes-de-la-Chaudière, south of Quebec City, Charny was incorporated as a village in 1924 and a town in 1965. The name was given in honour of Jean de Lauson de Charny (c.1620–1661), a son of New France Gov. Jean de Lauson (1583–1666). He was appointed by his father as the grand seneschal (judge) of New France and was killed by the Iroquois on Île d'Orléans.

Chase BC On Little Shuswap Lake, northwest of Salmon Arm, this village (1969) was named in 1908 by James A. Magee, secretary of the Adams River Lumber Company, after Whitfield Chase (1820–96), the first settler, who established a ranch here in 1865. An American, Chase joined the Cariboo Gold Rush in the early 1860s. He was brought here by Aboriginals, after having been rescued in the Adams River country, where he had gotten lost.

Châteauguay QC Situated at the mouth of the Rivière Châteauguay and in the regional county of Roussillon, southwest of Montreal, this city was created in 1975 through the merger of the towns of Châteauguay and *Châteauguay-Centre*. The name has its roots in the seigneury of Charles Le Moyne de Longueuil et de Châteauguay (1626–85), granted in 1673 by Comte Louis de Buade Frontenac, Governor General of New France.

Château-Richer QC A town (1968) in the regional county of La Côte-de-Beaupré, northeast of Quebec City, its post office was named in 1832. This name occurred on a 1641 map by Jean Bourdon, but its origin is uncertain.

Chatham NB Part of the city of Miramichi since 1 January 1995, it was named about 1800 by Francis Peabody after William Pitt, 1st Earl of Chatham (1759–1806), who was then the prime minister of Great Britain. Its post office opened in 1825, and it became an incorporated town in 1896.

Chatham ON In 1793 Lt.-Gov. John Graves Simcoe (1752–1806) proposed naming a town Chatham on the Thames, downriver from London, ON. **Chatham Township** in Kent County was named in 1794, and remained a separate municipality from the city. Incorporated as a village in 1851, Chatham became a town four years later, and finally a city in 1895. In 1998 the city and the township, along with the other towns, villages, and townships in Kent County, became the municipality of **Chatham-Kent**.

Chatham QC A township municipality (1845) in the regional county of Argenteuil, west of Lachute, it was named after the township of **Chatham**, proclaimed in 1799 and called after William Pitt, 1st Earl of Chatham (1708–78), the father of noted British prime minister William Pitt (1759–1806).

Chats, Lac des ON, QC The name of this 40-km enlargement of the Ottawa River at Arnprior reflects the description of *Chats Falls* (dammed in the 1930s for hydroelectric development), which either had the appearance of a wildcat's paw or sounded like hissing wildcats.

Chatsworth ON In 2000 the village of Chatsworth and the townships of Holland and Sullivan in Grey County became the township of **Chatsworth**. A village (1904) in Grey County, south of Owen Sound, it was named in 1857 by postmaster Henry Caldwell after his birthplace near Chatsworth House in Derbyshire, southwest of Sheffield, England.

Chaudière Falls ON, **Chaudières, Chute des** QC Located on the Ottawa River and between the cities of Ottawa and Gatineau, these falls were first described in 1613 by Samuel de Champlain (1567–1635). The Algonquin called its large deep basin, shaped by the swift eddies below the falls, Asticou, which Champlain interpreted as *chaudière* (kettle).

Chaudière, Rivière QC Rising in Lac Mégantic, near the border of Maine, this river flows almost 200 km to the north to empty into the St. Lawrence, upriver from Quebec City. Samuel de Champlain (1567–1635) called it *Rivière des Etechemins* on his 1612 and 1632 maps, but after 1650 it usually had a variation of Rivière Chaudière, referring to a deep circular hole in relatively soft rock surrounded by more resistant rock in the **Chutes de la Chaudière**, 3 km above the mouth of the river.

Chauvin AB Near the Saskatchewan border, southeast of Wainwright, this village (1912) was named by the Grand Trunk Pacific Railway in 1908 after George von Chauvin, a director of the Grand Trunk's parent, the Grand Trunk Railway. The post office opened the following year.

Cheadle, Mount BC This mountain (2660 m) in the Monashee Mountains, south of Valemount, was named in 1863 by Viscount Milton (1839–77) after Dr. Walter Butler Cheadle (1835–1910), who undertook an arduous journey through the western mountains in 1862–3.

Chedabucto Bay NS Separating the mainland from Isle Madame, this bay extends for 60 km from Cape Canso to the head of the bay at Guysborough. In Mi'kmaq it was called *Sedabooktook* ('a bay running far back').

Chelmsford ON In 2001 this urban centre became part of the city of Greater Sudbury, Sudbury Region. It was named in 1886 after Chelmsford in Sussex, England, northeast of London. It had been an incorporated town from 1910 to 1969, when it was transferred into the town of Rayside-Balfour.

Chelsea QC This municipality northwest of the city of Gatineau replaced *Hull-Partie-Ouest* in 1990. Chelsea was developed in 1819 at the present site of **Old Chelsea**, and was likely named by Thomas Brigham and his nephew Thomas Brigham Prentiss after Chelsea, VT, south of Barre.

Chemainus BC In the district municipality of North Cowichan, southeast of Ladysmith, this community was named in 1871 after the Tsiminnis, a Salish tribe. In Island Halkomelem it means 'bitten breast', in reference to the crescent shape of **Chemainus Bay,** which, legend claims, was a bite taken from a bystander by an excited shaman during a tribal ceremony.

Chemong Lake ON The name of this lake—one of the Kawartha Lakes, north of Peterborough—derives from the Ojibwa *Tchiman* ('canoe') in reference to its long curving shape. Curve Lake Indian Reserve is at its north end.

Chénéville QC The post office in this village, located in the regional county of Papineau, northeast of Buckingham, was called *Hartwell* from 1876 to 1884, when it was renamed after postmaster Hercule Chéné.

Chephren, Mount AB Named *Black Pyramid* by British climber Norman Collie (1859–1942) in 1898, this mountain northeast of Howse Pass was renamed in 1918 by the Alberta–British Columbia Boundary Commission. It was named after the son of King Khufu (Cheops), who was the builder of the Great Pyramid in 2565 BCE.

Chertsey QC Situated in the regional county of Matawinie, west of Joliette, this municipality was named in 1991 after the parish municipality, created in 1856. It took its name from the township, proclaimed in 1795, and named after Chertsey, in Surrey, England, southwest of London.

Chesley ON In 1999 this town became part of the municipality of Arran-Elderslie, Bruce County. The post office of the town (1906) was named in 1868 by the post office department after Solomon Yeomans Chesley (1795–1880), an official of the department in Ottawa. From 1820 to 1845 he was the Indian agent at the St. Regis Indian Reserve near Cornwall.

Chester NS Located on Mahone Bay, this village (1963) was first called Shoreham after Shoreham Township (created in 1759), named after Shoreham, Sussex, England. It was changed to Chester within a year, possibly after Chester, PA. Postal service was provided at Chester in 1832 and at nearby **Chester Basin** in 1855.

Chesterfield Inlet NU A hamlet (1980) on the south side of the mouth of **Chesterfield Inlet**, it was named in 1946. The inlet, which extends for 160 km to the mouth of the Thelon River, was named in 1747 by William Moor and Francis Smith after Peter Dormer Stanhope, 5th Earl of Chesterfield (1694–1773). Moor and Smith were sponsored by the North West Committee to seek a western outlet of the Northwest Passage.

Chestermere AB This town (1995) east of Calgary had been developed since 1959 as a summer community surrounding **Chestermere Lake**. The lake was created in 1906 by the Canadian Pacific Railway as a reservoir and may have been named after one of the railway's directors.

Chesterville ON In 1998 this village (1889) was transferred into the township of North Dundas, united counties of Stormont, Dundas and Glegarry. It was first known as *Armstrong's Mills* after miller Thomas Armstrong. In 1845 its post office was called *Winchester*, but in 1876 it was renamed for merchant and telegraph operator Chester Casselman. *See also* Winchester.

Chéticamp NS The name of this community, located on the west side of Cape Breton Island, is of French origin, and may mean 'poor' or 'miserable camping'. Its first post office opened in 1837, and the second was opened in 1868. **Chéticamp Island** is connected to Cape Breton Island by a narrow isthmus.

Chetwynd BC West of Dawson Creek, this district municipality (1983) was incorporated as a village in 1962. The post office here was called *Little Prairie* in 1949, but it was renamed in 1959 after Ralph L.T. Chetwynd (1890–1957), minister of railways, 1952–4. He had the Pacific Great Eastern Railway (now the British Columbia Railway) extended from Prince George to Dawson Creek and Fort St. John.

Chezzetcook Inlet NS East of Dartmouth, this inlet's name derives from the Mi'kmaq sesetcook ('flowing rapidly in many channels'). Among places surrounding the inlet, with postal

opening dates, are **West Chezzetcook** (1864 as *Chezzetcook*), **Head of Chezzetcook** (1880), **East Chezzetcook** (1880), and **Lower East Chezzetcook** (1897).

Chibougamau QC This town, located 200 km northwest of Lac Saint-Jean, was established as a mining centre in 1952. The name desrives from **Lac Chibougamau**, which in Cree may mean 'a lake crossed from side to side by a river', 'water blocked by a narrow outlet', or 'meeting place'.

Chic-Chocs, Monts QC This mountain chain in the Gaspé has several high summits, including Mont-Jacques Cartier, which rises to 1268 m. The Mi'kmaq word *sigsôg* signifies 'steep rocks' or 'rocky mountains'.

Chicoutimi QC Chicoutimi is one of the three boroughs in the city of Saguenay, which were established in 2002. The city of Saguenay is in the regional county of Le Fjord-du-Saguenay. **Chicoutimi** had its beginnings in 1845 in the township of Chicoutimi on the south bank of the Rivière Saguenay. In Montagnais, *chicoutimi* means 'the end of the deep water'.

Chidley, Cape NL, NU This place is the most northerly point of the province of Newfoundland and Labrador on Killinek Island, with Nunavut sharing Cape Chidley and the island. The cape was named in 1587 by explorer John Davis (c.1550–1605) probably after John Chidley (or Chudleigh), a friend and neighbour, near Exeter, in Devon, England.

Chignecto Bay NB, NS The northeastern head of the Bay of Fundy, this bay's name may derive from the Mi'kmaq *sigunikt* ('footcloth'). It may have applied originally to **Cape Chignecto** in Nova Scotia, which separates the bay from Minas Channel, or from *saukanicktook* ('forks at the mouth'), referring to the LaPlanche and Missaguash Rivers flowing together into the head of Cumberland Basin. Fr. Pierre Biard called it Chinictou in 1611. The 30-km-wide **Chignecto Isthmus** joins New Brunswick to Nova Scotia.

Chilcoot Pass BC This pass (1140 m) on the Alaska–British Columbia border, just west of White Pass, was named in the Alaska Coast Pilot of 1883 *Chilkoot Portage* and *Shasheki Pass*. The Chilcoot, a Tlingit tribe, live in the areas of Skagway and Haines.

Chilcotin River BC Rising 160 km west of Quesnel, this 235-km river flows southeast to join the Fraser River, 45 km southwest of Williams Lake. The area is occupied by the Chilcotin, an Athapaskan tribe. Their name means 'ochre river people', in reference to red and yellow mineralized substances valued as a base for dyes and paints. The area west of Williams Lake is commonly called 'the Chilcotin' and 'the Chilcotin country'.

Chilkat Pass BC North of the Alaska–British Columbia border, and midway between Haines, AK, and Haines Junction, YT, this pass was named in 1957 after the **Chilkat River**. The river, which rises east of the pass, was named in 1898 after a Tlingit tribe, whose name means 'salmon storehouse'.

Chilko Lake BC This lake, located in the Coast Mountains, is drained by the **Chilko River** northeast into the Chilcotin River. The river was identified on Joseph Trutch's 1871 map as *Chilcote*, but the Geographic Board of Canada authorized the present name in 1911. *Chilko* is a variant of Chilcotin, which means 'ochre river' in the Chilcotin language.

Chilliwack BC Chilliwack post office opened in 1872, a village was created in 1873, and the city in 1908. Since 1980, it has been a district municipality. The incorporated township (1873), which surrounded the city before 1980, was called *Chilliwhack*. The **Chilliwack River** rises to the east in **Chilliwack Lake**, and flows west to join the Vedder River, in the southern part of the district municipality. The name of the Chilliwack, a Salish tribe, means either 'quieter water on the head', or 'travel by way of a backwater or slough'.

Chinguacousy ON This township was named in 1819 by Lt.-Gov. Sir Peregrine Maitland (1777–1854) after the Mississauga name for the Credit River, which means 'young pine'. In 1974 it was divided equally between Brampton and Caledon in Peel Region. *See also* Albion, Brampton, *and* Caledon.

Chipman AB Northeast of Edmonton, the village (1913) was founded in 1905 by the Canadian Northern Railway. It was named after Clarence Campbell Chipman, private secretary to Sir Charles Tupper (1821–1915), when he was minister of railways and canals in 1882. He was appointed chief commissioner of the Hudson's Bay Company in 1891.

Chipman NB The post office in this village (1966) on the Salmon River, northeast of Fredericton, was named in 1865 after **Chipman Parish**. In 1835 the parish was called after Ward Chipman Jr. (1787–1851), chief justice of the province, 1834–50. About 1870 W.C. King tried to rename the place *Lillooet* after a schooner built by his brother George, which he had named after the place in British Columbia, but by 1903 that name had been almost forgotten.

Chiputneticook Lakes NB This series of lakes is located on the New Brunswick–Maine border and near the head of the St. Croix River. The name was taken from the Passamaquoddy word meaning 'great fork river', in reference to that part of the river above Grand Falls Flowage, a lake northwest of St. Stephen.

Chisasibi QC This Cree village—located at the mouth of La Grande Rivière, where the river flows into James Bay—was created in 1978 by Hydro-Quebec to provide a new community for the residents of Fort George. In Cree the name means 'grand river'.

Choiceland SK The post office for this town (1979), located west of Nipawin, opened in 1927. It was named by local resident Peter Rotz in recognition of the high quality of soils in the area.

Chomedey QC This town was created in 1961 by amalgamating Saint-Martin, Renaud, and L'Abord-à-Plouffe, and was named after Paul de Chomedey (1612–76), first governor of the Île de Montréal, 1641–65. In 1965 Chomedey was united with all municipalities on the Île Jésus to form the city of Laval. Chomedey is now a sector of Laval.

Chown, Mount AB Located in the northwestern part of Jasper National Park, this mountain (3381 m) was named in 1912 by Arthur Wheeler (1860–1945) after the Reverend Samuel Dwight Chown (1853–1933), a Winnipeg Methodist clergyman and founder of the United Church of Canada in 1925.

Christina Lake BC The post office in this community, located between Trail and Grand Forks, was named in 1912 after the adjacent lake. The lake was named in 1870 after Christina McDonald McKenzie Williams (1847–1925), daughter of Hudson's Bay Company trader Angus McDonald (1816–89). That year she had saved valuable HBC records during a rafting accident on the lake, and the following year the lake was identified on Joseph Trutch's map.

Christopher Lake SK Located north of Prince Albert, the post office of this village (1985) was named in 1925 after Christopher Graval. The nearby lake was named about 10 years earlier by his brother-in-law J.E. Morrier, the district surveyor.

Churchbridge SK This town (1964), southeast of Yorkton, was named in 1886, when the Manitoba and North Western Railway was built from Winnipeg to Saskatoon. The place was developed by the Church Colonization Land Society of the Anglican Church. The name was formed from the society's title and from the name of the Reverend John Bridger, a society director. Its post office opened in 1889.

Churchill MB Manitoba's seaport, and the Hudson Bay Railway's terminus, this community is located at the mouth of the **Churchill River** on Hudson Bay. Its post office was named in 1932 after Fort Churchill, constructed here in 1686 and named after John Churchill, the Duke of Marlborough (1650–1722). Churchill had been made a governor of the Hudson's Bay Company the previous year. The river was subsequently named after the fort, having been called *Danish River* and *Manoteusibi* (Cree for 'stranger's river'), in reference to a visit in 1619–20 by the Danish naval officer Jens Munk (1579–1628); *Missinipi* in 1714 (Cree for 'big river'); and *English River*, given by fur trader Joseph Frobisher in 1775.

Churchill PE The post office for this place, located west of Charlottetown, was named in 1900 after Sir Winston Spencer Churchill (1874–1965), who had then received considerable fame as a reporter of the South African War. Although the post office existed for only 13 years, its name was reinforced by a church built here on a hillside.

Churchill Falls NL Located on the **Churchill River** in Labrador, this set of falls (305 m) was called *Grand Falls* in 1839 by Hudson's Bay Company trader John MacLean (c.1798–1890). The falls were renamed on 4 February 1965 by Premier Joseph R. Smallwood (1900–91) after the British wartime leader Sir Winston Churchill (1874–1965), honouring a pledge made to Churchill to name a major feature after him. An unincorporated community called **Churchill Falls** was established at the falls. The river (335 km), also called after Sir Winston in 1965, had been named *Hamilton River* after Hamilton Inlet. This 215-km arm of the Atlantic Ocean was named after Sir Charles Hamilton (1767–1849), governor of Newfoundland, 1818–24.

Churchill Peak BC Located in the Sir Winston Churchill Range, Muskwa Ranges, Rocky Mountains, this mountain (2819 m) was named in 1944 by provincial minister of lands Edward T. Kenny (1888–1974) after British prime minister Sir Winston Churchill (1874–1965). It was one of the names given in the area to honour Allied leaders and victories of the Second World War.

Church Point NS On the southern shore of St. Marys Bay and southwest of Digby, this point of interest was named after a Catholic church first built in 1808, rebuilt in 1829, and replaced by the present church in 1905, which is the highest and largest wooden church in North America. Its spire rises 56.3 m above the ground, and its dimensions are 58 m long and 41 m wide. Church Point post office opened in 1857, but was changed to *Port Acadie* six years later. In 1893 the name Church Point was restored. The place is known to its Acadian residents as Pointe-de-l'Église.

Chutes-aux-Outardes QC A village beside rapids on the **Rivière aux Outardes**, southwest of Baie-Comeau, it was founded in 1951. In 1535 Jacques Cartier (1491–1557) identified the wild goose as an outarde, which is really the French word for a bird known in Europe as the bustard. The Rivière aux Outardes is a major river on the north shore, flowing south parallel to Rivière Manicouagan for almost 400 km, to enter the St. Lawrence just west of the latter. The village of **Pointe-aux-Outardes** was erected in 1964, taking its name from its post office, opened in 1901.

Clair NB The first post office of this village (1966) southwest of Edmundston was called *Middle St. Francis* in 1867. It was renamed in 1892 after Peter Clair (1817–1902), a native of County Clare, Ireland.

Claireville ON This community's post office, located at the point where the cities of Brampton and Vaughan meet, was named in 1853 by Upper Canada College French master Jean du Petit Pont de la Haye for his daughter Claire. Called John de la Haye by his neighbours, he had a farm here called Les Ormes ('the elms').

Clara ON This township in Renfrew County was named in 1863. As Herbert Gardiner wrote in *Nothing But Names* (1899), 'the most diligent inquiry has failed to discover a single person who knows Clara's other name'. For municipal purposes Clara Township is united with Head and Maria townships.

Clarence ON In 1998 Clarence township was amalgamated with the town of Rockland to become the city of **Clarence-Rockland**, the united counties of Prescott and Russell. The township was named in 1798 after Prince William Henry, Duke of Clarence (1765–1837), who was crowned William IV in 1830, and reigned for seven years. The community of **Clarence Creek** in the township was known as *New England* until 1848, when Clarence post office opened here. It was in the middle of Clarence Township and near the head of Fox Creek. To reflect the community's French character, it was renamed *Lafontaine* in 1935, but because of confusion with Lafontaine in Simcoe County, it was changed back to Clarence Creek the next year. Assuming the proper name of the creek was **Clarence Creek**, the Geographic Board of Canada officially approved the name in 1931.

Clarendon QC This municipal township in the regional county of Pontiac and adjacent to the town of Shawville was created in 1855, taking its name from the township, proclaimed in 1833. The township was named after Clarendon Park, an estate near Salisbury, Wiltshire, England.

Clarenville NL On the Northwest Arm of Random Sound, an extension of Trinity Bay, this town (1951) was named *Clarenceville* about 1892, possibly after the Prince William Henry, Duke of Clarence, the eldest son of the Prince of Wales (later Edward VII), who had died that year. The town had amalgamated the coastal settlements of *Brook Cove*, *Dark Hole*, *Lower Shoal Harbour*, *Broad Cove*, and *Red Beach*, and shortly after the name was changed to Clarenville.

Claresholm AB Northwest of Lethbridge, this town was named in 1891 by John Niblock, a Canadian Pacific Railway superintendent, after his home in Medicine Hat. His house was called 'Clare's Home', named after his wife. Its incorporation on 31 August 1905 was the last official act of the North-West

Territories administration, based in Regina; the following day Alberta became a province.

Clarington ON In 1993 the town of Newcastle became the municipality of Clarington, whose name derives from the townships of Clarke and Darlington. In 1974, on the creation of the regional municipality of Durham, the town of Bowmanville, the village of Newcastle, and the two townships had been united as Newcastle, named after Newcastle District, which existed from 1798 to 1850. Confusion between the new town and the former village, and displeasure by the residents of Bowmanville, resulted in a referendum in favour of a change, and a consultative process by a committee, which recommended Clarington.

Clark's Harbour NS This town (1919) on Cape Sable Island was named after a New England captain, who had his Nova Scotia headquarters here while on fishing expeditions. Its post office opened in 1858.

Clarke's Beach NL At the head of Bay de Grave and on the west side of Conception Bay, this town (1965) may have been named before 1800, although it was not noted in a census until 1857. John Clarke was a fisherman at Port de Grave in 1772.

Clark, Mount NT In the Franklin Mountains and on the east side of the Mackenzie River, this mountain (1462 m) was named before 1910 after chief factor John Clarke (1781–1852) of the Hudson's Bay Company. After he climbed it, he ate breakfast and deposited a flagon of brandy for future climbers.

Clavet SK The post office in this village (1978), southeast of Saskatoon, opened in 1904 as *French* after Daniel French, who had come from Kansas. When the Grand Trunk Pacific arrived in 1908, its name was changed to Clavet to maintain the alphabetical order of station names between Portage la Prairie and beyond Saskatoon.

Clayoquot Sound BC An intricate group of bays, channels, and inlets on the west coast of Vancouver Island, west of Port Alberni, it took its name from the Clayoquot, a Nootka tribe. The tribe's name may mean either 'different people', because they had become quarrelsome after having been once quiet and peaceful, or 'people of a place where it becomes the same even when disturbed'.

Clearview ON Created in 1994 in the reorganized Simcoe County, Clearview was the name chosen for the new municipal township when the town of Stayner, the village of Creemore, and the townships of Nottawasaga and Sunnidale were merged into a single municipality.

Clearwater BC This community is located at a bend of the North Thompson River, where the **Clearwater River** flows in from the north. The post office here was called *Clearwater Station* in 1925. It was changed to Clearwater in 1961.

Clemenceau, Mount BC This mountain (3658 m), the fourth highest in the Canadian Rockies, was named in 1919 by the Alberta–British Columbia Boundary Commission, after Georges Clemenceau (1841–1929), premier of France, 1906–09 and 1917–20. The **Clemenceau Icefield** extends east toward the Columbia Icefield.

Clementsport NS On the south side of Annapolis Basin, this place was first called *Moose River* after a river identified on Marc Lescarbot's 1609 map as *Rivière de l'Orignal* ('moose river'). Clements post office opened in 1840, taking its name from Clements Township. It was renamed Clementsport in 1852. The post office at nearby **Clementsvale** was opened in 1863. Clements was the family name of the mother of John Parr (1725–91), governor of Nova Scotia, 1782–91.

Clermont QC Located in the regional county of Charlevoix-Est, it was created as a village in 1949 and a town in 1967. It took its name from the municipal parish of *Saint-Philippe-de-Clermont,* established in the early 1930s by writer Félix-Antoine Savard (1896–1982), who may have had in mind Clermont-Ferrand, the French birthplace of celebrated writer Blaise Pascal (1623–62).

Cleveland QC This municipal township is located in the regional county of Le Val-Saint-François, adjacent to Richmond. It was named in 1855 after prominent landowner George Nelson Cleveland, the first mayor of the municipality.

Clifford ON A village (1873) in Wellington County, south of Hanover, it was named in 1856 by miller and innkeeper Francis Brown after his native village in West Yorkshire, England, northeast of Leeds.

Climax SK A post office opened in 1913 near the Montana border, southwest of Swift Current, and was named by Christ Fuglestad after Climax, MN. When the railway arrived in 1923, the office was moved 5 km to the present site of the village (1923).

Cline, Mount AB West of Rocky Mountain House, this mountain (3361 m) was named in 1902 by British alpinist Norman Collie (1859–1942). He named it after Michael Cline, who was in charge of the Hudson's Bay Company's Jasper House, 1824–5 and 1829–34.

Clinton BC A village (1963) north of Cache Creek, it was originally known as *Cut-Off Valley* and *47 Mile House*. On the completion of the Cariboo Road to Barkerville in 1863, it was named after Henry Pelham-Clinton, 5th Duke of Newcastle (1811–64), who was the British colonial secretary, 1859–64.

Clinton ON In 2001 this town (1874) became part of the municipality of Central Huron, Huron County. Located 19 km southeast of Goderich, it was named in 1853 by tavern keeper William Rattenbury after Sir Henry Clinton (1771–1829), who had served with Wellington in the Peninsular War in Spain. Rattenbury's father had been a tenant farmer on Lord Clinton's estate in Hampshire, England.

Clinton-Colden Lake NT Located northeast of Great Slave Lake, this lake (596 km²) was named in 1834 by explorer Capt. Sir George Back (1796–1872) 'as a mark of respect to the memory of those distinguished' American lawyers and statesmen De Witt Clinton (1769–1828) and Cadwaller David Colden (1769–1834).

Clive AB A village (1912) east of Lacombe, it was named in 1909 after Robert Clive, Baron Clive (1725–74), who took a large part in establishing British power in India.

Clutterbuck, Mount BC In the Purcell Mountains, northeast of Kaslo, this mountain (3063 m) was named in 1930 by climber Dr. James Monroe Thorington (1895–1989) after British author Walter John Clutterbuck (1853–1937), who had visited the area and wrote several travel books, including *B.C. 1887* and *The Glittering Mountains of Canada*.

Clyde AB A village (1914) north of Edmonton, its post office was named in 1905 after homesteader George Clyde, who settled here in 1900.

Clyde River NS Situated on the **Clyde River**, southwest of Shelburne, this place was founded in 1850. The river was called *Cape Negro River* in the latter half of the 1700s, but by 1785 Clyde River was being used after Scotland's River Clyde.

Clyde River NU Near the mouth of **Clyde Inlet** and on the northeastern coast of Baffin Island, this hamlet was established in 1978. The site was named *Clyde* in 1950 by Patrick D. Baird, and the post office was called Clyde in 1956, but preferred usage became Clyde River after a small river flowing into Patricia Bay on the north side of the inlet. The inlet was named in 1818 by Sir John Ross (1777–1856).

Clyde River PE A municipal community (1974) west of Charlottetown and on the **Clyde River**, a tributary of West River, it was created as a school district about 1864. Its post office opened in 1886. The river was formerly called *Dock River*, sometimes rendered as *Dog River*. In 1765 Samuel Holland (1728–1801) called it *Edward River* after Edward Eliot, 1st Baron Eliot (1727–1804).

Coachman's Cove NL This municipal community (1970) was first known as *Pot d'Étain* by the migratory French fishermen. It may have been named in English because the French hired English guards (or coaches) to maintain their fishing stages.

Coaldale AB East of Lethbridge, this town (1952) was named in 1909 by the Canadian Pacific Railway after Lethbridge's first residence of Elliott T. Galt (1850–1928). Galt was the general manager of the Alberta Railways and Irrigation Company.

Coalhurst AB A town (1995) northwest of Lethbridge, it took its name from the official designation of Lethbridge before 1885. Coal mining had begun in the area in 1872, with the first settlers describing it as Coalbanks.

Coast Mountains BC Extending from Vancouver north to the Yukon, this coastal chain of the Cordillera was named in 1902. Its highest peak is Mount Waddington (4019 m).

Coaticook QC This town (1883), located in the regional county of **Coaticook** south of Sherbrooke, was incorporated as a village in 1864. The name derives from the **Rivière Coaticook**, a tributary of the Saint-François. In Abenaki the name means 'river of the pine land'.

Coats Island NU Located at the north end of Hudson Bay, south of Southampton Island, this island (5498 km²) was named after Capt. William Coats (d.1752), who compiled valuable notes on the geography of Hudson Bay. He made several trips between 1727 and 1751 to supply the Hudson's Bay Company forts in the bay.

Cobalt ON A town (1906) in Timiskaming District, Cobalt was named in 1904 by provincial geologist Willet Green Miller. He had observed traces of cobalt in the silver ore that was discovered the previous year when the route of the Temiskaming and Northern Ontario Railway (now Ontario Northland) was being laid out.

Cobden ON In 2001 this village (1900) became a part of the township of Whitewater Region, Renfrew County. It was founded in 1849 by Jason Gould and named two years later after Richard Cobden (1804–65), a British pacifist and free trader admired by Gould.

Cobequid Bay NS One of the two heads of the Bay of Fundy (the other is Cumberland Basin), it extends for 50 km from Lower Truro to Economy Point. The name was noted as *Cocobequy* in a 1689 grant and as *Gobetick* in a 1738 report. It possibly derives from the Mi'kmaq *wakobetquick* ('end of flowing water'), referring to the extent that the tidal bore flows up the rivers on each side of the bay. The rugged terrain, rising to 373 m north of the bay and Minas Basin, is known as the **Cobequid Mountains**.

Coboconk ON In 2001 this place became part of the city Kawartha Lakes, Victoria County. Located 39 km north of Lindsay, it was named in 1859 after the Ojibwa *kakapikang* ('waterfalls' or 'swift water'), in reference to the Gull River. In 1873 the Toronto and Nipissing Railway named the station after its president John Shedden, who was accidentally killed that year at Cannington. However, eight years later local residents renamed Coboconk.

Cobourg ON This town (1850) in Northumberland County was first named *Buckville* for settler Elijah Buck; later, it became *Amherst*, after Jeffery Amherst (1717–97), commander-in-chief of the British forces in North America, 1760–3; and finally *Hamilton*, Hamilton Township. In 1819 it was named Cobourg in honour of the 1816 marriage of the future George IV's daughter, Charlotte (1796–1817), to Prince Leopold of Saxe-Coburg (1790–1865), Germany. She died in 1817, while Leopold became the King of the Belgians from 1831 to 1865. Coburg is in northern Bavaria, north of Nürnberg. The extra 'o' was apparently a clerical error.

Cocagne NB The post office in this place, situated on the **Cocagne River** 16 km northwest of Shediac, was named in 1837 after the river. The river was named *R de Cocanne* before 1672 by Acadian Gov. Nicolas Denys (c.1598–1688), following a pleasant sojourn here during an eight-day period of inclement weather. A thirteenth-century English satire called *Land of Cockayne* described a medieval land made of cakes.

Cochenour ON In Kenora District, north of Red Lake, this place was named in 1939 after brothers Bill and Ed Cochenour, who had staked mining claims here in 1924.

Cochrane AB Northwest of Calgary, this town (1971) was named in 1884 by the Canadian Pacific Railway after Senator Matthew Henry Cochrane. He established the Cochrane Ranche Company Limited nearby in 1881.

Cochrane ON When the Temiskaming and Northern Ontario Railway (now Ontario Northland) reached the site of this town (1910) in 1908, it was named after Frank Cochrane (1852–1919), then Ontario's minister of lands and forests, and an avid promoter of the railway's route to James Bay. In 1911 he was appointed the minister of railways and canals in Sir Robert Borden's federal government. **Cochrane District** was created in 1922.

Codette SK South of Nipawin, this village (1929) was named by the Canadian Pacific Railway in 1924 after the **Codette Rapids** in the Saskatchewan River, 6 km to the west. The rapids were named after Jean-Baptiste Cadotte (c.1723–1801), a partner in the late 1700s of Alexander Henry (1739–1824) the elder. In 1917 the post office was to be called Cadotte, but it came back as Codette, which moved to the CPR line.

Codette Station was a post office in 1924 at the former place. It was changed to *Elk Hill* in 1929, but was closed in 1957.

Colborne ON In 2001 this village (1858) became part of the township of Cramahe in Northumberland County. Colborne was named in 1829 for Sir John Colborne, 1st Baron Seaton (1778–1863), lieutenant-governor of Upper Canada, 1828–36.

Colborne Township ON In 2001 this township (1830) became part of the township of Ashfield-Colborne-Wawanosh, Huron County. The township was named after Sir John Colborne, 1st Baron Seaton (1778–1863), lieutenant-governor of Upper Canada, 1828–36.

Colchester NS This county was separated from Halifax County in 1835. It was named after the district of Colchester, used in the area of Truro as early as 1780. The district was likely named after Colchester, a borough in Essex, England.

Colchester ON The post office in the community of Colchester, west of Leamington, was named after **Colchester Township** in 1831. The township was established in Essex County in 1792 and called after the city of Colchester, in Sussex, England. It was divided into the municipal townships of **Colchester North** and **Colchester South** in 1880. In 1999 the two townships became part of the town of Essex.

Cold Lake AB The post office in this city (2000) on the southwestern shore of **Cold Lake** was named in 1910. In 1996 it annexed the town of Grand Centre. The lake, on the Saskatchewan border, was referred to as *Coldwater Lake* on a 1790 map by trader Philip Turnor (c.1751–99). The name likely derives from the cold temperature here year round.

Coldstream BC This district municipality (1906) in the Okanagan Valley, south of Vernon, was named after the Coldstream Ranch. The ranch was developed in 1863 by Col. Charles F. Houghton (1839–98) and named after cold springs that rise on **Coldstream Creek**. Its main urban centre is Lumby.

Coldwater ON On the **Coldwater River** and in Simcoe County, northwest of Orillia, this place was named in 1835. The river's name in Ojibwa is *Kassina Nibish* ('cold water'). Incorporated as a village in 1908, it was united in 1994 with the townships of Matchedash and Orillia to form the municipal township of Severn.

Colebrook ON In 1998 this place, located northeast of Napanee, became part of the township of Stone Mills, Lennox and Addington County. The post office here was named in 1851 after Cole Warner, in whose store the post office was located.

Coleman AB Located in the municipality of Crowsnest Pass, this urban centre was an incorporated town from 1910 to 1979. Its post office was named in 1904 after the 18-year-old Florence Coleman Flumerfelt, the youngest daughter of A.C. Flumerfelt, president of the International Coal and Coke Company.

Coleman, Mount AB This mountain (3135 m) was named in 1902 after Arthur Philemon Coleman (1832–1939), a professor at the University of Toronto and an alpinist in the Rocky Mountains after 1889.

Coles Island NB The post office at this place, located at the mouth of the Canaan River, northwest of Sussex, was named in 1858. The island, in the mouth of the river, was named after David Cole, a Loyalist who settled here in 1809.

Coleville SK A post office opened north of Kindersley in 1908, named after its first postmaster, Malcolm Cole. It was relocated to the present site of this village (1953) in 1913, when the Grand Trunk Pacific Railway was built southwest from Biggar.

Colinet NL This municipal community (1974) was named after **Great Colinet Island**. Recorded in the late 1600s on maps as *Collinett, Colonet Isle*, and *Collemot*, the island's name may have been given for a French or Channel Islands fisherman, or after the French word *curnett* ('place of little hills').

College Bridge NB On the west side of Memramcook River, southeast of Moncton, this community's post office was named in 1885 after the nearby Collège Saint-Joseph (now Memramcook Institute) in the village of Saint-Joseph.

Colliers NL Located at the head of **Colliers Bay**, on the southwest side of Conception Bay, this town (1972) may have been named because it was a site where wood was gathered to produce charcoal. Collier was a surname in Newfoundland as early as the mid-1700s, although there is no evidence that the town was named after a person.

Collingwood ON The township in Grey County was named in 1840 for Cuthbert Collingwood, Baron Collingwood (1748–1810), a British admiral who won a sea battle in 1797 off Cabo São Vicente, Portugal, and served as Lord Nelson's second-in-command off Cabo Trafalgar in 1804.

Collingwood ON This town (1858) in Simcoe County was named in 1853, when Frederic Cumberland, general manager of the Toronto, Simcoe and Lake Huron Railway, chose it as the terminus of its line on Georgian Bay. He named the town after the nearby Collingwood Township.

Collins Bay ON A community and a bay in Kingston, Frontenac County, both were named for Deputy Surveyor General John Collins (d.1795), who laid out the township in 1783 and was granted land on the bay. The post office opened in 1854.

Colonsay SK Located southeast of Saskatoon, this town (1977) was named by the Canadian Pacific Railway in 1906 after one of the Inner Hebrides Islands, off the west coast of Scotland. Its streets and avenues recall other islands in the group, including Jura, Islay, Oronsay, Bute, Skye, Torran, Kintyre, Staffa, and Tiree. Postal service was provided in 1908.

Colpoy's Bay ON The bay on the east side of the Bruce Peninsula was named in 1826 by Admiralty surveyor Henry W. Bayfield (1795–1885) after RAdm. Sir Edward Griffith Colpoys (d.1832). Colpoy's Bay post office was open from 1863 to 1917. The community's name was changed in 1946 to *Colpoy Bay*, properly spelled *Colpoys Bay* in 1950, and then changed to the locally preferred Colpoy's Bay in 1978. The bay's name was also changed to Colpoy's Bay the same year. In 1999 the community became part of the town of South Bruce Peninsula.

Columbia, Cape NU Canada's most northerly point of land (83° 06'41.35"N), this cape was named in 1876 by Sir George S. Nares (1716–86) of a British naval exploring expedition after the poetic name of the United States. Pelham Aldrich determined on 1 May of that year that it was the most northerly point of land. In 1987 the Mapping and Charting Establishment of the Department of National Defence ascertained its precise position.

Columbia, Mount AB, BC Located at the point on the continental divide where waters drain to three oceans—the Atlantic, the Arctic, and the Pacific—this mountain (3747 m) was named in 1898 by climbers Norman Collie and Herman Woolley after the Columbia River.

Columbia River BC Rising in **Columbia Lake**, in the Rocky Mountain Trench, this river (2044 km, 917 km in Canada) flows north then south to cross the British Columbia–Washington boundary at Waneta. It was named on 11 May 1792 by Capt. Robert Gray (c.1755–1806) of Boston, MA, after his ship *Columbia Rediviva*. The river drains the area of the **Columbia Icefield** into the Pacific Ocean.

Colville Lake NT Northwest of Great Bear Lake, this lake (452 km²) was named in 1857 by Hudson's Bay Company trader Roderick MacFarlane after Andrew Colvile, deputy governor of the HBC, 1839–52, and governor, 1852–6.

Colwood BC This city (1985) west of Victoria was named after one of the four farms of the Puget Sound Agricultural

Company, which belonged to the Hudson's Bay Company. Capt. Edward Edwards Langford (1809–95) arrived here in 1851 to manage it, naming it after a property of his in Sussex, England. The farm became better known as Esquimalt, with the Langford residence retaining the designation of Colwood. Its post office opened in 1881.

Combatant Mountain BC This mountain (3756 m) in the Coast Mountains, between Mount Waddington and Mount Tiedemann, was named in 1933 by climber Walter Alfred (Don) Munday (1890–1950), possibly after the difficulty in climbing it.

Combermere ON In Renfrew County, south of Barry's Bay, this community was first known as *Dennison's Bridge* after Capt. John Dennison (c.1799–1881). He renamed it in 1865 after Sir Stapleton Cotton, Viscount Combermere (1773–1865), with whom he may have served. Lord Combermere commanded calvary in the Peninsular War in Spain, 1808–14, was commander-in-chief in India, 1825–30, and became a field marshal in 1855. His home was Combermere Abbey in Cheshire, England. In 1999, the community became part of the township of Madawaska Valley.

Comeauville NS Located on the French Shore, southwest of Digby, this place's post office was first called *Clare* in 1841 after the municipality of Clare, which comprises the western part of Digby County. It was renamed in 1877 after its first postmaster, Augustin F. Comeau.

Come-By-Chance NL This town (1969) at the north end of the Isthmus of Avalon was named after an extension of Placentia Bay called **Come by Chance**. There is a reference to this bay as *Comby Chance* as early as 1706. It may have been named because it was a chancy proposition for fishermen to bring their boats to shore here during rough weather. In 1612 John Guy (d.1629) identified it as *Passage Harbour*.

Comfort Cove-Newstead NL This municipal community (1967), which extends into the Bay of Exploits, originally comprised the separate centres of Comfort Cove: **Comfort Head**, *New Harbour*, and *Turtle Cove*. *New Harbour*, the largest of the three, became Newstead in 1921.

Committee Punch Bowl AB, BC This basin, located on the continental divide at the head of Athabasca Pass, was named in 1824 by Sir George Simpson (1787–1860) after the Hudson's Bay Company's governing committee. The small basin, measuring 18 m across, impressed Simpson because it drained toward both the Pacific and the Arctic oceans.

Comox BC On the east coast of Vancouver Island and east of Courtenay, this town (1967) was named in 1868 after the Kamuckway, a Salish tribe. Comox means 'place of plenty', in

reference to the excellent game and berries in the Puntledge River valley and around **Comox Lake**.

Compton QC This village in the regional county of Coaticook, midway between Coaticook and Lennoxville, was named in 1893 after the township of **Compton**, proclaimed in 1802. Its name was possibly taken from a village in Surrey, England, southwest of London. Compton post office opened in 1829. **Compton Station**, an adjacent municipality, had a post office from 1890 to 1964.

Compton Mountain BC In the Coast Mountains, east of Bute Inlet, this mountain (2873 m) was named in 1933 by George G. (Ken) Aitken (d.2007), provincial member of the Geographic Board of Canada, after the birthplace in England of Sir Humphrey Gilbert (c.1539–1583). *See also* Gilbert, Mount.

Conception Bay NL This bay was named *baia da conceição*, possibly by the Portuguese in the early 1500s, in honour of the feast day (8 December) of Our Lady of the Immaculate Conception. As early as 1588 it was called Conception Bay, but only four years later it was identified as *Consumption Bay* on a map by Thomas Hood (1577–96), presumably after local usage. Possibly as early as 1497 it had been named *Assumption Bay*, after the feast day (15 August) of Our Lady of the Assumption, with the two names becoming confused. Conception Bay and *Consumption Bay* were used interchangeably during the 1600s, with the present name prevailing after 1700. Nevertheless some people were still calling it *Consumption Bay* after the turn of the twentieth century.

Conception Bay South NL This town (1971) on the eastern shore of Conception Bay and southwest of St. John's amalgamated the settlements of Topsail, Chamberlains, Codner, Long Pond, Manuels, Kelligrews, Upper Gullies, and Seal Cove. It took its name from the provincial electoral district of Conception Bay South.

Conception Harbour NL On **Conception Harbour** and at the head of **Conception Bay**, this town had been called *Cats Cove* (1830s) and *Avondale North* (1906), but was renamed in 1972 after the harbour.

Conche NL On the northeast side of the Northern Peninsula, this municipal community (1960) may have been named in the 1700s by fishermen after the shellfish, or after the shape of the peninsula, which is shaped like a conch shell. It may also have been named after a place on Guernsey in the Channel Islands.

Concord ON In the city of Vaughan, York Region, this place was named in 1854, possibly after Concord, VT, or perhaps as an antidote when people here could not agree on a name.

Coniston ON In 2001 this town (1934) became part of the city of Greater Sudbury, Sudbury Region. Coniston became part of the town of Nickel Centre in 1973. It had been named in 1903 by first postmaster Dennis O'Brien, on the suggestion of Canadian Pacific Railway engineer T.R. Johnson, who had been reading an English novel set in the Coniston Lake district of northwestern England.

Conne River NL On the south bank of the **Conne River**, where it flows into the Bay d'Espoir, this town (1972) was settled by the Mi'kmaq in the mid-1800s, after they had lived a nomadic existence for several years in the southern and central parts of the Newfoundland. The river was recorded as *rivière le con* by Capt. James Cook (1728–79) in the 1760s, and was subsequently anglicized to its present form. The meaning of the original name is not known.

Connolly, Mount YT Northeast of Faro, this mountain (2139 m) was named in 1976 after Thomas Osborne Connolly (1918–75), an outfitter and guide at Ross River, 1945–64.

Conquerall Mills NS On Fancy Lake, south of Bridgewater, this place was possibly named about 1805, when miller George Fancy was struck by the beauty of the lake and exclaimed 'this conquers all'. However, he may have used the word on his lumber to promote the quality of his sawmill. Its post office was established in 1882. In 1855 **Conquerall Bank** post office had opened on the south bank of the LaHave River, east of Bridgewater.

Conquest SK Southwest of Saskatoon, this village (1911) was founded in 1904 by pioneer settlers, who may have performed a 'conquest' of the South Saskatchewan by ferrying their families and possessions across it to Outlook. The Canadian Pacific Railway was built through it in 1908, with the post office opening in 1911.

Conrad, Mount BC This mountain (3252 m) in the Purcell Mountains, northwest of Invermere, was named in 1935 by British alpinist Igor Armstrong Richards (1893–1979) after climber and guide Conrad Kain (1833–1934). Kain, a native of Austria, had immigrated to Canada in 1909 and made the first ascent of Mount Robson.

Consort AB Southeast of Stettler, this village (1912) was named in 1911 by the Canadian Pacific Railway in honour of Queen Mary (1867–1953), the consort of recently crowned George V. Its post office was previously called *Sanderville*.

Constance Bay ON In 2001 this community became part of the city of Ottawa. Adjacent to the Ottawa River, it was named after **Constance Lake** and **Constance Creek**, both called after Constance Pinhey (1819–98), the wife of John Hamnett Pinhey (1827–1901) and the daughter of Hamnett

Kirkes Pinhey (1784–1857). The latter settled nearby on the Ottawa River in 1820. Developed as a summer-cottage community, most of Constance Bay's residents now live here year round.

Constantine, Mount YT This mountain in the St. Elias Mountains was named in 1900 by surveyor James J. MacArthur (1856–1925) after Charles Constantine (1849–1912), an inspector with the North-West Mounted Police. He established a NWMP post at Fortymile River in 1895 and represented Canadian law during the Klondike Gold Rush.

Contrecoeur QC The post office in this municipality, located in the regional county of Lajemmerais southwest of Sorel, opened in 1849 as Sainte-Trinité-de-Contrecœur, and shortened to Contrecoeur in 1955. In 1672 Antoine Pécaudy de Contrecoeur (1596–1688), an officer with the Carignan-Salières Regiment, was granted a seigneury here by Jean Talon (1625–94).

Contwoyto Lake NU Located north of Great Slave Lake, this lake (933 km²) was named in 1821 by Sir John Franklin (1786–1847) after a Chipewyan word for 'rum'. Samuel Hearne (1745–92) provided rum to his guide Mattonabee and his companions here in 1771.

Cook, Cape BC The northwestern point of Brooks Peninsula, and on the west coast of Vancouver Island, this cape was named in 1860 by Capt. George Richards (1620–96) after Capt. James Cook (1728–79), who in 1778 was the first British navigator to explore the West Coast. Cook had named it *Woody Point*.

Cook, Mount YT On the Yukon–Alaska boundary and in the St. Elias Mountains, this mountain (4194 m) was named in 1874 by William H. Dall of the United States Coast Survey after Capt. James Cook (1728–79), who explored the northwestern coast in 1778.

Cook's Bay ON The southern arm of Lake Simcoe, it was named in 1793 by Lt.-Gov. John Graves Simcoe (1752–1806) after Capt. James Cook (1728–79). Cook undertook hydrographic surveys on the east coast of North America, 1758–68, and served with Simcoe's father, after whom Lake Simcoe was named.

Cook's Harbour NL On the southeastern side of the Strait of Belle Isle, the inlet at this town (1956) was named in 1764 by Capt. James Cook (1728–79), who undertook a hydrographic survey of the coasts of Newfoundland from 1763 to 1768. After extensively exploring the Pacific Ocean during the following decade, he was killed on the Sandwich Islands (Hawaiian Islands).

Cookshire QC This town (1892) in the regional county of Le Haut-Saint-François, east of Sherbrooke, was founded in 1799 by Loyalists from Vermont and New Hampshire, and named after first settler John Cook (1770–1819). A post office opened here in 1851.

Cooksville ON In the city of Mississauga, Peel Region, this urban centre was named in 1836 after Jacob Cook, who bought land in 1814 at the corner of Dundas and Hurontario streets and settled here in 1819. The post office from 1826 to 1836 was called *Toronto*, after the township of *Toronto*.

Coombs BC South of Qualicum Beach and northwest of Nanaimo, this settlement was named in 1911 after Capt. Coombs of the Salvation Army, who helped labourers and their families from Leeds, England relocate to Vancouver Island.

Copper Cliff ON Originally on the west side of the city of Sudbury when it was founded in 1883, this urban centre became part of the city of Greater Sudbury, Sudbury Region in 2001. A mine was opened here in 1886 and a smelter was built two years later. Its post office was named in 1890. The place was incorporated as a town in 1901 and was annexed by Sudbury in 1973.

Coppermine River NT, NU Rising in Lac de Gras, north of Great Slave Lake, this river (845 km) flows northwest into Coronation Gulf. It was named in 1771 by Samuel Hearne (1745–92) who observed outcroppings of copper on its banks. In Inuktitut the river is called *Kugluktuk* ('big river'). The hamlet *Coppermine* was changed to Kugluktuk in 1996. *See also* Kugluktuk.

Coquitlam BC This district municipality (1891), east of Burnaby, and south of Port Moody, was named after the Coquitlam, a Salish tribe. Their name means 'stinking with fish slime', in reference to their butchering salmon for their masters, the Kwantlen, a Cowichan tribe. Their name may also mean 'small red salmon'. *See also* Port Coquitlam.

Coral Harbour NU This hamlet (1972), located on the south side of Southampton Island, was established in 1924 by the Hudson's Bay Company. The harbour was named in 1907–9 by Capt. George Comer (1858–1937) after the unusual 'red rock' he retrieved while taking soundings in the harbour.

Corbeil ON The post office here, located in East Ferris Township, Nipissing District, southeast of North Bay, was named in 1906 for lumber millers Jean-Baptiste and Joseph Corbeil. The Dionne Quintuplets were born on the west side of the community in 1934.

Corbyville ON In 1855 Henry Corby (1806–81) bought a mill north of Belleville and added a distillery in 1859. In 1882 the new post office was named in his honour.

Cordova Bay BC This community, located in the district municipality of Saanich, north of Victoria, was named in 1920 after the adjacent bay. The bay was named about 1842 by the Hudson's Bay Company. It transferred the name *Puerto de Cordova,* given in 1790 by Spanish SLt. Manuel Quimper to Esquimalt Harbour, west of Victoria. Quimper named it after the forty-sixth viceroy of Mexico, Don Antonio Maria Bucareli y Ursua Henestrosa Lasso de la Vega Villacis y Cordova.

Cormack NL Located north of Deer Lake, this municipal community (1964) was named in 1948 after William Epps Cormack (1796–1868), the first non-Aboriginal to travel by foot across Newfoundland in 1822.

Corner Brook NL This city (1956) on the south side of Humber Arm was created through the amalgamation of the towns of *Corner Brook, Corner Brook East, Corner Brook West,* and *Curling.* The city was named after the brook draining **Corner Brook Lake** into the Humber Arm of the Bay of Islands. The town of *Humbermouth* was annexed two years later. Capt. James Cook (1728–79) named **Corner Brook** in 1767, presumably because the shoreline took a sharp turn at its mouth.

Cornwall ON This city (1944) was named *New Johnstown* in 1789 after Johnstown, NY, which had been given in honour of Sir William Johnson (c.1715–74). His son, Sir John Johnson (1742–1830), brought many Loyalists to Upper Canada. It was renamed Cornwall in 1797.

Cornwall ON In 1998 the township of Cornwall and the township Osnabruck became the township of South Stormont, united counties of Stormont, Dundas and Glengarry. It was named in 1787 after a title of George III's eldest son, the Duke of Cornwall (1762–1830), who reigned as George IV, 1820–30.

Cornwall PE This town (1995), west of Charlottetown, was first established as a school district in 1849, with a post office opening in 1859. It was created as a village in 1966 and a municipal community in 1983. The name may derive from the Duke of Cornwall, a title received at birth by Albert Edward (1841–1910), the eldest son of Queen Victoria and the future Edward VII. In 1995 Cornwall annexed the adjoining municipal communities of North River and Eliot River.

Cornwall Island NU This island (2258 km²), the most north-eastern of the Parry Islands of the Queen Elizabeth Islands, was named in 1852 by Sir Edward Belcher (1682–1757) after Prince Edward, the Prince of Wales and Duke of Cornwall (1841–1910).

Cornwallis NS On the Annapolis Basin, east of Digby, this place was established during the Second World War as a Canadian military base. It took its name from Edward

Cornwallis (c.1712–76), the first governor of Nova Scotia, 1749–52.

Cornwallis Island NU The most southeastern of the Parry Islands of the Queen Elizabeth Islands, this island (6995 km²) was named in 1819 by Sir William Parry (1790–1855) after Adm. Sir William Cornwallis (1744–1819). Parry served with Cornwallis in the Channel Fleet in 1803.

Cornwallis Square NS This village (1977) west of Kentville, and on the Cornwallis River, is an amalgamation of the former villages of Cambridge, Grafton, and Waterville. It took its name from the **Cornwallis River**, which rises near Berwick and flows east into Minas Basin.

Coronach SK This town (1978) near the Montana border, southeast of Assiniboia, was founded by the Canadian Pacific Railway in 1926, and named by its English settlers after a horse that had won the Epsom Derby that year. Its post office opened in 1927.

Coronation AB Located southeast of Stettler, this town (1912) was named by the Canadian Pacific Railway in honour of the crowning of George V (1865–1936) on 22 June 1911. Its post office opened the same year.

Coronation Gulf NU Between the mainland and Victoria Island, this 290-km gulf was named *George IV's Coronation Gulf* in 1821 by Sir John Franklin (1786–1847) in honour of the king's coronation. The Geographic Board authorized Coronation Gulf in 1920.

Coronation Mountain AB, BC On the continental divide near the head of the North Saskatchewan River, this peak (3176 m) was named on 9 August 1902 by British climber Norman Collie on the day of the coronation of Edward VII and Queen Alexandra.

Coteau-Landing QC The post office in this village, located in the regional county of Vaudreuil-Soulanges and on the north shore of Lake St. Francis, was named in 1847, six years before the village was incorporated. The municipality of **Coteau-Station**, established as Coteau in 1855 on the Grand Trunk Railway line between Montreal and Toronto, was named *La Station-du-Coteau* in 1887 and changed to its present form in 1984. The municipality of **Coteau-du-Lac**, downriver, had a post office by that name in 1789. Each of the names recalls a hillside on the portage around rapids at the foot of the lake.

Côte-Saint-Luc QC In 2002 the city of Montreal embraced all of the cities and towns on the Île de Montréal. In 2006 Côte-Saint-Luc regained its municipal *cité*. One of two remaining *cités* in the province (the other is Dorval), it is located in the city of Montreal. The name was given for an

ancient shoreline terrace and for Luc de La Corne Saint-Luc (1711–84), military officer, merchant, interpreter, and legislative councillor.

Coulonge, Lac ON, QC This widening of the Ottawa River, east of Pembroke, was named after **Rivière Coulonge**, which enters the lake from the north. These features recall a noted family of the French regime, especially trader Nicolas d'Ailleboust de Manthet (1663–1709), whose grandfather was Nicolas d'Ailleboust de Coulonge-la-Madeleine. *See also* Fort-Coulonge.

Courcelette, Mount BC In the Rocky Mountains, east of Invermere, this mountain (3044 m) was named in 1918 after a village in northeastern France, where Canadian forces fought between 1916 and 1918.

Courtenay BC This city (1915) on the east coast of Vancouver Island was named in 1891 after the nearby **Courtenay River**. The river had been named about 1860 after Capt. George William Conway Courtenay (1793–1863), commander of HMS *Constance* on the Pacific station, 1846–9.

Courtenay Bay NB This inlet on the east side of Saint John Harbour was named *Courtney Bay* about 1775 by mapmaker Joseph Frederick Wallet DesBarres (1722–1824) after John Courtenay (1741–1816), master surveyor of the British ordnance.

Coutts AB On the Montana border, southeast of Lethbridge, this village (1960) was named in 1890 by the Alberta Railways and Irrigation Company. It was called after either Sir William Lehman Ashmead Bartlett Burdett-Coutts (b.1851), a British banker and director of the company, or his wife, Baroness Angela Georgina Burdett-Coutts (1814–1906), a stockholder of the company. *See also* Burdett.

Covehead Road PE The post office in this place, located north of Charlottetown, was named in 1856 after the road leading north to **Covehead Bay**. Called *Stanhope Cove* in 1765 by Samuel Holland (1728–1801) the bay likely acquired its present name after the locality of **Covehead**, which developed at the head of the bay.

Cowansville QC Located in the regional county of Brome-Missisquoi, it was created a village in 1876, and a town in 1931. It was first called *Nelsonville* and *Churchville*, before the Cowansville post office opened in 1841, and named after postmaster and merchant Peter Cowan (b.1818).

Cow Head NL On the northwestern coast of Newfoundland, and surrounded by Gros Morne National Park, this town (1964) may have been named after a boulder shaped like the profile of a cow's head.

Cowley AB The post office of this villiage (1906) east of Crowsnest Pass was named in 1900 by rancher Frederick Godsal (1853–1935), possibly inspired by the line 'The lowing herd winds slowly o'er the lea' in Thomas Gray's 'Elegy' (1751). Before the Canadian Pacific Railway had been built, the area was called *French Flats*.

Cox's Cove NL On the Middle Arm of the Bay of Islands, and on the west side Newfoundland, this town (1969) was settled about 1840 by fishermen George, John, and William Cox.

Crabtree QC This municipality (1945) in the regional county of Joliette was the site of a saw and pulp mill established in 1905 by Edwin Crabtree. **Crabtree Mills** post office opened a year later.

Craigellachie BC On 7 November 1885, Donald Smith, Lord Strathcona (1820–1914) drove the last spike of the Canadian Pacific Railway at this point, a railway siding in Eagle Pass, between Revelstoke and Salmon Arm. It was named after a prominent crag in Morayshire, Scotland. A post office operated here from 1912 to 1970.

Craighurst ON In Simcoe County, north of Barrie, this place was called *Flos*, after Flos Township, in 1837. In the 1850s it was renamed after pioneer settler Thomas Craig (1798–1876).

Craig, Mount YT This mountain (4039 m) was named in 1916 after John Davidson Craig (1875–1936), who surveyed the Yukon–Alaska boundary from Mount St. Elias north to the Beaufort Sea, 1905–10. From 1924 to 1931 he was Director of Surveys in the Department of the Interior.

Craik SK On a Canadian National Railway's line, but built for the Canadian Pacific in 1889–90, this town (1907) northwest of Regina was named in 1902 after Robert Craik, an engineer with the CPR's construction party. Its post office opened the following year.

Cramahe ON This township in Northumberland County was named in 1792 after Hector Theophilus Cramahé (1720–1788), a native of Dublin, Ireland. He administered the government of British North America in the absence of Sir Guy Carleton (1724–1808), 1770–74, and was lieutenant-governor of Quebec, 1771–82.

Cranberry Portage MB Southeast of Flin Flon, this place is located on a narrow portage separating the basins of the Saskatchewan and Nelson Rivers. Its post office was established in 1928. It was noted as *Cranberry Carrying Place* on a 1796 Arrowsmith map, and *Cranberry Lake* on David Thompson's map of 1812–3.

Cranbrook BC This city, the largest (1905) in the southeastern part of the province, was laid out in lots in 1897. Twelve years before, Col. James Baker (1830–1906) had settled here and named the ranch site Cranbrook farm, for an old family property in Kent, England, south of Maidstone. In 1898 it became a divisional point on the Canadian Pacific Railway's Crowsnest line.

Crapaud PE This municipal community (1983) on Westmoreland River, east of Borden-Carleton, was incorporated in 1950 as a village. Its name was first noted in 1832, and its post office opened in 1857. It took its name from the French designation of the river, Rivière aux Crapauds ('river of toads'), in reference to the *crapaud de mer* ('eel').

Craven SK A village (1905) in the Qu'Appelle River Valley, north of Regina, its first settlers wanted to call their post office Sussex. Postal authorities rejected it because that name was in use in New Brunswick, and sent a list from which the settlers chose Craven in 1884, after William Craven, Earl of Craven (1608–97), noted for his devotion to Elizabeth I.

Credit River ON During the 1700s French traders met with the Mississauga at the mouth of the *Rivière au Crédit* each spring, and extended credit for supplies until the following spring. *See also* Port Credit.

Creemore ON In Simcoe County, southeast of Collingwood, this urban centre was named in 1849 by Barrie judge Sir James Gowan (1815–1909) from the Gaelic words *creagh mhor* ('big heart'). Incorporated as a village in 1889, it was merged with the municipal township of Clearview in 1994.

Creighton SK A town on the Manitoba border, adjacent to the city of Flin Flon, its post office was named in 1958 after Tom Creighton (1874–1949), a prospector who staked claims in the area in 1915.

Creignish NS On the west coast of Cape Breton Island and northwest of Port Hawkesbury, this place was named after Loch Craignish, Argyllshire, Scotland. Creignish Station post office opened in 1913 at Craigmore, 5 km to the north.

Cremona AB Northwest of Calgary, this village (1955) was named in 1906 by the post office department, possibly after the city on the Po River in Italy, northwest of Bologna.

Creston BC This town (1924) south of Kootenay Lake and near the Idaho border was named in 1898 by the Canadian Pacific Railway after the Iowa hometown of settler Fred Little. Little agreed to sell land to the CPR after it consented to name its station Creston. The post office opened a year later. Creston, IA, is southwest of Des Moines.

Creston NL This place was proclaimed in 1914 by the government. Its name has no particular local connection. The communities known informally as Creston North and Creston South were annexed by the town of Marystown in 1967.

Crofton BC In the district municipality of North Cowichan, northeast of Duncan, it was named in 1902 after Henry Croft (1856–1917). A brother-in-law of coal magnate James Dunsmuir (1851–1920), he was appointed the manager of the Mount Sicker Copper Company in 1900. He developed the townsite as a location for a copper smelter.

Crossfield AB Between Airdrie and Carstairs, north of Calgary, this town (1980) was named in 1893 by the Calgary and Edmonton Railway Company after one of its engineers. The post office opened in 1902.

Cross Roads PE This part of the town of Stratford (since 1995) was created as a municipal community in 1972. It took its name from the crossing of the Old Georgetown Road (now the Trans-Canada Highway), by another road leading south over Tea Hill.

Crotch Lake ON On the Mississippi River and in Frontenac County, this cross-shaped reservoir was known as Crotch Lake in the mid-1800s, when surveyor John Harper gave it the euphemism *Cross Lake*. Crotch Lake was still well known in the 1960s, so the name was restored.

Crown Prince Frederik Island NU In the Gulf of Boothia and west of Fury and Hecla Strait, this island (401 km²) was named in 1922 by the Fifth Thule Expedition after a son of Christian X of Denmark. It was submitted to the Geographic Board in 1925 by Knud Rasmussen (1879–1933) and endorsed the following year. In 1911 explorer J.T.E. Lavoie had named it *Hall Island* after Charles Francis Hall (1821–71), who had explored the area in 1868.

Crowsnest Pass AB This municipality was named in 1979 through the amalgamation of the towns of Blairmore and Coleman, the villages of Bellevue, Frank, and Hillcrest Mines, and adjacent communities. The pass (1357 m) was explored in 1858 by Thomas Blakiston (1832–91). **Crowsnest Mountain** (2785 m) may have been named after a hill 30 km to the east, where the raven's nest of Blackfoot and Cree legends was located. The place names for the river, the pass, and the mountain translate as 'crow's nest' from Blackfoot and Cree.

Crysler ON In 1998 this place became part of the township of North Stormont, united counties of Stormont, Dundas and Glengarry. It was named in 1860 for miller John Crysler (1770–1852), who settled here on the South Nation River in 1843. He served in the House of Assembly of Upper Canada, 1808–26. In 1784, his father, John Crysler, had settled on the

St. Lawrence River east of present-day Morrisburg. During the War of 1812 his land was the site of the Battle of Crysler's Farm, where the British forces defeated the much larger American forces on 11 November 1813.

Crystal Beach ON In the town of Fort Erie, Niagara Region, this urban community was established in the 1890s as a summer resort and a religious meeting ground for the residents of Buffalo seeking peace and spiritual renewal.

Crystal City MB The post office in this village (1947), located near the North Dakota border and southeast of Brandon, was named in 1879 by Thomas Greenway (1838–1908), premier of Manitoba, 1888–90, who had settled here that year.

Cudworth SK Founded in 1911 by the Grand Trunk Pacific Railway, the post office of this town (1961) was also named in 1911. Located south of Prince Albert, it was named after Ralph Cudworth (1617–88), a noted English moralist and freethinker.

Culloden ON This community in Oxford County, northwest of Tillsonburg, was named in 1854 after the famous 1746 Battle of Culloden Moor in Inverness-shire, Scotland.

Culross ON In 1999 this township became part of the municipality of South Bruce, Bruce County. It was named in 1850 after the town of Culross in Scotland's Fifeshire, northwest of Edinburgh. Sir George Bruce built a palace in Culross at the beginning of the seventeenth century, and developed an export trade in salt and coal.

Cultus Lake On the north shore of **Cultus Lake** and south of Chilliwack, this community was named in 1913. The lake's name in Chinook jargon means 'worthless', 'foul', or 'anything bad'.

Cumberland BC A village (1958) south of Courtenay, it was first known as Union after the Union Coal Company. It was renamed in 1898 by coal mine owner James Dunsmuir (1851–1920) after Cumberland, England, from where many of the miners had come.

Cumberland ON In 2001 this city became part of the city of Ottawa. It had been named after **Cumberland Township**, established in 1799 and called after Prince Ernest Augustus (1771–1851), who was created that year the Duke of Cumberland and Teviotdale. The community of **Cumberland** was settled in 1801, with its post office opening in 1839. It was changed to Osborne in 1856, but Cumberland was restored seven years later.

Cumberland Basin NB, NS At the head of Chignecto Bay, this basin was called *Beau Basin* by the French. It was renamed in 1755 after Fort Cumberland, the name given that year by the captors of the French *Fort Beauséjour*. The fort was named after the Duke of Cumberland (1721–65), who won the decisive victory over the supporters of Bonnie Prince Charlie at Culloden, 16 April 1746. **Cumberland County**, NS, was established in 1759.

Cumberland House SK This community was founded in 1774 by Samuel Hearne (1745–92) as the Hudson's Bay Company's first inland post. Located on the south shore of **Cumberland Lake**, northeast of Nipawin, it was named after Prince Rupert, Duke of Cumberland (1619–82), first governor of the company. Postal service was established in 1891.

Cumberland Sound NU On the southeast side of Baffin Island, this 260-km sound was named in 1587 by explorer John Davis after George Clifford, 3rd Earl of Cumberland (1558–1605), a mathematician and navigator who became an admiral in 1598.

Cupar SK The post office in this town (1968) on the Canadian Pacific Railway, northeast of Regina, was called *Dalrymple* in 1903. It was renamed two years later after a burgh in Fifeshire, Scotland.

Cupids NL This town (1965) on the western side of Conception Bay has the distinction of being the first year-round British colony in what is now Canadian territory. It was founded in 1610 by Bristol merchant John Guy (d.1629), who arrived in 'Cuperres coue' with 39 carpenters, shipwrights, and stonemasons. *Cupers Cove*, as he later wrote it, likely took its name from the practice of fish packers sending coopers to the adjacent well-treed slopes to cut wood for staves to make barrels for the pickling of fish.

Curling NL A neighbourhood in the west side of the city of Corner Brook, it was formerly called *Birchy Cove*. It was named in 1904 by the Most Reverend Michael Howley (1843–1914), after the Reverend James Joseph Curling (1844–1906), who had been appointed the pastor of the Catholic St. Mary's Parish in 1873. Incorporated as a town in 1947, it was annexed to Corner Brook in 1956.

Cut Knife SK The post office in this town (1968), located west of Battleford, was established in 1905. It was named after a Tsuu T'ina (Sarsi) chief who was killed by a Cree party, possibly at the battle of Cut Knife Hill in 1885. The Cree were so proud of eliminating the famed Sarsi fighter that they thereafter called the hill after him. In 1990 the hill was named after Chief Poundmaker, who had helped Col. William Otter and his troops to escape from a fight on Poundmaker's reserve. Poundmaker is buried on the hill.

Cypress Hills AB, SK These hills were called by the French *Montagnes des Cyprès*, mistaking the lodgepole pines for the cypress trees of Eastern Canada. Attaining a height of 1460 m, the hills have the highest elevation between the Rocky Mountains and the Torngat Mountains on the Quebec–Newfoundland and Labrador boundary.

Cypress River MB Situated on a tributary of the Assiniboine, southeast of Brandon, this place was named in 1886, when the Canadian Pacific Railway was built west from Winnipeg toward Souris. Littleton post office was located here from 1881 to 1887, when it was changed to Cypress River.

Czar AB This village (1917) south of Wainwright was named in 1909 by the Canadian Pacific Railway, possibly as a recognition of the Anglo-Russian Treaty (1907), which resulted in the creation of the Allied forces during the First World War. It may have been given for a boss of the railway's construction workers, or after the nickname of Arthur Lewis Sifton (1858–1921), premier of Alberta, 1910–17.

Dacre ON This community in Renfrew County is located southwest of the town of Renfrew. The post office here was named in 1865, possibly after Dacre in Cumberland, England, southwest of Penrith. In 2001 it became a part of the township of Greater Madawaska.

Dagon, Mount BC In the Coast Mountains, southeast of Bella Coola, this mountain (2880 m) was named in 1953 by a member of the Alpine Club of Canada after the mythical chief lord of Satan.

Dalhousie NB This town (1905) at the mouth of the Restigouche River was named in 1826, probably by Lt.-Gov. Sir Howard Douglas (1776–1861) after Gen. George Ramsay, 9th Earl of Dalhousie (1770–1838), governor-in-chief of British North America, 1820–8.

Dalhousie ON This township in Lanark County was named in 1823 after Gen. George Ramsay, 9th Earl of Dalhousie, governor-in-chief of British North America, 1820–8. In 1998 it became part of the township of Lanark Highlands. *See also* Ramsay.

Dalkeith ON The post office here, located in the united counties of Stormont, Dundas and Glengarry (north of Alexandria) was named in 1867 after the title of the Duke of Buccleuch's eldest son. Dalkeith, the former seat of the dukes of Buccleuch, is southeast of Edinburgh, Scotland. In 1998 it became part of the township of North Glengarry.

Dalmeny SK North of Saskatoon, this town (1883) was founded by the Canadian Northern Railway in 1905. It was likely named after Dalmeny, West Lothian, west of Edinburgh. Its post office opened the following year.

Dalvay Beach PE Located at the east end of Prince Edward Island National Park, this beach was named after Dalvay-By-The-Sea, a summer home built in 1896 by Alexander MacDonald of Cincinnati, OH, vice-president of the Standard Oil Company. His home in Ohio was also named Dalvay, in commemoration of his original home in Scotland. The national park's headquarters is at **Dalvay by the Sea**.

Daniels Harbour NL This municipal community (1965), on the northwest coast of the Northern Peninsula, may have been named after Daniel Regan, an Englishman, who sought refuge in its harbour in the 1820s.

Danville QC This town in the regional county of Asbestos, north of Sherbrooke, was settled in 1801 by Loyalists from Danville, VT. That place northeast of Barre had been named in 1784 after French map-maker Jean-Baptiste Bourgignon d'Anville (1697–1782).

Darlington PE The post office in this municipal community (1983), northwest of Charlottetown, was named in 1870, possibly after Darlington, County Durham, England.

Dartmouth NS This metropolitan area in the regional municipality of Halifax since 1 April 1996 was created as a town in 1873 and a city in 1961. It was founded in 1750 by 355 settlers who came on the ship *Alderney* and was named after William Legge, 1st Earl of Dartmouth (1672–1750) who died that year, although he had not been involved in the affairs of state after 1714.

Dartmouth, Mount BC In the Coast Mountains, southeast of Mount Waddington, this mountain (2972 m) was named in 1958 by Capt. Dr. G.V.B. Cochran of the United States Air Force after Dartmouth College in Hanover, NH. He and English climbers A. Morrison and J. Rucklidge climbed the mountain in 1957.

Dashwood ON This community, located in Huron County, west of Exeter, was named *Friedsburg* in 1860 after brothers and millers Absolom and Noah Fried. In 1871 the post office was changed to Dashwood, possibly after Dashwood House in London, England, the British headquarters of Canada's Grand Trunk Railway. In 2001 it became part of the municipality of South Huron.

Dauphin MB This town (1910) is located north of Riding Mountain National Park and west of **Dauphin Lake**. The post office here was first called *Lake Dauphin* in 1890, with the present name being adopted in 1897, a year after the site was laid out in lots. The lake took its name from Fort Dauphin, founded by explorer Pierre Gaultier de la Vérendrye (1685–1755) in 1741 at present Winnipegosis, 55 km to the north. He named it after the Dauphin, the eldest son of Louis XV, who did not survive his father. The **Dauphin River** unites Lake Manitoba with Lake Winnipeg, via Lake St. Martin.

D'Autray QC This regional county on the north shore of the St. Lawrence, between the regional counties of L'Assomption and Maskinongé, was named in 1982 after military officer and explorer Jacques Bourdon d'Autray (1652–88).

Davidson SK The station in this town (1906), midway between Regina and Saskatoon, was named in 1902 after Col. Andrew Duncan Davidson of Minnesota, who organized the Saskatchewan Valley Land Company. He sold over 2,023,500 ha (5,000,000 a) to American settlers. Its post office opened in 1903.

Davis Inlet NL Now located on Iluikoyak Island on the Labrador coast, this place was formerly established as a Hudson's Bay Company trading post in 1831 on Ukasiksalik Island. It was named after the inlet, given after explorer John Davis (c.1550–1605), who entered it while exploring the coast in 1585. It had been the site of the Innu (Naskapi) settlement of Utshimassit ('storekeepers place') since 1967, but was relocated to Little Sango Pond on the mainland, 18 km to the south, in the late 1990s.

Davis Strait NU Separating southern Baffin Island from Kalaallit Nunaat (Greenland), this strait was possibly named in 1616 by William Baffin and Robert Bylot after John Davis (c.1550–1605), who had explored the area in 1585, 1586, and 1587.

Dawn ON In 1998 this township (1829) became part of the township of Dawn-Euphemia in Lambton County. Its name may have been given because surveyors encountered sombreness in Sombra Township, but found Dawn more pleasant. Perhaps fugitive slaves, who arrived here in 1828, expressed thanks for the 'dawn of liberty'.

Dawson YT After the discovery of gold on Bonanza Creek in early August 1896, Joseph Ladue started laying out a townsite at the junction of the Klondike and Yukon Rivers. The following January, William Ogilvie (1846–1912) agreed to survey the land into lots, on the condition that the place was named for the finest person he knew, George Mercer Dawson (1849–1901). At the time, Dawson was the director of the Geological Survey of Canada; despite physical disabilities he undertook incredible exploratory journeys as a brilliant and versatile scientist—traveling over 2200 km during one expedition. Dawson was declared the capital of the Yukon in 1897, but in 1951 the territory's government was moved to the larger centre of Whitehorse, and two years later Dawson ceased to be the capital. Commonly called *Dawson City*, it is incorporated in the statutes as the 'town of the City of Dawson'. It was an incorporated city from 1902 to 1904.

Dawson Creek BC The post office in this city (1958) on the Peace River country was named in 1921 after a small tributary of Pouce Coupé River. The creek was likely named in 1879 by Henry A.F. MacLeod, a Canadian Pacific Railway exploration

engineer, who met geologist George M. Dawson (1849–1901) that year. Dawson had undertaken an arduous reconnaisance from the mouth of the Skeena River to Edmonton. On his maps he called the creek *Dawson's Brook*.

Dawson, Mount BC In the Selkirk Mountains, east of Revelstoke, this mountain (3390 m) was named in 1888 by British alpinist William Green after geologist George M. Dawson (1849–1901). *See also* Dawson.

Dawson, Mount NB Located southwest of Nictau Lake, this mountain was named in 1899 by naturalist William F. Ganong (1864–1941) after geologist George M. Dawson (1849–1901). Although he was better known for his geological work in British Columbia and the Yukon, he also undertook some studies in New Brunswick.

Daysland AB This town (1907) southeast of Camrose was named in 1905 by the Canadian Pacific Railway after Egerton W. Day, who first settled here in 1888. He returned to Ontario soon after, coming back to central Alberta in 1904. Its post office opened in 1906.

Dease Lake BC In northwestern British Columbia, this place was established in 1834 by Hudson's Bay Company chief trader John McLeod (1795–1842) and named after fur trader Peter Warren Dease (1788–1863), Chief Factor of the Husdon's Bay Company who joined Franklin's British Arctic land expedition, 1825–7.

Dease Strait NU Uniting Coronation and Queen Maud gulfs, and between the mainland and Victoria Island, this strait was named in 1826 by Sir John Franklin (1786–1847) after Hudson's Bay Company Chief Factor Peter Warren Dease (1788–1863). Dease joined Franklin's British Arctic land expedition, 1825–7.

Deauville QC A village on the north shore of Lac Magog, southwest of Sherbrooke, it was known as *Petit-Lac-Magog* until 1952, when it was renamed by Mayor Edgar Genest after the prominent French resort community in Normandie, France.

Debden SK Northwest of Prince Albert, this village (1922) was founded by the Canadian Northern Railway in 1909. It was named after Debden in Essex, England, southeast of Cambridge. Postal service was established in 1912.

Debert NS The post office in this place, located northwest of Truro and on the **Debert River**, was called *River Debert* in 1855. In 1875 it became *Debert Station* and in 1963 it was given its present name. The river's name, noted as early as 1820, was adapted from *Rivière de Bourq*, its designation during the French period before 1755.

DeCew Falls ON On the southwest side of the city of St. Catharines, this mill site was settled by John DeCew (1766–1855) in 1788. It was to his home that heroine Laura Secord walked, in 1813 from Queenston, to warn the British of a possible American attack. After the first Welland Canal destroyed his mill site in 1825, DeCew moved in 1834 to Haldimand County, where he founded **DeCewsville**.

Deep River ON This town (1959) in Renfrew County was created in 1944 as the residential community for the families of scientists and other staff of the Chalk River Nuclear Laboratories. In 1686 Chevalier de Troyes (d.1688) named the 70-km stretch of the Ottawa River *rivière creuse*, which Alexander Henry (d.1814) the younger translated as 'Deep-river' at the end of the next century. The river is more than 75 m deep at its deepest point, 10 km downriver, near the site of the laboratories.

Deer Island NB The name of this island in Passamaquoddy Bay possibly derives from the Passamaquoddy *edokwemeneek* ('deer island'). There is a legend that wolves were chasing a moose and a deer, but they turned into rock, resulting in Moose Island in Maine, Deer Island, and The Wolves in the Bay of Fundy.

Deer Lake NL Located at the north end of **Deer Lake** and northeast of Corner Brook, this town (1950) was first known as *Nicholsville*. It was named after George Nichols, a native of Cape Breton Island who established a timber-cutting operation here in 1867.

Dégilis QC Located in the regional county of Témiscouata, southeast of Rivière-du-Loup, this place was known as *Sainte-Rose-du-Degelé* from 1879 to 1968, when it was modified to *Sainte-Rose-du-Dégilis*, and abbreviated the following year to Dégilis. The name derives from the unusual phenomenon of the adjacent Rivière Madawaska, where it does not freeze at the outlet of Lac Témiscouata during the winter. In French such a phenomenon is called a *dégilis*.

De Grau NL This place, on the south shore of the Port au Port Peninsula, was presumably named after a French phrase meaning 'we are finished', in reference to having completed a season of summer fishing. It has been part of the municipal community of Cape St. George-Petit Jardin-Grand Jardin-De Grau-Marches Point-Loretto since 1969.

Delaware ON This township in Middlesex County was named in 1798 after an Algonquian confederacy of tribes, which settled on the Thames River. The name is traced to the Delaware River, a major river in the eastern United States. The river and the state of Delaware are named after Thomas De La Warr (1577–1618), governor of Virginia, 1610–18.

The community of **Delaware**, southwest of London, ON, was named in 1820. In 1998 Delaware Township became part of the township of Middlesex Centre.

Delburne AB East of Red Deer, this village (1913) was named in 1911 by the Grand Trunk Pacific Railway. It may have been named after Della Mewburn, sister of pioneer medical doctor F.H. Mewburn, or the name may have been chosen by landowners M.J. Manning and W.C. Clendening from a GTP list.

Delhi ON This urban centre in Haldimand-Norfolk Region was known as *Sovereen's Corners* and *Fredericksburg* after innkeeper Frederick Sovereen, and as *Middleton* after the township, before it was named in 1853 in honour of the capital city of India. In 1974 it was united with parts of the townships of Charlotteville, Middleton, South Walsingham, and Windham to form the municipal township of **Delhi**.

Delia AB This post office in this village (1914) west of Hanna was named in 1909 after the wife of merchant A.L. Davis, who earlier operated Delia's Stopping House here. In 1913 the Canadian Northern Railway called its station *Highland*, as it was its highest point between Kindersley and Drumheller, with Delia post office being moved to the line. Subsequently, it was agreed to change the station name to Delia.

Delı̨nę NT Located near the point where Great Bear River flows west from Great Bear Lake, this charter community (1993) was the site of Fort Franklin, established by the Hudson's Bay Company in 1825 to serve an expedition led by Sir John Franklin (1786–1847). Its post office opened in 1965, with *Fort Franklin* becoming a hamlet in 1972. In 1993 it was renamed after the Slavey word for 'bear river'.

Delisle QC This municipality in the regional county of Lac-Saint-Jean-Est, north of Alma, was created as the township municipality of Delisle in 1890. The latter had been named after the township of De l'Île, itself named in 1857 after Île d'Alma, with the township's name being respelled Delisle in 1861.

Delisle SK Southwest of Saskatoon, the post office in this town (1913) was named in 1905; John Amos Delisle was the first postmaster. His three brothers, Edward Walter, Eugene, and Alfred also settled in the area. Delisle was moved to the line of the Canadian Northern Railway, when it was laid in 1907–8.

Della Falls BC The highest falls (440 m) in Canada, it is located on Vancouver Island, northwest of Port Alberni. It was named in 1948 after Della Drinkwater, whose husband, Jo, had been a prospector in the area. Jo Creek drains Della Lake into Drinkwater Creek.

Deloraine MB Located southwest of Brandon, near the North Dakota border, this town (1907) was founded in 1882 by Scots settlers and named that year by the first postmaster, after Deloraine, Roxburghshire, Scotland. Four years later, when the Canadian Pacific Railway arrived, the townsite was shifted south of the tracks.

Deloro ON This village (1919) in Hastings County, east of Marmora, was named in 1881 after the first discovery of gold in Ontario. Refining of gold, as well as silver and cobalt, after 1903 continued here until 1961. In 1998 Deloro became part of the township of Marmora and Lake. In 2001 it was changed to the municipality of Marmora and Lake.

Delphine, Mount BC In the Purcell Mountains and west of Windermere, this mountain (3399 m) was named in 1911 by climber Edward Harnden, after a mine opened by George Starke. The mine was named after his wife, Delphine Francour, who died in 1921 at Wilmer, where Starke had opened a hotel.

Delson QC The post office in this town (1957) in the regional county of Roussillon, south of Montreal, was named in 1912 by devising a name from Delaware and Hudson, the title of a railway company.

Delta BC This district municipality, south of Vancouver and between the Fraser River and Boundary Bay, was established as the corporation of Delta in 1879, taking its name from the flat deltaic land at the Fraser's mouth. Among its urban areas are North Delta and Ladner.

Delta ON This location in the united counties of Leeds and Grenville, west of Brockville, was known as *Stevenstown* after first settler Abel Stevens; *Stone Mills*, after Stevens's grist mill; and *Beverley*, for Chief Justice Sir John Beverley Robinson (1791–1863). The name derives from the location of Delta in combination with Upper and Lower Beverley lakes; the three together all form the triangular shape of the Greek capital letter 'delta'.

Deltaform Mountain AB, BC On the continental divide, south of Lake Louise, this mountain (3424 m) was named in 1898 by American writer and climber Walter Wilcox (1869–1949) after its distinctive shape reminded him of the Greek capital letter 'Delta'.

Demarcation Point YT This marks the most northwesterly point of Canada. Sir John Franklin (1786–1847) wrote in 1828, 'from its being situated in longitude 141°W, the boundary between the British and Russian dominions'.

Dempster Highway NT, YT Extending northeast from the Klondike Highway, 42 km east of Dawson, to Fort McPherson, NT, this highway was created after 1959. It was named in 1963 after William John Duncan 'Jack' Dempster (1876–1964), a Royal North West Mounted Police officer. He served in the Yukon from 1897 to 1934.

Denbigh ON In 1998 this township became part of the township of Addington Highlands, Lennox and Addington County. It was named in 1859 after Denbighshire in Wales. The post office in the community of **Denbigh** was named in 1864.

Denman Island BC On the east coast of Vancouver Island, and southeast of Courtenay, this island was named about 1864 by Capt. George Richards (1820–96) after RAdm. Joseph Denman (1810–74), who served on the Pacific station, 1864–6.

Denmark NS This place is located east of Tatamagouche, on property that once belonged to the Right Reverend Charles Inglis (1734–1816), bishop of Nova Scotia, 1787–1816. The perimeter of the property was identified with the dean's mark. The post office opened as *Denmark Road* in 1888, and became Denmark 10 years later.

Denys, Mount NB On the south side of the Nepisiguit River, this mountain was named in 1899 by naturalist William F. Ganong (1864–1941) after Nicolas Denys (c.1598–1688), who was governor of Acadia in the late 1600s, and author of a book published in 1672 on the geography and natural history of North America.

Denzil SK Located southwest of Battleford, this village (1911) was founded by the Canadian Pacific Railway in 1910. The post office opened in 1911.

Derby ON In 2001 this township became part of the township of Georgian Bluffs, Grey County. It was named in 1842 after Edward George Geoffrey Smith Stanley, 14th Earl of Derby (1799–1869), who was prime minister of Great Britain for three terms.

Derwent AB Northwest of Lloydminster, this village (1930) was named in 1928 by the Canadian Pacific Railway after the River Derwent in Cumberland, England. Its post office opened the same year.

DesBarres, Mount NB This mountain, on the south side of the Nepisiguit River, was named in 1899 by naturalist William F. Ganong (1864–1941) after Joseph Frederick Wallet DesBarres (1722–1824), producer of the hydrographic charts in the *Atlantic Neptune*, lieutenant-governor of Cape Breton, 1784–7, and of Prince Edward Island, 1804–12.

Desbiens QC This town is located in the regional county of Lac-Saint-Jean-Est and on the south shore of Lac Saint-Jean. The post office here was called *Moulin-Desbiens* in 1922 after early settler and miller Louis Desbiens; the name was shortened to Desbiens the following year. It was the village of *Saint-Émilien* from 1926 to 1960, when it became the town of Desbiens.

Desboro ON The post office of this community in Grey County, south of Owen Sound, was named in 1869 after Desborough in Northamptonshire, England, north of the city of Northampton. In 2000 it became part of the township of Chatsworth.

Deschaillons-sur-Saint-Laurent QC On the south shore of the St. Lawrence, east of Trois-Rivières, this municipality traces its origins to the seigneury of *Rivière-Duchesne* (or *Deschaillons*), granted in 1674 to Pierre de Saint-Just de Saint-Louis (1640–1724), a captain in the Carignan-Salières Regiment. Échaillon was a family estate near Grenoble, France.

Deschambault QC Located in the regional county of Portneuf and on the north shore of the St. Lawrence, southwest of Quebec City, this municipality was created in 1989 from the village of Deschambault and the parish municipality of *Saint-Joseph-de-Deschambault*. In 1683 Jacques-Alexis de Fleury Deschambault (c.1642–1715) became the seigneur of Chavigny, with his name superseding it in 1690.

Deschênes, Lac ON, QC The name of this widening of the Ottawa River, extending for 40 km northwest from the Ottawa city centre to Fitzroy Harbour, was taken from *Portage des Chênes* on the north side of the river, used during the French regime to bypass the **Deschênes Rapids**. The name of the portage means 'carrying place at the oak trees' in French.

D'Escousse NS On the north shore of Isle Madame, this place may have been named after Martin Descouts, a surgeon who was engaged in the fishery off the Atlantic coast from 1714 to 1725. He lost property at Canso in 1718, and spent the years from 1726 to 1745 at Port la Joie, on the southwest side of Charlottetown Harbour.

Deseronto ON This town (1889) is located on the north side of the Bay of Quinte, east of Belleville. In 1835 John Culbertson laid out village lots and named the site *Culbertson's Wharf*. In 1855 he named the place for his grandfather John Deserontyon (1740–1811), also known as Odeserundiye, who led some Mohawk here from Massachusetts in 1784. The Mohawk had been surrounded by white settlers. This place was known as Hugo Rathbun's *Mill Point* from 1851 to 1881. The postal and village names were changed to Deseronto in 1881.

Desjardins QC This regional county, centred on the city of Lévis opposite Quebec City, was named in 1982 after Alphonse Roy *dit* Desjardins (1854–1920), the founder in 1900 of the co-operative movement and the first *caisse populaire* ('people's bank') in Quebec.

Des Ruisseaux QC This municipality northwest of Mont-Laurier was created in 1974 and named after the numerous streams in the area. In 1897 it had been called the united townships of *Robertson-et-Pope*, named after Quebec Central Railway founder Joseph Gibb Robertson (1820–99) and former minister of railways and canals Joseph Henry Pope (1819–89).

Destruction Bay YT On the western shore of Kluane Lake, this place was named in 1942 after a construction camp built by United States Army engineers that had been destroyed by high winds.

Detroit River ON Antoine de la Mothe, Sieur de Cadillac (1658–1730) built Fort Pontchartrain du Détroit, commonly called Fort Détroit, on the Michigan side of the river in 1701. By 1744 *Rivière du Détroit* was commonly used on maps for the drainage connecting Lakes Huron and Erie, but the name Detroit River was restricted to the present river in English-language records after 1759. Although the name suggests that the French perceived the feature to be a strait (*étroit*), there is in fact a drop of 1 m from Lake Huron to Lake St. Clair, and 1.7 m from Lake St. Clair to Lake Erie.

Deux-Montagnes QC This town at the eastern end of **Lac des Deux Montagnes** and in the regional county of **Deux-Montagnes** was named in 1963. The regional county was created in 1983, taking its name from the former county. The lake's name first occurred on a 1684 map by Jean-Baptiste-Louis Franquelin (c.1653–1712). The two mountains in question may be Mont Rigaud on the south side and Mont Oka on the north, although claims for the two highest summits at Oka are often advanced.

Devon AB On the south bank of the North Saskatchewan, southwest of Edmonton, this town (1950) was established by the Imperial Oil Company in 1947. Its name was proposed by a Mr Johnson of Toronto after the Devonian formation, from which the Leduc No. 1 gushed forth. The post office opened in 1948.

Devon Island NU This island, the second largest (55,247 km²) of the Queen Elizabeth Islands, was named in 1819 by Sir William Parry (1790–1855) after Devon, England, the home county of his second-in-command, Lt. Matthew Liddon.

Dewberry AB The post office in this village (1957) northwest of Lloydminster was named in 1907. Difficulty in choosing a name was resolved when a woman brought a basket of dewberries into the store where the post office was to be located. The dewberry (*Rubus pubescens*) is a trailing raspberry common to the damp woods of the parkland country of central Alberta.

Dewdney, Mount BC In the Cascade Mountains, southeast of Hope, this mountain (2255 m) was named in 1936 after Edgar Dewdney (1835–1916), who built the Dewdney Trail in the mid-1860s from Fort Hope to present-day Trail. **Dewdney Creek**, which rises 14 km to the north and flows northwest into the Coquihalla River, was named when the trail was laid out.

Diadem Peak AB In the Winston Churchill Range, north of the Columbia Icefields, this peak (3371 m) was named in 1898 by British climber Norman Collie (1859–1942) after the band of snow around its crest.

Diadem Peak BC In the Coast Mountains, southeast of Mount Waddington, this mountain (2868 m) was named in 1982 by climber Bruce Fairley of the Alpine Club of Canada's Vancouver section. It was named because its profile reminded him of a crown.

Diamant, Cap QC On the heights at Quebec City, this name was given by Jacques Cartier (1491–1557) in 1541 after several stones he found upriver at Cap Rouge, which he concluded were diamonds. By the beginning of the 1800s the furthest east point of the heights was identified as Cap Diamant. A comment made around 1575 by French writer André Thevet provided the oft-repeated proverb, '*Voilà un diamant de Canada*' ('false as a Canadian diamond').

Diamond Jenness Peninsula NT A midwestern extension of Victoria Island, this 260-km peninsula was named in 1971 by William E. Taylor (1927–94) of the National Museum of Man after Diamond Jenness (1886–1969). Jenness joined the Geological Survey of Canada in 1913 as an anthopologist, and was the chief anthropologist at the museum from 1926 to 1948. He undertook extensive anthropological studies in Northern Canada and wrote a number of books on Aboriginal societies in Canada.

D'Iberville, Mont QC The highest point (1622 m) of a massif in the Torngats on the Quebec–Newfoundland and Labrador boundary was named in 1971 after Pierre Le Moyne d'Iberville (1661–1706), noted for expeditions to Newfoundland and Hudson Bay in the 1690s. The same mountain was named Mount Caubvick in 1981 by the Newfoundland Geographical Names Board.

Didsbury AB North of Calgary, this town (1906) was named by the Canadian Pacific Railway in 1892–3 after a southside district of Manchester, England.

Diefenbaker, Lake SK This enlargement of the South Saskatchewan River extends some 200 km upriver from the Gardiner and Qu'Appelle Dams. It was created in 1958 and named in 1967 after John George Diefenbaker (1895–1979), prime minister of Canada, 1957–63.

Dieppe NB On the east side of Moncton, this town (1952) was named in 1946 after Dieppe, France, where many Canadian troops were killed on 19 August 1942, while assaulting the German defences. The post office was called *Legere Corner* in 1896, and renamed *Leger Corner* in 1930.

Digby NS This town (1890) on the Annapolis Basin was settled by New Englanders in 1766 and named *Conway*, likely after Henry Seymour Conway (1721–95), British secretary of state for the southern department. It was renamed in 1783 after RAdm. Robert Digby (1732–1815), commander of HMS *Atlanta* (the flagship of the convoy that brought Loyalist settlers to the site in 1783). In 1782 Digby had been named a joint commissioner with Sir Guy Carleton (1724–1808) to reconcile the differences between Great Britain and its North American colonies. **Digby County** was separated from Annapolis County in 1837. **Digby Gut** is the narrow entrance into Annapolis Basin, and **Digby Neck** is a long peninsula extending southwest, between St. Marys Bay and the Bay of Fundy.

Digdeguash River NB Rising near McAdam, this river flows southeast into Passamaquoddy Bay. Of unknown meaning in Passamaquoddy, its current spelling appeared on various plans and maps in the late 1700s, but it is pronounced more like *Diggedeguash River*, shown on a 1799 map by Surveyor General George Sproule (1741–1817).

Dildo NL On the east side of Trinity Bay, this place was named after **Dildo Arm**. The arm was noted as *Dildo Harbour* as early as 1810 by hydrographer Michael Lane. Although its origin is unknown, it would seem plausible that the word describes the deep, narrow entrance into the arm, reflecting an old meaning of the word in England. Between New World Island and Newfoundland, **Dildo Run** unites the Bay of Exploits with Hamilton Sound. Its channel is quite narrow between several islands.

Dingwall NS On Aspy Bay and south of Cape Breton Island's Cape North, this place was first called *Young's Cove*. Its post office, called *Aspy Bay* in 1855, was renamed in 1883 after its postmaster, Robert Dingwall.

Dinorwic ON This place located at the north end of Dinorwic Lake and in Kenora District, southeast of Dryden, was named in 1897 by Canadian Pacific Railway superintendent Sir William Whyte (1843–1914) after Dinorwic in northwestern Wales.

Dinsmore SK In 1907 a post office opened at this village (1913) southwest of Saskatoon; the post office was named after farmer Robert Neilson Dinsmore. When the Canadian Northern Railway built a line through the area in 1913, it retained the name for its station.

Disraeli QC In the regional county of L'Amiante, south of Thetford Mines, this place was incorporated as the village of *D'Israëli* (or *d'Israëli*) in 1904, with the spelling modified to *Disraëli* in 1953, and incorporated as the town of Disraeli in 1969. The original parish municipality was created in 1882 and named after Benjamin Disraeli, 1st Earl of Beaconsfield (1804–81), prime minister of Great Britain, 1867–8 and 1874–80.

Dixon Entrance BC Separating the Queen Charlotte Islands from Alaska, it was named in 1788 by Sir Joseph Banks (1743–1820), president of the Royal Society of London, after Capt. George Dixon (c.1755–1800). Dixon explored the west coast with Capt. James Cook (1728–79) in 1778, and was the commander of the *Queen Charlotte*, 1786–8.

Dixville QC The post office in this village (1874), located in the regional county of Coaticook south of the town of Coaticook, was called *Drew's Mills* from 1835 to 1874. It was then renamed after pioneer miller and postmaster Richard (Dick) Baldwin, replicating a name 45 km to the southeast in New Hampshire.

Doaktown NB The post office in this village (1966) on the Southwest Miramichi River, was named in 1854 after Robert Doak (d.1857), who arrived from Scotland about 1812.

Dodsland SK This village (1913) northeast of Kindersley was established in August 1913, when the Grand Trunk Pacific Railway built a line southwest from Biggar. It was named after Dr. Dodds, who had come from Newport, NE, and acquired 810 ha (2000 a) of land in the area. The post office opened in 1914.

Dolbeau QC On the Rivière Mistassini, north of Lac Saint-Jean, and in the regional county of Maria-Chapdelaine, this town was named in 1927 after the township of **Dolbeau**, created in 1904 and named after Récollet missionary Jean Dolbeau (1586–1652).

Dollard-des-Ormeaux QC This city (1960) was established as a municipality in 1924. It became part of the city of Montreal in 2002 but recovered its city status in 2006. The name honours one of the most celebrated figures in early Canadian history, Adam Dollard Des Ormeaux (1635–60). In May 1660, with a group of armed defenders consisting of 16 French and several Huron, Dollard Des Ormeaux defended *Ville-Marie* (Montreal) by repelling an attack of some 800 Onondaga, Mohawk, and Oneida. The battle took place at Long Sault, on the Ottawa River, near present-day Hawkesbury.

Dolphin and Union Strait NU A shallow passage connecting Coronation Gulf with Amundsen Gulf, this strait was named in 1826 by Sir John Richardson (1787–1865) after the two little boats that transported Richardson and Edward Kendall along the coast from the Mackenzie Delta to the Coppermine River.

Dominion NS This urban community in the regional municipality of Cape Breton since 1 August 1995 was first incorporated as a town in 1906. It was named after the Dominion No. 1 coal shaft, which sunk into a seam in 1894, and had been incorporated earlier as the village of *Old Bridgeport Mines*. The post office was called *Bridgeport Mines* in 1886, *Old Bridgeport Mines* in 1887, and *Old Bridgeport* in 1906. It became Dominion in 1940.

Dominion City MB North of Emerson, this small community of some 385 people was first called *Roseau Crossing* after a tributary of the Red River. It was renamed Dominion City by the Canadian Pacific Railway in 1878, taking its name from the Dominion of Canada and from the hope it would become a large urban centre. Its post office opened two years later. Its population in 2008 was 1781.

Domremy SK This village (1921) south of Prince Albert was founded in 1895 by settlers from France, and named after their hometown Domrémy-la-Pucelle, Vosges, France, the birthplace of St. Joan of Arc. Postal service was set up the following year. It was moved 3 km to the south, when the Canadian Northern Railway was built in 1918.

Domville ON This place, located in the united counties of Leeds and Grenville north of Prescott, was named in 1880 by Augusta Township reeve John Dumbrille, who proposed the original French Huguenot form of his family name. Earlier, he had suggested Frogmore after one of Queen Victoria's homes, but the local residents thought he had the noisy frogs in nearby Long Swamp in mind.

Donalda AB Located southeast of Camrose, this village (1912) was named in 1911 by the Canadian Northern Railway after Donalda Crossway of Cobourg, ON, a niece of Sir Donald Mann (1853–1934), vice-president of the company. The post office was called *Harker* from 1907 to May 1911, when it was called *Eidswold* for just four months, before adopting Donalda.

Donjek River YT A tributary of the White River, this river rises in Kluane Lake. It was likely named by Dr. Charles Willard Hayes (1859–1916) during a trip in the area in 1891. In Gwich'in *donyak* or *donchek* means 'pea-vine', a good source of winter feed for game and domestic animals.

Don Mills ON Part of the city of Toronto in the early 1800s, this urban centre in the former city of North York, was farmland until 1954, when Canada's first large planned residential community was built. Mills were operated on the **Middle Don River** by James, William, and Alexander Gray. In 1998 Don Mills became again a part of the city of Toronto.

Donnacona QC Located in the regional county of Portneuf, southwest of Quebec City, this place became a village in 1915 and a town five years later. The name recalls the Iroquois chief of Stadaconé, who Jacques Cartier (1491–1557) met at the present site of Quebec City in 1535; Cartier took Stadaconé back to France the following year.

Donnelly AB In the Peace River country, between Falher and McLennan, this village (1956) was named in 1915 after an official of the Edmonton, Dunvegan and British Columbia Railway. The post office opened in 1917.

Don River ON Flowing into the east side of Toronto Harbour, this river was named by Elizabeth Posthuma Gwillim Simcoe (1762–1850), wife of Lt.-Gov. John Graves Simcoe (1752–1806), because it reminded her of the River Don in East Yorkshire, England.

Dorchester NB West of Sackville, this town (1911) was founded in 1801 and its post office opened in 1825. It was named after **Dorchester Parish**, established in 1787 and named after Sir Guy Carleton, 1st Baron Dorchester (1724–1808), who was then governor-in-chief of British North America.

Dorion ON This township in Thunder Bay District, northeast of Thunder Bay, was named in 1874 after Sir Antoine-Aimé Dorion (1818–91), co-premier of Canada for two terms between 1858 and 1864, and chief justice of the Court of Queen's Bench of Quebec from 1874. The post office was called *Dorion Station* in 1912, and shortened to Dorion in 1954.

Dorion QC This town (1916) in the regional county of Vaudreuil-Soulanges, west of Montreal, was was named in honour of Sir Antoine-Aimé Dorion (1818–91), member of the Legislative Assembly of Canada, 1854–67, and of the House of Commons, 1872–4. He was co-premier of the Province of Canada with George Brown for a few days in 1858, and with Sir John A. Macdonald in 1863–4. He was the chief justice of the Court of Queen's Bench of Quebec from 1874.

Dornoch ON In 2000 this place became a part of the township of Chatsworth. In 1852 the post office here was named *Glenelg* after the township of Glenelg in Grey County. Philip McIntosh renamed it Dornoch in 1880 after his father's birthplace at the mouth of Dornoch Firth, 50 km northeast of Inverness, Scotland.

Dorset ON Located in the district municipality of Muskoka, southeast of Huntsville, this community was first called *Colebridge* after the Coles family. It was named Dorset in 1880, possibly after Dorset, England. The adjacent townships of Ridout and Sherborne were named after Thomas Ridout

(1754–1829), surveyor general of Upper Canada, 1810–29, who was born in Dorset.

Dorval QC This is one of two municipalities still designated *cité* in the province (the other is Côte-Saint-Luc). In 1691 Jean-Baptiste Bouchard d'Orval (c.1658–1724) bought property in the area of the present Dorval. Dorval was created a village in 1892, a town in 1903, and a city in 1956. The post office was named in 1878. In 2002 Dorval became part of the city of Montreal. Four years later it recovered its status as a city.

Douglas MB Located east of Brandon, this place was first known as *Currie's Landing* after homesteader and ferry operator William Currie. It was moved north to the Canadian Pacific Railway's main line in 1882, and renamed Douglas after James Douglas Sutherland Campbell, Marquess of Lorne (1845–1914), governor general of Canada, 1878–83, who travelled on the newly laid track in 1881. Its post office was called *Douglas Station* in 1883.

Douglas ON On the Bonnechere River in Renfrew County, west of the town of Renfrew, it became a part of the township of Bonnechere Valley in 2001. Douglas was named in 1853 by Judge John Glass Malloch (1806–73) of Perth, who surveyed lots; he named it for Douglas in Scotland's Lanarkshire, southeast of Glasgow. His wife's father and Perth pioneer, the Reverend William Bell, was from Douglas, Scotland.

Douglas Channel BC Extending southwest from Kitimat Arm, this channel was named by Hudson's Bay Company officers after Sir James Douglas (1803–77), governor of Vancouver Island, 1851–63, and of British Columbia, 1858–64.

Douglas, Mount AB Northwest of Banff, this mountain (3235 m) was named in 1884 by geologist George M. Dawson after Scottish botanist David Douglas (1798–1834). He studied trees and plants during several trips through North America, and the Douglas fir—an evergreen closely related to the larch—was named after him. It is considered the most valuable timber tree in North America.

Douglastown NB The post office in this location within the city of Miramichi and between Newcastle and Chatham was named in 1835. It had been named about 10 years earlier by lumbermen Allan Gilmour and John Rankin after Sir Howard Douglas (1776–1861), lieutenant-governor of the province, 1823–32. It may have been named when Sir Howard was in Newcastle to lay a stone for a Presbyterian church, just before a great fire swept the area. It was also known in the early years as *Gretna Green*. Douglastown was an incorporated village from 1966 to 1995.

Douro ON This township in Peterborough County was named in 1821 after one of the titles of Arthur Wellesley, Duke of Wellington, Baron Douro (1769–1852). The duke was given the title after a victory over French forces after crossing the Rio Douro at Oporto, driving them from Portugal. In 1998 the township became part of the township of Douro-Dummer.

Dover NL On the northwest shore of Bonavista Bay, this town was first called *Shoal Bay* in the 1890s. In 1949 Dover had been selected by the local residents from a list submitted by the post office department of Canada, after *Wellington* had been rejected. The town was incorporated as *Wellington (Dover)* in 1971, but after a local petition it was shortened to Dover two years later.

Dover NS Southwest of Canso, this village (1969) was probably named in the 1820s after Dover, England. Its post office was called *Little Dover* in 1890.

Dover ON In 1998 this township became part of the municipality of Chatham-Kent, Kent County. It was named in 1794 after the seaport in Kent, England.

Dowling ON This township, northwest of the city of Sudbury, became part of the city of Greater Sudbury in 2001. It was named in 1885 after John F. Dowling, member for Renfrew South in the Ontario Legislature, 1884–6 and 1891–4. In 1973 most of the township became part of the new town of Onaping Falls. The community of **Dowling** is one of the main urban centres in the city.

Downie ON In 1998 this township became part of the township of Perth South, Perth County. It was named in 1830 for Robert Downie, a director of the Canada Company. The Canada Company was a British company established in 1826 to develop the Huron Tract, a large area of what is now Southwestern Ontario.

Downie Peak BC Located in the Selkirk Mountains, north of Revelstoke, this mountain (3015 m) was named in 1866 by surveyor Walter Moberly (1832–1915) after William Downie (1819–93), who prospected in the Goldstream River valley in 1865. Mountaineer Howard Palmer (1883–1944) called it *Mount Arrowhead* in 1912 and *Eldorado Mountain* in a 1914 report. Earlier in 1849 Downie had taken part in the gold rush to California, where Downieville is named for him.

Drake SK Located southeast of Saskatoon, between Lanigan and Nokomis, this village (1910) was founded by the Canadian Pacific Railway in 1907. It was named after Sir Francis Drake (1540–96), the famous English sea captain, who may have been the first European explorer to cruise the west coast of Canada. The post office opened in 1908.

Drayton ON This village (1873) in Wellington County, northwest of Fergus, was named in 1851 after Drayton

Manor, the English home of Sir Robert Peel (1788–1850) in Staffordshire, northeast of Birmingham. In 1999 it became part of the township of Mapleton.

Drayton Valley AB The post office in this town (1957) on the northwest side of the North Saskatchewan River, southwest of Edmonton, was named in 1920 after the hometown of the wife of postmaster W.J. Drake in Hampshire, England, a northern suburb of Portsmouth. Previously its post office had been called *Powerhouse*.

Dresden ON The post office in this town (1882) on the Sydenham River in Kent County was named in 1854 by postal authorities after the city in Germany. Fairport had been suggested for part of the town, but the name soon disappeared. Dresden was the end of the Underground Railway for Josiah Henson and other fugitive slaves from the US. It is the site of Josiah Henson's cabin, which inspired Harriet Beecher Stowe's *Uncle Tom's Cabin* (1852). In 1998 the town became part of the municipality Chatham-Kent.

Drumheller AB In 1998 this city (1930) became a town with the municipal district of Badlands. It is located on the Red Deer River, 95 km northeast of Calgary. The post office here was named in 1911 after Samuel Drumheller (1864–1925), who arrived in 1910 and developed the townsite in the centre of coal fields. The Canadian Northern Railway arrived in 1912.

Drummond NB The post office in this village (1967) located southeast of Grand Falls was named in 1891 after **Drummond Parish**, which had been established in 1872. It may have been named after Drummond Castle near Perth, Scotland, where various Barons Drummond were also called Lord Perth. Perth Parish is immediately south of **Drummond Parish**.

Drummond ON This township northeast of Perth in Lanark County was named in 1816 after Gen. Sir Gordon Drummond (1772–1854), administrator of Lower and Upper Canada, 1814–6.

Drummondville QC This city on the west bank of the Rivière Saint-François, and in the regional county of **Drummond** (1982), was named by Maj. Gen. Frederick Heriot (1786–1843) in 1815 after Gen. Sir Gordon Drummond (1772–1854), a native of Quebec City. The administrator of Lower and Upper Canada, 1814–16, Drummond had directed Heriot to organize a military agricultural establishment along the river.

Dryden ON In 1998 Dryden and the township of Barclay became part of the city of Dryden. A settlement here was first founded in 1895 by provincial Minister of Agriculture

John Dryden (1840–1909), who opened an experimental farm called New Prospect at nearby Wabigoon Lake. In 1910 Dryden became a town in Kenora District.

Dubawnt Lake NT, NU Midway between Great Slave Lake and Hudson Bay, this lake (3629 km²) was named in 1893 by geologist Joseph Burr Tyrrell (1858–1957) after the Chipewyan word *tobutua* ('water shore lake'), possibly because the lake remains ice-covered in the summer, except for a narrow fringe along the shore. Most of the lake is in Nunavut. The **Dubawnt River** rises north of Lake Athabasca and flows northeast to join the Thelon River, upstream from Aberdeen Lake.

Dublin ON The post office in this place, located in the township of West Perth, Perth County, northwest of Stratford, was named *Carronbrook* in 1854 after a tributary of the Bayfield River. It was renamed Dublin in 1878, after the birthplace in Ireland of merchant and miller Joseph Kidd.

Dublin Shore NS On the Atlantic coast, southwest of the mouth of the LaHave River, this community was named in 1857 after New Dublin Township. The township was established here in the 1760s and called after the capital of Ireland. The post office in **West Dublin**, west of Dublin Shore, opened in 1864.

Dubreuilville ON In Algoma District, northeast of Wawa, this community was founded in 1951 by brothers Napoléon, Joachin, Augustin, and Marcel Dubreuil, natives of Taschereau, Abitibi, QC. The post office here was called *Magpie Mine* in 1954, but it was renamed in 1961 after the founders of the lumbering community. It became a municipal township in 1989.

Duchess AB This village (1921), north of Brooks, was named in 1911 by the Canadian Pacific Railway after Duchess Louise Marguerite (1860–1917), wife of the Duke of Connaught and Strathearn, son of Queen Victoria, and Governor General of Canada, 1911–6.

Duck Lake SK This town (1911) southwest of Prince Albert was established in 1890 by the Canadian Northern Railway, and named after the lake to its west, made famous in 1885 when the first shots of the North-West Rebellion were fired. *Stobart* post office, named after merchant Frederick William Stobart, opened in the area in 1879 and was changed to Duck Lake in 1894. In 1907 the postmaster reported that 'The ducks are so plentiful that when generally disturbed by sportsmen the vibration of their wings sounds like thunder'.

Dufferin ON Provisionally created as a county in 1874 and legally established seven years later, its name was proposed in 1872 for Frederick Temple Blackwood, 1st Marquess of Dufferin and Ava (1826–1902), governor general of Canada, 1872–8 and viceroy of India, 1884–8. The title of Dufferin came from a barony in County Down, Ireland.

Dummer ON This township in Peterborough County was named in 1821 after William Dummer Powell (1755–1834), chief justice of Upper Canada and speaker of the Legislative Council, 1816–25. In 1998 it became part of the township of Douro-Dummer.

Duncan BC This city (1912) on Vancouver Island, northwest of Victoria, was first named *Duncan's* in 1887 by the Esquimalt and Nanaimo Railway after William Chalmers Duncan (1836–1919). He arrived to Victoria in 1862 from Ontario and settled at the site of the city shortly after. He named his farm and the new community *Alderlea. Duncan's Station* post office opened in 1889 and changed to Duncan in 1926.

Duncan, Mount BC North of Kootenay Lake, this mountain (3228 m) was named in 1890 by British alpinist Harold Topham after prospector John (Jack) Duncan. **Duncan Lake** and **Duncan River**, both north of Kootenay Lake, were also named for him.

Dundalk ON This village (1886) in Grey County, northwest of Shelburne, was named in 1874 by Elias Brabazon Grey after his hometown in County Louth, Ireland. In 2000 Dundalk became part of the township of Southgate.

Dundas ON This county, part of the united counties of Stormont, Dundas, and Glengarry since 1850, was named in 1792 after Henry Dundas, 1st Viscount Melville (1742–1811), who served in several British ministries and provided information about British North America.

Dundas ON In 2001 this town was annexed by the city of Hamilton. Dundas became a town in 1848 in the Hamilton-Wentworth Region. It had been named *Dundas Mills* in 1800 after its location at the east end of **Dundas Street**, and its post office opened in 1814. In 1793 Lt.-Gov. John Graves Simcoe (1752–1806) ordered the building of Dundas Street to the Forks of the Thames (London), naming it after Henry Dundas, 1st Viscount Melville, then secretary of state for the Home Department, 1791–1801. Dundas Street was subsequently extended to York (Toronto).

Dundas Peninsula NT A southwestern extension of Melville Island, this 140-km peninsula was named by Sir William Parry (1790–1855) after Robert Saunders Dundas, 2nd Viscount Melville (1771–1852), who was then the first lord of the Admiralty.

Dundela ON The post office in this place, located in the united counties of Stormont, Dundas, and Glengarry, northwest of Morrisburg, was named in 1866 after local resident Delia Dillabough. It was earlier called *McIntosh's Corners*, where pioneer settler John McIntosh discovered some wild apple trees, and his son Allen propagated the famous McIntosh apple. In 1998 it became part of the township of South Dundas.

Dundurn SK This town (1980) south of Saskatoon was named in 1894 by postmaster James Leslie after Dundurn Castle in Hamilton, ON, built by Sir Allan Napier MacNab in the 1830s.

Dunedin ON In Simcoe County, south of Collingwood, this place was named in 1866 by first postmaster John Carruthers, after the New Zealand city of Dunedin, which he had visited. In 1994 it became part of the township of Clearview.

Dungannon ON This community in Huron County, northeast of Goderich, was laid out in village lots in 1855 by William Mallough and named the next year after his hometown in County Tyrone, Ireland. In 2001 it became part of the township of Ashfield-Colborne-Wawanosh.

Dunham QC This town in the regional county of Brome-Missisquoi, south of Cowansville, was created a township municipality in 1845. The name comes from **Dunham Township**, proclaimed in 1796. It became a village in 1867 and a town in 1971.

Dunk River PE This river rises near the community of Hunter River and flows west into Bedeque Bay, south of Summerside. It was named in 1765 by Samuel Holland (1728–1801) after George Montagu Dunk, 2nd Earl of Halifax (1716–71), who was then British secretary of state for the southern department.

Dunlop ON Just north of Goderich, this place was named *Millburn* in 1878. Four years later it was renamed after Capt. Robert Graham Dunlop (1790–1841) and Dr. William 'Tiger' Dunlop (1792–1848). Robert served in the House of Assembly of Upper Canada, 1836–41, and was followed in the Legislative Assembly of the Province of Canada by his brother William, who became the superintendent of the Lachine Canal, at Montreal, in 1846. In 2001 Dunlop became part of the township of Ashfield-Colborne-Wawanosh.

Dunnottar MB Situated on Lake Winnipeg, south of Gimli, this village (1947) was named by Alex Melville, who united the resort developments of Whytewold, Ponemah, and Matlock. He chose the name after Dunnottar Castle at Stonehaven, south of Aberdeen, Scotland.

Dunnville ON In Haldimand-Norfolk Region, this town (1900) was named in 1830 for John Henry Dunn (1792–1854), receiver general of Upper Canada, 1820–43, and president of the Welland Canal Company, 1825–33. In 1974 the town was considerably enlarged by annexing the townships of Dunn, Canborough, Moulton, and Sherbooke.

Dunrobin ON In the city of Ottawa, this community was first called *Torbolton*, after the township, in 1864. Four years later it was named after Dunrobin Castle, the home of the Duke of Sutherland in Sutherlandshire, northeast of Inverness, Scotland. Dunrobin became part of the city of Ottawa in 2001.

Duntroon ON This community in Simcoe County, south of Collingwood, was known as *McNab's Corners*, *Scotch Corners*, *Nottawasaga* (after the township), and *Bomore*, before Presbyterian minister John Campbell renamed it in 1864 after Duntroon Castle in Argyllshire, northwest of Glasgow. In 1994 Duntroon became part of the township of Clearview.

Dunvegan NS The post office in this place, situated northeast of Inverness, was called *Broad Cove Marsh* in 1866. It was renamed 20 years later after Dunvegan Castle on the Isle of Skye, Scotland.

Dunvegan ON The post office in this place, located north of Cornwall, in the united counties of Stormont, Dundas and Glengarry, was first called *Kenyon*, after the township, in 1848. It was renamed in 1862 after Dunvegan on Scotland's Isle of Skye, the Clan Macleod home for over 700 years. In 1998 it became part of the township of North Glengarry.

Dunville NL Located on the north bank of the Northeast Arm of Placentia Harbour, this place is a neighbourhood in the town of Placentia. It had been incorporated as a town in 1963, but was annexed in 1994. It was first known as *North East Arm*. It was renamed Dunville about 1888, when a branch of the Newfoundland Railway was built to Placentia.

Dunwich ON In 1998 this township became the municipality of Dutton-Dunwich, Elgin County. It was named in 1792 after the village of Dunwich on the North Sea coast of Suffolk, England.

Duparquet QC The post office in this place, located in the regional county of Abitibi-Ouest, northwest of Rouyn-Noranda, opened in 1933, receiving its name from the **Duparquet Township**, created in 1916. The township's name honoured a captain in the La Sarre Regiment who was killed in a battle at Quebec City in 1760.

Durham ON Durham County was proclaimed in 1792 after England's County Durham. It was united with Northumberland County for municipal purposes from 1850 to 1974, when it annexed most of *Ontario County* (while losing three townships and the town of Port Hope to adjacent counties) to form the regional municipality of Durham.

Durham ON This town (1872) in Grey County was named in 1848 by George Jackson, when he moved the Crown lands office here from *Sydenham* (Owen Sound). Jackson was born in the city of Durham, County Durham, England. The post office here was *Bentinck*, after the township, from 1847 to 1857, when it was called Durham. In 2001 the town became part of the township of West Grey.

Durham-Sud QC In the regional county of Drummond, south of Drummondville, this municipality and its post office were first named *South Durham* in 1854. The present municipality merged the municipality of Durham-Sud (1865) and the village of Durham-Sud (1918) in 1975. The original township of Durham was named in 1795 after County Durham in England.

Dutton ON In 1998 this village became part of the municipality of Dutton-Dunwich, Elgin County. The village (1890), located southwest of St. Thomas, was named in 1872, after the Canadian Southern Railway's civil engineer.

Dyment ON In Kenora District, southeast of Dryden, the post office in this settlement was named in 1899, probably after Thessalon lumberman Albert Edward Dyment (1869–1944), a Liberal member of Parliament, 1896–1908.

Dysart ON This township surrounding the community of Haliburton, in Haliburton County, was named in 1860 after the town of Dysart in Fifeshire, Scotland, north of Edinburgh. Since 1874 it has been the senior member of the municipal township of Dysart, Bruton, Clyde, Dudley, Eyre, Guilford, Harburn, Harcourt and Havelock, which is frequently referred to as 'Dysart et al'.

Dysart SK Located northeast of Regina, the post office serving this village (1909) was named in 1906, after one of the surveyors of the Canadian Pacific Railway. The father of First World War flying ace Billy Bishop owned the land through which the line ran. He agreed to name the place after Dysart, if Dysart agreed to run the line through his land. He came from the town of Kirkcaldy, Fifeshire, Scotland.

Eagle Pass BC This pass (561 m) through the Monashee Mountains, and between Revelstoke and Salmon Arm, was named in 1865 by Canadian Pacific Railway explorer Walter Moberly (1832–1915), who was guided by two eagles up the valley of **Eagle River**. Twenty years later Donald Smith, Lord Strathcona (1820–1914), drove the Last Spike of the CPR at Craigellachie in the pass.

Ear Falls ON The post office in this municipal township in Kenora District, southeast of Red Lake, was named in 1948. Ear Falls in Ojibwa is called *Otak Powitik* after a rock ledge at the lip of the falls shaped like a huge human ear. French fur traders called it *Portage de l'Oreille*.

Earl Grey SK North of Regina, the post office at this village (1906) was opened in 1905 and called after Albert Henry George Grey, 4th Earl Grey (1851–1917), governor general of Canada, 1904–11. In 1909 he donated the Grey Cup for the Canadian football champions of each year. The Canadian Pacific Railway arrived here in 1907.

Earlton ON The post office in this place, located in Timiskaming District, north of New Liskeard, was named in 1905 for George Earl Brasher, the eldest son of postmaster Albert Edward Brasher.

East Angus QC A town (1912) northeast of Sherbrooke, its post office was named in 1882 after Montreal industrialist William Angus (d.1902), who built a sawmill and a pulp and paper mill here.

East Broughton QC This municipality in the regional county of L'Amiante, northeast of Thedford Mines, was first known as *Sacré-Coeur-de-Jésus*. It was renamed East Broughton in 1931 after **Broughton Township**, named in 1795 and proclaimed in 1800. The village of **East Broughton Station**, 1 km to the northwest, was created in 1954; the post office had been named in 1899.

Eastend SK Located on the east side of the Cypress Hills, southwest of Swift Current, the post office was first called *East End*, which took its name in 1900 from a North West Mounted Police post established here in 1877. In 1914 it was taken to the Canadian Pacific Railway, where the two words were tied into one. It became a town in 1920.

Eastern Kings PE A municipal community (1974) on the east side of Kings County, it embraces several localities, including Baltic, Bayfield, East Point, Elmira, Kingsboro, North Lake, and South Lake.

Easterville MB In 1964 a Manitoba Hydro dam at Grand Rapids raised the level of Cedar Lake and inundated the Aboriginal community of *Chemahawin*. The community was resettled on the south shore of the lake and named for Donald Easter, a former chief of the community. The post office opened the following year.

East Farnham QC This village in the regional county of Brome-Missisquoi, north of Cowansville, was established in 1914. The post office had been named in 1837. It is situated in the eastern part of the township of **Farnham**, proclaimed in 1798 and named after a village in Surrey, England, southwest of London.

East Ferris ON This municipal township in Nipissing District, southeast of North Bay, was created in 1921 when Ferris Township was divided into East and West Ferris municipal townships, with West Ferris being annexed by North Bay in 1968. **Ferris Township** was first named in 1880 after James M. Ferris, Liberal Member for Northumberland East in the Ontario Legislature, 1875–83.

East Garafraxa ON This municipal township in Dufferin County was separated from West Garafraxa Township in 1869 and added to Dufferin in 1874. There are many guesses as to the meaning of Garafraxa. It might be connected with an Irish estate, such as 'Garrafranes', or derive from the Irish *garry fraech* ('rough heath').

East Gwillimbury ON This town (1977) in York Region was created as a township in 1798. It was possibly named after Lt. Col. Thomas Gwillim (1721–1766), the father of Elizabeth Posthuma Simcoe (1762–1850).

East Hawkesbury ON This municipal township in the united counties of Prescott and Russell was separated in 1884 from Hawkesbury Township. The latter had been named in 1798, either for Charles Jenkinson (1727–1808), Baron Hawkesbury and Lord Liverpool, or for his son, Robert Banks Jenkinson (1770–1828), created Baron Hawkesbury in 1796. The son, who became Lord Liverpool in 1808, was prime minister of Great Britain, 1812–27. *See also* Hawkesbury *and* West Hawkesbury.

East Luther ON Luther Township, named in 1831 after Protestant reformer Martin Luther (1483–1546), was divided in 1879, with East Luther joining Dufferin County in 1883. In 1995 it was united with the village of Grand Valley to form the new municipal township of **East Luther Grand Valley**.

Eastmain QC This Cree village at the mouth of **Rivière Eastmain** (which flows for 700 km from central Quebec into the southeastern part of James Bay) is located at the site of the Hudson's Bay Company post of Eastmain, established in 1730. Taking its name from its location on the east side of James Bay's 'main' (water body), *East Main* was attached to the river in the late 1800s, and shortened to Eastmain in the early 1900s.

Eastman QC This post office in this municipality in the regional county of Memphrémagog, west of Magog, was called *Bolton Forest* after the township of Bolton, in 1865. It was renamed in 1881 after pioneer settler John Eastman. The municipality merged with the municipality of Stukley in 2001.

Eastport NL On **Eastport Bay**, an extension of Bonavista Bay, this town (1959) was established in the 1860s by families from nearby Salvage. The post office here was called *Salvage Bay* before 1900, when it was changed to *Brighton*. Because of duplication, *Salvage Bay* was restored in 1904. Eleven years later the residents asked for Eastview, but the Newfoundland Nomenclature Board imposed Eastport, although the place did not have harbour facilities.

East Redonda Island BC Between Vancouver Island and the mainland, northeast of Campbell River, this island was considered by Spanish explorers Dionisio Alcalá Galiano (1760–1805) and Cayetano Váldes y Bazan (1767–1835) in 1792 to be part of *Isla Redonda*, which included present West Redonda Island. The two names were endorsed in 1950. In Spanish *redonda* means 'round'.

East Riverside-Kingshurst NB This village (1966) is located 13 km northeast of the centre of Saint John. The first post office here from 1898 to 1901 was called *Riverside Beach*. It was reopened as East Riverside in 1911 and closed in 1969. Kingshurst was a former Canadian National Railway station.

East Royalty PE Within the eastern limits of Charlottetown, this locality—part of the original territorial division of Charlottetown Royalty—was a municipal community from 1983 to 1995.

East Wawanosh ON Wawanosh Township was named in 1840 for Chief Joshua Wawanosh of the Chippewas on the Sarnia Reserve. Wawanosh was one of the chiefs who transferred a large area of Southwestern Ontario to the British Crown in 1827. It was divided in 1867 into East Wawanosh and West Wawanosh municipal townships, with both remaining in

Huron County. In 2001 East Wawanosh became a part of the township of North Huron.

East Williams ON Williams Township, created in Middlesex County in 1830, was named after William Williams, a deputy governor of the Canada Company. This British company was established in 1826 to develop the Huron Tract—a large area of what is now Southwestern Ontario. It was divided into East Williams and West Williams municipal townships in 1860. In 2001 both of the municipal townships became part of the municipality of North Middlesex.

Eastwood ON In Oxford County, east of Woodstock, this place was named in 1853 after Eastwood Park, the home of RAdm. Henry Vansittart (1777–1843). Built here in the 1830s, the home was named after his widowed sister whose married name was East, who lived with him.

East York ON York Township was named in 1793, with East York Township being severed from it in 1924. It joined the town of Leaside in 1967 to form the borough of East York. In 1998 East York amalgamated into the city of Toronto.

East Zorra ON The original Zorra Township was named in 1819 by Lt.-Gov. Sir Peregrine Maitland (1777–1854) after the Spanish word *zorra* ('female fox'). It was divided into East Zorra and West Zorra municipal townships in 1845. In 1975 East Zorra was joined with the village of Tavistock to form the municipal township of **East Zorra-Tavistock**.

Eaton QC Located in the regional county of Le Haut-Saint-François, this township municipality east of Sherbrooke was named in 1855 after **Eaton Township**, named in 1795 and proclaimed in 1800. It may have been named after one of the places called Eaton in England. Eaton post office operated from 1825 to 1969.

Eatonia SK Southwest of Kindersley, this town (1954) was founded in 1917 by the Canadian Northern Railway, and named *Eaton* after Timothy Eaton (1834–1907), who founded the T. Eaton Company department store in Toronto in 1869. His son, Sir John Eaton was a shareholder of the Canadian Northern Railway. Timothy Eaton established the popular Eaton's catalogue, which allowed frontier communities access to a variety of merchandise. The first post office in the area was called *Cornfeld* in 1913 and was renamed Eatonia in 1921, amending the station's name to avoid confusion with nearby Eston.

Ebenezer SK North of Yorkton, the post office at this village (1948) was named *Ebenezer Valley* in 1891 and renamed Ebenezer in 1911. When the Grand Trunk Pacific Railway constructed a line though the area in 1909, it named its station *Anoka*. The German Baptist settlers disliked it, so the company agreed to call its station Ebenezer.

Eckville AB West of Red Deer, the post office in this town (1966) was named in 1905 after pioneer settler Andy E. Eckford. Presumably a naming contest was held, with Hattie Mitzner (later Stephens) winning with Eckville.

Eclipse Sound NU Located between Baffin and Bylot Islands, this sound was named in 1904, possibly by geologist Albert P. Low (1861–1942). He encountered the Scottish whaler *Eclipse*, under the command of Capt. W.F. Milne, working the waters west of Pond Inlet.

Economy NS The post office in Economy, located on the west side of **Economy Point** and west of Truro, was opened in 1836. It was an Acadian settlement called *Vil Conomie* in the mid-1700s. Its name was taken from the point, called by the Mi'kmaq *Kenomee* ('large point jutting out into the sea').

Ecum Secum NS The post office in this place, on the Eastern Shore between Sheet Harbour and Sherbrooke, opened in 1879. Its name possibly derives from the Mi'kmaq *megwasaagunk* ('red bank').

Edam SK The post office at this village (1911), settled in 1907 and located northwest of North Battleford, was named in 1908 after Edam in the Netherlands—famous for its cheese. In 1911 the Canadian Northern Railway established a station here, when a rail line was built through the Turtlelake River valley.

Edberg AB This village (1930) was named in 1902 by postmaster Johan Edstrom (1850–1910), who arrived here from Sweden not long before. He chose the name by joining the first syllable of his name with the Swedish *berg* ('hill').

Eden Mills ON East of Guelph and in Wellington County, this place was first called *Kribbs Mills* after David and Aaron Kribbs. Adam Argo bought the mills in 1846 and renamed the site Eden Mills after the garden where Adam and Eve first lived.

Edenwold SK Northeast of Regina, the first post office at this village (1912) was opened in 1890 and moved around among a number of farm residences. It was fixed at its present location in 1912, when the Grand Trunk Pacific Railway was built from Melville to Regina. The name was originally spelled *Edenwald*, from the Garden of Eden and the German for 'forest', but the postal officials misspelled it Edenwold, perhaps misreading the handwritten application.

Edgerton AB Southeast of Wainwright, this village (1917) was named in 1908 by the Grand Trunk Pacific Railway after H.H. Edgerton, a GTP engineer. The post office was also opened that year.

Edith Cavell, Mount AB, BC After English nurse Edith Cavell (1865–1915) was executed in Belgium by the Germans during the First World War, British Columbia premier Sir Richard McBride (1870–1917) and prime minister Sir Robert Borden (1854–1937) urged the naming of a mountain after her in Canada. In 1916 the Geographic Board chose this mountain (3363 m) south of Jasper, overlooking the valley of the Athabasca River.

Edmonton AB Edmonton House was established by the Hudson's Bay Company in 1795, 32 km downstream, near present-day Fort Saskatchewan. The name probably came from clerk John Peter Pruden's birthplace on the northeast side of London, England. The place was abandoned in 1807 and relocated near the present site of the city. In 1821 it was called Fort Edmonton, and was rebuilt in 1830 near the present legislative building. The city was incorporated in 1904. The summer village (1959) of **Edmonton Beach**, west of Edmonton, was created in 1926.

Edmundston NB At the confluence of the Madawaska and Saint John Rivers, this city (1952) was named in 1851 after Sir Edmund Walker Head (1805–68), lieutenant-governor of the province, 1848–54. It was originally called *Petit-Sault* after falls at the mouth of the Madawaska. The first post office, from 1847 to 1851, was *Little Falls*. The city's name is commonly misspelled Edmunston.

Edson AB This town (1911) on the McLeod River, west of Edmonton, was named in 1910 by the Grand Trunk Pacific Railway after Edson J. Chamberlain (1852–1924), then vice-president and general manager of the GTPR. He served as the company's president from 1912 to 1917. Earlier its post office was called *Heatherwood*.

Edwardsburgh ON In 2001 this township and the village of Cardinal became the township of Edwardsburgh/Cardinal. Located in the united counties of Leeds and Grenville, Edwardsburgh was named in 1787 after Prince Edward Augustus, Duke of Kent (1767–1820), the fourth son of George III and father of Queen Victoria.

Edwardsville NS The post office here, across Sydney Harbour from Sydney, was named in 1894 after nearby Point Edward. The point was called after Prince Edward, the Duke of Kent and Strathearn (1767–1820) and the father of Queen Victoria.

Edziza, Mount BC East of the Stikine River, this mountain (2480 m) was first called *Edziza Peak* on a Geological Survey map of 1926, and was shown as Mount Edziza in a GSC report the following year. It was named after Johnny Edzerza, who was killed by an avalanche while crossing the mountain. **Mount Edziza Provincial Park** embraces the area of the mountain where craters, reddish volcanic ash, and pumiceous sand are characteristics of the land.

Eel Ground NB Located southwest of Newcastle (part of the city of Miramichi) and on Eel Ground Indian Reserve, this place in Mi'kmaq was called *Nendookun* ('where eels are speared in the mud').

Eel River Crossing NB This village (1966), southwest of Dalhousie, was named after the river that flows northeast into Chaleur Bay. Its post office was *Eel River* from 1861 to 1886, when it was changed to its present name. In 1783 the river was referred to as *Longuil River*, a reference to the French word *anguille* ('eel').

Eganville ON In 2001 the village (1890) of Eganville became part of the township of Bonnechere Valley, Renfrew County. The post office here was named in 1852 after lumberman John Egan (1811–57), who bought a lumbering depot in 1837 at the Fifth Chute—the segment of the Bonnechere River where the village is located.

Eglinton Island NT Located in the Parry Islands of the Queen Elizabeth Islands, and between Melville and Prince Patrick Islands, this island (1541 km²) was named in 1853 by George F. Mecham after Archibald William Montgomerie, 13th Earl of Eglinton (1812–61), who was then Lord Lieutenant of Ireland.

Egmondville ON In 2001 this community became part of the municipality of Huron East, Huron County. South of Seaforth, its post office was named in 1855 after merchant Constant Van Egmond. He and his brothers Leopold, William, and August developed several businesses here. Their father, Anthony Van Egmond (1775–1838) built the road from Guelph to Goderich in 1832, but after a dispute with the Canada Company, he joined William Lyon Mackenzie's rebel forces in 1837 and was put in jail, where he died.

Egremont ON In 2000 this township became a part of the township of Southgate in Grey County. It was named in 1840 after George O'Brien Wyndham, 3rd Earl of Egremont (1751–1837), a brother-in-law of Gov. Gen. Lord Durham's mother.

Ekfrid ON In 2001 Ekfrid Township became a part of the municipality of Southwest Middlesex, Middlesex County. It had been named in 1821 after the Northumbrian king Egfrith, killed in 685 CE in a battle with the Picts near present-day Forfar, Scotland.

Elbow SK Located due south of Saskatoon, this site of this village is at a sharp turn of Lake Diefenbaker—described in 1804 as an 'elbow' in a journal by John McDonald of Garth—when ascending the South Saskatchewan River. The post

office was called *River View* in 1906, but it was renamed Elbow three years later, when the village was incorporated.

Elderslie ON In 1999 this township became part of the municipality of Arran-Elderslie, Bruce County. The township had been named in 1850 after the village of Elderslie, west of Glasgow, where the Scottish national hero Sir William Wallace (1270–1305) was born. *See also* Wallaceburg.

Eldon ON In 2001 this township became part of the city of Kawartha Lakes. The township was previously in Victoria County, having been named in 1823 after John Scott, 1st Earl of Eldon (1751–1838), who was then lord chancellor of Great Britain.

Eldorado Creek YT This tributary of Bonanza Creek was named in September 1896 by Knut Halstead, who had earlier prospected for gold on Fortymile River. It turned out to be one of the richest gold streams in the world, producing some $20 million of gold in a 5-km stretch.

Elfros SK This village on the Canadian Pacific Railway, northwest of Yorkton, and its post office were both established in 1909 and named after the Icelandic for 'garden of roses'. Some of the residents in the village believe that the name came from Norway.

Elgin ON This county was named in 1851 for James Bruce, Earl of Elgin, governor of the Province of Canada, 1847–54. The title was taken from the city of Elgin in Scotland's County Moray.

Elgin ON In 1998 this place became a part of the township of Rideau Lakes, the united counties of Leeds and Grenville. This community, southwest of Smiths Falls, was named in 1850 after James Bruce, Earl of Elgin, governor of the Province of Canada, 1847–54.

Elginfield ON In 2001 this place became part of the municipality of North Middlesex and part of the township of Lucan Biddulph in Middlesex County. Its post office was named in 1849 after James Bruce, Earl of Elgin, governor of the Province of Canada, 1847–54.

Elie MB Situated midway between Winnipeg and Portage la Prairie, this place was founded by the Canadian Northern Railway in 1888–9, and named after merchant Elie Dufresne—described on his tombstone as 'The Founder of Elie'. Its post office opened in 1898.

Eliot River PE Created as a municipal community in 1975, this place was annexed by the town of Cornwall in 1995. Samual Holland (1728–1801) took the name from *Elliot River* in 1765, itself called after Edward Eliot, 1st Baron Eliot

(1727–1804), then lord commissioner of trade and plantations. When the French occupied the island, they called this small stream *rivière de l'Ouest*. West River superseded *Elliot River* in 1970.

Elizabeth, Mount NB Southeast of Mount Carleton, this mountain (655 m) was named in 1903 by naturalist William F. Ganong (1864–1941) after Louise-Élisabeth de Joybert de Soulanges et de Marson (1673–1740), who was born near present-day Jemseg, 43 km east of Fredericton. Marson was the mother of Pierre de Rigaud de Vaudreuil de Cavagnial, Marquis de Vaudreuil, the last French governor of New France.

Elizabethtown ON In 2001 this township became part of the township of Elizabethtown-Kitley, united counties of Leeds and Grenville. It was named in 1787 for Princess Elizabeth (1770–1840), third daughter of George III.

Elkford BC This district municipality (1981) in the Elk River valley, north of Sparwood, is at an elevation of 1400 m—the highest populated place in Canada. It was established as a village in 1971, the same year that the post office opened. The name was composed from Elk River and its tributary, Fording River. Elkford was developed in 1971 by the Fording Coal Company.

Elkhorn MB Located northwest of Virden, near the Saskatchewan border, this village (1905) was established on the main Canadian Pacific Railway line in 1882. Surveyors had observed a large pair of elk horns on a nearby hill. Postal service was established the next year.

Elk Island National Park AB Located 45 km northeast of Edmonton, this park (194 km²) was created in 1913 as a fenced 'island' for elk, bison, mule deer, and other wildlife.

Elk Point AB This town (1962) on the north side of the North Saskatchewan River, northwest of Lloydminster, owes its name to Wilbur Higby from Elk Point, SD. He had moved first to Vegreville, but to escape the temptation of alcohol, he went down the river in 1905, and lived in a hole in the river bank near the site of the future town. Deeming the site to be promising, he persuaded others from Vegreville to homestead here the next spring.

Ellef Ringnes Island NU In the Sverdrup Islands of the Queen Elizabeth Islands, this island (11,295 km²) was named *Ellef Ringnes's Land* in 1900 by Otto Sverdrup (1854–1930), during his Norwegian Arctic expedition (1898–1902), after Ellef Ringnes, a Norwegian patron.

Ellerslie-Bideford PE North of Tyne Valley, this municipal community (1977) embraces the localities of **Ellerslie** and **Bideford**. Ellerslie was named before 1845 by a man called Wallace after Elderslie, Scotland, west of Glasgow, where the Scottish hero Sir William Wallace (c.1270–1305) was born. Bideford was named by William Ellis and Thomas Chanter, who had come from Bideford, Devon, England in 1818. First known as *New Bideford*, its post office opened as Bideford in 1912. In 1765 Samuel Holland (1728–1801) named the adjacent stream *Goodwood River* after a residence near Chichester, Sussex, England owned by the 3rd Duke of Richmond (1735–1806). By the late 1800s it had become better known as **Bideford River**.

Ellesmere Island NU Canada's third largest island (196,236 km²)—after Baffin and Victoria Islands—this island was named in 1852 by Sir Edward Inglefield (1820–94) after Francis Leveson-Gower, 1st Earl of Ellesmere (1800–57), who was then president of the Royal Geographical Society. **Ellesmere Island National Park Reserve** (37,775 km²) was established in 1988.

Ellice ON In 1998 this township became a part of the township of Perth East, Perth County. It was named in 1830 for Edward Ellice (1783–1863), a director of the Canada Company. This British company was established in 1826 to develop the Huron Tract, a large area of what is now Southwestern Ontario.

Elliot Lake ON This city (1991) in Algoma District is the site of a uranium ore discovery in 1948. Laid out as a planned community in 1955, its population fluctuated between 7000 and 25,000 over the next 30 years. Anticipating the closing of the mines, Elliot Lake has strongly promoted its potential as a retirement and recreation centre since 1983, resulting in a stable population of some 12,500. The lake may have been named by a geologist in the late 1800s.

Elliston NL This town (1965), southeast of Bonavista, was first known as *Bird Island Cove*. It was renamed in 1892 after the Reverend William Ellis (1780–1837), a Methodist missionary. He is believed to have held the first Protestant service here in 1812.

Elma ON In 1998 this township was taken into the township of North Perth, Perth County. It was named in 1849 after Lady Elma Bruce, daughter of James Bruce, 8th Lord Elgin (1811–63), governor of the Province of Canada, 1847–54.

Elmira ON The post office in this urban centre in Woolwich Township, in the regional municipality Waterloo, was called *West Woolwich* in 1849. It was renamed in 1867 after Elmira, NY.

Elmvale ON In Simcoe County, south of Midland, this former village was first called *Elm Flats* in the early 1850s, with Elmvale post office opening in 1859. It was united with Flos and Vespra townships in 1994 to form the municipal township of Springwater.

Elmwood ON In 2001 this community became part of the municipality of Brockton, Bruce County and part of the township of West Grey, Grey County. Its post office was named in 1864 after a giant elm tree in its main intersection, which had shattered into many pieces when it was cut down 10 years earlier.

Elnora AB Southeast of Red Deer, this village (1929) requested *Stewartville*, after a student minister, as a post office name in 1908, but it was turned down. A new name was then created from the first names of Elinor Hogg and Nora Edwards, whose husbands, Alex Hogg and William Edwards, were the first postmasters.

Elora ON In 1999 this village (1858) became a part of the township of Centre Wellington, Wellington County. It is located on the Grand River, northwest of Guelph. Founded in 1832 by retired British Capt. William Gilkison (1777–1833), the settlement was named after his brother John's ship *Ellora*. The ship itself was named after the famous cave temples and sculptures at Ellora, India, northeast of Mumbai.

Elphinstone MB Situated south of Riding Mountain National Park and northwest of Neepawa, this community was named in 1879 by Hudson's Bay Company factor John A. Lauder after the 15th Earl of Elphinstone. Elphinstone owned 13 sections south of the park, and actively promoted the settlement of Manitoba. The post office opened in 1887.

Elrose SK South of Rosetown, this town (1951) was founded about 1909 and named *Laberge* after a pioneer settler. When the Canadian Northern Railway arrived in 1913 it was renamed by contractor Louis Chirhart, possibly after a place in the United States, such as Elrosa (a village in central Minnesota). Its post office also opened that year.

Elsa YT East of Dawson, this incorporated hamlet was founded in 1929 as a residential community for miners at the Calumet silver-lead mine. Production did not get underway until 1937, and its post office was not opened until 1949. The reason for choosing the name Elsa is not available in official records.

Embree NL On the Bay of Exploits, northeast of Lewisporte, this town (1871) was first known as *Salt Pond*. It was renamed in 1931, possibly after the Reverend Jerimiah Embree (1844–90), a Methodist missionary who served on the north coast of Newfoundland from 1871 to 1888.

Embrun ON In the united counties of Prescott and Russell, southeast of Ottawa, this urban centre was named in 1858 by either Fr. François Coopman or Fr. François-Joseph Michel after Embrun in France's Hautes-Alpes, southeast of Grenoble.

Emerald Isle NT In the Parry Islands of the Queen Elizabeth Islands, this island (549 km²) was named in 1853 by Sir Francis McClintock after a poetic name for Ireland and because of its proximity to Prince Patrick Island.

Emerald Junction PE In the central part of the province, this place became the point where the Prince Edward Island Railway, originating in Borden, was built east to Charlottetown and west to Summerside. Located on the Prince–Queens County boundary, the post office was called *County Line* from 1875 to 1887. It was renamed in 1887 after the 'Emerald Isle', a poetic name for Ireland.

Emerson MB This town (1887), located at the point where the Red River flows north into Manitoba, was founded in 1879 by Thomas Carney and W.H. Fairbanks and named after American essayist Ralph Waldo Emerson (1803–83). West Lynne post office opened here in 1873 and was changed to Emerson in 1879; West Lynne remains a neighbourhood in the town.

Emily ON In 2001 this township became part of the city of Kawartha Lakes, Victoria. It was named in 1820 after Lady Emily Charlotte Berkeley, a sister of Charles Lennox, Duke of Richmond, the governor-in-chief of British North America, 1818–9. Her niece, Lady Sarah Maitland, was the wife of Sir Peregrine Maitland (1777–1854), lieutenant-governor of Upper Canada, 1818–28.

Emo ON This place in the municipal township of **Emo**, Rainy River District, west of Fort Frances, was first called *Emo River* in 1887 and shortened to Emo 10 years later. Alex Luttrell named it after Emo in Ireland's County Laois, southwest of Dublin, and near his birthplace in County Kildare.

Empress AB On the Saskatchewan border and near the junction of the South Saskatchewan and Red Deer Rivers, this village (1914) was named in 1913 by the Canadian Pacific Railway after Queen Victoria's title of Empress of India, proclaimed in 1876.

Endeavour SK Established in 1928 by the Canadian Northern Railway, this village (1953) was named after the first passenger aircraft to fly from England to the United States. Walter Hinchcliffe, a pilot, wanted to be the first to cross the Atlantic with a passenger; he bought a monoplane from the United States, and named it *The Endeavour*. He set off on the flight, taking with him a "secret" passenger, actress and co-pilot Elsie McKay. The plane however crashed into the ocean. The post office in this location was called *Annette* in 1915, after a Ukrainian settler, but was renamed Endeavour in 1929.

Enderby BC This city (1905) on the Shuswap River and at the north end of the Okanagan Valley first had a variety of names, including *Spallumcheen*, *Steamboat Landing*, *Fortune's Landing*, *Lambly's Landing*, and *Belvidere*. On a day in 1887, when the river was in flood, a lady at an afternoon tea party was inspired to recite Jean Inglelow's poem, 'The High Tide on the Coast of Lincolnshire'. The line 'Play uppe "the Brides of Enderby"' so caught the imagination of the others that Enderby was proposed as the name for the post office.

Engelfeld SK Situated east of Humboldt, the post office at this village (1916) was named in 1907 in honour of Abbot Peter Engel of St. John's Abbey, Collegeville, MN. He helped the Benedictines establish the parish of the Holy Guardian Angels of Engelfeld.

Englee NL The name of this town (1948), located on the north side of Canada Bay and on the east coast of the Northern Peninsula, possibly derives from *Éguillettes*, a French fishing station located here during the seventeenth and eighteenth centuries.

Englehart ON When the Temiskaming and Northern Ontario Railway was extended from New Liskeard in 1906, its station, 40 km to the north, was named after Jacob (Jake) Lewis Englehart (1847–1921), the popular chairman of the railway, 1906–21. Englehart became a town in 1908. In 1880 Jake Englehart had founded the Imperial Oil Company in Petrolia, selling it to Standard Oil (Esso) in 1898.

English Bay BC On the northwest side of Vancouver and at the entrance of Burrard Inlet, this bay (and nearby Spanish Bank) commemorate the friendly meeting on 22 June 1792 of Capt. George Vancouver (1757–98) and Spanish explorers Dionisio Alcalà Galiano (1760–1805) and Cayetano Valdés (1767–1835).

English Harbour East NL On the northeastern shore of Fortune Bay, this municipal community (1974) had its port recorded as English Harbour by Capt. James Cook (1728–79) in 1764. By the 1860s it was given its present name to distinguish it from another fishing port on the western side of Fortune Bay called **English Harbour West**, which was settled by English fishermen in the early 1800s. English Harbour West is a small community on Burin Peninsula.

English River ON Flowing west from Lac Seul to join the Winnipeg River at the Manitoba border, this river was part of the traditional British fur trade route from Lake Winnipeg to Hudson Bay.

Ennadai Lake NU The name of this lake (669 km²), located on the Kazan River and west of Arviat, derives from the Chipewyan word for 'slaughter'. Presumably the Cree

disguised themselves as stags in an attempt to ambush the Chipewyan, but the ruse was discovered and the Cree were slaughtered. Or, as legends often evolve, it may have been the Cree who slaughtered the Chipweyan.

Enniskillen ON This township in Lambton County was named in 1834 by Lt.-Gov. Sir John Colborne (1778–1863) in honour of Gen. Sir Galbraith Cole (1772–1842). A native of Enniskillen in Ireland's County Fermanagh, Cole was an associate of Colborne in the Peninsular War in Spain. The community of **Enniskillen** in the municipality of Clarington, Durham Region was first called *Charlesville*. It was renamed Enniskillen in 1851, possibly after the same place in Ireland.

Ennismore ON In 1998 this township became part of the township of Smith-Ennismore, Peterborough County. It was named in 1829 after William Hare, Viscount Ennismore, 2nd Earl of Listowel (1802–1856). A native of the townland of Ennismore near Listowel in County Kerry, Ireland, he was a member of the British Parliament, 1826–30.

Enterprise ON This location in Lennox and Addington County, north of Napanee, was first called *Thompson's Corners* after merchant Robert Thompson. When a visitor observed that it was an enterprising place, Thompson had its post office named Enterprise in 1854.

Entwistle AB In 2000 this village (1955) became a hamlet. Located on the Pembina River, 99 km west of Edmonton, it was named in 1908 after first postmaster James G. Entwistle. He had formerly been a locomotive engineer with the Grand Trunk Railway in Ontario and had lived in Winnipeg before moving to this area of Alberta about 1904–5.

Eramosa ON In 1999 this township and the township of Guelph became part of the township of Guelph/Eramosa, Wellington County. The township of Eramosa was named in 1822, possibly after *un-ne-mo-sah*, the Mississauga word for 'dog'. One of the first surveyors may have found a dead dog.

Erasmus, Mount AB Near the head of the North Saskatchewan River, this mountain (3265 m) was named in 1859 by Dr. Sir James Hector (1834–1907) after Peter Erasmus (1834–1931), a fur trader, interpreter, and noted guide. Erasumus assisted Hector in 1858–9, during the Palliser expedition's investigation of what is now Western Canada.

Erickson BC The post office of this community, located in the Kootenay River valley and adjacent to the town of Creston, was named in 1908 after E.G. Erickson (1857–1927), the Canadian Pacific Railway superintendent at Cranbrook, 1904–8.

Erickson MB Located south of Riding Mountain National Park, northwest of Neepawa, the post office in this village (1953) was first called *Avesta* in March 1908 but was renamed in August after postmaster E. Albert Erickson, who owned the site of the village.

Erieau ON In 1998 this village (1917) became part of the municipality of Chatham-Kent, Kent County. The village was located at the entrance of Rondeau Harbour in Kent County and was named in 1886 by joining 'Erie' to the last syllable of 'Rondeau'.

Erie Beach ON In 1998 this village became part of the municipality of Chatham-Kent, Kent County. The village was on the shore of Lake Erie and in Kent County. It was incorporated in 1916, but never had a post office. There was, however, an *Erie Beach* post office from 1913 to 1959, on the south side of the town of Fort Erie. **Erie Beach** remains as a subdivision of Fort Erie.

Erie, Lake ON The Erihon ('wildcat') clan of the Iroquois lived on the south shore of the lake. As early as 1650, the lake was shown on maps as *Lac du Chat*, but 20 years later René de Bréhant de Galinée (1645–78) identified it on a map as *Lac Érié*.

Eriksdale MB East of Lake Manitoba, and northwest of Winnipeg, this place was founded by the Canadian Northern Railway in 1911 and named after Swedish settler Jonas Erikson. Postal service was also established here that year.

Erin ON In 1998 the township and the village of Erin became the town of **Erin**, in Wellington County. The township was named in 1820 after the poetic name for Ireland. The village (1879) of Erin was first called *MacMillan's Mill* after Daniel MacMillan in 1824, but was renamed Erin in 1832.

Erindale ON This location on the Credit River and in the city of Mississauga was called *Credit* and *Springfield-on-the-Credit*, before being named in 1900 after Erindale Farm, established by James Magrath in 1827.

Erinsville ON In 1998 this place became part of the township of Stone Mills, Lennox and Addington County. This community was named in 1853 by settler John Murphy after the poetic title of Ireland, with 'ville' added because he believed it had the prospect of becoming a thriving village.

Ernestown ON In 1998 this township became a part of the Loyalist Township, Lennox and Addington County. It was named in 1784 for Prince Ernest Augustus, Duke of Cumberland and Teviotdale (1771–1851), fifth son of George III. The name was locally spelled *Ernesttown* until the 1950s, when the surveyor general of Ontario urged the municipality to abide by the original spelling.

Errol ON Laid out as a planned town in 1833 in Sarnia Township, Lambton County, this place was named after Errol in Scotland's Perthshire, east of Perth. A post office opened in 1837. With no harbour and poor land communications, it became a ghost town by the 1880s. New building has taken place in recent years, because of its desirable location on the Lake Huron shore, and in the city of Sarnia, which had annexed the township in 1991.

Erskine AB Located west of Stettler, this community became a hamlet in 1979. Its post office was named in 1905, possibly after Thomas Erskine (1750–1823), a British jurist. It may have been named after Millicent Fanny St. Clair-Erskine (1867–1955), wife of the 4th Duke of Sutherland (1851–1913) and eldest daughter of the 4th Duke of Rosslyn. Prior to 1905 its post office was called *Liberal*.

Escuminac QC This municipality (1912) in the regional county of Avignon and on the north side of the estuary of the Restigouche River took its name from the **Rivière Escuminac**, which flows into **Baie Escuminac** and is located in front of **Pointe d'Escuminac**. The sharp turn of the point replicates Point Escuminac on the southeast side of Miramichi Bay, NB, whose name derives from the Mik'maq *eskumunaak* ('lookout place').

Escuminac, Point NB At the northwestern end of Northumberland Strait, this point's name derives from the Mik'maq *eskumunaak* ('lookout place'). In 1685 map-maker Pierre Jumeau referred to it as *Pte echkoumenak*. The present spelling was established in 1791 on a map by Frederick Holland. The community of **Escuminac**, west of the point, had a post office from 1858 to 1968.

Eskasoni NS This location on the north shore of Bras d'Or Lake's East Bay and on the **Eskasoni Indian Reserve** derives from the Mi'kmaq *eskasoonig* ('green boughs').

Eskimo Lakes NT Situated southeast of Tuktoyaktuk, this chain of lakes was named in 1928 after the English-language designation of the local native people, the Inuvialuit. The form *Eskimo (Husky) Lakes* was authorized in 1957, but the original form was restored in 1968. The word 'Eskimo' is the English rendering of 'Esquimaux', acquired by the French from the Algonquian-speaking Montagnais or Naskapi on the north shore of the Gulf of St. Lawrence, with the meaning 'they who eat their fish raw'.

Espanola ON This town (1958) in Sudbury District was established in 1899 by the Spanish River Pulp and Paper Company. The feminine form of 'Spanish', the name was given to the planned community in 1902.

Espoir, Bay d' NL Penetrating the south coast of Newfoundland for some 45 km, this bay may be the same as Jacques Cartier's *hable du Sainct Esperit*, which he entered on 4 June 1536, the holy day of Whitsuntide. The French spelling and the former French pronunciation, which sounded like 'bay despair', have been maintained.

Esquesing ON Now divided between the towns of Halton Hills and Milton in Halton Region, this township was named in 1819 after the Mississauga *eshkwessing* ('the last in a row or a range'), presumably referring to the present Sixteen Mile Creek.

Esquimalt BC This district municipality on the west side of Victoria was incorporated in 1912 as a township. The post office here had been named in 1864 after Esquimalt Harbour. The harbour's name derives from Straits Salish, meaning 'place of gradually shoaling' in reference to the flats at the mouth of Mill Stream at the head of the harbour. The bay was named *Puerto de Cordova* in 1790 by Spanish SLt. Manuel Quimper (c.1757–1844). About 1842 the Hudson's Bay Company restored the Aboriginal designation and relocated Cordova Bay north of Victoria.

Essa ON This township in Simcoe County was named in 1822, but its origin is obscure. One tradition claims Shawnee chief Tecumseh had a wife called Essa; however, it is generally believed that this chief had only one wife, Mamate, who died after her only child was born. Other traditions point to the name of either an Aboriginal chief or to the daughter of a chief. Ojibwa chief Wasson (c.1730–1790) was the best-known Aboriginal in the period 1750–1820 with a name similar to Essa. He signed a peace treaty with the British at Detroit in 1764–5.

Essex ON The county was named in 1792 for Essex in England. *Essex Centre* became a railway station in 1872, but when it was incorporated as a town in 1890, the name was shortened to **Essex**.

Estcourt QC This community in the town of Pohénégamook, south of Rivière-du-Loup and on the border of the most northerly point of Maine, was called after the township of **Estcourt**, proclaimed in 1842. The township was named after British boundary commissioner Lt. Col. James Bucknall Bucknall Estcourt (1802–55).

Esterhazy SK Southeast of Melville, this town (1957) was named after Count Paul Oscar Esterhazy (1830–1912), who helped Hungarian coal miners in 1886 to move from Pennsylvania to this area north of the Qu'Appelle River. Hungarian migrants came directly to the settlement from Hungary two years later. *Esterhaz* post office opened in 1886, with both *Kolin* and Esterhazy replacing it in 1903.

Estevan SK This city (1957), just north of the North Dakota border, was founded in 1892, when the Soo Line was extended by the Canadian Pacific Railway from North Portal, on the border, to Moose Jaw. It was named after the registered telegraphic address *Estevan* of George Stephen, Baron Mount Stephen (1829–1921). He was the first president of the CPR, 1881–8.

Estevan Point BC On the south side of Nootka Sound and on the west coast of Vancouver Island, this point was the first feature to be named by a European explorer on Canada's west coast. It was named in 1774 by Spanish Lt. Cmdr. Juan Perez after his second lieutenant, Estevan Jose Martinez. Capt. James Cook (1728–79) named it *Breakers Point* four years later, but the earlier name was restored in 1849 by the British Admiralty.

Eston SK The post office in this town (1928), southeast of Kindersley, was named in 1912, presumably after the hometown of A.J. Harris in West Yorkshire, England.

Estrie QC An administrative region of southeastern Quebec since 1981, the name was devised in 1946 by Sherbrooke historian Maurice O'Bready as a French equivalent of 'Eastern Townships', which had been usually rendered as *Cantons de l'Est*. The region, embracing 10,698 km², is centred on Sherbrooke, with Stanstead on the south, Asbestos on the north, Magog on the west, and Thetford Mines and Lac-Mégantic on the east.

Ethelbert MB This village (1905), northwest of Dauphin, was named in 1898 by K.J. Mackenzie, construction supervisor of the Canadian Northern Railway. It was named after his niece, Ethel Bertha, a daughter of the company's president, Sir William Mackenzie (1849–1923). The post office here opened the following year.

Etobicoke ON The city of Etobicoke was laid out as a township in 1792 and was named after **Etobicoke Creek**. The creek's name is a variant of the Mississauga designation *Wah-do-be-kaung* ('place where the black alders grow'). The municipal township was united in 1967 with the towns of Mimico and New Toronto and the village of Long Branch to become the borough of Etobicoke, which was elevated to city status in 1983. In 1998 it became part of the city of Toronto.

Euphemia ON In 1998 this township and the township of Dawn became the township of Dawn-Euphemia, Lambton County. It was named in 1848 by Malcolm Cameron, the member for Kent in the Legislative Assembly of the Province of Canada, after his mother, Euphemia McGregor Cameron.

Euphrasia ON In 2001 this township and the townships of Artemesia and Osprey and the village of Markdale became part of the municipality of Grey Highlands, Grey County. Euphrasia was named in 1823 after the Greek word meaning 'delight' and a genus of flowers known as eyebright.

Eureka NS South of Stellarton, this community's post office was named in 1887 after the Eureka Milling Company, established here on the East River of Pictou five years earlier.

Eureka NU Located on the Fosheim Peninsula of Ellesmere Island, this site of a weather station was established in 1948 near **Eureka Sound**, which separates Ellesmere and Axel Heiberg Islands. The sound was named *Heureka Sund* in 1901 by Ivar Fosheim, a member of the Sverdrup expedition, who discovered the 280-km passage.

Eutsuk Lake BC This lake is located in Tweedsmuir Provincial Park, southeast of Kitimat. The name Eutsuk was adapted in 1910 by Frank Swannell (1880–1969), a provincial surveyor, from the Carrier word *teootsabungut*, which may have the meaning of 'far from Ootsa Lake'. Fr. Gabriel Morice (1859–1938) claimed in 1904 that a Carrier companion had named it after him, but his proposal had not been submitted to the provincial names authority for consideration.

Evansburg AB In 1998 this village (1953) became a hamlet. Located on the Pembina River, 105 km west of Edmonton, the post office here was named in 1914 after Henry Marshall Erskine Evans (1876–1973), who prospected for coal on the river in 1904. Subsequently he settled in Edmonton, where he became president of the board of trade and mayor of the city.

Evans, Mount AB Near the head of the North Saskatchewan River, this mountain (3210 m) was named in 1935 after Capt. Sir Edward Ratcliffe Garth Russell Evans (1880–1957), who had performed heroic exploits while commanding HMS *Broke* during the First World War.

Everett ON The post office in this place in Simcoe County northwest of Alliston was named in 1878. Local stories state that it was named by Thomas Gordon for his father's birthplace in England, called after the birthplace of Henry Baycroft in England, or given for a Mr Fisher's farm. No place in England is identified as Everett on the largest scale of ordnance survey maps.

Exeter ON In 2001 this town (1951) and the townships of Stephen and Usborne became part of the municipality of South Huron, Huron County. Exeter was first called *Francistown* and *Carling's Corners* before merchant James Pickard may have named it in 1851 after the city of Exeter in Devon, England.

Exploits River NL Rising in the central part of Newfoundland, this river (246 km) flows northwest into the **Bay of Exploits**, on the north coast of the island. Capt. James Cook recorded the name of the river on his 1774 chart. The origin and meaning of the name are not provided in various standard references.

Exshaw AB This community, located east of Canmore, was named in 1905 by Sir Sandford Fleming (1827–1915) after his son-in-law, William Exshaw (1866–1927). Both of them were directors of the Western Canada Cement and Coal Company. Exshaw managed the company's cement factory here.

Eyebrow SK This village (1909), located northwest of Moose Jaw, was named in 1907 when the Canadian Pacific Railway was built north to Outlook. It received its name from the outline of Central Butte, above Eyebrow Lake, on the south side of the village. Its post office was first called *Eyebrow Station* in 1908, but 'Station' was dropped later that year.

Eyebrow Peak BC In the Purcell Mountains, the name of this peak (3353 m) was proposed in 1910 by surveyor Arthur O. Wheeler (1860–1945) after the distinctive character of the peak that he observed. Subsequent investigation by geologist Peter Robinson revealed that Wheeler was really looking at Mount Farnham, 14 km to the east.

Faber Lake NT Situated between Great Bear and Great Slave Lakes, this lake was named in 1864 by Fr. Émile Petitot (1838–1916) after Fr. Frederick William Faber (1814–63), an English Catholic priest and orator.

Fair Haven NL On the east side of Placentia Bay and on the southwest side of the Isthmus of Avalon, this place was called *Famish Gut* and *Famish Cove* until June 1940, when the Newfoundland Nomenclature Board authorized the change to this more positive designation. In 1971 Edgar R. Seary (1908–84) suggested *Famishgut*, along with the adjacent settlement of *Pinchgut*, because the survey crew of hydrographer Michael Lane (d.1794) had become short of rations in the 1770s.

Fairmont Hot Springs BC In the Columbia River valley, 26 km southeast of Invermere, this resort community was named *Fairmont Springs* in 1888 after the Fairmont Hotel, established by Sam Brewer. Fairmount is a suburb of Philadelphia, PA. The hotel was closed in 1909, but reopened under its present name two years later.

Fairvale NB The first post office in this village (1966), 15 km northeast of Saint John, was called *Fairleigh*. It opened in 1885 and closed in 1890. *Fair Vale* post office served the area of the village from 1908 to 1946, and *Fairvale Station* post office was open from 1925 to 1970.

Fairview AB On the north side of the Peace River, north of Grande Prairie, this town (1949) was founded by the Edmonton, Dunvegan and British Columbia Railway in 1928, and named by E.J. Martin after the local municipal district. In 1910 Howard L. Propst had established a farm that he called Fairview. Four years later the municipal district of **Fairview** was created.

Fairweather Mountain BC This mountain (4663 m), situated on the British Columbia–Alaska boundary southwest of Whitehorse, YT, was named *Mount Fair Weather* in 1778 by Capt. James Cook (1728–79). It is the highest point in the province. *See also* Waddington, Mount.

Falconbridge ON In 2001 this town became part of the city of Greater Sudbury, Sudbury Region. The former township was named about 1885 after Sir William Glenholme Falconbridge (1846–1920), chief justice of the Supreme Court of Ontario, 1900–20. Falconbridge post office was named in 1930.

Falher AB West of Lesser Slave Lake, this town (1955) was named in 1915 by the Edmonton, Dunvegan and British Columbia Railway after Oblate missionary Fr. Constant Falher (1863–1939). A native of Bretagne, France, he had arrived at nearby Grouard in 1889, with the mission of Saint-Jean-Baptiste-de-Falher being established 5 km from the present town's site. Falher post office opened in 1923.

Fallowfield ON Located in the sector of Nepean in the city of Ottawa, this community was named as early as 1861, when Bishop Bruno Guigues (1805–74) inspected the ongoing building of the present handsome stone St. Patrick's Church. The name was likely inspired by a nearby field left fallow during a growing season. Its post office opened in 1872.

Fall River NS Located at the falls between Miller Lake and Lake Thomas, north of Dartmouth, this community became a station on the Intercolonial Railway in 1857. Fall River post office opened in 1878, but it was renamed Goffs the following year, after postmaster William Goff. The place called Goffs developed 12 km to the northeast.

Falmouth NS This place, located on the west side of the Avon River, was named after *Falmouth Township*, established in 1761. The township was named after Adm. Edward Boscawen, 2nd Viscount Falmouth (1711–61), who led the successful British naval attack on Louisbourg in 1758.

False Creek BC This small inlet in the city of Vancouver was named in the late 1850s by Capt. George Richards (1861–1950), who expected to find a stream flowing into it at the head of the inlet. However, he only found mud flats here.

Farnham QC This place, located in the regional county of Brome-Missisquoi, southeast of Granby, was first created as the village of *West Farnham (Farnham-Ouest)* in 1862 and became the town of Farnham in 1876. It took its name from the township of **Farnham**, proclaimed in 1798, and named after the town of Farnham in Surrey, England, southeast of London.

Farnham, Mount BC In the Purcell Mountains, west of Invermere, this mountain (3468 m) was named in 1911 by climber Edward Harnden after mine developer Paulding Farnham. A native of New York, Farnham spent a considerable fortune prospecting and developing mines in southeastern British Columbia.

Faro YT This town in the Pelly River valley, northeast of Whitehorse, was founded in 1969 to provide homes for the miners working at the Anvil lead, zinc, and silver mine. The name was probably first given by Dr. Aro Aho to the first claim staked here, choosing a word of a gambling card game that was popular in mining camps.

Farquhar, Mount AB, BC On the continental divide, north of Crowsnest Pass, this mountain (2905 m) was named in 1919 after Maj. Francis Douglas Farquhar (1874–1915), who was the commander of the Princess Patricia's Canadian Light Infantry in Europe, and was killed during the First World War.

Farrellton QC This community, located in the municipality of La Pêche 13 km north of Wakefield, was named *Farrelltown* in 1872 after first postmaster Patrick Farrell. The spelling was amended to Farrellton in 1887.

Fascination Mountain BC Situated in the Coast Mountains, southeast of Mount Waddington, this mountain (3048 m) was named about 1927 by climber Walter Alfred (Don) Munday (1890–1950), who found it a challenging and shapely mountain.

Fassett QC The post office of this municipality (1951), situated in the regional county of Papineau, east of Montebello, was named in 1906 after S. Jonathan Fassett, who established a lumber company here the previous year. It had been first called *Petite-Nation* in 1845, after the Rivière de la Petite-Nation, and was renamed the parish municipality of *Notre-Dame-de-Bon-Secours* 10 years later.

Fathom Five National Marine Park ON Located in Georgian Bay and on the northeast side of the Bruce Peninsula, this park (113 km²) was created in 1987 to protect valuable underwater sites and flowerpot formations. With a depth of five fathoms (about 9 m) its best known feature is Flowerpot Island.

Fatima QC Located in the regional county of Les Îles-de-la-Madeleine, this municipality was named in 1959. Ten years earlier its post office was called after the place in Portugal where three young children saw a vision of the Virgin Mary in 1917.

Fauquier BC The post office in this community, situated on the east shore of Lower Arrow Lake, was named in 1913 after F.G. Fauquier, an early rancher and fruit grower here who had previously worked as a customs officer, mining recorder, government agent, and police officer.

Fay, Mount AB, BC Situated on the continental divide and south of Lake Louise, this mountain (3234 m) was named in 1902 after American alpinist and editor Charles Ernest Fay (1846–1931), who had climbed several mountains in the Canadian Rockies.

Fenelon ON In 2001 this township and the village (1874) of **Fenelon Falls** became part of the city of Kawartha Lakes, Victoria County. The township was named in 1823 after Fr. François de Salignac de la Mothe Fénelon (1641–79). In 1668 Fénelon founded a mission on the Bay of Quinte, and spent the next year at Frenchman's Bay, in the present town of Pickering. **Fenelon Falls** was named in 1838 after the township. The village had been called *Cameron's Falls* after Duncan Cameron, provincial secretary of Upper Canada, who owned the area of the falls.

Fenwick NS South of Amherst, this place's post office was named in 1866 after Sir William Fenwick Williams (1800–83), a native of the province. He was the hero of the Russian siege of Kars (present-day Turkey) in 1855 and lieutenant-governor of Nova Scotia, 1865–7.

Fenwick ON This place in the town of Pelham, Niagara Region, was named in 1853, possibly by Pelham Township reeve Dr. John Fraser after his birthplace, northeast of Kilmarnock, Ayrshire, Scotland.

Fergus ON In 1999 this town (1952) became a part of the Centre Wellington, Wellington County. It was named in 1834 after Adam Fergusson (1783–1862), a native of Perthshire, Scotland, and a member of the Legislative Council of Upper Canada, 1839–62.

Ferguson Lake NU Southwest of Baker Lake, this lake was named in 1894 by Joseph Burr Tyrrell (1858–1957) after Robert Munro Ferguson, an aide-de-camp to Gov. Gen. Lord Aberdeen. The lake is drained by **Ferguson River** into Hudson Bay, northeast of Arviat. At his own expense, Ferguson accompanied Tyrrell on his geological reconnaissance through northern Manitoba and Keewatin District.

Ferme-Neuve QC This village north of Mont-Laurier was named in 1917 after a model farm that eight Montreal journalists established in 1902. The parish municipality of Ferme-Neuve was named in 1930. From 1902 to 1930 it was called the united township municipality of *Würtele-Moreau-et-Gravel*. The three separate townships were named in 1899 after legislator Jonathan S.C. Würtele and priests Louis-Zépherin Moreau and Elphège Gravel.

Fermeuse NL On the east coast of the Avalon Peninsula, the name of this municipal community (1967) was taken from **Fermeuse Harbour**. It was a name of Portuguese origin, having been recorded on a 1519 map as *R Fermoso* ('beautiful river').

Fermont QC Located some 300 km north of Sept-Îles, this town was founded in 1971 by the mining company Quebec Cartier on the Newfoundland and Labrador border, 23 km southwest of Labrador City. Its name means 'iron mountain'. Iron ore, mined at nearby Mont Wright, is shipped south by rail to the seaport of Port-Cartier. Fermont is the headquarters of the regional municipality of Caniapiscau.

Fernie BC The post office in this city (1904) in the Elk River valley, east of Cranbrook, was named in 1898 after William Fernie (1837–1921), who discovered coal in 1887 on a tributary of Michel Creek. He had been gold commissioner in the Kootenay district, 1873–82, and had become a director of the Crows Nest Pass Coal Company. After achieving considerable wealth in the coal fields, he retired in 1906 to Oak Bay, beside Victoria, and became a prominent philanthropist.

Ferryland NL This municipal community (1971) on the east coast of the Avalon Peninsula was named after the adjacent **Ferryland Head**. The head was named in Portuguese in the early 1500s as *Farilham* after *farelhão* ('steep rock'), in reference to the high cliffs on both the head and adjacent Bois Island, between which is the narrow passage leading to Ferryland's harbour. By the mid-1500s, the French had called it *Forillon*, and early in the following century it became Ferryland in English.

Feuilles, Rivière aux QC A major river in northwestern Quebec, it flows 480 km northeast from Lac Minto to Ungava Bay. Known by the Inuit as *Kuugaaluk* ('grand river'), it was well known in the late 1800s and early 1900s as *Leaf River*. In 1914 it was renamed *Rivière des Feuilles* and changed 11 years later to the present form. Since this river is located at the northern limit of tree growth, its name is probably derived from dwarf willow and birch.

Field BC This first Canadian Pacific Railway station west of the continental divide (in Yoho National Park) was named in 1884 after Cyrus West Field (1819–92), the founder of the American Telegraph Company. The ATC won the race in 1866 to connect North America with Europe, by laying the first successful transatlantic telegraph cable. **Mount Field** (2643 m) overlooks the station.

Field ON This township in Nipissing District was named in the 1880s after Corelli Collard Field (c.1830–98), Liberal member for Northumberland West in the Ontario Legislature, 1886–98. The post office in the community of **Field**, in the township, was named in 1899.

Fillmore SK Northeast of Weyburn, this village (1905) was named for Charles Wesley Fillmore, president of the Winnipeg Oil Company. Fillmore owned the site of the village at the time of the survey of the route of the Canadian Pacific

Railway, which was built through its site in 1900. The post office was named the following year.

Finch ON In 1998 this township and the village of **Finch** became parts of the township of North Stormont, the united counties of Stormont, Dundas, and Glengarry. The township was named in 1798, either after George Finch-Hatton (a son-in-law of the 7th Viscount Stormont), or after Lady Elizabeth Finch-Hatton (the viscount's aunt by marriage). The village (1906) of Finch was known as *South Finch* from 1856 to 1899, when it was changed to Finch. *See also* Berwick, ON.

Findlay, Mount BC In the Purcell Mountains, northeast of Kaslo, this mountain (3162 m) was named in 1954 after **Findlay Creek**. The latter was named in 1915 after George Finlay, who prospected the area in 1863. He was a son of John (or Jacques) Raphael 'Jaco' Finlay (1774–1833), a partner in the North West Company, who was in charge of the post on Lake Athabasca in the early 1800s and ran a trail through Howse Pass in 1806.

Finlay River BC Rising in the Omineca Mountains in the north central part of the province, this river was once one of the two major tributaries (the Parsnip is the other) of the Peace River, before the construction of the W.A.C. Bennett Dam in 1968–9 and the subsequent creation of Williston Lake. The river was named after John Finlay (1774–1833) of the North West Company, who had travelled along it in 1797.

Firth River YT Rising in the Davidson Mountains in Alaska, this river flows northeast through the British Mountains into the Beaufort Sea, opposite Herschel Island. The river was named *Mountain Indian River* in 1826 by Sir John Franklin (1786–1847) after some interior Aboriginals, who used to come to the coast to trade with the Inuit. It was renamed in 1890 by John H. Turner after John Firth, Hudson's Bay Company agent at Rampart House (on the Porcupine River where it flows west across the Alaska–Yukon border), who joined Turner in his trip along the coast.

Fisher Branch MB The post office in this place, located on the **Fisher River**, north of Winnipeg, opened in 1911. The French called the river *Rivière aux Pécans* ('river of the fisher') after a fur-bearing animal of the marten family, *Martes pennanti*.

Fisher, Mount BC In the Rocky Mountains, northeast of Cranbrook, this mountain (2846 m) was named about 1900 after Jack Fisher, who had found gold on nearby Wild Horse Creek in 1863. The mining camp that developed here was called Fisherville.

Fisher Ridge NB South of the Nepisiguit River, this ridge was named in 1964 by Arthur F. Wightman (1905–88), then the provincial names authority, after Charles Fisher (1808–80), premier of New Brunswick, 1854–61, and a Father of Confederation.

Fitzroy ON A part of the ward of West Carleton in the city of Ottawa, Fitzroy Township was named in 1823 after Sir Charles Augustus Fitzroy (1796–1858), a son-in-law of the Duke of Richmond, governor-in-chief of British North America, 1818–9. The community of **Fitzroy Harbour** was named in 1832.

Fitzwilliam, Mount BC On the south side of Yellowhead Pass, west of Jasper, this mountain (3385 m) was named in 1863 by Dr. Walter Butler Cheadle (1836–1910) after his companion, William Wentworth Fitzwilliam, Viscount Milton (1839–77).

Five Houses PE Located east of St. Peters Bay, this place was probably named after five French dwellings that had been destroyed. In 1765 Surveyor General Samuel Holland (1728–1801) wrote 'Ruined Village' on his map, and 'Ruined Village of 5 Houses' in his notes.

Flaherty Island NL This island is the largest of the Belcher Islands on the southeast side of Hudson Bay. It was named in 1919 by geologist G. A. Young after Robert Joseph Flaherty (1884–1951), who investigated the minerals of the islands in 1914. In 1922 Flaherty produced the documentary film *Nanook of the North*.

Flamborough ON In 2001 this town (1985) became part of the city of Hamilton. *Flamborough* had been formed as a municipal township in 1974, through the amalgamation of the village of Waterdown, the municipal township of Beverley, and parts of the municipal townships of *East Flamborough* and *West Flamborough*. *East Flamborough* and *West Flamborough* were named in 1792 after Flamborough Head and the town of Flamborough, East Yorkshire, England.

Flat Rock NL North of St. John's, this town (1975) was named after 'the thick red sandstone, which dips at a slight angle towards the sea, forming a long, smooth, sloping pavement', according to Joseph Beete Jukes (1811–69) in 1840. References to the place were made on maps as early as 1630.

Fleming SK Just west of the Manitoba border, this town (1907) is located on the main Canadian Pacific Railway line, between Winnipeg and Regina. Its station was named in 1882, after Sir Sandford Fleming (1827–1915), Canada's most distinguished railway engineer in the nineteenth century. Fleming initiated the system of time zones and designed Canada's first postage stamp. The post office here opened in 1884.

Fleming Peak BC This peak (3164 m) of Mount Rogers in the Selkirk Mountains, northeast of Revelstoke, was named in 1901 by surveyor Arthur O. Wheeler (1860–1945) after Sir

Sandford Fleming (1827–1915), first engineer-in-chief of the Canadian Pacific Railway. *See also* Sir Sandford, Mount.

Flesherton ON In 1998 this village (1912) became part of the township of Artemesia, Grey County. It was founded in 1853 by miller William Kingston Flesher (1827–1907). The post office was called *Artemesia*, after the township, from 1851 to 1867, when it was changed to Flesherton.

Fletchers Lake NS Located north of Dartmouth, this place was first settled by pioneer William Fletcher and his son Robert. William bought land at the head of the lake in the 1780s, and Robert received a grant of 101 ha (250 a) in 1812.

Fleur de Lys NL On the western side of Notre Dame Bay, and north of Baie-Verte, this town (1967) was a French fishing harbour from the 1500s to the 1700s, with its name being noted in 1640. It was given by French fishermen after a striking rock formation, rising to 249 m, said to resemble the national symbol of France.

Fleurimont QC On the north side of Sherbrooke, it was known as the municipality of *Ascot-Nord* from 1937 to 1971, when it became the town of Fleurimont. The name derives from Nicolas-Joseph de Noyelles de Fleurimont (1695–1761), who arrived in Canada at the beginning of the 1700s.

Flin Flon MB This unusual name of this city (1970) on the Saskatchewan border is rooted in Joyce Emerson Preston Muddock's dime novel, *The Sunless City* (1905). In the novel, Professor Josiah Flintabbatey Flonatin found a strange world under the Rocky Mountains paved with gold and ruled by strong women. The professor escaped through a hole of an inactive volcano. In the summer of 1915 several prospectors led by Tom Creighton (1874–1949) were searching for gold, when Creighton presumably fell through the ice. While drying off beside a fire, Creighton observed that the heat revealed gold at the bottom of a hole, prompting him to exclaim 'That must be the hole where old Flin Flon came up and shook his whiskers, so what do you say we call the discovery Flin Flon?' The post office opened as *Flinfon* in 1929, and was changed to Flin Flon in 1937.

Flinton ON In 1998 this community became part of the municipality of Tweed, Lennox and Addington County. It was named in 1858 after Belleville merchant and lumberman Billa Flint (1805–94). He was a member of the Legislative Assembly of Canada, 1847–51; of the Legislative Council, 1863–7; and of the Senate until his death.

Florence NS Northwest of Sydney Mines, this place's post office was called *Stubbert* in October 1904 and *Cantley* in December 1904. The following year it was named after Florence McKenzie, the wife of Daniel D. McKenzie, Liberal member for Cape Breton North-Victoria in the House of Commons, 1904–6 and 1908–23, and solicitor general of Canada, 1921–3.

Florence ON In 1998 this place became part of the township of Dawn-Euphemia, Lambton County. It was named *Zone Mills* in 1840, when it was in Zone Township. Postmaster George Pigeon Kirby wanted to call it *Victoria* in 1856 after the Queen, but postal authorities persuaded him to rename it after the city in Italy. It was likely merely a coincidence that Florence Nightingale became famous then as the heroine of the Crimean War.

Florenceville NB This village (1966) north of Woodstock was named in 1853 by Lt.-Gov. Lemuel Allan Wilmot (1809–78) after Florence Nightingale, the heroine of the Crimean War. Settled in 1832, it was first called *Buttermilk Creek*.

Flowers Cove NL This town (1961) on the northwestern coast of Newfoundland includes the nearby localities of Nameless Cove and Mistaken Cove. It was earlier called *French Island Harbour*, as the French continued to fish here well into the late 1800s. The cove was named in 1764 by Capt. James Cook (1728–79), who named it *Flour Cove* after the foam created by breakers. The word 'flour' is an old English word for froth formed by breaking waves on a shoreline.

Foam Lake SK This town (1924) northwest of Yorkton acquired its name from the nearby shallow lake, identified by early settler Joshua Milligan (1857–1931) because its shore always had a ring of foam around it. Its post office opened in 1900.

Foch, Mount AB Southwest of Calgary, this mountain (3180 m) was named in 1918 after Marshal Ferdinand Foch (1851–1929), supreme commander of the Allied forces at the end of the First World War.

Fogo NL The name of this town (1948) on **Fogo Island** derives from the Portuguese name of the island, *y do Fogo* ('fire island'), possibly referring to forest fires or to fogs that appeared to be smoke. It may also have been named after the island of Fogo in the Cape Verde islands, west of Dakar, Senegal.

Foleyet ON This station on the main line of the Canadian National Railways, and in Sudbury District, west of Timmins, was named accidentally in 1912, when Canadian Northern Railway president Sir Donald Mann (1853–1934) insisted on naming a station after contractor Timothy Foley. Having been told by superintendent A.J. Hills there was already a station called Foley, Mann blurted out 'I'll name that place Foley yet!' 'Foleyet will be fine, Sir', replied Hills, and the post office opened in 1916.

Foley Island NU In Foxe Basin and west of Baffin Island, this island was named in 1949 after John Hilliard Foley, the navigator of a special Royal Canadian Air Force flight, which had investigated the recently discovered islands in the basin the previous year. Foley was killed in 1949 in a flying accident, near Maxville, ON.

Fond du Lac SK West of the mouth of the **Fond du Lac River** and on the north shore of the east end of Lake Athabasca, this northern village was the site of a Hudson's Bay Company post built in 1851. There had been both HBC and North West Company posts nearby in the earlier part of the nineteenth century. A post office opened here in 1934. The French phrase *fond du Lac* means 'far end of the lake'.

Fonthill ON In the town of Pelham, Niagara Region, this community was first known as *Osborne's* and *Temperanceville*. When *Pelham* post office was located here in 1856, it was called Fonthill, either after Fonthill Abbey in Wiltshire, England or after a public reservoir and fountain on the road from here to Canborough, beside the Short Hills.

Forbes, Mount AB Northwest of Lake Louise, this mountain (3612 m) was named in 1859 by Dr. James Hector (1834–1907) after Edward Forbes (1815–54), professor of natural history at the University of Edinburgh, who was one of Hector's teachers.

Foremost AB Located southwest of Medicine Hat, this village (1950) was established in 1913 by the Canadian Pacific Railway. It was the 'foremost' point reached that year, and the railway was not extended farther east until two years later. Foremost post office opened in 1914, replacing *Webber*, opened four years earlier, 3 km to the south.

Forest ON This town (1889) in Lambton County, northeast of Sarnia, was named in 1859, when the Grand Trunk Railway was built through a heavily wooded area. Forest post office opened in 1862. To qualify as a town with 2000 people, the village delayed a Grand Trunk train for an hour in 1888 and registered the passengers and crew.

Forestburg AB Southeast of Camrose, this village (1919) was established in 1915 by the Canadian Northern Railway. It was likely named by a pioneer settler after Forestburg, SD, northwest of Sioux Falls. A claim that it may have been named after Forestburg in Ontario is doubtful, as this name has never been used for a place in that province.

Foresters Falls ON In 2001 this community became part of the township of Whitewater Region, Renfrew County. It was named in 1854 after first postmaster Oliver Forester.

Forestville QC This community on the north shore of the St. Lawrence, midway between Tadoussac and Baie-Comeau, was first called *Sault-au-Cochon* after the river that flows into the St. Lawrence. From 1870 to 1890 Price Brothers operated a sawmill here, and the place was called *Forrest-Ville* after the company's superintendent, Grant William Forrest. The town of Forestville was incorporated in 1944, seven years after the Anglo Pulp Company opened a mill here.

Forillon National Park QC Created in 1970 on the eastern end of the **Presqu'île de Forillon**, this became the first national park (240 km²) in Quebec. In 1626 Samuel de Champlain (1567–1635) noted that there was a *forillon* (rocky point extending into the sea), which looked like a mill wheel with a rock shaped like a hat on top.

Formosa ON In 1999 this community became part of the municipality of South Bruce, Bruce County. It was named about 1856 by the Reverend Fr. Gaspar Matoga of Guelph after the Asian island called Formosa ('beautiful') by the Portuguese in 1590, more commonly known as Taiwan. The post office opened in 1861.

Forres, Mount BC West of Williston Lake and on the north side of Ingenika River, this mountain (2072 m) was named in 1933 by surveyor James R. Mackenzie after his birthplace in Morayshire, Scotland, northeast of Inverness.

Fort Albany ON Near the mouth of Albany River, northwest of Moosonee, it was established in 1679 by the Hudson's Bay Company and named about 1683 after the Duke of York and Albany (1674–1728), who became King James II in 1685.

Fort Alexander MB Located 5 km above the mouth of the Winnipeg River, this was the site of the French Fort Maurepas, established in 1733–4 on the north side of the river, but abandoned in 1745. In 1792 the North West Company built Fort Bas de la Rivière (also called Winnipeg House) on the south side, which the Hudson's Bay Company called Fort Alexander in 1821. The post office was called *Pine Falls* in 1879 and was renamed Fort Alexander two years later.

Fort Assiniboine AB On the north bank of the Athabasca River, northwest of Edmonton, this community was the site of a Hudson's Bay Company post in 1823. Its post office opened in 1913, and it was an incorporated village from 1958 to 1991.

Fort Beauséjour NB Located on the boundary with Nova Scotia, it was declared a national historic site in 1926. Built by the French in the early 1750s, it was captured by Col. Robert Monckton (1726–82) in 1755 and renamed Fort Cumberland. The fort had been named after a nearby point, part of the property of Laurent Chatillon, Sieur de Beauséjour.

Fort Chipewyan AB On the north side of the west end of Lake Athabasca and at the point where the lake is drained by the Slave River, this place was the site of a North West Company post established in 1804. The post had been created on the south shore of the lake by explorer Alexander Mackenzie (c.1764–1820) and fur trader Roderick Mackenzie (c.1761–1844), naming it after the Chipewyan nation, whose name is Cree for 'pointed skins'. The post office here opened in 1912.

Fort-Coulonge QC Located in the regional county of Pontiac, this village is situated at the mouth of the Rivière Coulonge, where it flows into Lac Coulonge (a widening of the Ottawa River). Its post office took its name in 1853 from the trading post established here in 1784 by the North West Company. The river and the post office, and subsequently the lake, were named after Nicolas d'Ailleboust de Mathet (1663–1709), who was also called Sieur de Coulonge after a title of his grandfather, Nicolas d'Ailleboust de de Coulonge-la-Madeleine.

Forteau NL Located on **Forteau Bay**, and on the Labrador side of the Strait of Belle Isle, this municipal community (1971) was named after the bay. The bay's name is said to derive from either the strong (*fort*) southerly winds producing heavy swells, or the strong tide rips. In 1535 Jacques Cartier (1491–1557) called the bay *H de la Balaine* ('whale harbour').

Fort Erie ON The fort was established in 1764, and the post office was called Fort Erie in 1820. However, the town was only named in 1931, after the amalgamation of the village of *Waterloo*, named in 1857, and the village of *Bridgeburg*, named in 1895. In 1970 Fort Erie annexed Bertie Township and the village of Crystal Beach.

Fort Frances ON This town (1903) in Rainy River District was named in 1830 during a visit by Sir George Simpson (1787–1860) and his wife Lady Frances Simpson, when the fort was christened in her honour. Lady Frances (c.1812–53) was also the first cousin of Sir George, governor-in-chief of the Hudson's Bay Company, 1820–60. The post office opened in 1876.

Fort Fraser BC On the Nechako River, just east of Fraser Lake and west of Prince George, this place has its roots in the establishment of a North West Company trading post here in 1806 by Simon Fraser (1776–83). Its post office was called *Fraser Lake* in 1907, but was renamed Fort Fraser in 1913.

Fort Good Hope NT This settlement on the east bank of the Mackenzie River, just below the Arctic Circle, was initially established in 1804 as a trading post on the west bank by the North West Company. After a number of moves, the fort was re-established at the present site by the Hudson's Bay

Company in 1836. It was approved as *Good Hope* in 1915 by the Geographic Board, but the older name was restored in 1939.

Fortierville QC This village in the regional county of Bécancour, northeast of Trois-Rivières, was named in 1913 after a pioneer family.

Fort Lawrence NS West of Amherst and on the New Brunswick border, this place had postal service as early as 1825. The fort was built in 1750 by Lt. Col. Charles Lawrence (1709–60) to protect the province from invasion. Appointed governor of Nova Scotia in 1753, he directed the expulsion of the Acadians from the province two years later.

Fort Liard NT This hamlet (1987) on the Liard River, where the Petitot River flows in from the east, was the site of the Hudson's Bay Company post of Fort Rivière-au-Liard, established about 1800. It was familiarly called Fort Liard. The name of the place was approved by the Geographic Board as *Liard* in 1921, but Fort Liard was endorsed in 1944.

Fort MacKay AB On the west bank of the Athabasca River, north of Fort McMurray, this place was named about 1870 after Dr. William Morrison MacKay (1836–1917), a Hudson's Bay Company surgeon and fur trader. He settled in Edmonton in 1898, and was elected first president of the Northern Alberta Academy of Medicine in 1902.

Fort Macleod AB A town (1892) on the Oldman River, west of Lethbridge, it originated with the establishment in 1874 of the first North West Mounted Police fort in present-day Alberta. It was named after Lt. Col. James Farquharson Macleod (1836–94), who became commissioner of the NWMP from 1877 to 1880, and was made a judge of the supreme court of the North-West Territories in 1887.

Fort McMurray AB At the junction of the Athabasca and Clearwater Rivers, this urban service centre was established by the Hudson's Bay Company in 1870 at the site of the North West Company's Fort of the Forks (1788). It was named by factor H.J. Moberly after William McMurray (1822–77), chief factor at Île-à-la Crosse, which is located southeast on the Churchill River in present-day Saskatchewan. Incorporated as a city in 1980, it was joined with Improvement District No. 143 on 1 April 1995 to form the regional municipality of Wood Buffalo.

Fort McPherson NT On the Peel River, southwest of Inuvik, this hamlet (1986) was established in 1840 as a Hudson's Bay Company trading post. It was named in 1848 after Murdoch McPherson, a HBC chief trader.

Fort Nelson BC This town (1987) in the northeastern part of the province was founded as a trading post in 1805 by George Keith of the North West Company. It was likely named after Adm. Viscount Horatio Nelson, who died that year. It had been incorporated as a village in 1971.

Fort Providence NT On the north bank of the Mackenzie River, and 75 km downriver from the point where the river drains Great Slave Lake, this hamlet (1987) is the site of a fort built by the Hudson's Bay Company about 1850. In 1915 the Geographic Board authorized the name *Providence*, but the historic name was restored in 1945. In 1790 Alexander Mackenzie (c.1764–1820) had built another Fort Providence at the outlet of Yellowknife River, 210 km to the northeast.

Fort Qu'Appelle SK Northeast of Regina, this town (1951) is located in the valley of the Qu'Appelle River. It was the site of the Hudson's Bay Company's fort, established by Peter Hourie (c.1819–1910) in 1864. Its post office was called *Qu'Appelle* in 1880 and was renamed Fort Qu'Appelle in 1911. *See also* Qu'Appelle.

Fort Resolution NT On Great Slave Lake, south of the mouth of the Slave River, this settlement (1988) is the site of a Hudson's Bay Company trading post established in 1815. The name is suggestive of the hardships endured at the most northerly HBC post, before the union with the North West Company in 1821. The Geographic Board called it *Resolution* in 1815, but the older name was restored in 1940.

Fort St. James BC At the east end of Stuart Lake, northwest of Prince George, this village (1952) is the oldest continuously occupied community in the province. It was founded in 1806 by Simon Fraser (1776–83) as the North West Company trading post of *Stuart Lake*. The village was renamed Fort St. James in 1822, but the reason for the name change is not recorded in the official names records. Its post office opened in 1899.

Fort St. John BC On the Alaska Highway, north of the Peace River, this city (1975) is located near the original site of a trading post called Rocky Mountain House in 1799, and later called Fort St. John. The city's present site was fixed at *North Fort St. John* in 1942, when the Alaska Highway was built northwest from Dawson Creek.

Fort Saskatchewan AB The site of this city (1985) 25 km northeast of Edmonton was selected in 1875 for the first North West Mounted Police post north of Calgary. It was anticipated that the transcontinental Canadian Pacific Railway line would cross the North Saskatchewan River at this point, but it was subsequently decided to build the railway though the Kicking Horse Pass, west of Calgary, and not the Yellowhead Pass.

Fort Simpson NT This village (1973) on the Mackenzie River and on the west side of the mouth of the Liard River was established about 1820 by the North West Company as the site of *Fort of the Forks*. It was renamed in 1821 after Sir George Simpson (1787–1860), the governor of the Hudson's Bay Company after the union with the NWC, and its governor-in-chief after 1839. The Geographic Board approved the name *Simpson* in 1915, but Fort Simpson was restored in 1944.

Fort Smith NT This town (1966) on the Slave River just north of the Alberta border was established as a Hudson's Bay Company trading post in 1870. It was named after Donald A. Smith, 1st Baron Strathcona and Mount Royal (1820–1914). In 1871 he was appointed chief commissioner of the HBC.

Fortune NL A town (1946) on the west side of the Burin Peninsula, it took its name from **Fortune Bay**. The bay's name came from the Portuguese *fortuna* ('luck'), perhaps referring to an unknown incident of good fortune in the early 1500s. It is identified on the maps of Maggiolo (1527), Verrazzano (1528), and Ribiero (1529).

Fort Vermilion AB On the south bank of the Peace River, west of Lake Athabasca, this place was established about 1828 by the Hudson's Bay Company as a post at the mouth of **Vermilion River**. The fort had been built by the North West Company in 1788 farther downriver. Its post office opened in 1905.

Fort William ON A large sector of the city of Thunder Bay, this community was established in 1803 by the North West Company and named after William McGillivray (1764–1825), who was appointed the principal director of the company in 1804. Fort William, Port Arthur, and parts of Neebing Township and Shuniah Township were amalgamated in 1970 as the city of Thunder Bay.

Fortymile River YT Rising in Alaska, this river flows 100 km northeast across the Yukon border to enter the Yukon River, about 66 km (40 mi) below the site of the Hudson's Bay Company's Fort Reliance. The name was given about 1886 by prospectors, who found coarse gold on the river.

Fosheim Peninsula NU On the west side of Ellesmere Island, this 160-km peninsula was named before 1910 after Ivar Fosheim, a member of the Sverdrup expedition, 1898–1902. He and Oluf Raanes explored the west side of the island in 1901.

Foulon, Anse au QC Located at the foot of the cliff below Sillery, west of the city centre of Quebec, this was the site of two fulling mills in the early 1700s. Fulling (*foulon*) describes a process of cleaning and thickening cloth. The earliest written evidence of the cove is a reference to Gen. James Wolfe's ascent with his troops to the Plains of Abraham in 1759. Thereafter, the site became widely known in English as *Wolfe's Cove*.

Foxboro ON The post office in this location in Hastings County, northwest of Belleville, was called *Smithville* in 1851, after either pioneer settler Richard Smith or blacksmith Smith Demorest. Because of duplication, it was changed in 1861 to Foxboro. It may have been chosen by first postmaster William Ashley, possibly after Foxboro Hall in Suffolk, England, or after Foxborough Hall in County Roscommon, Ireland.

Fox Creek AB This town (1983) northwest of Whitecourt was established in 1967, and named after a stream flowing north into Iosegun Lake. The creek was noted in a surveyor's notes in 1901, but was portrayed on a 1928 map as *Fox Brook*.

Foxe Basin NU North of Hudson Bay, with Baffin Island on its east and Melville Peninsula on its west, this basin was named in 1921 after Capt. Luke Foxe (1586–1635). In 1631 Foxe explored Hudson Bay and the west coast of Baffin Island. **Foxe Peninsula**, which extends for 240 km from southwestern Baffin Island, was named *Fox Land* in 1905, and the present name was substituted in 1920. **Foxe Channel**, which unites Foxe Basin with Hudson Strait, was called *Fox Channel* in 1905. It was corrected to Foxe Channel in 1920.

Fox Harbour NL This municipal community (1964) on the east side of Placentia Bay and north of Placentia was first called *Little Glocester* after the fishing town of Gloucester, MA. It was known as Fox Harbour as early as 1836, possibly because foxes were observed eating fish drying on flakes.

Fox Valley SK Located near the Alberta border, west of Swift Current, this village was established in 1908. It received rail service in 1924–5 when the Canadian Pacific Railway extended a line from Pivot in Alberta. The name probably came from the occurrence of numerous red foxes in the area. Its post office opened in 1911.

Foymount ON This community was named in 1873 after tavern keeper and first postmaster John Foy. At 523 m, many people in the Ottawa Valley believe that Foymount is the province's most elevated community; however, the community of Dundalk, 38 km northwest of Orangeville, is 4 m higher than Foymount.

Frances River YT Draining **Frances Lake**, this river flows south to join the Liard River, upriver from Watson Lake. The river and the lake were named in 1840 by Hudson's Bay Company chief factor Robert Campbell after Lady Frances Simpson (c.1812–53), the wife of HBC governor Sir George Simpson.

Francheville QC This regional county on the north shore of the St. Lawrence, centred on the city of Trois-Rivières and extending between Portneuf and Maskinongé, replaced the county of Champlain in 1982. It was named after Montreal merchant and Saint-Maurice seigneur François Poulin de Francheville (1692–1733). Francheville developed the iron at the Forges du Saint-Maurice, a national historic site.

Francis SK Southeast of Regina, this town was named in 1900 after James Hervey Francis, who donated land for the town site. Earlier, the area was called *Wascana* after Wascana Creek, before the railway arrived.

François Lake BC South of Burns Lake and west of Prince George, this name resulted from a misinterpretation by French speakers of the Carrier name *Nitapoen* ('lip lake'), named because its two shores provide the outline of a smiling mouth. Believing the name was *Netapoen* ('white man's lake'), French traders translated it in the 1800s as *Lac des Français*, which was subsequently rendered in English as François Lake.

Frank AB In the municipality of Crowsnest Pass since 1979, this coal mining community was named in 1901 after A.L. Frank, a partner in the Canadian American Company. Nineteen months after it was founded, it was nearly destroyed by a massive rock slide on Turtle Mountain that killed 70 people.

Frankford ON In 1998 this village (1921) became part of the city of Quinte West, Hastings County. It was named in 1836, when a bridge was constructed across the Trent River. The name was suggested by Lt.-Gov. Sir Francis Bond Head (1793–1875), who had descended the river by canoe that year. The post office opened in 1838.

Franklin Mountains NT Extending over 400 km on the east side of the Mackenzie River, this range of mountains was named in 1944 after Sir John Franklin (1786–1847), who passed this way in 1825 during his second Arctic expedition.

Frankville ON In 2001 this place became part of the township of Elizabethtown-Kitley, the united counties of Leeds and Grenville, northwest of Brockville. It was first known as *Wilson's Corners*, *Brennan's Corners*, and *Brennanville*. Brandenburgh was suggested as a possible postal name, but Frankville was adopted in 1852. Claims that it was named after a Frank Wilson cannot be verified.

Fraser Lake BC The post office in this village (1966), on the south shore of **Fraser Lake** and west of Prince George, was named in 1920 after the lake. In 1806 Simon Fraser (1776–1862) established a North West Company trading post on the east end of the lake. *Fraser Lake* post office opened in 1907, but was renamed Fort Fraser in 1913.

Fraser, Mount AB, BC This mountain (3338 m) on the continental divide and near the head of the North Saskatchewan River was named in 1917 after Simon Fraser (1776–1862), a North West Company fur trader and discoverer of the Fraser River. **Simon Peak** (3322 m), just to the north on the divide, was also named after him.

Fraser River BC Rising in the Yellowhead Pass, west of Jasper, this river (1370 km) drains into the Strait of Georgia at Vancouver. In 1808, believing he was travelling down the Columbia, Simon Fraser (1776–1862) was so disappointed on reaching its mouth that he failed to name it. Five years later geographer David Thompson (1770–1857) named it after him. It had been previously called *Rio Floridablanca* by the Spanish, and *New Caledonia River* and *Jackanet River* by the fur traders.

Frayn, Mount BC In the Rocky Mountains, west of Sparwood, this mountain (2914 m) was named in 1964 after FO Richard P. Frayn of Fernie, who was killed in action in Europe on 8 January 1943.

Fredericton NB The capital of New Brunswick, this city (1848) was named in 1785 by Lt.-Gov. Thomas Carleton (1736–1817) after Prince Frederick (1763–1827), Bishop of Osnabrück and second son of George III. In a letter that year to Lord Sydney, Carleton called it *Fredericstown*, indicating an earlier elision of the 'k'. The French had named the site *Sainte-Anne*, with the Pre-Loyalists calling it *St. Anne's Point*. Briefly in the 1780s it was also called *Osnaburg*.

Fredericton Junction NB Located south of Fredericton, this village (1966) was first known as *Hartt's Mills* after Thomas Hartt, who established a lumber business here in 1804. Its post office opened in 1871, having been served by the Blissville way office from 1852.

Freels, Cape NL This cape, located on the northwestern side of Bonavista Bay, was named after a nearby island, which the Portuguese called *Ilha de frey luis* ('island of Brother Louis') in the early 1500s. Perhaps a brother accompanied one of the early expeditions, possibly even John Cabot's of 1497.

Freeport NS At the southwestern end of Long Island, and southwest of Digby, this village (1929) was first called *Lower Cove*. It was renamed Freeport in 1865, although its post office, opened as *Long Island* ten years before, was not changed to Freeport until 1883. It may have been named after Freeport, ME, northeast of Portland.

Frelighsburg QC This municipality (1985) in the regional county of Brome-Missisquoi, south of Cowansville, was settled in 1800 by Abram Freligh, a native of Clinton, NY, who managed a sawmill here for many years. The municipality annexed the village (1867) and the parish municipality (1967) of **Frelighsburg.**

Frenchman's Cove NL The harbour in this municipal community (1974), on the west side of the Burin Peninsula, was known by this name as early as the 1760s, when Capt. James Cook (1728–79) undertook hydrographic surveys here. It may have been named by English fishermen after one or more French fishermen, who continued to fish along the shore after the close of the French regime.

French, Mount AB At the head of the Kananaskis River, southwest of Calgary, this mountain (3234 m) was named in 1918 by surveyor Morrison Parsons Bridgland (1878–1948) after Sir John Denton Pinkstone French (1852–1925), commander-in-chief of the British Expeditionary Force in France during the First World War.

French River ON This important navigation route joining Lake Nipissing with Georgian Bay and Lake Huron was well known as *Rivière des Français* during the French regime. After 1759 it was first called *Frenchman's River* on English maps, with the current form becoming the only English name used on maps after 1847.

French Village NS On St. Margarets Bay, and west of Halifax, this place took its name from the descendants of French families who had been settled by Gov. Charles Lawrence (1709–60) in Lunenburg in 1753. They were encouraged in 1783 to resettle on the east side of the bay by Gov. John Parr.

Freshfield, Mount AB, BC On the continental divide and southwest of Howse Pass, this mountain (3336 m) was named in 1897 by British climber Norman Collie (1859–1942) after alpinist Douglas William Freshfield (1845–1934), president of the Alpine Club in England in 1893.

Freshwater NL This neighbourhood in the town of Placentia and on the north side of the Northwest River was incorporated as a town in 1950. Its name likely refers to the finding of a good supply of fresh water by fishermen. Locally, it is believed the site was named *Fontaine* by the French, in reference to the fresh water obtained from a brook draining from Larkins Pond.

Fresnoy Mountain AB, BC This mountain (3240 m) on the continental divide, southeast of the Columbia Icefield, was named in 1919 after a village in northeastern France, which had been captured by Canadian troops two years earlier.

Frobisher SK East of Estevan, this village (1904) was established by the Canadian Pacific Railway in 1884. Its post office was called *Frobyshire* on 1 February 1902, with the name being respelled Frobisher on 1 June 1902. In 1905 chief geographer

James White stated that it was named after Benjamin Frobisher (c.1742–87), a fur trader in the West, 1764–87, and a shareholder in the North West Company after 1779. The post office may have been named after the Elizabethan explorer Sir Martin Frobisher (1535–94).

Frobisher Bay NU On the southeast side of Baffin Island, this 240-km inlet was named in 1900 after Sir Martin Frobisher (1535–94), who assumed the bay was a strait when he explored the area in 1576. In 1587 John Davis called it *Lumley Inlet* after Lord Lumley, one of his patrons. *See also* Iqaluit.

Frontenac ON The county was named in 1792 after Fort Frontenac. It had been built as Fort Cataraqui in 1673, but was renamed soon after by René-Robert Cavelier de La Salle (1643–87) after Louis de Buade (1620–98), comte de Frontenac et de Palluau, governor of New France, 1672–82 and 1689–98. Col. John Bradstreet destroyed the fort in 1758.

Frontenac QC Located in the regional county of Le Granit, east of Lac Mégantic, this municipality replaced the united townships of *Spalding-et-Ditchfield* in 1959. It was named after Louis de Buade de Frontenac et de Palluau (1622–98), governor of New France, 1672–82 and 1689–98.

Frontier SK Near the Montana border, southwest of Swift Current, this village (1930) took its name from the rural municipality of **Frontier** (1912). The post office here opened in 1917, with a Canadian Pacific Railway branch line arriving in 1923.

Front of Escott ON In 2001 the Front of Escott became part of the township of Leeds and the Thousand Islands in the united counties of Leeds and Grenville. Escott Township was established in 1840, and was named after the family residence of Sir George Yonge (1732–1812) at Escott, near Honiton, Devon, England. In 1850 it became part of Front of Yonge and Escott Township. *See also* Rear of Yonge and Escot.

Front of Leeds and Lansdowne ON In 2001 Front of Leeds and Lansdowne became part of the township of Leeds and the Thousand Islands. This municipal township was created in 1850 from the front portions of the townships of Leeds and Lansdowne. They were named in 1788, the one for Francis Osborne, 5th Duke of Leeds (1751–99), secretary of state for foreign affairs, 1783–91; and the other for William Petty Fitzmaurice, 2nd Earl of Shelburne and Marquess of Lansdowne (1737–1805), prime minister of Great Britain, 1782–3. *See also* Leeds *and* Grenville, ON.

Front of Yonge ON Yonge Township in Leeds County was named in 1786 after Sir George Yonge (1732–1812), secretary of war, 1782–94. In 1850 it was divided between Front of Yonge and Escott and Rear of Yonge and Escott townships.

Front of Yonge was made a separate municipal township in 1905.

Fruitvale BC This village (1952) in the Beaver Creek valley, east of Trail, was named in 1907, when the post office opened.

Fryatt, Mount AB Northwest of the Columbia Icefield, this mountain (3361 m) was named in 1920 by the Alberta–British Columbia Boundary Commission after Capt. Charles Algernon Fryatt (1872–1916). He had rammed a German submarine with his unarmed merchant ship during the First World War and was subsequently shot by his captors.

Fullarton ON In 1998 this township became part of the township of West Perth, Perth County. It was named in 1830 for John Fullarton, a director of the Canada Company. This British company was established in 1826 to develop the Huron Tract, a large area of what is now Southwestern Ontario.

Fundy, Bay of NB, NS Separating the provinces of New Brunswick and Nova Scotia, this 50- to 70-km-wide inlet was called *La Baye Françoise* in 1604 by explorer Pierre du Gua de Monts (c.1558–1628). In 1624 Sir William Alexander (1567–1640) referred to it as *Argall's Bay* after a raider who was there 11 years before. On a 1679 map it was identified as *Bay of Funda*, with the present form appearing on a map in 1711. The name may derive from *Cap Fendu*, the French name of Cape Split, in reference to the prominent cape separating Minas Channel from Minas Basin. **Fundy National Park** (206 km^2), in Albert County, was created in 1948.

Fury and Hecla Strait NU Uniting Foxe Basin and the Gulf of Boothia, this strait was discovered and named in 1822 by Sir William Parry (1790–1855) after the two ships under his command, the *Fury* and the *Hecla*. Because the strait was icebound, he was unable to navigate through it, but a journey overland confirmed that a sea lay beyond.

Fusilier Peak BC In the Tower of London Range of the Muskwa Ranges of the Rocky Mountains, this mountain (2819 m) was named in 1960 by Capt. Michael Francis Richard Jones after the Royal Fusiliers in London and the Third Battalion Royal Canadian Regiment (London and Oxford Fusiliers). A party of British and Canadian fusiliers climbed this peak in 1960.

Gabarus NS The post office in this location on the south side of **Gabarus Bay** and southwest of Louisbourg was called *Gabarouse* in 1842, taking its spelling from the British Admiralty charts. The bay was identified as *Gabor* on Jean Guérard's map of 1631, and *Baye de Gabari* on Jacques-Nicolas Bellin's map of 1764. Jurist and writer Thomas Chandler Haliburton (1796–1865) used the present spelling in 1829. Although there has been much speculation on the linguistic origin of the name, its source and meaning remain uncertain.

Gabriola Island BC One of the Gulf Islands, offshore from Nanaimo, the island took its name from its eastern point, named *Punta de Gaviota* ('seagull point') in 1791 by Spanish explorer Jose Maria Narvaez (1768–1840). The island was later named *Punta de Gaviola*, and then changed again to Gabriola, possibly in 1859 by Capt. George Richards (1820–96).

Gads Hill ON In 1998 this community became a part of the township of Perth East, Perth County. Located northeast of Stratford, the community has a name of English literary origin, but there is no certainty as to its source. It may be from Shakespeare's *Henry IV Part I*, where it occurs in the form Gadshill, in reference to Gads Hill, northwest of Rochester, Kent, England (Charles Dickens lived in this location from 1857 to 1870).

Gagetown NB This village (1966) is located 45 km southeast of Fredericton, on the west bank of the Saint John River, and was named in 1825 after **Gagetown Parish**, established in 1786. The parish was named after *Gage Township*, which in turn was named in 1765 after Thomas Gage (1721–87). Gage was commander-in-chief of British forces in North America, 1764–75, and a grantee of land in the township. **Canadian Forces Base Gagetown** was established in 1952. It embraces 111,000 ha in Sunbury and Queens counties, between Fredericton and Saint John.

Gainsborough SK The province's oldest village (1894), it is located near both the Manitoba and North Dakota borders. It was named by Jesse Johnson Sadler (1846–1917), after Thomas Gainsborough (1727–88), the brilliant painter and landscape artist. Postal service was provided here the following year.

Galahad AB Located southeast of Camrose, this village (1918) was named after Galahad post office, established

in 1907 at present Alliance, 14 km to the southeast. After the name Alliance was instituted in 1916 by the Canadian Northern Railway, Galahad was reassigned to its present site. The name may have been given after the legendary thirteenth-century knight of the Round Table.

Galiano Island BC One of the Gulf Islands, northeast of Saltspring Island, this island was named in 1859 by Capt. George Richards (1820–96) after Dionisio Alcalá Galiano (1760–1805), who, as commander of the Spanish vessel *Sutil,* explored the waters of the Strait of Georgia in 1792.

Galt ON This city of 38,000 was united in 1973 with the towns of Preston and Hespeler, and part of the township of North Dumfries to form the new city of Cambridge. First called *Schade's Mill* after miller Absolom Schade, it was renamed in 1825 by legislative councillor and land developer William Dickson for John Galt (1779–1839), the founder of Guelph. Galt was the commissioner of the Canada Company, which developed the Huron Tract, a large part of what is now Southwestern Ontario. *See also* Cambridge.

Gambo NL This town (1980) is situated at the head of Freshwater Bay, the most westerly extension of Bonavista Bay. Its name—first given to **Gambo Ponds** and **Gambo Brook**—may derive from the word *gambo*, a type of sledge used to haul timber in the woods. It may have its origin in a Mi'kmaq word. A suggestion in the early 1900s by the Most Reverend Michael Howley (1843–1914) that the name might have originated in the sixteenth-century Spanish or Portuguese name *Baie de las Gamas*, 'bay of does', cannot be verified. The town also comprises the adjacent communities of Dark Cove and Middle Brook.

Gananoque ON Joel Stone founded the town of Gananoque at the mouth of the **Gananoque River** in 1791. Although Guy Carleton, Lord Dorchester (1724–1808), used the present spelling as early as 1788, it was not standardized until the 1820s. French surveyor Jean Deshayes (1668–1706) was told in 1685 that the river in Onondaga was called *Ganonocouy* ('flint at the mountain'), still the preferred meaning. Incorporated as a town in 1890, it became a separated town in 1922.

Gander NL Situated on the north shore of **Gander Lake**, this town (1959) took its name from the lake and the **Gander River** (156 km), which may have been named after wild geese. It had its beginnings in 1937–8, when a large airport was constructed to strengthen the transatlantic links between North America and Europe. The modern townsite was developed in the mid-1950s.

Ganges BC The post office in this main service centre of Saltspring Island was named in 1906. The village is located at the head of **Ganges Harbour**, which was named in 1859 by Capt. George Richards (1820–96) after HMS *Ganges*. The ship was built in 1821 at Bombay, India, and served on the Pacific station from 1857 to 1860.

Ganong, Mount NB This mountain (655 m), located northeast of Mount Carleton and 50 km southwest of Bathurst, was named in 1901 by American naturalist Mauran Furbish after William Francis Ganong (1864–1941). Ganong was a professor of botany at Smith College, Northampton, MA; he spent several summers exploring the geography, geology, and natural history of his native province. He wrote two monographs on New Brunswick's place names and several articles on Aboriginal names.

Gargantua, Cape ON Located on the eastern shore of Lake Superior, this cape was named during the French regime after the legendary giant in the tales of *Gargantua* and *Pantagruel* by François Rabelais (1494–1553). **Pantagruel Bay**, after Gargantua's son, and **Grangousier Hill**, after Gargantua's father, Grandgousier, are located nearby.

Garibaldi, Mount BC This mountain (2678 m), located northeast of Squamish in **Garibaldi Provincial Park** (1927), was named in 1860 by Capt. George Richards (1820–96) after Giuseppe Garibaldi (1807–82), an Italian patriot, who had a major role in achieving Italian unity.

Garnish NL Located on the west side of the Burin Peninsula, west of Marystown, this town (1971) is situated on **Garnish Barasway**, a small harbour protected by a bar. The town was identified in 1775 as *Little Garnish* by Capt. James Cook (1728–79), but neither the meaning of this name nor that of **Great Garnish Barasway** (found 3 km to the southwest) is known.

Garry Lake NU This lake on the Back River, northwest of Baker Lake, was named in 1834 by Capt. Sir George Back (1796–1872) after Nicholas Garry (c.1782–1856), who strongly supported research in the Arctic. After the Army Survey Establishment of the department of national defence found in 1959 that there were three different levels, it was divided into Garry, Upper Garry, and Lower Garry lakes. The present Garry Lake has an area of 916 km².

Garson MB Located midway between Selkirk and Beausejour, and northeast of Winnipeg, this village was incorporated in 1915 as *Lyall*, but in 1927 was renamed Garson after the Canadian Pacific Railway station, established in 1902.

William Garson (1856–1911) opened a quarry here about 1900 and **Garson Quarry** post office opened in 1908.

Gaskiers-Point La Haye NL This municipal community (1970) is located on the east shore of St. Mary's Bay. Gaskiers may derive from the French *casse-coeur*, a variant of *crève-coeur* ('heart-break'), or from a French family name such as Gasquié or Gascoigne. It could also be a variant spelling of the surname of the Marquis de Castries (1727–1801), who served as the French minister of marine in the 1760s. Both *Point La Haye* and *La Haye Point* are shown on Capt. James Cook's 1762 map. La Haye is both a French family name and place name. The 1869 census listed *Gaskin Point, La Haye*.

Gaspé A town (1959) near the inner part of the **Baie de Gaspé**, and not far from **Cap Gaspé** (the most eastern extremity of the **Péninsule de Gaspé**), it is near the site of Jacques Cartier's famous planting of his first cross in the New World in 1534. The name, most often spelled *Gaspay* or *Gaspei* until the late 1600s, first appears in records about 1590. Its exact origin remains uncertain. It seems likely that its form is associated with the Mi'kmaq root *kesp(i)-/gesp(i)-*, which conveys the meaning of 'end' and occurs in the names of other promontories within Mi'kmaq territory in the present-day Maritime provinces. Assuming that this is correct it could be concluded that it originally designated the headland of Cap Gaspé. However, one or more European languages almost certainly influenced the name through re-interpretation or outright creation, before the prevailing pronunciation, spelling, and the use of the name Gaspé were fixed. It is quite probable that Basque mariners, who were active in the Gulf of St. Lawrence in the late 1500s, adapted the final syllable to conform to the suffix *-pe* ('below') and, using it to refer to the bay and harbour, took the complete name to be a compound Basque word such as *gerizpe/kerizpe* ('harbour'). Documentary evidence is too scanty to either prove or disprove this theory.

Gatineau QC In 2002 this city became significantly larger by taking over the cities of Aylmer, Hull, and Buckingham, and the town of Masson-Angers. The original city of Gatineau was located at the mouth of the **Rivière Gatineau**. In 1975 it merged with the town of *Pointe-Gatineau*, the villages of *Touraine*, *Templeton*, and *Templeton-Est*, and the territory of the present municipality of Cantley, which separated from Gatineau in 1989. The river's name recalls the seventeenth-century fur trader Nicolas Gatineau (or Gastineau) *dit* Duplessis, who traded on the river between the Ottawa and the Saint-Maurice, and his sons, Louis and Jean-Baptiste, who had a trading post at the mouth of the river. **Gatineau Park** (363 km²) is located north of Canada's capital and is a popular all-season recreation area.

Gaultois NL On Hermitage Bay and on the southwestern coast of Newfoundland, this town (1962) took its name from

Havre le Galtois. In 1764 Capt. James Cook (1728–79) referred to it as Gaultois. It was possibly named by French or Jersey fishermen in the 1600s after the many rocky pinnacles found here, derived from the Norman French word *galtas* ('pinnacle').

Geddes, Mount BC In the Coast Mountains, northwest of Mount Waddington, this mountain (3223 m) was named in 1928 by Walter Alfred (Don) Munday (1890–1950) after climber M.D. Geddes of Calgary, who was killed the previous year while ascending Mount Lefroy in the Rockies.

George, Rivière QC This 563-km river rises north of Smallwood Reservoir and flows north to Ungava Bay. It was called *George River* in 1811 by Moravian missionaries Gottlieb Kohlmeister and George Kmoch after George III. They noted its local name was *Kangertlualuksoak*, which in modern Inuktitut is *Kangirsualujjuap Kuunga* ('river of the very great bay').

Georgetown ON This urban centre in the town of Halton Hills, Halton Region, was settled in 1821 by George Kennedy (1799–1870), who built several mills on Silver Creek. It was named in 1837 after Kennedy, who had been named for George III, the reigning monarch when he was born.

Georgetown PE Northeast of Montague, this town (1912) was created in 1765 by Samuel Holland (1728–1801) and named after George III. Its port was called *Three Rivers* in the early 1800s after the French *Trois Rivières*, describing the Brudenell, Cardigan, and Montague Rivers. Georgetown post office opened in 1827. The town is located in Georgetown Royalty, one of the 70 territorial divisions laid out by Holland.

Georgian Bay ON This large arm of Lake Huron was called *Mer Douce* ('freshwater sea') by Samuel de Champlain (1567–1635) in 1615. Admiralty surveyor Henry W. Bayfield (1795–1885) charted its shores in the 1820s and named it after George IV. The municipal township of **Georgian Bay** in the district municipality of Muskoka was created in 1971. **Georgian Bay Islands National Park** (14 km²) was created in 1929.

Georgia, Strait of BC Separating southern Vancouver Island from the mainland, this water body was named on 4 June 1792 the *Gulph of Georgia* by Capt. George Vancouver (1757–98) on the occasion of the birthday of George III. On 27 November 1858 Capt. George Richards (1820–96) informed the British Navy's hydrographer that he had changed *Gulf of Georgia* to Strait of Georgia, as 'it seemed a more appropriate name and I thought it better to alter it at once'. The Gulf Islands have remained as evidence of Vancouver's earlier name. In 1791 Spanish Lt. Francisco Eliza had named the gulf *Gran Canal de Nuestra Señora del Rosario la Marinera*, a name which Vancouver shifted to the channel (now Malaspina Strait) between Texada Island and the mainland.

Georgina ON The original township was named in 1815 after George III. Georgina was proposed in 1819 as a name for the new royal princess, the future Queen Victoria. In 1971 the municipal township of Georgina was united with the village of Sutton and the municipal township of North Gwillimbury to form the new municipal township of Georgina, which has been a town since 1986.

Gerald SK Located east of Esterhazy, this village (1953) was established by the Grand Trunk Pacific Railway in 1907. It was named after one of its officials, possibly Gerald Campbell, a GTP civil engineer. Its post office opened two years later.

Geraldton ON This town (1937) in Thunder Bay District was the site of a major gold strike in the early 1930s. In 1933 the Canadian National Railways proposed naming its new station Fitzgerald, after Stanley J. Fitzgerald, vice-president of the Little Long Lac Gold Mines Ltd. When informed that the name was already in use in Western Canada, the CNR proposed Geraldton, composed of syllables from Fitzgerald and Joseph Errington, the company's president.

Gesner Ridge NB Situated on the east side of Little Tobique River and west of Mount Carleton, this formation was named *Gesner Mountains* in 1902 by naturalist William F. Ganong (1864–1941). Named after geologist Abraham Gesner (1797–1864), the inventor of kerosene, it was renamed Gesner Ridge in 1975.

Gibbons AB This town (1977) northeast of Edmonton was first known as *Astleyville* and *Battenburg*. Its post office was named in 1920 after William Reynolds Gibbons, who moved to the area in 1892 from Orillia, ON.

Gibsons BC This town (1982) is located on the west side of Howe Sound, where it joins the Strait of Georgia. The post office was called *Howe Sound* in 1892, and was renamed *Gibson's Landing* in 1907 after George William Gibson (1829–1913). He and his sons settled here in 1866. In 1948 local businessmen persuaded the post office department to rename the office Gibsons.

Gilbert, Mount BC Located in the Coast Mountains, east of Bute Inlet, this mountain (3117 m) was named in 1933 by George G. Aitken (d.2007), provincial member of the Geographic Board of Canada, after Sir Humphrey Gilbert (c.1537–83). Gilbert had applied for a charter in 1566 to trade on the west coast of North America, and received it 12 years later. After taking possession of Newfoundland in 1583, he drowned in the Atlantic Ocean before attaining his goal of reaching the Pacific.

Gilbert Plains MB This village (1906) is located west of Dauphin. Its post office was named in 1892 after the adjacent plains, identified by residents of Dauphin with Métis scout Gilbert Ross.

Gillams NL On the north side of Humber Arm and northwest of Corner Brook, this municipal community (1971) was named after **Gillams Cove**. The cove, as noted in 1849, may have been named after a French settler, possibly Blanchard, whose forename was Guillaume ('William').

Gimli MB On the southwestern shore of Lake Winnipeg, this town (1947) was founded in 1875 by the first Icelandic settlers in Western Canada. The name derives from the Great Hall of Heaven, where all brave men gather with the Norse god Odin. Gimli post office opened at present Riverton in 1877 and transferred to its current site in 1886.

Girardville QC This municipality northwest of Lac Saint-Jean was named in 1921 after Joseph Girard (1853–1933), a member of the Legislative Assembly for Lac Saint-Jean, 1892–1900, and of the House of Commons for Chicoutimi, 1900–08.

Girouxville AB This village (1951) west of Falher in Peace River country was founded in 1915 by the pioneering Giroux family, with the post office opening two years later. Earlier it had been called *Fowler* by the Edmonton, Dunvegan and British Columbia Railway.

Gjoa Haven NT This hamlet (1981) on the southeast shore of King William Island was established in 1947. The haven was named in 1904 after the vessel *Gjoa*, under the command of Roald Amundsen (1872–1928). Amundsen wintered here from the fall of 1903 to the spring of 1905. In 1906 the *Gjoa* became the first vessel to complete the navigation of the Northwest Passage. It was anchored at San Francisco until 1972, when it was returned to Norway.

Glace Bay NS This urban community, in the regional municipality of Cape Breton since 1 August 1995, was incorporated as a town in 1901. Postal service was established at *Little Glace Bay* in 1864 and the name was changed to Glace Bay in 1902. During the French regime, the water body now known as **Big Glace Bay** was called *Baie de Glace* ('icy bay'). Samuel Holland (1728–1801) named it *Dyson Bay* in 1769, and Joseph Frederick Wallet DesBarres (1772–1824) referred to it as *Glass Bay* in 1786.

Glacier National Park BC Located in the Selkirk Mountains and on both sides of the Rogers Pass, this park (1350 km²) was established in 1886. Among its mountains are several glaciers and its valleys are often the scenes of avalanches.

Gladstone MB Located halfway between Lake Manitoba and Neepawa, this town (1882) was first called *Third Crossing*, because the old pioneer Carlton Trail to Edmonton had already crossed the Whitemud River twice. The post office here was called *Palestine* in 1872, because the bounty from the land recalled the biblical 'promised land'. It was renamed Gladstone in 1879 for William Ewart Gladstone (1809–98), prime minister of Great Britain, 1880–5, 1886, and 1892–4.

Glanbrook ON In 2001 this municipal township became part of the city of Hamilton. It was created in 1974 through the amalgamation of Binbrook and Glanford townships. **Glanford Township** was named in 1798 after the parish of Glanford Brigg in England's Lincolnshire, north of the city of Lincoln. **Binbrook Township** was named the same year after a town in England's Lincolnshire, northeast of the city of Lincoln.

Glaslyn SK North of North Battleford, this village (1929) was settled in 1908 by Welsh pioneers, who chose a name meaning 'clear water' in Welsh. The post office here was established in 1911.

Gleichen AB This town (1910) southeast of Calgary was named in 1883 by the Canadian Pacific Railway after Count Albert Edward Wilfred Gleichen (1863–1937), a financial supporter of the CPR who travelled on the line.

Glenavon SK Southeast of Regina, this village (1910) was first called *Kendal*. Its post office was named in 1908 by R.T. Young, possibly after Glendevon, in Perthshire, Scotland, southwest of Perth.

Glenboro MB Situated southeast of Brandon, this town (1949) was settled in 1879 and its post office opened in 1883. It was named by Scottish settler James Duncan after the glens of his homeland, with 'boro' being added to reflect the word 'town'.

Glenburnie-Birchy Head-Shoal Brook NF This municipal community (1978) on the South Arm of Bonne Bay is surrounded on the land side by Gros Morne National Park. **Glenburnie** was named by the first Scottish fishermen who settled here about 1800, likely after a community in Fifeshire, Scotland. The neighbourhoods of **Birchy Head** and **Shoal Brook** are located adjacent to physical features with those names.

Glencoe ON In 2001 this village (1873) became part of the municipality of Southwest Middlesex, Middlesex County. Southwest of London, this village was named in 1856 by surveyor A.P. Macdonald, after the vale of Glencoe in Argyllshire, Scotland, where the terrible massacre of Macdonalds took place in 1692.

Glendon AB The post office in this village (1956) southwest of Cold Lake was named in 1912 after the birth name of the mother of postmaster J.P. Spencer.

Glenelg ON In 2001 this township became a part of the township of West Grey, Grey County. It was named in 1840 after Charles Grant (1778–1863), Lord Glenelg in 1836, who chose his title after Glenelg on the Scottish mainland opposite the Isle of Skye. He was British secretary of state for war and the colonies, 1835–41.

Glen Ewen SK East of Estevan and between the towns of Oxbow and Carnduff, this village (1904) was named in 1884 by the Canadian Pacific Railway after Thomas Ewen (1844–1909), who had homesteaded here two years earlier. Ewen was its first postmaster in 1890.

Glengarry ON This county (since 1850) located within the united counties of Stormont, Dundas, and Glengarry was named in 1792 after the well-known glen in Inverness-shire, Scotland. The name was given in honour of Scottish Highlanders, who supported George III during the American Revolution, and received land grants in Glengarry through the intercession of Bishop Alexander McDonell (1798–1835).

Glen Robertson ON In 1998 this place became a part of the township of North Glengarry, united counties of Stormont, Dundas, and Glengarry. It was named in 1874, when the Canada Atlantic Railway was built across Alexander Robertson's farm.

Glenwood AB The post office in this village (1961) southwest of Lethbridge was named *Glenwoodville* in 1908 after Glen Wood, the son of Edward J. Wood, president of the Alberta stake of the Church of Jesus Christ of Latter-day Saints. In 1906 the stake acquired the Cochrane Ranche, whose headquarters were at the site of the village. The post office was changed to Glenwood in 1979.

Glenwood NL On the west bank of the Gander River, this town (1962) was founded in the 1890s by G.L. Phillips of Point Leamington, NL, and W.J. Sterritt, one of the owners of the Glenwood Lumber Company of Yarmouth, NS. The name was used for the sawmilling centre by 1901.

Gloucester NB In the northeastern part of the province, this county was named in 1826 after Princess Mary, Duchess of Gloucester and Edinburgh (1776–1857), fourth daughter of George III, and wife of her first cousin, William Frederick, 2nd Duke of Gloucester (1776–1834).

Gloucester ON In 2001 this city became a sector of the city of Ottawa. It had been created a township in Russell County in 1798, but was transferred that year to Carleton County. In 1981 Gloucester was converted into a city in the Ottawa-Carleton Region. It was named after Prince William Frederick, Duke of Gloucester (1776–1834), a nephew of George III, and husband of George III's daughter, Princess Mary.

Glovertown NL This town (1954) on the Middle Arm of Alexander Bay, an extension of Bonavista Bay, was first known as *Bloody Bay*, after an earlier name of Alexander Bay. It was renamed after Sir John Hawley Glover (1829–85), governor of Newfoundland, 1876–81 and 1883–5.

Godbout QC This municipality was created in 1933 at the mouth of Rivière Godbout in the regional county of Manicouagan, east of Baie-Comeau. The river, noted by Fr. Charles Albanel (1616–96) in 1670, and referred to by map-maker Jean-Baptiste-Louis Franquelin (c.1653–1712) in 1684 as *Godebou*, probably owes its name to Nicolas Godbout (1634–74), a navigator and pilot on the St. Lawrence.

Goderich ON The town (1850) and the municipal township of Goderich (1850) in Huron County were named in 1828 by John Galt (1779–1839) and Dr. William 'Tiger' Dunlop (1792–1848) after Frederick John Robinson, Viscount Goderich and Earl of Ripon (1782–1859). Robinson was British chancellor of the exchequer, 1823–7, secretary of state for war and the colonies, 1827, and prime minister of Great Britain, August 1827 to January 1828. In 2001 the municipal township of Goderich became part of the municipality of Central Huron.

Godmanchester QC This township municipality on the south side of Lake St. Francis, southwest of Salaberry-de-Valleyfield, was created in 1845 and named after the township of **Godmanchester**, proclaimed in 1811 and named after a town in Huntingdonshire, England, northwest of Cambridge.

Gods Lake MB Encompassing an area of 933 km², this lake—located in the east central part of the province—took its name from a translation of the Cree name honouring the great spirit Manitou. The Hudson's Bay Company established a trading post at **Gods Lake Narrows** in 1880. *God's Lake* post office opened in 1935 on an island in the lake. It was renamed God's Lake Narrows, when it was moved here in 1964.

Gold Bridge BC This place north of Pemberton was named in 1934 after the bridge over the Bridge River, which provided access to the gold mining country around Bralorne.

Golden BC In the Columbia River valley and at the mouth of the Kicking Horse River, this town (1967) was first known as *The Cache* and *Kicking Horse Flats*. In 1883, on learning about Silver City being developed west of Banff, surveying assistant Frederick W. Aylmer was inspired to call this place *Golden City*. Subsequently, 'City' was dropped from the name when the Canadian Pacific Railway arrived in 1885. The post office opened two years later.

Golden ON This municipal township north of Red Lake and in Kenora District was established in 1985 when the improvement district of Balmertown was renamed. The name reflects the gold-mining area of Red Lake, Balmertown, and Cochenour.

Golden Hinde BC Southwest of Campbell River, this mountain (2200 m)—the highest on Vancouver Island—was named in 1939 by R.P. Bishop after Sir Francis Drake's ship, the *Golden Hind*. It is possible Drake may have seen it during his voyage through the North Pacific in 1578, although accounts of his voyage suggest he did not get this far north.

Golden Lake ON In 2001 this community and **Golden Lake** became parts of the township of Bonnechere Valley, Renfrew County. Southwest of Pembroke, they were named possibly around 1830 by Hudson's Bay Company trader Charles Thomas, from the beauty of the sunlight's golden reflection upon the waters and sandy shore. However, the French may have earlier translated an Algonquin description as *Lac Doré*. Coincidentally, Lake Doré, located 10 km to the east, may mean 'golden lake', but may also mean 'yellow pike lake'.

Gold River BC This village (1981) on **Gold River**, southwest of Campbell River, was created as a district municipality in 1965. Its post office was named *Muchalat* in 1952 and changed to Gold River in 1961. The river flows south from Gold Lake into Muchalat Inlet, a southern arm of Nootka Sound. The name may refer to gold panners active on the river in the 1860s.

Gondola Point NB The post office in this village (1966) northeast of Saint John was named in 1883. The point, which extends into Kennebecasis River, was identified on a 1787 map. In the 1700s 'gondolas' were dugout canoes used for transporting people on rivers.

Good Hope Mountain BC In the Coast Mountains, southeast of Mount Waddington, this mountain (3240 m) was named *Mount Good Hope* before 1930 after HMS *Good Hope*, which sunk in action 1 November 1914 off Coronel, Chile. The current form of the name was adopted in 1950.

Good Neighbour Peak YT In the Centennial Range of the St. Elias Mountains, 3 km north of Mount Vancouver, this mountain (4785 m) was named in 1967 by the Yukon Alpine Centennial Expedition, which comprised four American and four Canadian climbers.

Goodsir, Mount BC In Yoho National Park, south of Field, this mountain (3581 m) was named in 1858 by Dr. James Hector (1834–1907) after Dr. John Goodsir (1814–67), professor of anatomy at the University of Edinburgh, where Hector studied medicine.

Goodsoil SK This village (1960) northwest of Meadow Lake was named in 1929, because the good soil of the surrounding farmland appealed to those suggesting it as a postal name.

Goose Cove East NL This municipal community (1971) is located on the eastern coast of the Northern Peninsula, just south of St. Anthony. The place was originally called *Les Petites Oies* ('little geese') by French migratory fishermen in the late 1600s.

Gordon, Mount NB 30 km Southwest of the city of Campbellton, this mountain was named in 1899 by naturalist William F. Ganong (1864–1941) after Arthur Charles Hamilton-Gordon, 1st Baron Stanmore (1829–1912), lieutenant-governor of the province, 1861–6. He visited the area in 1863.

Gore Bay ON This town (1890) on **Gore Bay** and in Manitoulin District was named in 1860 after the bay, which was named after the steamship *Gore*, a vessel frozen in the North Channel in the 1850s. The steamboat, which had run between Collingwood and Sault Ste. Marie until 1870, was named after Sir Charles S. Gore (1793–1896), who helped put down the Rebellion of 1837–8 in Upper Canada.

Gosfield North; Gosfield South ON In 1999 these municipal townships became parts of the town of Kingsville, Essex County. They were separated in 1887 from Gosfield Township, which had been named in 1792 after the village of Gosfield in Essex, England.

Gouin, Réservoir QC This huge reservoir covering an area of over 1300 km² at the head of Rivière Saint-Maurice was named in 1918 by the Shawinigan Water and Power Company after Sir Lomer Gouin (1861–1929), premier of Quebec, 1905–20.

Goulbourn ON In 2001 this township became a sector of the city of Ottawa. The original township was named in 1816 after Henry Goulburn (1784–1856), undersecretary of state for war and the colonies, 1812–26.

Goulds NL This neighbourhood in the city of St. John's since 1992, south of the city centre, was incorporated as a town in 1971. It is said to have been named after a farm that Joseph B. Jukes visited about 1840. He stated that the farm was named after a bright gold-coloured flower, common along the brooks of the Avalon Peninsula.

Govan SK North of Regina, the post office (1906) in this town (1911) was named after homesteader Walter Govan (1859–1926) when the Canadian Pacific Railway arrived here. Other names had been considered. The pioneers had wanted Richmond, but it was turned down by the postal officials.

Gracefield QC The post office in this village (1905) in the regional county of La Vallée-de-la-Gatineau, south of Maniwaki, was named in 1883 after Patrick Grace, the first merchant here and the subsequent mayor of the township municipality of Wright, 1885–90.

Grafton NB This place is situated on the east side of the Saint John River and opposite Woodstock. The post office here was named in 1875 by Sperry Shea and George Stickney after their extensive grafting and nursery operations. The form of the name may have been chosen to honour Crimean War general Augustus Fitzroy, 7th Duke of Grafton (1821–1918).

Graham Island BC This largest island in the Queen Charlotte Islands was named in 1853 by Cdr. James C. Prevost after Sir James Robert Graham (1792–1861), who was then the first lord of the Admiralty.

Graham Island NU In Norwegian Bay and between Ellesmere and Cornwall Islands, this island (1378 km²) was named in 1853 by Sir Edward Belcher after Sir James Robert George Graham, then the first lord of the Admiralty.

Granby QC This city (1916) in the regional county of La Haute-Yamaska, east of Montreal, was created a village in 1859. The latter was named after the township of **Granby**, proclaimed in 1803 and named after John Manners, 4th Duke of Rutland and Marquess of Granby (1721–70), who fought bravely during the Seven Years War in Germany and returned to England in 1763 to a hero's welcome. The township municipality of **Granby** totally surrounds the city.

Grand Bank NL The site of this town (1943) on the west side of the Burin Peninsula was a French fishing port in the 1600s, known as *Grand Banc* or *Grand Banq*. The name derives from a prominent bank on the west side, which extends from **Grand Bank Harbour** to L'Anse au Loup Point.

Grand Bay NB The post office in this village (1972) northwest of Saint John was named in 1869 after the large bay formed by the Saint John River at that point, which was named during the French regime. The bay was identified as *Le Grand Baye* by Robert Monckton in 1758, and as Grand Bay by Joseph Peach in 1762.

Grand Bend ON In 2001 this village became part of the municipality of Lambton Shores, in Lambton County. The village (1951) was named in 1872 after a sharp bend in the Ausable River. Twenty years later the bend was altered by diverting the river into Lake Huron at the village, rather than following its original course to enter the lake, 16 km to the south at Port Franks.

Grand-Calumet QC This township municipality, located in the regional county of Pontiac and surrounded by two branches of the Ottawa River, was created in 1847, a year after the township of Grand-Calumet was proclaimed. The name of

Grand Calumet Township recalls the Algonquin practice of smoking the pipe of peace, called *calumet* in French.

Grand Centre AB This place was incorporated as a town in 1958, but was annexed by the town of Cold Lake in 1996. Its post office was named in 1937, when it was perceived it would become an important centre in a prosperous agricultural area.

Grand Coulee SK The first Canadian Pacific Railway station west of Regina, this place was an incorporated village from 1907 to 1919, and was reincorporated in 1984. It was named after Cottonwood Coulee, 4 km to the west, which, as the largest coulee (valley) crossed by the line in 1883, was given the designation 'grand'. It received postal service in 1903.

Grande-Anse NB The post office in this village (1968) west of Caraquet was named *Grand Ance* in 1851, after a cove of Chaleur Bay. The post office name was respelled Grande-Anse by 1883.

Grande Cache AB This town (1983) northwest of Jasper was created as a coal mining 'new town' in 1966, with its post office opening three years later. Its name recalls the hiding of furs about 1820 by trader Ignace Giasson, who decided a load of furs he was carrying from the west of the Rocky Mountains down the Smoky River was too difficult to carry through deep snow, prompting him to leave them in a large hiding place, a '*grande cache*'.

Grande Prairie AB This city (1958) in the Peace River country was founded as the site of a Hudson's Bay Company fort in 1881 and named by Mgr. Émile-Jean-Marie Grouard, who identified the vast undulating landscape as a '*grande prairie*'. Promoted as a city as early as 1910, it did not develop as a regional centre until the Edmonton, Dunvegan, and British Columbia Railway arrived in 1916. The post office here opened in 1911.

Grande-Rivière QC This town in the regional county of Pabok, southwest of Gaspé, was created in 1967 through the merger of the village and the municipality of Grande-Rivière. The post office was called *Grand River* from 1853 to 1933, when it was changed to the French form. In 1697 the seigneury of **Grande-Rivière** was granted to Jacques Cochu. The river is rather less than grand, rising only 40 km to the northwest among many larger rivers.

Grande Rivière, La QC Rising in central Quebec, this river flows west for nearly 900 km before emptying into James Bay. It has three reservoirs, created by Hydro-Quebec in the 1970s and 1980s to harness its magnificent waterpower potential. It was known as *Big River* until the beginning of the twentieth century. Its Cree name is *Tschishasipi*, a name reflected in the Cree village of Chisasibi at its mouth.

Grandes-Bergeronnes QC This village in the regional county of La Haute-Côte-Nord, northeast of Tadoussac, was developed after 1845 when two sawmills were built at the mouth of the **Rivière des Grandes-Bergeronnes**. The village was incorporated in 1929. The river's name originated with Samuel de Champlain (c.1575–1635) in 1626, who likely mistook some plover for a type of sparrow, known in French as *bergeronnette*.

Grandes-Piles QC Located in the regional county of Mékinac, north of Shawinigan, this village's post office was called *Saint-Jacques-des-Piles* from 1882 to 1966, when it was changed to Grandes-Piles. The parish municipality of *Saint-Jacques-des-Piles*, created in 1885, became the village of Grandes-Piles in 1988. The name derives from the sedimentary beds along the banks of the Saint-Maurice, described locally as strata being piled one on top of another.

Grand-Étang NS South of Chéticamp, this place was settled in the 1790s by Acadians from Prince Edward Island. The name means 'big pond' in French. Its post office opened in 1871.

Grande-Vallée QC Located in the municipality of the region of La Côte-de-Gaspé, northwest of town of Gaspé, this municipality derives its name from a seigneury granted in 1691 to François Hazeur. The post office here opened in 1872. The valley's name, noted by explorer Louis Jolliet in 1699, reflects its larger river in contrast to the nearby Rivière de la Petite Vallée.

Grand Falls; Grand-Sault NB The post office in this town (1890) on the Saint John River opened in 1837. The town was laid out as *Colebrooke* that year, after Sir William MacBean George Colebrooke (1787–1870), lieutenant-governor of New Brunswick, 1841–7. The post office was called *Colebrooke* in 1848, but Grand Falls was restored soon after. **Grand-Sault** is also official for the town's name. In 1688 Mgr. Jean-Baptiste Saint-Vallier had called the falls *Grand Sault Saint Jean-Baptiste*. John Gyles, in his 1689 memoir of his life among the Maliseet, called it *Checanekepeag*, which means 'destroyer place', probably in reference to a legend where Malabeam, a Maliseet woman, led Mohawks to their death.

Grand Falls-Windsor NL The present town at the **Grand Falls** on the Exploits River was incorporated in 1991. **Grand Falls** was laid out as a planned town in 1909, when the Anglo-Newfoundland Development Company constructed a pulp and paper mill here. It was incorporated as a town in 1961. **Windsor** was founded in the early 1900s, because only the company's mill workers could live in Grand Falls. It had first been named *Grand Falls Station*, but was renamed in 1938 after the British royal family.

Grand Forks BC The post office in this city (1897) at the junction of the Kettle and Granby Rivers, near the Washington State border, was named in 1895. Earlier the place was called *Grande Prairie*.

Grand Harbour NB In the village of Grand Manan since 8 May 1995, this place had been incorporated as a village in 1968. Its post office was called *Grand Manan* in 1837 and was renamed Grand Harbour in 1868. The harbour was identified on maps in 1770.

Grand Lake NB The name of this lake—largest in the province—appeared on plans and maps in the 1770s. It was earlier known as *Grand Lac* in French. On a 1632 map it was named *Lac Freneuse* after Mathieu Damours, Sieur de Freneuse, who was then living in the area of Jemseg.

Grand Le Pierre NL The name of this municipal community (1969) on the northeastern shore of Fortune Bay may derive from *Grande Île à Pierre* ('great stone island'), possibly in reference to the steep cliff here.

Grand Manan Island NB The largest island in the Bay of Fundy, this island was known in Passamaquoddy, Maliseet, and Penobscot as *Munanook* ('island'). Samuel de Champlain (1567–1635) referred to it as *Menane* on his 1607–8 and 1632 maps. The French called it Grand Manan after 1686, to distinguish it from Petit Manan, on the Maine coast, east of Bar Harbor. The present name was established on English maps by 1755. On 8 May 1995 the whole island was incorporated as the village of **Grand Manan**, with North Head, Grand Harbour, and Seal Cove becoming urban communities.

Grand Marais MB Situated on the southeastern shore of Lake Winnipeg, this community takes its name from the French for 'big marsh'. Alexander Henry (d.1814) the younger referred to the place in his account of 1800. The post office here was established in 1923.

Grand-Mère QC This community on the right bank of the Saint-Maurice, north of Shawinigan, became a village in 1898, was elevated to city status in 1920, and became a town in 1970. Its post office opened in 1888 and was named after the Algonquin *kokomis* ('grandmother'), in reference to a split rock that resembled the profile of an aged woman. It has often been misspelled *Grand'Mère*.

Grand Pré NS Settled as early as the 1680s by Acadians from Port-Royal, this place was resettled by New Englanders in the 1760s. In French the name means 'big meadow', referring to the extensive dyked farmland created by the Acadians. The post office was first called *Lower Horton* in 1842, and was given its present name in 1879.

Grand-Remous QC On the Rivière Gatineau, west of Mont-Laurier, this township municipality was known from 1937 to 1973 as *Sicotte*, after Louis-Victor Sicotte, member of the Legislative Assembly, 1857–63. Its post office was also called *Sicotte* from 1927 to 1933, when it was changed to Grand-Remous, which describes the fast water and swirling eddies in the river.

Grand River ON The Grand River rises in Grey and Dufferin counties and drains into Lake Erie below the town centre of Dunnville after passing through Fergus, Kitchener, Cambridge, Paris, and Brantford. It was called *Grande Rivière* during the French regime. It was also called *Rivière d'Urfé*, probably after missionary François-Saturnin Lascaris d'Urfé (1641–1701). Lt.-Gov. John Graves Simcoe (1752–1806) tried in 1793 to impose Ouse River, after a tributary of England's River Humber, but Grand River prevailed.

Grand Tracadie PE The name of this municipal community (1984) northeast of Charlottetown was noted in the *Journal of the Assembly* in 1854, taking its name from Tracadie Bay on its east side. The post office here opened in 1871. The bay's name may derive from the Mi'kmaq *tulakadik* ('camping ground'). Samuel Holland called it *Bedford Bay*, with *Tracadi Harbour* as a secondary name. He named it after John Russell, 4th Duke of Bedford (1710–71), who was first lord of the Admiralty, 1744–8.

Grand Valley ON Situated on the Grand River and in Dufferin County, west of Orangeville, this location was called *Joice's Corners*, *Little Toronto*, *Manasseh*, and *Luther*, before its post office was called Grand Valley in 1883. Incorporated as a village in 1898, it merged with East Luther Township in 1995 to form the municipal township of **East Luther Grand Valley**.

Grandview MB Situated west of Dauphin and midway between Riding Mountain National Park and Duck Mountain Provincial Park, this town and its post office were both named in 1901, supposedly because a passenger on a Canadian Northern Railway train exclaimed that the place had such a 'grand view' of the Gilbert Plains to the south and west.

Granger, Mount YT Southwest of Whitehorse, this mountain (2035 m) was named after William P. Granger, who came to the Yukon to prospect in 1895. He died in the Copper King Mine in May 1907.

Granisle BC This village (1971) on the west shore of Babine Lake, northwest of Burns Lake, was founded in 1965 by the Zapata Granby Mining Company to exploit copper on Sterret Island in the lake. Its name was created by combining 'Gran,' from Granby, with 'isle'.

Grantham QC Located in the regional county of Drummond, west of the city of Drummondville, this municipality was created in 1936, taking its name from the township, proclaimed in 1800. The township was named after pioneer settler William Grant, and after the town of Grantham, in Lincolnshire, England.

Grant MacEwan Peak AB This peak (2075 m), located on Heart Mountain, was named for Grant MacEwan (1902–2000), lieutenant-governor of Alberta, 1966–74. He was born in Brandon, MB, studied at the Ontario Agricultural College and Iowa State College, and was a professor at the University of Saskatchewan from 1828 to 1946. He was the dean of agriculture at the University of Manitoba from 1946 to 1951.

Granton ON This place is part of the township of Lucan Biddulph, Middlesex County. It was named by the Grand Trunk Railway in 1864 after Granton, Scotland, on the northwest side of Edinburgh, and after farmers Alexander, William, and James Grant. Two other farmers, William Levitt and George Foreman, wanted to call it *Awmik*, from the Ojibwa word for 'beaver'. This name was selected at a public meeting, but both the railway and postal officials rejected it.

Granum AB The post office in this town (1910) between Claresholm and Fort Macleod was named in 1907 by Malcolm McKenzie, a member of the Alberta Legislative Assembly (1905–1913). Granum is the Latin for 'grain', a name chosen because the town was located in good grain-growing land. It was formerly called *Leavings* in 1904, because the trail from Fort Benton, MT, to Calgary left the banks of Willow Creek at that point.

Granville Ferry NS This place is located across the Annapolis River from Annapolis Royal, and its post office was established in 1836. It took its name from Granville Township, created in 1764 and named after John Carteret, Earl Granville (1690–1763), who had been president of the council in the British government, 1751–63.

Gras, Lac de NT Located 300 km northeast of Yellowknife, this lake (577 km²) was recorded in 1890 by British explorer and hunter Warburton Pike, who wrote in his *Barren Ground* (1892) that it was known as Lac de Gras by his companions, presumably his Métis assistants. The name was submitted for approval in 1924 by surveyor G.H. Blanchet. The reason a name meaning 'fat lake' was given to the lake is not explained in the official records.

Grassy Lake AB Midway between Lethbridge and Medicine Hat, this place, incorporated as a village from 1950 to 1996, was named in 1893 by the Canadian Pacific Railway after a nearby lake that had long since gone dry. The lake's name was known to the Blackfoot as *Moyi-kimi* ('grassy waters').

Grassy Narrows ON This location in Kenora District, northeast of Kenora, was named in 1960 after a thick growth of grass on the shore of **Grassy Narrows Lake**, an enlargement of the English River.

Grattan ON In 2001 this township became part of the township of Bonnechere, Renfrew County. It was named in 1851 after Henry Grattan (1746–1820), who promoted the independence of Ireland and encouraged the emancipation of Catholics.

Gravelbourg SK Southwest of Moose Jaw, this town (1916) was founded in 1906 by Fr. Louis-Joseph-Pierre Gravel (1868–1926) and four brothers: Dr. Henri Gravel, Sam Gravel (a member of the North West Mounted Police), Wilfred Gravel (a journalist), and Émile Gravel (the first postmaster in 1907). They promoted a colonization scheme to resettle Quebec and New England francophones in the West.

Gravenhurst ON This town (1887) on the southern end of Lake Muskoka in the district municipality of Muskoka was named in 1862 by William Dawson LeSueur (1840–1917). A secretary of the post office department, he took the name in reference to Gravenhurst in Washington Irving's novel, *Bracebridge Hall, or the Humorists* (1822).

Gray, Mount NB South of the Nepisiguit River, this mountain was named in 1964 by Arthur F. Wightman (1905–88), then the provincial names authority, after John Hamilton Gray (1814–89), a Father of Confederation and chief justice of the British Columbia supreme court, 1872–89.

Grayson SK Southeast of Melville, this village (1906) was first called *Nieven*. It was renamed in 1903 by the Canadian Pacific Railway after construction contractor Harry Grayson. Its post office opened the next year.

Great Bear Lake NT The largest lake (33,764 km²) entirely within Canada, and the fourth largest in North America, it was noted in 1783–4 by fur trader Peter Pond (1740–1807). The name derives from the river, which flows west for 90 km into the Mackenzie River. The river was then known to the Dene as *Sacschohetha*, in reference to the bears in the area.

Greater Sudbury ON This city is the largest incorporated city (2001) in area of 3300 km² in Canada. It has a population of 160,000. The official name in French is **Grand-Sudbury**. Timmins was the largest incorporated city in area of 3000 km² in Canada. The site of the city of **Sudbury** (1930) was named in 1883 by the Canadian Pacific Railway superintendent of construction James Worthington. It was given in honour of his wife's birthplace in Suffolk, England, west of Ipswich. **Sudbury District** was created from Nipissing District in 1894. In 1873 the regional municipality of **Sudbury** was severed from the district and divided into the city of Sudbury and the towns of Capreol, Nickel Centre, Valley East, Rayside-Balfour, Onaping Falls, and Walden. *See also* Sudbury.

Great Harbour Deep NL Located on the eastern coast of the Northern Peninsula, this municipal community (1971) was known to French fishermen as *Baie l'Orange*. A 1693 British marine chart labelled it *Harver Deep*. The harbour is surrounded on three sides by steep cliffs leading to the plateau of the Long Range Mountains.

Great Slave Lake NT The second-largest lake (27,048 km²) in Canada, it was known to Samuel Hearne (1745–92) as *Arabasca Lake* when he travelled to the mouth of the Coppermine River, 1770–2. The present name was noted on a map of John Franklin's 1819–22 expedition, and was named for the Slavey, an Athapascan tribe.

Great Village NS On the north side of Cobequid Bay and west of Truro, this place was the site of an Acadian settlement before 1755. Its post office opened in 1855. It may have been named because it was judged to be a great site to establish a village.

Greely ON In 2001 this community became a part of the city of Ottawa. It was named *Greeley* in 1885 after American explorer Adolphus Washington Greely (1844–1935), who sailed into the Canadian Arctic in the 1880s. It was correctly spelled Greely in 1903.

Greely Fiord NU On the western side of Ellesmere Island, this fiord was named in 1883 by Lt. James B. Lockwood after Adolphus Washington Greely (1844–1935), who led the United States Polar Year expedition to Ellesmere Island, 1881–4.

Greenfield Park QC In 2002 this city became a borough in the city of Longueuil. Created in 1911, this city in the regional county of Champlain, east of Montreal, was possibly named after its green and park-like surroundings, although it has also been suggested that its name was a translation of Parc des Prés-Verts.

Green Gables PE This name was given in 1953 to the post office in Cavendish. It was taken from the book *Anne of Green Gables*, published in 1908 by internationally acclaimed author Lucy Maud Montgomery.

Green Lake SK A village at the north end of **Green Lake** and northwest of Prince Albert. The Métis received a post office here in 1901. The lake was named after a water plant, whose leaves gave the lake a very green colour, especially in summer.

Green, Mount YT In the St. Cyr Range, south of Ross River, this mountain (2033 m) was named in 1951 after Lt. A.D. Green, who was killed in action during the Second World War.

Greenmount-Montrose PE Located between Alberton and Tignish, this municipal community (1977) comprises the localities of **Greenmount** and **Montrose**. The former had a post office from 1895 to 1914. The latter was named in 1864 by Donald McIntyre after Montrose, Angusshire, Scotland, and its post office was open from 1871 to 1913.

Greenock ON In 1999 this township became part the municipality of Brockton, Bruce County. It was named in 1850, possibly after Charles Cathcart, 2nd Earl Cathcart and 2nd Earl Greenock (1783–1859), who commanded the British forces in North America in the 1840s and administered the government of the Province of Canada for 14 months. His title was taken from the great Scottish seaport on the Firth of Clyde, northwest of Glasgow.

Green's Harbour NL On the eastern shore of Trinity Bay and southwest of Harbour Grace, this harbour was noted on maps as early as 1775. It has been speculated locally that the harbour may have been named after trees found here, providing lumber for boat building. It may, however, have been named after an English family.

Greenspond NL On **Greenspond Island**, and on the northwest side of Bonavista Bay, this town (1951) was settled by the Green and Pond families soon after 1697, with Thomas Green and Edward Pond listed here in 1800. The place is identified on Herman Moll's map of 1801.

Greenwich NS This community is located between Kentville and Wolfville. The post office here was named in 1857, possibly after Greenwich, CT. It was called *Port Williams Station* from 1870 to 1970 until the original name was restored.

Greenwood BC Canada's least populous city (656 in 2008), it was established by American prospectors as a mining community in 1895, and named after the Greenwood mining camp in Colorado, west of Pueblo. It was incorporated in 1897.

Greenwood NS In the Annapolis Valley, southwest of Kentville, this village (1961) was first known as *Greenwood Square*. Its post office opened in 1874 and closed in 1916. It reopened in 1966 after the closing of the *RCAF Station Greenwood* office.

Greenwood ON This location in the city of Pickering, Durham Region, was first called *Norwood* but was renamed in 1852 after miller Frederick Green.

Grenfell SK This town (1911) is located on the main Canadian Pacific Railway line east of Regina. The station and post office here were named in 1883 after CPR director Pascoe du Prés Grenfell (1828–96).

Grenfell Heights NL On the Exploits River, east of Grand Falls-Windsor, this place was developed in the 1960s. It was named after Sir Wilfred Thomason Grenfell (1865–1940), a Methodist medical missionary who served on the Labrador coast from 1892–6 and 1899–1939. Sir Wilfred Grenfell College in Corner Brook was named after him in 1975.

Grenville ON The county was named in 1792 after Lord William Wyndham Grenville (1759–1834), secretary of state for foreign affairs, 1791–1801. The municipality of the united counties of **Leeds and Grenville** was formed in 1852.

Grenville QC The township municipality of Grenville was created in 1845, abolished in 1847, and reinstated in 1855, taking its name from the township. **Grenville Township** was named in 1795 and proclaimed in 1808 after Lord George Grenville (1712–70), British prime minister, 1763–5. The village of **Grenville** was separated from the township municipality in 1876.

Grenville, Mount BC In the Coast Mountains, east of Bute Inlet, this mountain (3079 m) was named in 1933 by George G. Aitken (d.2007), provincial member of the Geographic Board of Canada, after Sir Richard Grenville (1542–91). Grenville had been granted the first English charter to create a settlement in the Pacific. He submitted a proposal to search for the Northwest Passage, a mission later undertaken by Sir Francis Drake.

Gretna MB This village (1896) on the North Dakota border, west of Emerson, is the site of a Canadian Pacific Railway station that was named in 1882 after Gretna Green, the place on the Scottish border noted for its many marriages of eloping couples. The post office here opened in 1884.

Grey ON The county was named in 1852 after Henry George Grey, 3rd Earl Grey (1802–94), secretary of state for war and the colonies, 1846–52. **Grey Township** in Huron County was named in 1848, either for Henry George Grey, 3rd Earl Grey, or for Charles Grey, 2nd Earl Grey (1764–1845), and prime minister of Great Britain, 1830–4.

Grey, Point BC West of Vancouver and extending into the Strait of Georgia, this point was named in 1792 by Capt. George Vancouver (1757–96) after Capt. Sir George Grey (1767–1828) of the Royal Navy. He commanded HMS *Victory*, Sir John Jervis's flagship at the Battle of St. Vincent in 1797. In 1791 Spanish Lt. Francisco Eliza named the point *Punta de Langara* after Spanish Adm. Langara (d.1806).

Grimsby ON The town (1921) in Niagara Region was named in 1816 after **Grimsby Township**. The township, originally in Lincoln County, was named in 1792 after the town of Grimsby in England's Lincolnshire. It was divided into the municipal townships of *North Grimsby* and *South Grimsby* in 1882. When the region was formed in 1970, *North Grimsby* was merged with the town of Grimsby, and *South Grimsby* was annexed by the municipal township of West Lincoln.

Grimshaw AB This town (1953) north of the Peace River and west of the town of Peace River was founded in 1921 by the Edmonton, Dunvegan, and British Columbia Railway. It was named in honour of Dr. Matthew William Edward Grimshaw (1880–1929), who established a medical practice in 1914 at Peace River and served as the mayor of that town in 1922.

Grinnell Peninsula NU The northwestern extension of Devon Island, this peninsula was named in 1851 by William Penny after Henry G. Grinnell (1799–1874), an American philanthropist. He fitted out two expeditions in 1850 and 1853 to search for Sir John Franklin (1786–1847).

Grise Fiord NU Located at the mouth of **Grise Fiord** and at the south end of Ellesmere Island, this hamlet (1987) is the farthest north of any permanent community in Canada. It was founded in 1953 by the government of Canada as a suitable location for the resettlement of impoverished Inuit on the eastern shore of Hudson Bay. It was named *Grisefjorden* by explorer Otto Sverdrup in 1899, with *grise* meaning 'pig' in Norwegian.

Gros Morne NL On the west coast of Newfoundland, this peak is one of the highest points (806 m) in the Long Range Mountains, and its name in French means 'great height'. The word *morne* may derive from the Spanish *morro* ('mound'). **Gros Morne National Park** (1943 km²) was established in 1970.

Grosse Île, La QC Located in the St. Lawrence River, southeast of Île d'Orléans, this small 3-km-long island gained notoriety from 1832 to 1937 as a quarantine station, where more than 10,000 immigrants, mostly Irish, died from cholera, typhus, and malnutrition. It was called *Île de Grâce* when it was ceded to Gov. Charles Huault de Montmagny in 1646. The name was transformed in 1662 into *Grosse-Île* in a reference to the seigneury of Noël Jérémie *dit* Lamontagne. In 1984 the island became a national historic site.

Grouard AB The post office in this place, located on the northwest side of Lesser Slave Lake, was first called *Lesser Slave Lake* in 1903. In 1909 it was renamed after Mgr. Émile-Jean-Marie Grouard (1840–1931), vicar apostolic of the diocese of Athabasca, 1890–1929. The adjacent community on the Freeman Indian Reserve is called **Grouard Mission**.

Grouse Mountain BC In the district municipality of North Vancouver, this mountain (1221 m) was named by a climbing party that shot a blue grouse here in 1894.

Guelph ON The city (1879) and the township were founded in 1827 by Canada Company general agent John Galt (1779–1839), who chose the name Guelph in honour of the royal family. The directors of the company wanted the name *Goderich*, after Lord Goderich, then the British prime minister. The conflict between Galt and the directors led to the erroneous story that the plans for Guelph and Goderich, on Lake Huron, had been switched.

Guernsey SK This village (1908) is located east of Saskatoon, near Lanigan. The post office here was named in 1907 after Guernsey, in the Channel Islands. Some of the street names recall places on the island of Guernsey. The Canadian Pacific Railway was built through the village in 1908.

Guillaume-Delisle, Lac QC Named in 1744 *Sir Atwell's Lake* after Hudson's Bay Company governor Sir Atwell Lake, this saltwater body (712 km²) was also known as *Winipeq*, *Artiwinipeck*, *Baie Winipeke*, *Golfe de Hazard*, *Golfe de Richmond*, and *Baie de Richmond* before it was officially named *Richmond Gulf* in 1905, a name of uncertain origin. In 1962 it was renamed after Guillaume Delisle (1675–1726), the great French map-maker, who was the first geographer to the King in 1718.

Gull Lake SK Southwest of Swift Current, this town (1911) was named in 1883 by the Canadian Pacific Railway. The nearby lake was named in 1879 by John Macoun, who provided agricultural advice to the CPR to justify the route chosen to cross the prairies. The name was a translation of the Cree *kiaskus*. The post office here opened in 1889.

Gunningsville NB In the town of Riverview, across the Peticodiac River from Moncton, Gunningsville was the name of a post office from 1910 to 1919 and 1939 to 1958. It was an incorporated village from 1966 to 1973. The first settler here was Hazen Gunning.

Guysborough NS At the head of Chedabucto Bay, this place was founded by disbanded troops and their families in 1784, and named after Sir Guy Carleton (1724–1808), who was then commander-in-chief of British forces in North America. The founders had settled the previous year at Port Mouton, in the southwestern part of the province, and called the place *Guysborough*, but moved to the eastern part of the province after it was wiped out by a fire. Postal service was established here in 1825. **Guysborough County** was created in 1836.

Gwaii Haanas National Park Reserve BC Located at the south end of Moresby Island of the Queen Charlotte Islands, this park (1470 km²) was established as the *South Moresby National Park Reserve* in 1988 to preserve its wilderness and ancient Haida cedar villages. It was called *South Moresby/ Gwaii Haanas National Park Reserve* the following year, and the present name was confirmed in 1993. In Haida the name means 'islands of wonder and beauty'.

Gypsumville MB This place between Lake Manitoba and Lake Winnipeg was the site of a gypsum mine in 1890, but it did not develop as a community until the post office opened in 1905 and the Canadian Northern Railway was built to it in 1912.

Hafford SK East of North Battleford, this town (1981) was established in 1912–13 by the Canadian Northern Railway, and may have been named after a survey engineer, who later died in an accident in Blaine Lake. *Redberry* post office had been opened on 1 September 1906, but it was changed to *Luxemburg* on 1 December 1906. There is another story about how Hafford received its name. In 1913 the CNR offered farmer Henry Francis Hudek (1879–1959) $20 an acre for his land but he could not afford to sell it at that price. A land agent took the word 'afford' and combined with the first letter of Hudek's name.

Hagar ON In 1999 Hagar Township became part of the municipality of Markstay-Warren. The township's name was given in 1882 for Albert Hagar (1827–1924), Liberal member for Prescott in the Ontario Legislature, 1880–6. The Hager post office was named in 1927.

Hague SK Established in 1890 by the Canadian Pacific Railway, this village (1903) was named after bridge and railway engineer Jenkins Harry Hague (d.1962) during a meeting of CPR railway engineers in Prince Albert. The line became part of the Canadian Northern Railway in 1906 and of the Canadian National Railways in 1923. Its post office opened in 1896.

Ha! Ha!, Baie des QC Appearing as though it is an extension of the impressive Saguenay fiord, this bay east of Chicoutimi comes to an abrupt end only 10 km above the point where the Saguenay appears to divide in two rivers of equal size. *Haha* is an old French word describing an unexpected barrier blocking progress or penetration. At the head of this bay are two coves that give the illusion of leading to other waterways, thus explaining its plural form. The exclamation marks came about when surveyors, historians, and others presumed in the nineteenth century that the phrase represented a shriek of surprise by travellers. *See also* Saint-Louis-du-Ha! Ha!.

Haileybury ON This town (1904) in Timiskaming District, was named in 1889 by developer Charles C. Farr after the exclusive Haileybury public school in Hertfordshire, England. In 2004 the towns of New Liskeard and Haileybury, with the township of Dymond, became the city of Temiskaming Shores.

Haines Junction YT At the junction of the Haines and Alaska highways, this village was created in 1942, when the Alaska Highway was connected with Haines, AK, on Lynn Canal, an extension of the Pacific Ocean. The Alaska village was named about 1881 by Presbyterian missionary S. Hall Young after Francine E. Haines, secretary of the Committee of Home Missions.

Haldimand ON The county was named in 1783 after Sir Frederick Haldimand (1718–91), a native of Switzerland and a British Army officer, who was governor of Quebec from 1778 to 1786. The county was united in 1974 with Norfolk County to form the regional municipality of **Haldimand-Norfolk**. The town of **Haldimand** was also formed in 1974 by merging the town of Caledonia, the villages of Cayuga and Hagersville, the municipal townships of North Cayuga, Oneida, Seneca, and South Cayuga, and parts of the municipal townships of Rainham and Walpole. **Haldimand Township**, in Northumberland County, was named in 1792 after Sir Frederick Haldimand.

Haliburton ON The community in **Haliburton County** was named in 1864 after Nova Scotia humorist Thomas Chandler Haliburton (1796–1865), who had been a judge of the Nova Scotia Supreme Court. He had moved to England in 1842 and in 1859 he was elected to the British House of Commons. He was also appointed chairman of the London-based Canadian Land and Emigration Company, which in 1861 bought a million acres in central Canada West, embracing nine townships. The county was created as a provisional county in 1874 and did not achieve full county status until 1983.

Halifax NS Originally incorporated as a city in 1841 on the west side of **Halifax Harbour**, it became the regional municipality of Halifax in 1996, embracing all of the former municipal county of Halifax, extending east to Ecum Secum Bridge and west to Hubbards. It was named in June 1749 by Gov. Edward Cornwallis after George Montagu Dunk, 2nd Earl of Halifax (1716–71), then British secretary of the southern department. In July of that year the seat of Nova Scotia government was moved here from Annapolis Royal. During the French regime the harbour was called *Chebucto* from the Mi'kmaq *chebookt* ('great long harbour').

Halkirk AB East of Stettler, this village (1912) was named in 1910 by pioneer settlers from a list provided by the Canadian Pacific Railway. It was named after Halkirk, Caithness, Scotland, south of Thurso.

Hall Beach NU This hamlet (1978) on the eastern side of Melville Peninsula was founded in 1970. It took its name from nearby **Hall Lake**. The lake (474 km²) was named by the Fifth Thule expedition in 1921–4 after Charles Francis Hall (1821–71), who explored the area, 1864–9.

Hallowell ON In 1998 this township became part of the municipality of Prince Edward County. The township was named in 1797 after Benjamin Hallowell (1724–99), a Loyalist who had been granted 486 ha (1200 a) at the head of Picton Bay. He lived in England until his son-in-law, John Elmsley, became chief justice of Upper Canada in 1796, when he joined the Elmsley family in York (Toronto) in 1797 and died there two years later.

Hall Peak BC Located in the Purcell Mountains, northeast of Kaslo, this mountain (3040 m) was named in 1961 after Canadian Army private John H. Hall of Marysville, BC, who was killed in action on 24 May 1945.

Hall Peninsula NU On the east side of Baffin Island and northeast of Iqaluit, this 280-km peninsula was named by the Geographic Board in 1901 after Christopher Hall, the master of the vessel *Gabriel* during the 1576 voyage by Sir Martin Frobisher. Frobisher had named *Hall Island* in Frobisher Bay in 1576 and this was endorsed by the board in 1928. It was changed to **Christopher Hall Island** in 1961.

Hallville ON In 1998 this community became part of the township of North Dundas, united counties of Stormont, Dundas, and Glengarry. This place was named in 1879 after the hall of the local lodge of the Orange Order.

Halton ON The county was named in 1816 after Maj. William Halton (d.1821), secretary to Lt.-Gov. Francis Gore, 1806–11 and 1815–7. In 1974 it became the regional municipality of **Halton**. The town of **Halton Hills** in Halton Region was created in 1974 by amalgamating the towns of Georgetown and Acton, most of the municipal township of Esquesing, and a small part of the town of Oakville.

Halvorson, Mount BC In the Cariboo Mountains, west of McBride, this mountain (2782 m) was named in 1965 after Tpr. Frank Halvorson of McBride, who was killed in action on 29 October 1944.

Hamill, Mount BC In the Purcell Mountains, northeast of Kaslo, this mountain (3243 m) was named in 1911 after prospector Thomas Hamill. Hamill was murdered in 1885 by Robert Evan Sproule, a fellow prospector who accused him of jumping his claim. Sproule was hanged the following year in Victoria.

Hamilton ON The city (1846) was founded and named by George Hamilton, a native of Queenston and the son of Robert Hamilton (1787–1851), the founder of the city of St. Catharines. He represented Wentworth in the House of Assembly of Upper Canada from 1820 to 1830. **Hamilton Harbour** was proclaimed *Burlington Bay* in 1792 by Lt.-Gov. John Graves Simcoe (1752–1806), but by provincial Order-in-Council in 1919, it was renamed Hamilton Harbour. The high-level bridge carrying the Queen Elizabeth Way over the harbour entrance is called the Burlington Bay James N. Allan Skyway, retaining its original designation, and adding the name of a former provincial minister of highways. In 2001 Hamilton amalgamated in the regional municipality of Hamilton-Wentworth of the city of Stoney Creek, the towns of Ancaster, Dundas and Flamborough, and the township of Glanbrook to become a much larger city of Hamilton.

Hamilton ON This township in Northumberland County was named in 1792 after Henry Hamilton (c.1734–96), lieutenant-governor of Quebec, 1781–5, and administrator of British North America, 1784–5. Subsequently, he was governor of Bermuda, where the capital bears his name. Fort Henry at Kingston was also named for him.

Hamilton Inlet NL This extended entrance (212 km to the head of Lake Melville) into the coast of Labrador was named after Sir Charles Hamilton (1767–1849), governor of Newfoundland, 1818–24. Earlier, the inlet was called in French *Baie des Esquimaux*, *Baie des Sauvages*, and *Baie Saint-Louis*. Churchill River, which flows into the inlet, was officially called *Hamilton River* until 1965. **Hamilton Sound**, between Fogo Island and Newfoundland, was also named after Sir Charles Hamilton.

Hamiota MB Situated northwest of Brandon, the post office at this village (1906) was first called *Hamilton* in 1882 after first postmaster Thomas Hamilton, but confusion with the Ontario city prompted the selection of another name. In devising a new postal name in 1884, Hamilton may have been inspired by the rural municipality of Miniota, 30 km to the west, which was named in 1883 from the Sioux words for 'plenty' and 'water'.

Hammond, Mount BC In the Purcell Mountains, southwest of Invermere, this mountain (3368 m) was named in 1910 by mine developer Charles Ellis after Toronto financier Herbert Carlyle Hammond (1844–1909).

Hampden NL At the head of White Bay, northeast of Deer Lake, this municipal community (1959) was known as *Riverhead* before 1911. It may have been named after Hampden House in Buckinghamshire, England, built by Member of Parliament John Hampden (c.1595–1643).

Hampshire PE The post office of this municipal community (1974) northwest of Charlottetown was named in 1897, probably after the English county.

Hampstead QC In 2002 this town became a part of the city of Montreal, but regained its town status in 2006. It was developed at the beginning of the First World War, although by 1932 it only had a population of less than 800. The name was inspired by the wealthy district northwest of the centre of London, England.

Hampton NB The first post office in this village (1966) on the Kennebecasis River, northeast of Saint John, opened in 1831. It was named after **Hampton Parish**, created in 1795 and possibly called after Hampton, southwest of London, England. In 1859 its European and North American Railway station was named *Ossekeag* after the Ossekeag River. It was renamed *Hampton Station* in 1916.

Haney BC Situated in the district municipality of Maple Ridge and on the north bank of the Fraser River, the post office here was named in 1936 after Thomas Haney (1841–1916), who had settled in 1876. In its early years it was known as *Haney's Landing*. *Port Haney* post office was also opened in 1936 and was renamed Maple Ridge in 1970.

Hanley SK Located south of Saskatoon, this town (1906) was established in 1890 by the Qu'Appelle, Long Lake and Saskatchewan Railway and Steamboat Company, and became part of Canadian Northern Railway in 1906. Postal service was provided here in 1903. The source of Hanley's name is a village on the north side of the city of Stoke-on-Trent, Staffordshire, England.

Hanmer ON Gilbert Hanmer moved north from Brant County about 1900 and settled in what is now the town of Valley East, north of Sudbury. Hanmer post office opened in 1904. In 2001 Hanmer and Valley East became part of the city of Greater Sudbury.

Hanna AB This town (1914) northeast of Calgary was named in 1913 by the Canadian Northern Railway after David Blythe Hanna (1858–1938), then third vice-president of the railway. After the Canadian government bought the railway in 1918, he became the first president of the Canadian National Railways, 1918–22.

Hanover ON This town (1904) in Grey County was first known as *Buck's Crossing* and *Adamstown*. Most residents disliked *Adamstown*, so in 1856 first postmaster Abraham Gottwals proposed Hanover, because many of the first settlers came from the area of Germany now known as Hanover.

Hansen ON This township in Sudbury District, southwest of Sudbury, was named in 1986 after Rick Hansen, whose Man in Motion world tour focused on the need for research into spinal cord injuries. It had been named *Stalin Township* during the Second World War after Joseph Stalin, whose perceived villainy led to a unanimous vote in the Ontario Legislature to change it.

Hants NS This county in central Nova Scotia was named in 1781 after the colloquial name of England's Hampshire. For municipal purposes, it is divided into the districts of **East Hants** and **West Hants**.

Hants Harbour NL On the east shore of Trinity Bay and north of Carbonear, this town (1970) was named after the harbour, which was identified in the 1697 report by Abbé Jean Baudoin as *Lance arbe* and *Anse Arbre* ('tree cove'). By 1775 it had become known by its present name.

Hantsport NS This town (1895) on the west side of the Avon River, north of Windsor, was first called *Halfway River*, as it was midway between *Pisiquid* (Windsor) and Grand Pré. It was named in 1849 by Ezra Churchill, because it was the chief seaport of Hants County. Postal service was established here that year.

Happy Adventure NL This municipal community (1960) on **Happy Adventure Bay** may have been named after an incident when a fishing ship eluded pirates in the adjacent maze of channels and coves. The place was first recorded in the 1869 census of the province.

Happy Valley-Goose Bay NL This town at the mouth of the Churchill River was incorporated in 1974 by amalgamating the town of **Happy Valley** (1961) and the local improvement district of **Goose Bay** (1970). In 1941 an airport had been established at Goose Bay, at the river's mouth, to provide a shorter transatlantic link with the British Isles. Happy Valley, a name suggesting pleasure and contentment, was created as the residential community of *Refugee Cove* in 1942, and was renamed in 1955.

Harbour Breton NL On the south coast of Newfoundland and on the north side of Fortune Bay, this town (1952) was likely named after fishermen from Bretagne, France in the 1600s, although it was also noted as *Havre Bertrand* during those years.

Harbour Grace NL This town (1945) on the west side of Conception Bay was named after its harbour, called *Havre de Grâce* by the French in the 1600s. It was likely named after the earliest name of Le Havre, at the mouth of the Seine, in France, which François I created as the port of *Havre de Grâce* in 1517. The English form of the name came into use as early as 1681.

Harbour Main-Chapel Cove-Lakeview NL Near the head of Conception Bay, this town (1964) comprises three separate built-up centres. **Harbour Main**, which occurred on a 1630s map as *Harbour Maine*, may have been called after a French family surname. **Chapel Cove**, which was first noted in the 1830s, may have been given for an English surname, either Chappel or Chapple. **Lakeview** was developed inland in the 1930s on the west side of First Pond, Second Pond, and Third Pond.

Harcourt NB This place was named in 1869 when the Intercolonial Railway was built northwest of Moncton. It was called after **Harcourt Parish**, named in 1826 after William Harcourt, 3rd Earl of Harcourt (1743–1830), field marshal of British forces in 1820, and a friend of Lt.-Gov. Sir Howard Douglas (1776–1861). The post office here was named *Weldford* in 1871 after Weldford Parish, and was called Harcourt in 1894.

Hardisty AB Southwest of Wainwright, this town (1911) was named in 1906 by the Canadian Pacific Railway after Richard Charles Hardisty (c.1832–89), the last chief factor of the Hudson's Bay Company at Fort Edmonton, 1872–88. Appointed to the Senate in 1888 by Sir John A. Macdonald (1815–91), he died the next year in Winnipeg after being accidentally thrown from his buggy at Broadview, SK.

Hardwicke Island BC Between Vancouver Island and the mainland, and north of Campbell River, this island was named in 1792 by Capt. George Vancouver (1757–98) after Philip Yorke, 3rd Earl of Hardewicke (1757–1834), lord lieutenant of Ireland, 1801–04, and promoter of Catholic emancipation. He encouraged the naval career of Spelman Swaine, Vancouver's master's mate on the *Discovery*.

Hare Bay NL This town (1964) on the northwestern side of Bonavista Bay was possibly named in the 1860s, when a trapper caught hares in the rabbit snare he had set. There is also a **Hare Bay** on the northeastern side of the Northern Peninsula. It was identified on seventeenth century French maps as *B. aux Lievres* ('bay of hares'), with Hare Bay occurring on several eighteenth-century maps.

Harkin, Mount BC In the Rocky Mountains, northeast of Invermere, this mountain (2938 m) was named in 1923 by surveyor Morrison Bridgland (1878–1948) after James Bernard Harkin (1875–1955), Dominion Commissioner of Parks, 1911–36.

Haro Strait BC The main channel uniting the Strait of Georgia to Juan de Fuca Strait, this strait was named *Canal de Lopez de Aro* in 1790 by SLt. Manuel Quimper (c.1757–1844)

after his first mate on the captured British vessel *Princess Royal*, Gonzalez Lopez de Haro. The present form was adopted by the British Admiralty, possibly on the recommendation of Capt. George Richards (1820–96) in 1859.

Harper, Mount YT In the Ogilvie Mountains, northwest of Dawson, this mountain (1874 m) was named in 1887–8 by surveyor William Ogilvie (1849–1912) after Arthur 'Cariboo' Harper (1835–98), one of the earliest (1873–4) prospectors in the Yukon.

Harricana, Rivière QC Rising just west of the city of Val-d'Or, this river flows north for 480 km to James Bay, crossing the Ontario border 30 km above its mouth, where it becomes the **Harricanaw River**. In Algonquin the name means 'river of biscuits', in reference to the hardtack carried by exploration parties and troops.

Harris SK The post office at this village (1909) southwest of Saskatoon was originally established 3 km to the north in the home of Richard Harris in 1906. Harris had arrived here from Huron County, ON, two years earlier. When the Canadian Northern Railway passed through in 1908, the post office was moved to the rail line.

Harris, Mount AB North of Lake Louise, this mountain (3299 m) was named in 1957 after L. Edward Harris, a surveyor with the Topographical Survey of Canada, who had climbed the mountain in 1919.

Harris, Mount BC On the British Columbia–Alaska boundary and in the Coast Mountains, this mountain (1948 m) was named by the United States Geographic Board in 1923, and by the Geographic Board of Canada in 1924, after Dennis R. Harris (1851–1932), who participated in the survey of the boundary in 1904. He was a son-in-law of Sir James Douglas (1803–77), a chief trader of the Hudson's Bay Company, the second governor of Vancouver Island, and the first governor of British Columbia.

Harrison Hot Springs BC The post office in this village (1949) at the south end of Harrison Lake, northeast of Chilliwack, was named in 1889. In 1828 Hudson's Bay Company governor Sir George Simpson (1787–1860) named the lake after Benjamin Harrison, then a director of the company, and later its deputy governor, 1835–9.

Harrison, Mount BC In the southern Rocky Mountains, this mountain (3359 m) was named in 1964 after PO Francis A. Harrison of Cranbrook, who was killed 14 October 1944 while serving overseas.

Harriston ON In 1998 this town (1878) became a part of the town of Minto, Wellington County. Its post office was named in 1856 after miller Archibald Harrison and first postmaster Joshua Harrison.

Harrow ON In 1999 this town (1930) became part of the town of Essex, Essex County. It was named in 1857 by John O'Connor (1824–87), a member of Parliament, 1867–82, and postmaster-general, 1873–82. It was named after the exclusive public school in Harrow, within Greater London, England, northwest of the city of London.

Hartland NB The post office in this town (1918) on the east bank of the Saint John River, north of Woodstock, was first called *Beckaguimeck* in 1852, and changed the following year to *Becaguimic*, both after the adjacent Becaguimec Stream. It was renamed Hartland in 1868, possibly for its central location in Carleton County, although claims have been made for James R. Hartley, a member of the Legislative Assembly, and the Reverend Samuel Hartt.

Hartney MB The post office in this town (1905) in the Souris River valley, southwest of Brandon, was named in 1885 after postmaster and farmer James H. Hartney. He was later an immigration agent in Toronto.

Harvey NB This village (1966) southwest of Fredericton was named in 1837 by Andrew Inches after Sir John Harvey (1777–1852), lieutenant-governor of New Brunswick, 1837–41). Its post office was named in 1842, but was closed in 1873, because of confusion with **Harvey** in Albert County. **Harvey Station** post office in the village had been opened in 1870. **Harvey Mountain** (260 m) is 5 km north of the village. **Harvey Lake** and **Second Harvey Lake** are just west of the village.

Harvey ON In 1998 this township became a part of the township of **Galway–Cavendish and Harvey**, Peterborough County. The township was named in 1821 for Sir John Harvey (1778–1852), who had a distinguished military career, including service in Upper Canada during the War of 1812. Between 1836 and 1852, he served as lieutenant-governor of Prince Edward Island, New Brunswick, and Nova Scotia, as well as governor of Newfoundland.

Harwich ON In 1998 this township became a part of the municipality of Chatham-Kent, Kent County. It was named in 1794 after the town of Harwich in Sussex, England, on the North Sea coast.

Hastings ON The county was named in 1792 after Francis Rawdon-Hastings, Baron Rawdon, Earl of Moira (1754–1826), who became the Marquess of Hastings in 1817.

Hastings ON This village (1874) on the Trent River and in Northumberland County was named in 1851 by miller Henry

Fowlds after Flora Muir Campbell, the Countess of Loudoun (1780–1840), wife of the Marquess of Hastings. In 2001 the village became part of the municipality of Trent Hills.

Havelock ON This village (1892) in Peterborough County and east of the city of Peterborough was named in 1859 after Sir Henry Havelock, who fought with distinction in various wars in Asia. During the Sepoy Mutiny in India in 1857, Havelock was besieged at Lucknow. A township in Haliburton County was also named for him in 1872.

Havre-aux-Maisons QC The post office in this location, a municipality since 1875 in the regional county of Les Îles-de-la-Madeleine, was called *House Harbour* from 1870 to 1964, when it was changed to its present name, taken from the name of the island. In the eighteenth century the island had been called *Allright* and *Alright*, and in the nineteenth century it was known as *Saunders*, after Adm. Charles Saunders (1713–75), who accompanied Gen. James Wolfe (1727–59) to the capture of Quebec City in 1759.

Havre Boucher NS East of Antigonish, the site of this village (1960) was occupied in the winter of 1759 by Capt. François Boucher, according to an 1812 report by Mgr. Joseph-Octave Plessis. In 1785 John and Paul Bushee were reported as being here and in 1811 Paul Boucher was recorded as living at *Havre au Bouchee*. The post office was called *Harbour Au Bouche* in 1854, and was renamed Havre Boucher in 1909.

Havre-Saint-Pierre QC Located 200 km east of Sept-Îles, this municipality was settled in the 1850s by Acadian families from the Îles de la Madeleine. Incorporated as *Pointe-aux-Esquimaux* in 1873, it was renamed Havre-Saint-Pierre in 1927, three years after *Esquimaux Point* post office had been changed to reflect the importance of the place's harbour and the name of its religious parish.

Hawke's Bay NL At the head of Ingornachoix Bay and on the northwestern coast of the Northern Peninsula, this town (1956) was called after the adjacent bay. The bay was named in 1767 by Capt. James Cook (1728–79) after Adm. Edward Hawke, 1st Baron Hay (1705–81). Two years later Cook assigned the same name on the east coast of New Zealand's North Island.

Hawkesbury ON This town (1896) in the united counties of Prescott and Russell was first known as *Hawkesbury Mills* and *Hamilton's Mills* before Hawkesbury post office was named in 1819. The original **Hawkesbury Township** was created in 1798, and named either for Charles Jenkinson, Baron Hawkesbury and Lord Liverpool (1727–1808), or for his son, Robert Banks Jenkinson (1770–1828), who as Lord Liverpool, was prime minister of Great Britain, 1812–27. *See also* East Hawkesbury *and* West Hawkesbury.

Hay ON In 2001 this township became part of the municipality of Bluewater, Huron County. It was named in 1835 after R.W. Hay, then a joint secretary of state for the colonies. The other secretary of state was Lord Stanley, after whom the adjacent Stanley Township was named.

Hayes Peak YT On the west side of Teslin Lake, southwest of Whitehorse, this peak (1849 m) was named in 1897 by surveyor Arthur St. Cyr after Dr. Charles Willard Hayes (1859–1916). A geologist with the United States Geological Survey, Hayes explored southwestern Yukon in 1891 with US Army Lt. Frederick Schwatka (1849–92).

Hayes River MB Rising in Molson Lake, northeast of Norway House, this river flows 420 km northeast into Hudson Bay, just east of the mouth of the Nelson. Its lowest part was named by Pierre Radisson (1636–1710) in 1684 after Sir James Hayes (c.1676–1731), Prince Rupert's secretary and a charter member of the Hudson's Bay Company. In 1901 the name was extended to its head.

Hay Lakes AB The post office in this village (1928) southeast of Edmonton was named in 1913 after nearby lakes, known in Cree as *Apichikoo Obiwas* ('little swamp'). The lush grass of such lakes was called 'prairie wool' by the pioneer settlers.

Hay River NT Originally established on Vale Island at the mouth of **Hay River**, the centre of the town (1980) was moved 6 km upriver to its present site, after severe flooding in 1963. The river (702 km), identified on an Arrowsmith map of 1854, was called after grass along its banks.

Hazelton BC This village (1956) at the north side of the junction of the Skeena and Bulkley Rivers was developed in 1871 by Edgar Dewdney (1835–1916), and named by Thomas Hankin when he found a large amount of hazelnuts ripening. A post office opened in 1899. **South Hazelton**, on the south side of the junction, received its own postal service in 1923. The district municipality of **New Hazelton** (1980) is located east of Hazelton, in the Bulkley River valley. New Hazelton post office opened here in 1912.

Hazen, Lake NU In northern Ellesmere Island, this lake (537 km²) was named in 1882 by explorer Adolphus Greely (1844–1935) after Gen. William Babcock Hazen (1830–87), chief signals officer of the United States Army, 1880–7.

Hazen Strait NT, NU Between Melville and Mackenzie King Islands, this strait was named in 1917 by Vilhjalmur Stefansson (1879–1962) after Sir John Douglas Hazen (1860–1937), who was then the minister of both the marine and fisheries and of the naval service.

Headingley MB This rural municipality west of Winnipeg was united with Winnipeg from 1972 to 1992. It was named about 1853 by the Reverend Griffith Owen Corbett after his former parish in Leeds, West Yorkshire, England. *Headingly* post office opened in 1871. In 1951 the name was respelled Headingley.

Head-Smashed-In Buffalo Jump AB West of Fort Macleod, this provincial historic site and interpretative centre is designated a UNESCO World Heritage Site. Buffalo jumps were part of the ancient hunting culture of Plains Aboriginals. This particular one recalls the story of a curious Aboriginal warrior who was trapped on a ledge as the buffalo plunged over the jump, and was subsequently found with his skull crushed.

Hearst ON In Cochrane District and at the point where the main line of the Canadian National Railways meets the Algoma Central Railway, this town (1922) was founded shortly after 1900. First named *Grant*, it was renamed in 1912 after Sir William Howard Hearst (1864–1941), minister of lands, forests and mines, 1911–4, and premier of Ontario, 1914–9.

Heart's Content NL Located on the eastern shore of Trinity Bay and northwest of Carbonear, this town (1967) was identified by John Guy (d.1629) in 1612 as *Hartes content*, and by Abbé Jean Baudoin in 1697 as *Havre-Content*. Its name may have been given by English fishermen either after a ship or as a place of relaxation and protection from stormy seas.

Heart's Delight-Islington NL This town (1972) on the eastern shore of Trinity Bay and west of Carbonear comprises the separate communities of **Heart's Delight** and **Islington**. Heart's Delight may have been named in the early 1800s, because the first settlers to arrive were delighted with its beauty. First known as *Island Cove*, Islington was named in 1911, possibly after the district in London, England.

Heart's Desire NL This local improvement district on the eastern shore of Trinity Bay and west of Carbonear was named in the 1700s, possibly because its pleasant site fulfilled the 'desires' of its first settlers.

Hebbville NS Southwest of Bridgewater, this village (1975) may have been named after pioneer settler John George Hebb. George, Adam, and Nicholas Hebb bought land here in 1805. Its post office opened in 1913. **Hebbs Cross**, 7 km to the southwest, had a post office in 1873.

Hébertville QC This municipality east of Lac Saint-Jean was created in 1859 and named after Nicolas-Tolentin Hébert (1810–88), who led settlers here from Kamouraska in 1849 and founded the parish of Notre-Dame-d'Hébertville in 1857. The village of **Hébertville-Station**, 3 km to the north, was incorporated in 1903, eight years after its post office had been opened.

Hebron NS Located north of Yarmouth, this place was developed around a house built by pioneer settler and shoemaker Anthony Landers, and named by him after the biblical Hebron. Postal service was established here in 1838.

Hecate Strait BC Separating the Queen Charlotte Islands from the mainland, this water body was named about 1862 by Capt. George Richards (1820–96) after his Royal Navy survey ship *Hecate*, which he commanded in 1861 and 1862.

Hector, Mount AB North of Lake Louise, this mountain (3394 m) was named in 1884 by geologist George M. Dawson (1849–1901) after Dr. Sir James Hector (1834–1907), the surgeon and geologist with the Palliser Expedition, 1857–60. Hector named many geographical features in Western Canada, including Castle Mountain and Kicking Horse Pass. He headed the Geological Survey of New Zealand from 1865 to 1903.

Hedley BC In the Similkameen River valley, east of Princeton, this place was named in 1898 by prospector Peter Scott after Robert R. Hedley, manager of the Hall Mines smelter at Nelson. Hedley had provided financial help to Scott to stake some of the earliest claims in the area of the community. The post office here opened in 1903.

Heisler AB A village (1961) southeast of Camrose, its post office was named in 1915 after pioneer settler Martin Heisler.

Hemmingford QC Located south of Montreal, near the New York state border, the municipal township of Hemmingford was established in 1845. It took its name from **Hemmingford Township**, proclaimed in 1799, and named after Hemingford in Huntingdonshire, England, northwest of Cambridge. The village of **Hemmingford** was separated from the township municipality in 1878.

Henrietta Maria, Cape ON The point where the west side of James Bay meets Hudson Bay was named in 1631 by explorer Thomas James (c.1593–1635) after his ship the *Henrietta Maria*, which was named after the wife of Charles I of England.

Henryville QC Situated east of the Richelieu, and south of Saint-Jean-sur-Richelieu, this village's post office was called *Saint-Georges* in 1827, taking its name from the Anglican parish of St. George, established in 1794 and named after George III. The office was renamed Henryville in 1927. The parish municipality of *Saint-Georges*, established in the 1840s, was called **Henryville** in 1957. In 1815 Napier Christie Burton, the seigneur of Noyan, appointed Edmund Henry (1760–1841) to develop his lands on both sides of the Richelieu.

Hensall ON In 2001 this village (1896) became part of the municipality of Bluewater, Huron County. Its post office was named in 1876 after Hensall in West Yorkshire, England. Brothers George and James Petty had migrated from that place, southeast of Leeds, in 1851.

Hepburn SK North of Saskatoon, this village (1919) was named about 1908, when the Canadian Northern Railway was built from Dalmeny to Carlton. Gordon Hepburn gave 16 ha (40 a) for the village centre. Rowat Hepburn was the first postmaster of the post office in 1909.

Hepworth ON In 1999 this village (1907) became part of the town of South Bruce Peninsula, Bruce County, northwest of Owen Sound. It was named in 1866 after Epworth in Lincolnshire, England, 40 km southwest of Kingston upon Hull, which was the birthplace of John Wesley, the founder of Methodism. The Reverend Josias Greene proposed the name, and prominent resident William Plows's mispronunciation resulted in Hepworth.

Herbert SK East of Swift Current, this town (1912) was founded by the Canadian Pacific Railway in 1883 and named after English diplomat Sir Michael Henry Herbert (1857–1903). Its post office was established in 1904.

Hermitage-Sandyville NL On the south coast of Newfoundland and northwest of Harbour Breton, this municipal community (1963) comprises **Hermitage**, a settlement on **Hermitage Bay**, and **Sandyville**, a second settlement on Connaigre Bay. Hermitage Bay was possibly named by Channel Islands fishermen, who perceived that a small island in the bay resembled the Hermitage, an island outside the port of St. Helier, Jersey. Sandyville was first called *Dawson's Cove*, noted by Capt. James Cook (1728–79) in 1765 as *Dawsson's Cove*. There is a wide sandy beach at the head of Sandyville's harbour.

Herring Cove NS The post office of this place south of Halifax was named in 1875 after the cove. The cove was identified as *Ance du Hareng* on a 1779 French marine chart. In 1779 Charles Morris Sr. (1711–81) showed it on a map as *Dunk alias Herring Cove*. He may have named it after George Montagu Dunk, 2nd Earl of Halifax (1716–71), who had been British secretary of state for the southern department when Halifax was founded.

Herschel Island YT Off the north coast of Yukon, this island was named in 1826 by Sir John Franklin (1786–1847) after Sir William Herschel (1738–1822), the noted British astronomer.

Hewitt Bostock, Mount BC In the Cascade Mountains, southwest of Merritt, this mountain (2179 m) was named in 1932 by Charles Taggart after Hewitt Bostock (1864–1930), a Cambridge graduate who had settled on a ranch east of Kamloops in 1893 and was elected to the House of Commons three years later. Appointed to the Senate in 1904, he served as both its Liberal leader and speaker.

Hibbert ON In 1998 this township became a part of the township of West Perth, Perth County. It was named in 1830 after William T. Hibbert Jr., a director of the Canada Company. This British company was established in 1826 to develop the Huron Tract, a large area of what is now Southwestern Ontario.

Hibbs Cove NL This small fishing centre on Bay de Grave, northeast of Bay Roberts, was founded in the mid-1700s as *Hibbs Hole*. It may have been named a century earlier for Thomas Hibbs, one of the earliest settlers in Conception Bay. Although the word 'hole' has been long established in the English language as a small cove, it acquired an indelicate connotation in the twentieth century. The name was changed to Hibbs Cove in 1969.

Hickman's Harbour NL On the southern side of Random Island and on Random Sound, an inlet on the western side of Trinity Bay, this place's harbour may have been named in 1770 by Capt. James Cook (1728–79) after Jonathan Hickman (1747–1847), the pilot of Cook's survey vessel in Trinity Bay.

Hickson, Mount BC In the Coast Mountains, north of Mount Waddington, this mountain (3170 m) was named in 1928 by Walter Alfred (Don) Munday (1890–1950) after climber J.W.A. Hickson.

Highgate ON In 1998 this village (1917) became part of the municipality Chatham-Kent, Kent County. It was named in 1865 after Highgate in north central London, England.

High Level AB This town (1965), located in northwestern Alberta and at the height of land separating the Peace and Hay Rivers, had its post office named in 1958. Its site was known to the Slavey as *Tloc-Moi* ('hay meadow').

High Prairie AB This town (1950) west of Lesser Slave Lake was first known as *Prairie River*. Its post office was named in 1910, five years before the Edmonton, Dunvegan and British Columbia Railway arrived.

High River AB Located on the **Highwood River**, south of Calgary, this town (1906) was first called *The Crossing*. It was named High River by the Canadian Pacific Railway in 1892. The river's name, identified as *High Woods River* by Thomas Blakiston (1832–91) in 1858, was a translation of Blackfoot *ispitsi* ('tall timbers'), in reference to the trees along its banks that were taller than those found along rivers flowing from the Rocky Mountain Foothills.

Hillier ON In 1998 this township became part of the municipality of Prince Edward County. It was named in 1824 after Maj. George Hillier (d.1840), aide-de-camp and secretary to Lt.-Gov. Sir Peregrine Maitland (1777–1854).

Hillsborough NB The post office in this village (1966) on the west bank of the Petitcodiac River, southeast of Moncton, opened in 1842 and was named after **Hillsborough Parish**. The parish, named in 1786, was created as a township the year before, and called after Wills Hill, Earl of Hillsborough (1718–93), then lord commissioner of trade and plantations.

Hillsborough River PE Rising at the community of **Head of Hillsborough**, southwest of Morell, this river flows into **Hillsborough Bay**, on the south side of Charlottetown. The names of the river and the bay were given in 1765 by Samuel Holland (1728–1801) after Wills Hill, Earl of Hillsborough (1718–93), lord commissioner of trade and plantations, 1763–6. The French knew the river as *Rivière du Nord-Est*. It has been commonly called the *East River* during the twentieth century, as a counterpoint to the North and West Rivers.

Hillsdale NL Located between Witless Bay and Cape Broyle on the Avalon Peninsula, this place was originally called *Brigus South*. The roots of that name may be traced to a 1636 map, where its harbour is identified as *Abra de Brigas*, likely a Portuguese description of its rough waters. Because of confusion with Brigus in Conception Bay, the place was renamed Hillsdale in the 1960s.

Hill Spring AB The post office at this village (1961), located southwest of Lethbridge, was named in 1911 after a large spring on the north end of a hill, which provided water for the village. It had been traditionally called *Spring Hill*, but as that name had already been taken for a post office elsewhere in Canada, the two words were reversed.

Hilton ON This township on St. Joseph Island, in Algoma District, was named in 1887. *Marksville* post office opened in 1879 and changed to *Hiltonbeach* in 1928. **Hilton Beach** became a village in 1923 and the postal name was amended in 1956.

Himsworth North; Himsworth South ON Himsworth Township in Parry Sound District was named in 1876 after William Alfred Himsworth (1820–80), clerk of the Queen's Privy Council, 1872–80. The township was divided into the municipal townships of Himsworth North and Himsworth South in 1886. The township of Himsworth North is between the city of North Bay and the municipality of Powassan. In 2001 the township of Himsworth South became part of the municipality of Powassan.

Hinchinbrooke ON In 1998 this township became part of the **Central Frontenac**, Frontenac County. It was named in 1798 after Viscount Hinchinbrooke, 5th Earl of Sandwich, who as a member of Britain's Parliament, voted for the Canada Bill in 1791.

Hinchinbrooke QC This municipal township south of Salaberry-de-Valleyfield was first created in 1845, abolished in 1847, and re-established in 1855. The name derives from **Hinchinbrooke Township**, named in 1795 and proclaimed in 1799, taken from an estate in Huntingdonshire, England.

Hines Cree AB North of the Peace River and west of the town of Peace River, the post office at this village (1951) was named in 1928 after **Hines Creek**. It was relocated 5 km when the Edmonton, Dunvegan and British Columbia Railway arrived later that year. The creek may have been named after an Anglican missionary, who served in the area from 1875 to 1888.

Hinton AB The post office in this town (1958) in the Athabasca River valley and between Edson and Jasper was named in 1910 after the Hinton Trail, which led from Jasper to the Yukon. The trail was named after William Pitman Hinton, who became president and general manager of the Grand Trunk Pacific Railway in 1917.

Hinton, Mount YT Northeast of Mayo, this mountain (2059 m) was named in 1904 after Thomas Hinton, a mining recorder in the early 1900s at both Dawson and Mayo.

Hobbema AB This urban community serving several adjacent Indian reserves south of Wetaskiwin was named in 1891 by the Canadian Pacific Railway after the Dutch landscape painter Meyndert Hobbema (1638–1709). CPR president Sir William Van Horne (1843–1915) collected his paintings.

Hodgeville SK Southeast of Swift Current, the post office at this village (1921) was named in 1908. It was named after the first postmaster, Arthur Hodge. The Canadian Northern Railway arrived here in 1921.

Hodnett, Mount YT South of Whitehorse, this mountain (1993 m) was named in 1906 after David Hodnett, who discovered lode gold near it that year.

Holden AB The post office at this village (1909) southeast of Edmonton was named in 1907 after James Bismark Holden (1876–1956), who settled at Vegreville in 1900. He was a member of the Alberta Legislature, 1906–13, and served as mayor of Vegreville from 1921 to 1945. The post office here had been earlier called *Vermilion Valley*.

Holdfast SK Located northwest of Regina, this village (1911) was named in 1910, when farmer John A. Fahlman declined to let the Canadian Pacific Railway go through his land, forcing it to go farther west, before turning north. Because he was determined to 'hold fast', the CPR named the station after his obstinacy. However, these details may be folklore, and the name may have derived from the CPR's list of suggested names. *Frohlich* post office had opened in 1907, with G. Frohlich as the postmaster. It was changed to Holdfast in 1912.

Holland ON In 2000 this township became a part of the township of Chatsworth, Grey County. It was named in 1840 after Henry Richard Vassall Fox, 3rd Baron Holland (1773–1840), a minister in the 1830s in the governments of Lord Grey and Lord Melbourne. *Williamsford Station* post office opened in 1874, but was changed to **Holland Centre** in 1886.

Holland Landing ON On the **Holland River East Branch** and in the town of East Gwillimbury, York Region, this place was an important transfer point before the availability of reliable land and rail transportation. Lt.-Gov. John Graves Simcoe (1752–1806) named it *Gwillimbury* after his wife's father, Lt. Col. Thomas Gwillim (d.1762). It was also known as *St. Albans* and *Beverley*, before Holland Landing post office opened in 1831.

Holland River ON Flowing north into Lake Simcoe, this river was named in 1793 by Lt.-Gov. John Graves Simcoe (1752–1806) after Samuel Holland (1728–1801), surveyor general of Quebec from 1764 and of the northern district of North America, 1764–78. Its west branch (officially *Schomberg River*, 1927–65), now the head of the river, is the location of the **Holland Marsh** market gardens, first developed in 1927.

Holway, Mount BC Located in the Selkirk Mountains, north of Revelstoke, this mountain (3047 m) was named in 1912 by climber Howard Palmer (1883–1944) after Ewart Willett Dorland Holway (1853–1923), a botany professor at the University of Minnesota who led the first ascent of this mountain.

Holyrood NL At the head of Conception Bay, this town (1962) was named after **Holyrood Bay**. The bay may have been named after Holyrood, in the parish of Crewkerne, Somerset, England. It was noted as *Hollyrude* as early as the 1630s.

Homathko River BC Rising northeast of Mount Waddington, this river flows southwest into Bute Inlet. It was named in 1911 after the Mainland Comox word for 'swift'. **Homathko Icefield**, east of the river, rises to an elevation of 2400 m. In the 1860s Alfred Waddington (1801–72) pursued financing to build a railway through the river's valley in order to connect Victoria with Eastern Canada.

Honey Harbour ON In the township of Georgian Bay, district municipality of Muskoka, this resort community was developed with tourist facilities after 1900, with its post office being named *Royal Honey Harbour* in 1910. 'Royal' was dropped from the name in 1912, when the post office was moved to the mainland.

Honeywood ON In Dufferin County, north of Shelburne, this community was settled in the 1840s by young men from Yorkshire, England, who bought the land from a Mr. Wood of Toronto. *Rosewood*, composed from Mr. Wood's surname and his wife's first name, was not accepted as a postal name, but Honeywood was approved in 1865.

Honguedo, Détroit d' QC The large channel at the mouth of the St. Lawrence River, between Île d'Anticosti and Péninsule de Gaspé, was first noted by Jacques Cartier (1491–1557) in his *Relation* of 1535–6. However, it was not portrayed on a map until the twentieth century. It may mean 'gathering place' in Mi'kmaq, or it may be connected to *hehonguesto* ('his own nose'), a word listed in Cartier's vocabulary from an Iroquoian tribe's language.

Hooker, Mount AB, BC This mountain (3286 m) east of Athabasca Pass was named in 1827 by Scottish botanist David Douglas (1799–1834) after one of his patrons, Sir William Jackson Hooker (1785–1865), English botanist and director of Kew Museum and the Royal Botanical Gardens, southwest of London.

Hope BC This district municipality (1992) is located at the confluence of the Fraser and Coquihalla Rivers. It was the site of the Hudson's Bay Company's Fort Hope, established in 1848–9 after an all-British route from Fort Kamloops to Fort Langley was found north of the forty-ninth parallel, answering a 'hope' of the company. O.J. Travaillot and Corp. William Fisher laid out the townsite in 1858 and the post office opened the same year. It was incorporated as a village in 1929 and a town in 1965.

Hope ON In 2001 this township became part of the municipality of **Port Hope and Hope**, Northumberland County. The township had been in the county since 1974. The township was named in 1792 for Henry Hope (c.1746–89), lieutenant-governor of Quebec, 1785–9.

Hopedale NL On the coast of Labrador and due north of Happy Valley-Goose Bay, this municipal community (1969) was founded in 1774 by Moravian missionaries, and named after their ship *Hope*. Settlement began here in 1781, with 25 missionaries assigned to the station the following year.

Hopes Advance, Cap QC One of the most northerly points of Quebec, at the northwestern side of Ungava Bay, it had been named *Prince Henries Foreland* by Henry Hudson in 1610.

Two years later Thomas Button (c.1601–34), while searching for the abandoned Hudson, made references to *Hopes Checked* and *Hopes Advance*. While on board the *Advance* in 1850–1 in search of Sir John Franklin (1786–1847), Capt. Henry Grinnell (1799–1874) may have assigned Hopes Advance to this particular cape.

Hopewell Cape NB South of Hillsborough, this place's post office was named *Hopewell 'The Cape'* in 1846 after the cape extending into Shepody Bay. In the mid-1700s the cape was called *Cap des Demoiselles* after the shape of the Cape Rocks, whose curvaceous outlines probably reminded those who named them of the figures of young women (*demoiselles*). English speakers call similar rocks 'flowerpots'.

Hornby Island BC One of the Gulf Islands, southeast of Courtenay, this island was named about 1850 by the Hudson's Bay Company after RAdm. Phipps Hornby (1785–1867), commander-in-chief of the Pacific Station, 1847–51, and a lord of the Admiralty, 1851–2.

Hornepayne ON In Algoma District, southwest of Hearst, this municipal township (1986) was first named *Fitzback* in 1916. It was renamed in 1920 after British financier Robert M. Horne-Payne (d.1929), an advisor to Canadian Northern Railway builder Sir William Mackenzie (1849–1923).

Horning's Mills ON This community in Dufferin County, north of Shelburne, was founded in 1830 by Lewis Horning, far from the other settlements in Ontario. He built mills on the Pine River, but returned to his native Hamilton in 1838, a few years after his son Lewis and three children of other families were lost in the woods.

Horton ON This township in Renfrew County was named in 1826 for Sir Robert John Wilmot Horton (1784–1841), under-secretary of state for war and the colonies, who corresponded about the union of Upper and Lower Canada. Born Robert John Wilmot, he married Anna Beatrix Horton in 1823, and added her surname to his.

Horton River NT Rising north of Great Bear Lake, this river flows northwest to Harrowby Bay, part of Beaufort Sea. It was named in 1826 by Sir John Richardson (1787–1865), who was a member of the British Arctic Land expedition, which explored the lands north of the lake. He named it after Sir Robert Wilmot Horton (1784–1841), under-secretary of state for the colonies.

Horwood NL On Dog Bay of Hamilton Sound and on the north coast of Newfoundland, this place was formerly called *Dog Bay*. It was renamed about 1914 after William Frederick Horwood (1856–1927), president of the Horwood Lumber Company in St. John's, 1902–27.

Hottah Lake NT South of Great Bear Lake, this lake (840 km²) was named before 1910 after the Slavey word for 'two-year-old moose'.

Houston BC This district municipality (1957) in the Bulkley River valley was first called *Pleasant Valley*. A newspaper contest was held in 1910 to choose a new name, and John Houston (1850–1910), Prince Rupert's first newspaperman and a railway surveyor, won the contest. Previously he had lived in Golden and Nelson, where he edited newspapers, served as the mayor of Nelson, and had been elected to the provincial legislature. A creek, pass, and glacier, west of the head of Duncan River and north of Kootenay Lake, were also named for him.

Howard ON In 1998 this township became a part of the municipality of Chatham-Kent, Kent County. It was named in 1794 after Thomas Howard, 2nd Earl of Effingham and 8th Baron Howard (1714–91). His daughter, Lady Mary Howard, was the wife of Sir Guy Carleton, Lord Dorchester, governor-in-chief of British North America, 1786–96.

Howe Island ON In 1998 this township became part of the township of Frontenac Islands, Frontenac County. One of the Thousand Islands, it became a township in Frontenac County in 1792. It was named for Gen. William Howe, 5th Earl Howe (1729–1814), who was commander-in-chief of the British forces in North America, 1776–8.

Howe Sound BC Extending 40 km north from the Strait of Georgia, this water body was named in 1792 by Capt. George Vancouver (1757–98) after Adm. Richard Scrope, Earl Howe (1726–99), who won a decisive victory over the French in 1794. The victory was thereafter called 'The Glorious First of June'.

Howick ON This township in Huron County was named in 1850 after Henry George Grey, 3rd Earl Grey and Viscount Howick (1802–94), under-secretary of state for the colonies. His father, the 2nd Earl Grey, was prime minister of Britain, 1830–3, and secretary of state for the colonies, 1846–52. The 3rd Earl Grey was born and died at Howick, Northumberland, north of Newcastle-upon-Tyne.

Howick QC This village in the Châteauguay valley, southeast of Salaberry-de-Valleyfield, was called *Howick Village* by English settlers about 1833 after Henry George Grey, 3rd Earl Grey and Viscount Howick (1802–94), British under-secretary of state for the colonies, 1830–3, and secretary of war and the colonies, 1846–52. The post office here was named in 1851 and the village was incorporated in 1915.

Howley NL At the foot of Grand Lake and east of the town of Deer Lake, this town (1958) was named after geologist James Patrick Howley (1847–1918), author of the *Geography of*

Newfoundland (1877) and *The Beothucks or Red Indians* (1915). His brother was the Most Rev Michael Francis Howley (1843–1914), who wrote about Newfoundland's history and place names, and was the first Catholic archbishop of St. John's, 1904–14.

Howse Pass AB, BC Hudson's Bay Company explorer and fur trader Joseph Howse (1773–1852) crossed this pass on the continental divide, northwest of Kicking Horse Pass, in 1810. **Howse Peak** (3290 m) is on the east side of the pass.

Howser Spires BC North of Kootenay Lake, these spires (3339 m) are spectacular granite walls. They were named after **Howser Creek**, which in turn was called after the locality of **Howser** on the west side of Duncan Lake. Howser replaced *Duncan* in 1900, when mail was frequently misdirected to the city of Duncan on Vancouver Island. Howser was named after a prospector whose surname was Hauser.

Hubbard, Mount YT On the Yukon–Alaska border, and in the St. Elias Mountains, this mountain (4577 m) was named in 1890 by American explorer and geologist Israel C. Russell (1852–1906) after Gardiner Green Hubbard (1822–97), founder and president of the National Geographic Society. The Society was a joint sponsor, along with the United States Geological Survey, of Russell's 1890–91 expeditions.

Huber, Mount BC This mountain (3368 m) in Yoho National Park, east of Field, was named in 1903 by American writer Walter Wilcox (1869–1949) after Emil Huber (1865–1939), a noted Swiss alpinist, who also climbed in the Canadian mountains.

Hudson QC In the regional county of Vaudreuil-Soulanges and on the south shore of Lac des Deux Montagnes, this became a town in 1969 through the merger of the villages of Hudson and **Hudson Heights**. *Pointe-à-Cavagnol* post office was renamed Hudson in 1865 after Elisa Hudson, the wife of George Matthews, who established a glassworks here 20 years earlier.

Hudson Bay NU This massive interior sea (637,000 km²) is united to the Atlantic Ocean by **Hudson Strait**. Henry Hudson (c.1565–1611) explored the Hudson River, in present-day New York, as far as Albany in 1609. The following year he and his crew sailed into the strait and the bay, and wintered at the bottom of James Bay. Most of his crew abandoned him and seven other explorers on present-day Charlton Island on 24 June 1611; eight of the mutineers were able to return to London. The fate of Hudson and his companions is not known. The Hudson's Bay Company was created in London in 1670, and is one of the oldest merchandising companies in the world. In 1900, following a standard then used throughout the English-speaking world, the Geographic Board modified the names of the bay and the strait by lopping off the apostrophe and the 's'. Attempts to rename the bay Canada Sea during the twentieth century were not widely supported.

Hudson Bay SK The post office in this town (1947) was named *Hudson Bay Junction* in 1909, after plans were made to connect the Canadian Northern Railway with a seaport on Hudson Bay. The line was built as far as The Pas before 1915, but it was not until 1931 that it reached Churchill. 'Junction' was dropped from the postal designation in 1947.

Hudson's Hope BC A district municipality (1965) on the Peace River, west of Fort St. John, it was named after the Hudson's Bay Company's post called Hudson's Hope, established in 1873. The name may have been given as an ironic comment on the poor prospects of success at this seasonal trading post. Since 1913 its post office has been called **Hudson Hope**.

Hughenden AB South of Wainwright, this village (1917) was named by Charles E. Stockdill of the Canadian Pacific Railway after Hughenden, north of High Wycombe, Buckinghamshire, England. This location was the estate of Benjamin Disraeli, Earl of Beaconsfield, prime minister of Great Britain, 1867–8 and 1874–80.

Hull QC In 2002 this city (1875) became a sector of the city of Gatineau. The Gatineau city hall is on Laurier Street in Hull. Its post office was named in 1819, taking its name from the township of **Hull**, noted on a map as early as 1795, and proclaimed in 1806. This name was probably proposed by lumber king Philemon Wright (1760–1839), who was born in Woburn, MA. He founded Wrightville, near the Chaudière Falls in the Ottawa River.

Hullett ON In 2001 this township became part of the municipality of Central Huron, Huron County. It was named in 1830 after John Hullett, a director of the Canada Company. This British company was established in 1826 to develop the Huron Tract (a large area of what is now Southwestern Ontario). Hullett was a hops supplier based at Sillery, a suburb of Quebec City.

Humber River NL Draining Grand and Deer lakes, this river (153 km) drains into the **Humber Arm** of the Bay of Islands. The river was named after England's River Humber, which flows into the North Sea. It was named by Capt. James Cook (1728–79), who charted Humber Arm in 1767.

Humber River ON Rising in Dufferin County, this river flows southeast to enter Lake Ontario on the western boundary of the city of Toronto. It was known as *Rivière Taronto* after the French name of Lake Simcoe, *Lac de Taronto*, and *St.*

John's River after trader Jean-Baptiste Rousseau (1758–1812). The river was named about 1793 by Lt.-Gov. John Graves Simcoe (1752–1806) after the River Humber, which separates the English counties of Yorkshire and Lincolnshire.

Humboldt SK East of Saskatoon, this town (1907) was named as early as 1870, when the Dominion Telegraph established an office nearby. It was named after Baron Alexander von Humboldt (1769–1859), a German natural scientist who had investigated the geography of North and South America, 1799–1804. Postal service was established in 1905, after the Canadian Northern Railway was built from Winnipeg to Edmonton.

Hungabee Mountain AB, BC On the continental divide and west of Lake Louise, this mountain (3492 m) was named in 1894 by climber Samuel Allen after the Stoney word for 'chieftain'.

Hungerford ON In 1998 this township became part of the municipality of Tweed, Hastings County. It was named in 1798 after one of the titles of Sir Francis Rawdon-Hastings (1754–1826). The title of Baron Hungerford was granted to Edward Hastings in 1482 and derives from the town of Hungerford in Berkshire, England, west of Reading.

Hunker Creek YT A tributary of the Klondike River, this creek was named after prospector Andrew 'Old Man' Hunker, who discovered gold here in September 1896. A native of Germany, Hunker prospected for gold in the Cariboo, BC, and on the Fortymile River near the Alaska border.

Hunter River PE In the central part of the province and at the head of Hunter River, the post office in this municipal community (1983) was named in 1875. The community was incorporated as a village in 1974. The post office was called *Hunter's River* from 1901 to 1967. The river was named in 1765 by Samuel Holland (1728–1801) after Thomas Orby Hunter, lord of the Admiralty in 1761. During the nineteenth century the river was also known as *Clyde River* and *New Glasgow River*.

Huntingdon ON In 1998 this township became a part of the municipality of Centre Hastings, Hastings County. It was named in 1798 after the 11th Earl of Huntingdon (1728–1804), the father-in-law of Sir Francis Rawdon-Hastings (1754–1826). The title was taken from Huntingdonshire in east central England.

Huntingdon QC Situated on the Rivière Châteauguay, south of Salaberry-de-Valleyfield, this town's post office was named in 1830 after the county of **Huntingdon**, created in 1792 and named after Huntingdonshire in England. It became a village in 1848 and a town in 1921.

Huntley ON In 2001 this ward (1974) of the municipal township of West Carleton became part of the city of Ottawa. It was named as a township in 1823 after the Huntly estate in Scotland. The estate was inherited by the wife of the Duke of Richmond (1764–1819), governor-in-chief of British North America, 1818–9. Huntly Castle is a grand ruin, northwest of the city of Aberdeen.

Huntsville ON The post office in this town (1901) in the district municipality of Muskoka was named in 1870 after Capt. George Hunt (1830–82), a British military officer who had settled at Huntsville the previous year, and was appointed the first postmaster.

Huron ON The county was named in 1841 after the Huron Tract, which was established by the Canada Company in 1826 on the eastern shore of **Lake Huron**. The lake was named by the French after a confederacy of five Iroquoian tribes, with the name signifying 'boar's head' or 'ruffian', because their hair stood up in bristles. After the closing in 1966 of the Royal Canadian Air Force Station Centralia, south of Exeter, the civilian community was renamed **Huron Park** after the county. *See also* Centralia.

Huron Township ON In 1999 this township became part of the township of **Huron-Kinloss**, Bruce County. Huron Township was named in 1849.

Hythe AB The post office in this village (1929) northwest of Grande Prairie was named in 1914 by Mr. and Mrs. Harry Hartley after their hometown of Hythe, Kent, England, southwest of Dover.

Iberville QC This town opposite the city of Saint-Jean-sur-Richelieu was called the village of *Christieville* in 1846 in honour of seigneur Napier Christie Burton, who had donated land for a church and presbytery. When it became a town in 1859, it was renamed after Pierre Le Moyne d'Iberville (1661–1706), described in the *Dictionary of Canadian Biography* as 'the most renowned son of New France'.

Ibex Valley YT This hamlet on the Alaska Highway, west of Whitehorse, was named in 1990 after the valley of the **Ibex River**. The river was named in 1947 after wild goats found in its valley.

Iconoclast Mountain BC In the Selkirk Mountains, northwest of Rogers Pass, this mountain (3240 m) was named in 1902 by surveyor Arthur O. Wheeler (1860–1945) after its steep black face. Five years later surveyor Percy Carson described it as a very prominent majestic mountain whose name was quite suitable.

Igloolik NU On **Igloolik Island**, at the east end of Hecla and Griper Strait and offshore of Melville Peninsula, this hamlet (1976) was named in 1951 after the Inuktitut for 'there are houses'. Archaeological studies reveal the site has been continuously occupied for 4000 years.

Ignace ON This location in Kenora District, southeast of Dryden, was named in 1879 by Sir Sandford Fleming (1827–1915) after Ignace Mentour, a Mohawk from the *Caughnawaga* (now Kahnawake) Reserve, south of Montreal, who guided him across Canada in 1872. After it became a municipal township in 1908, an effort was made to rename it *Elmsdale*, but the original name was retained to respect the place's historical significance.

Île-à-la-Crosse SK This place is situated on the west side of the cross-shaped **Lac Île-à-la-Crosse**, an enlargement of the Churchill River, northwest of Prince Albert. North West Company trader Roderick McKenzie (1772–1859) based his headquarters here in 1830. The first mission was founded in 1846 at this northern village by Fr. (later Bishop) Alexandre Taché (1823–94) and Fr. (later Bishop) Louis-François Laflèche (1818–98). Its post office opened in 1910.

Illecillewaet River BC Rising in the Selkirk Mountains, this river (77 km) flows southwest into the Columbia River at Revelstoke. It was named in 1865 by explorer Walter Moberly (1832–1915), adapting its Okanagan name ('swift water').

Imperial SK Northwest of Regina, this town (1962) was founded by the Canadian Pacific Railway in 1910 and was likely named by an admirer of the monarchy. The town's streets have names such as Royal, King, Queen, Prince, and Princess. Its post office was first called *Harkness* in 1907 and was renamed Imperial in 1911.

Incomappleux River BC Rising in the Selkirk Mountains, south of Rogers Pass, this river flows southwest into the Northeast Arm of Upper Arrow Lake. The name derives from the Okanagan word for 'head of lake' or 'end of the water'.

Indian Bay (Parson's Point) NL Located on the northwestern side of Bonavista Bay and northeast of Gambo, this municipal community (1971) was probably settled soon after 1800 by William Parsons. Although Parson's Point is considered a former name of the place, the province authorized the double name for the municipality.

Indian Head SK This town (1902) east of Regina was founded by the Canadian Pacific Railway in 1882 and named after an Aboriginal's skull found near the site of the railway station by the CPR survey crew. The skull was still in the possession of a farmer in 1905. In 1854, a missionary referred to a hill called Indian Head, noting its Aboriginal name was *Ustiquanuci*.

Ingenika River BC Rising west of Williston Lake and on the west side of the **Ingenika Range**, this river was named after the Sekani word for 'bearberry'. The low bearberry bush is also known as kinnikinnick.

Ingersoll ON In 1817 Charles Ingersoll (1791–1832) settled at *Oxford-upon-the-Thames* and became the first postmaster of *Oxford Centre* in 1821. It was incorporated as the village of Ingersoll in 1852, in honour of his father Thomas, and the postal name was also changed the same year. In 1795 Thomas Ingersoll (1749–1812) was granted 486 ha (1200 a) here, where he lived from 1797 to 1799. Established as a town in 1860, it became a separated town in 1914 and reverted to a town in 1975.

Ingleside ON In the united counties of Stormont, Dundas, and Glengarry, west of Cornwall, this planned community was created in 1955 for the residents of *Aultsville, Farrans Point, Dickinson Landing*, and *Wales*, flooded in 1957 by the St. Lawrence Seaway project. Osnabruck Township reeve Thorold Lake observed the name Ingleside on a house and the township council endorsed it for the new community.

Inglewood ON In the town of Caledon, northwest of Brampton, this place was named *Riverdale* in 1860. Because of confusion with Riversdale in Bruce County, residents asked Sir Thomas White (1866–1955), their member of Parliament, to suggest a new name. He proposed Inglewood in 1885, possibly after the old tale *The Farmer of Inglewood Forest*. Two years later the name inspired the naming of a new community in California, southwest of the centre of Los Angeles. Inglewood, CA, is now a city of 115,000.

Ingonish NS Located on the north side of **North Bay Ingonish** and on the northeast coast of Cape Breton Island, this place was noted by Samuel de Champlain (1567–1635) in 1632 as *Niganis*, and by Nicolas Denys (c.1598–1688) in 1672 as *Niganiche*. The present form of the name may have been a misprint in Thomas Chandler Haliburton's *Nova-Scotia* (1829). Ingonish post office opened in 1846. The name is likely of Mi'kmaq origin, but its meaning is not noted in official names records. **Ingonish Centre** is at the head of North Bay Ingonish, and **Ingonish Beach** is on the north side of South Bay Ingonish.

Ingornachoix Bay NL This bay is located south of Port au Choix, and its name derives from the Basque *aingura charra* ('bad anchorage'). In the late 1500s many of the bays on the west coast of Newfoundland were either unprotected or too deep for the small Basque fishing craft to anchor.

Ingram, Mount YT West of Whitehorse, this mountain (2158 m) was named in 1897 by surveyor James J. McArthur (1856–1925) after he discovered the gravesite headboard of a prospector, inscribed 'Ingram'. The prospector had apparently drowned in the Takhini River and was buried beside the Dalton Trail.

Innisfail AB The post office in this town (1903) south of Red Deer was named in 1892 by Estella (Wildman) Scarlett after the poetic name for Ireland, *Innis Vail* ('isle of destiny'). It was previously called *Poplar Grove*.

Innisfil ON This town in Simcoe County was created in 1991 by uniting the municipal township of Innisfil, the village of Cookstown, and parts of the municipal townships of West Gwillimbury and Tecumseth. Innisfil Township had been named in 1822 after *Innis Vail* ('isle of destiny'), a poetic name of Ireland.

Innisfree AB This village (1911) is situated between Vegreville and Vermilion. Its post office was first called *Delnorte* but was renamed in 1909 on the suggestion of Sir Edmund Walker (1846–1924), president of the Canadian Bank of Commerce. The area of Birch Lake reminded him of the view from his summer residence of Innisfree on Lake Simcoe, ON. Having been offered a bank in their community, the residents agreed to the change.

Inukjuak QC Located on the east coast of Hudson Bay and at the mouth of **Rivière Innuksuac**, this place was first named *Port Harrison* in 1901 by geologist Albert Peter Low (1861–1942) in honour of a shareholder of a mining company. *Port Harrison* post office opened in 1935 and was renamed *Inoucdjouac* 30 years later. The spelling was modified in 1980, after the residents were consulted on their preference for the newly incorporated northern village.

Inuvik NT On the East Channel of the Mackenzie River, the site of this town (1967) was selected in 1955 as an alternate community for the residents of Aklavik, and was first called *Aklavik East Three* and *New Aklavik*. Inuvik, from the Inuvialuktun for 'place of man', was proposed 1 May 1958 by Graham Rowley (1912–2003), who was then the secretary-coordinator of the Advisory Committee on Northern Development in the northern affairs and natural resources department. It was adopted by the Northwest Territories Council on 18 July 1958.

Inverary ON In 1998 this community became a part of township of South Frontenac, Frontenac County. It was named *Storrington* in 1841 after the township of Storrington. It was renamed in 1856 after Inveraray in Argyllshire, Scotland, northwest of Glasgow.

Invermay SK Located west of Canora, this village (1908) was named in 1904 when the Canadian Northern Railway arrived here. *Tullock* post office had opened the year before, 5 km to the southeast, and was named after Walter Tulloch. It was moved to the proposed station, which was first called *Inverness*. As there was already another Inverness post office in Canada, the name Invermay was put forward and accepted. Invermay is in Perthshire, Scotland, southwest of Perth.

Invermere BC Located at the point where the Columbia River flows northwest from Windermere Lake, this district municipality (1984) was first called *Copper City* by prospector Edmund T. Johnson in 1890. It was renamed *Canterbury* in 1900 by the Canterbury Townsite Company after the famous cathedral city in Kent, England. The name was changed again in 1912 to Invermere by Randolph Bruce (1863–1942) after the Irrigated Fruit Lands Company bought the site. The name means 'at the mouth of a lake'. Randolph Bruce was a lieutenant-governor of British Columbia, 1926–31.

Inverness NS In **Inverness County** on the west side of Cape Breton Island, this town (1904) was first known as *Broad Cove Marsh* in 1838. It was renamed after the county in 1903. The county was named after Inverness-shire, Scotland, in 1837 by Sir William Young (1799–1887), its first member in the Legislative Assembly, 1837–59. It had been called *Juste au Corps County* two years earlier.

Inverness QC Located northwest of Thetford Mines, this village was incorporated in 1900. The post office here was named in 1832 after the township of **Inverness**, which was proclaimed in 1802 and named after the Scottish royal burgh, where many of the first settlers came from. The township municipality of **Inverness** was established in 1845, abolished two years later, and re-established in 1855.

Iona ON In 1998 this place southwest of St. Thomas became part of the municipality of Dutton/Dunwich, Elgin County. The community's name was proposed in 1848 by Duncan McCormick after the holy isle of Iona in Scotland and the post office opened four years later. In 1872 a railway bypassed Iona 3 km to the northwest and the new community here was named **Iona Station** three years later.

Ipperwash Beach ON In 2001 this resort centre became a part of the municipality of Lambton Shores, Lambton County. It was developed in the 1920s around the Ipperwash Hotel. The hotel's name may derive from the Norwegian *yppare vass* ('better water').

Iqaluit NU Located at the head of Frobisher Bay, this city (2001) was established in 1949 as *Frobisher Bay*, when the Hudson's Bay Company moved its post here from a site 70 km southeast. It became a municipal hamlet in 1971, a village in 1974, and a town in 1980. In December 1984 its residents voted 310 to 213 to rename the town Iqaluit, meaning 'place of fish' in Inuktitut. Its population in 2006 was 6184.

Irishtown-Summerside NL On the north side of Humber Arm, opposite Corner Brook, this town was incorporated in 1991. **Irishtown** was settled by Irish in the early 1800s. **Summerside** was named because it was on the north, or sunny, side of Humber Arm.

Irlande QC This municipality in the regional county of L'Amiante, west of Thetford Mines, was established as *Ireland* in 1845 by merging the townships of Ireland and Wolfestown. It was abolished two years later, and then re-established in 1855. It took its name from the township of *Ireland*, proclaimed in 1802. Both the township and the municipality were renamed Irlande in 1985.

Irma AB The post office in this village (1912) 25 km northwest of the town Wainwright was named in 1909 after a

daughter of William Wainwright (1840–1914), second vice-president of the Grand Trunk Pacific Railway.

Iron Bridge ON This village (1960) in Algoma District, west of Blind River, was named in 1886, two years after a steel bridge over the Missisagi River replaced a wooden one. In 1949 a concrete structure replaced the old iron bridge.

Iroquois ON In 1998 this village (1857) became a part of the township of South Dundas, the united counties of Stormont, Dundas, and Glengarry. It was named in 1857 after nearby **Point Iroquois**, a name dating from the French regime, and said to be a site where the Iroquois held councils. In 1958 the entire village was relocated when the St. Lawrence Seaway project inundated the old site.

Iroquois Falls ON This town (1915) in Cochrane District was founded in 1912 by Montreal businessman Frank Anson, who developed the Abitibi Pulp and Paper Company at a falls on the Abitibi River. There is a legend of Huron women cutting loose the canoes of Iroquois men and sending them to their death over the falls, as retaliation for the Iroquois killing all the Huron men.

Irricana AB In 2005 this village (1911) became a town, located 32 km northeast of Calgary. Its post office was established in 1909 and took its name from the words 'irrigation' and 'canal'. In 1894 the Dominion government granted the Canadian Pacific Railway a block of land on condition that an irrigation system, drawing on the waters of the Bow River, be developed. The system was abandoned before reaching the village's site, but Irricana remains as a memory of it.

Irvine AB Located east of Medicine Hat, this place's post office was named in 1883 by the Canadian Pacific Railway after Col. Acheson Gosford Irvine (1837–1916), commissioner of the North-West Mounted Police, 1880–6, and a member of the council of the North-West Territories. It was an incorporated town from 1909 to 1996.

Isachsen, Cape NU At the northwestern point of Ellef Ringnes Island, this cape was named *Kap Isachsen* in 1901 after cartographer Gunerius Ingvald Isachsen (1868–1939), a member of the Sverdrup expedition, 1898–1902. **Isachsen** weather station, on the south side of **Isachsen Peninsula**, was established in 1949. The peninsula was named in 1959.

Ishpatina Ridge ON Ontario's highest elevation, with summits of 670 m to 690 m in Timiskaming and Sudbury districts, it is located north of Sudbury and west of New Liskeard. It was named in 1972 from the Ojibwa word *ishpadina* ('it is high'), used in reference to a hill or mountain.

Island Lake MB Located near the Ontario border and due east from the north end of Lake Winnipeg, this lake (1425 km²) was crossed by Samuel Hearne (1745–92) in 1772. He reported that it was entirely full of islands, making it appear to be a jumble of separate rivers and creeks. Island Lake post office opened in 1905.

Island View NB West of Fredericton, this place's post office was named in 1908 after its view of Savage, Sugar, and Keswick Islands, at the head of tide in the Saint John River.

Islands, Bay of NL Located on the west coast of Newfoundland and north of Corner Brook, this bay was named *Baie St-Jullian* by Jacques Cartier (1491–1557) in 1534. He found it full of islands, calling them *Les Coulombiers*, from *colombier* ('little dovecote'). Capt. James Cook (1728–79) recorded the present name in 1767, and repeated the name two years later on the northeast coast of New Zealand's North Island.

Isle aux Morts NL Located on the southwestern coast of Newfoundland and east of Channel-Port aux Basques, this town (1956) was likely named after an island where bodies had been discovered after a shipwreck, near the mouth of **Isle aux Morts River**.

Ituna SK Located northwest of Melville, this town (1961) was named by the Grand Trunk Pacific Railway in 1908. It may have been chosen by a railway official familiar with the Celtic name for the Solway Firth, used by Rudyard Kipling (1865–1936) in one of his books. The firth is the wide bay that separates northwestern England from southwestern Scotland. The town's post office opened in 1909.

Ivujuvik QC The most northerly of Quebec's northern villages, at the most northeasterly point of Hudson Bay, this was the site of the Hudson's Bay Company post *Wolstenholme*, established in 1909 and named after the nearby cape. It was renamed Ivujuvik in 1981 from the Inukititut word for 'place where the ice is carried by strong currents'.

Ivvavik National Park YT This park (10,168 km²) on the shore of the Beaufort Sea was called the *Northern Yukon National Park* in 1984, and 10 years later was given its present name. It was created to protect the migratory route of the Porcupine herd of the barren-ground caribou. In Inuvialuktun the name means 'place of giving birth and raising young'.

Jackson's Arm NL Located on a small arm of White Bay at the bottom of the Northern Peninsula, this municipal community (1982) was settled in the mid-1800s and was possibly named after one of the first settlers.

Jacksons Point ON In the town of Georgina, York Region, this resort community's post office was named in 1902 after John Mills Jackson, who had settled here in 1812.

Jacobsen, Mount BC In the Coast Mountains, southeast of Bella Coola, this mountain (3027 m) was named after Thorwald Jacobsen in 1948 by surveyor Maj. F.V. Longstaff. Jacobsen and the Reverend Mr Saugstad brought Norwegian settlers to the area about 1892.

Jacques-Cartier, Détroit de QC Located at the mouth of the St. Lawrence River, between the north shore and Île d'Anticosti, this passage was named in 1934 to celebrate the epic voyage by Jacques Cartier (1491–1557) 400 years earlier. Cartier himself had called it *Détroit Saint-Pierre*, because he discovered the passage on 1 August, the feast day of St. Peter.

Jacques-Cartier, Mont QC This highest point (1268 m) in the Monts Chic-Chocs, west of the town of Gaspé, was named in 1934 in memory of the four hundredth anniversary of Cartier's discovery of Canada.

Jacques-Cartier, Rivière; Jacques-Cartier, Lac QC The river flows into the St. Lawrence River at the town of Donnacona. It drains the lake 100 km north of Quebec City.

Jacquet River NB The post office in this village (1966), southeast of Dalhousie, was named *Jacquet River Station* in 1892 after the adjacent river. It was renamed *Durhamville* in 1892 after the parish and became Jacquet River in 1898. The river was identified on Thomas Sproule's 1799 map as *River Jaques*, suggesting it was named after a local French resident. It was called *Jacket* in 1803, with the present form occurring in Robert Cooney's 1832 history. The river may have been named after pioneer James 'Jock' Doyle, who settled here about 1790.

Jaffray BC On the Canadian Pacific Railway, southwest of Fernie, this place was named in 1901 after Toronto businessman and senator Robert Jaffray (1832–1914), who was the president of the Crows Nest Pass Coal Company.

Jaffray Melick ON In 2000 this town became part of the city of Kenora (2004). Located on the far eastern side of the city, it was created as the municipal township of *Jaffray and Melick* in 1908, and became a town in 1988, with the name being amended to Jaffray Melick in 1991. **Jaffray Township** was named after businessman and senator Robert Jaffray (1832–1914). **Melick Township** was named after the parish of Meelick in County Mayo, Ireland.

Jakes Corner YT On the Alaska Highway southeast of Whitehorse, this community was named in the 1940s, either after a Teslin called Jake Jackson, who had camped near here, or after Capt. 'Jake' Jacoby (or Jacobson) of the United States Army engineers. The engineers were responsible for the construction of the highway through this area in 1942.

James Bay NU This 460-km extension of Hudson Bay was named before 1662 after explorer Thomas James (c.1593–1635), who had been seeking the Northwest Passage on behalf of Bristol merchants. He wintered in the bay in 1631–2, returning to Bristol in July 1632.

Jansen SK This village is located on the Canadian Pacific Railway, between Wynyard and Lanigan. Both the village and its post office were named in 1908 after Peter Jansen (1852–1923), the vice-president of the Saskatchewan and Manitoba Land Company. He came from Jansen, NE, to settle Mennonites in the area southwest of Big Quill Lake.

Jasper AB At the junction of Athabasca and Miette Rivers, this resort centre owes its name to the North West Company's Jasper House, located on the west side of Brûlé Lake in 1817 and run by Jasper Hawes. It was rebuilt in 1829 by the Hudson's Bay Company 20 km northeast of the present community, but was abandoned in 1884. Named *Fitzhugh* in 1911 by the Grand Trunk Pacific Railway, the present place was renamed Jasper the next year. **Jasper National Park** (10,878 km²) was established as a park reserve in 1907.

Jasper ON In 2001 Jasper became part of the township of Elizabethtown-Kitley, the united counties of Leeds and Grenville. Located 13 km southeast of Smiths Falls, it was known for most of the 1800s as *Irish Creek* after a tributary of the Rideau River. When a railway was built from Brockville to Smiths Falls in 1859, railway officials refused to use *Irish Creek*, and urged the adoption of a new name. Jasper was selected in 1864 from a list provided by a postal inspector.

Jean Marie River NT On the west bank of the Mackenzie River, 60 km southeast of Fort Simpson, this settlement was established after 1884 and named for Bro. Jean-Marie Beaudet (1866–1949), a native of Bretagne, France. He became a missionary among the Dene in 1884 and was based at Fort Resolution, 380 km to the east.

Jeckell, Mount YT Northeast of Dawson, this mountain (1951 m) was named about 1957 after George Allan Jeckell (1880–1950), comptroller of the Yukon from 1932 to 1947. He performed the duties of commissioner during those years.

Jeddore Harbour NS East of Dartmouth, this harbour was described by Nicolas Denys (c.1598–1688) in 1672 as *Riviere de Theodore*. Some maps in the 1700s called it *R St. Theodore* and *Riviere Peliodore*. It was known as *Jedore Harbour* by 1769 when John Perceval, the 2nd Earl of Egmont (1711–70), advertised for settlers, with its identity becoming *Egmont Harbour, Jedore*. Among the post offices here were **Jeddore** (1862), **East Jeddore** (1865), **Head of Jeddore** (1875), **West Jeddore** (1878), and **Jeddore Oyster Ponds** (1884).

Jeddore Lake NL North of Bay d'Espoir, this reservoir may have been named after Noel Jeddore (1865–1944), the chief of the Mi'kmaq at Conne River, 1918–25. A defender of the traditional life of the Mi'kmaq, he left Conne River in 1925 after a dispute with Fr. Stanley St. Croix.

Jellicoe, Mount This mountain (3246 m) southwest of Calgary was named in 1919 after Adm. John Rushforth, 1st Earl Jellicoe (1859–1935), commander of the British grand fleet during the First World War, and victor over the Germans at the Battle of Jutland in 1916.

Jemseg NB Located 7 km northeast of Gagetown on **Jemseg River**, the drainage of Grand Lake, this community was the site of a trading post in the mid-1600s and the French capital of Acadia in the late 1600s. Its post office was open from 1850 to 1969. The river's name derives from the Maliseet *kadjimusek* ('jumping across place'), referring to the narrowness of Grand Lake at the river's head.

Jenny Lind Island NU Located in Queen Maud Gulf, southeast of Victoria Island, this island (420 km²) was named *Lind Island* in 1851 by explorer John Rae (1813–93) after the Swedish singer Johanna Maria Lind (1820–87), popularly known as Jenny Lind, 'whose sweetness of voice and noble generosity have been the theme of every tongue'. It was amended to Jenny Lind Island in 1946.

Jenpeg MB Situated on the south end of Cross Lake, north of Norway House, this place was named in 1973 by Jack Verner of Manitoba Hydro after Jennie Kitoski and Peggy Johnston,

employees of the Winnipeg office of the water resources branch, department of mines and natural resources.

Jens Munk Island NU At the northwest side of Foxe Basin, this island (920 km²) was named in 1921–4 by the Fifth Thule expedition after Danish explorer Jens Munk (1579–1628). Commissioned to find the Northwest Passage in 1619 by Christian IV of Denmark, Munk spent the following winter at the mouth of Churchill River, on the west side of Hudson Bay, returning across the ocean the following summer.

Jerseyside NL Located on the north side of Placentia Harbour, this place has been a neighbourhood in the town of Placentia since 1994. A former town (1950), it was named in the mid-1800s after fishing families from Jersey, in the Channel Islands, who had settled here after 1713.

Jervis Inlet BC Extending 90 km inland from Malaspina Strait, east of Powell River, this fiord-like inlet was named in 1792 by Capt. George Vancouver (1757–98) after RAdm. Sir John Jervis, Earl of St. Vincent (1735–1823). He won considerable fame in 1797 for his victory over the stronger Spanish fleet off Portugal's Cabo São Vincente.

Jésus, Île QC Located north of Montreal and embracing the city of Laval, it was named in 1636 when it was granted to the Jesuits by the Company of New France. Although it was only considered a temporary description, and the Jesuits themselves called it *Isle de Montagny* after the governor, the original designation prevailed.

Jetté, Mount YT Located at the point where the Yukon, British Columbia, and Alaska meet, this mountain (2579 m) was named in 1905 after Sir Louis-Amable Jetté (1836–1920), lieutenant-governor of Quebec, 1898–1908, and Canadian member of the Canada–Alaska Boundary Tribunal in 1903.

Joe Batt's Arm-Barr'd Islands-Shoal Bay NL A town (1989) on the north side of Fogo Island, the first two places had been joined as a rural district in 1972 and became a town in 1980. **Joe Batt's Arm** took its name from a small bay, on the west side of **Joe Batt's Point**. The arm and the point may have been named after the same Joe Batt 'who was sentenced to receive fifteen lashes for stealing a pair of shoes and buckles valued at 7s 6p about 1754 at Bonavista'. He may have worked with Capt. James Cook (1728–79) during his hydrographic survey of the north coast, before settling on Fogo Island in 1765, and was possibly a native of Ringwood, Hampshire, England. In 1901 it was renamed *Queenstown*, but the local people resented the change. **Barr'd Islands**, which was probably settled before 1800, may have been named after the narrow necks of land which formed its harbour. Shoal Bay is on a long but shallow indentation of the island.

Joffre, Mount AB This mountain (3449 m) southeast of Banff was named in 1818 by the Alberta–British Columbia Boundary Commission after Joseph-Jacques-Césaire Joffre (1852–1931), commander-in-chief of the French armies in the First World War, 1914–16.

Joggins NS On Chignecto Bay and southwest of Amherst, this place derives its name from the Mi'kmaq *chegoggin* ('fish weir place'), and it appeared on maps as early as 1750. Its post office opened as *Joggins Mines* in 1856 and became Joggins in 1937. Coal was mined here commercially from 1847 to 1961.

John Oliver, Mount BC In the Premier Range, west of Valemount, this mountain (3120 m) was named in 1928 after John Oliver (1856–1927), premier of British Columbia, 1918–27.

Johnson, Mount NB South of Nepisiguit River, this mountain was named in 1964 by Arthur F. Wightman (1905–88), then the provincial names authority, after John Mercer Johnson (1818–68), a Father of Confederation.

Johnstone Strait BC This passage, which links the Strait of Georgia with Queen Charlotte Sound and the open Pacific, was named in 1792 by Capt. George Vancouver (1757–98). He named it after James Johnstone, master of the tender *Chatham*, who discovered that year that Vancouver Island was separated from the mainland.

Johnstown ON In 2001 this community became part of the township of Edwardsburgh-Cardinal, in the united counties of Leeds and Grenville. It was named about 1790 after Sir William Johnson (c.1715–74), superintendent of the northern Indians in the American colonies, who died at Johnstown, NY, northwest of Albany. His son, Sir John Johnson, acquired land on the St. Lawrence River at Johnstown, which became the administrative centre of Upper Canada's Eastern District, 1793–1808.

Joliette QC This city in the regional county of Joliette, northeast of Montreal, was founded in 1823 by Barthélemy Joliette (1789–1850), who built a gristmill, sawmill, and foundry here, and called the place *L'Industrie*. It was renamed Joliette in 1864 after the county, the judicial district, and the post office had been called Joliette. The regional county was named in 1982, embracing the area of the former county, established in 1853.

Jones Sound NU Separating Ellesmere and Devon Islands, this 275-km body of water was named *Alderman Jones Sound* in 1616 by Robert Bylot (d.1622) and William Baffin (1837–1915). They named it after Sir Francis Jones, a London merchant and lord mayor, who was a generous patron of their expedition. The name was subsequently shortened to Jones Sound.

Jonquière QC In 2002 this city became a part of the city of Saguenay. It was named in 1866 after the township of **Jonquière**, which was proclaimed in 1850 and named after Jacques-Pierre de Taffanel, Marquis de Jonquière (1685–1752), governor of New France, 1746–52. In 1975 it annexed the adjoining towns of Kénogami and Arvida and the parish municipality of *Saint-Dominique-de-Jonquière*.

Jordan Falls NS The post office in this place on the Jordan River, northeast of Shelburne, was named *Head of Jordan River* in 1857. Its present name was adopted in 1913. Portuguese maps published in the mid-1500s identified *Ribeira de jardines* in this area, and it evolved into *R des Jardins* during the French regime and **Jordan River** after 1783.

Joseph, Lake ON This lake, one of the three largest of the Muskoka Lakes, was named in 1860–1 after Joseph Dennis, the father of surveyor John Stoughton Dennis Sr. (1820–85). Joseph Dennis, who was then living in Weston, ON, was captured during the War of 1812 while captain of a boat on Lake Ontario.

Jourimain, Cape NB Extending into Northumberland Strait, north of Cape Tormentine, this cape may have been named after an Acadian settler or after pioneer Germain Allen. Referred to as *Jeauriman* in an 1809 land petition, its present form was established on John Wilkinson's 1859 map.

Joyceville ON In 1998 this community became part of the city of Kingston, Frontenac County. The post office here was named *Bermingham* in 1852, and changed in 1855 to *Birmingham*, after postmaster and hotel keeper James Birmingham. In 1901 it was named Joyceville after postmaster Luke J. Joyce and the many Joyces living in the area.

Juan de Fuca Strait BC Separating Vancouver Island from the state of Washington, this 23-km-wide entrance to Puget Sound and the Strait of Georgia was named in 1787 by fur trader Charles W. Barkley (1759–1832) after a Greek sea captain known as Juan de Fuca (1525–1602). He had told a tale in 1596 of having discovered a wide inlet four years earlier, between the forty-seventh and forty-eighth parallels, while sailing under the instructions of the Viceroy of Mexico. Although the navigator's Greek name has been rendered as Apostolos Valerianos in various accounts, his real Greek name was Iwannis Phokas. He came from Valerianos on the island of Kefallinía (Cephalonia) in the Ionian Sea, west of Athens. *See also* Barkley Sound.

Judique NS This place is located on the southwestern coast of Cape Breton Island. Its post office was named in 1832 after the Judique River. The river's name may have evolved from *jou-jou-dique* (from the French words *jouer* and *dique*), in reference to the river playfully cutting through the sandbar at **Judique Harbour** after storms closed the entrance.

Jules-Léger, Lac QC Situated in north central Quebec near Mont Otish, this place was named in 1982 after Jules Léger (1913–80), governor general of Canada, 1974–9, and brother of Paul-Émile Cardinal Léger (1904–91).

Jumbo Mountain BC In the Purcell Mountains, west of Invermere, this mountain (3399 m) was named in 1911 by climber Edward Harnden after the Jumbo Mine, staked in 1890 and named after the famous elephant of P.T. Barnum's circus. At that time Jumbo's body was on display in the museum of Boston's Tufts University.

Kahnawake QC The name of this Mohawk community and reserve, south of Montreal, was spelled *Caughnawaga* from 1716 to 1980, when the preferred Mohawk form was acknowledged. The name means 'at the rapids', in reference to the Rapides de Lachine.

Kakabeka Falls ON Located in Thunder Bay District and on the Kaministiquia River, west of Thunder Bay, these falls plunge down a 47-m cliff. The name in Ojibwa is *Kakabika* ('steep rock with a waterfall'). The post office in the community of **Kakabeka Falls** was named in 1906.

Kaladar ON In 1998 this township became part of the township of Addington Highlands, Lennox and Addington County. It was named in 1820. The origin is uncertain, but the name may derive from John Campbell, Baron Cawdor of Castlemartin (1753–1821), a Conservative member of Britain's Parliament, who took his title from the Scottish parish of Cawdor in Nairn, Scotland. A post office called *Cawdor* in the township from 1865 to 1869 suggests a connection between Cawdor and Kaladar. The post office at the present community of Kaladar was called *Kaladar Station* from 1889 to 1950.

Kaministiquia River ON Rising 120 km west of Thunder Bay, this river flows east over Kakabeka Falls and enters Lake Superior in the Fort William sector of Thunder Bay. The name in Ojibwa means 'island river'. The post office at **Kaministiquia**, northwest of Thunder Bay, was established in 1875.

Kamloops BC This city (1893), at the forks of the South and North Thompson Rivers, is located at the site where fur trader David Stuart established Fort Kamloops for the Pacific Fur Company in 1812. The post office here opened in 1870. The Shuswap called the place *Kahmoloops* ('meeting of the waters').

Kamouraska QC This regional county, fronting on the St. Lawrence upriver from Rivière-de-Loup, was named in 1982 after the former county of Kamouraska. The name goes back to 1674 when Olivier Morel de la Durantaye (1640–1716) was granted the seigneury of Kamouraska. **Kamouraska** post office opened in 1816. Created as a village in 1858, it was united in 1987 with the parish municipality of *Saint-Louis-de-Kamouraska* to form the municipality of Kamouraska. The name derives from

Algonquin, meaning 'where there are reeds along the edge of the water'.

Kamsack SK This site of this town (1911) on the Assiniboine River and near the Manitoba border was created in 1904 by the Canadian Northern Railway. Its post office was established nearby in 1888 and named after a Saulteaux man. The man was apparently short, and nicknamed Kamsack ('big man') in Fort Pelly in the 1860s. He helped the settlers when they arrived in the Kamsack area and died about 1896.

Kananaskis River AB In 1858 explorer John Palliser (1817–87) named this river, and the **Kananaskis Pass** over the continental divide, southeast of Banff, after a Cree man called Kineahkis, who was said to have recovered from an axe blow to the head. Subsequently the name was given to **Kananaskis River, Kananaskis Lakes, Kananaskis Falls, Kananaskis Range, Kananaskis Provincial Park, Kananaskis** hamlet near Exshaw, and **Kananaskis Country** with **Kananaskis Village** in Peter Lougheed Provincial Park.

Kanata ON In 2001 this city (1978) became a part of the city of Ottawa. It was named by Bill Teron in the 1960s because its clusters of neighbourhoods replicated the sector concept of *Kanata*, meaning 'a cluster of dwellings' in an Iroquoian language. It was a word encountered by Jacques Cartier (1491–1557) in the 1530s, which eventually evolved into the name for our country.

Kane Basin NU On the east side of Ellesmere Island and extending for 220 km from Cape Sabine to Cape Lawrence, this basin was named after Dr. Elisha Kent Kane (1820–57), who commanded the second Grinnell expedition in search of Sir John Franklin (1786–1847). He explored the Kalaalluit Nunaat (Greenland) and Ellesmere Island coasts north of Baffin Bay, 1853–5.

Kanesatake QC Formerly called *Oka*, the Mohawk community on the north shore of Lac des Deux Montagnes was officially named Kanesatake in 1986. In Mohawk the name means 'at the bottom of the hill'. *See also* Oka.

Kangiqsualujjuaq QC This northern village at the mouth of Rivière George in northeastern Quebec is near the site of the Hudson's Bay Company's George River trading post, which operated from 1869 to 1952. The place was called *Port-Nouveau-Quebec* in 1961, an unpopular choice among the local Inuit. The present name, given in 1980, means 'the very large bay' in Inuktitut.

Kangiqsujuaq QC Located in northern Quebec, this northern village was the site of the Stupart meteorological station, established in 1884 and named after meteorologist Sir Frederic Stupart (b. 1857). In 1897 geologist Albert Peter Low (1861–1942) named the inlet here *Wakeham Bay* after Capt. William Wakeham, the commander of his vessel. Fur traders Revillon Frères opened their post at *Wakeham Bay* in 1910. In 1965 it was renamed *Maricourt* after Paul Le Moyne de Maricourt (1663–1704), who took part in an expedition to Hudson Bay in 1686, but the name was not accepted by the local Inuit. It was officially renamed Kangiqsujuaq in 1980, after the Inuktitut for 'the big bay'.

Kangirsuk QC Located at the mouth of Rivière Arnaud on the west side of Ungava Bay, this northern village, where the Hudson's Bay Company established a post in 1920, was first called *Payne River*. In 1961 the place was named *François-Babel* after a missionary, and was renamed *Bellin* the following year after the famous French hydrographer and map-maker Jacques-Nicolas Bellin (1703–72). The place was then called *Bellin (Payne)* until 1980, when it was renamed Kangirsuk, which is Inuktitut for 'the bay'.

Kapuskasing ON The post office of this town (1921) in Cochrane District was named in 1917 after the **Kapuskasing River**, which rises in **Kapuskasing Lake** and flows north to join the Mattagami River. The name derives from the Cree *kepuskaskikwa* ('it branches from a river').

Kasba Lake NT, NU This lake (1341 km²) is located north of the point on the sixtieth parallel where the provinces of Manitoba and Saskatchewan meet. Its name was ascertained in 1894 by geologist Joseph Burr Tyrrell (1858–1957). In Chipewyan the name means 'small ptarmigan'.

Kaslo BC This village (1893) on the west bank of Kootenay Lake, northeast of Nelson, was first called *Kane's Landing* after George and David Kane, who settled here in 1889. Its post office was named in 1892 after **Kaslo Creek**. David Kane, who was the village's second mayor in 1894, claimed the creek was named after Johnny Kasleau, who had prospected for lead for the Hudson's Bay Company many years before. According to William Cockle, the postmaster in 1905, the creek's name derives from the Kootenay *cassoloe* ('blackberry'). However, some claim that blackberries have never grown on the creek's banks.

Kativik QC Embracing 500,164 km² of northern Quebec, this regional territory was created in 1978 to supervise the

northern villages and to manage the health, welfare, economic development, and environment of the province's region north of the fifty-fifth parallel. In Inuktitut the name means 'the place where they go to assemble'.

Kaumajet Mountains NL On the coast of northern Labrador, these mountains rise some 1300 m straight from the sea. In Inuktitut, the name means 'shining top'.

Kawartha Lakes ON These lakes, north of Peterborough and on the Trent Canal/Severn Canal system, were named *Kawatha* in 1895 by Martha Whetung, a resident of the Curve Lake Indian Reserve, who said it meant 'land of reflections'. Resort promoters respelled it Kawartha, and claimed it meant 'bright waters and happy lands'.

Kawartha Lakes ON In 2001 all of the municipalities of Victoria County became the city of **Kawartha Lakes**. This joined the town of Lindsay, the villages of Fenelon Falls, Omemee, Sturgeon Point, and Woodville, the municipality of Bobcaygeon/Verulam, and the townships of Bexley, Carden and Dalton, Digby and Longford, Elson, Emily, Fenelon, Laxton, Manvers, Mariposa, and Ops and Somerville.

Kazabazua QC This municipality in the regional county of La Vallée-de-la-Gatineau is located midway between Gatineau and Maniwaki. It was named in 1976 after the well-known community of Kazabazua, a name in use before 1873. The municipality was named after **Rivière Kazabazua**, whose name in Algonquin means 'water flowing underground', in reference to the river flowing under a natural stone bridge near its mouth.

Kearney ON This town (1907) in Parry Sound District, north of Huntsville, was settled in 1879 by William Patrick Kearney. The post office adopted his name the next year.

Kedgwick NB The post office in this village (1966) northeast of Edmundston was called *Richards Station* in 1912. It was renamed three years later after the **Kedgwick River**, which rises in Quebec and flows 70 km southeast into the Restigouche River, west of the village. Its name derives from the Mi'kmaq *madawamkedjwik* ('large branch' or 'flowing underground in many places'). The name was spelled many ways until the Geographic Board standardized it in 1901.

Keele Peak YT North of Macmillan Pass, this peak (2975 m) in the Hess Mountains of the Selwyn Mountains was named in 1909 by geologist R.G. McConnell (1857–1942) after Joseph Keele (1863–1923), who extensively surveyed the Yukon and the western Northwest Territories. In 1911 geologist D.D. Cairnes (1879–1917) named **Keele Range**, on the Yukon–Alaska boundary, south of Porcupine River, for him.

Keele River NT This tributary of the Mackenzie River rises in the Mackenzie Mountains. It was named by the Geographic Board in 1924, after geologist Joseph Keele (1863–1923), who had explored this river and the Ross River in the Yukon. It was approved in 1909 as *Gravel River*, shown on an 1887–8 map and recommended by Keele. In Slavey it was known as *Mbekonityeh* ('dried meat river').

Keewatin ON In 2000 this town (1908) became part of the city of Kenora. It was called Keewatin Mills in 1880, after John Mather's sawmill and the District of Keewatin, established in 1876, then occupying the northwest of Ontario and the north of Manitoba. The name was soon shortened to Keewatin. The name is from the Ojibwa for 'north wind', in reference to all cold winds.

Kejimkujik Lake NS In south central Nova Scotia, this lake is midway between Digby and Liverpool. In Mi'kmaq, its name may mean 'swelled private parts', in reference to the exertion required to row across the lake, or 'attempting to escape', or 'fairy lake', as it was formerly called *Fairy Lake*. **Kejimkujik National Park** (382 km²) was created in 1968.

Kelligrews NL In the town of Conception Bay South, southeast of St. John's, this built-up centre was named after nearby **Kelligrew's Point**. The point was likely named after a Kelligrew family, who established a store here in the early 1800s. The family may have come from Port de Grave, across Conception Bay.

Kelliher SK Established in 1908, this village (1909) northwest of Melville was named after Grand Trunk Pacific Railway chief engineer Bartholomew Brosman Kelliher. The name preserves the alphabetical arrangement of stations from Portage la Prairie to Edmonton, with Jasmin to the east, and Leross to the west. Its post office opened in 1908.

Kelowna BC On the eastern shore of Okanagan Lake, this city (1905) was named in 1892 after the Okanagan word for 'female grizzly bear'. With the largest beach on the lake, it was early known as *L'Anse au Sable* by French-speaking trappers and fur traders.

Kelvington SK The post office in this town (1944) northeast of Wadena opened in 1905 and was named after Baron William Thomson Kelvin (1824–1907), a famed physicist and inventor, who lived at Largs on the Firth of Clyde, west of Glasgow. Mary McQuarrie (1858–1930), the wife of the postmaster, was raised on the estate of the Lord Kelvin, which she had thought was called Kelvington, but was really called Kelvingrove.

Kempenfelt Bay ON This western arm of Lake Simcoe was named by Lt.-Gov. John Graves Simcoe (1752–1806) in 1793 after RAdm. Richard Kempenfelt (1718–82). He commanded the Blue Squadron of His Majesty's Fleet, and died when his ship *Royal George* went down off Spithead, a channel between Portsmouth and the Isle of Wight.

Kemptville ON In 1998 this town (1963) became part of the township of North Grenville, united counties of Leeds and Grenville. It was named in 1828 after Sir James Kempt (1764–1854), lieutenant-governor of Nova Scotia, 1820–8, and administrator of the government of Canada, 1828–30. It was earlier called *Clothier's Mills* after Lyman Clothier and his four sons, who settled here in 1812.

Kenaston SK This village (1910) was founded as *Bonnington* in 1890 by the Qu'Appelle, Long Lake and Saskatchewan Railway and Steamboat Company, which became part of Canadian Northern Railway in 1906. *Bonnington* post office opened in 1904, but because of confusion with Bonnyville, AB, it was renamed Kenaston in 1906. It was named after F.E. Kenaston of Minneapolis, vice-president of the Saskatchewan Land Valley Company, which developed the area between Davidson and Hanley.

Kennebec ON In 1998 this township became part of the township of Central Frontenac, Frontenac County. It was named in 1823, possibly after the Ojibwa word *kenibig* ('snake') or after the Kennebec River in Maine, where in Penobscot it means 'long bay place'.

Kennebecasis River NB Rising east of Sussex, this river flows southwest to empty into **Kennebecasis Bay**, an arm of the Saint John River. In Mi'kmaq the name means 'little bay place', suggesting the lower Saint John River may have been once called Kennebec ('big bay place') as far as the head of tide west of Fredericton. Many spellings were used after 1686, with the present one being adopted by surveyor Joseph Bouchette (1774–1841) in 1815.

Kennedy SK The post office at this village (1907) was named in 1904 after Findlay Kennedy, who previously carried the mail from Whitewood on the main Canadian Pacific Railway line, 35 km to the north. The CPR built a line through Kennedy in 1907, and, choosing from a list of names, named the station for J. Ashmore Kennedy, without having any information about him.

Kennedy Channel NU Between Ellesmere Island and Kalaalluit Nunaat (Greenland), this channel unites Kane Basin with Hall Basin. It was named in 1854 by explorer Dr. Elisha Kent Kane (1820–57) after John Pendleton Kennedy (1795–1870), secretary of the United States Navy.

Kennedy, Mount YT The proposal to name this mountain in the St. Elias Mountains, east of Mount Alverstone, was made in December 1964 by Walter Wood (1907–93), president of the

American Geographical Society, after John Fitzgerald Kennedy (1917–63), the thirty-fifth president of the United States. A few weeks earlier the Canadian government had named another peak after him, but Wood pointed out that it was only a lower part of the uplift of Mount Logan.

Kénogami QC This sector of the city of Saguenay was an incorporated town from 1958 to 1975. It was named after **Rivière Kénogami**, which drains **Lac Kénogami** north to the Rivière Saguenay. Fr. Charles Albanel (1616–96) made reference to the lake in 1672. The name in Montagnais means 'long lake'.

Kenora ON In 2000 this town became a city, amalgamating the towns of Keewatin and Jaffray Melick in Kenora District. It became the Manitoba town of *Rat Portage* in 1882, when the British Privy Council awarded it to that province, reversing Canada's decision from the previous year. But in 1884 the Privy Council put it back into Ontario, where it became an incorporated town in 1892. The place took its name from the abundance of muskrat in the Winnipeg River basin. It was renamed in 1905, taking the first two letters of each of Keewatin, *Norman*, and *Rat Portage*. *Norman*, a locality midway between Kenora and Keewatin, had been named after the son of a lumber company manager.

Kenosee Lake SK The post office of this village (1987) within Moose Mountain Provincial Park and north of Carlyle was called *Kenosee Park* in 1923. It was renamed Kenosee Lake in 1974. In Ojibwa *kenosee* means 'long creek'.

Kensington PE The name of this town (1914) east of Summerside was chosen about 1863 for a school district after Kensington in London, England. First called *Glover's*, its post office was *Barretts Cross* from 1851 to 1886, when it was changed to its present name. *Barretts Cross* may have been named after a Miss Barrett, who operated a tavern here.

Kent BC This district municipality (1895) on the north side of the Fraser River, northeast of Chilliwack, was likely named after Kent in southeastern England.

Kent NB Established in 1826, this county was named after Prince William, the Duke of Kent (1765–1837), who became William IV, 1830–7.

Kent ON In 1998 this county became part of the municipality of Chatham-Kent in Kent County. It took the city of Chatham, the towns of Blenheim, Bothwell, Dresden, Ridgetown, Tilbury, and Wallaceburg, the villages of Erie Beach, Erieau, Highgate, Thamesville and Wheatley, and the townships of Camden, Chatham, Dover, Harwich, Howard, Orford, Raleigh, Romney, Tilbury East, and Zone. Kent County was named in 1792 after the southeastern county in

England. Its territory then went all the way to Hudson Bay, but was confined to Southwestern Ontario in 1800 and to its present area in 1850.

Kent Peninsula NU This peninsula is part of the mainland south of Victoria Island and the gulfs between Coronation and Queen Maud. It was named in 1838 by explorer Thomas Simpson (1808–40) after Mary Louise Victoria, the Duchess of Kent (1786–1861), mother of Queen Victoria.

Kentville NS This town (1886) was named in 1826 after Prince Edward, the Duke of Kent and Strathearn (1767–1820), father of Queen Victoria. He visited the place in 1794, while he was the commander of the British forces in Halifax. The town was earlier called in Mi'kmaq *Penooek* ('crossing place'), and *Horton Corner* after **Horton Township**.

Kenyon ON In 1998 this township became a part of the township of North Glengarry, united counties of Stormont, Dundas, and Glengarry. It was named in 1798 after Lloyd, Lord Kenyon (1732–1802), a chief justice of England's Court of King's Bench.

Keppel ON In 2001 this township became part of the township of Georgian Bluffs, Grey County. It was named in 1855 by William Coutts Keppel, Viscount Bury (1832–94), superintendent of Indian affairs in Canada, after his uncle Henry Keppel (1809–1904). Keppel wrote an account of his voyage as captain of the ship that took James Brooke, the future rajah, to Sarawak in 1841.

Keremeos BC In the Similkameen River valley, southwest of Penticton, this village (1956) served as the site of the Hudson's Bay Company's Fort Okanagan from 1860 to 1872. Its post office opened in 1887 and was named after **Keremeos Creek**; this name in Okanagan means either 'land cut across in the middle', or 'flat cut through by water'.

Kerrobert SK Located west of Biggar, this town (1911) was founded in 1911 by the Canadian Pacific Railway and named after Robert Kerr (1845–1916), the CPR's traffic manager. The post office was called *Kerr-Robert* in 1910 and was changed to Kerrobert in 1924.

Keswick NB West of Fredericton, this community is located at the mouth of the **Keswick River**. Its post office was called *Mouth of Keswick* in 1849. The river's name derives from the Maliseet *nookamkeechwak* ('gravelly river'). Its present name occurred in a land petition of 1811, but for many years between 1783 and 1820 it was called *Madamkeswick River*. Nearby **Keswick Ridge** was named after Maliseet *quesawednek* ('the end hill'), and its spelling was adjusted to agree with the name of the river.

Ketepec NB The name of this neighbourhood in the city of Saint John and on the west side of the Saint John River was created in 1902 by naturalist William F. Ganong (1864–1941) for a Canadian Pacific Railway station. He adapted it from Maliseet *pekwitepekek* ('grand bay'), which may have been a Maliseet translation of the French name.

Kicking Horse Pass AB, BC In 1858 Dr. James Hector (1834–1907), after ascending a tumultuous tributary of the Columbia River, was kicked by a horse and knocked senseless near the summit of the pass (1627 m). By association, the river was named **Kicking Horse River**.

Kidd, Mount AB This mountain (2958 m) in the Kananaskis Range, southeast of Banff, was named in 1907 by geologist Donaldson B. Dowling (1858–1925) after trader Stuart Kidd (1883–1956). Kidd managed posts at Morley and Nordegg, and became fluent in the language of the Stoney, who made him Honorary Chief Tah-Osa ('moose killer') in 1927.

Kilbride NL Located on the south side of the city of St. John's, this urban centre may have been named about 1860 after Kilbride Falls on the Waterford River. Kilbride may have inspired the naming of St. Bridget's Church in 1863. The Irish for Kilbride, *Cill-Bhrigde*, means 'Brigid's church'.

Killaloe ON The original Killaloe in Renfrew County was named in 1850 by lumberman James Bonfield (1825–83) after his birthplace in County Clare, Ireland. In 1894 the railway passed 2 km to the north, where the post office (1896) and new village (1911) were named *Killaloe Station*. The post office was changed to Killaloe in 1961, and the village became Killaloe in 1989, while the original community was renamed **Old Killaloe** in 1990.

Killam AB The station in this town (1965) southeast of Camrose was named in 1906 by the Canadian Pacific Railway after Albert Clements Killam (1949–1908), Western Canada's first appointment to the Supreme Court of Canada, 1903–4, and chief commissioner of the Board of Railway Commissioners, 1904–8. The post office opened in 1907.

Killarney MB The post office in this town (1907), southeast of Brandon and near the North Dakota border, was named in 1883 by John O'Brien after the town and lakes in County Kerry, Ireland. It was previously called *Oak Lake* after the adjacent lake, but O'Brien thought it was a pity that such a beautiful gem of water should go by such a plain name.

Killarney ON The post office in this community, situated on the north shore of Georgian Bay in Manitoulin District, was named in 1854 after the town in County Kerry, Ireland. **Killarney Provincial Park** was created in 1964.

Kimberley BC This city (1944) northwest of Cranbrook was named in 1897 by Col. William Ridpath of Spokane, WA. He likely chose the name in the hope that the mines, which he had bought the previous year for his syndicate, would produce riches similar to those of South Africa's Kimberley. The South African diamond centre was named in 1873 after John, the 1st Earl of Kimberley (1826–1902), then British secretary of state for the colonies, who placed the mines under British protection.

Kimmirut NU On the south coast of Baffin Island and southwest of Iqaluit, this hamlet (1982) was first called *Lake Harbour*. In Inuktitut, Kimmirut means 'looks like a heel', because a nearby large rock resembles an upturned heel. *Lake Harbour* was the site of an Anglican mission in 1910 and a Hudson's Bay Company store in 1911. A Royal Canadian Mounted Police post and a post office were established here in 1927.

Kinbasket Lake BC Impounded by the Mica Dam on the Columbia River, this reservoir was created in 1973 and first named after Gen. A.G.L. McNaughton (1887–1966), commander of the Canadian forces in Britain, 1939–43, and chairman of the Canadian section of the International Joint Commission, 1950–62. In 1980 the name was restored to Kinbasket Lake, which was a small lake named officially in 1912 and later submerged by the reservoir. In 1866 surveyor Walter Moberly (1832–1915) had named it *Kinbaskit Lake* after Shuswap chief Paul Ignatius Kinbaskit, who provided much appreciated assistance to Moberly.

Kincaid SK This place west of Assiniboia was reached by the Canadian Pacific Railway in early July 1913 and the village was promptly incorporated that month. The village and the post office were named after William Kincaid, a CPR officer.

Kincardine ON In 1999 the township of Kincardine (1849) and the town of Kincardine (1875) became parts of the municipality of Kincardine, Bruce County. The township was named after a title of James Bruce, 8th Earl of Elgin and 12th Earl of Kincardine (1811–63), governor of the Province of Canada, 1846–54. The town was first called *Penetangore* in 1851, after the Penetangore River.

Kindersley SK This town formed midway on a line run by the Canadian Northern Railway in 1909 from Rosetown to Alsask on the Alberta border. The post office in the town (1910) was named in 1909 after Sir Robert Molesworth Kindersley (1871–1954), a prominent stockholder in the Canadian Northern Railway. Kindersley has grown into the largest urban centre between Saskatoon and Medicine Hat.

King ON This township in York Region was named in 1798, probably after John King, then the British under-secretary of state for the colonies. The post office at **King City** was called

King from 1853 to 1953, when local residents persuaded the postal authorities to accept King City, then the name of the police village.

King Christian Island NU In the Sverdrup Islands of the Queen Elizabeth Islands and south of Ellef Ringnes Island, this island (645 km²) was named *King Christian Land* in 1901 by Otto Sverdrup (1854–1930) after Christian IX (1818–1906), who became king of Denmark in 1863.

King Edward, Mount AB, BC On the contintental divide and near the head of the Athabasca River, this mountain (3490 m) was named in 1906 by climber Mary Schäffer after Edward VII (1841–1910), who succeeded his mother, Queen Victoria, in 1901.

King George IV Lake NL In the southwestern part of Newfoundland, this lake was named in 1822 by William Eppes Cormack (1796–1868) after the reigning monarch.

King George, Mount BC This mountain (3422 m) in the Royal Group of the Rocky Mountains, east of Invermere, was named in 1916 by the Alberta–British Columbia Boundary Commission after George V (1865–1936), the first sovereign of the House of Windsor (1917), who ascended the throne in 1910. Other peaks in the group were named at the same time after Queen Mary, Princess Mary, and the princes Albert, Edward, George, Henry, and John.

King George, Mount YT Located north of Mount Vancouver in the St. Elias Mountains, this mountain (3734 m) was named in 1935 by the National Geographic Society Yukon Expedition after George V, on the occasion of the twenty-fifth anniversary of his accession to the throne.

King, Mount YT Near the Alaska border and west of Mount Logan, this mountain (5173 m) was named about 1918 after William Frederick King (1854–1916), chief astronomer of Canada (1890–1905), director of the Dominion Observatory (1905–16), and member of the International Boundary Commission, 1892–1916.

King Peak BC In the Muskwa Ranges of the Rocky Mountains, this mountain (2972 m) was named in 1967 by W.R. Young, provincial member of the Canadian Permanent Committee on Geographical Names, after William Lyon Mackenzie King (1874–1950), prime minister of Canada during the Second World War. This name and several others were given that year to honour world leaders, places, and battles associated with the war.

Kings NB This county north of the city of Saint John was named to express loyalty to George III, who had become the monarch in 1760. The county was established in 1785.

Kings NS This county in the eastern part of the Annapolis Valley was named in 1786 after George III.

Kings PE In the eastern county of the province, this location was named in 1765 by Samuel Holland (1728–1801) after the monarch, George III.

Kingsclear NB Located west of Fredericton, this community was named in 1849 after **Kingsclear Parish**. The parish was established in 1786 and was possibly named by Edward Winslow (c.1746–1815), the surveyor of the king's woods, devising the name from the clearings made in the woods to provide masts and timber for the King's navy.

King's Cove NL The name of this municipal community (1966), located on the south side of Bonavista Bay and southwest of the town of Bonavista, is likely a variant of *Canning's Cove*, an eighteenth-century name. It was settled in the early 1800s by English and Irish immigrants, who pursued the local inshore and Labrador fishery and sealing.

Kingsey Falls QC Located in the regional county of Arthabaska, south of Victoriaville, the municipality was erected in 1865, taking its name from the township of **Kingsey**. The township was named in 1792, proclaimed in 1803, and likely named after a village in Oxfordshire, England. The post office in the village (1922) of **Kingsey Falls** opened in 1849. The western part of the township was incorporated as the township municipality of **Kingsey** in 1845; its post office opened in 1836.

Kingsmere QC This community in Gatineau Park, north of Aylmer, was named in 1879 after a small lake, which was earlier named after nearby **Mont King**. It is reported that the mountain was named after an early settler in the area of the present park. Dr. William Frederick King (1854–1916), who was appointed the Dominion Astronomer in 1905, established the first geodetic triangulation station that year on the mountain, and subsequently it was incorrectly assumed the mountain had been named after him.

King Solomon Dome YT The highest point (1234 m) in the Klondike area, this mountain was initially called *The Dome*, because of its shape. Recognizing some of the richest goldfields in the world radiated from it, the miners named it after the biblical king's lost gold mines.

Kingsport NS The post office in this village, located north of Wolfville on the shore of Minas Basin, was named in 1874 after its situation as a port in Kings County. It was earlier known as *Indian Point* and *Oak Point*.

Kingston NS The first post office of this village (1957), located west of Kentville in the Annapolis Valley, was called

Kingston Station in 1869, when the Dominion Atlantic Railway was built from Digby to Halifax, and was renamed Kingston in 1922. **Kingston Village** post office was established in 1842, 3 km to the south. Both post offices were named after Kings County.

Kingston ON The township and townsite of the city (1846) of Kingston were surveyed in 1783 and were first named *King's Town* after George III, but were soon shortened to Kingston. The French had built Fort Cataraqui in 1673 at the mouth of the Cataraqui River. It was renamed Fort Frontenac that year by Sieur de La Salle in honour of Louis de Buade (1620–98), comte de Frontenac et de Palluau, governor of New France, 1672–82 and 1689–98. Kingston was the capital of the Province of Canada from 1841 to 1843, when it was moved to Montreal.

Kingston PE The school district in this place west of Charlottetown was called *South Wiltshire* in 1864. Its post office opened as *South Wiltshire* in 1870, renamed Kingston in 1898. This place became a municipal community in 1974, and it embraces the area of Emyvale.

Kingsville ON This town (1901) in Essex County, west of Leamington, was named in 1843 by developer Andrew Stewart after Col. James King, who took up Stewart's offer to have the place named after the first person to build a house here. King was later a customs collector and court clerk here.

King William Island NU Between Boothia Peninsula and Victoria Island, this island (13,111 km²) was named in 1830 by explorer Sir John Ross (1777–1856) after William IV (1765–1837), who became the king of Great Britain and Ireland that year.

Kinistino SK The area of this town (1952) west of Melfort was known as the *Carrot River Settlement* in the 1870s. Its post office was named *Kinisteno* in 1883, likely taken from the Cree name Kenistin. Four years later it was respelled Kinistino.

Kinkora PE This municipal community (1983) northeast of Borden-Carleton was incorporated as a village in 1955. Its school district was called *Somerset* about 1841. Its post office opened as *Somerset* in 1867 and was changed 20 years later to Kinkora after the ruins of the palace of Irish king Brian Boru (926–1014), near Killaloe, County Clare, Ireland. The area of Kinkora was settled by Irish immigrants about 1841.

Kinlock PE Formerly part of the municipal community of Keppoch-Kinlock, this place south of Charottetown became part of the town of Stratford in 1995. It was named after Kinloch, Isle of Skye, Scotland.

Kinloss ON In 1999 this township became part of the township of Huron-Kinloss in Bruce County. Kinloss in Scotland is northeast of Inverness.

Kinuso AB This village (1949) south of Lesser Slave Lake was first known as *Swan River*, but its post office was named Kinuso in 1915 after the Cree word for 'fish'.

Kipawa, Lac QC This lake with a vast labyrinth of arms and bays is located near the town of Témiscaming in northwestern Quebec. The name in Algonquin means 'it is closed' or 'it is blocked', possibly in reference to the lake's outlet at Laniel, where **Rivière Kipawa** carries it waters to Lake Timiskaming.

Kipling SK This town (1954) southwest of Grenfell was founded in 1909 by the Canadian Northern Railway, and was named after popular writer Rudyard Kipling (1865–1936). The post office was named *Kipling Station* that year, with the name being shortened to Kipling in 1955.

Kippens NL Located on St. George's Bay and on the southwestern coast of Newfoundland, this town (1968) may have been named after a Capt. Kippen, who was shipwrecked here in the 1840s, or after a local Keeping family.

Kirkfield ON In 2001 this community became a part of the city of Kawartha Lakes, Victoria County, northwest of Lindsay. Its name was selected by residents in 1864 from a list of eight names provided by the post office department. As most of the area's settlers were Highland Scots, it appropriately reflected the Scottish kirk (church) and the farming community.

Kirkland QC In 2002 this city became part of the city of Montreal. In 2006 Kirkland recovered its status as a city. It was named in 1961 after Dr. Charles-Aimé Kirkland (1896–1961), member of the Legislative Assembly, 1939–61.

Kirkland Lake ON In 1907 surveyor Lewis Rorke named a small lake in Timiskaming District after Winifred Kirkland, a secretary in the provincial department of mines. Gold was discovered here four years later, and a mining community quickly developed. In 1972 the municipal township of Teck, which included this urban centre as well as the communities of Swastika and Chaput Hughes, was incorporated as the town of Kirkland Lake.

Kirkton ON In 2001 this place, 28 km located west of Stratford, became part of the boundary of the townships of South Huron and Perth South. Five Kirk brothers settled here in the 1840s. In 1856 Presbyterian minister John Fotheringham named the post office after many places Kirktons in Scotland.

Kisbey SK Situated northeast of Estevan, this village (1907) was established by the Canadian Pacific Railway in 1905 and named after Richard Claud Kisbey (1862–1941), then the agent of the Crown Lands Department in Alameda.

Kitchener ON This city (1912) in the regional county of Waterloo was named *Berlin* in 1833 after the capital of Prussia. Because patriotism of local residents was doubted during the First World War and because of fear of business losses from products labelled 'made in Berlin', the city was renamed in 1916 after British military hero Lord Horatio Herbert Kitchener, who was drowned that year off the Orkney Islands. In the early years, it had been known as *Sandhills*, and also *Ben Eby's* and *Ebytown* after Mennonite bishop Benjamin Eby.

Kitchener, Mount AB This mountain (3480 m) on the north side of the Columbia Icefield was named in 1919 after Horatio Herbert Kitchener, 1st Earl Kitchener (1850–1916), a prominent British military leader, who was lost at sea when the HMS *Hampshire* struck a mine north of Scotland. There are three mountains named after him in British Columbia, one south of Kootenay Lake, a second in the Coast Mountains, near Knight Inlet, and a third in the northwest, near the Stikine River.

Kitimat BC This district municipality (1953) southeast of Prince Rupert and at the head of Kitimat Arm was founded in 1951 by the Aluminum Company of Canada. **Kitimat Arm** was named in 1837 by the Hudson's Bay Company after the Kitamaat, a Kwakiutl tribe whose name in Coast Tsimshian means 'people of the falling snow'.

Kitley ON In 2001 this township became part of the township of Elizabethtown-Kitley, united counties of Leeds and Grenville. It was named in 1798 after the Bastard family home in Devon, England. The Bastard family acquired the Kitley estate in 1710. John Pollexfen Bastard (1756–1816) was a British member of Parliament (1784–1800) when Kitley Township was named. The family name is pronounced as 'bahs-TARD'. *See also* Bastard.

Kitscoty AB The post office in this village (1911) west of Lloydminster was named in 1907 after Kit's Coty House in Kent, England, north of Maidstone. The name may have been given by Canadian Pacific Railway contractor George Still. The ancient English 'house' is a Neolithic structure comprising three large upright stones with a fourth balanced over them.

Kitwanga BC The post office in this place at the confluence of the Skeena River and **Kitwanga River** was named *Gitwangak* in 1910. It was changed to Kitwanga in 1917. The river's name in Gitksan means 'people of the place of rabbits'.

Klahowya Mountain BC This mountain (2922 m) in the Purcell Mountains, northeast of Kaslo, was named in 1931 after **Klahowya Creek**. The creek was named after a riverboat built

in 1910 by Capt. Francis P. Armstrong, who had operated boats on the upper Columbia River between 1885 and 1914. In Kootenay the name means 'greetings friend'.

Kleefeld MB West of Steinbach, this Mennonite community was established in 1896, and its post office was named that year after a village in Ukraine, where locals had previously lived. In German the name means 'clover field'. It had been briefly called *Gruenfeld* ('green field').

Kleinburg ON This place in the city of Vaughan, northwest of Toronto, was named in the 1830s after John Nicholas Klein Sr., who built a sawmill, a grist mill, and a cooperage on the West Humber River. The post office was called *Klineburg* in 1852, and corrected to Kleinburg five years later.

Kliniklini River BC Rising northeast of Mount Waddington, this river flows west and then south into the head of Knight Inlet. In Kwakwala the name means 'eulachon grease', a valuable component in the diet of both coastal and interior Aboriginal tribes. The oily eulachon is also called 'candle-fish'. The river provided a 'grease-trail' route into the interior, where the Kwakwala traded with the Chilcotin and other tribes. The post office at **Kleena Kleene**, where the Chilcotin–Bella Coola Highway crosses the river, was named in 1927.

Klondike River YT Rising in the Ogilvie Mountains, this river flows west into the Yukon River at Dawson. The name derives from the Gwich'in *Thronduik* ('hammer water') and recalls their practice of driving stakes into the river's bottom to trap migrating salmon. On learning of the discovery of gold on Bonanza Creek, a tributary of the Klondike, North West Mounted Police Insp. Charles Constantine (1846–1912), the mining recorder at Fortymile River, rendered the name in 1896 as *Klondyke*. Two years later the Geographic Board of Canada made the present spelling official.

Kluane Lake YT Northwest of Whitehorse, this lake (405 km²) was named in 1882 by Aurel Krause, who undertook an expedition on behalf of the Bremen Geographical Society. In Tlinkit the name means 'whitefish place'. **Kluane National Park Reserve** (22,015 km²) was established in 1972 in the area of Mount Logan and the St. Elias Mountains.

Knight Inlet BC This deep 95-km fiord extending inland from Queen Charlotte Strait was named in 1792 by Lt. Cmdr. William Broughton (1762–1821) after Capt. (later Adm. Sir) John Knight (c.1748–1831). Broughton and Knight had served together in 1775–6.

Knowlton QC Established as a village in 1888, it became part of the town of Lac-Brome in 1971. It was named after Paul Holland Knowlton (1787–1863), who settled on a farm on the south shore of Lac Brome in 1815, built a store and a distillery, and exercised considerable influence in the area. The post office opened in 1851.

Knutsford PE West of O'Leary, this place was established as a school district in 1869. It may have been named after Knutsford, on the southwest side of Manchester, England. Its post office from 1871 to 1913 was called *O'Leary Road*.

Koch Island NU In the north part of Foxe Basin and southwest of Baffin Island, this island (458 km²) was named in 1921–4 by the Fifth Thule expedition after Danish polar explorer Johan Peter Koch.

Koksoak, Rivière QC Flowing into the south side of Ungava Bay, this wide river is the main outlet for several rivers draining north from central Quebec. The name derives from the Inuktitut for 'big river' and was known in the early 1800s, but was not made official until 1916 after being called *Big River* or *South River* for many years.

Kootenay River BC Rising in the Rocky Mountains, southeast of Field, this river (780 km) flows south, crossing the border into Montana, northeast of Libby, and recrossing the border from Idaho, 100 km to the west. After flowing into **Kootenay Lake** (407 km²), it turns west to join the Columbia at Castlegar. The river and the lake were named after the Blackfoot pronunciation of the name of the Kootenay, a distinct linguistic group, whose name means 'water people'. In 1808 geographer David Thompson (1770–1857) named the river *McGillivray's River* after brothers Duncan and William McGillivray, North West Company traders. **Kootenay National Park** (1378 km²) was created in 1920.

Kouchibouguac River NB This river flows northeast into Northumberland Strait. Its name derives from the Mi'kmaq *pijeboogwek* ('river of the long tideway'). Nearby is the **Kouchibouguacis River**, whose Mi'kmaq name means 'little river of the long tideway'. Extending along the shore of the strait is **Kouchibouguac National Park** (225 km²), established in 1969.

Krestova BC This community north of Castlegar was named by Peter Veregin Sr. (d.1924), who led Doukhobors from Saskatchewan in 1908 to the Slocan River valley. The name in Russian means 'place of the cross'.

Kugluktuk NU Situated on Coronation Gulf at the mouth of the Coppermine River, this hamlet (1981) was officially given this name on 1 January 1996. First known as *Coronation*, it was established as a trading post by Charles Klengenberg in 1916. It was renamed *Coppermine* in 1930. The name Kugluktuk means 'place of rapids' in Inuktitut, probably in reference to Bloody Fall, where a group of Chipewyan, accompanying Samuel Hearne (1745–92), massacred a group of Inuit 17 July 1771. *See also* Coppermine River.

Kuujjuaq QC Located on the west bank of Rivière Koksoak, this largest of Quebec's northern villages became the site in 1830 of the Hudson's Bay Company's Fort Chimo. The word *chimo* in Inuktitut means 'greeting', in the sense of 'are you friendly?' The community of *Fort-Chimo* was renamed Kuujjuaq in 1979, using the contemporary spelling of Koksoak ('big river').

Kuujjuarapik QC Situated at the mouth of the Grande rivière à la Baleine in northwestern Quebec, this location was first known during the Second World War as *Great Whale River*. By 1960 the Inuit residents started calling it *Kuujjuaq*, but they were persuaded by the residents of Fort-Chimo (Kuujjuaq) on the larger 'grand river' to call their place Kuujjuarapik ('the little grand river'). In 1961 the Quebec government changed the name to *Grande-Baleine*, and the following year it became Poste-de-la-Baleine, which remains the postal name. Kuujjuarapik was recognized as the name of the northern village in 1980, and the Cree name Whapmagoostui was also authorized. In English the place is commonly called Great Whale.

Kyle SK Located north of Swift Current and Lake Diefenbaker, the post office in this town (1959) was called *Kyleville* in 1909 after early settler Jerry Kyle. When the Canadian Pacific Railway built its line south from Rosetown in 1923, it shortened the name to Kyle, and the postal name was shortened the following year. There had been another Kyle post office (1905–1918) northwest of Melfort, which was named after *Kyle* in Ayrshire, Scotland, near the birthplace of poet Robert Burns.

La Baie QC In 2006 this city became part of the city of Saguenay, regional county of Le Fjord-du-Saguenay. Located at the head of the Baie des Ha! Ha!, this city was created in 1975 through the merger of the towns of Bagotville, Grande-Baie, and Port-Alfred, and the parish municipality of Bagotville. Grande-Baie had been incorporated as a town in 1859. The town of Port-Alfred, created in 1919, was named after Julien-Édouard-Alfred Dubuc (1871–1947), who founded a pulp company here at the beginning of the century. The town of Bagotville was named after the township of Bagot, proclaimed in 1848 and named after Sir Charles Bagot (1781–1843), governor of the Province of Canada, 1841–3.

Labelle QC This municipality in the regional county of Les Laurentides, west of Mont Tremblant, was created in 1973 through the amalgamation of the village of Labelle and the township municipality of *Joly*. The post office was called *Chute-aux-Iroquois* from 1881 to 1902, when it was changed to Labelle the year that the village was incorporated. It took its name from the township, proclaimed in 1894, and named in honour of Mgr. Antoine Labelle (1833–91), who promoted settlement in the area north of Montreal.

Laberge, Lake YT A widening of the Yukon River, directly north of Whitehorse, this lake was named *Lake Lebarge* in 1870 by American naturalist William H. Dall (1845–1927), who was working on behalf of the Western Union Telegraph Company in choosing a route for a line from the United States to Russia. The United States Board on Geographic Names adopted it in 1890, noting it was named after 'Michael Lebarge'. This and other decisions made for names on Canadian territory prompted Canada in 1897 to set up its own names board in 1898. The Canadian board consulted church officials in Chateauguay, QC, and learned that Michel Laberge was still living there. The name was corrected to Lake Laberge. Michel Laberge was born in 1836 in Chateauguay and died there in 1909.

Labrador NL The province of Newfoundland and Labrador was renamed from *Newfoundland* in 2001 to include this mainland district. An amendment was made in the Constitution of Canada. The name may be traced to the Portuguese *lavrador* ('small landholder') João Fernandes. Fernandes explored the coasts of North America at the end of the 1400s and beginning of the 1500s. In 1500 he identified Kalaallit Nunaat (Greenland) as *Tiera del Lavrador*

and the present Labrador as *Tiera del Corte Real*, given for another *lavrador*, Gaspar Corte-Real. About 1560, after the name 'Greenland' was found to be in general use, mapmakers shifted the name 'Labrador' to the mainland.

Labrador City NL In western Labrador, this town (1961) was founded as *Carol Lake* in 1959 by the Iron Ore Company of Canada. It has the distinction of being the most populous incorporated municipality in Canada with the word 'City' as the terminal part of its name.

La Broquerie MB East of Steinbach, this place's post office was named in 1882 by Mgr. Alexandre Taché (1823–94) after his uncle, Joseph B. La Broquerie (1759–1830). The rural municipality of **La Broquerie** was erected a year earlier.

L'Acadie QC Situated west of Saint-Jean-sur-Richelieu and on the **Rivière L'Acadie**, this municipality's post office was called L'Acadie in 1835. The municipality was incorporated as *Lacadie* in 1926 and was changed to L'Acadie in 1976. Acadians settled here in 1768, a few years after their expulsion from Acadia.

Lac-à-la-Tortue QC This municipality east of Grand-Mère was created in 1981, taking its name from the post office, which had opened in 1882. The name likely reflected the presence of many turtles (*tortues*) here.

Lac-au-Saumon QC Situated in the regional county of La Matapédia and midway between the towns of Causapscal and Amqui, this village was named in 1905 after Lac au Saumon, an enlargement of the Rivière Matapédia. Its post office had opened eight years earlier.

Lac-Baker NB The post office in this village (1967) west of Edmundston was named *Lake Baker* in 1893 after the 8-km-long lake, which extends into Quebec. It was renamed Lac-Baker in 1938. The lake was named after John Baker (1796–1868), who strenuously resisted having his land being considered British territory in the 1820s, which inflamed a boundary dispute between New Brunswick and Maine, and was not resolved until the Webster-Ashburton Treaty of 1842. *See also* Baker Brook.

Lac-Beauport QC This municipality north of Quebec City, and inland from the borough of Beauport, was named in 1989 after the parish municipality of *Saint-Dunstan-du-*

Lac-Beauport, created in 1855. The area is a popular all-season resort centre.

Lac-Bouchette QC Located south of Lac Saint-Jean, this municipality was established in 1930, taking its name from the post office that opened in 1902. The lake was named in 1828 after survey party leader Joseph Bouchette (1774–1841), who was surveyor general of Lower Canada, 1801–40.

Lac-Brome QC This town in the regional county of Brome-Missisquoi was created in 1971 through the merger of the villages of Knowlton and Foster, and the township municipality of *Brome*. The township municipality had been created in 1845, abolished in 1847, and re-established in 1855, and took its name from **Brome Township**, proclaimed in 1797.

Lac-Carré QC This village south of Mont Tremblant was named in 1947 after a small square-shaped (*carré*) lake. It was established as the municipality of *Saint-Faustin-Station* in 1922. This name was the postal designation from 1900 to 1946, at which point it was changed to Lac-Carré.

Lac-des-Écorces QC Located on the east side of Mont-Laurier, this village was created in 1955, with its post office having been opened in 1903. The name of the nearby lake relates to bark (*écorce*) stripped from birch trees.

Lac-Drolet QC This municipality north of Lac-Mégantic was named in 1968 after the nearby lake, called after pioneer settlers. In 1885 it had been created as the township municipality of *Saint-Samuel-de-Gayhurst*, which was also the postal name from 1879 to 1969.

Lac du Bonnet MB The post office in this village (1947) on the Winnipeg River, northeast of Winnipeg, was named in 1900 after the **Lac du Bonnet**, a widening of the river. The lake's name recalls the practice of Aboriginals laying stones in a circle and crowning them with a wreath of plants and branches.

Lac-Etchemin QC The post office in this town, located in the regional county of Les Etchemins, southeast of Quebec City and at the head of Rivière Etchemin, was called *Lake Etchemin* in 1866 and was changed to Lac-Etchemin in 1920. Lac-Etchemin was established as a village in 1960 and became a town six years later. In Abenaki the name means 'where there is leather for snowshoes'.

Lachenaie QC This town (1972) fronting on Rivière des Mille-Îles, northeast of Montreal, was created as a municipality in 1845, abolished two years later, and re-established in 1855 as the parish municipality of *Saint-Charles-de-Lachenaie*. The name derives from fur trader Charles Aubert de La Chesnaye (1632–1702).

Lachine QC In 2002 this city became a borough in the city of Montreal. The **Rapides de Lachine** may be traced to René-Robert Cavelier de La Salle (1643–87), who had planned an expedition to China in 1669. After returning that year far short of his objective, his land, which had been granted to him in 1667, derisively became known as La Chine. The religious parish of Saints-Anges-de-la-Chine was created in 1678. Lachine post office opened in 1829; the place became a village in 1848 and a city in 1909.

Lachute QC A town (1885) in the regional county of Argenteuil, west of Montreal, it is located at falls (*chute*) on the Rivière du Nord. Known as *La Chute Settlement* in the late 1700s, its post office opened in 1835, although between 1880 and 1957 it was called *Lachute Mills*.

Lac-Kénogami QC In 2002 this township municipality became part of the city of Saguenay. It took its name from the township of **Kénogami**, proclaimed in 1865, with its name meaning 'long lake' in Montagnais. Its post office opened in 1899 and it became a municipality in 1986.

Lac La Biche AB This town (1950) on the south shore of **Lac la Biche**, northeast of Edmonton, was established in 1798 as a North West Company trading post by geographer David Thompson (1770–1857). The lake's name, which translates from French to mean 'red doe lake', was recorded in 1790 by Hudson's Bay Company surveyor Philip Turnor (c.1751–99).

Lac La Hache BC On the east shore of **Lac la Hache**, northwest of 100 Mile House, this place's post office was named *Lake La Hache* in 1864 and renamed *Lac La Hache* 10 years later. The present form was confirmed in 1955. The lake was named after an incident in the nineteenth century when a Hudson's Bay Company fur brigade lost a load of axes (*haches*) or hatchets after a horse carrying them broke through the ice and drowned.

Lac-Mégantic QC In the regional county of Le Granit, east of Sherbrooke, this place became the town of *Mégantic* in 1907 through the merger of the villages of *Mégantic* (1885) and *Agnès* (1895). The present name was adopted in 1958. The town is located at the north end of **Lac Mégantic**, the source of Rivière Chaudière; its name has its roots in the Abenaki *namagôtegw* ('at the camp of the salmon trout').

Lac-Nominingue QC This municipality east of Mont-Laurier was created in 1971 through the merger of the municipalities of *Loranger* (1896), *Loranger-Partie-Sud-Est* (1920), and *Nominingue* (1904). The post office, called *Nominingue* in 1887 and changed to Lac-Nominingue in 1986, has its roots in the Algonquin *Onamani Sakaigan* ('vermilion lake').

Lacolle QC This village south of Saint-Jean-sur-Richelieu and near the New York border was named in 1920. It was severed from the municipality of *Saint-Bernard-de-Lacolle*, created in 1855; ten years earlier it was called Lacolle, but abolished in 1847. The name may be traced to the seigneury of La Colle, granted in 1743 to Daniel-Hyacinthe-Marie Liénard de Beaujeu (1711–55). The name may also derive from a hill (*colline*) 7 km to the southwest, where Rivière Lacolle was first identified as *Rivière à la Colle*.

Lacombe AB The post office in this town (1902) north of Red Deer was named in 1891 after Fr. Albert Lacombe (1827–1916), an Oblate missionary to the Cree, Blackfoot, and Métis from 1849. The post office was earlier called *Barnett. See also* St. Albert.

La Côte-de-Beaupré QC This regional county northeast of Quebec City was named in 1982. The name has its roots in the early seventeenth-century phrase *le beau pré* ('the pretty meadow'), which was blended into Beaupré by 1657.

La Côte-de-Gaspé QC A regional county embracing an area of nearly 4000 km² centred on the town of Gaspé, it takes its name from the town, the peninsula, and the bay. It is usually called simply La Côte.

Lac-Saint-Charles QC In 2002 this municipality became a sector of Quebec City. Located 16 km northwest of the centre of Quebec City, this municipality was named in 1947 after the lake. Along with **Rivière Saint-Charles**, both places were named in the early 1700s by Récollet missionaries after Charles Desboues (or de Boves), the vicar of Pontoise, 30 km northwest of Paris. The post office was called *Lake St. Charles* from 1905 to 1936, when it was changed to its current form.

Lac-Saint-Jean-Est QC Located on the east side of Lac Saint-Jean, this regional county (1982) is centred on the city of Alma, and embraces 2709 km².

Lac-Supérieur QC This municipality east of Mont Tremblant was first named *Wolfe* in 1881 after Wolfe Township, which was named in honour of Gen. James Wolfe (1727–59), the British commander at the Battle of the Plains of Abraham in September 1759. In 1944 it was renamed *Saint-Faustin* after the parish founded in 1878. It was changed to its present name in 1957, which had been its postal name since 1913.

Ladner BC This place is located in the district municipality of Delta, south of Vancouver, and on the south bank of the Fraser River. William Henry Ladner (1826–1907) and his brother, Thomas Ellis Ladner (1836–1922) traveled to California in 1852, then went to the Cariboo Gold Rush in 1858. In 1867 William pre-empted land in Delta, with the post office on his property. It was called *Ladner's Landing* in 1876, and was shortened to Ladner in 1895.

La Doré QC Located northwest of Lac Saint-Jean, this parish municipality was called *Saint-Félicien-Partie-Nord-Ouest* in 1906, renamed *Notre-Dame-de-la-Doré* in 1915, and given its present name in 1983 after the Rivière au Doré. *Doré* is the French word for 'pickerel'.

Ladysmith BC A town (1904) on the east coast of Vancouver Island and on the forty-ninth parallel, it was originally called *Oyster Harbour*. When coal-mine owner, politician, and premier of British Columbia James Dunsmuir (1851–1920) received word on 1 March 1900 that Ladysmith in South Africa had been relieved the previous day, he decided to call the place Ladysmith. The post office was renamed the following January. The original Ladysmith had been named in 1850 after Lady Juana Smith (1798–1872), the wife of Sir Harry Smith (1787–1860), governor of Cape Colony and high commissioner to South Africa, 1847–52. He had rescued her in 1812, when she was 13, after the British had overrun Badajos in Spain, and married her the same year.

Ladysmith QC This community north of Shawville in the regional county of Pontiac was named on 28 February 1900 in honour of the lifting of the siege of Ladysmith in Natal, South Africa. That town had been named after Lady Juana Smith (1798–1872), the wife of Sir Harry Smith, governor of the Cape Colony, 1847–52.

Lafleche SK A town (1953) west of Assiniboia, its post office was named in 1909 after Mgr. Louis-François-Richer Laflèche (1818–98), a missionary in the West, 1844–54, and bishop of Trois-Rivières, QC, from 1869.

Lafontaine QC This village (1958), on the north side of the city of Saint-Jérôme was named after Sir Louis-Hippolyte LaFontaine (1807–64), a prominent Reformer after the union of Canada in 1841, who formed union governments with Robert Baldwin (1804–58), 1842–3, and 1848–51.

La Guadaloupe QC This village in the regional county of Beauce-Sartigan, southwest of the city of Saint-Georges, was known as the village of *Saint-Évariste-Station* from 1929 to 1949, when it was changed to La Guadaloupe. It was named after the religious parish of **Notre-Dame-de-la-Guadaloupe**, created in 1945 and named in commemoration of the 400th anniversary of three apparitions of the Virgin Mary to Mexican Juan Diego. The place in Mexico had been named in honour of Our Lady of Guadaloupe, whose image had been found by a shepherd in Spain's Extramadura.

La Haute-Côte-Nord QC Located between Tadoussac and Betsiamites, this regional county, embracing over 12,500 km², was named in 1982 after its location on the upper north shore of the St. Lawrence River.

La Haute-Yamaska QC In the upper watershed of the Rivière Yamaska, and centred on the city of Granby, this regional county was named in 1982.

LaHave River NS Rising within 20 km of the Bay of Fundy, this river (75 km) flows southeast to the Atlantic Ocean. It was named after **Cape LaHave**, at the outer side of **Cape LaHave Island** and 12 km south of the river's mouth. The cape was named *Cap de la Hève* in 1604 by Pierre Du Gua de Monts after Cap de la Hève, at the entrance to the port of La Havre, France, where his voyage had originated.

Laird SK The post office at this village (1911) north of Saskatoon was named *Tiefengrund* in 1900. It was renamed nine years later after David Laird (1833–1914), first resident lieutenant-governor of the North-West Territories, 1876–81, and Indian commissioner for the West, 1898–1909.

La Jacques-Cartier QC Extending north of Quebec City, this regional county was named in 1981 after its central feature, the **Rivière Jacques–Cartier**, named in homage to the explorer who discovered of Canada.

Lajemmerais QC This regional county fronting on the St. Lawrence from Boucherville to Contrecoeur was named in 1982 after Marie-Marguerite Dufrost de Lajemmerais (1701–71), also known as Marguerite d'Youville, the founder of the Grey Nuns in 1753.

Lake ON In 2001 this township became a part of the municipality of Marmora and Lake, Hastings County. It was named in 1822 for Viscount Gerard Lake (1744–1808), who conquered Delhi in India in 1803.

Lake Cowichan BC This village (1944) west of Duncan is located at the point where the **Cowichan River** flows east from **Cowichan Lake**. The Cowichan, a Salish tribe that once occupied a large area on both sides of the Strait of Georgia, took their name from an Island Halkomelem word meaning 'land warmed by the sun'. The name referred to a rock formation on the side of Mount Tzuhalem that resembled a frog basking in the sun. The Cowichan called the lake *Kaatza* ('big lake'). *See also* North Cowichan.

Lakefield ON North of the city of Peterborough, this village (1874) was variously known as *Nelson's Falls*, *Thompson's Rapids*, *Herriot's Falls*, and *Selby*. By 1853 it had been laid out and named Lakefield, and the *North Douro* post office, named in 1856, became Lakefield in 1875.

Lake Lenore SK Located between Humboldt and Melfort, the post office at this village (1921) was named *Lenora Lake* in 1906 after the lake 5 km to the north. The lake had been named after surveyor Theodore Fawcett's daughter Lenora, but it became **Lake Lenore** after the village was incorporated. The postal name was changed to Lake Lenore in 1939.

Lake Louise AB This resort community northwest of Banff was named in 1916 after the lake, which had been named in 1884 after Princess Louise Caroline Alberta (1848–1939), fourth daughter of Queen Victoria and wife of the Marquess of Lorne (1845–1914), governor general of Canada, 1878–83. First known in 1883 as *Holt City*, the station was renamed *Laggan* that year by Lord Strathcona after Laggan, Inverness-shire, Scotland.

Lakelse Lake BC Located south of Terrace and on the eastern shore of **Lakelse Lake**, this place's post office was called *Lakelse* from 1913 to 1935. The lake's name in Tsimshian means 'fresh water mussel'.

Lake of Bays ON This municipal township created in 1971 in the district municipality of Muskoka was named after its main feature, itself named in 1853 by geologist Alexander Murray (1810–84) after its numerous coves and bays. The lake had been earlier identified as *Lake Baptiste*, *Trading Lake*, and *Forked Lake*.

La Loche SK On the east shore of **Lac La Loche** and east of Fort McMurray, AB, this settlement was established by the Chipewyan in the early 1800s. The French word *loche* identifies a fish called 'burbot' or 'freshwater cod'. When Peter Pond (1740–1807) travelled in 1778 over the 20-km Methy Portage, separating the waters of the Mackenzie and Churchill basins, the lake was called *Methy Lake*. The North West Company had a post here in 1808, and the Hudson's Bay Company opened the Portage La Loche post here in 1853. La Loche post office opened in 1926.

La Macaza QC Erected in 1930 as a municipality northwest of Mont Tremblant, this place took its name from **Lac Macaza**, which may have been named after an Algonquin chief or after an Aboriginal who camped on its shore.

La Malbaie QC In 1608 Samuel de Champlain (1567–1635) named the **Rivière Malbaie** because the bay at its mouth had insufficient depth to anchor vessels. Incorporated as a village in 1896, it became a town in 1958. In 1762 John Nairne and Malcolm Fraser, retired officers from Gen. James Wolfe's army, received grants at the mouth of the river, and named the river, the bay, and the settlement *Murray Bay* after Gen. James Murray (c.1721–84), Wolfe's successor. *Murray Bay* was the post office from 1832 to 1914, when it was changed to La Malbaie, although *Murray Bay* continued to have wide international usage well into the latter half of the twentieth century.

Lamaline NL On the south side of the Burin Peninsula, this town (1963) may have been named after the dangerous shoals offshore, described by the French as *La Maligne* ('the evil one'). A map of 1750 identified *cap de la Meline*, with islands offshore called *Isles de la Meline*.

La Matapédia QC Embracing the central valley of **Rivière Matapédia**, this regional county was named in 1982. It encompasses 20 municipalities, including the towns of Amqui and Causapscal.

La Mauricie National Park QC Established in 1970 on the west side of the Rivière Saint-Maurice and in the regional county of Le Centre-de-la-Mauricie, this national park (544 km²) took its name from the regional designation, Mauricie, proposed in 1931 by Mgr. Albert Tessier (1895–1976).

Lambart, Mount YT Situated in the St. Elias Mountains, this mountain (3269 m) was named in 1918 after geodesist Howard Frederick John Lambart (1880–1946). From 1906 to 1917 he worked on the Yukon–Alaska boundary, and determined the position and height of this mountain. He led a United States-Canada expedition to climb the mountain in 1925.

Lambeth ON In 2000 Lambeth became a part of the city of London, located southwest of the city centre. It was named *Westminster*, after Westminster Township, in 1840. In 1857 it had been called after the district of Lambeth in Greater London, England, on the south side of the River Thames.

Lambton ON This county was named in 1849 by Malcolm Cameron (1808–76), assistant commissioner of public works in the Province of Canada, for Sir John George Lambton, Earl of Durham (1792–1840), governor-in-chief of British North America, 1838.

Lambton QC A municipality on the east side of Lac Saint-François and north of Lac-Mégantic, it was created a township municipality in 1845 and a municipality in 1913, taking its name from **Lambton Township**. The township was proclaimed in 1848 and named after Lord Durham, governor-in-chief of British North America, 1838. The author of the famous Durham Report, he recommended the union of the two Canadas under a single government.

Lamèque NB The post office of this town (1982) on **Île Lamèque**, east of Caraquet, opened in 1867. In 1672 Acadia Gov. Nicolas Denys (c.1598–1688) referred to the island as *Grande Ile de Miscou*. It was identified in 1777 as *Shippegan Island* by map-maker Joseph Frederic Wallet DesBarres. After a local petition in 1974, the present name of the island was officially acknowledged.

L'Amiante QC This regional county centred on the city of Thetford Mines was named in 1982 after the principal industrial activity of the area, the extraction of asbestos (*amiante*).

La Mitis QC Situated on the south shore of the St. Lawrence and centred on the **Rivière Mitis**, east of Rimouski, this regional county was established in 1982. The name of the river has its roots in the Mi'kmaq *miti sipo* ('poplar river').

Lamont AB The post office in this town (1968) northeast of Edmonton was named in 1906 after John Henderson Lamont (1865–1936), who moved from Toronto to Prince Albert in 1899 to practice law. He served in both the House of Commons and the Saskatchewan Legislature before being appointed to the Supreme Court of Saskatchewan in 1907 and to the Supreme Court of Canada in 1927.

Lampman SK This town (1963) northeast of Estevan was established by the Canadian Northern Railway in 1909 as a station on its Poet's Line. It was named after poet Archibald Lampman (1861–99). Postal service was set up here in 1910.

Lanark ON The village (1862) of Lanark was founded by Scottish settlers in 1820, who named it *New Lanark* for the county and town east of Glasgow. That year **Lanark Township** surrounded the village, but in 1998 they became parts of the township of **Lanark Highlands**. Lanark post office was established in 1824 at the village. The following year, **Lanark County** was separated from Carleton County.

Lancaster ON Ontario's most easterly township, it was named in 1787 after the Duke of Lancaster, one of the titles of George III. Lancaster post office was first located in 1789 at the mouth of the Raisin River, now the site of **South Lancaster**. When the Grand Trunk Railway was built from Montreal to Brockville in 1855, its station, 2 km to the north, was called *New Lancaster*. It soon became simply Lancaster, and became a village in 1887.

Lancaster Sound NU Between Baffin and Bylot Islands on the south, and Devon Island on the north, this 350-km-long entrance to Parry Channel was named *Sir James Lancaster Sound* by explorers Robert Bylot (d.1622) and William Baffin (1837–1915) in 1616. The place was named after Sir James Lancaster (c.1554–1618), a trader for the East India Company. The place name was subsequently shortened to Lancaster Sound.

L'Ancienne-Lorette QC In 2002 this city became part of Quebec City; but in 2006, it recovered its city status. Located 11 km west of Quebec City, it was incorporated as the village of *Notre-Dame-de-Lorette* in 1948. Its post office was called *Ancienne-Lorette* in 1854, in contrast to *Nouvelle-Lorette*, the present city of Loretteville, to the north. In 1673 the Huron settlement here was placed under the protection of Notre-

Dame de l'Annonciation, whose order was modelled on the Holy House of the Virgin, established in 1295 in Loreto on Italy's east coast.

Landis SK Located northwest of Biggar, this village (1909) was founded by the Grand Trunk Pacific Railway in 1908, and named after the American judge Kenesaw Mountain Landis (1866–1944). Landis was well known as the commissioner of baseball, 1920–44. The post office had been opened as *Daneville* in 1907 and was changed to Landis in 1909.

Lang SK Situated northwest of Weyburn, this village (1906) was established by the Canadian Pacific Railway's extension of the Soo Line in 1893 and named after its resident engineer G.M. Lang, who was living in Moose Jaw. The post office here opened in 1904.

L'Ange-Gardien QC Located northeast of Quebec City, this parish municipality was established in 1845, abolished two years later, and re-established in 1855. *Ange-Gardien* post office opened in 1861. Its area was the site of the religious parish of Saints-Anges-Gardiens, erected here in 1664. The village of **L'Ange-Gardien**, southwest of Granby, was long known as *Ange-Gardien-de-Rouville*, *Saint-Ange-Gardien*, and *Canrobert*. The municipality of **L'Ange-Gardien** on the Ottawa River was created in 1980, having been part of the town of Buckingham since 1975. Its roots may be traced to the religious parish, created in 1861, which became the parish municipality in 1881.

Langenburg SK This town (1959), southwest of Yorkton and near the Manitoba border, was established by the Manitoba and North Western Railway in 1886. It was named by German settlers after Prince Hermann Ernst Hohenlohe Langenburg (1832–1913), who visited the Canadian prairies in 1883. The post office was first called *Hohenlohe*, but it was renamed Langenburg in 1888.

Langford BC A former district municipality, this city (2003) is located west of Victoria. Its post office was named *Langford Station* in 1911 after **Langford Lake**. The lake received its name from Capt. Edward E. Langford, who came to Victoria in 1851 to manage the Esquimalt farm of the Puget Sound Agricultural Company, which was owned by the Hudson's Bay Company. He returned to England 10 years later.

Langham SK Located near the east bank of the North Saskatchewan, northwest of Saskatoon, this town (1907) was founded in 1905 by the Canadian Northern Railway and named after E. Langham, then general passenger agent for the line.

Langley BC The district municipality (1936) and the city (1955) of Langley took their names from Fort Langley.

The fort was established in 1827 on the Fraser River, opposite the site of Haney, by the Hudson's Bay Company and named after HBC director Thomas Langley (d.1829). Twelve years later, the fort was relocated 4 km upriver to better agricultural land. Abandoned in 1896, the fort was restored in the 1950s as a national historic site.

Lanigan SK Southeast of Saskatoon, the site of this town (1908) was established by the Canadian Pacific Railway in 1905 and named after the CPR's freight traffic agent, W.B. Lanigan. Its post office also opened in 1907.

L'Annonciation QC This village northwest of Mont Tremblant was first known as *Ferme-du-Milieu*, because it furnished provisions for the surrounding timber shanties in the woods. L'Annonciation became a village in 1908, its name having been chosen by Fr. Antonio Labelle in 1880 for the religious parish in honour of the annunciation by the Angel Gabriel that the Virgin Mary would be the mother of Christ.

Lanoraie-d'Autray QC This municipality on the St. Lawrence, southeast of Joliette, was established in 1948. The double name honours two seigneurs, Jacques Bourdon d'Autray (1652–88) and Louis de Niort de La Noraye (1639–1708).

La Nouvelle-Beauce QC This regional county (1982) is centred on the town of Sainte-Marie, south of Quebec City. The county of Beauce had been established in 1829 in the valley of the Rivière Chaudière, taking its name from the valley's regional designation, La Beauce, in use as early as 1739.

Lansdowne ON In 2001 this community became part of the township of Leeds and the Thousand Islands, united counties of Leeds and Grenville. Its post office was named in 1852 after **Lansdowne Township**, itself given for William Petty-Fitzmaurice, Earl of Shelburne (1780–1863), who was made the Marquis of Lansdowne in 1784. When the Grand Trunk Railway was built in 1856 from Montreal to Kingston, the place was relocated 2 km to the north.

L'Anse-Amour NL On the north side of the Strait of Belle Isle, this place was named after *L'Anse-aux-Morts,* adjacent to Pointe aux Morts ('dead man's point'), because of the many shipwrecks here. The first reference to 'Amour' ('love') as part of the name was recorded in 1820. A burial mound dating from 5500–5000 BCE is located here.

L'Anse-au-Clair NL On the north side of the Strait of Belle Isle and just east of the Quebec–Newfoundland/Labrador boundary, it is believed this cove was first known as *L'Anse à l'Eau Claire* ('clear water cove'). It was used by the French as a fishing and sealing station in the 1700s.

L'Anse-au-Loup NL On the north side of the Strait of Belle Isle, this place's name means 'wolf cove'. Augustin Le Gardeur de Courtemanche (1663–1717) built a fort here in the early 1700s, and a French migratory fishery was established here later that century. Permanent settlement took place after the 1830s.

L'Anse aux Meadows NL At the northern end of the Northern Peninsula and on the south side of the Strait of Belle Isle, this place is the site of a Norse settlement, established about 1000 CE. The name derives from *Anse aux Meduses* ('jellyfish cove'), not from 'grassy meadows'.

L'Anse-Saint-Jean QC This municipality is located on the south side of the Saguenay River and east of the city of Saguenay. It was named in 1981, having been created the township municipality of *Saint-Jean* in 1859, with the religious parish having been called Saint-Jean-Baptiste-de-l'Anse-Saint-Jean in 1839.

Lantz NS Located on the Shubenacadie River, northeast of Halifax, this place was named *Lantz Siding* about 1898, when Harvey and Croft Lantz built a brick factory here. The post office here opened as *Lantz Siding* in 1913 and was shortened to Lantz in 1967.

Lantzville BC Northwest of Nanaimo, this community was named in 1923 after Harry Lantz, an American investor who financially supported the mining of coal at nearby Nanoose.

La Patrie QC This village east of Sherbrooke was named in 1941 after the newspaper *La Patrie*, founded about 1870 by Jérôme-Adolphe Chicoyne, and after the religious parish, named Saint-Pierre-de-Ditton ou La Patrie in 1878, given in honour of Québécois repatriating from the United States. Miller Pierre-V. Vaillant was one of the first to return from New England, with the first post office here being called *Vaillantbourg* in 1875.

La Pêche QC This municipality, north of the city of Gatineau, was created in 1975 through the merger of the township municipalities of Wakefield and Aldfield, the village of Wakefield, and the municipality of Sainte-Cécile-de-Masham. The name was taken from the **Rivière la Pêche**, which drains **Lac la Pêche**, noted for its good quality of fish (*pêche*).

La Plaine QC Located east of Saint-Jérôme, this parish municipality was first named *Sainte-Anne-des-Plaines* in 1922, and shortened to La Plaine in 1969, the name given to its post office in 1879. The flat land here was described as 'la plaine' in the 1700s by the first seigneur of Terrebonne, Louis Lepage de Sainte-Claire (1656–1718), with an addition to his seigneury being called Belle Plaine in 1731.

La Pocatière QC Established as a town in 1961, in the regional county of Kamouraska, it had been erected as the village of *Sainte-Anne-de-la-Pocatière* the previous year. The name derives from the first seigneur, François Pollet de La Combe-Pocatière (1650–72), who was granted the land in 1672. His widow called her property Sainte-Anne-de-la-Pocatière, which became the name of the religious and civil parishes.

La Prairie QC On the southeast side of the St. Lawrence, opposite Montreal, the area of this town was known as a 'prairie' in the mid-1600s, and the parish of Notre-Dame de Laprairie de la Magdelaine was established in 1692. The village of *Laprairie de la Magdelaine* was incorporated in 1846, became the town of *Laprairie* in 1909, and adopted the present spelling in 1972.

La Présentation QC Located northwest of Saint-Hyacinthe, this parish municipality was named in 1845, abolished two years later, and re-established in 1855. The name derives from the religious parish of La Présentation-de-la-Vierge, named in 1806 in honour of the presentation of the Virgin Mary in the temple. The post office of La Présentation opened in 1857.

Lardeau BC The post office of this community on the west shore of Kootenay Lake, just south of the mouth of Lardeau River, was named *Lardo* in 1899 after prospector Johnny Lardeau. It was renamed Lardeau in 1947.

Larder Lake ON This municipal township in Timiskaming District, east of Kirkland Lake, was laid out in 1907, after a nearby gold strike, and called *Larder City* after the nearby lake. Larder Lake was a town from 1938 to 1946, when it became a municipal township. The lake was known to the Ojibwa as *Asandjikaning* ('hanging storehouse'), a container where fish and game are hung to dry.

L'Ardoise NS On the south coast of Cape Breton Island, this community was named during the French regime after the slate (*ardoise*) cliffs. Postal service was established here in 1838, followed by **Lower L'Ardoise** (1865), **L'Ardoise Highlands** (1904), and **L'Ardoise West** (1912).

La Rivière MB Situated on the Pembina River, west of Morden, this community's post office was named in 1887 after Alphonse Alfred Clément La Rivière (1841–1925), who served in both the provincial legislature and the House of Commons, before being appointed to the Senate in 1911. In 1964 the Winnipeg radio station CKY offered to advertize its ski resort for free if the name could be changed Seekayewye. It was vigorously opposed by the Manitoba government, especially when it was learned that, by sheer coincidence, the station's call letters also meant 'he who urinates' in Cree.

La Rivière-du-Nord QC Created in 1983, this regional county embracing the area of Saint-Jérôme was named after the river, which flows southwest to the Ottawa River, south of Lachute.

Lark Harbour NL On the southwest side of the Bay of Islands and northwest of Corner Brook, this municipal community (1974) was named after the harbour. The harbour was named in 1767 by Capt. James Cook (1728–79) after HMS *Lark*, which he used during his hydrographic surveys of the coasts of Newfoundland.

La Ronge SK Located on the west shore of **Lac La Ronge**, 205 km north of Prince Albert, this town (1976) was named after the lake. It may have been named because either the jagged shoreline had the appearance of having been gnawed by *Kitchi Amik* (the Great Beaver), or because early voyageurs discovered trees along its shoreline gnawed by beavers. Its post office was called *Lac la Ronge* in 1911, and was changed to La Ronge in 1949.

Larrys River NS On Tor Bay and south of Guysborough, this place's post office was named in 1869. The small river had been named after Lawrence (Larry) Keating of Halifax, who hunted moose here during winter.

Larsen Sound NU Surrounded by Boothia Peninsula and Victoria, King William, and Prince of Wales Islands, this body of water was named in 1965 after Henry Asbjorn Larsen (1899–1964). A member of the Royal Canadian Mounted Police, Larsen commanded the patrol vessel *St. Roch* from 1928 to 1948. He made the first east-to-west traverse in 1940–2 through the Northwest Passage, and in a single season (1944) made the return west-to-east voyage.

La Salle MB On the **La Salle River**, south of Winnipeg, this place may have been named about 1882 after René-Robert Cavelier, Sieur de La Salle (1643–87), the noted explorer of the Mississippi. Its post office was named in 1891. The place's name was inspired by the original designation of the river, *Rivière Salé* ('foul river'), because of its smell and alkaline taste. The river was officially renamed after the place in 1975.

LaSalle ON This town in Essex County, on the west side of Windsor, was originally named in 1924 to honour explorer René-Robert Cavelier, Sieur de La Salle (1643–87). It was annexed in 1959 by the municipal township of *Sandwich West*, which became the town of LaSalle in 1992.

LaSalle QC In 2002 this city became part of the city of Montreal, and became a borough of Montreal in 2006. It was named in 1912 after René-Robert Cavelier de La Salle (1643–87), the noted explorer of the Mississippi, 1681–2 and 1684–7. It was previously called the parish municipality of *Saint-Michel-de-Lachine* (1845) and *Saints-Anges-de-Lachine* (1855).

La Sarre QC In the regional county of Abitibi-Ouest, this community became a village in 1937, and a town in 1949, taking its name from the township of La Sarre, proclaimed in 1916. The township was named after the La Sarre Regiment, which came to New France in 1756. The township municipality of La Sarre was established in 1917 and united with the town in 1980.

L'Ascension-de-Notre-Seigneur QC This parish municipality in the regional county of Saint-Jean-Est, north of Alma, was named in 1919 after the religious parish, which was established on 8 June 1916, the day of the ascension of Christ. It is usually shortened to L'Ascension.

La Scie NL On the north coast of Newfoundland and east of Baie-Verte, this town (1955) was named in the 1700s by the French for the serrated landscape surrounding the harbour, which reminded them of a saw (*scie*).

Lashburn SK Southeast of Lloydminster, the first post office in this town (1979) was called *Wirral* in 1905 after Wirral Peninsula in Cheshire, England, opposite Liverpool. The Canadian Northern Railway arrived that year and the following year renamed it after Zebulon Aiton Lash (1846–1920), the company's solicitor, and after the Scottish word *burn* ('small stream').

Lasqueti Island BC In the Strait of Georgia and south of Texada Island, this island was named in 1791 by Spanish sailing master Jose Maria Narvaez (1768–1840) after Juan Maria Lasqueti, a prominent naval officer.

L'Assomption QC The names of the town and the regional county of L'Assomption may be traced to the Rivière l'Assomption and the seigneury of L'Assomption, established in 1647 and granted to Pierre Legardeur de Repentigny (c.1608–48). The present area of the town was created in 1992 through the merger of the parish municipality of L'Assomption (1855) and the town of L'Assomption (1888). The regional county was incorporated in 1983.

La Tabatière QC This fishing community on the lower north shore of the Gulf of St. Lawrence was founded in 1820 and was first known as *Spark Point*. In 1885 the mission of Saint-Joseph-de-la-Tabatière was established here, with the La Tabatière post office opening in 1907. The word *tabatière* has its roots in a Montagnais word meaning 'sorcerer', with Montagnais who visited the mission calling upon their *tabatière* before returning to their camps.

Latchford ON This town (1907) with the lowest population in Ontario (363 in 2001) is located in Timiskaming District, southwest of New Liskeard. It was named in 1903 after Francis R. Latchford (1854–1938), then Ontario minister of public works, who turned the first sod of the Temiskaming and Northern Ontario Railway in North Bay that year, and drove the last spike at Moosonee in 1932.

Laterrière QC In 2006 this town became part of the city of Saguenay. It was erected in 1989, having merged the municipal parish of Laterrière (1883) and the village of Laterrière (1921) in 1983. The original township of Laterrière was proclaimed in 1850, after Marc-Pascal de Sales Laterrière (1792–1872), the member for Saguenay in the Legislative Assembly of the Province of Canada, 1845–51.

La Tour, Mount NB North of the Nepisiguit River, this mountain was named in 1899 by naturalist William F. Ganong (1864–1941) after Charles de Saint-Étienne de la Tour (1593–1666), governor of Acadia, 1651–66.

La Tuque QC This town on the Rivière Saint-Maurice, midway between the St. Lawrence and Lac Saint-Jean was created in 1911 through the merger of the villages of La Tuque (1909) and *La Tuque Falls* (1910). As early as 1806 a portage at La Tuque was mentioned by Jean-Baptiste Perrault. Explorer François Verreault explained in 1823–4 that the name had its roots in a nearby high mountain, shaped like the knitted hat called a tuque.

Laurentides QC Located in the regional county of Montcalm, northeast of Saint-Jérôme, this town—formerly called the village (1856) of Saint-Lin—and its post office were named in 1883. It took its name from the vast mountain complex north of Montreal, which was named in 1845 by historian François-Xavier Garneau (1809–66). In English the popular all-season tourist destination is widely known as the Laurentians. North of Quebec City is the 8706-km² Laurentides fish and game reserve, established in 1981, replacing a park created in 1895. The regional county of **Les Laurentides** was created in 1983.

Laurier MB Located east of Riding Mountain National Park, southwest of Dauphin, this place's post office was first called *Fosbery* in 1896. It was renamed the next year by settlers from Quebec after Sir Wilfrid Laurier (1841–1919), prime minister of Canada, 1896–1911. He donated instruments to the local band.

Laurier, Mount YT Located east of Lake Laberge, this mountain (1779 m) was first named in 1888 by surveyor William Ogilvie (1849–1912) after geologist George M. Dawson (1849–1901). However, Dawson asked Ogilvie to

rename it after Sir Wilfrid Laurier (1841–1919), who was then the leader of the Liberal Party of Canada.

Laurier-Station QC This village southwest of Quebec City was incorporated in 1951. Its post office was named in 1900 in honour of Sir Wilfrid Laurier (1841–1919), prime minister of Canada, 1896–1911.

Laurierville QC A village (1902) 20 km south of Laurier-Station, and 35 km northeast of Victoriaville, it was named after Prime Minister Sir Wilfrid Laurier (1841–1919). Its post office opened in 1903.

Laussedat, Mount BC In the Rocky Mountains, north of Golden, this mountain (3059 m) was named in 1911 by surveyor Arthur O. Wheeler (1860–1945) after Col. Aimé Laussedat (1819–1907), a French officer who developed photographic surveying techniques during the latter half of the 1800s.

Lauzon QC The name of this sector of the city of Lévis recalls the first grantee of the seigneury of Lauzon (Lauson, Loson), Jean de Lauson (1584–1666), who acquired the seigneury in 1636. Erected as a village in 1867, it became a town in 1910 and a city in 1957. It was united with Lévis to become the city of *Lévis-Lauzon* in 1989, but two years later Lauzon was dropped from the city's designation.

Laval QC Île Jésus was granted in 1675 to Mgr. François Laval (1623–1708), apostolic vicar of New France, 1658–74, and the first bishop of Quebec, 1674–88. The island became the county of Laval in 1853 and the regional county of Laval in 1979. In 1965 all the municipalities in the county were united as the city of Laval, making it the province's second most populous city after Montreal.

La Vallée-de-la-Gatineau QC This regional county in the valley of the Rivière Gatineau extends north from Farrelton to Réservoir Cabonga. It replaced the former county of *Gatineau* in 1983.

La Vallée-du-Richelieu QC Centred on the valley of the Richelieu, and extending north from Chambly, this regional county was created in 1982.

Lavaltrie QC Located on the north side of the St. Lawrence, downriver from Montreal, and opposite Contrecoeur, this village was erected in 1926. The seigneury of Lavaltrie was granted in 1672 to Séraphin Margane, Sieur de Lavaltrie (1644–99), a lieutenant in the Carignan-Salières Regiment.

L'Avenir QC This municipality southeast of Drummondville was created in 1862. It was named after *L'Avenirville* post office, itself named in 1853 after the newspaper *L'Avenir*, founded in Montreal in 1847 by Jean-Baptiste-Éric Dorion (1826–66). Dorion was also a member for Drummond in the Legislative Assembly of the Province of Canada, 1854–7, and 1861–6.

Lawn NL This town (1952) at the south end of the Burin Peninsula was named after **Lawn Bay**, which was identified by the French in the 1600s as *L'Anse Sauvage* ('wild cove'). The bay was called *Great Lawn* by William Tavener in 1714, and Capt. James Cook (1728–79) adapted it in the 1760s for the present bay's name. Suggestions that a French fisherman named it *l'ane* ('the donkey') after a doe caribou seen here, or that Cook was inspired by the lushness of grass to call it Lawn, are probably just speculative.

Lawrencetown NS In the Annapolis Valley, between Bridgetown and Middleton, this village (1953) was named after Lt. Col. Charles Lawrence (1709–60), governor of Nova Scotia, 1753–60. Its post office opened in 1836. In 1862 a second post office, east of Dartmouth, was named **Lawrencetown** after him, but was changed to *East Lawrencetown* in 1924. **Upper Lawencetown**, between Lawencetown and Dartmouth, had a post office from 1907 to 1960.

Lawrenceville QC The post office in this village (1905) in the regional county of Le Val-Saint-François, midway between Sherbrooke and Granby, was named in 1859 after Isaac Lawrence, a native of Connecticut who settled here in 1794.

Lax Kw'alaams BC On the Tsimpsean Peninsula, north of Prince Rupert, this Tsimpsian name meaning 'place of the wild rose with small hips' was adopted in 1986 in place of *Port Simpson*. Fort Simpson had been established further up the Nass River in 1831 by Hudson's Bay Company trader Capt. Aemilius Simpson. He died here later that year. The fort was moved in 1834 to the site of *Port Simpson*. It was closed in 1913, and was burned the next year. *Port Simpson* post office was named in 1900.

Leacock, Mount YT In the St. Elias Mountains, this peak (3109 m) was named in 1970 by the Stephen Leacock Centennial Committee after Stephen Leacock (1869–1944), the noted Canadian humorist. He had been a professor of economics at McGill University in Montreal.

Leader SK Situated south of the South Saskatchewan River and near the Alberta border, the post office at this town (1917) was first called *Happyland* in 1908. It was renamed *Prussia* in 1912 by the first German settlers, but it was changed to Leader in 1917, as the connection with Germany was deemed offensive.

Leading Tickles West NL On an island off the north coast of Newfoundland, and encompassing **Leading Tickles**

South on the mainland, this municipal community (1961) took its name from a rock called The Ladle, and from the very narrow tickles (channels) between the islands and the mainland, which were difficult for fishing boats to pass through. The community was first called *Ladle Tickles* (1836) and *Lading Tickles* (1845).

Leaf Rapids MB Situated at **Leaf Rapids** and on the south bank of the Churchill River, northwest of Thompson, this town (1974) was established in 1970 as a mining community, and its post office opened in 1972. In 2006 its population was 539.

Leamington ON In 1999 this town (1890) and the township of Mersea became part of the municipality of Leamington, Essex County. It was named in 1854 by miller William Gaines after his hometown, Royal Leamington Spa, a borough on the east side of the borough of Warwick in Warwickshire, England.

Leaside ON In 1998 this place became part of the city of Toronto. It was named *Leaside Junction* by postmaster J.H. Lea in 1893, and the name was shortened to Leaside in 1915. His father, William Lea, built a brick house, 1851–4, and called it Leaside.

Leask SK This village southwest of Prince Albert was founded by the Canadian Northern Railway in 1912 and incorporated that year. Its post office also opened then and was named after homesteader Robert Leask (1867–1943), who had settled here in 1903.

Leaskdale ON In Uxbridge Township, Durham Region, northeast of Newmarket, this location was settled in 1847 by Peter Leask of Banffshire, Scotland, who built a sawmill, which his son, James, managed. Another son, George, built a grist mill in 1854 and was appointed the first postmaster three years later.

Le Bas-Richelieu QC This regional county in the area of the mouth of the Richelieu and centred on the city of Sorel was named in 1982.

Lebel-sur-Quévillon QC Located on the western shore of Lac Quévillon, northeast of Val-d'Or, this town (1965) was founded in 1948. It owes its name to pioneer Jean-Baptiste Lebel (1887–1966), who built a sawmill on nearby Rivière Bell. The lake was named after noted architect, sculptor, and master cabinetmaker Louis-Amable Quévillon (1749–1823).

Le Bic QC The present form of the name of this municipality located southwest of Rimouski was established in 1987. The municipality of *Bic* had been created in 1972 through the merger of the village of *Bic* and the parish municipality of *Sainte-Cécile-du-Bic*. In 1603 Samuel de Champlain (1567–1635) named a nearby mountain *Pic*, which became *Bic* when the seigneury was created in 1675. Bic continued in the postal name, established in 1832.

Lebret SK East of Fort Qu'Appelle, this village (1912) was named in 1886 by Senator Marc-Amable Girard (1822–92) after its first postmaster, Fr. Louis Lebret (d.1903), who established a residential school here in 1884 for Métis.

Le Centre-de-la-Mauricie QC Centred on the city of Shawinigan and the Rivière Saint-Maurice, this regional county was named in 1982.

LeClercq, Mount NB North of the Nepisiguit River, this mountain was named in 1899 by naturalist William Francis Ganong (1864–1941) after Fr. Chestien LeClercq (c.1641–1700), a Recollet missionary to the Mi'kmaq.

Le Domaine-du-Roy QC This regional county northwest of Lac Saint-Jean and centred on the town of Roberval was named in 1983. The name recalls a vast domain, including the whole area of Lac Saint-Jean, which was established in 1674 for the sole pleasure of the King. The special lease was only suspended in 1842, when the lands were opened for settlement.

Leduc AB South of Edmonton, this city (1983) was named about 1890 by Edgar Dewdney (1835–1916) when he established a Dominion Telegraph station here, and named it after Fr. Hippolyte Leduc (1842–1918), an Oblate missionary who served in Western Canada after 1865. The famous Imperial Leduc No 1 oil well came into production in 1947 at Devon in **Leduc County**, 18 km to the northwest.

Leeds ON The county was named in 1792 by Lt.-Gov. John Graves Simcoe (1752–1806) after Francis Godolphin Osborne, 5th Duke of Leeds (1751–99), secretary of state for foreign affairs, 1783–91. The municipality of the united counties of **Leeds and Grenville** was formed in 1852. *See also* Front of Leeds and Lansdowne *and* Rear of Leeds and Lansdowne.

Le Fjord-de-Saguenay QC This regional county centered on the city of **Saguenay** was established in 1983, taking its name from the submerged glacial valley between Chicoutimi and Tadoussac. The valley with its vertical escarpment walls is the only true fiord on the southern edge of the Canadian Shield.

Lefroy ON In the town of Innisfil, Simcoe County, southeast of Barrie, this community was named by Sir John Beverley Robinson (1791–1863) in 1852 after his son-in-law, Sir John Henry Lefroy (1817–90), superintendent of the magnetic observatory in Toronto, 1842–53.

Lefroy, Mount AB This mountain (3423 m) near Lake Louise was named in 1858 by Dr. James Hector (1834–1907) after Sir John Henry Lefroy (1817–90), an astronomer noted for his studies of magnetism. Insp. Gen. Lefroy performed measurements at Fort Edmonton in 1844.

Legal AB In 1998 this village (1914) became a town. Located 45 km north of Edmonton, the community was named in 1900 after Mgr. Émile-Joseph Legal (1849–1920), who arrived in Western Canada in 1881 as a missionary, and subsequently became bishop of St. Albert (1902) and archbishop of Edmonton (1912).

Le Gardeur QC Located in the regional county of L'Assomption, this town was named in 1978. It replaced the town of *Saint-Paul-l'Ermite*, erected five years earlier, which had been established as a parish municipality in 1857. The post office had been called Le Gardeur in 1957 to reduce the confusion among the many places called Saint-Paul in the province. In 1647 Pierre Legardeur de Repentigny (1632–1709) was granted the vast seigneury of La Chesnaye, but he died the following year and was succeeded by his son Jean-Baptiste.

Le Goulet NB The post office of this village (1986) southeast of Caraquet was called *Shippigan Gully* from 1904 to 1955 and *Shippegan Gully* until 1961, when it was renamed Le Goulet. The name refers to the narrow entrance to the harbour at Shippagan, between the mainland and Île Lamèque, which is officially called Shippegan Gully.

Le Granit QC This regional county in the southeastern part of the province, surrounding the town of Lac-Mégantic, was named in 1982 after the granitic mountainous relief that rises to 1105 m at Mont Mégantic.

Le Haut-Richelieu QC Based on the upper reaches of the Richelieu, with Saint-Jean-sur-Richelieu as its main urban centre, this regional county was named in 1982.

Le Haut-Saint-François QC This regional county was created in 1982 and embraces the upper part of the Rivière Saint-François and several small towns, including East Angus, Cookshire, Scotstown, and Ascot Corner.

Le Haut-Saint-Laurent QC Located south and west of Salaberry-de-Valleyfield, with Huntingdon, Ormstown, and Saint-Chrysostome as its main centres, this regional county was named in 1982 after its location at the upper part of the St. Lawrence that is within the territory of Quebec.

Le Haut-Saint-Maurice QC Located in the upper reaches of the Rivière Saint-Maurice, and centered on the town of La Tuque, this regional county was named in 1982.

Lemberg SK Southwest of Melville, this town (1907) was established by the Canadian Pacific Railway in 1903 and its post office opened in 1904. It was named after Lemberg, then the chief centre of Galicia, but now L'viv in Ukraine.

LeMoyne QC In 2002 this town (1949) became part of the city of Longueuil, the regional county of Champlain. LeMoyne post office existed from 1910 to 1921. The name recalls Charles Le Moyne (1626–85), the first seigneur of Longueuil in 1657. Among his 12 sons was the noted Pierre Le Moyne d'Iberville (1661–1706), the founder of Louisiana, 1700–2.

Lempriere, Mount BC This mountain (3208 m) in the Monashee Mountains was named in 1863 after Lt. (later Maj. Gen.) Arthur Reid Lempriere (1835–1927), an English military engineer who helped lay out wagon roads in the province's interior between 1858 and 1863.

Lennox and Addington ON These places were created as separate counties in 1792, each only having three townships near the Lake Ontario shore. They were joined temporarily in 1798, but in 1860 their union as a single county was affirmed, with several townships to the rear added. Lennox was named after Charles Lennox, 3rd Duke of Richmond (1734–1806), the uncle of the 4th Duke of Richmond, governor-in-chief of British North America, 1818–9. Addington was named after Henry Addington, Viscount Sidmouth (1755–1844), a British politician.

Lennox Island PE In the northern end of Malpeque Bay, this island was named *Lenox Island* in 1765 by Samuel Holland (1728–1801) after Charles Lennox, 3rd Duke of Richmond (1734–1806), who had served as the British ambassador to France. It was established as a Mi'kmaq reserve in 1840, although the Mi'kmaq had long been living here.

Lennoxville QC Situated next to the city of Sherbrooke, this town was first known as *Petites-Fourches* and *Little Forks* for its location at the junction of the Saint-François and Coaticook Rivers. It was named about 1820 after Charles Lennox, 4th Duke of Richmond and Lennox (1764–1819), governor-in-chief of British North America, 1818–9. It became a village in 1871 and a town in 1920.

Leoville SK Located northwest of Prince Albert, the post office at this village (1944) was established in the 1930, taking its name from first homesteader Leo Carpenter.

L'Épiphanie QC This parish municipality in the regional county of L'Assomption south of Joliette was named in 1853 in honour of the three wise men's visit to the Christ child. The village of **L'Épiphanie** was separated from it in 1921 and became a town in 1967.

Lepreau, Point NB Extending into the Bay of Fundy, southwest of Saint John, this point is identified on Jean-Baptiste-Louis Franquelin's map of 1686 as *Pointe aux Napraux*. The origin and meaning of the name is unknown. Variations of 'Little Pro' appeared on several English-language maps between 1711 and 1772, suggesting the name may relate to the point resembling a little sailing boat (*proe* in French). The post office in the community of **Lepreau**, at the mouth of the **Lepreau River**, was named *Lepreaux* from 1850 to 1854, when it was changed to Lepreau.

Lequille NS Southeast of Annapolis Royal, this place's post office was named in 1860 after the *Rivière à l'Anguille*, a former name of Allains River. The river had been named after the French word *anguille* ('eel'), possibly by Samuel de Champlain (1567–1635). Allains River was called after Louis Allain, a miller here before 1755.

L'Érable QC Located in the middle of the province's important maple syrup and sugar area, northeast of Victoriaville, this regional county was named in 1982. The word *érable* means 'maple'.

Leroy SK The post office in this town (1963) northeast of Lanigan was first named Bog End in 1909. In 1919, when the Canadian Pacific Railway was built from Lanigan, it was called Onwa, a name disliked by the local people. They suggested commemorating local soldier Jack LeRoy, who was killed during the First World War. Jack spelled his name as LeRoy, and the local residents wanted that spelling. The Rural Telephone Company spelled the name as Leroy in 1921. The postal authorities spelled the post office as Leroy when it was opened later in 1921.

Léry QC This town on the shore of Lac Saint-Louis, southwest of Montreal, was created before the First World War. Its roots can be traced to the religious parish of Saint-Cyprien-de-De Léry, established in 1831. The town was named by one of its leading citizens after his wife's ancestor, perhaps Gaspard-Joseph Chaussegros de Léry (1716–56), who designed several public buildings during the eighteenth century.

Les Basques QC Located between Rivière-du-Loup and Rimouski and centred on the town of Trois-Pistoles, this regional county was founded in 1981. It took its name from Île aux Basques, where Basques dried fish and extracted whale oil during the first half of the seventeenth century.

Les Cèdres QC On the north shore of the St. Lawrence, northeast of Salaberry-de-Valleyfield, the abundant cedars, after which this municipality owes its name, were noted as early as 1695. The municipality was created in 1985, having been incorporated as the village of *Cèdres* in 1967. *Cèdres* itself had been created in 1852 from the village of *Soulanges* and the parish municipality of *Saint-Joseph-de-Soulanges*. It has been widely identified in English as Cedars.

Les Chutes-de-la-Chaudière QC Located at the mouth of the Rivière Chaudière, southwest of Quebec City, this regional county was created in 1982.

Les Collines-de-l'Outaouais QC North of the city of Gatineau, this regional county was created in 1991 by severing seven municipalities from the Communauté-Urbaine-de-l'Outaouais. West of Aylmer, it fronts on the Ottawa River, officially called Rivière de l'Outaouais in French. East of Gatineau, the town of Thurso fronts on the Ottawa River.

Les Éboulements QC This municipality in the regional county of Charlevoix is located east of Baie-Saint-Paul. It received its present name in 1956; however, the name's roots can be traced to the seigneury of Éboulements granted to Pierre Lessard in 1683. Éboulements post office opened in 1832. The name relates to a massive landslide (*éboulement*) as the result of an earthquake in February 1663.

Les Escoumins QC References were made to the site of this municipality, on the north shore of the St. Lawrence and northeast of Tadoussac, as early as 1603 by Samuel de Champlain (1567–1635). It was called *Les Escoumains* in 1863 and amended to the present form in 1957. The name derives from the Montagnais *iskomin* ('place of wild fruit').

Les Etchemins QC This regional county to the rear of Bellechasse, and centred on the town of **Lac-Etchemin** and the upper reaches of **Rivière Etchemin**, was named in 1982. The name in Abenaki means 'where there is leather for snowshoes'.

Les Jardins-de-Napierville QC Located south of Montreal and on the New York border, this regional county was named in 1982 after the former county of *Napierville* and the rich agricultural lands of the area.

Les Maskoutins QC This regional county surrounding the city of Saint-Hyacinthe, east of Montreal, was named in 1982. The name describes the people living along the Rivière Yamaska, which flows north to the St. Lawrence, some 20 km east of the Richelieu.

Les Méchins QC The name of this municipality in the regional county of Matane, northeast of the town of Matane, derives from a legendary evil monster called *Matsi* by the Mi'kmaq, which was rendered by the French as *méchant* and later deformed to *méchin*.

Les Moulins QC Located north of Laval and centred on the towns of Mascouche and Terrebonne, this regional county

was created in 1982. The name recalls the ancient flour, saw, carding, and fulling mills (*moulins*) that were built here in the early 1700s.

Les Pays-d'en-Haut QC Centred on the all-season recreational centres of Sainte-Adèle and Saint-Sauveur, this regional county was created in 1983. The name essentially means 'the highlands', an apt description of the rugged hills and valleys between Saint-Jérôme and Mont Tremblant.

Lesser Slave Lake AB This lake (1168 km^2), in the north central part of the province, was named *Slave Lake* in 1792 by Sir Alexander Mackenzie (c.1764–1820) after the Cree word *Awonak*, their name for any strangers, but which translated literally as 'slaves'. It was not the Slavey, a major group of the Dene people living farther north, that they had in mind, but another people, perhaps either the Blackfoot or the Beaver. 'Lesser' was subsequently added to distinguish it from Great Slave Lake.

Lester Pearson, Mount BC In the Premier Range, west of Valemount, this mountain (3060 m) was named in 1973 after Lester Bowles Pearson (1897–1972), prime minister of Canada, 1963–8.

Lestock SK Northwest of Melville, this village (1912) was established by the Grand Trunk Pacific Railway in 1908, taking its name from land surveyor John Lestock Reid (1841–1911). As part of the alphabetical list of names given by the GTP, it was first called *Mostyn*, as it was the station following Leross. Mostyn is a place in Wales, west of Liverpool. The post office opened as *Lestock Station* in 1911 and was changed to Lestock in 1947.

Letang NB Located on **Letang Harbour**, south of St. George, its post office was named in 1892. The original French name was *Havre à L'Étang* ('harbour at the pond'). The name is still commonly spelled *L'Etang*.

L'Étang-du-Nord QC Located in the regional county of Les Îles-de-la-Madeleine, on the north side of a small harbour, this municipality was named in 1875. The name derives from the religious parish of Saint-Pierre-de-l'Étang-du-Nord, established in 1848.

Letellier MB On the Red River, north of Emerson, this community was first known as *Catherine* after Catherine Wright, a local landowner. It was named in 1880 after Luc Letellier de Saint-Just (1820–81), lieutenant-governor of Quebec, 1876–9.

Letete NB The post office of this community situated on **Letete Passage**, southwest of St. George, was called *L'Etete* from 1856 to 1941. The name may derive from French *la tête* ('the head'), possibly in reference to a high hill on Macs Island or to a white ledge at Greens Point.

Lethbridge AB This city (1906) on the Oldman River was first known as *The Coal Banks* in 1872 after a coal mine that had been developed here. It was renamed Lethbridge about 1882 after William Lethbridge (1824–1901), first president of the North Western Coal and Navigation Company, which was created that year, and a partner in the London-based booksellers W.H. Smith and Son. As the name had already been allotted to a rural office in Ontario, the post office department called the new office *Coalhurst*. However, three years later, it consented to Lethbridge for the office in Alberta.

Lethbridge NL On Goose Bay, which is united to Bonavista Bay by Chandler Reach, this city was first known as *Southeast Arm* and *Hopevale*. It was renamed in 1912 after James Lethbridge, the city's oldest resident at the time.

Levack ON In 2001 this community in the town of Onaping Falls became part of the city of Greater Sudbury, Sudbury Region. This place was named in 1914 after **Levack Township**. The township was created in 1885, and named in honour of Mary Levack, the mother of Sir Oliver Mowat (1820–1903), then premier of Ontario.

Le Val-Saint-François QC Located between Sherbrooke and Drummondville, this regional county in the valley of the Rivière Saint-François was named in 1982.

Lévis QC This city across the St. Lawrence from Quebec City has an indirect association with Pointe de Lévy, noted as early as 1629 by Samuel de Champlain (1567–1635). That name was given in honour of Henri de Lévis (or Lévy), Duc de Ventadour (1596–1651), who was the viceroy of New France, 1625–7. The former county of Lévis and the post office were named in 1854. The city itself was known as the *Ville-d'Aubigny* from 1849 to 1861, after Duc de Richmond et d'Aubigny. In 1860, in honour of the 100th anniversary of the heroism of François-Gaston de Lévis, Duc de Lévis (1719–87) at the Battle of Sainte-Foy in 1760, it was renamed after him. In 1989 Lévis and Lauzon became the city of *Lévis-Lauzon*. When the town of Saint-David-de-l'Auberivière was annexed in 1990, Lévis became the name of the new city.

Lewin's Cove NL Located at the north end of Burin Inlet and southwest of Marystown, this municipal community (1973) was identified as *Lunes Cove* on an 1860 Admiralty chart and as *Loon's Cove* in the 1891 census. The present form of the name occurred for the first time in a 1945 provincial census. The adjacent cove may have called after the common loons that nest around nearby ponds.

Lewisporte NL On Burnt Bay, an extension of the Bay of Exploits, this town (1946) was originally named *Burnt Bay* (1857) and *Marshallville* (1891). It was renamed Lewisporte in 1900, after the Scottish firm of Lewis Miller and Company, which was involved in lumbering in the area until 1903. *See also* Millertown.

Liard River BC, NT, YT Rising in the Yukon, northwest of Watson Lake, this river flows generally southeast to its confluence with the Fort Nelson River, where it runs generally northeast to enter the Mackenzie River at Fort Simpson. French voyageurs, who accompanied John McLeod (1836–94) of the Hudson's Bay Company in 1834, called it *Rivière aux Liards*, *liard* being the French word for the cottonwood (poplar) trees lining its banks. Four years later Robert Campbell (1808–94) of the HBC called it *Bell River* after chief trader John Bell (c.1799–1868), but Liard River eventually prevailed.

Likely BC At the west end of Quesnel Lake, southeast of Quesnel, this place's post office was named in 1923 after gold miner John Likely (1842–1929), who was known as 'Plato John' for his lectures on the Greek philosophers.

L'Île-d'Orléans QC Embracing the entire island, downriver from Quebec City, this regional county was named in 1982. *See also* Orléans, Île d'.

L'Île-du-Havre-Aubert QC This municipality in the county of L'Île-de-la-Madeleine was created in 1875 as *Havre-Aubert* and was changed to *Bassin* in 1959. The municipality of *Havre-Aubert-Est* (1951) became *Havre-Aubert* in 1964, merging with *Bassin* in 1971 under the present name. The name's origin is uncertain, with some pointing to a sixteenth-century sailor, and others to a seventeenth-century pilot or ship's master.

L'Île-Perrot QC This town (1955) is located on Île Perrot, at the point where the Ottawa River drains Lac des Deux-Montagnes into Lac Saint-Louis. The island was named in 1672 after its seigneur, François-Marie Perrot (1644–91), a captain in the Picardie Regiment and governor of Montreal, 1670.

Lillooet BC This village (1946) on the Fraser River, west of Kamloops, was named after the Lillooet, a Salish tribe that occupied the valleys to the west and the south. It received its name because the village was the end of the trail leading from **Lillooet Lake**, 65 km to the southwest, near Mount Currie. The meaning of the name is unknown, with the usual interpretation, 'wild onion', considered incorrect. The site of the village was earlier called *Cayoosh Flat* after a dead cayuse (pony) found in Cayoosh River. The **Lillooet River** (165 km) rises in the Coast Mountains and flows southeast through Lillooet Lake to Harrison Lake. **Alouette Lake**, to the south near Mission, was officially called *Lillooet Lake* until 1914, when it was renamed after the French word for 'lark'.

Limerick SK West of Assiniboia, the post office at this village (1913) was named in 1908 by first postmaster Edward Lossing (d.1964) for his grandmother, a native of Limerick, Ireland.

Linacy NS East of New Glasgow, this place was founded in the 1800s. Among its early settlers was Edward Linacy.

Lincoln NB The post office in this place, on the southeast side of Fredericton and along the Saint John River, was named in 1867. It took its name from **Lincoln Parish**, established in 1786 and probably named by the Loyalist Glasier family, who came from Lincoln, MA. In 2001 its population was 2850, and likely to have more than doubled in 2008.

Lincoln ON The county was named by Lt.-Gov. John Graves Simcoe (1752–1806) in 1792 after Lincolnshire, England. In 1970 it was merged into the regional municipality of Niagara. The town of **Lincoln** in Niagara Region was created in 1970 by uniting the town of Beamsville with the municipal township of Clinton and part of the municipal township of Louth.

Lincolnville NS North of Guysborough, this place was founded in the late 1800s by descendants of African-Americans who had come to Guysborough as Loyalists in 1784. The place was named after Abraham Lincoln (1809–65), the American president, who freed his nation's slaves.

Linden AB Northeast of Calgary, this village (1964) was named after a school established in 1904. The post office here opened in 1949. The name had been given by a strict Mennonite sect from Europe called Holdemanites after the linden tree, widely used in the northern hemisphere for its shade and fragrant flowers.

Lindsay ON In 2001 this town (1857) became part of the city of Kawartha Lakes, Victoria County. Chosen as a townsite in 1825, the town was first called *Purdy's Mills* and *Purdy's Rapids* after millers William, Jesse, and Hassard Purdy. When John Huston surveyed the townsite in 1834, a man named Lindsay was presumably shot by accident. He subsequently died of infection and was buried in the river bank. Huston made no mention of the incident in his diary of July 1834, although he inscribed the name Lindsay on the cover page of his diary. Lt.-Gov. Francis Bond Head (1793–1875) authorized Lindsay as the postal name in 1836.

Linière QC The post office in this village in the regional county of Beauce-Sartigan, south of Saint-Georges, was named in 1875 after the township of Linière. The township was created in 1852 and named after a family of seigneurs, who went by the surname of Linière.

Linkletter PE This municipal community (1972) west of Summerside was settled in 1786 by George Linkletter, a Loyalist from Connecticut, and his sons George, John, and James. Its post office opened in 1896.

Lintlaw SK Southeast of Kelvington, this village (1921) was named when the first school opened here in 1909. The post office opened the following year, and the Canadian Northern Railway arrived in 1919. The name was proposed by John McChesney, likely after Lintlaw in Berwickshire, Scotland, west of Berwick-upon-Tweed.

Lions Bay BC On the east shore of Howe Sound, northeast of Vancouver, this village (1971) and the bay took their names from two mountains directly to the east that had earlier been called *The Sisters* and *Sheba's Paps*. From Vancouver they look like a pair of crouching lions, and about 1890 **The Lions** were named by Judge John Hamilton Gray (1814–89), who suggested the narrow entrance into Burrard Inlet be called **Lions Gate**. The Lions Gate Bridge, uniting the north shore with downtown Vancouver, through Stanley Park, was built in 1938.

Lion's Head ON In 1999 this village (1917) became a part of the municipality of Northern Bruce Peninsula, Bruce County. It was named in 1875 after a rock formation on a nearby headland that had the profile of a lion's head. Much of the headland collapsed into Isthmus Bay in the early 1900s.

Lipton SK North of Fort Qu'Appelle, this village (1905) was first called *Miles* in 1904 by the Canadian Pacific Railway after surveyor Miles Patrick Cotton. The pioneer settlers, having been here since 1883, objected, proposing Lipton after Sir Thomas Lipton (1850–1931). A famous Scottish provisions merchant, Lipton made five unsuccessful attempts to win the America's Cup, emblematic of the international yachting championship. Lipton post office was named in 1905, replacing *Hayward*, given in 1884 after Henry Hawksworth Hayward (d.1904).

Lisle ON In Simcoe County, southwest of Barrie, this place was named in 1879 after either the popular song *Annie Lisle*, a favourite of lumberman Thomas H. Wilmott's daughter, or after a village in the southern United States where Wilmott had lived as a boy.

L'Islet QC The seigneury of L'Islet was granted in 1677 to Geneviève Couillard, and the seigneury of L'Islet-de-Bonsecours was granted the same year to François Bellanger, taking their names from a rock offshore in the St. Lawrence (with the dimensions of 244 m by 45 m), downriver from Montmagny. The municipality of **L'Islet-sur-Mer** was created in 1989 by merging the village of L'Islet and the parish municipality of *Notre-Dame-de-Bon-Secours-de-L'Islet*. The town of

L'Islet, created in 1966, was earlier called *L'Islet-Station* (1950) and *L'Isletville* (1954). The regional county of **L'Islet** was established in 1982.

L'Isle-Verte QC This village (1955) downriver from Rivière-du-Loup was named as a municipality in 1845 after an offshore island noted in the Jesuit *Relations* of 1664. Later it became *Saint-Jean-Baptiste-de-l'Isle-Verte* in 1855.

Listowel ON In 1998 this town (1874) became part of the town of North Perth, Perth County. It was named *Listowell* by the post office department in 1856, when the residents could not agree on either Mapleton or Windham. Ten years later it was respelled Listowel, when the place was incorporated as a village. Listowel is a town in County Kerry, Ireland.

Little Bay Islands NL In the southwest side of Notre Dame Bay, this municipal community (1955) on Little Bay Island and on adjacent Mack's Island was first settled in the early 1800s.

Little Britain ON In 2001 this community became part of the Kawartha Lakes, Victoria County. It was named in 1855 by merchant Robert Ferguson Whiteside after his birthplace in the township of Little Britain, Lancaster County, PA.

Little Burnt Bay NL The name of this town (1975) on Southern Head, where it extends into the Bay of Exploits, north of Lewisporte, was first recorded in 1901, although settlement had taken place here as early as the 1830s.

Little Catalina NL This town (1965) is located 5 km northeast of Catalina. Efforts in the 1930s to get out from under the shadow of Catalina by renaming it *Orangeville* or *Dayton* were rejected by the Newfoundland Nomenclature Board.

Little Current ON This town (1890) in Manitoulin District was known to the Aboriginals as *Waibejewung* ('where the waters flow back and forth'), and to the French as *Le Petit Courant*. Shaftesbury was proposed in 1865, but the translation of the French name was adopted.

Little Heart's Ease NL On the Southwest Arm of Random Sound, a western extension of Trinity Bay, this location was named either after the small secluded cove where fishermen could find comfort from stormy waters or after a fishing vessel.

Lively ON In 2001 this urban centre in the town of Walden became part of the city of Greater Sudbury, Sudbury Region. It was created in 1950 by the International Nickel Company for its workers at nearby Creighton Mine. It was named in 1951 after Charles Lively, a long-time INCO employee. Incorporated as a town in 1953, it was merged into Walden in 1973.

Liverpool NS This urban community (1996) in the regional municipality of Queens and at the mouth of the Mersey River was incorporated as a town in 1897. It was founded in 1761 and named after *Liverpool Township*, which had been named a year earlier by the governor and council in Halifax, presumably after the British port city. In 1604 Pierre Du Gua de Monts (c.1558–1628) called the site *Port Rossignol* for a French captain who was undertaking a fur trade in the territory granted to de Monts. Postal service was established at Liverpool in 1802. *See also* Rossignol, Lake.

Livingstone, Mount BC In the Clemenceau Icefield of the Rocky Mountains, southeast of Athabasca Pass, this mountain (3094 m) was named in 1927 by alpinist James Monroe Thorington (1894–1989) after explorer David Livingstone (1813–73), who was found in Africa by Henry Stanley in 1871. **Mount Livingstone** (3090 m) and **Livingstone Range** in Alberta, northwest of Claresholm, were named in 1858 by Capt. Thomas Blakiston (1832–91) of the Palliser Expedition.

Lloyd George, Mount BC In the Muskwa Ranges of the Rocky Mountains, this mountain (2972 m) was named in 1916 by American explorer Paul L. Haworth (1876–1938) after David Lloyd George (1863–1945), prime minister of Great Britain, 1915–22.

Lloydminster AB, SK This city (1958) on the Saskatchewan–Alberta border was conceived in 1902 by Anglican cleric Isaac M. Barr to develop a British presence in the area of the North Saskatchewan River, northwest of Saskatoon. The following year 2000 settlers arrived in Saint John, NB, and came by train to Saskatoon, where their chaplain, the Reverend George Exton Lloyd (1861–1940) took over the project and led it to the *Britannia Settlement*. In 1930 the Saskatchewan town and the Alberta village were united as the town of Lloydminster by orders in council passed by both provinces.

Lloydtown ON In York Region, west of Aurora, this community was settled in 1812 by Pennsylvania Quakers Jesse and Phoebe Lloyd and named in 1831. Jesse Lloyd (1786–1838), a supporter of William Lyon Mackenzie (1795–1861), fled to the United States in 1837 after the defeat of the rebels; he died the next year in Tippecanoe, IN. His wife remained at Lloydtown.

Lobo ON In 1998 this township became part of the township of Middlesex Centre, Middlesex County. It was named in 1821 by Lt.-Gov. Sir Peregrine Maitland (1777–1854) after the Spanish word for 'wolf'.

Lochaber NS South of Antigonish, this community on **Lochaber Lake** was founded in 1808 by Scots from Lochaber, Inverness-shire, Scotland. Lochaber post office opened in 1852, with subsequent offices being located at **Lochaber West**

Side (1861), **South Lochaber** (1877), and **North Lochaber** (1885).

Lochiel ON In 1998 this township became part of township of North Glengarry, the united counties of Stormont, Dundas, and Glengarry. The name was given in 1816 after the Scottish home of the Clan Cameron, Lochiel Castle, which overlooks Loch Lochy in Inverness-shire.

Lockeport NS On the South Shore and east of Shelburne, this town (1907) was named after Jonathan Locke (1717–99), a native of Rhode Island who acquired land in *Liverpool Township* in 1764. Shortly after, he and other New England planters and fishermen founded the settlement of *Locke's Island*, which was given its present name in 1870.

Lockport MB On the Red River, southwest of Selkirk, this community was first called *Little Britain* by the first settlers from England and Scotland. The post office here was then named *St. Andrews North* in 1894 after the St. Andrews Rapids, given by the Selkirk settlers after the patron saint of Scotland. When a lock was constructed in 1902 to allow boat traffic to pass the rapids, the place and post office were renamed Lockport.

Logan ON In 1998 this township became part of the township of West Perth, Perth County. It was named in 1830 after Hart Logan, a merchant from London, England and a director of the Canada Company. This British company was established in 1826 to develop the Huron Tract (a large area of what is now Southwestern Ontario). Sir William Edmond Logan (1798–1875) worked in Hart Logan's business in London for some 20 years before returning in 1842 to his birthplace, Montreal, and founding the Geological Survey of Canada.

Logan Lake BC Southwest of Kamloops, this district municipality (1984) was previously incorporated as a village in 1970, which was named after a small lake here. The lake was named after an Aboriginal called Tslakan who raised horses and traded furs, but his name was badly rendered as 'Logan'.

Logan, Mont QC Forming one of the highest points (1135 m) of the Monts Chic-Chocs, east of Matane, this mountain was named after an exploratory mineral survey of the mountains in 1844 by geologists Sir William Edmond Logan (1798–1875) and Alexander Murray (1810–1903).

Logan, Mount YT This mountain—the highest (5959 m) in Canada—was named in 1890 by American explorer and geologist Israel C. Russell (1852–1906) after Sir William Edmond Logan (1798–1875), the founder of the Geological Survey of Canada in 1842. He served as its director until 1869, undertaking several geological expeditions in present Ontario

and Quebec. The **Logan Mountains** in southeastern Yukon and southwestern Northwest Territories, and on the eastern side of Frances Lake, were named in 1887 after Sir William Logan by geologist George M. Dawson (1849–1901).

Loggieville NB Located east of Chatham, this place was settled about 1790 by Robert Logie (later Loggie). Its first post office was *Black Brook*, 1861–95, with Robert Blake as the first postmaster. It was renamed Loggieville in 1895. Incorporated as a village in 1966, it was annexed by the city of Miramichi in 1995.

Loki, Mount BC In Purcell Mountains, northeast of Nelson, this mountain (2771 m) was named before 1890 after a poker game played by miners. The name may derive from Loki, the Norse god of fire, strife, and humour.

Lombardy ON In 1998 this community became part of the township of Rideau Lakes, united counties of Leeds and Grenville. Located southwest of Smiths Falls, it was settled in the 1820s by Francis Lombard (d.1864), who operated an inn here. It was called *Lombard Corners* until 1853, when the *South Elmsley* post office opened. Twenty years later local residents requested Lombardy after the first resident and the area's resemblance to the plain of Lombardy in Italy.

Lomond AB This village (1916) southeast of Calgary was named in 1914 by the Canadian Pacific Railway after Loch Lomond, northwest of Glasgow, Scotland.

Londesborough ON In 2001 this place became part of the municipality of Central Huron, Huron County. Located east of Goderich, the name was given by Thomas Hagyard (1841–99) in 1861 after the East Yorkshire estate of Albert Denison, 1st Baron Londesborough (1805–60), midway between the cities of York and Kingston upon Hull, where Hagyard had lived.

London ON In March 1793, before arriving in Canada, Lt.-Gov. John Graves Simcoe (1752–1806) considered the forks of the Thames as a possible location for the capital of Upper Canada, which he had called Georgina. After looking at the site, he renamed it New London. Lord Dorchester, the governor-in-chief, disallowed Simcoe's choice but consented to his proposal to move the capital to Toronto (renamed York later that year). London post office had been established 5 km west of the forks in 1825, but it was moved here the next year, when London became the administrative capital of London District. It became a city in 1855. **London Township** was named in 1798. In 1998 this township became part of the township of Middlesex Centre.

Longlac ON This town in Thunder Bay District, east of Geraldton, is situated at the north end of **Long Lake**. Founded as a Hudson's Bay Company post in 1800, *Long Lake* was a busy settlement and trading centre when the Canadian Northern Railway arrived in 1914 and proposed Longlac for its station. The post office opened in 1919. Set up as an improvement district in 1952, it became a municipal township in 1964 and a town in 1982.

Long Point ON Stretching for 35 km into Lake Erie, this peninsula was crossed in 1670 by explorers François Dollier de Casson (1636–1701) and René de Bréhant de Galinée (1645–78), who called it *La Longue Pointe*. After 1759 it was called Long Point.

Long Range Mountains NL Extending for 500 km from Cape Ray to the northern end of the Northern Peninsula, these mountains achieve heights of 559 m in the Anguille Mountains, 814 m in the Lewis Hills, 806 m in Gros Morne National Park, and 606 m northeast of Port au Choix.

Long Sault ON In 1998 this community became part of the township of South Stormont, united counties of Stormont, Dundas, and Glengarry. It was created in 1956 to accommodate the residents of *Mille Roches* and *Moulinette*, inundated during the construction of the St. Lawrence Seaway. Taken from a historic stretch of the St. Lawrence River, the name was spelled Longue Sault by English-speaking settlers. However, the names authorities and French-language purists insisted on spelling it Long Sault.

Longstaff, Mount BC Northwest of Mount Robson, this mountain (3180 m) was named in 1911 by surveyor Arthur O. Wheeler (1860–1945) after Dr. Thomas George Longstaff (1875–1964), who made several climbs around the world, including an early attempt on Mount Everest.

Longueuil ON In 1998 this township became part of the township of Champlain, united counties of Prescott and Russell. It was known as the seigniory of *Pointe-à-l'Orignal* until 1798, when it was renamed after Baron Joseph-Dominique-Emmanuel Le Moyne de Longueuil (1738–1807), who had become its seigneur in 1778.

Longueuil QC The largest city in the regional county of Champlain, across the St. Lawrence from Montreal, Longueuil was created a parish municipality in 1845, abolished in 1847, and recreated as a village in 1848. It became a town in 1874 and a city in 1920, when it annexed the town of *Montréal-Sud*. In 1974 it further annexed the city of *Jacques Cartier* (1947) and the parish municipality of *Saint-Antoine-de-Longueuil* (1855). Charles Le Moyne (1626–85) became the seigneur in 1657, and then a barony in 1700. He was born in Longueuil, near Dieppe, France, and came to New France in 1641. In 2002 the city of Longueuil took over the cities of Boucherville, Brossard, Greenfield Park, LeMoyne, Saint Bruno-de-Montarville, and Saint-Hubert. In 2006 Boucherville, Brossard,

Saint Bruno-de-Montarville, and Saint-Lambert recovered their status as cities.

Longview AB South of Calgary on the Highwood River, the post office at this village (1964) was named in 1905 after the good view of the mountains and after first postmaster, Thomas Long, who settled in the area of Okotoks in 1895. Thomas and his brother Oliver moved to the *Big Hill* for their homestead. That hill is now called **Longview Hill**.

Loon Lake SK West of Meadow Lake, this village (1950) is 2 km east of **Loon Lake**, near Makwa Lake. The Cree word *makwa* means loon. It received a post office in 1923.

Lord's Cove NL On the south end of the Burin Peninsula, this municipal community (1966) was established in the latter half of the 1800s and named after the cove. The origin of the cove's name is unknown, although there may be a connection with harlequin ducks, called lords and ladies in Newfoundland.

Loreburn SK The post office at this village (1909) on the Canadian Pacific Railway line, uniting Moose Jaw with Outlook, was established in 1908 and named after Sir Robert Reid, 1st Earl of Loreburn (1846–1923). A British politician, he was created Baron Loreburn in 1905, when he was appointed lord chancellor.

Lorette MB The post office in this community between Winnipeg and Steinbach was named *Loretto* in 1875 after Loretteville, northwest of Quebec City. It was renamed Lorette in 1939.

Loretteville QC In 2002 this city became part of Quebec City. It was named in 1913 and became a town in 1947. Its territory was formerly part of the parish municipality of *Saint-Ambroise-de-la-Jeune-Loretteville*, incorporated in 1845. The original religious parish was created in 1676 to serve the Huron, who had gathered here in the middle of the 1600s. They were placed under the protection of Notre-Dame de l'Annonciation, modelled on the Holy House of the Virgin, founded in 1295 in Loreto on the east coast of Italy.

L'Orignal ON In 1998 this village (1876) became a part of the township of Champlain, united counties of Prescott and Russell. The name derives from the seigniory of *Pointe-à-l'Orignal*, granted to François Prévost (1810–91) in 1674. The seigniory was named after *Pointe à l'Orignal* (now Grants Point), where moose (*orignal*) historically crossed the Ottawa River.

Loring ON In Parry Sound District, north of the town of Parry Sound, it was named in 1884 by Member of Parliament William Edward O'Brien (1831–1914) after his wife, Elizabeth (Loring) Harris, whom he married in 1864. The nearby community of **Port Loring** was named in 1922. She was the daughter of Robert R. Loring (1790–1848) and the widow of Dr. J.F. Harris of London, ON.

Lorne NB Southeast of Dalhousie, this place's post office was named in 1893 after Sir John Douglas Sutherland Campbell, 9th Duke of Argyll and Marquess of Lorne (1845–1914), governor general of Canada, 1878–83.

Lorne, Mount YT On the west side of Marsh Lake, and south of Whitehorse, this mountain (1951 m) was named in 1887 by surveyor William Ogilvie (1846–1912) after the Marquess of Lorne (1845–1914), governor general of Canada, 1878–83. The hamlet of **Mount Lorne**, west of the mountain, was named in 1990.

Lorne Valley PE The post office in this municipal community (1978) north of Montague was named in 1878 after a property in Argyllshire, Scotland, owned by the Marquess of Lorne (1845–1914), governor general of Canada, 1878–83.

Lorneville ON In 2001 this community became a part of the city of Kawartha Lalkes, Victoria County. Located northwest of Lindsay, it was named in 1874 after Marquess of Lorne (1845–1914), governor general of Canada, 1878–83, who had married Princess Louise in 1871.

Lorraine QC This town in the regional county of Thérèse-De Blainville and on the north shore of the Rivière des Mille-Îles was created in 1960. The name derives from the historic region of eastern France.

Lorrainville QC The post office in this village, located in the regional county of Témiscamingue, east of Ville-Marie, was named in 1889 after Mgr. Narcisse-Zéphirin Lorrain (1842–1915), apostolic vicar of the Pontiac, 1882–98, and bishop of Pembroke, 1898–1915. The village was incorporated in 1930.

Lotbinière QC This regional county on the south shore of the St. Lawrence, southwest of Quebec City, was named in 1982 after the former county. The municipality of **Lotbinière** was created in 1978 through the merger of the village of Lotbinière and the parish municipality of *Saint-Louis-de-Lotbinière*. A post office opened here in 1831, taking its name from the seigneury of René-Louis Chartier de Lotbinière (1641–1709), who was granted the seigneury in 1672. The name derives from Chartier's ancestral home of Binière in western France.

Loudon, Mount AB South of Abraham Lake and the North Saskatchewan River, this mountain (3220 m) was named in 1956 after William James Loudon (1860–1951), a professor of mechanics at the University of Toronto.

Loughborough ON In 1998 this township became part of the township of South Frontenac, Frontenac County. It was named in 1798 after Alexander Wedderburn, Baron Loughborough and Earl of Rosslyn (1733–1805). His title was taken from the borough of Loughborough in Leicestershire, England.

Lougheed AB Southeast of Camrose, this village (1911) was first named *Holmstown*. It was renamed in 1906 by the Canadian Pacific Railway after Sir James Alexander Lougheed (1854–1925), who had set up a law practice with Viscount Richard B. Bennett (1870–1947) in Calgary in 1882. He was appointed in 1889 to the Senate, where he served as its Conservative leader from 1906 to 1921. The next station to the east was named after his father-in-law, William Hardisty. **Mount Lougheed** (3105 m), between Calgary and Banff, was named after him in 1928. It had been named *Windy Mountain* in 1858 by botanist Eugène Bourgeau (1813–77) and called *Wind Mountain* by geologist George M. Dawson (1849–1901) in 1886.

Lougheed Island NU In the Parry Islands of the Queen Elizabeth Islands, this island (1308 km²) was named in 1917 by Vilhjalmur Stefansson (1879–1962) after Sir James Alexander Lougheed (1854–1925). He was called to the Senate in 1889, and from 1911 to 1918 served as a minister without portfolio in Sir Robert Borden's cabinet.

Louisbourg NS This urban community, in the regional municipality of Cape Breton since 1 August 1995, is located on the north side of **Louisbourg Harbour**. It was founded by the French on the south side of the harbour on 2 September 1713, following the awarding of Cape Breton Island to France by the Treaty of Utrecht. The harbour was then known as *Havre à l'Anglois* after English fishermen. The place was first called *Port St-Louis* after Louis XIV. The site of the French fortress, captured and destroyed by the British in 1758, was declared a national historic park in 1931. Since 1961 the area of the fortress has been reconstructed. The post office opened as *Louisburg* in 1835, with the current spelling adopted in 1955. The town, incorporated as *Louisburg* in 1901, was renamed Louisbourg in 1966.

Louisdale NS On The post office in this location on Cape Breton Island and east of Port Hawkesbury was called *Barachois St. Louis* in 1893 after a local cove. It was renamed Louisdale in 1905 by postmaster J. Nelson Scott, retaining part of the original name.

Louise, Lake AB In 1884 this lake was named for Princess Louise Caroline Alberta (1848–1939), the fourth daughter of Queen Victoria and the wife of the Marquess of Lorne (1845–1914), governor general of Canada, 1878–83. George M. Dawson (1849–1901) had also named the lake in 1884 after the daughter of Sir Richard Temple (1826–1902), an international alpinist. Tom Wilson (1859–1935) named the lake after *Emerald Lake* before 1884. The local people had called it *The Lake of the Little Fishes. See also* Lake Louise.

Louiseville QC This town in the regional county of Maskinongé, southwest of Trois-Rivières, was created as a village in 1878 and named the following year after Princess Louise Caroline Alberta (1848–1939), the wife of the Marquess of Lorne (1845–1914), governor general of Canada, 1878–83. Its post office was known as *Rivière-du-Loup-en-Haut* from 1816 to 1880, when it was renamed after the village.

Louis St-Laurent, Mount BC In the Premier Range, west of Valemount, this mountain (3018 m) was named in 1964 after Louis Stephen St-Laurent (1882–1973), prime minister of Canada, 1948–57.

Lourdes NL On the northwest side of the Port au Port Peninsula, this municipal community (1979) was formerly called *Clam Bank Cove*. It was renamed in the 1930s after Lourdes in southwestern France, where the Virgin Mary revealed herself in 1858 as the Immaculate Conception to Marie Bernarde Soubirous (St. Bernadette).

Lower Arrow Lake BC The lower of the two Arrow lakes, this narrow 95-km-long widening of the Columbia River was named in the early 1800s after Arrow Rock. Before the flooding of the lake behind the Keenleyside Dam, the rock was a steep cliff on the east side of the lake where the arrows of Aboriginal warriors were lodged. Arrows that remained lodged in the rock were believed to bring good luck to the brave.

Lower Mazinaw Lake ON On the Mississippi River system, north of Kaladar, this body of water was considered part of *Mazinaw Lake* until 1981, when it was divided at The Narrows into Lower and Upper Mazinaw Lakes. *Mazinaw* is an Algonquin word meaning 'picture', recalling pictographs on the face of **Mazinaw Rock**, on the east shore of Upper Mazinaw Lake.

Lower Montague PE A municipal community (1974) east of the town of **Montague** and on the south side of the **Montague River**, its post office served the area from 1871 to 1913 and from 1916 to 1946.

Lucan ON In 1999 this village (1871) became part of the township of Lucan Biddulph, Middlesex County. Located northwest of London, it was named in 1857 by 'Dublin' Tom Hodgins (1828–1910) after the estate of the 4th Earl of Lucan (1830–1914) at Lucan in County Dublin, west of the Dublin, Ireland city centre.

Lucania, Mount YT In the St. Elias Mountains, this mountain (5227 m) was named in 1897 by Italian explorer and mountaineer Luigi Amedeo Abruzzi, the Duke of Abruzzi (1873–1933) after the Cunard liner on which he and his expedition members crossed the Atlantic.

Luceville QC This village in the regional county of La Mitis, northeast of Rimouski, was created in 1918. Its post office was called *Sainte-Luce-Station* in 1883 and renamed Luceville in 1917. The name may have its roots in the eighteenth-century grantee of a seigneury, Gertrude-Luce (or Luce-Gertrude) Drapeau.

Lucifer, Mount AB The most northwesterly point of Jasper National Park, this mountain (3060 m) was named in 1956 after one of the titles of the devil.

Lucknow ON In 1999 this village (1873) became part of the township of Huron-Kinloss, Bruce County. Located southwest of Walkerton, it was planned in 1858 and named by James Somerville (1826–98) in honour of a fellow Scot, Sir Colin Campbell (1792–1863), who the previous year had led the relief of Lucknow in India.

Lucky Lake SK The post office in this village (1920) north of Lake Diefenbaker and northwest of Moose Jaw was named in 1908. It took its name from a lake 10 km to the north, which had been named by settler Jock Swansen. He considered it lucky to retrieve his team of oxen, which had fallen into what had been previously called *Devil's Lake*. The lake is officially called **Luck Lake**.

Lulu Island BC Part of the city of Richmond and comprising a large part of the delta of the Fraser River, this island was named in 1862 by Col. Richard C. Mayne (1835–92) after Lulu Sweet, an actress with the first theatrical company to visit the province.

Lumby BC The post office in this village (1955) east of Vernon was called *White Valley* in 1889. It was named in 1894 after Moses Lumby (1842–93), who had been appointed a government agent in Vernon in 1891. After migrating from England in 1862, Lumby became a miner in the Cariboo, a farmer at Monte Creek near Kamloops, a mail carrier on the upper Columbia, a farmer again in the north end of the Okanagan Valley, and a vice-president of the Shuswap and Okanagan Railway.

Lumsden NL This town (1968) on the northeastern coast of Newfoundland was first known as *Cat Harbour*. It was renamed in 1917 after the Reverend James Lumsden (1854–1915), a Methodist minister in Newfoundland, 1881–3, and 1885–92, who was affectionately called the 'skipper parson'. He later became sheriff of Queens County, NS, and the member for Queens in the provincial legislative assembly.

Lumsden SK Located in the Qu'Appelle River valley, north of Regina, this town (1905) was named in 1890, when the Qu'Appelle, Long Lake and Saskatchewan Railway and Steamboat Company line reached that point. It was named after Hugh D. Lumsden (1844–1928), the railway's supervising engineer. Its post office opened in 1892.

Lunenburg NS This town (1888) was founded in 1753 by Gov. Charles Lawrence (1709–60) for the settlement of Protestants from Germany, France, and Switzerland. It took its name from the British royal house of Brunswick-Lüneburg, and its post office opened in 1819. The site had been occupied by Acadians until 1749, which they called *Merligueshe*, a Mi'kmaq word that is said to mean 'milky bay'. **Lunenburg County** was created in 1759.

Lunenburg ON In 1998 this community became part of the township South Stormont, united counties of Stormont, Dundas, and Glengarry. It was named in 1858 after Lunenburg District, given in 1788 out of respect for George III's German roots, but it was renamed Eastern District in 1792 by Lt.-Gov. John Graves Simcoe (1752–1806).

Luseland SK This town was established in 1908 by the Luse Land Development Company of St. Paul, MN, and managed by John R. Luse. The town was located northwest of Kerrobert and was relocated in 1910 to the new Canadian Pacific Railway line, built northwest from Rosetown to Macklin. The post office also opened in 1910

Lushes Bight-Beaumont-Beaumont North NL This municipal community (1968) on Long Island in Notre Dame Bay comprises three separate built-up areas. **Lushes Bight** may have been named after William Lush of nearby Burlington, who fished here seasonally. **Beaumont**, first called *Ward's Harbour*, was named in 1918 after Beaumont Hamel, France, where many soldiers of the Newfoundland Regiment lost their lives in April, 1916, during the First World War.

Luskville QC This community in the municipality of Pontiac, northwest of Aylmer, was named in 1884 after pioneer Joseph Lusk (1783–1879), who settled here in 1832.

Łutselk'e NT On the southeast shore of Great Slave Lake, this settlement was named *Snowdrift* in 1936. It was renamed Łutselk'e in 1992 after the Chipewyan word for 'place of small fish'.

Lyall, Mount AB, BC On the continental divide, north of Crowsnest Pass, this mountain (2952 m) was named in 1917 after Dr. David Lyall (1817–95), a surgeon and naturalist who had served on the International Boundary Commission between the Rockies and the Pacific Ocean, 1858–62.

Lyell, Mount AB, BC On the continental divide and near the head of the North Saskatchewan River, this mountain (3504 m) was named by Dr. James Hector (1834–1907) in 1858 after British geologist Sir Charles Lyell (1795–1875).

Lyn ON In the united counties of Leeds and Grenville, west of Brockville, this community was named *Lowell* in 1839 after the Massachusetts city north of Boston, from where the settlers had come. Fearing confusion with similar names in Upper Canada, it was renamed after Lynn, MA, a city northeast of Boston.

Lynn Lake MB Located north of Flin Flon, this community has its roots in the discovery in 1941 of copper and nickel deposits. The deposits were developed in 1947. Its post office was named in 1951 after Lynn Smith, chief engineer of the Sherritt Gordon Mining Company.

Lyster QC This municipality in the regional county of L'Érable, northeast of Victoriaville, was created as a village in 1912. In 1976 it became a municipality by merging with the municipality of *Sainte-Anastasie-de-Nelson*. Lyster post office was named in 1862 and renamed *Sainte-Anastasie* in 1898, but Lyster was restored in 1981. The name was given by lumber merchant Charles King after his birthplace of Lister in Essex, England.

Lytton BC At the confluence of the Fraser and Thompson Rivers, this village (1945) was named in 1858 by Gov. James Douglas (1803–77) after Sir Edward Bulwer-Lytton (1803–73), author and British secretary of state for the colonies. Before the first detachment of Royal Engineers sailed in 1858 from Cowes, England, he joined them on board and wished them well in the new colony.

M

MacAlpine Lake NU On the Arctic Circle, northwest of Baker Lake, this lake (421 km²) was named in 1929 by geologist G.H. Blanchet (1884–1966) after Col. C.D.H. MacAlpine, president of Canadian Explorers Ltd. Learning in 1930 that North West Mounted Police inspector F.H. French had named the lake in 1918 after NWMP (RCMP from 1919) Commissioner Aylesworth Bowen Perry (1860–1956), the Geographic Board changed it to *Perry Lake*. In 1932 the board reversed its decision, restored MacAlpine Lake, and named the 140-km river draining the lake north to Queen Maud Gulf after Perry.

Macamic QC Located on the south shore of **Lac Macamic** in the regional county of Abitibi-Ouest, north of Rouyn-Noranda, this community became a village in 1919 and a town in 1955. The name of its post office was spelled *Makamik* from 1915 to 1949. In Algonquin *makamik* means 'crippled beaver'.

Macaulay, Mount YT In the St. Elias Mountains, this mountain (4663 m) was named in 1958 after territorial judge Charles Daniel Macaulay.

MacCarthy, Mount BC Located in The Bugaboos of the Purcell Mountains, west of Invermere, this mountain (3062 m) was named in 1954 by climber Peter Robinson after alpinist Albert Henry MacCarthy (1876–1955), who had climbed in the Purcells and had led the first ascent of Mount Logan in the Yukon in 1925.

Macdonald, Mount BC In the Selkirk Mountains, directly south of Rogers Pass, this mountain (2893 m) was named in 1897 by Order-in-Council after Sir John A. Macdonald (1815–91), prime minister of Canada, 1867–73 and 1878–91.

Maces Bay NB Adjacent to the Bay of Fundy, southwest of Saint John, this bay may have been named by map-maker Joseph Frederric Wallet DesBarres (1722–1824) after Benjamin Mace, surgeon with the 22nd Regiment. The name may also derive from the Passamaquoody *musquasikik* ('place for Indian beans'), a reference to Salkeld Island. The community of **Maces Bay**, north of Point Lepreau, had a post office from 1855 to 1918.

MacGregor MB West of Portage la Prairie, this village (1947) was named in 1881 by the Marquess of Lorne (1845–1914) after his chaplain, the Reverend James MacGregor (1759–1830) of St. Cuthbert's Church, Edinburgh, who accompanied him west. Its post office was called *MacGregor Station* in 1883, with 'Station' being dropped in 1900.

Machias Seal Island NB In the Bay of Fundy and south-east of Machias Bay, ME, this island was known to the Passamaquoddy as *Menascook* ('at the grassy island'). Map-maker Herman Moll (d.1732) called it *Seal I* in 1715. The present name was noted in 1876 by historian J.G. Lorimer.

MacKay Lake NT Northeast of Great Slave Lake, this lake (977 km²) was named *Lake Mackay* in 1892 by explorer Warburton Pike. In 1924 geologist G.H. Blanchet (1884–1966) recommended MacKay Lake, as it was named after Dr. William Morrison MacKay (1836–1917), a Hudson's Bay Company surgeon and fur trader.

Mackenzie BC This district municipality (1966) on the eastern shore of Williston Lake was created as a centre for the exploitation of the rich forest and mineral wealth of the area. It was named after explorer Sir Alexander Mackenzie (1764–1820), who passed by the future site of the munici-pality in 1793. **Mount Mackenzie**, northeast of Bella Coola, was named in 1953 by the department of national defence, also after the explorer. *See also* Sir Alexander, Mount.

Mackenzie King Island NT In the Parry Islands of the Queen Elizabeth Islands, this island (5048 km²) was named in 1949 after William Lyon Mackenzie King (1874–1950), prime minister of Canada, 1921–26, 1926–30, and 1935–48. Until a Royal Canadian Air Force aerial survey in 1947, it had been considered part of Borden Island.

Mackenzie King, Mount BC Located in the Premier Range, west of Valemount, this mountain (3280 m) was named in 1962 after William Lyon Mackenzie King, prime minister of Canada, 1921–26, 1926–30, and 1935–48. *See also* King, Mount.

Mackenzie, Mount BC Located in the Selkirk Mountains, southeast of Revelstoke, this mountain (2456 m) was named in 1887 after Alexander Mackenzie (1822–92), prime minister of Canada, 1873–8.

Mackenzie Mountains NT, YK Located on the border of the Yukon and Northwest Territories, this system of several ranges of mountains was named in 1944 by the Geographic Board after Alexander Mackenzie, prime minister of Canada, 1873–8. The name had occurred as early as 1927 on a map of northwestern Canada.

Mackenzie River AB, BC, NT, YT The longest river system (4241 km, to the head of the Finlay River, northern British Columbia) entirely within Canada, this river was named by Sir John Franklin (1786–1847), who explored the river to its mouth in 1789. Discouraged that he had not arrived at the Pacific Ocean, he called it River Disappointment. In 1825 he renamed the river after Sir Alexander Mackenzie (c.1764–1820).

Macklin SK Southwest of Battleford, near the Alberta border, this town (1912) was established in 1906 by the Canadian Pacific Railway and named after E.H. (Harry) Macklin. A Winnipeg *Free Press* executive, he was following the progress of the railway's construction. Its post office opened in 1908.

Macmillan River YT Rising in the **Macmillan Pass**, and in the Mackenzie Mountains, the **South Macmillan River** joins the **North Macmillan River** north of Faro. The main river then flows west to join the Yukon River at the site of Fort Selkirk, west of Pelly Crossing. Hudson's Bay Company trader Robert Campbell (1808–94) named it in 1843 after HBC chief factor James McMillan (1783–1858). The name's official spelling was made by the Geographic Board in 1898.

Macoun SK Northwest of Estevan, this village (1903) was named after John Macoun (1831–1920), a field naturalist who had persuaded Canadian Pacific Railway officials in the early 1880s that the southern prairies were ideally suited for agriculture. Its post office also opened in 1903.

Macoun, Mount BC In the Selkirk Mountains, southeast of Rogers Pass, this mountain (3049 m) was named in 1889 by climber William S. Green (1847–1919) after naturalist John Macoun (1831–1920). Earlier alpinist Harold Topham had called it *North Sentinel*.

Mactaquac Lake NB Extending from a dam west of Fredericton up the Saint John River valley to Woodstock, this reservoir was created by the New Brunswick Electric Power Commission in 1967. It was named after **Mactaquac Stream**, which rises south of Millville. This name may be Mi'kmaq for 'big branch', possibly in reference to the Saint John River itself, and subsequently applied to the first stream above the head of tide.

Madame, Isle NS On the south side of Cape Breton Island, this island was known to Acadian Gov. Nicolas Denys (c.1598–1688) in the 1660s as *Isle Ste-Marie*, which was rendered by map-makers as early as 1684 as *Isles Madame*. It was called

I. de Maurepas in the early 1700s after Comte Jean Frédéric Phélypeaux Maurepas (1701–81), a French secretary of state and minister of the marine and colonies. Samuel Holland (1728–1801) introduced *Richmond Island* in 1767 after Charles Lennox, 3rd Duke of Richmond (1734–1806), a British official who served as ambassador to France. However, the name Isle Madame was not supplanted.

Madawaska River NB, QC This river drains Lac Témiscouata in Quebec southeast into the Saint John River at Edmundston. The name derives from the Maliseet *medaweskak* ('porcupine place') or ('murmuring at the mouth'). It was noted in a seigneury grant of 1683 as *Madouesca*, with the present spelling being established in 1778 by map-maker James Peachey. **Madawaska County** was created in 1873.

Madawaska River ON Rising in Algonquin Park, this river flows southeast to the Ottawa River at Arnprior. The name may derive from an Algonquin band that Samuel de Champlain (1567–1635) met in 1613, which he called *Matouoüescarini* ('people of the shallows'). The post office in the community of **Madawaska**, on the river and in Nipissing District, west of Barry's Bay, was named in 1900.

Madeira Park BC On the Sechelt Peninsula, northwest of Vancouver, this community's post office was named in 1946. The name was proposed by Joseph Gonsalos after his native Arquipélago da Madeira, a Portuguese possession in the Atlantic Ocean, west of Casablanca, Morocco.

Madeleine, Îles de la QC Located in the southern part of the Gulf of St. Lawrence, and 250 km southeast of Gaspé, this archipelago was visited in 1534 by Jacques Cartier (1491–1557). Two years later he called them *Les Araynes*, signifying 'the sandy ones'. During the 1600s the group was called *Ramea*, *Ramée*, and *Ramées*, names suggesting branches united by strips of sand. On his 1632 map, Samuel de Champlain (1567–1635) called the largest island *La Magdelene*. In 1663 their second proprietor, François Doublet, was authorized to rename the group Îles de la Madeleine after his wife, Madeleine Fontaine. The regional county was created in 1981, embracing the Îles de la Madeleine. Until about 1980 they were commonly called the Magdalen Islands in English. However, the print media have almost entirely accepted the official designation.

Madoc ON The township of **Madoc** was named in 1820 after the Welsh Prince Madoc, who reputedly discovered America in 1170. In 1998 this village became a part of the township of Centre Hastings, Hastings County. The post office in the village (1877) was named after the township in 1836. In 1855 the police village was called *Hastings*, in the hope it would become the county seat of Hastings County. Ten years later it was renamed **Madoc** and was incorporated as a village in 1877.

Mafeking MB The post office and station of this community west of Lake Winnipegosis, and between Swan River and The Pas, were named in 1904 in honour of the brilliant defence in 1900 of Mafeking (now Mafikeng), South Africa, by Col. Robert Baden-Powell (1857–1941). The next two Canadian Northern Railway stations were called Baden and Powell.

Magaguadavic River NB This river drains **Magaguadavic Lake** southeast into the Bay of Fundy at St. George. Its name derives from the Mi'kmaq, through Passamaquoddy, *Mageecaatawik* ('river of the big eels'). Spelled many ways in the late 1600s and throughout the 1700s, its present spelling was set by 1859, although some earlier references used *Macadavic*, reflecting its pronunciation.

Magnetic Hill NB In Moncton, 10 km northwest of the city centre, this site of an illusory phenomenon of vehicles seeming to roll up a hill was discovered in 1933 by Muriel Lutes Sikorski on the side of a hill called Lutes Mountain. She opened an ice cream stand called 'The Shanty' on the top of the hill. Her discovery was promoted by several writers throughout North America. Many drivers from the Canadian provinces and the United States still come to the Magnetic Hill to roll up the hill in their cars.

Magog QC Located at the north end of **Lac Memphrémagog**, which is drained by **Rivière Magog** northeast to the Saint-François at Sherbrooke, its present form can be traced to the township of **Magog**, proclaimed in 1849. The township took its name from the lake, which in Abenaki had the significance of 'place where there are salmon trout'. Magog was incorporated as a village in 1888, and was upgraded to a town less than two years later. *See also* Memphrémagog.

Magrath AB This town (1907) south of Lethbridge was named in 1899 after Charles A. Magrath (1860–1949), who had been a Dominion land surveyor from 1878 to 1885. Settling in Lethbridge, he managed the Canadian North Western Coal and Irrigation Company, 1885–1906, served as the city's first mayor, 1891, represented Lethbridge in the North-West Territories Assembly, 1891–1902, and was a member of Parliament for Medicine Hat, 1908–11.

Mahone Bay NS Situated on the west side of the 20 km² **Mahone Bay**, this community was founded in 1754, with its post office being established in 1848. An attempt in 1857 to rename it *Kinburn*—after the fortress at the mouth of the Dneiper in present Ukraine, attacked by the British and the French during the Crimean War—was not accepted. The bay had been called *Baie de la Mahonne* in French, after low-lying vessels used by pirates.

Maidstone ON In 1999 this township became part of the town of Lakeshore, Essex County. It was named in 1792 after the county town of Kent in England, southeast of London. The post office at the community of **Maidstone**, southeast of Windsor, was named in 1837, but its postmaster was not appointed until 1851.

Maidstone SK Located southeast of Lloydminster, this town (1955) was named in 1905 by the Canadian Northern Railway after Maidstone in Kent, England, southeast of London. The post office had been called *Sayers* that year and was renamed Maidstone in 1906.

Main-à-Dieu NS On the east coast of Cape Breton Island, this place's name derives from the Mi'kmaq *Menadou* ('the spirit of evil'). In 1786 Joseph Frederic Wallet DesBarres (1722–1824) interpreted it as *Main a Dieu* ('hand of God'), and this became its postal name in 1837. The Geographic Board amended it to *Mainadieu* in 1909. Assuming it was a French name, the Canadian Board on Geographical Names changed it to its present form in 1954.

Main Brook NL On the south side of Hare Bay, southwest of St. Anthony, this town (1948) was founded in the 1920s, becoming one of the first 11 towns incorporated in the province before 1949.

Mainland NL Located on the west side of Port au Port Peninsula, this place was called in French *Grand'Terre* ('mainland'), as seen by French-speaking fishermen from Red Island (*Île Rouge*), offshore. Basque fishermen may have earlier called it *certan*, their word for mainland.

Main Point-Davidsville NL This local service district (1984) is located on the east side of Gander Bay and on the north coast of Newfoundland. **Main Point** was named after a nearby point. **Davidsville**, known as *Mann Point* until 1956, was named after the St. David's Anglican Church.

Maisonnette NB This village (1986) northwest of Caraquet was noted on a survey map of 1755 as *Maisonette* ('little house'). Its post office opened as *Mizonette* in 1885, became *Ste Jeanne d'Arc* in 1919, and changed to its present name in 1936.

Maitland NS On the west side of the mouth of the Shubenacadie River and west of Truro, this settlement was named in 1832 by Judge Charles R. Fairbanks after Sir Peregrine Maitland (1777–1854), lieutenant-governor of Nova Scotia, 1828–34. It had been earlier called *Beaver River Settlement* and *Port Shubenacadie*. A second **Maitland**, between Mahone Bay and Bridgewater, was likely named for the lieutenant-governor as well. *See also* Port Maitland.

Maitland ON This community northeast of Brockville in the united counties of Leeds and Grenville was named in 1824, possibly by settler Ziba Marcus Phillips. It was named after Sir Peregrine Maitland (1777–1854), lieutenant-governor of Upper Canada, 1818–28, who may have stopped here that year. The post office opened in 1828.

Maitland River ON Rising in Wellington County, this river flows west to Goderich on Lake Huron. Earlier called *Red River* and *Menesetung* (Ojibwa for 'healing waters' or 'windings'), it was named by the Canada Company about 1822 after Sir Peregrine Maitland (1777–1854), lieutenant-governor of Upper Canada, 1818–28.

Majestic Peak BC In the Coast Mountains, southeast of Mount Waddington, this mountain (2911 m) was named in 1958 by Capt. Dr. G.V.B. Cochran of the United States Air Force.

Makkovik NL On the Labrador coast, northeast of Happy Valley-Goose Bay, this community is located on **Makkovik Bay**. The origin of the name is uncertain, with the possibility that it was named after an Inuit family or after a French trader, possibly Pierre Marcoux. It was founded in the mid-1800s and was known among fishermen from Newfoundland as *Flounders Bight*. It became a Moravian mission in 1896.

Malagash NS Located northwest of Tatamagouche, this community's name derives from either the Mi'kmaq *malegawate* (possibly 'mocking place') in reference to games played in the area, or *muligech* ('milk'), referring to the appearance of the water when it is stirred up. Its post office was established in 1855. Other places in the area with former post offices include **Malagash Point** (1877), **Upper Malagash** (1877), **Malagash Centre** (1901), **Malagash Station** (1937), and **Malagash Mine** (1938).

Malahide ON In 1998 this township, with the township of South Dorchester and the village of Springfield, became part of the township of Malahide, Elgin County. It was named in 1810 after Malahide Castle in the village of Malahide, County Dublin, Ireland, where Col. Thomas Talbot (1771–1853) was born. Col. Talbot built his Castle Malahide at Port Talbot in Dunwich Township.

Malarctic QC This town in the regional county of Vallée-de-l'Or, west of the city of Val-d'Or, was incorporated in 1939, taking its name from the township of **Malarctic**, proclaimed in 1916. The township was named after Anne-Joseph-Hippolyte de Maurès de Malarctic (1730–1800), who fought in both the battles of the Plains of Abraham (1759) and Sainte-Foy (1760).

Malaspina, Mount YT In the St. Elias Mountains, this mountain (3886 m) was named in 1890 by explorer and geologist Israel C. Russell (1852–1906) after navigator Alexandro Malaspina (1754–1810). The Italian-born Malaspina explored the northwestern coast of North America in 1791 on behalf of Spain.

Malaspina Strait BC Separating Texada Island from Powell River on the mainland, this channel was named in 1859 by Capt. George Richards (1820–96) after Capt. Alexandro Malaspina (1754–1810), an Italian who explored the west coast of Vancouver Island in 1791 for Spain. **Malaspina Inlet** and **Malaspina Peninsula** are northwest of Powell River.

Malcolm Island BC Between Vancouver Island and the mainland, and at the head of Queen Charlotte Strait, this island was named in 1846 by Cdr. George T. Gordon of HMS *Cormorant* after Adm. Sir Pulteney Malcolm (1758–1838), commander-in-chief of the St. Helena station in 1816–7 where Napoleon Bonaparte spent his last days.

Malden ON In 1998 this township became part of the town of Amherstburg, Essex County. It was named in 1792 after the town of Maldon in Essex, England, east of London. Fort Malden, named after the township, was constructed from 1797 to 1799 at Amherstburg.

Maligne, Lake AB In Jasper National Park, southeast of Jasper, this lake took its name from the **Maligne River**, a tributary of the Athabasca. It had been called *Sore-foot Lake* by railway surveyor Henry MacLeod in 1875. The name of the river, given in 1846, means 'malignant' in French. **Maligne Mountain** (3220 m) was named in 1911 by Mary Schäffer after the name of the lake.

Maliotenam QC Situated on the north shore of the St. Lawrence River, east of Sept-Îles, this Indian reserve was established in 1949. In Montagnais the name means 'village of Mary'.

Mallery Lake NU Located west of Baker Lake, this lake (467 km²) was named in 1945 by surveyor Walter Stilwell after Mr. and Mrs. H.A. Mallery of Calgary, AB.

Malpeque Bay PE On the north side of the province, this bay was referred to as *Magpec* by Jacques Nicolas Bellin in 1744. Its name derives from the Mi'kmaq *makpaak* ('big bay'). In 1765 Samuel Holland (1728–1801) named it *Richmond Bay*, with *Malpeck Bay* as a secondary name, after Charles Lennox, 3rd Duke of Richmond (1734–1806), who served as the British ambassador to France. *Richmond Bay* continued to be used into the twentieth century for the west side of the bay and provided the name Richmond for a municipal community to the west. **Malpeque** is in the municipal community (1973) of

Malpeque Bay, on the east side of the bay. It was originally called *Princetown* after the original *Princetown Royalty,* which served as its post office from 1827 to 1945, but Malpeque was used for the place as early as 1775 and became the postal name in 1945. The municipal community of Malpeque Bay embraces several localities, including Indian River, Hamilton, Spring Valley, and Darnley.

Malton ON On the northeast side of Mississauga, this place was named in the 1830s by Richard Halliday after his birthplace in North Yorkshire, England, northeast of the city of York. Lester B. Pearson International Airport (1983) was long known as Malton Airport after it opened in 1937.

Mamquam Mountain BC In the Coast Mountains, northeast of Squamish, this mountain (2595 m) was named by a group of climbers of the British Mountaineering Club in 1911 after the **Mamquam River**. The river was named by the Squamish after its smooth and murmuring characteristics in lower stretches.

Manicouagan QC This regional county, on the north shore of the St. Lawrence and centred on the city of Baie-Comeau, was named in 1981. It took its name from the **Rivière Manicouagan**, which drains the **Réservoir Manicouagan**, 210 km north of Baie-Comeau. In 1664 missionary Henri-Nouvel referred to a *grande rivière de Manicouaganistikou* and the following year called it *rivière Manicoüagan*. In Montagnais the name means either 'where birch bark is gathered to repair canoes', or 'place where they get a drink'.

Manilla ON The post office of this community on the border of Victoria County and in Durham Region, west of Lindsay, was called *Mariposa* in 1836 after the township of Mariposa. In 1851 it was renamed Manilla after a village in Rush County, IN, which was probably named for the city of Manila in the Philippines.

Manitoba The name of the province derives from the Ojibwa *Manito-Bah* or Cree *Manito-Wapow* ('the strait of the spirit'), in reference to noisy sounds made by pebbles on a beach of **Manitoba Island** in The Narrows of **Lake Manitoba**. The name is less likely from the Assiniboine *Mini-Tobow* ('lake of the prairie'). Pierre Gaultier de La Vérendrye (1685–1755) called it *Lac des Prairies* in 1730.

Manitoba, Mount YT In the Centennial Range of the St. Elias Mountains, this mountain (3399 m) was named in 1967 after the province.

Manitou MB This village (1897) west of Morden was first called *Manitoba City* but was renamed Manitou by the Canadian Pacific Railway in 1883, selecting a word meaning 'great spirit' in Ojibwa and other Algonquian languages. Its

post office was called *Archibald* in 1879 and was changed to Manitou 10 years later.

Manitou, Lake ON This lake on Manitoulin Island was named after the great spirit of the Ojibwa. It is believed to be the world's largest lake on an island that is itself located in a freshwater lake.

Manitoulin Island ON The largest island in a freshwater lake in the world, its name originated in the Ojibwa, Ottawa, and Algonquin concept of the great spirit Manitou, the master of life and ruler of all things. The island is a sacred place for the First Nations.

Manitouwadge ON This township in Thunder Bay District, southeast of Geraldton, was developed in the 1950s as a mining centre on the shores of **Manitouwadge Lake**. In Ojibwa the name of the lake means 'cave of the great spirit'.

Maniwaki QC A town (1957) in the regional county of La Vallée-de-Gatineau, this place was incorporated as a municipal township in 1904 and a village in 1930. The post office here was called River Desert from 1854 to 1875, when it was renamed Maniwaki. In Algonquin the name means 'place of Mary', in reference to the mission established among the Algonquin in 1849 by the Oblate fathers. The reserve was established in 1851 and its limits were set two years later.

Mankota SK This village (1941) southwest of Assiniboia was established by early settlers from Mankato, MN, southwest of Minneapolis, and its post office was named in 1911. The settlers had travelled through North Dakota and Manitoba and combined these names to form Mankota. The Canadian Pacific Railway arrived here in 1928.

Mannheim ON The post office of this community in the regional county of Waterloo, southeast of Kitchener, was named in 1863 after Mannheim on the Rhine in Germany.

Manning AB Originally called *Aurora*, this town (1957) was named after Ernest Charles Manning (1908–96), premier of Alberta, 1943–68, and a member of the Senate, 1970–96.

Mannville AB This village (1906), between Vegreville and Vermilion, was named in 1905 by Winnipeg land agents Davidson and McRae after Sir Donald D. Mann (1853–1934), who was then vice-president of the Canadian Northern Railway.

Manor SK Northeast of Estevan, this village (1902) was named in 1900, when the Canadian Pacific Railway was built from Souris, MB, to Arcola, SK. It took its name from *Cannington Manor*, 16 km to the northwest, established in the 1880s by English capitalists who dreamed of a gracious community on the frontier. A post office opened here in 1901.

Manotick ON In 2001 this community became part of the city of Ottawa. It is partly on Long Island, in the Rideau River, with the main centre on the west side of the river and with subdivisions on the east side of river. Its population in 2008 was about 8000. This community was named in 1864 by miller Moss Kent Dickinson, who devised the name from the Ojibwa words for 'long island'.

Manseau QC This village in the regional county of Bécancour, north of Victoriaville, was named in 1922 after Fr. Martial Manseau (b. 1870), who was the parish priest here from 1899 to 1907.

Mansel Island NU This island (3180 km²) in the north-eastern part of Hudson Bay was named *Mancel Island* in 1613 by explorer Thomas Button (c.1601–34) after VAdm. Sir Robert Mansel (1573–1653), treasurer of the Navy. Button's wife was Sir Robert's niece. It was corrected to Mansel Island by the Geographic Board in 1908, after it had been shown as *Mansfield Island* on some British Admiralty charts.

Mansfield ON The post office in this community in Dufferin County, northeast of Shelburne, was named in 1858 after the local Presbyterian church's glebe (field) and residence (manse).

Mansons Landing BC Located on Cortes Island, east of Campbell River, this settlement was named in 1941 after Michael Manson, a Shetlander who operated a trading post here from 1887 to 1895 with his brother John. In 1893 Michael Manson was the first postmaster of *Cortez Island* at the same location.

Mansonville QC The post office in this community west of Lac Memphrémagog, near the Vermont border, was named in 1837 after miller Robert Manson, a Scot who settled here in 1811.

Manvers ON In 2001 this township became part of the city of Kawartha Lakes, Victoria County. It was in Durham County when it was named in 1816, but it was transferred to Victoria County in 1974. It was named for Charles Pierrepoint, Baron Pierrepoint (1737–1816), who was created Earl Manvers in 1806.

Maple ON In the city of Vaughan, York Region, this urban centre's post office was called *Rupert* in 1852, but it was changed in 1855 to Maple. From 1851 to 1904, its railway station was known as *Richmond Hill* after Richmond Hill on Yonge Street, 7 km to the east. It was still a town of 178,000 in 2008. The population of Maple was 55,000 in 2008.

Maple Creek SK This town (1903) southwest of Swift Current originated in 1882–3, when construction of the Canadian Pacific Railway east from Calgary was halted near here, and the crew remained for the winter. A post office opened here in 1883. **Maple Creek** rises in the Cypress Hills and flows north to Bigstick Lake. It was named after the fringe of box elder (Manitoba maple) trees along its banks.

Maple Grove QC Located in the regional county of Beauharnois-Salaberry, southwest of Montreal, this town was named in 1918 after the estate of Robert Howden Norval (c.1798–1855), who purchased the land in 1828 and named the estate about 1840. Maple Grove post office operated here from 1854 to 1954.

Maple Ridge BC This district municipality (1974) is located on the north side of the Fraser River, east of Vancouver. Its post office was named in 1876 but it was closed 10 years later. It was restored in 1959 and replaced *Port Haney* in 1970.

Maquapit Lake NB The name of this lake on the west side of Grand Lake and east of Fredericton derives from the Maliseet *maquahpak* ('red lake place'). It was variously called *Quacopeck*, *Oquapo*, and *Maquako*; the present name was established by 1859 on John Wilkinson's map of the province.

Marathon ON When the Canadian Pacific Railway was built in 1883–4 along the shore of Lake Superior, the site of this town (1988) was called *Peninsula* after a prominent point extending into Peninsula Harbour. In 1917 *Peninsula* post office opened here. General Timber Company of Port Arthur (now part of the city of Thunder Bay), a subsidiary of Marathon Paper Mills of Rothschild, WI, built a paper mill here in 1936. A request in 1944 to rename the post office Everest (after the company's president) was rejected by the post office department, but the parent company's name was accepted.

Marbleton QC The post office in this village (1895) in the regional county of Le Haut-Saint-François, northeast of Sherbrooke, was named in 1855 after a local marble quarry. A request in 1979 to rename it Saint-Adolphe-de-Marbleton was rejected because it would be confused with the nearby locality of Saint-Adolphe-de-Dudswell.

Marcelin SK Southwest of Prince Albert, this village (1911) was settled in 1902 by Antoine Marcellin (1842–1915). Five years later the first school opened and was named after him. When the Canadian Northern Railway arrived in 1912, he proposed St. Albert for the station, but was persuaded to accept Marcellin. The post office opened in 1904.

Marchand QC This municipality west of Mont Tremblant was named in 1886 after the township of **Marchand**, which was named after 1880 and proclaimed in 1892. The township was called after Félix-Gabriel Marchand (1832–1900), who became the premier of Quebec, 1897–1900.

Marconi, Mount BC In the Rocky Mountains, southeast of Invermere, this mountain (3105 m) was named in 1919 after Guglielmo Marconi (1974–1919), noted for his experiments with wireless telegraphy.

Margaree River NS The name of this river on the west coast of Cape Breton Island was shown on a 1685 French map as *R de Magre* and possibly derives from the name *Marguerite*, noted on later maps. It was also called *R au Saumon* and *Salmon R.* A post office opened at Margaree in 1824, and other offices opened later at **Margaree Forks** (1859), **Margaree Harbour** (1876), **South West Margaree** (1876), **East Margaree** (1877), **Margaree Island** (1894), **Margaree Ford** (1901), **North East Margaree** (1901), **Margaree Brook** (1930), **Margaree Valley** (1961), and **Margaree Centre** (1961).

Margo SK The post office in this village (1911) northwest of Canora opened in 1905; the name was taken from a nearby lake. **Margot Lake** had been named after a Métis's daughter called Margot, who had been murdered in the late 1900s. The Canadian Northern Railway was constructed through the village in 1906.

Maria QC The name of this municipality (1977), situated on the north shore of Chaleur Bay, west of New Richmond, was noted as early as 1815. It was given after Lady Maria Howard (1754–1836), the wife of Sir Guy Carleton, Lord Dorchester (1724–1808), governor-in-chief of Quebec, 1768–78, and 1786–96. Nearby Carleton was named after him. Maria was a township municipality from 1845 to 1977.

Maria-Chapdelaine QC This regional county north of Lac Saint-Jean was named in 1983 after the celebrated 1913 novel by Louis Hémon (1880–1913), who wrote about the difficult pioneer life in the area.

Marieville QC This town in the regional county of Rouville, east of Chambly, traces its roots to the French seigneury of *Saint-Nom de Marie de Monnoir*, granted to Gov. Claude de Ramezay (1659–1724) of Montreal. He was granted the seigneury of Monnoir in the area of the town in 1708, with the religious parish of Sainte-Marie-de-Monnoir being established in 1801. The same name was given to the parish municipality in 1845, and the town was incorporated in 1905, seven years after the Marieville post office (1897) opened.

Maringouin, Cape NB Extending into Chignecto Bay, southwest of Sackville, this cape's name derives from the French word for 'mosquito'. Jean-Baptiste-Louis Franquelin (c.1653–1712) called it *C des maringouins* on his map of 1686,

and *Mosquito Point* occurred in a 1704 report. However, most English-language maps and reports used variations on the French name, such as *Cape Marangouin*.

Mariposa ON In 2001 this township became part of the city of Kawartha Lakes, Victoria County. It was named by Lt.-Gov. Sir Peregrine Maitland (1777–1854) after the Spanish word for 'butterfly'. Stephen Leacock's fictional town of Mariposa in *Sunshine Sketches of a Little Town* (1912) is believed to have been modelled on Orillia, where he had spent his summers after 1928 in a grand residence. In 1978 his house became a national historic site and museum, open in the summer.

Markdale ON In 2001 this village (1888) became a part of the municipality of Grey Highlands, Grey County. Located southeast of Owen Sound, it was called *East Glenelg* in 1851 after Glenelg Township. In 1864 it was renamed *Cornabuss* after Cornabus on Scotland's Isle of Islay. It was renamed again in 1873, when Mark Armstrong sold land for a railway, stipulating its station be named after him.

Markham ON This township was laid out in 1792 and named after the Right Reverend William Markham (1720–1806), archbishop of York, 1777–1806. The township's largest urban centre was called Markham in 1828. When regional government was established in 1969, Markham Township became a town. With a population of 175,000 in 2008, it is the province's most populous town.

Markstay ON In 1999 Markstay amalgamated with the villages of Warren and Hagar, and with adjacent townships, to become the municipality of Markstay-Warren. Markstay was named in 1892 after Marks Tey in Sussex, England, 18 km southeast of Sudbury in Suffolk.

Marmora ON In 2001 this township, the township of Lake, and the village of **Marmora** became part of the municipality of **Marmora and Lake**, Hastings County. Marmora Township was named in 1820 after a huge marble rock on Crowe Lake, taking the Latin plural for 'marble'. The post office at the village (1901) of Marmora was first called *Marmora Iron Works* in 1821 and was shortened to Marmora in 1823.

Marmot Towers BC Located in the Coast Mountains, northwest of Pemberton, this mountain (3124 m) was named in the 1950s by climbers of the Alpine Club of Canada. Earlier they had ascended its Desperation, Deviation, and Inspiration peaks, and at first used the name Desperation Towers for the mountain. They renamed it after the marmots encountered during an ascent.

Marsden SK Located west of Battleford, the area of this village (1931) was first known as *Manitou*, after a lake to the south. In 1907 Marsden post office opened and was named after the birthplace in England of postmaster Alex Wright's wife. Marsden is in West Yorkshire, southwest of Bradford. The Canadian Pacific Railway adopted the name in 1923.

Marshall SK Southeast of Lloydminster, the post office at this village (1906) was called *Stringer* in 1904 after homesteader Lewis Stringer. When the Canadian Northern Railway arrived in 1905, its station was named Marshall after Noel Marshall, an associate with Sir William Mackenzie (1795–1861), one of the founders of the railway.

Marsh Lake YT A widening of the Yukon River, southeast of Whitehorse, this community was first called *Mud Lake* by the early miners. In 1883 American Army officer Lt. Frederick Schwatka (1849–92) named it after paleontologist Othniel Charles Marsh (1831–99). He was a professor of vertebrate paleontology at Yale University, 1866–99, and honorary curator of vertebrate paleontology at the United States National Museum, 1887–99.

Marsoui QC This village (1950) is located on the south shore of the St. Lawrence, northwest of Gaspé. Noted on maps as early as 1755, the name derives from the Mi'kmaq *malseoui* ('flint'), which they used to produce tools and ignitors.

Martensville SK Located just north of Saskatoon, this town (1969) had its beginnings when Isaac Martens and his son Dave subdivided their farm into building lots in the 1960s. Its post office was established in 1963.

Martha Black, Mount YT This mountain (2496 m) in the St. Elias Mountains, south of Haines Junction, was named in 1945 by geologist Hugh Bostock (1901–94) after Martha Munger Black (1866–1957). The wife of Yukon commissioner George Black (1872–1965), she replaced him as the Yukon member of Parliament, 1935–40, while he was ill. *See also* Black, Mount.

Martinon NB In the city of Saint John, west of the city centre, this neighbourhood was named in 1902 for a Canadian Pacific Railway station by naturalist William F. Ganong (1864–1941) after Martin d'Aprendestiguy, Sieur de Martignon (c.1616–89). A son-in-law of Gov. Charles de Saint-Étienne de la Tour (c.1595–1665), he had a seigneury here about 1660–2.

Martintown ON In 1998 this community became part of the township of South Glengarry, united counties of Stormont, Dundas, and Glengarry. Located northeast of Cornwall, it was first called *MacMartin Mills* after miller Malcolm MacMartin and was renamed Martintown in 1824.

Martre, Lac la NT This lake (1687 km²) was described as both *Martin Lake* and *Marten Lake* by Sir Alexander Mackenzie (c.1764–1820) in 1801, and *Great Marten Lake* by Sir John Franklin (1786–1847) in the journal of his trip to the polar

seas, 1819–22. It appeared on various maps before 1900 as Lac la Martre, the French form of 'marten lake', and may have resulted from the writings of Fr. Émile Petitot (1838–1916). The lake is drained into the North Arm of Great Slave Lake by **Rivière la Martre**. *See also* Whati.

Marwayne AB This village (1952) northwest of Lloydminster was named in 1906 after W. Creasey Marfleet's farm. He arrived here in 1901 and named the farm after his family name and after his hometown, Wainfleet All Saints, Lincolnshire, England, near the North Sea coast.

Maryborough ON This township in Wellington County was named in 1840 after William Wellesley-Pole, 1st Baron Maryborough (1763–1845), a brother of the Duke of Wellington (1769–1852). His daughter, Mary Charlotte Anne, was the wife of Sir Charles Bagot (1781–1843), governor of the Province of Canada, 1841–3. The title was from the Irish town of Maryborough (now Port Laoise) in County Queens (now County Laois), Ireland.

Maryfield SK Southeast of Moosomin and near the Manitoba border, this village (1907) was named after the school district, which had been created in 1883 and called after John Young McNaught's farm. When he left Scotland, he had promised his sister Mary that he would name his farm after her. He moved to Harrison Hot Springs, BC, in 1881, but still provided $10 for the building of the local school in Maryfield. Postal officials adopted the name in 1896 and the Canadian Northern Railway accepted it in 1907.

Mary Henry, Mount BC In the Muskwa Ranges of the Rocky Mountains, this mountain (2972 m) was named in 1931 by surveyor K.F. McCusker after botanist Mary Gibson Henry (1884–1967), who led an expedition to the area that year.

Maryhill ON Located in the regional municipality of Waterloo, east of the city of Waterloo, this community was called *Freiburg* from 1851 to 1941, when it was renamed after the Virgin Mary, whose shrine was on the nearby hill.

Mary March's Brook NL Rising west of Badger, this brook flows south into the northeast end of Red Indian Lake. It was named after Demasduit, called Mary March, the wife of Beothuk chief Nonosbawsut. She had been captured and died in captivity 8 January 1820.

Marystown NL The area of this town (1951) on the east side of the Burin Peninsula was known as *Mortier Bay* until the first half of the twentieth century. The name first occurred in the 1845 census and was possibly given in honour of the Virgin Mary.

Marysvale NL Located on the southwest side of Conception Bay, this place was known as *Turks Gut* until 1919, when it was renamed Marysvale. The cove here retained the name Turks Gut, and a nearby pond is still called Turks Gut Long Pond. Presumably the gut was called after Barbary pirates who plundered Newfoundland's coasts in the seventeenth century.

Marysville ON In 1998 this place on Wolfe Island became part of the township of Frontenac Islands, Frontenac County. This community was named in the 1820s for Mary Hitchcock, who was the postmistress of Wolfe Island from 1845 to 1877. Marysville was officially accepted as the community name in 1977, while maintaining Wolfe Island as the postal name. There is another **Marysville** in Hastings County, 55 km to the west, which was named in 1851 after the local Catholic parish of St. Mary's.

Mary Vaux, Mount AB This mountain (3027 m) near Lake Maligne was named in 1908 by climber Mary Schäffer after Mary Vaux Walcott (1870–1940) of Philadelphia, who performed extensive glaciological studies in the mountains of Canada.

Mascouche QC This town (1971) on the **Rivière Mascouche**, north of the city of Laval, was a parish municipality from the mid-1800s. The river's name, which occurred in records as early as 1772, means 'little bear' in Algonquin.

Maskinongé QC This village (1931) in the regional county of **Maskinongé**, midway between Joliette and Trois-Rivières, took its name from the parish municipality of *Saint-Joseph-de-Maskinongé*, created in 1845. In the early 1700s, the religious parish of Saint-Joseph-de-Maskinongé was formed here. The regional county was established in 1982. **Rivière Maskinongé**, which occurred as early as 1672 as *Masquinongé* in reference to a seigneury, means 'big pike'.

Masset BC The post office in this village (1961) at the north end of Graham Island, the largest of the Queen Charlotte Islands, was named in 1909 after a Haida village on the shore of **Masset Harbour**, 3 km to the northwest. Two years earlier it had been named *Graham City* after Benjamin Graham, the president of Graham Steamship, Coal and Lumber Company. After adopting the name Masset, the older place became *Old Masset*, and later was named Haida. The Haida believe the name Masset came from the burial of a white officer called Massetta on a small island, which they called *Mahsht* after him. George M. Dawson (1849–1901) recorded the island's name in 1878 as *Maast*.

Massey ON This town (1904) in Sudbury District, west of Espanola, was named *Massey Station* in 1889 after Hart Almerrin Massey (1823–96), founder of the Massey Manufacturing Company in Newcastle in 1870, which relocated to Toronto nine years later. The postal name was shortened to Massey in 1939.

Massey Island NU One of the Parry Islands in the Queen Elizabeth Islands, this island (423 km²) was named in 1961 after Charles Vincent Massey (1887–1967), Canada's first native-born governor general, 1952–9.

Massiwippi, Lac QC This lake is located 20 km southwest of the city of Sherbrooke, with **Rivière Massiwippi** draining the lake to the Rivière Saint-François at Lennoxville. The lake is 15 km², with a depth of 75 m. In Abenaki, Massiwippi means 'very good clear water'.

Masson-Angers QC In 2002 this town (1992), located southwest of Buckinham, became a sector of the city of Gatineau. It was named after consulting the residents of the town of Masson, which included the area of Angers. From 1975 to 1980, the two had been parts of the town of Buckingham. Masson had been incorporated as a village in 1897 and a town in 1966. The township of **Masson** was proclaimed in 1894 and named after Louis-François-Rodrigue (or Roderick) Masson (1833–1903), member of the House of Commons, 1876–82, and lieutenant-governor of Quebec, 1884–7. The **Angers** post office was named in 1869 after the birthplace in western France of Fr. Eugène Trinquier, first parish priest of L'Ange-Gardien. Angers became a village in 1915.

Massueville QC Located southeast of Sorel, this village was named in 1903 after its principal benefactor, Gaspard-Aimé Massue (1812–75).

Matachewan ON This township in Timiskaming District, southwest of Kirkland Lake, was the site of the Hudson's Bay Company's Fort Matachewan trading post in 1850. Matachewan post office opened in 1935. In Ojibwa, the word *matadjiwan* means 'meeting of the currents'.

Matagami QC Situated just south of **Lac Matagami** and in northwestern Quebec, this town (1963) became a village in 1961 to exploit the nearby rich reserves of copper and zinc. The lake was named in the late 1800s after the Algonquin for 'junction of waters', in reference to the Bell, the Waswanipi, and the Allard Rivers all flowing into it. The present Rivière Harricanaw was identified on a 1703 map as *R. Matagami*, although the lake is drained north to James Bay by the Rivière Nottaway.

Matane QC Located on the south shore of the St. Lawrence, northeast of Rimouski, this town (1937) was created as the village of *Saint-Jérôme-de-Matane* in 1893. In 1603, Samuel de Champlain (1567–1635) identified the Rivière Matane as *Mantanne*, which derives from the Mi'kmaq *mtctan* ('beaver pond'). The regional county of **Matane** was established in 1982.

Matapédia, Rivière NB, QC Rising in Lac Matapédia, south of Matane, this river flows 70 m south to join the Restigouche, west of Campbellton, NB. The meaning of the name in Mi'kmaq is 'river that forks'.

Matawinie QC This regional county northwest of Joliette was created in 1982. It is centred on the **Rivière Matawin**, which in Algonquin means 'meeting of the waters'.

Matheson ON This township in Cochrane District was named in 1903 for Arthur James Matheson (1842–1913) member for Lanark South in the Legislative Assembly of Ontario, 1895–1913, and provincial treasurer, 1905–13. It forms part of the municipal township of **Black River-Matheson**. The post office in the community of Matheson was first named *McDougall Chute* in 1907, was renamed *Matheson Station* in 1911, and was changed to Matheson in 1949.

Matilda ON In 1998 this township became part of the township of South Dundas, united counties of Stormont, Dundas, and Glengarry. It was named in 1787 for Princess Charlotte Augusta Matilda (1766–1828), the eldest daughter of George III.

Matsqui BC The post office in this community, located in the north side of the city of Abbotsford, was named in 1903. Until 1995 it was part of the district municipality of Matsqui, which had been created in 1892. **Matsqui**, **Matsqui Prairie**, and **Matsqui Island** in the Fraser River take their names from a Halkomelem word for 'easy portage', possibly referring to the ease of travelling overland to Sumas Lake (now dry), or to the Nooksak River in the state of Washington.

Mattagami River ON Rising in **Mattagami Lake** at Gogama, this river flows north through Timmins and Smooth Rock Falls to join the Moose River, upriver from Moosonee. The lake's two long arms provide the meaning of the name in Ojibwa and Cree ('forked lake').

Mattawa ON This town (1892) is in Nipissing Disrict, and at the point where the **Mattawa River** flows into the Ottawa. The river's name in Algonquin and Ojibwa means 'meeting of waters'. The North West Company founded Mattawa House here in 1784, which continued as a Hudson's Bay Company post from 1821 to 1915.

Mattice ON On the Missinaibi River and in Cochrane District, east of Hearst, this place was first called *Missinaibi*. With the coming of the railway in 1915, the post office was called Mattice, possibly after a member of an Eastern Ontario family. Since 1983 it has been part of the municipal township of **Mattice-Val-Côté**.

Matty Island NU Between Boothia Peninsula and King William Island, this island (477 km²) was named on 23 May 1830 by James Clark Ross (1800–62) after the family that donated the expedition's silk colours. The colours were flown that day in honour of the first anniversary of the expedition's departure from London.

Maugerville NB The post office in this community on the north side of the Saint John River and opposite Oromocto was open from 1800 to 1812 and from 1854 to 1966. It was named after **Maugerville Parish**, created in 1786. It took its name from Maugerville Township, established in 1765 and named after Halifax merchant Joshua Mauger (1725–88). Appointed Nova Scotia's agent in England in 1762, his name was the first on the list of grantees of the township.

Maurelle Island BC Between Vancouver Island and the mainland, northeast of Campbell River, this island was named in 1903 by Capt. John Walbran (1848–1913) after Francisco Antonio Maurelle (1754–1820). Maurelle was the second-in-command of the *Sonora* in 1775, when Juan Francisco de la Bodega y Quadra (1744–94) undertook an exploratory voyage along the northwest coast. Until 1903 the island was considered part of *Valdes Island*, but it is now divided among Maurelle, Sonora, and Quadra Islands.

Maxville ON In 1998 this village (1891) north of Cornwall became part of the township of North Glengarry, united counties of Stormont, Dundas, and Glengarry. Its post office was called *Macs Corners* from 1847 to 1852 after the many people with surnames beginning with 'Mac' or 'Mc'. When the railway arrived in 1880, postmaster John McEwan reopened the office as Maxville.

Mayerthorpe AB The post office of this town (1961) northwest of Edmonton was named in 1910 after first postmaster Robert I. Mayer and a schoolteacher called Thorpe.

Maymont SK The Canadian Northern Railway station and the post office at this village (1907) southeast of North Battleford were named in 1905 after May Montgomery, the second wife of Hugh John Montgomery. Hugh John was the father of the noted writer Lucy Maud Montgomery (1874–1942), whose mother died in 1876. Sir William Mackenzie (1795–1861) liked May and arranged to have a station named for her.

Mayne Island BC One of the Gulf Islands, east of Saltspring Island, it was named about 1859 by Capt. George Richards (1820–96) after RAdm. Richard Charles Mayne (1835–92), who served on Richards's survey vessels, 1857–61.

Mayo QC This municipality in the regional county of Papineau, northeast of Buckingham, was created in 1954, having been called the parish municipality of *Saint-Malachy* 100 years before. Mayo post office was open from 1866 to 1926.

Mayo YT This village (1984) on the Yukon River, southeast of Dawson, was founded in 1902–3 and named after nearby **Mayo Lake**. The lake was named in 1887 by prospector Alexander 'Klondike King' MacDonald (1854–1909) after trader and steamboat captain Alfred Henry Mayo (d.1924).

McAdam NB This village (1966) southwest of Fredericton and near the Maine border was established in 1869 as a station on the St. Andrews and Quebec Railway. When a railway was built in 1870 across Maine to Saint John, the post office here opened as *McAdam Junction*, shortened to McAdam in 1940. It was named after lumberman John McAdam (1807–93), a member of the provincial legislature, 1854–66 and 1882–6, and a member of the House of Commons, 1872–4.

McArthur, Mount BC In Yoho National Park, north of Field, this mountain (3015 m) was named in 1886 by astronomer Otto Klotz (1852–1923) after surveyor James Joseph McArthur (1856–1925), who surveyed the forty-ninth parallel through the Rocky Mountains in 1887 and undertook several other surveys. **Lake McArthur**, southeast of Field, was discovered and named by him.

McArthur Peak YT This peak (4344 m) in the St. Elias Mountains, and north of Mount Logan, was named in 1918 after James Joseph McArthur (1856–1925). McArthur was the leader of the Canadian surveyors of the Alaska–British Columbia–Yukon boundary survey, 1901–24, and commissioner of the Yukon, 1917–24.

McBride BC This village (1932) on the Fraser River, southeast of Prince George, was named in 1913 by the Grand Trunk Pacific Railway after Sir Richard McBride (1870–1917), who became premier of the province in 1903, at the age of 33.

McCoubrey, Mount BC Located in the Purcell Mountains, west of Invermere, this mountain (3216 m) was named *McCoubrey Mountain* in 1918 by Alexander Addison McCoubrey (1885–1942) of Winnipeg. A location engineer for the Canadian Pacific Railway, he made several ascents in the Purcells. It had previously been called *Peacock Mountain* on a 1915 map because pools of water on a glacier reflected like the eyes of a spreading peacock's tail. McCoubrey had also proposed Silverhorn or Silverspire for it. It was renamed Mount McCoubrey in 1960.

McCoubrey, Mount YT In the St. Elias Mountains, this mountain (3124 m) was named in 1970 by the Alpine Club of Canada after Alexander Addison McCoubrey (1885–1942), a surveyor and president of the club, 1932–4.

McCreary MB Located east of Riding Mountain National Park, the post office at this village (1964) was first called *Chamberlain* in August 1897. It was renamed *Elliott Station* two months later after homesteader George Elliott, but because of similar names in Canada, it was changed to McCreary in 1899. Its Canadian Northern Railway station was named in 1897 after William Forsythe McCreary (1855–1904), a member for Selkirk in the House of Commons. He promoted the settlement of Ruthenians and Doukhobors in the area.

McKellar ON This township in Parry Sound District was named in 1869 after Archibald McKellar (1816–94), member of the Legislative Assembly of Canada, 1857–67, and of the Ontario Legislature, 1867–75. **McKellar** post office opened in the township in 1870.

McKillop ON In 2001 this township became part of the municipality of Huron East, Huron County. It was named in 1830 after James Mackillop (1839–1922), a director of the Canada Company. This was a British company established in 1826 to develop the Huron Tract, a large area of what is now Southwestern Ontario.

McLean SK The Canadian Pacific Railway station at this village (1966) east of Regina was named for William J. McLean (d.1927) about 1883. Its post office opened in 1884, closed in 1889, then reopened 1893. McLean became the manager of Fort Pitt, north of Lloydminster. In 1885 he distinguished himself during the North West Rebellion.

McLennan AB Northwest of Lesser Slave Lake, this town (1948) was named in 1915 after Dr. J.K. McLennan, then secretary of the Edmonton, Dunvegan and British Columbia Railway, and later its vice-president. A post office opened here in 1915.

McLeod Lake BC Located north of Prince George, this lake was named about 1806 by Simon Fraser (1776–1862) after chief trader Archibald Norman McLeod (1781–1839) of the North West Company. Previously the lake was called *Trout Lake*, where trader James McDougall had built Trout Lake House the previous year. The post office was first called *Fort McLeod* here in June 1952 and became McLeod Lake two months later to avoid confusing the place with Fort Macleod in Alberta.

M'Clintock Channel NU Between Victoria and Prince of Wales Islands, this 400-km channel was named *Lady Franklin Channel* in 1859 by Capt. Allen Young. Lady Jane Franklin (1791–1875), the widow of Sir John Franklin (1786–1847), requested the naming of the channel after Sir Francis Leopold McClintock. In 1859 McClintock had discovered the fate of Franklin's expedition in the area of King William Island.

Long spelled M'Clintock Channel, its name was confirmed by the Canadian Board on Geographical Names in 1950.

McLure BC On the east bank of the North Thompson River, north of Kamloops, this community's post office was named in 1920 after John McLure (1849–1933), who arrived here in 1906.

M'Clure Strait NT Separating Banks Island on the southwest and Melville, Eglinton, and Prince Patrick Islands on the northeast, this 300-km strait was named after Robert John Le Mesurier McClure (1807–73). McClure explored the islands and waters of the western Arctic extensively in 1850–1, but his vessel *Investigator* became frozen in ice on the Banks Island side of the strait from 1851 to 1853. Spelled M'Clure Channel on many navigation charts and maps, the name was confirmed by the Canadian Board on Geographical Names in 1950.

McMasterville QC Located in the regional county of La Vallée-du-Richelieu and on the west bank of the Richelieu, east of Montreal, this village was created in 1917. It was named after William McMaster, the first president of Canadian Explosives, which became Canadian Industries Limited (C-I-L) in 1927.

McNab ON In 1998 this township became part of the township of **McNab/Braeside**, Renfrew County. It was named in 1825 after Archibald McNab (1775–1860), who was granted the township by the government of Upper Canada. Bitter strife with the tenants he had brought from Scotland in 1823 resulted in the government buying him out in 1842. After living for 10 years in Hamilton, he returned to Scotland to manage an estate in the Orkneys.

McNabs Island NS Situated in the entrance to Halifax Harbour, this island was called *Île de Chibouqueto* during the French regime. In 1749 it was named in honour of the Reverend Frederick Cornwallis (1713–83), who was appointed the archbishop of Canterbury in 1768. The island was purchased by John McNab in 1783, and thereafter it was known by his name.

McNair, Mount NB South of Mount Carleton, this mountain was named in 1969 by director of surveys Willis F. Roberts after John Babbit McNair (1889–1968), premier, 1940–52, chief justice, 1952–65, and lieutenant-governor of New Brunswick, 1965–8.

McNaughton Lake NU Northwest of Baker Lake, this lake was named in 1969 by the Army Survey Establishment after Gen. Andrew George Latta McNaughton (1887–1966), commander of the Canadian forces in Britain, 1939–43, and chairman of the Canadian section of the International Joint Commission, 1950–62.

McWatters QC This municipality east of Rouyn-Noranda was established in 1981; it had previously been called *Kinojévis* in 1979. McWatters Gold Mine opened in 1932, named after prospector David McWatters, who made its discovery two years earlier. The post office was called *McWaters* from 1936 to 1986, when it was corrected to McWatters.

Meadowbank PE This municipal community (1974) southwest of Charlottetown and on the north bank of the West River was named after the school district of *Meadow Bank*, established about 1877.

Meadow Lake SK Located on the west shore of **Meadow Lake**, this town (1936) was first settled in 1910, and its post office opened in 1911. Its development was slow until the arrival of the Canadian Pacific Railway in 1936. The lake was known to French traders as *Lac des Prairies*.

Meadows NL On the north side of Humber Arm, northwest of Corner Brook, this municipal community (1970) was established at **Meadows Point** in the late 1800s. The point may have been named because of its grassy cover, when it was encountered by the first explorers or hydrographic surveyors.

Meaford ON On 1 January 2001 this town (1874) became a part of the town of Georgian Highlands, Grey County, but restored its status as a town on 5 March 2001. It was named in 1858 after Meaford Hall, the birthplace in Staffordshire, England, of John Jervis, Earl of St. Vincent (1735–1823). He defeated superior Spanish forces in 1797 off Cabo de São Vincente, Portugal. Earlier the place had been called *Peggy's Landing*, *Stephenson's Landing*, and *Purdytown*.

Meaghers Grant NS In the Musquodoboit River valley, northeast of Dartmouth, this place was named after Martin Meagher, a Loyalist from North Carolina who received a 2024 ha (5000 a) grant on 7 June 1783. The federal place names office indicates that the grant was made after the War of 1812. Its post office opened in 1856.

Meath Park SK Northeast of Prince Albert, this village (1938) was developed 5 km to the south at Janow Corners before 1932, when the Canadian Pacific Railway arrived at the present site. Its post office opened in 1913 and was possibly named after County Meath in Ireland.

Medenagan Mountain BC In the Purcell Mountains, west of Invermere, this mountain (3295 m) was named *Meden Agan Mountain* in 1971 by climber Curt Wagner after the message recorded at the oracle of Delphi and meaning 'nothing too much'. He named it after climbing Mount Delphine, 6 km to the southeast. The spelling was altered to Medenagan in 1973.

Medicine Hat AB This city (1906) was named in 1882 by Corp. Walter Johnson of the North-West Mounted Police. Johnson may have simply translated the Blackfoot *saamis* ('headdress of a medicine man'), in reference to the shape of a small hill. However, at least 13 legends relating to the naming of the place have evolved over the years. Linguistic experts agree that the Blackfoot's *saamis* provides the details of a medicine man being killed during a battle with the Cree. After the battle the Blackfood fled, with the man's war bonnet floating down the South Saskatchewan. When some suggestions were made in 1910 to give the city a more prosaic name, such as Gasburg or Smithville, the calamity was averted after famous British writer Rudyard Kipling (1865–1936) sharply rebuked the thought of such insolence.

Medonte ON Now part of the municipal township of **Oro-Medonte**, Simcoe County, it was created as a township in 1822. It took its name from Ojibwa *nin mâdondan* ('I carry it away on my back on a portage strap'), referring to a portage route from Orillia to Georgian Bay.

Medstead SK North of North Battleford, a post office opened near this village (1931) in 1911. Sylvester Perry, the first postmaster, wanted to call it Medford after Medford, WI, northwest of Wausau. Believing it could be confused with Melfort, postal authorities modified it to Medstead, and Perry accepted it. The Canadian Northern Railway built its line through Medstead in 1927.

Meductic NB The post office in this village (1966) on the south side of the Saint John River, and southeast of Woodstock, was named in 1896 after the former Maliseet village of *Medoctec*. The name means 'the end', referring to the end of a portage from the Eel River to the Saint John River. Its former post office was called *Canterbury* from 1860 to 1897. The straight stretch of Mactaquac Lake here is called **Meductic Reach**. Before the lake was created in 1970, the rapids at the village was called *Meductic Falls*. *See also* Canterbury.

Meduxnekeag River NB Rising in the state of Maine, this river flows into the Saint John River at Woodstock. The name derives from the Maliseet *medukseneekik* ('rough at the mouth'). After 1689 several different spellings were used until the Geographic Board confirmed the present spelling in 1901.

Meech, Lac QC Congregational minister Asa Meech (1775–1849), a native of Brockton, MA, settled here in 1822. The lake is 10 km northwest of the city of Gatineau. Following an 1870 survey, the lake's name was misspelled *Meach*, and this was confirmed in 1931, based on long-established use on maps. The spelling was corrected in 1982.

Meelpaeg Lake NL In the south central part of Newfoundland, this lake's name derives from the Mi'kmaq *Makpaq* ('lake of many bays').

Meighen Island NU In the Sverdrup Islands of the Queen Elizabeth Islands, this island (955 km²) was named in 1916 by Vilhjalmur Stefansson (1879–1962) after Arthur Meighen (1874–1960), who was then solicitor general in Sir Robert Borden's cabinet. He followed Sir Robert as the prime minister in 1920. Defeated the next year, he returned briefly as prime minister in 1926.

Mékinac QC This regional county, north of Shawinigan, was named in 1982 after 15 places associated with the name, including **Lac Mékinac** and **Saint-Roch-de-Mékinac**. The name means 'turtle' in Algonquin.

Melancthon ON A township in Dufferin County, it was named in 1821 after the Protestant reformer Philip Melanchthon (1497–1560), Martin Luther's co-worker. His German surname was Schwarzerd, which an uncle translated into Greek *melan chthon* ('black earth').

Melbourne ON In 2001 this community became part of the municipality of Southwest Middlesex, Middlesex County. Located southwest of London, it was called *Ekfrid* from 1832 to 1857, when it was changed to *Longwood*. That name was changed to *Wendigo* in 1882, and changed again five years later to Melbourne. It was named after William Lamb, 2nd Viscount Melbourne (1779–1848), British prime minister, 1834–41.

Melbourne QC On the **Melbourne Ridge**, this village (1860) midway between the cities of Sherbrooke and Drummondville, was separated from the parish municipality of **Melbourne**, erected five years earlier. A post office opened here about 1834. The name of the township of **Melbourne**, given in 1795 and proclaimed in 1802, may reflect one of the two English places: one of these is located in Hampshire and the other in Derbyshire.

Melfort SK The post office in this city (1980) was named in 1892 by Mary (Campbell) Beatty, who was born on the Melfort estate at the head of Melfort Loch, 15 km south of Oban in Argyllshire, Scotland. The Canadian Northern Railway was built through it in 1909.

Melita MB In 1884 the name *Manchester* was first proposed for the post office in this town (1906) in the Souris River valley, southwest of Brandon. That name was refused on the grounds of duplication. The community was then inspired by Acts 28:1, 'When we were safe on land, we found that the island was called Melita', in reference to Malta in the Mediterranean. The hardships of Paul's travels likely resonated with the settlers in their difficulties of carving out a living in the wilderness.

Melocheville QC This village in the regional county of Beauharnois-Salaberry, southwest of Montreal, was called *Lac-Saint-Louis* from 1919 to 1953, when it was renamed after its post office. The latter was called after pioneer merchant Joseph Meloche in 1863.

Melrose NL South of Catalina, this municipal community (1971) was incorporated as a village in 1968. It was known as *Ragged Harbour* until 1904 when it was renamed, likely after Melrose, Roxburghshire, Scotland, near the birthplace of William MacGregor (1846–1919), governor of Newfoundland (1904–09).

Melville SK Founded in 1907–8, this city (1960) was established as a divisional point on the Grand Trunk Railway. It was named after Charles Melville Hays (1856–1912), the railway's general manager, 1896–1909, and its president from 1909 until 16 May 1912, when he went down on the *Titanic*. Its post office opened in 1908.

Melville Island NT, NU The largest of the Parry Islands of the Queen Elizabeth Islands, this island (42,149 km²) was named in 1819 by Sir William Parry (1790–1855) after Robert Dundas, 2nd Viscount Melville (1771–1851), then first lord of the Admiralty. Parry named **Melville Peninsula**, which separates Foxe Basin from the Gulf of Boothia, in 1822. **Viscount Melville Sound** is south of Victoria Island. **Melville Sound**, between the mainland and Kent Peninsula, was named in 1821 by Sir John Franklin (1786–1847).

Melville Lake NL The upper part of Hamilton Inlet, and east of Happy Valley-Goose Bay, this body of water was named after Henry Dundas, 1st Viscount Melville (1742–1811), first lord of the Admiralty, 1804–05.

Memphrémagog QC This regional county centred on the town of Magog was named in 1982 after **Lac Memphrémagog**. The name of the lake, which extends for 44 km from Newport, VT, to Magog, derives from Abenaki and means 'at the great stretch of water'.

Memramcook River NB Rising east of Moncton, this river flows into Shepody Bay, west of Sackville. The name derives from the Mi'kmaq *Amlamkook* ('variegated' or 'all spotted yellow'), in reference to the rock with variegated colours at Cape Maringouin. The community of **Memramcook**, midway between Moncton and Sackville, was identified in 1755 as *Mameramecou* on a French map. A post office opened here in 1845.

Meota SK Northwest of North Battleford, this village (1911) is located on the west shore of Jackfish Lake. In 1894 Arthur Mannix proposed the name Meotate from the Cree *mewasinota* ('good place to camp' or 'it is good here') for a post office near the present village. Postal officials shortened it to Meota. It was closed in 1897 and reopened in 1904 at the present-day Prince, 6 km to the southeast. After the Canadian Northern Railway was built through the area in 1910, Meota was restored the next year near its former location.

Mercier QC Located in the regional county of Roussillon, south of Châteauguay, this town was named in 1968, having been erected as the town of *Sainte-Philomène* four years earlier. *Sainte-Philomène* was the name of the parish municipality and the post office from the mid-1800s, but it was dropped because of its lack of commercial appeal, and because church authorities had declared that there was no certainty the saint ever existed. The new name reflected the nearby bridge crossing the St. Lawrence, which was named in honour of Honoré Mercier (1840–94), premier of Quebec, 1887–91.

Merigomish NS On **Merigomish Harbour** and east of New Glasgow, this place's name derives from the Mi'kmaq *malegomich* (possibly 'merrymaking place'). Postal service was established here in 1838.

Merlin ON In 1998 this community became part of the municipality of Chatham-Kent, Kent County. South of the centre of Chatham, this community was named *Smith's Corners* in 1855 after a local family. It was changed in 1868 to Merlin after a place near Edinburgh, Scotland.

Mermaid PE East of Charlottetown and on the east bank of the Hillsborough River, this place's post office was named *Mermaid Farm* in 1870 by first postmaster John Farquharson. He named his farm after HMS *Mermaid*, which was commanded by Capt. William Johnston at the mouth of the river in 1764–5.

Merrickville ON A Loyalist from Massachusetts, William Merrick (1760–1844) settled on the Rideau River in 1793 and built mills at what became *Merrick's Mills*. Merrickville post office opened in 1829 and the village was incorporated in 1860. In 1998 the village and the township of Wolford became the village of Merrickville-Wolford.

Merritt BC Located on the Nicola River, southwest of Kamloops, this city (1911) was laid out in 1906 by the Nicola, Kamloops and Similkameen Railway, and named after William Hamilton Merritt Jr., one of the city's promoters. Earlier names for the place were *Forksdale* and *Diamond Vale*. Its post office opened in 1907.

Merritton ON Within the city of St. Catharines since 1961, this urban centre was named after William Hamilton Merritt (1793–1862), an owner of the Welland Canal Loan Company who was a major promoter of a canal joining Lake Ontario to Lake Erie. It was called *Welland City* in 1829, but in 1858 it was exchanged with *Merrittsville*, now the city of Welland.

Mersea ON In 1999 this township became a part of the municipality of Leamington, Essex County. It was named in 1792 after Mersea Island on the east coast of Essex, England.

Mersey River NS Draining several lakes in south central Nova Scotia, this river flows into the Atlantic at Liverpool. It was called *Liverpool River* until 1937, when it was renamed after the River Mersey in England, which empties into the Irish Sea at Liverpool.

Merville BC On Vancouver Island, between Courtenay and Campbell River, this community's post office was named in 1919 by returned soldiers from the First World War. They gave the name after Merville, France, near the Belgian border, the site of Canada's first field headquarters during the war.

Mervin SK Northwest of North Battleford, the post office in this village (1920) was named in 1908 by postmaster Archie Gemmell after his son Mervin Gemmell (1895–1967). The Canadian Northern Railway arrived here in 1912.

Mesilinka River BC Rising west of Williston Lake, this river flows east into the Omineca Arm of the lake. In Sekani the word means 'stranger'.

Messines QC Located in the regional county of La Vallée-de-la-Gatineau, south of Maniwaki, it was named *Messine* in 1921 in honour of distinguished service by Canadian soldiers in capturing Messines in western Belgium during the First World War. The spelling was corrected to Messines in 1986, in conformity with the post office name, established in 1920. It replaced the postal name *Burbidge*, given in 1907 after the federal deputy minister of justice, George Wheelock Burbidge (1847–1908).

Métabetchouan QC This town on the southeast shore of Lac Saint-Jean was created in 1975 through the merger of the village of *Saint-Jérôme* and the parish municipality of *Saint-Jérôme*. Its name derives from the post office, opened in 1860, and the township, proclaimed in 1857. **Rivière Métabetchouan**, which flows north for 128 km, was first noted in the late 1600s. Its name in Montagnais may mean 'flowing down rapids to a lake'.

Meta Incognita Peninsula NU This most southeasterly peninsula of Baffin Island was named in 1957 by the Canadian Board on Geographical Names. The board was inspired by remarks made by Queen Elizabeth I about 1578, when she described the new-found lands of Sir Martin Frobisher (1535–94) as *meta incognita* ('limits unknown').

Metcalfe ON In 2001 this place became part of the city of Ottawa. This community's post office was called *Osgoode* from 1838 to 1877, when it was changed in honour of Charles Theophilus Metcalfe, 1st Baron Metcalfe (1785–1846), governor of the Province of Canada, 1843–6.

Metcalfe Township ON In 2001 this township became a part of the township of Adelaide-Metcalfe, Middlesex County. It was named in 1847 after Charles Theophilus Metcalfe, 1st Baron Metcalfe (1785–1846), governor of the Province of Canada, 1843–6.

Metchosin BC The name of this district municipality (1984) southwest of Victoria was mentioned as early as 1842 by Hudson's Bay Company chief trader James Douglas (1803–77), when he chose the site for Fort Victoria to the east. The name derives from Straits Salish and may relate to 'the oil of a beached dead whale'. Its post office opened in 1881.

Meteghan NS The name of this place on the French Shore, north of Yarmouth, derives from the Mi'kmaq *Muntoogun* ('blue stone'), referring to the blue-tinged stones along the shore of St. Marys Bay. Its post office opened in 1851, and other offices opened later include **Meteghan River** (1871), **Meteghan Station** (1883), and **Meteghan Centre** (1911).

Methuen ON This township in Peterborough County was named in 1823 after a Scottish title of Charles Lennox, 4th Duke of Richmond and Baron Methuen (1764–1819), governor-in-chief of British North America, 1818–9. His title is from the village of Methven, west of Perth, Scotland. **Belmont and Methuen** comprise a single township municipality. In 1998 this township became part of the township of **Havelock-Belmont-Methuen**, Peterborough County.

Métis-sur-Mer QC This village in the regional county of La Mitis was named in 1921, succeeding *Petit-Métis*, created as a village in 1850. Its name, and those of the regional county and Rivière Mitis, derives from the Mi'kmaq *miti sipo* ('poplar river'). Well known in English as *Metis Beach*, its site has long been renowned as a holiday destination.

Miami MB This place northwest of the town of Morden was named by the post office department in 1878, likely after the Aboriginal tribe that was once based in the present states of Ohio and Indiana. The tribe's name may mean 'all friends' in Delaware or 'pigeon' in Ojibwa. Miami County in southeastern Indiana had been named in 1834. Manitoba's Miami predates Miami in Florida by 18 years.

Michener, Mount AB In the upper reaches of the North Saskatchewan River, this mountain (2545 m) was named in 1979 after Daniel Roland Michener (1900–91), governor general of Canada, 1967–74. Noted for his fitness and vigour, he climbed to its summit in his eighty-third year, accompanied by two mountain guides.

Michipicoten ON A township in Algoma District, it was created in 1952 and named after nearby **Michipicoten River**, **Michipicoten Bay**, and **Michipicoten Island**. In Ojibwa it means 'great bluff'. The township's main urban centre is Wawa.

Midale SK Midway between Estevan and Weyburn, the name of the Canadian Pacific Railway station at this town (1962) was created in 1893 from the surnames of Dr. Robert M. Mitchell and Ole Dale, who were pioneers here. A post office opened here in 1903.

Middle Arm NL Located on the **Middle Arm** of Green Bay, a westerly extension of Notre Dame Bay, this municipal community (1966) was established in the late 1800s as a fishing and logging centre.

Middle Lake SK Southeast of **Middle Lake**, which is centrally located between the larger Basin Lake and Lake Lenore, the post office at this village (1963) was named in 1909. Its station was founded in 1929, when the Canadian Pacific Railway built a line from Humboldt to Prince Albert.

Middlesex ON Created from *Suffolk County* in 1796, this county was named after Middlesex, England, now organized as Greater London. The county of Middlesex has one city (London), four townships (*Middlesex Centre*, Lucan Biddulph, Strathroy-Caradoc, and Adelaide Metcalfe), and three municipalities (*North Middlesex*, *Southwest Middlesex*, and *Thames Centre*.)

Middleton NS This town (1909) in the Annapolis Valley is located midway between Kentville and Annapolis Royal. It was also in the centre of the former *Wilmot Township* and was previously called *Wilmot Corner* and *Fowlers Corner*. Its post office opened in 1855.

Midland ON This town (1890) in Simcoe County was developed in 1872–3 by the Midland Railway of Canada. The first train arrived in 1879, and the place became the main shipping centre at the south end of Georgian Bay. It had been called *Mundy's Bay* and *Aberdare*, but the railway company president Baron Adolf von Hugel insisted that it be called Midland.

Midnight Dome YT Overlooking Dawson, this elevation was early called *Moosehide Hill* and *Mooseskin Mountain* because of its shape. On the evening of the longest day of the year, 21 June, people have been gathering on the dome since the early 1900s to watch the sun almost set, before it rises again.

Midway BC This village (1967) on the Washington state border, west of Grand Forks, was first named *Boundary City* in 1893. It was renamed in 1894 by Capt. R.C. Adams of Montreal after the Midway Pleasance at the 1893 Chicago World's Fair, and after its location halfway between the Rocky Mountains and the Pacific Ocean.

Milden SK Southwest of Saskatoon and midway between Rosetown and Outlook, the post office at this village (1911) was named by Charles Mills in 1907, deriving it from his surname and the surname of neighbour Robert Bryden. They were the first settlers here. The Canadian Pacific Railway arrived the following year.

Mildmay ON In 1999 this village (1918) became part of the municipality of South Bruce, Bruce County. Located south of Walkerton, it was named in 1867, possibly after Mildmay Park near Islington in Greater London, England. For many years it was informally called *Mernersville* after Samuel Merner, who laid out a street plan in 1867.

Milestone SK South of Regina, this town (1906) was established in 1893 by the Canadian Pacific Railway. It was named after C.W. Milestone, CPR superintendent of the extension of the Soo Line from North Portal to Moose Jaw. Its post office opened in 1900.

Milford Station NS Between Elmsdale and Shubenacadie, this place's post office was named *Wickwire Station* in 1866, six years after the Intercolonial Railway was built to Halifax. It was renamed Milford Station in 1875, possibly after a mill at a crossing of the Shubenacadie River.

Milk River AB The post office in this town (1956), southeast of Lethbridge, was named in 1908 after the **Milk River**, a tributary of the Missouri. The river was named in 1805 by American explorers Meriwether Lewis (1774–1809) and William Clark (1770–1838) when they noted it looked like 'a cup of tea with the admixture of a tablespoon of milk'.

Millbrook ON In 1998 this village (1879) became part of the township of **Cavan-Millbrook-North Monaghan**, Peterborough County. Located southwest of the city of Peterborough, it was named in 1846 after a mill built by John Deyell on Baxter Creek, a tributary of the Otonabee River.

Mille-Îles, Rivière QC Uniting Lac des Deux Montagnes with the St. Lawrence and passing north of Île Jésus, this river was first noted in the Jesuit *Relation* of 1674 as *rivière Jésus*, with the additional observation that 'one only finds submerged shoals sprinkled with a thousand islands'.

Mille Lacs, Lac des ON This large lake northwest of Thunder Bay was named during the French regime, when its complex network of islands, peninsulas, bays, and coves gave it the appearance of a large number of small lakes.

Millertown NL This municipal community (1959) on the east side of Red Indian Lake, east of Buchans, was named after Lewis Miller (1848–1909), who established a lumbering operation here in 1900. *See also* Lewisporte.

Millet AB Between Leduc and Wetaskiwin, the station in this town (1983) was named about 1892 by the Canadian Pacific Railway. One story states that the name was given by Sir William Van Horne (1843–1915), who was an admirer of the paintings of Jean-François Millet (1815–75). A second suggests Van Horne asked Fr. Albert Lacombe (1827–1916) for a suggestion, and he proposed naming it after fur buyer August Millet, his frequent canoeing companion, who had drowned in the Red Deer River.

Millidgeville NB The post office of this place located on the north side of Saint John was named in 1864 after merchant and legislator Thomas Millidge (1776–1838) and his son, shipbuilder Thomas Edward Millidge (1814–94). The name of the post office was spelled *Milledgeville* from 1864 to 1963.

Milltown NB Part of the town of St. Stephen since 1973, Milltown was incorporated as a town in 1878. Known in the late 1700s as *Christie Town* and *Stillwater*, its post office was named Milltown in 1839.

Milltown-Head of Bay d'Espoir NL Near the head of Bay d'Espoir, this town (1952) comprises the separate population centres of **Head of Bay d'Espoir**, a fishing community established in about 1850, and **Milltown**, a sawmilling community created in the late 1800s. *See also* Espoir, Bay d'.

Millville NB East of Woodstock, this village (1966) was established about 1860 as a New Brunswick and Nova Scotia Land Company settlement. A Mr Hayes built a mill here, and Millville post office opened in 1866.

Milton NS Located at falls on the Mersey River, upriver from Liverpool, this municipal community (1996) was the site of three sawmills in 1762. When postal service was provided in 1855, it was given its present name.

Milton ON Jasper and Sarah Martin built a grist mill in 1822 on Sixteen Mile Creek, northwest of Oakville, and the site was called *Martin's Mills*. At a meeting in 1837 it was renamed Milton after English poet John Milton (1608–74) and after its many mills. The post office was *Milton West* from 1836 to 1962. It became a town in 1857 and annexed Nassagaweya Township, along with parts of Esquesing Township and Oakville, in 1974.

Milton, Mount BC This mountain (3185 m) in the Cariboo Mountains, south of Valemount, was named in 1863 by Dr. Walter Cheadle (1836–1910) after his travelling companion, William Wentworth Fitzwilliam, Viscount Milton (1839–77).

Miltonvale Park PE The name of this municipal community (1974) northwest of Charlottetown is a composite of **Milton** and **Springvale**. Milton's post office was called *Milton Station* in 1878. Noted on an 1830s plan, Milton may have been named after a place on South Uist, Scotland, where Scottish nationalist Flora Macdonald (1722–90) was born, or it may have been proposed after the many mills here. Springvale had been established as a school district about 1862.

Milverton ON In 1998 this village (1881) became a part of the township of Perth East, Perth County. Located north of Stratford, it was called *West's Corners* from 1854 to 1871 after shoemaker Andrew J. West. In 1871 Presbyterian minister the Reverend Peter Musgrave proposed renaming the post office after his birthplace of Milverton in Somerset, England, southwest of Bristol.

Mimico ON Located on the shore of Lake Ontario and at the mouth of **Mimico Creek**, this urban centre was named in 1857 after the creek, whose name in Mississauga is *Omimeca* ('place of wild pigeons'). Incorporated as a village in 1911 and a town in 1917, it was annexed by the borough of Etobicoke in 1967. In 1998 Mimico became part of the city of Toronto.

Miminegash PE A municipal community (1968) on the northwestern coast of the province, its name may derive from the Mi'kmaq *m'negash* ('portage place'). Its post office opened in 1861, closed in 1921, and reopened in 1967. *Ebbsfleet* post office opened here in 1894 and continued until 1967. The school district was called *West Port* in 1882 and changed to *Ebbsleet* in 1904. *Ebbsfleet* may have been named after the ebb tides and the local fishing fleet, replicating the same name in Kent, England.

Minaki ON In Kenora District, northwest of the town of Kenora, this settlement was known as *Winnipeg River Crossing* in 1870. In 1912 Minaki post office opened, and the National Transcontinental Railway built a luxury summer lodge here in 1914. In Ojibwa *minaki* means 'blueberry ground'.

Minas Basin NS With dimensions of 25 km by 38 km, this basin was called *Bassin des Mines* by Samuel de Champlain (1567–1635) in 1604 after the discovery of copper at Cape d'Or, on the north side of **Minas Channel**. The latter, extending for 45 km from Cape Chignecto to Cape Sharp, is the southern arm of the Bay of Fundy. *See also* New Minas.

Minden ON Both the township and the community in Haliburton County were named in 1858 after a town in

Prussia, southwest of Hamburg, where the British forces and Prince Ferdinand of Brunswick's forces defeated the French in 1759. In 2001 the municipal township of **Anson, Hindon and Minden** became part of the township of **Minden Hills**.

Mingan, Archipel de QC Located on the north shore of the St. Lawrence, east of Sept-Îles, this group of 47 islands, islets, rocks, and reefs became the **Mingan Archipelago National Park** (94 km²) in 1984. The name was long thought to be Montagnais for 'wolf', but the current preference is that it is a Breton word for 'white stone'. The regional county of **Minganie**, which embraces the archipelago and the north shore of the Gulf of St. Lawrence all the way to the Newfoundland–Labrador border, was created in 1982.

Miniota MB Located on the east bank of the Assinboine River, northwest of Brandon, this community was named after the rural municipality (1883) of **Miniota**. The municipality's name was adapted by W.A. Doyle, postmaster of nearby Beulah, from the Assiniboine *mini-ota* ('plenty of water'), after hearing a surveyor announce that some water he drank from a local spring creek was the best he had ever had. The post office was called *Parkismo* in 1885 and was changed to Miniota five years later.

Ministers Island NB In Passamaquoddy Bay, northeast of St. Andrews, this island was named after Samuel Andrews (c.1736–1818), a St. Andrews minister who lived on the island after 1791. Sir William Van Horne (1843–1915) purchased the island in 1890 and named it *Covenhoven* in honour of his father. Although it has also been called *Van Hornes Island*, the earlier name has prevailed. In 1977 the island was established as a provincial historic site.

Minitonas MB East of Swan River, the post office at this village (1901) was named in 1900 after a Cree word meaning 'home of the little god'.

Minnedosa MB This town (1883) on the Little Saskatchewan River, west of Neepawa, was first called *Tanner's Crossing* after ferry operator John Tanner. Its post office was called Hallsford in 1876. In 1879 the first postmaster J.S. Armitage, who built the first grist and sawmills here, suggested Minnedosa from the Sioux *minne duza* ('fast water'). His wife's name was Minnie, and they named a daughter Minnedosa in 1880, the same year it was adopted for the post office. The river was identified as both *Rapid River* and Little Saskatchewan River in the early 1800s, but *Minnedosa River* was adopted in 1911. Local appeals persuaded the Manitoba names authority to restore Little Saskatchewan River in 1978.

Minto NB The post office in this village (1905) east of Fredericton was named in 1905 after Gilbert John Elliot, 4th Earl of Minto (1845–1914), governor general of Canada, 1898–1904.

Minto ON In 1988 this township became part of the towns of Palmerston and Harriston and the village of Clifford of the town of Minto, Wellington County. It was named in 1840 after Gilbert Elliot Murray Kynynmound, 1st Earl of Minto and Viscount Melgund (1751–1814), governor general of India, 1806–13. His great-grandson, the 4th Earl of Minto, was governor general of Canada, 1898–1904, and viceroy of India, 1905–10. The name was taken from a village in Roxburghshire, Scotland.

Minto, Lac QC Situated at the head of Rivière aux Feuilles in northwestern Quebec, and covering an area of nearly 600 km², this lake was named in 1898 by geologist Albert Peter Low (1861–1942) after Gilbert John Elliot, 4th Earl of Minto, who was named Canada's governor general that year.

Mira Bay NS At the mouth of the **Mira River**, north of Louisbourg, this bay's name may have a Portuguese origin, perhaps given for a place south of Oporto. Pierre Jumeau identified it as *Baye de Miray* on his 1685 map, and Mgr. Joseph-Octave Plessis (1763–1825) described the settlement here as *Miré* in his 1815 journal. The Mira River flows northeast into the bay.

Mirabel QC This town was named in 1973, succeeding the town of *Sainte-Scholastique*, created two years earlier through the amalgamation of eight municipalities, together covering almost 500 km². The name was chosen in 1972 through public consultation to describe the new international airport, opened three years later. A post office called Mirabel had served part of its area from 1880 to 1914. It is said to have been devised from the names Miriam and Isabelle, daughters of a Scottish settler. It could also have been from a small plum called a *mirabelle*.

Miramichi NB On 1 January 1995 the city of Miramichi was established by amalgamating the towns of Chatham and Newcastle; the villages of Douglastown, Loggieville, and Nelson-Miramichi; and the surrounding area. Long proposed, it took its name from the region commonly called The Miramichi. The region is centred on the **Miramichi River**, which rises as three main branches called the **Southwest**, the **Northwest**, and the **Little Southwest Miramichi Rivers**. **Miramichi Bay** may have been named by Jacques Cartier (1491–1557) in 1535, after the Montagnais—living on the north shore of the Gulf of St. Lawrence—observed that he had been in *Maissimeu Assi* ('Mi'kmaq land'). In 1632 Samuel de Champlain (1567–1635) called it *Baie de Petit Misamichy*. The same year map-maker Jean Guérard identified it as *Petit Miramichi*, and this spelling was subsequently adopted.

Mirror AB In 2004 this village (1912) became a hamlet. Located 47 km east of Lacombe it was named in 1911 by the Grand Trunk Pacific Railway after *The Daily Mirror* of London, England. In its 10 August 1911 edition, the newspaper ran a headline reporting 'Mirror — Alberta / Rising Township Named after London Journal'.

Miscou Island NB The name of this island located on the northeast coast of the province derives from the Mi'kmaq *susqu* ('wet bog'). It was identified by Samuel de Champlain (1567–1635) in 1632 as *I de Miscou*.

Miscouche PE This municipal community (1983) northwest of Summerside was incorporated as a village in 1957. It was named after nearby **Miscouche Cove**, whose name in Mi'kmaq, *Menisgotjg*, means 'little marshy place'. Called *Belle Alliance* about 1824, it was noted as *Mascouche* in 1835. Miscouche post office opened in 1866.

Missaguash River NB Part of the boundary between New Brunswick and Nova Scotia, this river flows into Cumberland Basin. Its name likely derives from the Mi'kmaq *muskwash* ('muskrat'). After 1731 there were many different forms of the name, with the Geographic Board confirming the present spelling in 1901.

Mission BC This district municipality (1892) on the north side of the Fraser River, and east of Vancouver, was named after the St. Mary's Indian mission established in 1861 by Oblate Fr. Léon Fouquet. The urban centre on the Fraser River was called *Mission Junction* after the arrival of railways between 1885 and 1891 and was incorporated as the village of Mission in 1922. When it became the first incorporated town in the province in 1950, it adopted the name *Mission City*, the name it retained until 1973. *Mission City* was the name of the post office from 1891 to 1973.

Mississagi River ON Rising in Algoma District, this river flows south into Lake Huron's North Channel, just west of Blind River. The name derives from the Ojibwa *missi-sauk* ('large outlet').

Mississauga ON This city in Peel Region is on land surrendered in 1805 by the Mississauga to William Claus (1763–1826), Deputy Superintendent of Indian Affairs. Much of the area of the present city was organized that year as *Toronto Township*, which became the town of Mississauga in 1967 and a city in 1974, when it annexed the towns of Port Credit and Streetsville. An Ojibwa band, the Mississauga were first encountered in 1634 by French explorer Jean Nicolet (c.1598–1642) at the mouth of Mississagi River, in Algoma District. In the 1700s they occupied a large part of present Southern Ontario. They were located at the mouth of the Credit River from around 1720 to about 1850, when they moved to the New Credit Reserve on the Grand River.

Mississippi River ON Rising in Lennox and Addington County, this river flows east to the Ottawa River, close to the mouth of the Madawaska River at Arnprior. The first reference to it was in 1816 by government surveyor William Graves, while the nearby Madawaska and Bonnechere Rivers were recorded over a century before. The name means 'big river' in Cree and other Algonquian languages; this name, however, is not appropriate, since it is smaller than the nearby Madawaska. Graves may have misinterpreted what an Algonquin said, such as *Mazinaw-sippi* after the pictographs on the east side of Upper Mazinaw Lake, near the head of the river.

Mistassini QC Located on the east bank of the **Rivière Mistassini**, north of Lac Saint-Jean, this town (1947) was founded in 1930 as the village of Mistassini. It annexed the parish municipality of *Saint-Michel-de-Mistassini* (1897) in 1976. The river rises east of **Lac Mistassini**, which is drained west into James Bay by the Rivière Rupert. *Mistassini* means 'big rock' in Montagnais. The Cree village of **Mistissini**, at the extreme southeastern end of Lac Mistassini, has had several names since the establishment of the Hudson's Bay Company post of Canadian House in 1775, including *Mistassini Post* and *Baie-du-Poste*.

Mitchell ON In 1998 this town (1874) became part of the township of West Perth, Perth County. Located northwest of Stratford, it was first settled in the 1830s by a man by the name of Mitchell (first name not recorded), who provided lodging for travellers. Originally called *Big Thames*, it was renamed in 1847 by postmaster John Hicks, who arrived here in 1837 and had presumably met Mitchell.

Mitchell, Mount NB South of the Nepisguit River, this mountain was named in 1964 by Arthur F. Wightman (1905–88), then the provincial names authority, after Peter Mitchell (1824–99), premier of New Brunswick, 1866–7, and a Father of Confederation.

Moira River ON Flowing into the Bay of Quinte at Belleville, this river was known as *Sagonaska*, *Singleton's Creek*, and *Meyers' Creek*, before it was named Moira River in 1807 after Francis Rawdon-Hastings (1754–1826), who succeeded his father as the Earl of Moira in 1793. The title was taken from a village in County Down, Ireland, southwest of Belfast.

Moisie QC Situated at the mouth of the **Rivière Moisie**, east of Sept-Îles, this town was created in 1984 through the merger of the municipalities of Moisie, *De Grasse*, and *Rivière Pigou*. Under the form of *Moisy*, the river was identified on a 1685 map, and its name may be from the old French word *moise* or *moyse* ('wet river bank'), which describes the area of its marshy sand and clay plain, where there are several meanders and serpentine streams at its mouth.

Monarch Mountain BC In the Coast Mountains and at the southern edge of Tweedsmuir Provincial Park, this mountain

(3459 m) was named in the early 1930s by Walter Alfred Don Munday (1890–1950) in honour of Canada's head of state, George V.

Monashee Mountains BC Bounded by the Columbia River on the east, and by the Kettle, Shuswap, and the upper North Thompson Rivers on the west, these mountains extend 440 km from the Washington state border to Valemount. The name is from Scots Gaelic *monadh sith* ('mountain of peace'). It was given about 1880 by prospector Donald McIntyre to his mine in the Gold Range, south of Revelstoke. He coined the name after a particularly peaceful sunset over a nearby mountain.

Moncton NB This city (1890) was named in 1854 after **Moncton Parish**, which had been established in 1786. The parish was named after *Monckton Township*, created in 1765 and called after Gen. Robert Monckton (1726–82), who captured Fort Beauséjour on the Chignecto Isthmus in 1755 and renamed it Fort Cumberland. Its post office was called *Bend of Petitcodiac* from 1833 to 1865, when it was named Moncton. In 1930 the city council voted to restore the spelling *Monckton*, but universal public opposition resulted in a reversal of the vote.

Monkland ON In 1998 this place became part of the township of South Stormont, united counties of Stormont, Dundas, and Glengarry. Located northwest of Cornwall, this community may have been named after Old Monkland, east of Glasgow, Scotland, or after Monkland, near Leominster, Herefordshire, England. The post office was called *Monckland* in 1862, possibly influenced by the name of Lord Monck, appointed the governor general a year earlier. It was called *Monckland Station* from 1888 to 1966, when it was changed to Monkland, the name of the police village.

Monkman Pass BC This pass (1082 m) through the Rocky Mountains, northeast of Prince George, was discovered in 1921–2 by hunter and trapper Alexander Monkman (1870–1941).

Monmouth Mountain BC In the Coast Mountains, northwest of Whistler, this mountain (3194 m) was named in 1924 after HMS *Monmouth*, sunk in action 1 November 1914 off Coronel, Chile.

Mono ON This township in Dufferin County was named in 1821, possibly by Lt.-Gov. Sir Peregrine Maitland (1777–1854), and possibly after the Spanish for 'monkey'. Its name may also derive from other sources: a daughter of Shawnee chief Tecumseh; an Aboriginal word for 'let it be so' or 'little ironwood tree'; the Roman name for the Welsh Isle of Anglesey; the Gaelic word for 'hilly'; or from the Monach Islands or the Monadhliath Mountains in Scotland. **Mono Mills**, partly in the township, but mainly in the town of

Caledon, Peel Region, was named in 1839 after mills built on the Humber River about 20 years earlier by Michael, Francis, and Daniel McLaughlin.

Montague ON This township in Lanark County was named in 1798 for Adm. Sir George Montague (1750–1829), who was a British naval commander during the American Revolution.

Montague PE The post office in this town (1917) on the **Montague River** opened about 1854 and was named *Montague Bridge*. Samuel Holland (1728–1801) named the river in 1765, possibly for George Brudenell, 4th Earl of Cardigan (1712–90), who was created the Duke of Montagu in 1766.

Montcalm QC This regional county, situated between the cities of Saint-Jérôme and Joliette, was created in 1982, taking its name from the former county of Montcalm. It was named after Gen. Louis-Joseph, Marquis de Montcalm (1712–59), commander of the French forces in New France, 1756–9, who lost his life at the Battle of the Plains of Abraham.

Monteagle ON In 2001 this township became part of the municipality of Hastings Highlands, Hastings County. It was named in 1857 after Thomas Spring-Rice, Lord Monteagle (1790–1866), who had served as British Secretary of the Treasury, Secretary for the Colonies, and chancellor of the exchequer.

Montebello QC Located in the regional county of Papineau, east of Buckingham, this village was named in 1878 after the residence of Louis-Joseph Papineau (1786–1871). He had named it *Monte-Bello* in 1854 after Napoléon-Auguste Lannes, Duc de Montebello (1801–74), French minister of foreign affairs in 1839. Papineau met him in France during his exile from 1839 to 1845.

Mont-Joli QC This town—the largest in the regional county of La Mitis, northeast of Rimouski—was created in 1945, having been a village since 1880. Its post office was called *Sainte-Flavie-Station* from 1877 to 1914. The name is descriptive of its pretty (*joli*) view from its location on top of a hill (*mont*).

Mont-Laurier QC At the end of the nineteenth century, this town 160 km north of Buckingham was known as *Rapide-de-l'Orignal*, named, according to legend, after a prodigious leap by a moose (*orignal*) over a falls of the Rivière du Lièvre. Mont-Laurier was named in 1909 after Sir Wilfrid Laurier (1841–1919), prime minister of Canada, 1896–1911.

Montmagny QC This town on the south shore of the St. Lawrence, downriver from Quebec City, was incorporated as a village in 1845 and as a town in 1883. The name honours Charles Huault de Montmagny (c.1583–1653), the first governor of New France, 1636–48, who was granted the seigneury of Rivière-du-Sud in the area of the present town in 1646. The regional county of **Montmagny** was established in 1982.

Montmartre SK The post office at this village (1908) southeast of Regina was named in 1894, taking its name from the famed 'mount of martyrs' in Paris, France. It was proposed by a number of French settlers from Paris who arrived here in 1893, sponsored by a French colonization society called La Société foncière du Canada.

Montmorency, Chute QC At a height of 85 m, this pretty waterfall 13 km northeast of Quebec City was named as early as 1608 by Samuel de Champlain (1567–1635) after French Adm. Charles de Montmorency (1537–1612).

Montreal QC The largest city in Quebec, it traces its roots to 1535 when Jacques Cartier (1491–1557) named it Mont Royal, either in honour of François I or as a feature worthy of the King. The evolution of Mont Royal to Montreal may be explained by sixteenth-century evidence that *royal* and *real* had the same meaning, and that map-maker Belleforest used an Italian translation of Cartier's writings to identify the mountain in 1575 as *Monte Real* and the place as *Montreal*. In 1612 Samuel de Champlain (1567–1635) referred to the mountain as *montreal*, and 20 years later wrote about the *Isle de Mont-real*. In 1642 Paul de Chomedey de Maisonneuve (1612–76) founded the colony of *Ville marie en l'isle de Montréal*. By the early 1700s *Ville-Marie* was superseded by Montreal. The city of **Montréal-Nord**, on the north side of the island, was named in 1915. The post office of the town (1897) of **Montréal-Ouest**, southwest of the centre of Montreal, was called *Montreal West* from 1894 to 1913. The industrial town of **Montréal-Est** was founded in 1910 on the southeastern shore of the island. In 2002 the city of Montreal took over all of the municipalities on the Île de Montréal. Four years later 15 of the municipalities recovered their status as cities. Among them were Montréal-Nord, Montréal-Ouest, and Montréal-Est.

Montreal River ON Rising west of Kirkland Lake, this river flows into the Ottawa River at the south end of Lake Timiskaming. It was named in 1686 by French military commander Chevalier de Troyes (d.1688) on his way to Hudson Bay to seize British forts. A second **Montreal River** rises southwest of Chapleau, and flows southwest into Lake Superior. It was probably named in the early 1700s by French explorers and voyageurs in honour of the historic island in the St. Lawrence, where they planned their trips to the Northwest.

Mont-Rolland QC Located in the regional county of Les Pays-d'en-Haut, north of Saint-Jérôme, this village was founded in 1881 by papermaker Jean-Baptiste Rolland (1815–88). Created in 1918 as the parish municipality of *Saint-Joseph-de-Mont-Rolland*, the parish municipality's name was abbreviated to Mont-Rolland in 1967, following the postal name established in 1905. In 1981 it became a village after annexing the town of Mont-Gabriel.

Montrose BC The post office in this village (1956) east of Trail was named *Beaver Falls* in 1949. It was renamed in 1953 by Trail lawyer A.G. Cameron after his hometown of Montrose, Angusshire, Scotland.

Mont-Saint-Hilaire QC Located on the east side of the Richelieu, and in the shadow of the Monteregian hill called **Mont Saint-Hilaire**, the town's roots may be traced to the mission of Saint-Hilaire, established in 1799, and the religious parish of Saint-Hilaire, created in 1827. The mountain was known as both *Beloeil* and *Rouville* until 1916, when it was called *Montagne Saint-Hilaire*, with 'mont' being substituted five years later. Mont-Saint-Hilaire became a town in 1950 and annexed *Saint-Hilaire-sur-Richelieu* in 1966.

Mont Tremblant QC This municipality (1940) is one of the province's most popular all-season tourist destinations northwest of Montreal. The post office opened in 1902 and was called Mont-Tremblant. It took its name from the 968-m mountain known in Algonquin as *Manitou Ewitchi Saga* ('the mountain of the formidable spirit') or *Manitonga Soutana* ('mountain of the spirits or of the devil'), with the *manitou* (the god of nature) having a reputation of making mountains tremble. The name was rendered first in French as *Montagne Tremblante* but became Mont Tremblant in 1936.

Monument Peak BC In the Purcell Mountains, west of Invermere, this mountain (3094 m) was named in 1910 when geologists with the Geological Survey of Canada observed that its summit was shaped like a gravestone.

Moonbeam ON This community is located in the municipal township of **Moonbeam**, Cochrane District, southeast of Kapuskasing. Its railway station was named in 1913 after **Moonbeam Creek**, called after a splash of moonlight that was observed in the creek. Its post office was named in 1915.

Moore ON In 2001 this township became part of the township of St. Clair, Lambton County. It was named in 1829 by Lt.-Gov. Sir John Colborne (1778–1863) after Sir John Moore (1761–1809), one of his commanders in the Peninsular War, who was killed at La Coruña, Spain. It was named *St. Clair Township* about 1820. The post office at **Mooretown** was called *Moore* from 1837 to 1906.

Moore, Mount BC In the Coast Mountains, east of Mount Waddington, this mountain (3041 m) was named in 1960 after pioneer rancher Ken Moore, who had settled in the Tatlayoko Lake area about 1915.

Moose Creek ON In 1998 this community became part of the township of North Stormont, united counties of Stormont, Dundas, and Glengarry. Located northwest of Cornwall, and on a tributary of the South Nation River, the community was named in 1864 after the creek, which had been observed to rarely freeze at a small waterfall, providing a place for moose to gather in the winter.

Moose Factory ON A Hudson's Bay Company trading post founded in 1671 on an island in **Moose River**, this place was captured by the French in 1686. It was recovered by the British in 1730, and after it was rebuilt, Moose Factory became the company's main post in the James Bay area.

Moose Jaw SK This city (1903) is located on a bend of the **Moose Jaw River**. Its station was established by the Canadian Pacific Railway in 1883 and the post office was named the same year. Although some fanciful stories have been told about the origin of the name, it is generally accepted that the Cree gathered in winter camps in the sheltered valley of the river. The Cree called the warm breezes here *môso-tâpiskanihk*. First recorded by John Palliser (1817–87) as *Moose Jaw Creek* in 1857, its name may have been a translation of its Cree name. The Geographic Board called the place *Moosejaw* and the river *Moosejaw creek* in 1901 but accepted the city's name in 1931; the river's name was authorized in 1967.

Moose River ON A large river with several major tributaries, it drains northeast into the south end of James Bay. Identified on a map in 1679 as *R. des Monsonis*, the river was named after the Monsoni tribe, whose totem was the moose. The French also called it *Rivière des Orignaux* ('moose river'). After the Treaty of Utrecht in 1713, the English called it Moose River.

Moosomin SK Established by the Canadian Pacific Railway in 1882, this town (1889) near the Manitoba border was named after *moosomin*, a Cree word meaning 'high bush cranberry'. Another story states it was named after Chief Moosomin (d.1903), who lived northwest of Battleford, about 450 km away from the town. It is likely that the chief never went to the area of the town.

Moosonee ON On the west bank of the Moose River, this was the site in 1903 of a Revillon Frères trading post. In 1932 it became the end of the line of the Temiskaming and Northern Ontario Railway. The name was devised from Moose River and *Rivière des Monsonis*, named after the Monsoni, the first Algonquian tribe met by French explorers and traders in the area of James Bay.

Moraviantown ON In 1998 this community became part the municipality of Chatham-Kent, Kent County. It was first established at *Fairfield* on the north side of the Thames River in 1792 by the Delaware nation. They were survivors of a former active Moravian church in the United States, who sought asylum in Canada. Two years after their settlement was destroyed in 1813 by American forces, *New Fairfield* mission was established on the south side of the Thames and renamed Moraviantown. The **Moravian Indian Reserve 47** covers an area of 13 km².

Morden MB The name of this town (1903) originated in 1882, when the Canadian Pacific Railway was built west, 20 km north of the North Dakota border. It was named after Alvey Morden (d.1891), who had moved west from Bruce County, ON, in 1874. It was adopted for the post office in 1884.

Morell PE This municipal community (1983) northeast of Charlottetown and at the mouth of the **Morell River** was incorporated as a village in 1953. Its post office was called *Morell Station* in 1884 and was changed to its present form in 1916. The river was named after Jean-François Morel, who was living here in 1752.

Moresby Island BC This island—the second largest of the Queen Charlotte Islands—was named in 1853 by Cdr. James Charles Prevost (1810–81) after his father-in-law, Adm. Sir Fairfax Moresby (1786–1877), commander-in-chief of the Pacific station, 1850–3.

Morice River BC Rising in **Morice Lake**, east of Kitimat, this river flows east and north to join the Bulkley River at Houston. It was named after Fr. Adrien Gabriel Morice (1859–1938), an Oblate missionary among the Aboriginals of the north-central part of the province. Between 1885 and 1905 Fr. Morice explored, mapped, and named the geography centred on the basins of the Skeena and Nechako Rivers, but was much distressed when the province did not consult with him. He viewed the Morice River as the main source of the Bulkley River, rather than the smaller river now considered the head of the Bulkley, rising east of Houston, but authorities in Victoria recognized the latter as the natural valley of the Bulkley.

Morigeau, Mount BC This mountain (3155 m) in the Purcell Mountains, east of Kootenay Lake, was named in 1884 by geologist George M. Dawson (1849–1901) after François Baptiste Morigeau, a native of Saint-Martin, QC, who settled in the East Kootenay about 1819.

Morin-Heights QC Located in the regional county of Les Pays-d'en-Haut, west of Sainte-Adèle, this municipality owes its name to Augustin-Norbert Morin (1803–65), member for Bellechasse in the Legislative Assembly of the Province of Canada, 1830–8 and 1844–51. He developed a farm, a sawmill, and a flour mill here during the mid-1800s. In 1852 the township of **Morin** was proclaimed, with the township municipality of *Morin-Partie-Sud* being erected three years later. It became the municipality of Morin-Heights in 1950, adopting the name given several years before to its railway station.

Morinville AB The post office in this town (1911) north of Edmonton was named in 1893 after Fr. Jean-Baptiste Morin (1852–1911), who founded the francophone community here two years earlier.

Mornington ON In 1998 this township became part of the township of Perth East, Perth County. It was named in 1845 for Richard Wellesley, Marquess of Wellesley, 2nd Earl of Mornington (1760–1842). His younger brother, William, Baron Maryborough, was made 3rd Earl of Mornington (1763–1845) in 1845. Both were brothers of the Duke of Wellington (1768–1852). Mornington is a village in Ireland's County Meath, near Drogheda.

Morpeth ON In 1998 this place became part of the municipality of Chatham-Kent, Kent County. This community was named *Howard,* after Howard Township, in 1832. When a new name was considered at a meeting in 1851, *Jamesville* was proposed after pioneer James Coll. However, others preferred Morpeth after George Howard, Earl of Morpeth (1802–64), who was travelling in the area. Morpeth is in Northumberland, England, north of Newcastle upon Tyne.

Morrin AB This village (1920) north of Drumheller was named in 1911 by the Canadian Northern Railway. Locally it is believed the village was named after the locomotive engineer who brought the first train through the commnity. Records of the Canadian National Railways suggest it may have been named after Dr. Joseph Morrin (1794–1861), a native of Dumfriesshire, Scotland, who practised medicine in Quebec City after 1815, served as the city's mayor in the 1850s, and was the first president of the medical board of Lower Canada. The place was earlier called *Blooming Prairie*.

Morris MB The post office in this town (1883) on the Red River, south of Winnipeg, was named in 1881 after Alexander Morris (1826–89), lieutenant-governor of Manitoba, 1872–6. Morris River was called *Scratching River* in 1874. *Scratching River* was shown on the 1865 Palliser expedition map, but it was officially called Morris River in 1901. It was earlier called by the French *Rivière aux Gratias*, referring to thorns that tore clothes and slashed flesh.

Morris ON In 2001 this township became part of the municipality of **Morris-Turnberry**, Huron County. It was named in 1850 after William Morris (1786–1858), receiver general of the Province of Canada, 1844–7, and president of the Executive Council, 1846–8.

Morrisburg ON Called *Williamsburg West* from 1830 to 1851 after the township of Williamsburgh, the post office in this village (1860) was renamed in 1851 after James Morris (1798–1865), Canada's first postmaster general, 1851–3. In 1998 the village became part of the township of South Dundas, united counties of Stormont, Dundas, and Glengarry.

Morriston ON This place in Wellington County, southeast of Guelph, was named in 1854 after merchant R.B. Morison, who arrived here in 1847. He was still the postmaster in 1905, when he provided the details about the naming of the place, but he did not comment on the misspelling.

Morrisville NL Near the head of Bay d'Espoir and east of St. Alban's, this municipal community (1971) was first known as *Lynch Cove*, presumably after a fisherman who drowned here. It was renamed in 1910 after Edward Patrick Morris (1859–1935), prime minister of Newfoundland, 1909–17.

Morro, Mount BC In the Rocky Mountains, northeast of Cranbrook, this mountain (2912 m) was named in 1964 after Flt. Sgt. Frank P. Morro of Cranbrook, who was killed in action in Europe, 4 December 1943.

Morse SK East of Swift Current, the station at this town (1912) was established by the Canadian Pacific Railway in 1883. It was not developed as an urban centre until 1908, two years after its post office opened. It was named after Samuel Finley Breese Morse (1791–1872), the American inventor of the telegraph and of the Morse code in the 1830s.

Mortlach SK West of Moose Jaw, the station at this village (1949) was named in 1883 by the Canadian Pacific Railway, likely after the parish of Mortlach in the area of Dufftown, Banffshire, Scotland. The post office was named in 1905, the same year the first house was built here.

Mosa ON In 2001 this township became part of the municipality of Southwest Middlesex, Middlesex County. It was named in 1821 by Lt.-Gov. Sir Peregrine Maitland (1777–1854) after the Latin and Spanish form of the River Meuse in Belgium. Prussian forces of Gen. Gebhard von Blücher (1742–1819) were drawn up here before the historic Battle of Waterloo in 1815.

Moser River NS On the Eastern Shore, between Sheet Harbour and Sherbrooke, this place was founded in 1809 by Henry Moser Sr. He had migrated to the province from Germany in 1751. Mosers River post office opened in 1873.

Mossbank SK Southwest of Moose Jaw, the post office of this town (1959) was named in 1909 by Robert Jolly, modifying Mossgeil, the name of a farm north of Mauchline, Ayrshire,

Scotland. The Canadian Pacific Railway was built through it in 1914.

Mountain ON In 1998 this township became part of the township of North Dundas, united townships of Stormont, Dundas, and Glengarry. It was named in 1798 after the Right Reverend Jacob Mountain (1750–1825), who became the first Protestant Bishop of Quebec in 1793. The post office in the community of **Mountain** was named in 1888.

Mount Albert ON In the town of East Gwillimbury, York Region, northeast of Newmarket, this community was first called *Birchardtown* and *Newland*. After Prince Edward Albert, the Prince of Wales (1841–1910) visited Newmarket in 1860, the residents of *Newland* decided to rename the community after him, and the name was changed to Mount Albert in 1864.

Mount Carmel NL On the north side of the mouth of Salmonier River, where it flows southwest into St. Mary's Bay, this urban centre in the municipal community of **Mount Carmel-Mitchell's Brook-St. Catherine's** was called *Salmonier North* until 1930, when it was renamed after the local Our Lady of Mount Carmel Catholic Church.

Mount Carmel PE Located west of Summerside and on the shore of Northumberland Strait, this place's first post office was called *Fifteen Point* in 1858 after a point in Lot 15, one of the province's 70 divisions. It was renamed Mount Carmel in 1899 after the local parish church, Notre-Dame-du-Mont-Carmel.

Mount Currie BC In the Lillooet River valley, northeast of Whistler, this Lillooet community was named after John Currie (d.1910), who became a rancher at nearby Pemberton about 1885.

Mount Elgin ON The post office in this community in Oxford County, southeast of Ingersoll, was named in 1851 after James Bruce, 8th Earl of Elgin (1811–63), governor of the Province of Canada, 1847–54.

Mount Forest ON In 1999 this town (1879) became part of the township of Wellington North, Wellington County. Located on the South Saugeen River, the town was named *Maitland River* in 1849, in the mistaken belief that it was at the head of that river. Four years later it was renamed Mount Forest after the townland of Mountforest, near Gorey in County Wexford, Ireland.

Mount Moriah NL On the west side of Corner Brook, this town (1971) was named after the adjacent rounded hill, called earlier from the reference in the Bible to *Moriah* ('land of hills'). The place was formerly called *Giles Point*, likely after Joseph Giles, who was living here in 1871.

Mount Pearl NL This city (1988) on the west side of St. John's was developed after 1829 by retired British naval officer Sir James Pearl (1790–1840) and was called *Mount Cochrane* after Sir Thomas John Cochrane (1789–1872), governor of Newfoundland 1825–34. In 1837 he renamed it Mount Pearl. It was subdivided into building lots after the death of Pearl's widow in 1860. The town of *Mount Pearl-Glendale* was incorporated in 1955, and Glendale was dropped in 1958.

Mount Pleasant ON In 1999 this community became part of the County of Brant. Located south of Brantford, this place was named about 1800 by Loyalist Henry Ellis (1745–1831) after his birthplace in Flintshire, Wales. The post office was named Mount Pleasant in 1823, but it was called *Mohawk* from 1836 to 1922, when it reverted to Mount Pleasant.

Mount Royal / Mont-Royal QC This city on the northwest side of **Mont Royal** was incorporated in 1912 as both Mont-Royal and Mount Royal, and both names continue as official. It is widely known in English as Town of Mount Royal, and by the initials TMR. In 2002 Mount Royal / Mont-Royal became part of city of Montreal, but recovered its status as a city in 2006. The 223-m mountain called Mont Royal was named by Jacques Cartier (1491–1557) in 1535, either directly in honour of the king or indirectly as a feature worthy of the king.

Mount Sir Richard BC In the Coast Mountains, northeast of Squamish, this mountain (2728 m) was named in 1930 after Sir Richard McBride (1870–1917), premier of British Columbia, 1912–15. It was previously called *Pyramid Mountain*.

Mount Stewart PE This municipal community (1983) northeast of Charlottetown was incorporated as a village in 1953. Its post office was named about 1867 after John Stewart (1758–1834), the place's founder and author of *Account of Prince Edward Island* (1806).

Mount Uniacke NS Located midway between Halifax and Windsor, this place was named after the country residence of Richard John Uniacke (1753–1830), solicitor general of Nova Scotia, 1781–97, and attorney general, 1797–1830. The residence was built in 1813–15, taken over by the province in 1949, and opened to the public in 1952.

Mousseau, Lac QC Located above Lac Meech, northwest of the city of Gatineau, this lake is well known as the site of the Harrington Lake residence of the prime minister of Canada. Among early settlers on the lake were John Hetherington (a son-in-law of Asa Meech) and Louis Mousseau. Although a survey plan of 1850 called it *Harrington's Lake*, and official maps had *Harrington Lake* until 1962, it was locally called *Lac Mousseau* and *Mousseau Lake*. It was offically called Lac Mousseau (Lac Harrington) in 1962, with *Lac Harrington* being dropped in 1987 by the Commission de toponymie du Quebec.

Muenster SK Located east of Humboldt, this village (1908) became the site of the first Benedictine monastery in Canada. It was established in 1903, and its post office was first called *St. Peters Monastery* on 1 January 1904. It was renamed on 1 August 1904 after Münster (now in North Rhine-Westphalia, Germany), whose name derives from the Latin *monasterium* ('monastery').

Mulgrave NS On the mainland side of the Canso Causeway, this town (1923) was first called *McNair's Cove* and *Wylde's Cove* before being named *Port Mulgrave* in 1859 after the 2nd Earl of Mulgrave (1797–1863), the father of George Augustus Augustine Phipps, 3rd Earl of Mulgrave (1819–90), lieutenant-governor of Nova Scotia, 1858–63. *Port Mulgrave* post office,(opened in 1860) and *Port Mulgrave Station* post office (opened in 1893) were united as Mulgrave post office in 1897.

Mulmur ON This township in Dufferin County was named in 1821. Suggestions that it was named after a son of Shawnee chief Tecumseh or after the ninth-century Irish poet Maolmura are questionable. If it has a Gaelic origin, it may derive from Maol Mhor ('big hill') in Scotland, where there is an elevation with that name on the island of Mull.

Mummery, Mount BC Southwest of Howse Pass, this mountain (3328 m) was named in 1898 by British climber Norman Collie (1859–1942) after alpinist Albert Frederick Mummery (1855–96), who died climbing Nanga Parbat in the Himalayas.

Mundare AB The station in this town (1951) east of Edmonton was named in 1906 by the Canadian Northern Railway after station agent William Mundare. Its post office opened in the same year.

Munday, Mount BC Southeast of Mount Waddington, this mountain (3367 m) was named in 1928 after climber Walter Alfred 'Don' Munday (1890–1950), who led a survey party to the area of Mount Waddington in 1926–7.

Munson AB Between Drumheller and Morrin, this village (1911) was founded in 1911 by the Canadian Northern Railway, and was likely named after John Hnery Munson of the Winnipeg law firm Munson, Allan, Laird & Davis.

Murchison, Mount AB Near the head of the North Saskatchewan River, this mountain (3333 m) was named in 1858 by Sir James Hector (1834–1907) after Sir Robert Impey Murchison (1792–1871). He was a noted English geologist, who had recommended Hector for the position of geologist with the Palliser expedition, 1857–60.

Murdochville QC This town, almost 100 km west of Gaspé, was incorporated in 1953. It was named after James Y. Murdoch (1890–1960), the first president of Noranda Mines, which started mining the copper ore here in 1950.

Murillo ON This place in Thunder Bay District, west of the city of Thunder Bay, was called *Murillo Station* in 1880 and shortened to Murillo 10 years later. It was given for the celebrated Spanish painter Bartolomeo Estaban Murillo (1617–82).

Murray ON In 1998 this township became part of the city of Quinte West, Hastings County. It was named in 1792 after James Murray, 4th Baron Elibank (1721/22–94), a senior officer at the Battle of the Plains of Abraham, 1759, military governor of the district of Quebec, 1760–3, and governor of Quebec, 1763–8.

Murray Harbour PE This municipal community (1983) south of Montague, and on the south side of Murray Harbour, was incorporated as a village in 1953. The municipal community (1983) of **Murray River**, west of Murray Harbour, was incorporated as a village in 1955. It was first known as *Cambridge Mills* and then *Murray Mills*. Both the harbour and the river were named in 1765 by Samuel Holland (1728–1801) after James Murray (1719–94), governor of Quebec, 1763–8.

Musgrave Harbour NL On the north coast of Newfoundland, this town (1954) was first called *Muddy Hole*, until it was renamed in the 1860s after Sir Anthony Musgrave (1828–88), governor of Newfoundland, 1864–9.

Musgravetown NL This town (1974) on the west side of Goose Bay—an arm of Chandler Reach, which is a south-western extension of Bonavista Bay,—was once known as *Goose Bay*. It was renamed before 1869 after Sir Anthony Musgrave (1828–88), governor of Newfoundland, 1864–9.

Muskoka ON The district was created in 1851 and separated from Simcoe County in 1888. In 1970 it became the province's only district municipality, divided among three towns and three municipal townships. The municipal township of **Muskoka Lakes**, west of Gravenhurst and Bracebridge, was created in 1971. **Lake Muskoka** and the **Muskoka Lakes** recall Chief Yellowhead and his son William Yellowhead (1769–1864), also known as Mesqua Ukie and Musquakie, who were chiefs of the Ojibwa around Lake Simcoe and Lake Huron and had their favourite hunting grounds between Lake Muskoka and Lake of Bays. The name Yellowhead derives from the Ojibwa *mesqua* ('red') and *ahkees* ('ground'). The **Muskoka River** is comprised of two main branches, the **North Branch** and the **South Branch**, which join at Bracebridge.

Muskwa River BC Rising in the Muskwa Ranges of the Rocky Mountains, this river flows east and then north into the Fort Nelson River, east of the town of Fort Nelson. In Cree *muskwa* means 'black bear'.

Musquodoboit River NS Rising southeast of Truro, this river flows into the Atlantic at **Musquodoboit Harbour**, east of Dartmouth. The name derives from the Mi'kmaq *mooskudoboogwek* ('rolling out in foam at its mouth'). **Middle**

Musquodoboit, southeast of Stewiacke, had postal service in 1821; **Upper Musquodoboit**'s post office opened 10 years later; and **Musquodoboit Harbour**'s post office was established in 1855.

Myrnam AB The post office of this village (1930) northeast of Vegreville was named in 1908 after the Ukrainian words *myr nam* ('peace to us'). Many of the early settlers came from Ukraine.

Nackawic NB This town (1976) on the Saint John River and at the mouth of **Nackawic Stream** was established in 1970 as a residential community for the families of employees of the new St. Anne Pulp and Paper Company. The mill was closed in 2004. The stream's name in Maliseet was *Nelgwaweegek*, possibly meaning 'straight stream', referring to the fact that its lower part, before flooding by the waters of Mactaquac Lake, was in a direct line with the Coac Reach of the Saint John River. There was a *Nackawick* post office at Upper Queensbury, 3 km to the east, from 1862 to 1914.

Nahanni Butte NT Situated at the mouth of the South Nahanni River, where it flows into the Liard River, this settlement was named in 1958 after the nearby imposing hill. The butte, which is not in fact a flat-topped butte, rises to 1372 m. It was named before 1910 after the Nahanni, an Athapascan tribe in the northern Rocky Mountains and the southern Mackenzie Mountains. **Nahanni National Park Reserve** (4766 km²) was established on both sides of the South Nahanni River in 1972.

Naicam SK Northwest of Humboldt, this town (1954) was established in 1920, when the Canadian Pacific Railway line was surveyed from Watson to Melfort. Its name derives from the names of two railway contractors who built the line, Naismith and Campbell. A post office was also opened that year.

Nain NL This town (1970) on the Labrador coast was named in 1771 by Moravian missionaries, who chose the site as their first mission among the Inuit. It was the first settlement in Labrador and is now the most northerly one.

Nairn ON This community in **Nairn Township**, Sudbury District, is southwest of the city of Sudbury. Its post office was named **Nairn Centre** in 1897 after a Canadian Pacific Railway engineer who had named a station Nairn in 1886 for his birthplace in Nairnshire, Scotland, northeast of Inverness. The post office at Nairn in Middlesex County, northwest of London, was named in 1857.

Nakusp BC The post office in this village (1964) on the eastern shore of Upper Arrow Lake, south of Revelstoke was named in 1892. In the Okanagan language the name may mean 'lake narrowing', a description of the lake 10 km to the south.

Nalaisk Mountain NB Southeast of Mount Carleton, this mountain (785 m) was named in 1901 by naturalist William F. Ganong (1864–1941) after the Maliseet *Nalaisk* ('snake'), their name for the Serpentine River.

Nampa AB This village (1958) southeast of the town of Peace River was first called *Tank* in 1916 by the Edmonton, Dunvegan and British Columbia Railway. Confusion with Frank, AB, prompted local merchant Robert 'Pa' Christian to suggest naming it after his native Nampa, ID, west of Boise.

Namur QC This municipality (1964) in the regional county of Papineau was settled in 1865 by Belgian Protestants from the province of Namur. Its post office was named in 1874.

Nanaimo BC This second largest city (1874) on Vancouver Island was founded in 1852 at *Winthuysen Bay* to exploit the coal resources of the area. Hudson's Bay Company chief factor James Douglas (1803–77) noted that year that the bay was commonly called *Nanymo Bay*. The growing settlement was called *Colviletown* in 1854 after HBC governor Andrew Colvile, but that name's use was discontinued by 1860. The bay was named after a confederacy of Coast Salish called *Snenéymexw*, whose pronunciation approximated 'na-NY-mo'. In Halkomelem the name means 'the great and mighty people'.

Nanga Parba, Mount AB, BC On the continental divide and west of Howse Pass, this mountain (3240 m) was named by British climber Norman Collie (1859–1942) after Nanga Parbat in present-day Pakistan, the world's ninth highest peak. The latter was associated with climber Albert Mummery (1855–96), who was killed while ascending it in the Himalayas. The peaks surrounding Mount Nanga Parbat are part of the Mummery Group.

Nanisivik NU The site of a lead-zinc mine on northern Baffin Island, it was founded in 1976 as Canada's first commercial mine in the Arctic. In Inuktitut the name means 'place where people find things'.

Nantes QC Located in the regional county of Le Granit, northwest of Lac-Mégantic, this municipality was called *Whitton* in 1874 after the township of Whitton, proclaimed in 1863. The township was probably named after a suburb of London, England. It was renamed Nantes in 1957 in honour of settlers from Nantes, France, who arrived in this part of the province in the late 1800s.

Nanticoke ON Although mostly rural in character, Nanticoke was created a city in 1974 in Haldimand-Norfolk Region through the amalgamation of several municipalities, including the towns of Port Dover and Waterford and the village of Jarvis. Believed to mean 'crooked creek' in an Aboriginal language, it was taken from the small community of Nanticoke, on **Nanticoke Creek**, near the Lake Erie shore. In Maryland, the name of the Nanticoke nation is interpreted as 'tidewater people'.

Nanton AB Located midway between Calgary and Fort Macleod, this town (1907) was first called *Mosquito Creek*. It was renamed in 1893 by the Canadian Pacific Railway after Sir Augustus Meredith Nanton (1860–1925), a partner of the Winnipeg financial office of Osler, Hammond and Nanton, and a director of the CPR. His firm had a contract with the CPR to lay out townsites along the line south of Calgary.

Napanee ON In 1998 this town (1864) became the town of **Greater Napanee**, Lennox and Addington County. It took its name in the 1820s from **Napanee River**, originally called *Appanea*, whose meaning is unknown (but it is not 'flour', as often **claimed**). In the 1780s the mill site on the south side of the river was developed by millwright Robert Clark and government agent James Clark, and became known as *Clarkville*. In 1799 Richard Cartwright (1759–1815) of Kingston built a mill on the north side, and that area became known as *Cartwrightville*.

Napierville QC The post office in this village (1873) in the regional county of Les Jardins-de-Napierville, southwest of Saint-Jean-sur-Richelieu, was named in 1832. It was named in honour of Lt. Gen. Napier Christie Burton (1759–1835). In 1766 his father, Gabriel Christie (1722–99), purchased the seigneury of Léry, which included the area of Napierville.

Naramata BC On the eastern shore of Okanagan Lake, north of Penticton, this place was established in 1907 by John Moore Robinson (1855–1934). He reported that a spiritualist named the place after Narramattah, the wife of an Aboriginal chief. He had earlier planned to call the place *Brighton Beach*.

Nashwaak River NB This river flows into the Saint John River, opposite the city centre of Fredericton. The name is derived from the Maliseet *Nahwijewauk*, possibly meaning 'winding among others'—a reference to how it interlaces with the head of the Southwest Miramichi. Noted in a 1676 French grant as *Nachouac*, the name had several spellings until 1901, when Surveyor General Thomas Loggie (1854–1931) used the present form on a map.

Nashwaaksis NB This neighbourhood in the city of Fredericton and on the north side of the Saint John River is located at the mouth of **Naskwaaksis Stream**, whose name means 'little Nashwaak'. Its post office was *Naswaaksis* from 1854 to 1857, when it was changed to its present form. It was an incorporated village from 1966 to 1973, when it was annexed by Fredericton.

Naskaupi River NL Rising adjacent to Smallwood Reservoir, this river flows southeast into Lake Melville, part of Hamilton Inlet. The river took its name from the Naskapi, an Algonquian tribe related to the Montagnais. Their name was taken from a derisive Montagnais word, while calling themselves Nanénot ('true, real men'). Both the Naskapi and the Montagnais in Labrador are now called Innu ('people'). The river is also known as *North West River*.

Nass River BC Rising in the Skeena Mountains, northeast of Stewart, this river flows southwest into Portland Inlet. The name was given by the Tlingit, and literally means 'stomach' in their language. They came from southern Alaska to obtain their supplies of salmon and eulachon (a fish valued for its rich oily flesh) at the mouth of the river. Capt. George Vancouver (1757–98) established the spelling in 1793, after consulting the Tlingit. The Nisga'a, who occupy its basin, call it *K'alii Aksim Lisims*.

Natashquan QC Situated on the north shore of the Gulf of St. Lawrence and at the mouth of **Petite rivière Natashquan**, just west of the mouth of **Rivière Natashquan**, this township municipality was erected in 1907, taking its name from the township, proclaimed in 1869. Explorer Louis Jolliet (1645–1700) identified the larger river as *R. noutasquan* in 1684. In Montagnais *Nutahquaniu Hipu* means 'river where they caught the black bear'.

Nation River BC Flowing east into the Parsnip Reach of Williston Lake, this river was mentioned by Simon Fraser (1776–1862) in 1806 as *River au Nation*. He said it was named after the nation of Big Men (the Sekani) who were different from the nation of Little Men (the Carrier) at Trout Lake (renamed McLeod Lake about 1806).

Naughton ON Andrew McNaughton, the first judge in Sudbury, became lost in the woods in 1883, but found some railway engineers camped at this site, now in the area of Walden and the city of Greater Sudbury, Sudbury Region. First called *McNaughtonville*, it was shortened to Naughton when the post office opened in 1902.

Navan ON In 2001 this community in the township of Cumberland became part of the city of Ottawa. Its post office was named in 1861 after the town of Navan (An Uaimh), in County Meath, Ireland, northwest of Dublin.

Navy Peak BC In the Coast Mountains, east of Mount Waddington, this mountain (2941 m) was named in 1985 by Lt. Cmdr. Dave Redmond, who led a party into the **Naval Anniversary Range** that year. These names were given in honour of the seventy-fifth anniversary of the founding of the Royal Canadian Navy.

Nechako River BC Rising in Tweedsmuir Provincial Park, north of Bella Coola, this river flows northeast, and then east into the Fraser River at Prince George. In the Carrier language, *Nechako* means 'big river'. When the Kenney Dam was built in 1956 to provide power for aluminum production at Kitimat, it inundated several lakes (Natalkuz, Eutsuk, Ootsa, Whitesail, Tetachuck) to form **Nechako Reservoir**.

Necum Teuch NS The post office in this place, on the Eastern Shore and west of Ecum Secum, was established in 1855. The name of the adjacent **Necum Teuch Bay** derives from the Mi'kmaq *Noogoomkeak* ('soft sand place').

Neebing ON This municipal township in Thunder Bay District, on the west side of the city of Thunder Bay, was named about 1860 after the Ojibwa for 'summer'.

Neepawa MB This town (1883), northeast of Brandon, was named in 1873 after the Ojibwa *nibiwa* ('plenty' or 'abundance'), and its post office opened in 1882. The name was chosen by its promoters on account of the rich and productive agricultural land surrounding the town. It adopted the cornucopia (the horn of plenty) as its emblem.

Neguac NB Southwest of Tracadie, this village (1967) was first noted in various sources in the 1780s. Its post office was called *Niguac* in 1857 and was changed to its present form in 1873. The name may derive from the Mi'kmaq *Annikeooek* ('improperly situated'), referring to Hay Island in **Neguac Bay**.

Neilburg SK West of Battleford, the post office at this village (1947) was established in 1908 and named after first postmaster Clifford O'Neill. The Canadian Pacific Railway arrived here in 1923.

Nelson BC This city (1897) on the West Arm of Kootenay Lake was named in 1888 after Hugh Nelson (1830–93), lieutenant-governor of British Columbia, 1887–92. Previously it was called *Salisbury*, after the 3rd Marquess of Salisbury (1830–1903), prime minister of Great Britain for three terms between 1885 and 1902, and *Stanley*, after Frederick Arthur Stanley, Baron Stanley of Preston (1841–1908), governor general of Canada, 1888–93.

Nelson-Miramichi NB Located in the city of Miramichi and opposite to Newcastle, this settlement was incorporated as a village in 1967. Its post office was called *Nelson* in 1842 after

Nelson Parish, established in 1814 and named after Adm. Viscount Horatio Nelson (1758–1805), the victor in 1805 of the Battle of Trafalgar, off the coast of southwest Spain. *South Nelson* post office opened in 1853 and changed to Nelson-Miramichi in 1968.

Nelson, Mount BC This mountain (3294 m) in the Purcell Mountains, west of Invermere, was named in 1807 by geographer David Thompson (1770–1857) after Adm. Viscount Horatio Nelson (1758–1805).

Nelson River MB This 540-km river was named in 1612–3 by Sir Thomas Button (c.1601–34) after Robert Nelson, the ships master of the *Resolution*, who died near the river's mouth, where Sir Thomas had spent the winter.

Nemiscau QC This Cree village on the north shore of **Lac Nemiscau**, east of Fort Rupert, was an important fur trade site at various times between 1685 and the present. The name means 'where there is plenty of fish', in reference to the fact that five rivers flow into the lake, which is drained into James Bay through the Rivière Rupert.

Nepean ON This community was a city in Ottawa-Carleton Region from 1978 to 2001, when it became part of the city of Ottawa. Laid out as a township in 1792, it was named two years later after Sir Evan Nepean (1751–1822), British undersecretary of state for the home office. The area of the city of Ottawa west of the Rideau River was originally part of Nepean Township. **Nepean Point** is located near the mouth of the Rideau Canal, where it flows into the Ottawa River.

Nepisiguit River NB On the eastern flank of Mount Carleton, this river rises in the **Nepisiguit Lakes** and flows east, then north, into Bathurst Harbour and **Nepisiguit Bay**. It was named after the Mi'kmaq designation *Winpegijooik* ('river that dashes roughly along'). The river was noted by Acadian Gov. Nicolas Denys (c.1598–1688) in 1672 as both *Nepegiguit* and *Nepiziguit*, and its present spelling was not established officially until 1935. In various spellings, Nepisiguit Bay applied to Bathurst Harbour until 1777, when map-maker Joseph Frederic Wallet DesBarres (1772–1824) applied it beyond the sand bars that almost enclosed the harbour.

Neptune Peak BC Located in the Selkirk Mountains, north of Revelstoke, this mountain (3185 m) was named in 1939, likely by N.E. McConnell after the Roman god of fresh water, the equivalent of the Greek god Poseidon.

Nettilling Lake NU The name of this largest lake (5063 km²) on Baffin Island was recorded by anthropologist Franz Boas (1858–1942) in 1884. The name may derive from the Inuktitut *netsek*, in reference to the ringed seal, which has its only permanent freshwater habitat in this lake. In 1897 geologist

Robert Bell (1841–1917) was informed by his Inuk guide that the name meant 'flat floor', referring to the flat beds of rocks extending to Amadjuak Lake and Foxe Basin.

Neudorf SK Southwest of Melville, this village (1905) was founded by German settlers. Ludwig Jacob Wendel Sr. (1842–1909) became the postmaster in 1895, naming it after his hometown in southwestern Ukraine. The Canadian Pacific Railway was built through here in 1903.

Neustadt ON In 2001 this village (1907) became part of the township of West Grey, Grey County. South of Hanover, it was founded by several German immigrants in 1855. Its post office was called *Newstead* in 1856, but it was amended the following year to Neustadt, German for 'new town'.

Neuville QC Located in the regional county of Portneuf, southwest of Quebec City, this village was named in 1919 after the seigneury of Neuville. The seigneury was given its name in 1680 by Nicolas Dupont de Neuville (1632–1716), member of the King's council and keeper of the seals. The name may have come from a village in France, north of Paris, whose name means 'new estate'.

Newboro' ON In 1998 this village, located on the Rideau Canal, became part of the township of Rideau Lakes, united counties of Leeds and Grenville. It was first called *New Borough*, which was shortened to Newboro' for the post office in 1836, and for the incorporated village in 1876. Although the apostrophe is legally part of the name, it is rarely used.

New Brunswick The province was separated from Nova Scotia in 1784, and named after the House of Brunswick of the British royal family. Sir William Alexander (1567–1640) wanted to call the area New Alexandria in 1624. In 1784 British Under-Secretary of State William Knox proposed the name New Ireland, to complement New England and Nova Scotia, but Ireland was then out of favour with George III. Pittsylvania was also suggested as a compliment to William Pitt, the prime minister.

New Brunswick, Mount YT This mountain (3388 m) in the Centennial Range of the St. Elias Mountains was named in 1967 after the province.

Newburgh ON In 1998 this village (1859) became part of the township of Stone Mills, Lennox and Addington County. Located northeast of Napanee, it was named in 1839 by Isaac Brock Aylesworth (1812–88) after Newburgh on the Hudson River, in New York. The postal name was called *Newburg* in 1846 and altered to Newburgh in 1862.

Newbury ON In 2001 this village (1872) became part of the municipality of Southwest Middlesex, Middlesex County.

It was named in 1854 after a place in England, possibly Newbury in Berkshire, west of Reading.

New Carlisle QC Located on the north shore of Chaleur Bay, southwest of Gaspé, this municipality (1877) was founded by Loyalists in the late 1700s. The name, which appeared on maps as early as 1815, may have been given after Carlisle in Cumberland County, PA, which was named after Carlisle in Cumberland, England.

Newcastle NB In the city of Miramichi since 1995, this urban centre was incorporated as a town in 1899. The post office opened in 1823 and was named after **Newcastle Parish**, created in 1786 and possibly named by Benjamin Marston (1730–92) after Thomas Pelham Holles, Duke of Newcastle (1693–1768), prime minister of Great Britain, 1754–62.

Newcastle Village ON The post office in this location, in the municipality of Clarington, Durham Region, was named *Newcastle* in 1845. In 1857, this became the name of the village. When regional government was introduced in 1974, the village, the town of Bowmanville, and the townships of Clarke and Darlington became the town of *Newcastle*, taking its name from Newcastle District, which existed from 1798 to 1850. The former village became Newcastle Village in 1985 to distinguish it from the town. *See also* Clarington.

New Denver BC The name of this village (1929) on the eastern shore of Slocan Lake, north of Nelson, was proposed in 1892 by Thomas Latheen after Denver, CO. The year before it was called *El Dorado* (after the mythical city of gold) by a surveyor named Perry, but when it turned out that silver and lead, not gold, comprised the mineral wealth of the area, a meeting was called to choose an alternate name.

New Ferrolle Peninsula NL Situated on the northwestern coast of Newfoundland and north of Port au Choix, this peninsula was named by the Basques in the late 1500s *Ferrolgo Amuixco Punta*, probably after El Ferrol in Spain's Galicia, where the Basque whalers spent the winter. It was called 'new' to distinguish it from the original harbour of Ferrolle, called *Ferrol Çaharra*, at the present-day Plum Point to the north.

Newfoundland The Portuguese identified the island in the 1500s as *Tierra de Bacalaos* ('land of the codfish'). In 1497 John Cabot (c.1450–98) called it the *new founde isle*, and by 1502 *New found launde* was being used in British documents. Giovanni da Verrazzano (c.1485–1528) referred to it as *Terra Nova* in 1529. The coast of Labrador became part of Newfoundland in 1809, and its boundary with Quebec was defined by the Imperial Privy Council in 1927. In 1964 the province designated its administration as the government of the Newfoundland and Labrador. In 2001 the Constitution of Canada was amended for the province's name to be **Newfoundland and Labrador**.

Newfoundland, Mount YT Located in the Centennial Range of the St. Elias Mountains, this mountain (3670 m) was named in 1967 after the province.

New Germany NS Northwest of Bridgewater, this place on the LaHave River was settled in 1785 by immigrants from Germany. Its first post office in 1855 was *Chesleys Corner* and it was given its present name in 1901. In 1854 the post office 5 km to the east was called *New Germany*, but that was changed to Barss Corner in 1882.

New Glasgow NS This town (1875) in Pictou County was founded in the 1780s and named by surveyor William Fraser. He perceived the East River of Pictou as being akin to Scotland's River Clyde, and the new settlement akin to Glasgow. Postal service was established here in 1834.

New Glasgow PE This place between Hunter River and North Rustico was named in 1819 after Glasgow, Scotland. Its postal service began about 1834. The post office at nearby **New Glasgow Mills** was established in 1908.

New Harbour NL The place northeast of Dildo was named after its adjoining harbour. The harbour may have been named because it was established about 1750 as the first harbour on the east side of Trinity Bay, developed from the base at Trinity on the west side.

New Haven-Riverdale PE This municipal community (1974) west of Charlottetown is comprised of the localities of **New Haven**, **Riverdale**, and Churchill. New Haven's post office was named in 1872, possibly after Newhaven, a suburb of Edinburgh, Scotland. The place may have been named because it was a shipping port for some years. Riverdale is located in the deep valleys of West River and Howells Brook. Its post office opened in 1885.

New Liskeard ON This town (1903) in Timiskaming District was called *Liskeard* in 1896 after a town in Cornwall, England, but it was renamed *Thornloe* that year after newly ordained Anglican bishop George Thorneloe (1896–1926), because of confusion with Leskard, in the present Durham Region. In 1898 George Paget, a native of Cornwall, persuaded the province to restore *Liskeard*, and 'New' was added three years later for the post office and the town. In 2004 the towns of New Liskeard and Haileybury, with the township of Dymond, became the city of Temiskaming Shores.

Newmarket ON This town (1880) in York Region was named about 1816, when William Roe established a 'new

market' for Aboriginals to sell furs and trade for other goods. The post office opened in 1823.

New Maryland NB This village (1998) south of Fredericton was named by Benedict Arnold (c.1741–1801), who had come from the state of Maryland about 1817. It was first called *Maryland*, but New Maryland was in use by 1825. **New Maryland Parish** was established in 1850.

New Minas NS Between Kentville and Wolfville, the post office in this village (1968) was named in 1858 after the nearby **Minas Basin**.

New Norway AB The post office at this village (1910) southwest of Camrose was named in 1903 after some of the early settlers from their homeland of Norway.

Newport NS In 1761 Newport Township was established across the St. Croix River from *Pisiquid* (Windsor) at present-day Avondale. It was named by Nova Scotia Surveyor General Charles Morris (1731–1802) possibly after Newport, RI. The **Newport** post office was established in 1831 in the township at Brooklyn. Post offices were also opened at **Newport Corner** (1850), **Newport Landing** (1851), and **Newport Station** (1863).

Newport QC On the north shore of Chaleur Bay, south of Gaspé, this municipality was created in 1845, abolished two years later, and re-established in 1855, taking its name from the township of **Newport**, proclaimed in 1840. The name, also spelled *New Port* in the early days, was given by the Loyalists, who settled here at the beginning of the nineteenth century, perhaps recalling Newport, RI.

New Richmond QC This most populous town on the north shore of Chaleur Bay was first called *Richmond* in the early years of the 1800s. The township of **New Richmond** was identified on a map in 1803, but was not proclaimed until 1842. It became a township municipality in 1845, was abolished two years later, and was re-established in 1855. The name was likely given by Loyalists after a place they left in the American colonies, such as Richmond, the borough embracing Staten Island in New York city, or Richmond, VA.

New Sarepta AB The post office in this village (1960) southeast of Edmonton was named in 1905. It is believed Moravian bishop Clement Hoyler named it after the settlement of Sarepta in Vohlynia, Russia. That name may have been given for the ancient city of Sarepta (later Sidon, now Sayda in Lebanon). The Alberta village was formerly called *Little Hay Lakes*.

New Tecumseth ON Created as a town in Simcoe County in 1992, it comprises the former town of Alliston, the villages of Tottenham and Beeton, and the municipal township of Tecumseth. 'New' was added to distinguish it from the town of Tecumseh in Essex County.

Newton, Mount YT In the St. Elias Mountains, this mountain (4210 m) was named in 1890 by explorer and geologist Israel C. Russell (1852–1906) after Henry Newton (1845–77), a professor at the Columbia School of Mines in Columbia, MO, and a member of the United States Geological Survey.

Newton Robinson ON In Simcoe County, northwest of Newmarket, this settlement was first called *Latimer's Corners* and *Springville*. It was renamed in 1852 after one of the Newtowns in Ireland, and after William Benjamin Robinson (1797–1873), Conservative member for Simcoe in the House of Assembly of Upper Canada, 1830–41, and in the Legislative Assembly of the Province of Canada, 1844–57.

Newtown NL This neighbourhood (1996) in the town of New-Wes-Valley was first known as *Inner Pinchard's Islands*. It was named in 1874, and became a municipal community in 1954.

New Westminster BC The site of this city (1860) on the north bank of the Fraser River, southeast of Vancouver, was selected in 1858 by Col. Richard Clemen Moody (1813–87) as an appropriate location for the capital of British Columbia. He proposed calling it Queensborough. In 1859 Gov. James Douglas championed the name, but the colonial secretary, W.A.G. Young, stated Victoria was the 'Queen's borough'. To ensure that a suitable name was chosen, Douglas consulted Sir Edward Bulwer-Lytton, who responded 'that Her Majesty has been graciously pleased to decide that the capital of British Columbia shall be called "New Westminster"'. But in 1867, when the colonies of Vancouver Island and British Columbia were united, Victoria became the capital. New Westminster is still known as 'The Royal City'.

New-Wes-Valley NL This town (1996) on the northwest side of Bonavista Bay comprises three separate populated areas. Four years earlier it was incorporated as the town of Badger's Quay-Valleyfield-Pool's Island-Wesleyville-Newtown. The new name is a composite of the names Newtown, Wesleyville, and Valleyfield.

New World Island NL Between Twillingate Island and the island of Newfoundland, this island may have an indirect connection with *Novus Mundus*, noted on the Girolamo da Verrazzano map of 1529. It was not occupied by permanent settlements until after 1783.

Niagara ON The regional municipality of Niagara was created in 1970 through the amalgamation of Lincoln and

Welland counties, and the restructuring of the municipalities within the region. **Niagara Peninsula** is a misnomer, as it is really an isthmus, extending from Hamilton to Niagara-on-the-Lake. **Niagara Escarpment**, although really geological in structure, has acquired geographical significance between Queenston Heights and Tobermory, Bruce County.

Niagara Falls ON Arguably the most famous set of waterfalls in the world, they and the **Niagara River** are said to be named after the Neutral word *Onghiara* ('neck'), referring to the **Niagara Peninsula**'s being cut across by a river. The city of **Niagara Falls** was created in 1903 through the amalgamation of the town of *Clifton* and *Niagara Falls Village*. In 1963 the city annexed the municipal township of *Stamford*, and in 1970 absorbed parts of the municipal townships of *Crowland*, *Willoughby*, and *Humberstone*.

Niagara-on-the-Lake ON In 1792 Lt.-Gov. John Graves Simcoe (1752–1806) made *West Niagara* the capital of Upper Canada, and renamed it *Newark*, as it provided an ark of safety for the Loyalists, as well as recalling Newark upon Trent in Nottinghamshire, southwest of the city of Lincoln, England. Also in 1792 Niagara Township was renamed *Newark Township* by Simcoe, but the former name was reinstated in 1798. In 1970 the township was united with the town (1850) of *Niagara* to form the town of Niagara-on-the-Lake, which had been made the postal name in 1902.

Nichol ON In 1999 this township became a part of the township of Centre Wellington, Wellington County. It was named in 1822 after Robert Nichol (c.1780–1824), who was killed accidentally at Queenston on returning from his duties as a judge at *Niagara* (now Niagara-on-the-Lake).

Nicholas Denys NB The post office in this community northwest of Bathurst was named in 1940, misspelling it after Acadian Gov. Nicolas Denys (c.1598–1688), who lived in the area of present-day Bathurst after 1669.

Nickel Centre ON In 2001 this town became part of the city of Greater Sudbury, Sudbury Region. The town was created in 1973, when the town of Coniston, the townships of Falconbridge and Maclennan, and most of the township of Garson were amalgamated.

Nicola River BC Rising west of Kelowna, this river flows west through **Nicola Lake** to enter the Thompson River, midway between Lytton and Ashcroft. It was named by fur traders after a strong Thompson chief called Nukuala (c.1785–1865), interpreted as Nicola, but whose Aboriginal name was *Hwistemexe'quen* ('walking grizzly bear'). An 1849 map identified *R. Nicholas* and *Lac de Nicholas*.

Nicolet QC A town at the mouth of **Rivière Nicolet**, where it flows north into the east end of Lac Saint-Pierre, this settlement was erected in 1872. The river, identified on a 1641 map, was named after Jean Nicolet (or Nicollet) de Belleborne (c.1598–1642), who came to New France with Samuel de Champlain (1567–1635), and explored the area of the Great Lakes. The regional county of **Nicolet-Yamaska** was created in 1982.

Nictau Lake NB North of Mount Carleton, this lake is situated near the heads of several river systems. Its name in Maliseet means 'forks', referring to the confluence of the Little Tobique, Mamozekel, and Right Hand Branch Tobique Rivers, where they unite to form the Tobique River.

Nictaux NS On the **Nictaux River**, south of Middleton, this place was named for the river, called after the Mi'kmaq word *niktawk* ('river forks'), referring to the confluence of the Nictaux with the Annapolis River. Among places with post offices opened in the area are **Nictaux Falls** (1848), **Nictaux West** (1889), and **Nictaux South** (1896).

Nigadoo NB The post office in this village (1967) northwest of Bathurst was named in 1889 after the **Nigadoo River**. An 1807 land petition referred to Nigadoo. The name of the river derives from the Mi'kmaq *anigadoo* (meaning unknown).

Nigel, Mount AB This mountain (3211 m) in the area of Maligne Lake was named in 1898 by British climbers Hugh Stutfield (1858–1929) and Norman Collie (1859–1942), after their guide Nigel Vavasour.

Nipawin SK The post office in this town (1937) on the Saskatchewan River, east of Prince Albert, was named in 1910 after a Cree word meaning 'place where one stands', in reference to the site's broad outlook over the river and surrounding country.

Nipigon ON Now a municipal township in Thunder Bay District, and at the mouth of **Nipigon River**, it was known as *Red Rocks* in 1872, but it was renamed *Nepigon* in 1889 and changed to Nipigon in 1912. The river drains **Lake Nipigon**, whose name derives from the Ojibwa *anemebegong* ('continous water'), referring either to being unable to see the far side of the lake or to the straight route from Lake Superior up the river to the lake.

Nipissing ON The district was named in 1858 after **Lake Nipissing**, and the **Nipissing Township** on the south shore of the lake was named in 1879 after the lake. The lake's name derives from an Algonquin word meaning 'little body of water', referring to its size compared to the Great Lakes, or in contrast to the vast area of Georgian Bay.

Nippers Harbour NL Located on the western side of Notre Dame Bay and southeast of Baie Verte, this municipal community (1964) was first settled in the late 1700s by English immigrants. Although its name may derive from a Nippard family on Fogo Island, as early as 1854 Bishop Edward Feild wrote that the 'Nipper is the largest and most formidable of the mosquitoes' here.

Niut Mountain BC In the Coast Mountains, northeast of Mount Waddington, this mountain (2911 m) was named in 1925 by surveyor V. Dolmage after a Chilcotin legend of a woman who was banished with her husband Tzelos for cannabilism during a time of famine. Subsequently they acquired potatoes from Ashcroft and planted them along the tribe's migration route. They were readmitted to the tribe, and when they died they were turned into the mountains west of Tatlayoko Lake. Potato Range east of the lake recalls the same legend. **Niut Range**, southwest of the mountain, was named in 1910.

Nivelle, Mount BC Near the continental divide and at the head of the Elk River, this location was named in 1918 after Gen. Robert Georges Nivelle (1856–1924), First World War commander of the French armies until 1917.

Niverville MB The name of this town (1993) on the east side of the Red River, south of Winnipeg, was given to a station by the Canadian Pacific Railway in 1877 after Joseph Boucher de Niverville (1715–1804). He had set out from Montreal in 1750 to find the 'Western Sea', returning home four years later without achieving his goal. Postal service was provided in 1879.

Nobel ON The post office in this community in Parry Sound District, northwest of the town of Parry Sound, was named in 1913 by Canadian Industries Limited. The name was after Alfred Bernhard Nobel (1833–96), who invented dynamite in 1866 and established the Nobel prizes for peace, physics, chemistry, physiology and medicine, literature, and economics. The post office here was called *Ambo* from 1911 to 1913.

Nobleford AB A village (1918) northwest of Lethbridge, it was first called *Noble*, after Charles Sherwood Noble (1873–1957), a native of Iowa who homesteaded in 1902 near Claresholm. He accumulated 14,164 ha (35,000 a) of land for the Noble Foundation, which became the largest and highest-yielding farmland in the British Empire. The post office was named in 1918.

Noel NS This community is situated on **Noel Bay** and on the south side of Cobequid Bay in Nova Scotia. The post office here was named in 1832. There were also post offices at **Noel Shore** (1855), **Noel Road** (1883), and **North Noel Road** (1922). The bay was likely named after Acadian settler

Noel Pinet (c.1683–1738), who moved to Île Saint-Jean (now Prince Edward Island) in 1738. The community of **Pinette**, **Pinette River**, and **Pinette Point** in Queens County, southwest of Charlottetown, were named for him.

Nokomis SK Located between Regina and Humboldt, this town (1908) was named in 1906 by postmistress Mrs Thomas Halstead, who admired the name in Longfellow's *Hiawatha*, and related it to the romantic landscape long occupied by the Aboriginals. The town was positioned at a major crossing of the Canadian Pacific Railway's line from Humboldt to Virden, MB, with the Grand Trunk Pacific Railway's line from Winnipeg to Saskatoon. The CPR wanted to call it *Blaikie* in 1907 and the GTP proposed *Blakemore* in 1908, but Nokomis was accepted by both.

Nonacho Lake NT The name of this lake (698 km²) south of Great Slave Lake was approved in 1926. Meaning 'big point lake' in Chipewyan, it was submitted as *Nonachoh Lake* by surveyor G.H. Blanchet (1884–1966). On an earlier map it was identified as *Lady Grey Lake* and on a 1926 map it was called *The Big Lake*.

Nootka Sound BC This large bay on the west coast of Vancouver Island was named *King George's Sound* in 1778 by Capt. James Cook (1728–79), but he changed it to Nootka Sound in the belief that this was the Aboriginal name for it. Cook had asked the Aboriginals what they called it, but they interpreted the sweep of his arms to refer to his trip around the bay, and they responded with something like *nootk sitl* ('to go around'). Claims that it was named *Boca San Lorenzo* four years earlier by Spanish explorer Juan Perez (c.1725–75) appear to be unfounded. It is likely Perez was referring to another bay near Estevan Point, to the southwest, and later explorers equated it with Nootka Sound. **Nootka Island**, to the northwest of Nootka Sound, is the largest island on the west coast of Vancouver Island.

Norfolk ON Lt.-Gov. John Graves Simcoe (1752–1806) named the county in 1792 after the English county. It was united in 1974 with Haldimand County to form the regional municipality of Haldimand-Norfolk. The municipal township of **Norfolk** was also created the same year by amalgamating the village of Port Rowan, the municipal townships of Houghton and North Walsingham, and parts of the municipal townships Middleton and South Walsingham.

Norland ON In 2001 this place north of Lindsay became part of the city of Kawartha Lakes, Victoria County. This place's name was proposed in 1862 by the Reverend Bayard Taylor after Nordland, a village in Africa where he had been working. The 'd' was intentionally omitted, leading to the impression it was located at the end of civilization in the county.

Normanby ON In 2001 this township became a part of the township of West Grey, Grey County. It was named in 1840 after Constantine Henry Phipps, Marquis of Normanby (1797–1863), secretary of state for the colonies in 1839.

Normandin QC This town northwest of Lac Saint-Jean had its beginnings in 1878, when a colony was planted here by businessmen living in Quebec City. The township of Normandin was proclaimed nine years later and named after Joseph-Laurent Normandin, who explored the region in 1832 to determine the limits of the Domaine du Roy, 'the territory reserved exclusively for the King'. The town was formed in 1979 though the merger of the township municipality of Normandin (1899) and the village of Normandin (1926).

Norman Wells NT On the east bank of the Mackenzie River and west of Great Bear Lake, this town (1992) was developed in 1944 after the discovery of oil here. It took its name from *Fort Norman*, now known as Tulita, 75 km upriver at the mouth of Great Bear River.

Normétal QC Located in the regional county of Abitibi-Ouest, near the Ontario border, this municipality was incorporated in 1945. It was named in 1931 by blending the words *nord* and *métallurgique*, an appropriate description of the copper and zinc mines developed here in 1925.

Norquay SK Northeast of Canora, the post office in this town (1963) was named in 1907 by Hugh Wylie, who greatly admired John Norquay (1841–89), premier of Manitoba, 1878–87.

Norquay, Mount AB This mountain (2522 m) on the north side of Banff was named in 1904 after John Norquay, (1841–89), premier of Manitoba, 1878–87, who climbed it in 1888.

Norris Arm NL Located on **Norris Arm** at the southern end of the Bay of Exploits, this town (1971) was permanently settled after 1871. The arm, noted on an 1811 map by Capt. David Buchan, was named after pioneer settler James Norris, whom Lt. John Cartwright mentioned in his book, *A Sketch of the River Exploits*, 1768.

Norris Point NL This municipal community (1960) in Bonne Bay, on the northwestern coast of Newfoundland, was named after the point. The point and the adjacent Neddy Harbour were named after trapper Neddy Norris, who lived here about 1790.

North Battleford SK When the Canadian Northern Railway reached this site on the north bank of the North Saskatchewan River in 1905, opposite the historic town of Battleford, it wanted to call its station Riverview. However, much to the distress of residents of Battleford, the station and the post office were called North Battleford. Created as a village in 1906, it became a town in 1907 and a city in 1913. There is a subdivision in the city called Riverview.

North Bay ON This city (1925) in Nipissing District became a divisional point of the Canadian Pacific Railway in 1881. Although located over 35 km east of the **Great North Bay**, it was identified that year as the 'north bay' of Lake Nipissing, and the post office opened in 1884.

North Bend BC Located in the Fraser Canyon, almost opposite Boston Bar, this settlement was first called *Yankee Flats* and *Yankee Town*, but was renamed by the Canadian Pacific Railway. When the CPR built its transcontinental line from west to east through the province, it had to make a 150-km 'north bend' at Hope, with its easterly direction only restored at Ashcroft. The site of *Boston Bar* post office in 1884, it was renamed North Bend three years later.

North Burgess ON In 1998 this township became part of the township of Bathurst Burgess Sherbrooke. North Burgess was named in 1798, possibly for James B. Burgess, a British member of Parliament, who voted in 1791 for the Canada Bill. In 1841 the part of Burgess Township north of Big Rideau Lake was joined to Lanark County. *See also* South Burgess.

North Buxton ON In 1998 this community became part of the municipality of Chatham-Kent, Kent County. In 1849 this place was founded south of Chatham as a settlement of black Americans and named *Elgin Settlement* after Lord Elgin, the governor of the Province of Canada. It was renamed in 1874 after Sir Thomas Fowell Buxton (1837–1915), a British member of Parliament, who promoted the passing of the 1833 Emancipation Act. *See also* South Buxton.

North, Cape NS This location—the most northerly point of Cape Breton Island—was identified as *Le Çap de Nort* by Nicolas Denys (c.1598–1688) in 1672 and *C. de Nort* by Vincenzo Coronelli (1650–1718) on his map of 1698. *North Cape* occurred on English maps in the mid-1700s, with mapmaker Joseph Frederic Wallet DesBarres (1722–1824) establishing the present form in 1775.

North Cape PE This most northwesterly point of the province was named by Samuel Holland (1728–1801) in 1765. Jacques Cartier (1491–1557) referred to it as *Cap dez Sauvages* in 1534, as he observed an Aboriginal fleeing when his vessel approached the shore. Jacques Nicolas Bellin (1781–1836) called it *Pointe du Nord* in 1744 and subsequent English references called it *North Point*, but North Cape became the traditional usage.

North Cayuga ON Part of the town of Haldimand in Haldimand-Norfolk Region since 1974, the township was named in 1835 after the Cayuga tribe of the Six Nations confederacy. The name has many interpretations, including 'place where the canoes are drawn out', 'mountain rising from the water', and 'advising nation'. *See also* South Cayuga.

North Cowichan BC This district municipality (1873) on Vancouver Island, extending north from Duncan to Chemainus, was named after the Cowichan River and Cowichan Bay. The Cowichan, a Salish tribe that once occupied a large area on both sides of the Strait of Georgia, owe their name to an Island Halkomelem word meaning 'land warmed by the sun', referring to a rock formation on the side of Mount Tzuhalem resembling a frog basking in the sun.

North Crosby ON Crosby Township was created in 1798, and probably named after Brass Crosby (1725–93), Lord Mayor of London, a member of Parliament and a friend of Lt.-Gov. John Graves Simcoe (1752–1806). North Crosby was separated from South Crosby in 1806, with both of them becoming parts of the township of Rideau Lakes in 1998.

North Dorchester ON *Dorchester Township*, created in 1798 in Middlesex County, was named after Sir Guy Carleton, Baron Dorchester (1724–1808), governor of Quebec, 1768–78, commander-in-chief of forces in North America, 1782–6, and governor-in-chief of British North America, 1786–96. It was divided in 1851, with North Dorchester remaining with Middlesex County and South Dorchester transferring to Elgin County. In 2001 North Dorchester Township became part of the municipality of Thames Centre, Middlesex County.

North Dumfries ON This township in the regional municipality of Waterloo is the north half of *Dumfries Township*, named in 1816 by Niagara merchant William Dickson after his birthplace of Dumfries, in Dumfriesshire, Scotland. *See also* South Dumfries.

North Easthope ON Easthope Township in Perth County was named in 1830 for Sir John Easthope (1784–1865), a director of the Canada Company, a British company established in 1826 to develop the Huron Tract, a large area of what is now Southwestern Ontario. It was divided into North Easthope and South Easthope townships in 1843. In 1998 the two townships became parts of the township of Perth East.

North Elmsley ON Elmsley Township was named in 1798 after Upper Canada's chief justice John Elmsley (1762–1805). In 1841 the part of the township north of the Rideau River was attached to Lanark County, with South Elmsley Township remaining in Leeds and Grenville. In 1998 North Elmsley Township became part of the township of Drummond/North Elmsley.

Northern Peninsula NL This 35-km-wide peninsula extends for 225 km from the head of White Bay to L'Anse aux

Meadows. Since the 1960s it has become more commonly called the Great Northern Peninsula.

North Fredericksburgh ON Fredericksburgh Township was named in 1784, likely after Prince Augustus Frederick (1773–1843), sixth son of George III. Frederick's next older brother was honoured in the naming of Ernestown Township to the east, and his next younger brother was honoured in the naming of Adolphustown Township to the west. Since the townships named after the royal children were given in order of birth, it is unlikely that the township was named for George III's second eldest son, Prince Frederick, who was commemorated elsewhere, in Osnabruck Township. Fredericksburgh Township was divided in 1858 into North Fredericksburgh and South Fredericksburgh townships in Lennox and Addington County. In 1998 both of the townships became parts of the town of Greater Napanee.

North Gower ON Gower Township was created in 1798 in Grenville County and was divided into two townships in 1850. North Gower Township became part of Rideau Township in the regional municipality of Ottawa-Carleton in 1974. The original township was named after John Levenson Gower (1740–92), lord of the Admiralty, 1783–89. The post office in the community of **North Gower** was named in 1847. In 2001 Rideau Township became part of the city of Ottawa.

North Hatley QC This village at the north end of Lac Massawippi, southwest of Sherbrooke, was named in 1897 after the municipal township of **Hatley**, erected in 1845. The township of **Hatley** was proclaimed in 1803 and named after a village in Cambridgeshire, England.

North Head NB At the north end of Grand Manan Island, this community was an incorporated village from 1966 to 1995, when it became an urban community in the village of Grand Manan. Its post office opened in 1859. The port here connects the island with the mainland at Blacks Harbour.

North Kent Island NU Located between Ellesmere and Devon Islands, this island (590 km²) was named *Kent Island* in 1853 by Sir Edward Belcher (1682–1757) after Prince Edward Augustus, Duke of Kent (1767–1820), the fourth son of George III and father of Queen Victoria. It was renamed North Kent Island in 1939, but the reason for modifying the name is not apparent in the official records.

North Marysburgh ON In 1998 this township became part of the municipality of Prince Edward County. It was named in 1786 for Princess Mary (1776–1857), fourth daughter of George III and the wife of the Duke of Gloucester, her first cousin. North Marysburgh was separated from South

Marysburgh in 1871. In 1998 both of these townships became parts of Prince Edward County.

North Monaghan ON Monaghan Township in Peterborough County was named in 1820 after County Monaghan, in north central Ireland. In 1850 Monaghan Township was divided into North Monaghan and South Monaghan.

North Nahanni River NT Rising in the Mackenzie Mountains, this river flows into the Mackenzie River, 110 km downriver from Fort Simpson. It was named before 1910 after the Nahanni, an Athapascan tribe in the northern Rocky Mountains and the southern Mackenzie Mountains. *See also* Nahanni Butte *and* South Nahanni River.

North Pender Island BC One of the Gulf Islands, east of Saltspring Island, this island and adjacent South Pender Island were jointly named Pender Island (originally named 'Plunder Island') in 1859–60 by Capt. George Richards (1820–96) after Daniel Pender, who was then master of the survey vessel *Plumper*.

North Plantagenet ON The original Plantagenet Township was named in 1798 after the royal family surname from 1154 to 1485. North Plantagenet was separated from South Plantagenet in 1850, and both remained in the united counties of Prescott and Russell. In 1997 North Plantagenet became part of the township of Alfred and Plantagenet.

North Pole Mountain NB In north central New Brunswick, and adjacent to **North Pole Stream**, this mountain was named in 1964 by Arthur F. Wightman (1905–88), then the provincial names authority. Inspired by the Christmas spirit inherent in the stream's name, Wightman also named mountains after St. Nicholas, and after the eight reindeer (Blitzen, Comet, Cupid, Dancer, Dasher, Donder, Prancer, Vixen) in Clement Moore's 1823 poem *A Visit from Saint Nicholas*. The stream was named by lumbermen in the 1840s, possibly because it was the farthest north they had cut trees, or because the weather was especially cold.

North Portal SK Southeast of Estevan, this village (1903) was created in 1893, when the Soo Line connected with the Canadian Pacific Railway at the forty-ninth parallel. It took its name from the idea of being the entrance to north of the border. A post office opened here in 1894. Portal is on the south side of the boundary of North Dakota.

North River NL On the west side of Conception Bay and south of Bay Roberts, this municipal community (1964) is located on the northwest bank of the river, and extends southwest as far as The Pond That Feeds the Brook. Both the place and the river were earlier known as *Northern Gut*.

North River PE This locality in the town of Cornwall since 1995 was created as a municipal community in 1983. It was named after a school district, established about 1864, and its post office, opened in 1872. They were named after the adjacent river, which was called *Rivière du Nord* by the French. Samuel Holland (1728–1801) named the river in 1765 after John Yorke (1728–69), then lord commissioner of plantations. *Yorke River* remained official until 1966, when it was changed to *North (Yorke) River*, and changed again in 1971 to North River. During the 1800s North River was used interchangeably with *York River*. York Point, at the river's mouth, was named after the river's variant name in the mid-1800s.

North Rustico PE Located northwest of Charlottetown, this municipal community (1983) in the Rustico district was incorporated as a village in 1954. The post office here was named in 1855. The post office at **South Rustico** was called *Rustico* from 1852 to 1967, when it was changed to South Rustico, but closed the following year. **Rusticoville**, situated between the two, had postal service from 1886 and 1947. *See also* Rustico Bay.

North Saanich BC This district municipality (1965) at the north end of the Saanich Peninsula, north of Victoria, takes the second part of its name from the Saanich tribe. Its name in Straits Salish means 'elevated', in reference to Mount Newton (307 m), whose profile looks like a raised rump. *See also* Saanich *and* Central Saanich.

North Saskatchewan River AB, SK Rising in the Columbia Icefield and adjacent to **Mount Saskatchewan** (3342 m), this river (1287 km) flows northeast to Edmonton, where it takes a generally eastern course to join the South Saskatchewan River, 50 km east of Prince Albert, SK. *See also* Saskatchewan River *and* South Saskatchewan River.

North Shore PE This municipal community (1974) north of Charlottetown extends for 6 km along the north shore of the province. It embraces the localities of Covehead Road, West Covehead, Stanhope, and Stanhope by the Sea.

North Sydney NS An urban community in the regional municipality of Cape Breton since 1 August 1985, it was incorporated as a town in 1885. It was named after its location on the north side of **Sydney Harbour**. Postal service was established here in 1837.

Northumberland ON The county was named in 1792 by Lt.-Gov. John Graves Simcoe (1752–1806) after the county of Northumberland in the north of England. In 1850 it was united with Durham County for municipal purposes, but it became an independent county in 1974.

Northumberland Strait NB, NS, PE Located in the southern part of the Gulf of St. Lawrence, this strait was named about 1777 by map-maker Joseph Frederic Wallet DesBarres (1722–1824), after HMS *Northumberland*, the flagship of Adm. Lord Colville (1717–70). In 1765 Samuel Holland (1728–1801) observed that 'the sea betwixt the island and the continent is frequently of a red hue ... by many people called the Red Sea'. Lord Colville undertook a survey of Nova Scotia's North Shore in 1764. **Northumberland County**, NB, was named in 1785, likely after the strait.

North Vancouver BC A district municipality (1891) and a city (1907) on the north shore of Burrard Inlet, they were named for their location relative to the city of Vancouver. The site of the city was called *Moodyville* in 1872 after Sewell Prescott Moody (c.1835–75), who bought a sawmill here in 1864. It was renamed North Vancouver in 1902.

Northwest Miramichi River NB This principal tributary of the Miramichi River rises in north central New Brunswick. Its name in Mi'kmaq, *Elmunokun*, means 'a beaver hole', in reference to Big Hole, at the mouth of the Big Sevogle River. Variant forms of the Aboriginal name appeared on maps between 1686 and 1755, but the lumbermen's descriptive name ultimately prevailed.

Northwest Territories When Canada acquired the Hudson's Bay Company's Rupert's Land and The North-Western Territory from Great Britain in 1870, the combined lands were called North-West Territories. Ten years later Great Britain transferred its rights to the Arctic Archipelago. Meanwhile parts of the present province of Manitoba (1870) and the district of Keewatin (1876) were separated from the territories, and in 1897 the territory of Yukon was taken from it. In 1905 the provinces of Alberta and Saskatchewan were severed from the newly named territory of the Northwest Territories, with Keewatin being restored to it as one of its four districts (the others were Ungava, Mackenzie, and Franklin). In 1912 Ontario and Quebec took away parts of its territory by extending to the shores of Hudson and James bays. Nunavut separated from it in 1999. The residents of the remaining territory had the preference to retain the misnomer, Northwest Territories.

Northwest, Mount YT This mountain (3216 m) in the Centennial Range of the St. Elias Mountains was named in 1967 after the Northwest Territories.

North West River NL This town (1958), northeast of Happy Valley-Goose Bay, is situated on the east side of the mouth of the Naskaupi River, where it flows into Lake Melville. The town was named after an earlier name of the river. A French trading post was established here in 1742, and a Hudson's Bay Company post was opened in 1836.

North Wiltshire PE This community is located south of Hunter River in the Wiltshire district. The school district here was called *New Wiltshire* from about 1846 to about 1875, when it became North Wiltshire, the name of the railway station. The post office opened as *New Wiltshire* in 1863, and was only changed to North Wiltshire in 1967, with this becoming the name of the municipal community in 1974. The school district was likely named after the English county.

North York ON Separated from York Township in 1922, North York Township became a borough in Metropolitan Toronto in 1967, and then a city in 1979. In 1998, along with the other boroughs in the Metropolitan area, North York became part of the city of Toronto.

Norton NB The post office in this village (1966), southwest of Sussex, was called *Fingerboard* in 1840. It was changed to *Norton Station* in 1869 and became Norton in 1900. It was named after **Norton Parish**, created in 1795 and named after Norton, MA, near Taunton.

Norway House MB Located on the eastern shore of Little Playgreen Lake, an enlargement of the main channel of the Nelson River, this Cree reserve has its roots in the building of a winter road from York Factory to the Red River Settlement in 1814 by Norwegian axemen employed by the Hudson's Bay Company. First located at the Lake Winnipeg outlet, 25 km to the south, the community was moved to its present site in 1826 to avoid the possibility of its original location being destroyed by a flood. Its post office opened in 1904.

Norwegian Bay NU Surrounded by Ellesmere, Devon, Cornwall, and Axel Heiberg Islands, this water body was named *Norske Bugten* in 1900 by Otto Sverdrup (1854–1930), after his fellow countrymen.

Norwich ON This township in Oxford County was named in 1795, when it was part of Norfolk County, and took its name from the largest city in Norfolk, England. When Oxford County was restructured in 1975, the municipal townships of North and South Norwich (created in 1856), the village of Norwich (incorporated in 1876), and the municipal township of East Oxford were united as the municipal township of Norwich.

Norwood ON This village (1877) in Peterborough County, east of the city of Peterborough, was named in 1841 by Harriet Maria (Keeler) Groves, who was reading a book about a suburb called Norwood on the south side of London, England. She also noted that its site was in the woods, north of the family's former home of Colborne.

Notre Dame Bay NL On the north coast of Newfoundland, this large bay extends from Cape St. John, east of Baie Verte, to Joe Batt's Point on Fogo Island. The bay was likely named by French explorers in the 1500s after the Virgin Mary. It

was generally known to the Portuguese as *baia verde*, which has survived in the name Green Bay, a small bay on its south-western side.

Notre-Dame-de-Bon-Secours QC Located east of Chambly, this municipality was created in 1989, having been made a parish municipality in 1869. The name celebrates the feast day (24 May) of Our Lady of Perpetual Help. Its post office has been called Village-Richelieu since 1864.

Notre Dame de Lourdes MB A post office at this village (1963), south of Portage la Prairie, was opened in 1892. In the 1880s a seminary was founded here for the training of priests of the new order of Canons Régulaires, which was later broken up after a decree from Rome changed its rules. Lourdes in southwestern France is where the Virgin Mary revealed herself as the Immaculate Conception to Marie Bernarde Soubirous (St. Bernadette) in 1858.

Notre-Dame-de-Lourdes QC This parish municipality north of Joliette was named in 1925. It was given in honour of the sanctuary of Lourdes, in France's Hautes-Pyrénées, where the Blessed Virgin appeared to Marie Bernarde Soubirous (St. Bernadette) in 1858. The post office here has been called Lourdes-de-Joliette since 1930.

Notre-Dame-du-Bon-Conseil QC This village northeast of Drummondville was named in 1957. The religious parish of Notre-Dame-du-Bon-Conseil was created in 1895, and the municipal parish of the same name followed three years later. The original parish may have been named after the Sisters of Our Lady of Good Counsel, which provided Christian education and instruction here.

Notre-Dame-du-Lac QC Located on the western shore of Lac Témiscouata, southeast of Rivière-du-Loup, this community was created a parish municipality in 1871, became a village in 1949, and was elevated to town status in 1968. The religious parish was named in 1869.

Notre-Dame-du-Laus QC Situated north of Buckingham, this municipality was created in 1946, taking its name from its post office, opened in 1878. The religious parish, established in 1873, was named after Laus in France's Hautes-Alpes, where there were some 600 apparitions of the Virgin Mary between 1664 and 1718.

Notre-Dame-du-Mont-Carmel QC This parish municipality between Trois-Rivières and Shawinigan was erected in 1859, a year after the religious parish was established. The name may be traced to an order of monks established in the twelfth century at the foot of Mount Carmel in the Holy Land, where an order of Carmelite nuns was permitted to affiliate in the fifteenth century.

Notre-Dame-du-Nord QC Located at the head of Lake Timiskaming, this municipality was established in 1928, taking its name from the religious parish, created in 1895.

Notre-Dame-du-Portage QC Situated on the south shore of the St. Lawrence, southwest of Rivière-du-Loup, this municipality was created in 1856 and named after the religious parish. The parish was named by Mgr. Charles-François Baillargeon, who had a considerable devotion to the Immaculate Conception of the Virgin Mary. The portage is in reference to the point where the land route from Halifax reached the St. Lawrence in the 1780s.

Notre-Dame, Monts QC These mountains, part of the continental Appalachian chain, extend from Sherbrooke to Gaspé. Jacques Cartier (1491–1557) may have named them on 15 August 1535, the feast day of the Assumption of the Blessed Virgin Mary. In 1544 pilot Jean Alfonse *dit* Fonteneau mentioned the *montz Nostre Dame* four times in his *Cosmographie*.

Nottawasaga ON The township in Simcoe County was named in 1832 after the **Nottawasaga River**, which rises in Dufferin County, north of Orangeville. The river's name was taken from Ojibwa *Nahdowasaga* ('outlet of the river of the Iroquois'). In 1994 the municipal township, the town of Stayner, the village of Creemore, and the municipal township of Sunnidale were merged to form the municipal township of Clearview. *See also* Wasaga Beach.

Nouvelle QC This municipality north of the mouth of the Restigouche River was named in 1953, recalling the names of the mission (1834), the religious parish (1868), and the post office (1881). It was given in memory of Jesuit Fr. Henri Nouvel (c.1621–1702), who was a missionary among the Aboriginals of the north shore of the St. Lawrence and the Gaspé from 1663 to 1669, after which he went to the Great Lakes area to minister in several missions for the following 32 years.

Novar ON Located in Parry Sound District, north of Huntsville, a post office here was named in 1887 by miller Alexander McGillivray after his birthplace in Ross and Cromarty, Scotland, northeast of Dingwall.

Nova Scotia The province was named on 29 September 1621 in the grant to Sir William Alexander (1567–1640) of the 'lands lying between New England and Newfoundland ... to be known as Nova Scotia, or New Scotland'. At that time it included the areas of present-day Prince Edward Island (separated in 1769) and New Brunswick (1784).

Nova Scotia, Mount YT This mountain (3292 m) in the Centennial Range of the St. Elias Mountains was named in 1967 after the province.

Nueltin Lake MB, NU On the sixtieth parallel, this lake (2033 km²) was identified as *Nu-thel-tin-tu-eh* by geologist Joseph Burr Tyrrell in 1894. Tyrrell determined that in Chipewyan the name meant 'sleeping island lake'.

Nunavut This new territory was created in 1993, to come into being on 1 April 1999. It consisted of the administrative regions of Keewatin, Baffin, and Kitikmeot, which together comprise all the former district of Keewatin, the northeastern part of the district of Mackenzie, and most of the Arctic Archipelago in the district of Franklin, except Banks and Prince Patrick Islands and parts of Victoria and Melville Islands, with some smaller islands in the Northwest Territories. In Inuktitut Nunavut means 'our land'.

Nyland, Mount BC This mountain (2789 m) in the Coast Mountains, southeast of Bella Coola, was named in 1962 after Pvt. Arthur W. Nyland of Bella Coola, who was killed in action on 19 February 1945.

Oak Bay BC This district municipality (1906) on the east side of Victoria was named after the adjacent **Oak Bay**, identified on Capt. Henry Kellett's 1847 chart.

Oak Bay NB The name of this bay east of St. Stephen derives from the Passamaquoddy *Wahquaeek* ('head of the bay'). The name changed from *Waughweig* in the 1780s through *Aouk Bay* to *Oak Point Bay* before 1800. Waweig River flows into the east side of the bay. There were post offices in the communities of Oak Bay (1847) and Waweig (1859), but both closed in 1969.

Oak Island NS On the west side of Mahone Bay, this 1.3 km² island has been the legendary site of hidden treasure since 1795, when three men uncovered a shaft dug into the ground. Subsequent digging to 29.5 m and lowering of a camera to a depth of 60 m have failed to reveal any buried treasure.

Oak Lake MB Located 10 km northeast of **Oak Lake** and west of Brandon, the Canadian Pacific Railway established a station here in 1882, at what is now the smallest (population 359) town (1907) in the province. The town was earlier called *Flat Creek*. The lake was known as *Lac des Chênes*, named for the mature oak trees that lined the east side of the lake, conspicuous from the more commonly seen scrub oak.

Oakland ON This township in Brant County was named in 1821 after the ridge of oak trees extending through the area. The community of **Oakland** was first called *Perth* and *Malcolm's Mills*, and its post office was named Oakland in 1840. In 1999 the township became part of the County of Brant.

Oakville ON On the Lake Ontario shore, this town (1857) in Halton Region was founded in 1827 by Col. William Chisholm (1788–1842), and named in 1835 by his friend Robert Baldwin Sullivan (1802–53) after the great white oaks which supported the local oak stave industry. Sullivan was then the mayor of Toronto, and was later appointed to the Executive Council.

Oakwood ON In 2001 this place became part of the city of Kawartha Lakes, Victoria County. West of Lindsay, this community's post office was named in 1843 by Joseph Pearson after the extensive oak woods in the area.

Observatory Inlet BC Extending 70 km from the head of Portland Inlet, northeast of Prince Rupert, this inlet was named in 1793 by Capt. George Vancouver (1757–98), who set up his chronometers at its mouth and amended his latitude and longitude positions.

Odessa ON In 1998 this community became part of the Loyalist Township, Lennox and Addington County. West of Kingston, its post office was called *Mill Creek* in 1838 after mills built on what is now Millhaven Creek. The community was renamed in 1855 after the city in present-day Ukraine, then under siege by the British during the Crimean War.

Odessa SK This village (1911) southeast of Regina was founded in 1904 by settlers from the area of Odessa in Ukraine. The Canadian Northern Railway station was established here in 1907. Its post office was called *Magna* in 1908, *Odessa Station* in 1910, and simply Odessa in 1938.

Ogema SK This town (1913) west of Weyburn was named in 1910 when the post office opened and the Canadian Pacific Railway's survey for a line was laid out. Settlers here wanted to call it Omega, which is Greek for 'end', referring to the fact that it was at the end of the line. They were told Omega was already in use, so the letters were jumbled to form Ogema, which coincidentally is also the word in Cree and Saulteaux for 'chief'.

Ogidaki Mountain ON This elevation rising to 665 m in Algoma District, northeast of Sault Ste. Marie, was named in 1966 after the Ojibwa for 'high ground'. It was then believed to be the highest point in Ontario, but in 1972 Ishpatina Ridge, north of Sudbury, was discovered to be the highest point in the province at 685 m.

Ogilvie Mountains YT In the west central part of the territory and northeast of the Yukon River, this chain of mountains was named *Ogilvie Range* in 1898 after William Ogilvie (1846–1912), and was changed to its present name in 1948. Ogilvie made the first survey of the Yukon–Alaska boundary in 1887–8 and laid out the townsite of Dawson in 1896. He was the commissioner of the Yukon from September 1898 to April 1901.

Ogre Mountain BC Located in the Coast Mountains, southeast of Bella Coola, this mountain (2880 m) was named in 1960 because its profile resembled that of Mont Ogre in Switzerland.

Oil City ON In 2001 this community became part of the township of Brooke-Alvinston, Lambton County. Located southeast of Sarnia, this community's post office was named in 1874 after the oil boom 15 years earlier. Never incorporated, its population was about 270 in 2001.

Oil Springs ON The post office in this village (1864) in Lambton County, southeast of Sarnia, was named in 1859, when North America's first commercial oil field was developed here. Its population was 758 in 2001.

Oka QC Located on the north shore of Lac des Deux Montagnes, west of Montreal, Oka describes both a municipality and a parish municipality, each with nearly identical populations of some 1660. The municipality was erected as the parish municipality of *L'Annonciation* in 1875, and the current name was adopted in 1953 to match the postal name, given in 1867. The parish municipality was called the municipality of *L'Annonciation-Partie-Nord* in 1918, and was changed to its present name in 1977. It annexed the town of *Oka-sur-le-Lac* (1942) in 1982. Oka is said to derive from the name of an Algonquin chief, who is named after a variety of pike.

Okanagan Lake BC This lake (361 km²) in the southern interior of the province was noted in 1811 as *Ookanawgan* by geographer David Thompson (1770–1857). The origin of the name is uncertain. It may refer to the 'farthest point' on the **Okanagan River**, near **Okanagan Falls** and south of Penticton, which was as far upstream as salmon ascended. The river (314 km) drains south into the state of Washington, where the Okanogan River joins the Columbia, 83 km south of the border. The Okanogan, an important division of the Interior Salish, occupied a large territory in the Okanagan and Columbia River valleys. In the late 1860s, Gov. Frederick Seymour (1820–69) of British Columbia decided on the spelling Okanagan to differentiate it from Okanogan south of the border.

Okotoks AB This town (1904) south of Calgary was named *Dewdney* in 1894 by the Canadian Pacific Railway after Sir Edgar Dewdney (1835–1916), lieutenant-governor of the North-West Territories, 1882–8, minister of the interior, 1888–92, and lieutenant-governor of British Columbia, 1892–7. It was renamed in 1897 after the Blackfoot designation of a glacial erratic called the Big Rock, 8 km west of the town.

Old Crow YT This community at the junction of the **Old Crow** and Porcupine Rivers was founded in 1911 by the Gwitch'in. They had moved in 1869 from Fort Yukon, on American territory in Alaska, to Old Rampart House, which they assumed was in British territory. When it was found in

1889 to be in Alaska, they moved again to Rampart House, just east of the border, and, after a smallpox epidemic, they moved yet again to the present site. The place was named after a respected chief called Tshim-Gevtik, which meant 'Walking Crow'.

Olden ON In 1998 this township became a part of the township of Central Frontenac, Frontenac County. It was named about 1823 after John Olden, its first surveyor, who carved his name and the date 'June 12, 1831' in a tree.

Oldman River AB Rising in the Rocky Mountains west of Claresholm, this river flows south and then east through Fort Macleod and Lethbridge. Joining the Bow River west of Medicine Hat, the two continue east as the South Saskatchewan River. At the point where Livingstone River joins the Oldman, northwest of Pincher Creek, was 'Old man's playing ground', marked by a cairn of rocks, each one placed there as a sign of good luck before its bearer entered the mountains. The mythical 'Old man' was called *Apistoki* by the Blackfoot, and *Wisukishak* by the Cree. *See also* Belly River.

Old Perlican NL The name of this place, located northeast of Carbonear on the southeast shore of Trinity Bay, was recorded as early as 1597 as *Parlican*, with *Le Vieux Perlican* occurring 100 years later. Jacques Nicolas Bellin (1703–72) identified a small island offshore as *I du Vieux Perlican* in 1754. A community 35 km southwest on the same shore was recorded as *Little Pernocan* as early as 1669, but eight years later was referred to by its present name, **New Perlican**. The meaning of 'perlican' as a designation for geographical features is possibly related to the 'pelican', perhaps an erroneous description of another bird encountered here.

Olds AB South of Red Deer, this town (1905) was named in 1892 by the Canadian Pacific Railway after George Olds, a CPR traffic manager. It was previously called *Lone Pine* and *6th Siding*.

Old Wives Lake SK Located 37 km southwest of Moose Jaw, this lake recalls a story of Cree hunters and their families being pursued in the early 1800s by the Blackfoot, after the Cree had a successful hunt for buffalo meat. To allow the men, younger women, and children to escape, the older women hatched a plan to give the appearance that the entire party remained camped at the lake overnight. However, the next morning the Blackfoot found that only the older women had tended the fires, and in their fury they killed them all. About 1900 the lake was named after Sir Frederick John W. Johnstone (1715–74), who had hunted in the area. Nevertheless, the name Old Wives Lake persisted in local use and was officially restored in 1953.

O'Leary PE This municipal community (1983) in the western part of the province was incorporated as a village in 1951.

It was named after the road, which had been named after Michael O'Leary, who came from Ireland in 1837 and lived at the West Cape end of O'Leary Road. The community's post office was called *O'Leary Station* in 1877, and received its present name in 1967.

Oliver BC The post office in this town (1991) on the Okanagan River, south of Penticton, was named in 1921 after John Oliver (1856–1927), premier of the province, 1918–27. It was during his administration that an extensive irrigation project was undertaken in the area to provide land for returning First World War veterans. *See also* John Oliver, Mount.

Oliver ON This township in Thunder Bay District, west of the city of Thunder Bay, was named in 1874 after Adam Oliver (1823–82), a member of the Legislative Assembly of Ontario, 1867–75, and an owner of the Fort William (now part of Thunder Bay) lumbering firm Oliver, Davidson and Company.

Omemee ON In 2001 this village (1873) became part of the city of Kawartha Lakes, Victoria County. Southeast of Lindsay, it was first called *Williamstown*, *Emily*, and *Metcalfe*, before the post office was renamed Omemee in 1857, after the Omemee (Pigeon) subtribe of the Mississauga who once hunted here.

Omerville QC This village in the regional county of Memphrémagog, on the north side of the town of Magog, was erected in 1945. Its post office was open from 1950 to 1974. It was named after Magog butcher Omer Gaudreau, who acquired a farm here in 1932, divided it into village lots in 1945, and became the village's first mayor.

Omineca Mountains BC Located west of Williston Lake, this group of mountains was named before 1910 after the **Omineca River**, which rises in the Hogem Ranges and flows east into the lake, opposite its Peace Arm. In Sekani its name may mean 'sluggish river', or 'lake-like'.

Onaping Falls ON In 2001 this town became part of the city of Greater Sudbury, Sudbury Region. It was created in 1973 by amalgamating the townships of Levack and Dowling, as well as the improvement district of Onaping, which had been laid out as a township in 1911, and named after **Onaping Lake**. The name may derive from the Ojibwa word *onapina* ('I harness it'), possibly referring to the Onaping Dam.

Onderdonk, Mount BC Located in the Selkirk Mountains, north of Revelstoke, this mountain (2694 m) was named in 1971 by mountaineers William Lowell Putnam and Roger W. Laurilla after Andrew Onderdonk (1849–1905), a railway engineer who supervised the construction of the Canadian Pacific Railway through the Fraser Canyon in the early 1880s.

100 Mile House BC This district municipality (1991) in the Cariboo was established in 1862 on the Cariboo Road, 100 miles (161 km) northeast of Lillooet. A post office opened here in 1916, and the community became a village in 1965.

Oneida ON This township in the regional municipality of Haldimand-Norfolk was named in 1835 after the Oneida tribe of the Six Nations confederacy. Oneida may be an ancient name meaning 'upright stone', after a syenite boulder near their early home in central New York.

Onondaga ON In 1999 this township became part of the county of Brant. It was named in 1840 after the Onondaga nation, a member of the Six Nations confederacy, originally from the Lake Oneida and Syracuse area of New York. The name means 'on the mountain'.

Onoway AB In 2005 this village (1923) located 45 km northwest of Edmonton became a town. Its post office was named in 1904. It may have been named after the singer Onaway in Longfellow's *Hiawatha*. Alternatively, the name may derive from the Ojibwa for 'good meadow', chosen by first postmaster W.P. Beaupre, because he could not call the post office Beaupre ('good meadow') since Beaupré was already in use in Quebec.

Onslow NS Located on the north side of Truro, this place was named after Onslow Township, established in 1759. The township was named after Arthur Onslow (1691–1768), speaker of the British House of Commons, 1727–54. Onslow post office opened in 1855, with subsequent offices in the area called **Onslow Upper** (1854), **Central Onslow** (1866), **Onslow Mountain** (1884), **Onslow Station** (1884), and **Lower Onslow** (1884).

Ontario Ontario Ontario was first used for the lake in the Jesuit *Relation* of 1641. In 1656 map-maker Nicolas Sanson (1600–67) described it as *Ontario, ou Lac de St Louys*. René de Bréhant de Galinée (1645–78) in 1670 referred to it simply as *Lac Ontario*. Three years later explorer Louis Jolliet (1645–1700) called it *Lac Frontenac ou Ontario*, and explorer René-Robert Cavelier de La Salle (1643–87) in 1684 described it only as *Lac Frontenac*, given in honour of the colonial governor. By the mid-1700s only *Lac Ontario* was shown on maps, with **Lake Ontario** being adopted by the British. In 1683 Fr. Louis Hennepin (1626–c.1705) said it meant 'beautiful lake'. The Huron word for 'lake' is *ontare*, and similiar words are used in the other Iroquoian languages. The main islands at the eastern end of Lake Ontario formed the first *Ontario County* in 1792. The second was created in 1849 from the east side of York County, and separated from it in 1853. In 1974 all of *Ontario County*, except Mara and Rama townships (now Ramara Township in Simcoe County), was transferred to the regional municipality of Durham.

The province was officially named in 1867, and extended to its present limits in the north in 1912.

Ontario, Mount YT This mountain (3719 m) in the Centennial Range of the St. Elias Mountains was named in 1967 after the province.

Ootsa Lake BC The name of this part of the Nechako Reservoir, on the north side of Tweedsmuir Provincial Park, derives from the Carrier *yootsoo* ('very low down' or 'way down towards the water').

Ops ON In 2001 this township became part of the city of Kawartha Lakes, Victoria County. It was named in 1821, likely by Lt.-Gov. Sir Peregrine Maitland (1777–1854), after the Roman goddess of plenty and fertility. She was the wife of Saturn and the mother of Jupiter.

Orangeville ON This town (1873) in Dufferin County was named about 1845 for Orange Lawrence (1796–1861), a Connecticut native who developed mills at the site and was the first postmaster in 1851. It was earlier called *The Mill*.

Or, Cape d' NS Extending into Minas Channel, this cape was named *Cap d'Or* by Samuel de Champlain (1567–1635) in 1604, when he discovered outcroppings of copper here. He called the southern arm of the Bay of Fundy *Bassin des Mines*, which resulted in the names Minas Basin and Minas Channel.

Orford ON In 1998 this township became part of the municipality of Chatham-Kent, Kent County. It was named in 1794 after the town of Orford in Suffolk, England, and near the North Sea.

Orford, Mont QC Located northwest of the town of Magog, this 850-m mountain dominates the landscape of the township municipality of **Orford**, which was created in 1855. It took its name from the township, proclaimed in 1801 and named after a village in Suffolk, England. The area of the mountain was set aside as a 60-km² recreational park in 1933.

Orillia ON The township in Simcoe County was named by Lt.-Gov. Sir Peregrine Maitland (1777–1854) in 1822 after the Spanish *orilla* ('bank' or 'shore'). In 1994 it was united with the village of Coldwater and the municipal township of Matchedash to form the municipal township of Severn. The village (1867), the town (1874), and the city (1969) of **Orillia** were first known as *Invermara*, *The Narrows*, and *Newtown*, and its post office was called Orillia in 1836.

Orléans ON Since 2001 the sector of **Orléans** has been in the city of Ottawa. Before 2001 it was divided between the city of Gloucester and the municipal township of Cumberland, Ottawa-Carleton Region. Its post office was named in 1860,

probably by first postmaster Théodore Besserer (1785–1861), after his birthplace on Île d'Orléans, downriver from Quebec City.

Orléans, Île d' QC Considered one of the continent's prettiest pastoral landscapes, this island was named by Jacques Cartier (1491–1557) in 1536, likely after Henri II, Duc d'Orléans (1595–1663), the second son of François I (1494–1547), king of France (1515–47). A year earlier Cartier had called it *Isle de Bascuz* (recalling Bacchus, the Roman god of wine) for the strong vines he found here.

Ormstown QC Located southwest of Montreal, this village was incorporated in 1889, taking its name from its post office, opened in 1836. The origin of the name is uncertain, though the most common explanation is that it was named after the son of merchant Alexander Ellice (1743–1805), who bought the seigneury of Beauharnois in 1795. However, Ellice did not have a son called Orm. In 1905 the village clerk said that the name was chosen 20 years before for a station name, from a road that was named in the 1820s after a noted person called Ormiston in Britain. It may have had a connection with Ormiston Corners in New York.

Oro ON This township in Simcoe County was named in 1820 by Lt.-Gov. Sir Peregrine Maitland (1777–1854) after the Spanish word for 'gold'. In January 1994 Oro was joined with the township of Medonte to form the municipal township of **Oro-Medonte**.

Oromocto NB This town (1956) southeast of Fredericton was laid out in the 1950s to accommodate the headquarters and residential areas of Canadian Forces Base Gagetown, although Oromocto post office opened over a century earlier in 1843. **Oromocto River** has North and South branches that rise in **Oromocto Lake** and **South Oromocto Lake** respectively, and its name derives from the Maliseet *Welamooktook* ('fine river'), in reference to how easily it is navigated by canoe. In the late 1600s the river's name was usually spelled as variations of *Ramouctou*, with the present form being introduced by surveyors general Charles Morris (1731–1802) and Thomas Sproule (1741–1817) in the late 1700s.

Osgoode ON In 2001 this township became part of the city of Ottawa. It was named in 1798 after William Osgoode (1754–1824), chief justice of Upper Canada, 1792–4, and of Lower Canada, 1794–1801. The post office in the community of **Osgoode** was called *Osgoode Station* in 1880, and was shortened to Osgoode in 1962. Osgoode Hall, the Toronto headquarters of the Law Society of Upper Canada, was constructed in 1829–32. *See also* Metcalfe.

Oshawa ON This city (1924) in Durham Region was first known as *Skae's Corners*, after merchant Edward Skae. At a meeting in 1840, the name *Sydenham* was chosen in honour of Charles Edward Poulett Thomson, Baron Sydenham (1799–1841), governor-in-chief of British North America, 1839–41. Local trader Moody Farewell invited two Mississauga friends from Rice Lake to propose a more original name. They suggested *ajawi*, signifying 'crossing to the other side' or 'shore of a river or lake', and the name Oshawa evolved from it.

Osler SK North of Saskatoon, this town (1985) was named in 1890 after Sir Edmund Boyd Osler (1845–1924), member for West Toronto in the House of Commons, 1896–1917, president of the Dominion Bank from 1901, and a founder of the financial firm of Osler, Hammond and Nanton in Winnipeg. The firm contracted to build the Canadian Pacific Railway lines in western Canada.

Osnabruck ON In 1998 this township became part of the township of South Stormont, united counties of Stormont, Dundas, and Glengarry. It was named in 1787 after a title of the second son of George III, Frederick, the Duke of York and Albany (1763–1827). A year after his birth, he was appointed to the hereditary office of bishop of Osnabrück, which he abandoned in 1803. Osnabrück is a city in Germany's Lower Saxony.

Oso ON In 1998 this township became a part of the township of Central Frontenac, Frontenac County. It was named in 1823 by Lt.-Gov. Sir Peregrine Maitland (1777–1854) after the Spanish word for 'bear'.

Osoyoos BC On the eastern shore of **Osoyoos Lake** and near the Washington state border, this town (1983) was established in 1865 as a customs post. It took its name from the Okanagan *sooyoos* ('sand bar across'), referring to a bar that almost cuts the lake in half. Peter O'Reilly of Hope may have suggested adding 'O' to the name to give it dignity.

Osprey ON In 2001 this township became part of the municipality of Grey Highlands, Grey County. It was named in 1822, likely by Lt.-Gov. Sir Peregrine Maitland (1777–1854), after the osprey, a large bird of prey.

Otonabee ON In 1998 this township became part of the township **Otonabee–South Monaghan**, Peterborough County. It was named in 1820 after the **Otonabee River**, which flows southwest from Katchewanooka Lake through the city of Peterborough to Rice Lake. The name is from an Ojibwa word, such as *odonimaseebi* ('mouth water'), in reference to the place where the river empties into Rice Lake through a delta.

Ottawa ON Queen Victoria chose Ottawa as the capital of Canada in 1857, after being advised by Gov. Gen. Sir Edmund Head (1805–68) and Henry Labouchere (1798–

1869), secretary of state for the colonies. It had become a city two years earlier, having been incorporated as the town of *Bytown* in 1850. The name Ottawa was chosen in 1854 in honour of the two hundredth anniversary of the first flotilla of furs brought from the west side of Lake Michigan by the Ottawa and other Aboriginals to trade with the French. The townsite was developed in 1827 by Lt. Col. John By (1781–1836) on the instructions of Lord Dalhousie (1812–60), governor-in-chief of British North America. By 2001 the city of Ottawa had taken over the cities of Kanata, Vanier, Nepean, Gloucester, and Cumberland, the townships of West Carleton, Goulbourn, Osgoode, and Rideau, and the village of Rockcliffe Park. These municipalities were in the regional municipality of *Ottawa-Carleton*, which no longer existed after 2001.

Ottawa River ON Samuel de Champlain (1567–1635) referred to the river in 1613 as *Rivière du Nord* and *Grande rivière des Algommequins*. By the late 1600s it was called *Rivière des Outaouacs*, which was subsequently rendered as *Rivière de l'Outaouais* by the French, and as Ottawa River by the British. The Ottawa, an Algonquian nation, were known to the Huron as *Andatahouats*, noted as early as 1623–4 by Récollet brother Gabriel Sagard (c.1599–1636), and referred to as *Ondataouaouat, Outaouacs*, and *Outaouak* in the Jesuit *Relations* of the mid-1800s. Ottawa has been interpreted as being from *adawe*, used in Algonquin, Cree, Ojibwa, and other Algonquian languages to mean 'trade' and 'buy and sell'.

Otterburn Park QC Located on the east bank of the Richelieu, south of Mont-Saint-Hilaire, this place became a municipality in 1953 and a town in 1969. It was named after a Grand Trunk Railway station, which was named in 1871 for Otterburn in Northumberland, England, the birthplace of Sir Joseph Hickson (1830–97), general manager of GTR, 1874–97.

Ouimet Canyon ON Located northeast of Thunder Bay, this gorge was named after the nearby Canadian Pacific Railway station of Ouimet. The station was named for Joseph-Aldéric Ouimet (1848–1916), who served in a military expedition sent to the West in 1885 to subdue the North-West Rebellion. He was the minister of public works in Ottawa, 1892–6.

Outaouais, Communauté-Urbaine-de-l' QC The urban community is coextensive with the city of Gatineau, having embraced the cities Hull and Aylmer, and the towns Buckingham and Masson-Angers in 1995. The urban community was created in 1991. In 1971 the *Communauté regionale de l'Outaouais* was established, which then also included the present regional county of Les Collines-de-l'Outaouais, the territory immediately north of the city of Gatineau. *See also* Ottawa River.

Outardes, Rivière aux QC This major river on the north shore of the St. Lawrence flows south parallel to Rivière Manicouagan for almost 400 km. Identified on the mid-1700 maps of Jacques Nicolas Bellin (1703–72), its name originates from the Canada goose. The bird was described as an *outarde* in 1535 by Jacques Cartier (1491–1657), presuming it to be the equivalent of the European bustard, which is not native to North America.

Outhouse Point NB Extending into the Petitcodiac River, opposite Moncton, this point was likely named after Edwin Outhouse. An early settler in Coverdale Parish, his father was a Loyalist who received a land grant in Sackville Parish.

Outlook SK This town (1909) south of Saskatoon and on the east bank of the South Saskatchewan River was founded in 1908 by J.L. Doupe, a land commissioner for the Canadian Pacific Railway. Presumably the commissioner was impressed with the views up and down the river, and off toward the horizon, and proposed the name. Its post office was established that year as well.

Outram, Mount AB This mountain (3240 m), near the head of the North Saskatchewan River and north of Howse Pass, was named in 1921 by the Alberta–British Columbia Boundary Commission after climber Sir James Outram (1864–1925), grandson of Gen. Sir James Outram, who served in India. Settling in Victoria in 1900, he made many first ascents in the Rocky Mountains, including Mount Assiniboine.

Outram, Mount BC Located in the Cascade Mountains southeast of Hope, this mountain (2454 m) was named about 1858 by Hudson's Bay Company factor Alexander C. Anderson after his uncle, Gen. Sir James Outram (1803–63). Outram was one of the relievers of Lucknow, India, in 1857.

Outremont QC In 2002 this city became a borough of the city of Montreal. Located on the north side of Mount Royal, this city's name means literally 'beyond the mountain'. The Le Bouthillier family called their residence Outremont before the place was incorporated as a village in 1875, and as a town 20 years later.

Owen Sound ON This city (1920) in Grey County was called *Sydenham* in 1840 after the adjoining bay, which had been named after Charles Edward Poulett Thomson, Baron Sydenham (1799–1841), governor-in-chief of British North America, 1839–41. However, two decades before, Admiralty surveyor Henry W. Bayfield (1795–1885) had named the harbour after Adm. Sir Edward Campbell Rich Owen (1771–1849). Navigators called the harbour *Owen's Sound*, and this name was chosen for the post office in 1846. *Sydenham* was named the county seat in 1854, but three years later it became the town of Owen Sound, with the post office changing to this form.

Oxbow SK This town (1904) was named in 1884 by Mary (Stalker) Baird for the Canadian Pacific Railway. It is located at a pronounced 'ox bow' of the Souris River, having the appearance of part of a yoke used to harness a pair of draft oxen.

Oxford ON This county was created in 1798 and named after the English city and county west of London, following Lt.-Gov. John Graves Simcoe's proposal in 1793 that Oxford be established up the Thames River from London. **Oxford Township** was also created 1798. In 1845 it was divided into the municipal township of *East Oxford* (part of Norwich Township since 1975) and the municipal township of *West Oxford* (part of South-West Oxford Township, also since 1975). On the north side of the river, the municipal township of *North Oxford* was organized in 1850, but was merged with the municipal township of Zorra in 1975.

Oxford House MB Located on the north shore of **Oxford Lake**, at the point where Hayes River flows toward the north, this community was the site of a Hudson's Bay Company post established by William Sinclair in 1798. The post office here opened in 1950. The lake was called by the Cree *Pethapaw Nipi* ('lake with bottomless hole'), which was misleadingly rendered as *Holy Lake*.

Oxford-on-Rideau ON In 1998 this township became a part of the township of North Grenville, united counties of Leeds and Grenville. It was named in 1798 after the English city and county west of London. To differentiate it from Oxford County, and East, North, and West Oxford townships, it became the municipal township of Oxford-on-Rideau in 1850. **Oxford Mills**, southwest of Kemptville, was named in 1852.

Oyen AB This town (1965), east of Hanna and near the Saskatchewan border, was named in 1912 by the Canadian Northern Railway after settler Andrew Oyen (1870–1937). He arrived here in 1909 from the United States, having left Norway in 1887.

Pabok QC On the north shore of Chaleur Bay and south of Gaspé, this regional county was named in 1981. An earlier form of the name Pabos occurred in a 1753 register of births, marriages, and burials. The municipality of **Pabos** was erected in 1876. Several meanings have been advanced for both Pabok and Pabos, with the most convincing being the Mi'kmaq word *papôg* ('calm waters').

Pacific Rim National Park BC Located on the west coast of Vancouver Island, this national park (389 km²), created in 1970, comprises three distinct parts between Tofino, on the northwest, and Port Renfrew, on the southeast—a distance of 105 km. It also extends offshore to the 10-fathom line.

Pacquet NL Located on the north coast of Newfoundland and midway between Baie Verte and La Scie, this municipal community (1962) on the northern arm of **Pacquet Harbour** became a base for French migratory fishing after 1713. The name derives from the French word *paquet* and may mean 'big wave', perhaps a common feature of the harbour.

Paddockwood SK Northeast of Prince Albert, this village (1949) was named in 1912 by Francis Pitts after her birthplace of Paddock Wood in Kent, England, southwest of Maidstone. Its post office opened the following year. She had come from England in 1909.

Pagoda Peak In the Coast Mountains, northeast of Mount Waddington, this mountain (3215 m) was named in 1947 by mountaineer Fred W. Beckey because of its resemblance to a Chinese pagoda.

Pain Court ON In 1998 this community became part of the municipality of Chatham-Kent, Kent County. Its post office was named *Dover South* in 1860. At that time the place was also known as Pain Court, either because they had often become short of bread (*pain deviendrait court*) or the loaves were smaller than baked elsewhere. Pain Court became the postal name in 1911, but from 1916 to 1991 the words were fused as *Paincourt*.

Paipoonge ON This township in Thunder Bay District and on the southwest side of the city of Thunder Bay was named in 1889 after the Ojibwa word for 'winter'.

Paisley ON In 1999 this village (1873) became a part of the municipality of Arran-Elderslie, Bruce County. Located

northwest of Walkerton, it was founded in 1851. Three names were considered for the place: Orchardville, Forfar, and Roweville. A surveyor observed the close connections in Scotland of several local names in the county and suggested Paisley, which was adopted in 1856.

Pakenham ON In 1998 this township became a part of the town of Mississippi Mills, Lanark County. It was named in 1823 after Gen. Sir Edward Michael Pakenham (1778–1815), who was killed at the Battle of New Orleans. The community of **Pakenham** was first known as *Harvey's Mills* and *Pakenham Mills*, before Pakenham post office opened in 1832.

Palliser Range AB North of Banff, this range commemorates Capt. John Palliser (1817–87), who led an expedition in the late 1850s to investigate the geography of Canada between the Red River and the Rocky Mountains, and between the forty-ninth parallel and the North Saskatchewan River. His resulting reports on the people and land capability set the direction for much of the agriculture, communication, and settlement policies and practices that followed. A vast area of semi-arid land in southwestern Saskatchewan and southeastern Alberta is unofficially known as the Palliser Triangle. **Palliser River**, a tributary of the Kootenay in British Columbia, rises northeast of Windermere.

Palmerston ON In 1998 this town (1874) became part of the town of Minto, Wellington Country. Located northeast of Listowel, it was named in 1872 after Henry John Temple, 3rd Viscount Palmerston (1784–1865), prime minister of Great Britain 1855–65.

Pambrun, Mount BC In the Purcell Mountains, east of Kootenay Lake, this mountain (3063 m) was named in 1937 after Pierre Chrysologue Pambrun (1792–1840), a chief trader for the Hudson's Bay Company.

Pamdenec NB This neighbourhood is located in the village of Grand Bay, west of Saint John. From the Maliseet for 'small mountain', its name was chosen for a Canadian Pacific Railway station in 1902 by historian William Odber Raymond (1853–1923) and Maliseet-speaker Sabatis Paul to replace *Hillside*. Pamdenec was incorporated as a village in 1966, but was annexed by Grand Bay in 1972.

Panache, Lake ON Located southwest of Sudbury, this lake was commonly called *Lake Penage* before the present name was authorized in 1927. Panache is the French word for 'feather' or 'plume'. The lake's outline resembles a feather with a main stem and many little branches.

Pangnirtung NU Located on the south side of Cumberland Peninsula, Baffin Island, and at the mouth of **Pangnirtung Fiord**, this hamlet (1972) was established in 1921 as a Hudson's Bay Company post. The name in Inuktitut means 'place of many buck deer', although the occurrence here of deer and caribou since the beginning of the twentieth century has been rare.

Papineau QC The regional county was erected in 1983, succeeding the former county of Papineau. The latter was named after the celebrated politician Louis-Joseph Papineau (1786–1871), who lived in exile in Paris from 1839 to 1845 for his role in the aborted Rebellion of 1837–8. The village of **Papineauville** was erected in 1896, taking the name from its post office, opened in 1855. There is a claim that it was named after Louis-Joseph's father, Joseph Papineau (1752–1841), who was granted the seigneury of Petite-Nation in 1801. There is another claim that Louis-Joseph's brother, Denis-Benjamin Papineau (1789–1854), also a prominent politician, founded the place about 1850 and named it after himself.

Paquetville NB The post office in this village (1966) southwest of Caraquet was named in 1878 after Fr. Joseph-Marie Paquet (1804–69), the parish priest at Caraquet, 1848–69. It was established as a free-grant settlement in 1866.

Paradise NL The name of this town (1971) west of St. John's may have been chosen in the 1890s to suggest it was an inviting place to live and raise a family. It may have been given by the Reverend Mr Colley of Topsail or by a politician. In 1992 it annexed the area of St. Thomas, which was first called *Horse Cove*. It was renamed in 1922 in honour of Fr. Thomas O'Connor. St. Thomas was created a municipal community in 1977.

Parent QC The post office in this village (1947) on a line of the Canadian National Railways, northwest of La Tuque, was named in 1915, three years after a division point was established by the Transcontinental Railway here. It was named after Simon-Napoléon Parent (1855–1920), mayor of Quebec City, 1894–1906, premier of Quebec, 1900–5, and president of the Transcontinental Railway Company, 1905–11.

Paris ON In 1999 this town (1856) became part of Brant County. It was founded in 1829 by Hiram 'King' Capron, who named it three years later after the extensive plaster of Paris gypsum beds. Plaster of Paris was first recognized near Paris, France, as a valuable ingredient for luxuriant crop growth. The use of gypsum for plastering buildings was common some 9000 years ago in the Middle East.

Parkers Cove NL Located on the western shore of Placentia Bay and northeast of Marystown, this municipal community (1966) may have been named after a migratory fisherman, or after surveyor William Parker (1743–1802), who prepared maps and the ship's log and journal in the 1760s for Capt. James Cook (1728–79).

Parkhill ON In 2001 this town (1886) became part of the municipality of North Middlesex, Middlesex County. Located 35 km northwest of the London city centre, it was founded in 1860 and first named *Westwood* and *Swainby*. Its post office was named in 1864 after Parkhill in the parish of Logie, Ross and Cromarty, Scotland, the birthplace of resident Simon McLeod.

Parksville BC This city (1986) on the east coast of Vancouver Island, northwest of Nanaimo, was first called *Englishman's River* after the local river named for English settlers who had arrived in the late 1880s. Its post office was named in 1887 after first postmaster Nelson Parks, the earliest settler in the area.

Parrsboro NS On the north shore of Minas Basin, this town (1884) was named after John Parr (1725–91), governor of Nova Scotia, 1782–91. Its post office was named *Parrsborough* in 1812, with the present form adopted about 1895.

Parry Channel NT, NU This channel, from the entrance of Lancaster Sound in the east, to the outlet of M'Clure Strait in the west, was named in 1956 by geologist Yves Oscar Fortier after Sir William Edward Parry (1790–1855). He commanded four Arctic expeditions between 1818 and 1825. By penetrating Lancaster Sound, Barrow Strait, and Viscount Melville Sound as far as the 110°W on 6 September 1819, he was awarded £5,000 by a King's Order-in-Council.

Parry Islands NT, NU This group of islands in the Queen Elizabeth Islands (embracing Melville, Byam Martin, Bathurst, Cornwallis, Prince Patrick, Eglinton, Mackenzie King, Brock, Borden, and Lougheed Islands) was called the *Parry Group* before 1910. It was named after Sir William Edward Parry (1790–1855), who discovered and named the individual islands. In 1939 the group was given its present designation.

Parry Sound ON The harbour was named by Admiralty surveyor Henry W. Bayfield (1795–1885) during his 1822–5 survey. The name recalled northern Canada's *Parry Sound* (now Viscount Melville Sound), named in 1819 after Sir William Parry, who took the first ship west to the 110th meridian. The post office in the town (1887) was named in 1865, and **Parry Sound District** was created five years later.

Parsnip River BC Rising in the Hart Ranges of the Rocky Mountains, this river flows northwest into Williston Lake. Before the creation of the lake in 1968, it formed one of the two main sources of the Peace River (the other was the Finlay). It took its name from giant cow parsnips growing along its banks.

Parson's Pond NL Located on the northwestern coast of the Northern Peninsula, this municipal community (1966) is located at the outlet of **Parsons Pond**. Parsons is a common surname on the coast, with a family having settled in 1878 on Bonne Bay, 50 km to the south. It may have been called after the Reverend Isaac Parsons, who visited the settlement. Capt. James Cook (1728–79) called the pond *Sandy Bay* in 1768.

Partridge Island NB In Saint John Harbour, this island was noted in a French grant of 1672 as *Isle au Perdrix* ('partridge island'). By 1711 it was described by Nathaniel Blackmore as *Partridge I.*

Pasadena NL Located on the southeast side of Deer Lake, and northeast of Corner Brook, this town (1955) took its name in the late 1930s from a farm established in 1933 by Lawrence Earle. The farm was called after the city in southern California, where Earle's wife once lived. The city's name was devised in 1874 from Chippewa (Ojibwa) words meaning 'crown of the valley'.

Paspébiac QC The post office in this municipality, located on the north shore of Chaleur Bay, east of New Carlisle, opened in 1832, and the municipality was established in 1877. In 1672 Acadian governor and author Nicolas Denys (c.1598–1688) mentioned a cape called *Paspec-biac* in his *Description géographique et historique*. In 1707 the seigneury of Paspébiac was granted to Pierre Haimard (1674–1724). The municipality of **Paspébiac-Ouest** was created in 1922.

Passamaquoddy Bay NB On the southwestern side of the province, this bay's name derives from the Passamaquoddy *Peskutumaquadik* ('place where pollock are'), which is also the source of the Aboriginal tribe's name. Occurring as early as 1675–7 in the Jesuit *Relations* as *Pessemouquote*, its present spelling was established by map-maker Joseph Frederic Wallet DesBarres (1722–1824) in 1776.

Patapedia River NB, QC Rising in Quebec, this river flows southeast into the Restigouche River, west of Campbellton. It forms part of the boundary between New Brunswick and Quebec, where it is officially Rivière Patapédia. The name derives from the Mi'kmaq *Patawegeok* (possibly 'running through burnt land' or 'place to peel birch bark and build a canoe').

Patricia Portion ON In 1912 this portion of Canada (north of the Albany River, west of James Bay, east of Manitoba, and south of Hudson Bay) was attached to Ontario. It was named after Princess Patricia Ramsay (1886–1974), the daughter of

the Governor General of Canada, the Duke of Connaught and Strathearn (1850–1942). For judicial purposes, it was joined to the district of Kenora in 1927. In 1914 the Princess Patricia's Canadian Light Infantry became the infantry regiment in the Canadian Forces, Princess Patricia having been the colonel-in-chief. The regiments have served in the First World War, the Second World War, the Korean War, and the war in Afghanistan.

Patterson, Mount YT Located in the St. Elias Mountains, this mountain (3444 m) was named in 1970 after John Duncan Patterson (1864–1940), a former president of the Alpine Club of Canada.

Pattullo, Mount BC In the Coast Mountains and northeast of Stewart, this mountain (2729 m) was named in 1927 after Thomas Dufferin Pattullo (1873–1956), premier of British Columbia, 1933–41. Previously he was an alderman in Dawson, YT, a mayor of Prince Rupert, and a minister of lands in British Columbia.

Paul Lake BC Located east of Kamloops, this lake's name was proposed in 1925 by surveyor C.H. Taggart after Jean Baptiste Lolo, who was commonly called St. Paul.

Paynton SK Northwest of Battleford, this village (1905) was first settled about 1885 by three North West Mounted Police constables, including Peter Paynter (d.1934). Its post office opened in 1904, and the postmaster reported the next year that Paynter was farming 2000 a (809 ha) and was 'known for his kindly assistance to one and all'.

Peace River AB, BC One of Canada's major rivers, the Peace River rises in Williston Lake in British Columbia and flows east, north, and then east again to enter the Slave River, north of Fort Chipewyan. The name derives from a point near its mouth, where the Cree and Beaver reached an accord on their respective territories, which explorer Alexander Mackenzie (1764–1820) described in his *Voyages from Montreal* (1801). The town (1919) of **Peace River** is located at the junction of the Peace and Smoky Rivers, northeast of Grande Prairie. Known as *Peace River Crossing* until 1916, its development was assured when the Edmonton, Dunvegan and British Columbia Railway crossed the river here the previous year.

Peachland BC On the western shore of Okanagan Lake, southwest of Kelowna, this district municipality (1955) was named in 1898 by John Moore Robinson (1791–1863), probably after the first peach orchards planted here by the Lambley family. Earlier it was called *Camp Hewitt* after Gus Hewitt, who prospected here about 1890.

Peary Channel NU The entrance between Ellef Ringnes and Meighen Islands was named *Peary Strait* by Vilhjalmur Stefansson (1879–1962) in 1917 after Adm. Robert Edwin

Peary (1856–1920). The Geographic Board did not accept the proposal in 1921, but authorized Peary Channel in 1939. Peary led the United States Polar Expedition, 1898–1902, which explored the lands and waters on the east side of Ellesmere Island. Peary set out to reach the North Pole, getting as far as 84°17'27"N in 1902, reaching 87°06'N in 1906 and attaining the vicinity of the pole in 1909.

Peawanuck ON After the community of Winisk, near the mouth of Winisk River, was destroyed by ice and water in 1986, its residents were relocated 32 km upriver. The name of the new community possibly derives from the Cree *payuk-wunok* ('in one place').

Peck, Mount BC In the Rocky Mountains, north of Sparwood, this mountain (2921 m) was named in 1919 after H.M. Peck, a Geological Survey assistant who was killed in action in Europe.

Peck, Mount BC In the Muskwa Ranges of the Rocky Mountains, this mountain (2750 m) was named in 1987 after Don Peck (1920–80), a long-time guide, outfitter, and rancher in Fort St. John, and earlier at Trutch. It was named *Mount Stalin* in 1944 after Marshal Joseph Stalin (1879–1953), leader of the Union of Socialist Soviet Republics after 1925. The name was given in this area where other Allied leaders of the Second World War were honoured, but was changed as a result of several petitions to expunge the name of a man deemed to be a notorious criminal. *See also* Roosevelt, Mount *and* Churchill Peak.

Peel ON Peel County was named in 1849 after Sir Robert Peel (1788–1850), who held many senior posts in the British government, including prime minister, 1834–5 and 1841–6. It was reorganized as a regional municipality in 1974 with three municipalities: the cities of Brampton and Mississauga and the town of Caledon. In 1999 **Peel Township** became part of the township of Mapleton, Wellington County. It was named after Sir Robert Peel in 1835, during his first term as prime minister.

Peel River NT, YT Rising at the confluence of the Ogilvie and Blackstone Rivers, in north central Yukon, this river (684 km, to the head of the Ogilvie) flows northeast, then north, to flow into the Mackenzie River, north of Fort MacPherson, NT. It was named in 1826 by Sir John Franklin (1786–1847) after Sir Robert Peel (1788–1850). Peel was then the secretary of the home department and later served as the British prime minister, 1834–5 and 1841–6.

Peel Sound NU Located between Prince of Wales and Somerset Islands, this channel was likely named in the 1830s after Sir Robert Peel, prime minister of Great Britain, 1834–5 and 1841–4.

Peggys Cove NS At the eastern entrance to St. Margarets Bay, southwest of Halifax, this fishing community may have been named after Margaret (Peggy) Rodgers (Rogers), who with her husband, William, emigrated from Ireland about 1770, lived here for six years, and then moved to Caribou Island, north of Pictou.

Pelee ON This township, embracing **Pelee Island** in Essex County, was named in 1868. The island was called after **Point Pelee**, named *Pointe Pelée* during the French regime after the bare appearance on its east side. **Point Pelee National Park** (16 km²) was established in 1918.

Pelham ON A town in the regional municipality of Niagara since 1970, it was organized as a township in Lincoln County in 1790. It was named after Henry Fiennes Pelham Clinton, 9th Earl of Lincoln and 2nd Duke of Newcastle under Lyme (1720–94). His mother was the sister of two prime ministers, Sir Henry Pelham and Thomas Pelham-Clinton, the 3rd Duke of Newcastle, and his wife was Catherine Pelham, whose surname he adopted.

Pelly SK Located north of Kamsack, this village (1911) was named by the Canadian Northern Railway in 1910 after nearby Fort Pelly. The fort was established in 1824 by the Hudson's Bay Company and named after Sir John Henry Pelly (1777–1852), a governor of the company. Its post office also opened in 1910.

Pelly River YT Rising in the Mackenzie Mountains, south of Macmillan Pass, this river (608 km) flows northwest to join the Yukon River at the site of Fort Selkirk. It was named in 1840 by Hudson's Bay Company trader Robert Campbell (1808–94) after Sir John Henry Pelly (1777–1852), a governor of the company. **Pelly Crossing** is a small community at the point where the Klondike Highway crosses the river. The ferry crossing was replaced by a bridge in 1958. The **Pelly Mountains**, which extend for 375 km along the northwest side of the river, were named in 1887 by geologist George M. Dawson (1849–1901).

Pemberton BC This village (1956) in the Lillooet River valley, northeast of Whistler, was founded about 1911. Its post office was called *Agerton* in 1912 but was changed to Pemberton in 1931. It was named after Joseph Despard Pemberton (1821–93), who was engaged by the Hudson's Bay Company as the surveyor of Vancouver Island, 1851–59. After leaving the HBC, he was the surveyor general of Vancouver Island until 1864, and also conducted surveys on the mainland, including one in the Pemberton area.

Pembina River MB Rising in the area of Turtle Mountain Provincial Park, south of Boissevain, this river flows east, crossing into North Dakota, south of Morden. The name derives from the Ojibwa *nepemenah* ('summerberry'), an ingredient—along with lard and buffalo meat—in the preparation of pemmican.

Pembroke ON In 2000 the province's smallest township municipality became part of the township of Laurentian Valley, Renfrew County. It was named about 1835 after George Augustus Herbert, 11th Earl of Pembroke (1759–1827). The site of the present city of **Pembroke** (1971) was developed in the 1820s, with parts of it being called *Miramichi, Campbelltown, Lowertown, Moffat*, and *Sydenham*, before it became the village of Pembroke in 1857.

Pend-d'Oreille River BC This river rises in Pend Oreille Lake in Idaho; crosses into Pend Oreille County, WA; and flows north into British Columbia to enter the Columbia River, south of Trail. It was named after the Pend d'Oreille, an Aboriginal group now known as the Kalispell. They were named Pend d'Oreille by French traders, who called the ornaments in their ears *pendants d'oreilles*.

Penetanguishene NL On the north side of St. John's, and part of the city since 1982, this place was established in 1942 and took its name from the town in Ontario. It is reported that Stan Condon had then found a board attached to a farmer's fence with the name inscribed on it, and thereafter it was called Penetanguishene.

Penetanguishene ON This town (1882) in Simcoe County was named in 1793 as the Georgian Bay terminus of a road from Lake Simcoe. In Ojibwa it means 'place of the white rolling sands'. Its post office was called *Penetanguichine* in 1829 and was changed to Penetanguishene in 1833. The name is often shortened to Penetang.

Penhold AB The Canadian Pacific Railway originally intended to call the station in this town (1980), south of Red Deer, Essexville in 1892. However, when one of the railway officials accidentally dropped his pen, and it became stuck in their route map, one of them coined the name Penhold.

Pennant SK Northwest of Swift Current, this village (1912) was given its name in 1911, when the Canadian Pacific Railway started to construct a line south of the South Saskatchewan River. It was named when a surveyor found a pennant nearby. The post office was called *Pennant Station* in 1912.

Penobsquis NB East of Sussex, this place's name was coined in 1857 by Moses Henry Perley (1804–62) for a European and North American Railway station. It was called *Stones Brook* after a local stream. Perley blended the name from Maliseet *penobsq* ('stone') and *sips* ('brook'). The post office, called *Upper Sussex* in 1852, was renamed Penobsquis in 1865.

Pense SK Located between Regina and Moose Jaw, this village (1904) was named by the Canadian Pacific Railway in 1883 after Edward John Barker Pense (1848–1910). While he was president of the Canadian Press Association, he followed the laying of the CPR's track and was later publisher of the Kingston *Whig*. A post office also opened here in 1883.

Penticton BC The post office in this city (1948) at the south end of Okanagan Lake was named in 1889 after Tom Ellis's ranch. He choose the name from the Okanagan word *pentaktin* ('always place'), likely suggesting the site was permanently occupied. It is also said its name came from *snpnpiniyatn* ('place where the deer net was used'), from the extinct Nicola-Similkameen language. The townsite was laid out in 1892.

Percé QC Located at one of the continent's prettiest land and sea settings, this town overlooks the hauntingly beautiful **Rocher Percé**, widely known in the English-speaking world as Percé Rock. It was noted by Samuel de Champlain (1567–1635) in 1603 as *Isle Percée*, but one of its two arches collapsed in 1845. Percé was created a township municipality in 1845 and became a town in 1971 when it annexed the municipalities of Barachois (1953), Bridgeville (1933), Cap-d'Espoir (1935), and *Saint-Pierre-de-la-Malbaie-Nº2* (1876).

Percy ON In 2001 this township became a part of the municipality of Trent Hills, Northumberland County. It was named in 1798 after Lady Elizabeth Seymour (1685–1734), who became Baroness Percy after the death in 1786 of her husband, the Duke of Northumberland.

Perdue SK West of Saskatoon, this village (1909) was established in 1908 by the Canadian Pacific Railway, and named after Judge William Egerton Perdue (1850–1933) of Winnipeg. Postal service was also established in 1908.

Péribonka QC Situated at the mouth of **Rivière Péribonka**, on the north side of Lac Saint-Jean, this municipality was erected in 1926, and its post office opened in 1898. The river, which rises east of Lac Mistassini, was noted as early as 1679. In Montagnais the name expresses the idea of a 'river cutting through sand'.

Perkins QC This community in the regional county of Les Collines-de-l'Outaouais, north of the city of Gatineau, was established as a village in 1866 and its post office opened the same year. Lumberman John Adams Perkins arrived here in 1845 and built a sawmill. In 1975 the village was annexed by the new municipality of Val-des-Monts.

Perth ON Created as a district in 1847 and a county in 1850, this community was named in honour of Perthshire settlers from Scotland, the first to occupy its eastern townships of North Easthope and South Easthope. In 1998 the towns and townships of the county became four municipalities: the town of North Perth and the townships of West Perth, Perth East, and Perth South.

Perth ON This town (1853) in Lanark County was founded in 1816 by Scottish settlers, mainly families of disbanded officers and soldiers, and took its name from the Scottish city of Perth on the River Tay. It was called *Perth-on-Tay* in 1816 and shortened to Perth four years later.

Perth-Andover NB In 1966 the communities of *Perth*, on the east side of the Saint John River, and *Andover*, on the west, were united as the village of Perth-Andover. Perth post office opened in 1857, south of the village, and was called after **Perth Parish**, created in 1833 and named by Lt.-Gov. Sir Archibald Campbell (1769–1843) after his birthplace of Perth, Scotland. *Perth Centre* post office was opened in the village in 1879 and became Perth in 1902, after the older office was changed to *Coronation*. Andover post office was named in 1846 after Andover Parish, established in 1833, and possibly given for Andover, Hampshire, England.

Pétain, Mount AB, BC On the continental divide and at the head of the Kananaskis River, this mountain was named in 1922 after Marshal Henri Philippe Pétain (1856–1951), a military hero in France during the First World War and commander-in-chief of the French armies, 1917–18.

Petawawa ON In 1998 this township and the village of Petawawa became parts of the town of **Petawawa**, Renfrew County. The village of **Petawawa**, near the mouth of the river, was incorporated in 1961. The township was named in 1857 after the **Petawawa River**, a major tributary of the Ottawa River. The river's name is said to mean in Algonquin 'a noise is heard far away'. **Canadian Forces Base Petawawa** was established as a military base in 1904. In 2008 **Canadian Forces Command** at Petawawa is responsible for special forces units: Joint Task Force 2 (JTF2), the newly formed Canadian Special Operations Regiment (CSOR), the Joint Nuclear Biological and Chemical Defence Company (JNBCD), and the special operations aviation unit.

Peterborough ON The county was created in 1849 and named after the town of **Peterborough** (a city since 1905). The post office was named in 1825 after Peter Robinson (1785–1838), who organized the settlement here of 2024 Irish immigrants that year. Robinson was an Upper Canadian politician, commissioner of Crown lands, and surveyor general of woods.

Peter, Mount BC Located in the Purcell Mountains, southwest of Invermere, this mountain (3338 m) was named in 1924 after alpinist Peter Kerr, who climbed in the area in 1914 and was killed in France during World War I.

Peterview NL Located in the south side of Peters Arm of the Bay of Exploits and at the mouth of Peters River, northeast of Grand Falls–Windsor, this town (1962) may have been named after a Peters family, established here in the early 1800s. It was called *Peters Arm* until about 1949. Capt. David Buchan referred to Peters Arm in 1811, when he dropped anchor here.

Petitcodiac NB The first post office in this village (1966), southwest of Moncton and near the head of the **Petitcodiac River**, was called in 1848 *Head of Petitcodiac* and was renamed Petitcodiac in 1865. The river's name derives from the Mi'kmaq *Epetkutogoyek* ('river that bends around back'). It was identified as *Petcoucoyec* by map-maker Jean-Baptiste-Louis Franquelin (c.1653–1712) in 1686; its present form occurred on a map of 1799.

Petit-de-Grat NS On **Petit-de-Grat Island**, east of Isle Madame, this place's name derives from the Basque word for 'fishing station', with the French *petit* denoting it as small. Its post office, opened in 1866, was called *Petit-de-Grat Bridge* between 1894 and 1953.

Petite Rivière NS Located at the mouth of **Petite Rivière**, south of Bridgewater, this place's post office was called *Petite Rivière Bridge* in 1852. The river's name, meaning 'little river' in English, may have been given by the French during the early years of the seventeenth century.

Petitot River AB, BC, NT Rising in northwestern Alberta, this river flows northwest through northeastern British Columbia to empty into the Liard River at Fort Liard, NT. It was named after Fr. Émile Petitot (1838–1917), a missionary in the Mackenzie River valley, 1862–86, who produced a dictionary and a grammar of Dene languages and other important studies of the Dene.

Petit-Rocher NB The post office in this village (1966) northwest of Bathurst was called *Madisco* in 1850. It was given its present name, which means 'little rock', in 1877.

Petrolia ON The post office in this town (1874) in Lambton County, southeast of Sarnia, was named *Petrolea* in 1859, after the discovery of oil and the building of a refinery. Through a clerical mistake, the name was spelled Petrolia when the place was incorporated as a village in 1866. Postal authorities relented 40 years later, and respelled the office's name Petrolia.

Petty Harbour-Maddox Cove NL Located 10 km south of St. John's Harbour, this town (1969) is at the head of **Petty Harbour**. The harbour may have been named *Petit Havre* in French, in contrast to the larger harbour at St. John's. It may have had a Basque name before that. As early as 1675 there were people with variant spellings of the surname Maddox on the east coast of the Avalon Peninsula.

Philipsburg QC This village in the regional county of Brome-Missisquoi, southwest of Cowansville, was incorporated in 1846, having been noted in 1815 by surveyor Joseph Bouchette (1774–1841) as *Phillipsbourg*. Its post office was called *Philipsburg East* from 1812 to 1922. The village was named after the son of John Ruiter (Johannes Ruyter), who purchased land here in 1809.

Phillips, Mount AB, BC On the continental divide, northwest of Mount Robson, this mountain (3249 m) was named in 1910 after climber and guide Donald 'Curley' Phillips (1884–1938), who was the best authority on the mountains in the area of Jasper.

Piccadilly NL On the north side of Port au Port Peninsula, this place's name is an English interpretation of a local description of a hill, *Pic à Denis*, after an Acadian who settled here. The road leading to Abrahams Cove, on the south side of the peninsula, is called **Piccadilly Slant**, with 'slant' being an old English word for a slope.

Pickering ON The township, originally called *Edinburgh*, was renamed in 1792 after the town of Pickering in North Yorkshire, England, northeast of the city of York. It was part of York County until 1849, when it was transferred to Ontario County. On the creation of the regional municipality of Durham in 1974, the township was divided between the towns of Ajax and **Pickering**. The community of *Pickering*, where a post office opened in 1829, became part of the town of Ajax in 1974, and was renamed **Pickering Village** in 1987 to differentiate it from the town of Pickering.

Pickle Lake ON This municipal township in Kenora District, northeast of Sioux Lookout, was developed as a mining site in the 1930s. Its post office was first called Pickle Crow in 1935, but was known as Central Patricia from 1937 to 1977, when it was changed to Pickle Lake.

Picton ON In 1998 this town (1850) became part of the municipality of Prince Edward County. It was named in 1837 after Lt-Gen. Sir Thomas Picton (1758–1815), who served in the Peninsular War in Spain, 1810–14, and was killed at the Battle of Waterloo. In 1820 its post office was called *Hallowell* after the township, but its name was changed to Picton in 1840.

Pictou NS This town (1873) is located on the north side of **Pictou Harbour** and in **Pictou County**. It was settled in 1767 by Pennsylvanians and in 1773 by Scots from ports on the River Clyde. It was named after the harbour, identified in 1662 by Nicolas Denys (c.1598–1688) as *Rivière de Pictou*. The name derives from the Mi'kmaq *piktook* ('explosion of gas'). The three rivers entering the harbour are called **West River of Pictou**, **Middle River of Pictou**, and **East River of**

Pictou. Pictou County was named in 1835. The community of **Pictou Landing**, across the harbour from Pictou, received postal service in 1867. **Pictou Island** in Northumberland Strait was named in the 1760s by map-maker Joseph Frederic Wallet DesBarres (1722–1824).

Picture Butte AB The post office in this town (1960) north of Lethbridge was named in 1912 after petroglyphs on a butte (an isolated hill with a flat top). The butte was subsequently excavated for its gravel and became the site of a subdivision.

Piedmont QC Established in 1923, this municipality adjacent to Saint-Sauveur-des-Monts and north of Saint-Jérôme was named after its post office, which was named in 1875 for its location at the foot (*pied*) of Mont Olympia.

Pierceland SK Near the Alberta border and west of Meadow Lake, the post office at this village (1973) was named in 1932. There is no information about how Pierceland received this name; however, to the north is an enlargement of Waterhen River called **Pierce Lake**.

Pierrefonds QC In 2002 this city became part of the borough of Pierrefonds-Roxboro in the city of Montreal, but in 2006 it recovered its status as a city. Pierrefonds was incorporated as a village in 1904. It was called after the residence of Joseph-Adolphe Chauret (1854–1918), secretary-treasurer from 1880 to 1904, and member of the Legislative Assembly, 1897–1908. Built in 1902, the residence's design was inspired by a castle in Pierrefonds, near Compiègne, northeast of Paris. The parish municipality of *Sainte-Geneviève*, created in the mid-1800s, became the city of Pierrefonds in 1958, with the village of *Pierrefonds* becoming the town of Sainte-Geneviève the following year. *See also* Sainte-Geneviève.

Pierreville QC This village in the regional county of Nicolet-Yamaska, near where the Rivière Yamaska flows into Lac Saint-Pierre, was created in 1887. The name comes from the post office, opened in 1853. It was severed from the parish municipality of *Saint-Thomas-de-Pierreville*, created in 1855. The name has its roots in the seigneury of *Pierreville*, created in 1723, whose name may derive from the lake's name.

Pierson MB Located near the southwest corner of the province, this place's Canadian Pacific Railway station was named in 1886 after Jan Lodewijk Pierson (1854–1945) who was then a partner in the Amsterdam firm of Adolphe Boissevain and Company, which sold shares of the CPR in the European financial markets. Its post office opened in 1892. In 1925 Pierson wrote a book about Sir William Van Horne (1843–1915) and the CPR.

Pigeon River ON Part of the boundary separating Ontario from Minnesota, this river was known during the French regime as *Rivière aux Groseilles* ('gooseberry' or 'currant river') and *Rivière aux Tourtes* ('wild pigeon river'). Pigeon River was adopted about 1826.

Pilkington ON In 1999 this township became part of the township of Centre Wellington, Wellington County. It was named in 1851 after Robert Pilkington (1765–1834), an officer with the Royal Engineers, 1790–1802. In 1799 he bought the area of the township, and subsequently arranged for some emigrants from Northamptonshire and Warwickshire to settle here.

Pilkington, Mount On the continental divide, west of Howse Pass, this mountain (3285 m) was named in 1898 after climber Charles Pilkington (1850–1919).

Pilley's Island NL Located on **Pilley's Island** and in Notre Dame Bay, this municipal community (1975) embraces the entire island, which is connected by a bridge to Newfoundland. There were several Pelly, Pilly, and Pilley families living along the north coast in the 1840s, but the island was not settled until after 1887.

Pilot Butte SK This town (1980) 15 km east of Regina, was established in 1882 by the Canadian Pacific Railway and named after one of three nearly flat-topped hills, which provided extended views of the area's flat land. The post office opened in 1903.

Pilot Mound MB The post office in this village (1904) west of Morden was named in 1880 after an Aboriginal burial mound, which acted as a guide for travellers. When the Canadian Pacific Railway was built through the area in 1884, the post office was moved 3 km southeast to the line.

Pinawa MB The post office in this local government district (1962) on the Winnipeg River, northeast of Winnipeg, was named in 1910. In Ojibwa, its name means 'quiet waters'. Atomic Energy of Canada constructed the Whiteshell Research Establishment here in 1960.

Pincher Creek AB This town (1906) southwest of Lethbridge was named about 1878 after a tributary of the Oldman River. There are four different stories on the name's origin, all involving the loss of a pair of pinchers (an older form of pincers). One states some American Fur Company prospectors mislaid a pair of pinchers here in 1867, and Joseph Kipp was sent back to recover them. A second story relates the loss of a pair of pinchers by a group of prospectors, and the North West Mounted Police found them rusty and old in 1875. A third tale suggests Leonard Harnois lost them about 1870. A fourth story has prospectors being killed by Aboriginals, and the pinchers were found later at the grisly site.

Pincourt QC The post office in this town, located in the regional county of Vaudreuil-Soulanges and on the west side of Île Perrot, was named in 1932; the name derives from the short pines (*pins courts*) in nearby woods. It became a village in 1950 and was incorporated as a town in 1959.

Pine, Cape NL Extending into the Atlantic Ocean, southwest of Trepassey, this cape was called *c de pena* ('cape of sorrow') by the Portuguese in the early 1500s. By the 1670s, maps portrayed it as *C de Pine* and *C Pine*.

Pine Falls MB Situated 11 km above the mouth of the Winnipeg River, this place was founded by the Manitoba Pulp and Paper Company in 1925. Its post office was located at the site of Fort Alexander from 1879 to 1881, when it was moved upriver to its present location, on the south side of the falls.

Pinehouse SK Located on the western shore of **Pinehouse Lake**, and east of Île-à-la-Crosse, the post office of this northern village (1983) was known as *Snake Lake* from 1949 to 1955. In 1954 the residents requested the renaming of the lake and the post office.

Pine River BC Rising in the Rocky Mountains, this river flows northeast into the Peace River, opposite the district municipality of Taylor. Several species of pine trees, including the white, the lodgepole, the limber, and the whitebark support a thriving timber industry on the eastern flank of the mountains. **Pine Pass** (874 m), at the head of the river, is the lowest of the passes through the Rockies and was discovered in 1808 by one of Simon Fraser's men.

Pine River MB Located on the North Pine River, northwest of Dauphin, this place was founded by the Canadian Northern Railway about 1904. Its post office was called *Pine River Station* from 1904 to 1915, when 'Station' was dropped from the name.

Pintendre QC The post office in this municipality in the regional county of Desjardins, south of Lévis, was named in 1900. The municipality was established in 1986, having been earlier called *Saint-Louis-de-Pintendre*. The name probably has its roots in the area's soft white pines (*pins tendres*).

Pinware NL Located on the north side of the Strait of Belle Isle, and at the mouth of the **Pinware River**, this municipal community (1971) and the river were named after a rock in **Pinware Bay**, called by French fishermen *Pied Noir* ('black foot').

Pipestone MB South of Virden, this place's post office was named in 1884. It is located south of **Pipestone Creek**, which rises south of Grenfell, SK. The name of the creek, shown on the 1865 Palliser's expedition map, is said to have been transferred by Aboriginals from Pipestone, in the southwestern part of Minnesota.

Pitt Island BC South of the mouth of the Skeena River, this island (1375 km²) took its name from *Pitt Archipelago*, given in 1792 by Capt. George Vancouver (1757–98) after William Pitt the younger (1759–1806), prime minister of Great Britain, 1783–1801 and 1804–6. The present name was established in the 1920s.

Pitt Meadows BC This district municipality (1914) located at the confluence of the Pitt and Fraser Rivers, and between Port Coquitlam and Maple Ridge, was named after the river. Noted in 1827 as *Pitt's River* by James McMillan, the founder of Fort Langley, the river was likely named after William Pitt the younger (1759–1806), prime minister of Great Britain for 20 years between 1783 and 1806.

Pittsburgh ON In 1998 this township became part of the city of Kingston, Frontenac County. It was named in 1787 after William Pitt the younger (1759–1806), prime minister of Great Britain, 1783–1801 and 1804–6.

Placentia NL This town (1945) on the east side of **Placentia Bay** was the site of an important land base for the Basque fishery in the late 1500s. It was likely named by the Basques after their seaport of Plentzia, in the Basque country of Spain. It was renamed *Plaisance* by the French, and served as their capital on Newfoundland after 1624. The present spelling was adopted after 1713, when Newfoundland became British territory.

Plaisance QC Located in the regional county of Papineau, midway between Thurso and Papineauville, it was erected in 1931, having been called *Coeur-Très-Pur-de-la-Bienheureuse-Vierge-Marie-de-Plaisance* in 1900. The post office was named in 1882, possibly for a small house built about 1803 at the mouth of the Rivière de la Petite-Nation by Joseph Papineau (1752–1841), the local seigneur. The name of the house may derive from its attractive setting or from a similar place in France.

Plamondon AB In 2002 this village (1965) became a hamlet. Located 25 km northwest of the town of Lac La Biche, its post office was named in 1909 after postmaster Joseph Plamondon (1861–1923), who homesteaded here the year before.

Plantagenet ON In 1997 this village (1963) became part of the township of **Alfred and Plantagenet**, united counties of Prescott and Russell. Its post office was named in 1838 after **North Plantagenet Township**. *See also* South Plantagenet.

Plaster Rock NB Southeast of Grand Falls and on the Tobique River, this village (1966) was named in 1900 by Henry Day after the red gypsum hills and river banks. In 1841 Edmund Ward described the area as an 'immense body of Plaister of Paris'.

Pleasant Grove PE The post office in this municipal community (1980) northeast of Charlottetown was called *Suffolk Road* in 1870. Postmaster W.W. Duck renamed it in 1885 after someone observed a 'pleasant grove' of beech trees here.

Plenty SK Located northwest of Rosetown, this village (1911) was founded by the Canadian Pacific Railway in 1910. Presumably it was named by a railway engineer, because the only crops that he encountered on his survey between Rosetown and Kerrobert were at Plenty. The post office was called *Boraston*, after Shropshire, England, in 1907 and was renamed Plenty in 1911.

Plessisville QC Created as a village in 1855 and as a town 100 years later, Plessisville is located northeast of Victoriaville. The name was proposed by Fr. Charles Trudelle after Mgr. Joseph-Octave Plessis (1763–1825), 11th bishop of Quebec City, who became its first archbishop in 1818. The parish municipality of **Plessisville** was established in 1946 through the merger of the township municipalities of *Somerset-Nord* and *Somerset-Sud*.

Plevna ON In 1998 this place became part of the township of North Frontenac, Frontenac County. Located 34 km northwest of Sharbot Lake, this community's post office was named *Buckshot* in 1872 after Buckshot Creek and nearby Buckshot Lake. Local residents did not like the name, but quarrelled over a suitable substitute. When postal authorities threatened to impose a name in 1877, Sam Barton Sr. proposed Plevna after a place (now Pleven) in Bulgaria where many battles and quarrels took place.

Plumas MB This place, northeast of Neepawa, was first called *Richmond* in 1879. Because of confusion with other places called Richmond in Canada, postmaster James Anderson, who arrived here in 1878 from Plumas County, CA, proposed renaming it Plumas in 1888. In Latin the name means 'feather'. Plumas County has many birds with beautiful plumage.

Plum Coulee MB This village (1901) east of Winkler was named by Mennonites in the 1880s after the normally dry bed (coulee) of **Plum Creek**. In the 1800s its banks had wild plum trees. Its post office opened in 1890.

Plymouth NS Located on the south side of Stellarton, this community's post office was called *Plymouth Road* in 1884. First called *Irishtown* and *Churchtown*, it may have been named after Plymouth, England. There is another **Plymouth** between

Yarmouth and Wedgeport, probably named after the city of Plymouth, MA.

Plympton NS On the east side of St. Marys Bay, and southwest of Digby, this community was first called *Everette* after pioneer Jeremiah S. Everett (1771–1870). It was named Plympton in 1885 by Judge Alfred Savary (1830–1920) after his family's ancestral home in Massachusetts.

Plympton ON In 2001 this township became a part of the municipality of Lambton Shores, Lambton County. It was named in 1834 by Lt.-Gov. Sir John Colborne (1778–1863) after Plympton near Plymouth, Devon, England, not far from the childhood home of his wife, Elizabeth Yonge, Lady Colborne (1790–1872).

Poboktan Mountain AB In Jasper National Park, southeast of Maligne Lake, this mountain (3323 m) was named by geologist Arthur P. Coleman (1852–1939) after the Stoney word for 'owl'.

Pocologan NB East of St. George, this place's post office opened in 1883, closed in 1898, reopened in 1929, and closed again in 1948. It took its name from **Pocologan Harbour** and **Pocologan River**. In Passamaquoddy *pekelugan* means 'enclosed harbour' or 'it opens out across'.

Pohénégamook QC This town surrounding **Lac Pohénégamook**, adjacent to the most northerly point of Maine, was created in 1973 through the merger of three villages, Saint-Éleuthère (1903), Saint-Pierre-d'Estcourt (1922), and Sully (1916) to become the municipality of **Saint-Éleuthère-de-Pohénégamook**. The township of **Pohénégamook**, proclaimed in 1872, was called after the lake, whose name derives from an Abenaki word meaning 'winter camp'.

Poilus, Mont des BC In Yoho National Park, this mountain (3161 m) was named *Mount Habel* in 1900 by British climber Norman Collie (1859–1942) after German geographer Jean Habel (1839–1902). The mountain was renamed by Order-in-Council in 1916 to remove an obvious German name from the Canadian Rockies. The new name was given in honour of the heroic foot soldiers of the French Army during the First World War.

Point de Bute NB The post office in this community east of Sackville opened as *Pointe de Bute* in 1886. Settled by New Englanders in 1761, they adapted the name from *Pont à Buot*, a bridge over the Missaguash River. Pierre Buhot was a French-speaking settler here about 1700.

Pointe-à-la-Croix QC This municipality opposite the city of Campbellton was created in 1970, having been called the township municipality of *Mann* in 1845. Its post office was called *Cross Point* from 1846 to 1952. The name recalls a cross, probably erected by the Mi'kmaq.

Pointe au Baril ON Located in Parry Sound District, northwest of the town of Parry Sound, this place's post office was named in 1892 after a whiskey barrel that had been mounted on a pole as a beacon. The barrel of whiskey had been lost many years before and was found by French traders who consumed its contents before putting the barrel on the pole. The postmaster in 1905 recalled having seen the barrel in 1873. **Pointe au Baril Station**, 10 km to the east on the Canadian Pacific Railway line, was named in 1923.

Pointe-au-Père QC Located just east of Rimouski, this town was created in 1988. Noted as early as 1696 as *Sainte-Anne-de-la-Pointe-au-Père*, it took its name from the celebration of the first mass on 8 December 1663 by Fr. Henri Nouvel on the south side of the St. Lawrence. Its post office was called *Father Point* from 1863 to the early 1970s, when it became Pointe-au-Père. *See also* Nouvelle.

Pointe-au-Pic QC In the regional county of Charlevoix-Est, just west of La Malbaie, this village was incorporated in 1876. Its post office was named six years earlier after a peak (*pic*) on a point here, noted as *Point au Pic* in 1776 by map-maker Joseph Frederic Wallet DesBarres (1722–1824). Widely known as a restful place to get away from the continent's summer heat, it has been frequently called Murray Bay by English-speaking visitors.

Pointe-aux-Trembles QC Located in the regional county of Portneuf, between Neuville and Donnacona, this parish municipality was called *Saint-François-de-Sales* in 1855, although the popular name was Pointe-aux-Trembles. In the early 1700s the religious parish was identified as *Saint-François-de-Sales*, with Pointe aux Trembles describing the nearby point covered with aspen (*trembles*) and birch. In 1912 the town of **Pointe-aux-Trembles** was incorporated at the northeast end of Île de Montréal but was annexed by the city of Montreal in 1982. The trees have long since disappeared from the point.

Pointe-Calumet QC This village near the east end of Lac des Deux Montagnes was erected in 1953. The word *calumet* means 'peace pipe', with a local tradition that the Abenaki and the Iroquois settled their differences by exchanging peace pipes on the point about 1720.

Pointe-Claire QC In 2002 this city became part of the city of Montreal. In 2006 Pointe-Claire recovered its status as a city. Pointe-Claire was created as a municipality in 1845, abolished two years later, and re-established in 1855. It became the village of *Saint-Joachim-de-la-Pointe-Claire* in 1854 and the town of Pointe-Claire in 1911. Its post office was named in 1835, taking its name from **Pointe Claire**, identified on maps as early as 1686.

Pointe-des-Cascades QC Located at the east end of the regional county of Vaudreuil-Soulanges, where the St. Lawrence and Ottawa Rivers unite, this village was created in 1961. The name reflects the fast water at that point, noted on maps of the late 1600s as *Cascades*. The post office was called *Cascades Point* from 1893 to 1951, when it was changed to the present name.

Pointe-du-Lac QC This municipality is located on the north side of Lac Saint-Pierre, where the St. Lawrence continues its journey to the Atlantic. It was created in 1978 through the merger of the municipal parishes of *La Visitation-de-la-Pointe-du-Lac* (1855) and *Pointe-du-Lac* (1928). The prominent sandy point was mentioned as early as 1656.

Point Edward ON This village (1878) in Lambton County, where Lake Huron empties into the St. Clair River (and where it is surrounded on the south and east by the city of Sarnia) was called *Huron* in the early days, but it was renamed in 1865, after a visit in 1860 by Albert Edward, the Prince of Wales (1841–1910).

Pointe-Fortune QC This village on the Ontario border, northwest of Rigaud, was incorporated in 1881. Its post office was called *Point Fortune* from 1851 to 1954, when the present form was adopted. The point was named after Col. William Fortune (1748–1821), a native of County Wexford, Ireland, who lived in South Carolina before coming to Canada. He was granted large areas of land on both sides of the Ottawa River, and was living here as early as 1796. He surveyed many of the townships of Eastern Ontario.

Pointe-Lebel QC Located at the mouth of Rivière Manicouagan, southwest of Baie-Comeau, this village was incorporated in 1964. It was named in 1902 after Norbert Lebel, the first settler on the Pointe Lebel.

Pointe-Sapin NB Located on Northumberland Strait and north of Kouchibouguac National Park, this place's post office was called *Point Sapin* in 1873 after the local fir trees. It was renamed Pointe-Sapin in 1962.

Pointe-Verte NB Northwest of Bathurst, this village (1966) was named after a small point extending into Chaleur Bay. The post office was called *Green Point* in 1883 and was renamed Pointe-Verte in 1938.

Pokemouche NB South of Caraquet, this place was named after **Pokemouche River**, whose name in Mi'kmaq may mean 'salt water extending inward'. Its post office opened as Pokemouche in 1845, but was renamed *Pockmouch* in 1854. The original spelling was restored in 1940.

Pokiok NB The post office of this place on the Saint John River and at the mouth of **Pokiok Stream** was called *Poquiock* from 1854 to 1917. Pokiok is located 5 km southwest of the town of Nackawic. The stream's name, taken from Maliseet *Pokweok* ('runs out through narrows'), was recorded in 1762 by map-maker Joseph Peach as *R. Bogwiack*.

Pollard's Point NL Situated on the southwest side of White Bay and northeast of Deer Lake, this place was settled by Pollard families in the mid-1800s. It was named in the 1950s after the point. Droverville was rejected that year for a postal name, because Sam Drover—after whom it was to be named—was still living. Drover then represented the White Bay district in the House of Assembly.

Pomquet NS In 1761 five Acadian families returned to Acadia from Saint-Malo, France, and settled at Pomquet. The name derives from the Mi'kmaq *pogumkek* ('sandy beach'). Its post office, called *Pomquet Chapel* in 1864, was renamed Pomquet in 1900. There were other post offices at **Pomquet Forks** (1856), **Pomquet Station** (1897), and **Pomquet River** (1911).

Pond Inlet NU This hamlet (1975) on the north side of Baffin Island was established in 1922 as a Royal Canadian Mounted Police post. It took its name from the **Pond Inlet** that separates Baffin and Bylot Islands. The inlet was named in 1818 by Sir John Ross (1777–1856) after John Pond (1767–1836), who was then the astronomer royal.

Ponoka AB Midway between Red Deer and Wetaskiwin, this town (1904) was first called *Siding 14* in 1891 by the Canadian Pacific Railway. It was named Ponoka in 1897 after the Blackfoot word *ponokaii* ('elk').

Ponteix SK Southeast of Swift Current, this town (1957) was named in 1913 by the Canadian Pacific Railway after the hometown in France of Fr. Albert Royer, who founded the mission of Notre Dame d'Auvergne just to the north. The post office had been called *Notre Dame d'Auvergne* in 1908 and was renamed Ponteix in 1914.

Pontiac QC This regional county extending along the Ottawa River from west of Quyon to Rapides-des-Joachims, and covering an area of nearly 13,900 km² in western Quebec, was named in 1983 after the former county of Pontiac (1853). The county was named after noted Ottawa chief Pontiac (c.1712–69), who supported the French during the Seven Years' War (1756–63). The municipality of **Pontiac**, embracing the original townships of Onslow and Eardley, was created in 1975. It has been part of the regional county of Les Collines-de-l'Outaouais since 1991.

Pont-Rouge QC In 2002 this village became part of Quebec City. Four years later it became a sector of Quebec City. It was in the regional county of Portneuf, 12 km west of the Quebec City centre. Incorporated as the village of *Sainte-Jeanne-de-Pont-Rouge* in 1911, Pont-Rouge and adopted its present name seven years later. The bridge (*pont*) that the village was named after was built over the Rivière Jacques-Cartier in 1838, when it was entirely painted red (*rouge*).

Pool's Island NL This neighbourhood (1996) in the town of New-Wes-Valley is located offshore from Badger's Quay on **Main Pool's Island**. The island may have been named after a fisherman.

Poplar Point MB Located northeast of Portage la Prairie, this place's post office opened in 1871. It took its name from a bluff (a Western Canadian word for 'grove') of poplar trees growing further out from the belt of trees along the Assiniboine River.

Porcher Island BC This island, south of Prince Rupert, was named about 1867 by Capt. Daniel Pender after Cdr. Edwin Augustus Porcher (d.1878), who served on the west coast, 1865–8.

Porcupine Plain SK This town (1968), southeast of Tisdale, was founded by the Canadian National Railways in 1929. Richard Cooper proposed naming its post office Porcupine, but because that name was already in use in the Timmins area of Ontario, it was amended to Porcupine Plain that year.

Porcupine River YT Rising in the Ogilvie Mountains, north of Dawson, this major river (721 km) crosses the Yukon–Alaska border, west of Old Crow, and flows into the Yukon River at Fort Yukon. It was possibly named in 1844 by John Bell (c.1799–1868), a chief trader of the Hudson's Bay Company.

Porquis Junction ON Located in the town of Iroquois Falls, southwest of the town centre, this junction was named in 1910, when two branch lines of the Temiskaming and Northern Ontario Railway were built: one east to the new Abitibi Pulp and Paper company town of Iroquois Falls and another west to Porcupine.

Portage la Prairie MB This city (1907) on the Assiniboine River, 25 km south of Lake Manitoba, acquired its name from the practice of fur traders, travellers, and Aboriginals crossing the flat land from the river to the lake. Pierre Gaultier de La Vérendrye (1685–1755) noted in his 1739 journal that the Assiniboine carried their canoes over the portage on their way to the English posts on Hudson Bay. Its post office opened in 1871, nine years before the Canadian Pacific Railway arrived.

Portage-du-Fort QC This village in the regional county of Pontiac, west of Shawville, was incorporated in 1863, 16 years after its post office opened. Several possible origins have been suggested, the most likely being a place where supplies were kept for shantymen portaging around a series of rapids.

Port Alberni BC At the head of **Alberni Inlet**, this city (1912) was amalgamated with the city (1945) of **Alberni** in 1967. The first post office was *Sayward-Alberni* in 1886, which was changed to Alberni in 1891 and closed in 1962. *New Alberni* post office opened on the city's south side in 1900, and was changed to Port Alberni in 1910. The inlet was named *Canal de Alberni* in 1791 by Lt. Francisco Eliza after Don Pedro Alberni (1747–1802), captain of a company of soldiers accompanying Eliza. *Alberni Canal* was adopted in 1861 by Capt. George Richards (1820–96). Its narrow 45-km-long channel was reminiscent of other 'canals' (e.g., Portland, Gardner) on the west coast, but the Geographic Board changed it to Alberni Inlet in 1945.

Port Alice BC On the eastern shore of Neroutsos Inlet, an extension of Quatsino Sound on the northwest coast of Vancouver Island, this village (1965) was founded in 1917 by the Whalen Pulp and Paper Company. The Whalen brothers, who established the company, named the place after their mother, Alice.

Port Anson NL On Sunday Cove Island, in Notre Dame Bay, this municipal community (1961) was earlier called *Sunday Cove Tickle* and *Newtown* before the present name was adopted in 1903. It is said that local resident Josiah Ryan proposed Port Handsome to the Nomenclature Board.

Port Arthur ON This main urban sector of the city of Thunder Bay began in the late 1850s as a transfer point between Lake Superior and the West. Col. Garnet Wolseley (1833–1913) was sent to put down the North–West Rebellion and named the place *Prince Arthur's Landing* in 1870 after Queen Victoria's third son, Prince Arthur, Duke of Connaught (1850–1942), who became governor general of Canada, 1911–6. Its post office was called Thunder Bay in 1869 but changed to Port Arthur in 1883, 11 years after it was incorporated as a village. It became a town in 1884 and a city in 1907. Port Arthur, Fort William, and parts of Neebing Township and Shuniah Township were amalgamated in 1970 to become the city of Thunder Bay.

Port au Bras NL Located on the western shore of Placentia Bay and northeast of Burin, the narrow coves at this municipal community (1971) were likely named *Port au Bras* ('port of arms') by fishermen from Saint-Malo, France. The name was adopted by English fishermen in the late 1700s.

Port au Choix NL On the northwestern coast of Newfoundland, this town (1966) is located on a narrow isthmus joining Point Riche Peninsula to the mainland. Its name derives from the Basque *Portuchua*, a description of a little harbour on the outside of the peninsula. The present Back Arm, on the inside of the peninsula, was called *Portuchua Çaharra* ('old little port'). Capt. James Cook adopted the French form of the name in 1767.

Port au Port Bay NL In the late 1500s Basque fishermen named this place *Ophorportu* ('port of relaxation'), suggesting a place of calm waters. The bay is protected by the **Port au Port Peninsula**. Its name, rendered as Port au Port by the French, was transferred to the 500-km² triangular peninsula and adopted by Capt. James Cook (1728–79) in 1767.

Port au Port West-Aguathuna-Felix Cove NL This town (1975) was created by joining three separate communities. **Aguathuna** was first known as *Jack of Clubs Cove*. After a petition in 1911, it was renamed by the Most Reverend Michael Howley (1843–1914) after a Beothuk word he believed meant 'white rock', but it more likely meant 'grindstone'. **Felix Cove** was called after the cove, named about 1850 after French settler Harry Felix.

Port Blandford NL At the head of Clode Sound, a southwesterly extension of Bonavista Bay, this town (1983) was named in the 1890s after Capt. Samuel Blandford (1840–1909), who was a member of the House of Assembly, 1889–93, and a legislative councillor, 1893–1909. Another seaman of note was Capt. Darius Blandford, who lived at Greenspond.

Port Burwell ON In 1998 this village (1949) became part of the municipality of Bayham Elgin County. It was surveyed in 1830 by Col. Mahlon Burwell (1783–1846). A native of New Jersey, Burwell settled in the area in 1810 and served three terms in the House of Assembly of Upper Canada between 1812 and 1840.

Port-Cartier QC Situated on the north shore of the St. Lawrence, southwest of Sept-Îles, this town was established in 1959 by Quebec Cartier Mining as its trans-shipment point for its iron ore from Lac Jeannine near Gagnon and Mont Wright near Fermont. Previously the town was the site of *Shelter Bay*, where the Ontario Paper Company produced paper for the *Chicago Tribune*, but the mill was closed in 1955.

Port Clements BC Located on the eastern shore of Masset Inlet and on Graham Island, one of the Queen Charlotte Islands, this village (1975) was first called *Queenstown*. When postal authorities declined to accept that name, it was named in 1914 after Herbert Sylvester Clements (1865–1939), member for Kent West, ON, 1904–8, Comox-Atlin (1911–7), and Comox-Alberni (1917–21) in the House of Commons.

Port Colborne ON In the regional municipality of Niagara and at the Lake Erie entrance to the Welland Canal, this city (1966) was named in 1832 by William Hamilton Merritt (1793–1862) after Sir John Colborne (1778–1863), lieutenant-governor of Upper Canada, 1828–36.

Port Coquitlam BC This city (1913) at the confluence of the Pitt and Fraser Rivers took its name from the adjacent district municipality of **Coquitlam**. The latter was named after the Coquitlam, a Salish tribe. Their name means either 'small red salmon' or 'stinking with fish slime', in reference to their butchering salmon for their masters, the Kwantlen, a Cowichan tribe.

Port Credit ON Located at the mouth of the **Credit River** this post office was named Port Credit in 1842. Incorporated as a village in 1914 and a town in 1961, it was annexed by the city of Mississauga in 1974.

Port-Daniel QC Located on the north shore of Chaleur Bay, southwest of Gaspé, this municipality was created in 1990 through the merger of the township municipalities of *Port-Daniel-Partie-Est* and *Port-Daniel-Partie-Ouest*, both established in 1882. The township of **Port-Daniel**, proclaimed in 1839, was named after the harbour known as Port Daniel, which had been named after Dieppe sea captain Charles Daniel (d.1661), a contemporary of Samuel de Champlain (1567–1635). He made several ocean crossings to Acadia and New France, spending some 10 years in the New World.

Port Dalhousie ON Annexed by the city of St. Catharines in 1961, this urban centre was named in 1829, when it became the Lake Ontario outlet of the Welland Canal. This name was given in honour of Gen. George Ramsay, 9th Earl Dalhousie (1770–1838), who promoted the construction of the canal, while he was governor-in-chief of British North America, 1820–8.

Port de Grave NL Located on the west side of Conception Bay and on **Bay de Grave**, this place's name was taken from the French *baie de grève* ('bay with shingle beach'), where they dried their cod. The shingle beach is not at the present site of Port de Grave, but at the town of Clarkes Beach, at the head of Bay de Grave.

Port Edward BC Near the mouth of the Skeena River and south of Prince Rupert, this district municipality (1991) was established in 1908 as a possible rail terminus on the west coast and named after Edward VII (1841–1910). It became an important fish canning centre, but the last cannery closed in 1983.

Port Elgin NB The post office in this village (1922) northeast of Sackville was named in 1854 after James Bruce, 8th Earl of Elgin (1811–63), governor of the Province of Canada, 1846–

54. It was previously called *Gaspereau* after the Gaspereau River and the French Fort Gaspereau.

Port Elgin ON In 1999 this town (1949) became part of the town of Saugeen Shores, Bruce County. It was named *Normanton* in 1854, possibly after James Ellis, 3rd Earl Normanton (1818–96). The earl's wife was related to Viscount Bury, who had named several of Bruce County's townships. The residents did not like the name and had it changed in 1873, when it was incorporated as a village. It was named after James Bruce, 8th Earl of Elgin, governor of the Province of Canada, 1847–54.

Porters Lake NS East of Dartmouth, this place's post office was named in 1855 after **Porters Lake**. William Porter, one of the grantees of land at the lake in 1784, built a sawmill at the head of the lake in 1790. He was deputy commissary general of musters to the foreign troops serving with British armies during the American Revolution.

Port Hardy BC On the northeastern coast of Vancouver Island, this district municipality (1966) was founded in 1904. It took its name from **Hardy Bay**, named in 1860 by Capt. George Richards (1820–96) after Vice-Adm. Sir Thomas Masterman Hardy (1769–1839), the captain of Lord Nelson's *Victory* at the Battle of Trafalgar, 1805.

Port Hawkesbury NS The first post office in this town (1889) on the Cape Breton side of the Strait of Canso was named *Ship Harbour* in 1823. It was renamed in 1868, likely after Robert Banks Jenkinson, Baron Hawkesbury and Lord Liverpool (1770–1828), prime minister of Great Britain, 1812–27. He succeeded his father as Baron Hawkesbury in 1796.

Port Hood NS This community on the west coast of Cape Breton Island was known as *Juste-au-Corps* during the French regime. Samuel Holland (1728–1801) called its harbour *Port Barrington* in 1767, but it was renamed Port Hood by mapmaker Joseph Frederic Wallet DesBarres (1722–1824) about 10 years later. He called it after Adm. Samuel Hood (1724–1816), who served in the Caribbean Sea during the American Revolution. Port Hood received postal service in 1829.

Port Hope ON In 2001 this town (1850) and **Hope Township** became part of the town of Port Hope and Hope, Northumberland County. Port Hope was known as both *Smith's Creek* (after Elias Smith) and *Toronto* in 1817. Because of confusion with the Toronto post office (after *Toronto Township*) at present-day Erindale in Mississauga, a special meeting was called in 1819, resulting in renaming it after Hope Township, named in 1792 after Col. Henry Hope (c.1746–89), lieutenant-governor of Quebec, 1785–9.

Port Hope Simpson NL Located on the south bank of the Alexis River and in southeastern Labrador, this municipal community (1973) was established as a lumbering centre in 1934 by J.O. Williams of Wales and was named after Sir John Hope Simpson (1868–1961), commissioner of natural resources, 1934–6.

Portland ON In 1998 this community became part of the township of Rideau Lakes, united counties of Leeds and Grenville. Located on Big Rideau Lake, its post office was named in 1833 after William Henry Cavendish Bentinck, 3rd Duke of Portland (1738–1809), British secretary of the home department and for the colonies, 1794–1801. The title was taken from the Isle of Portland in Dorset, offshore from Weymouth.

Portland Canal BC This narrow 145-km-long channel, extending from the north side of Wales Island to Stewart, became part of the boundary between British Columbia and Alaska in 1903. It was named in 1793 by Capt. George Vancouver (1757–98) after William Henry Cavendish Bentinck, 3rd Duke of Portland (1738–1809), British home secretary, 1794–1801. Capt. Vancouver gave the name *Brown Inlet* to the present **Portland Inlet**, extending for 50 km from the south side of Wales Island to the mouth of the Nass River. The present name was adopted in 1920, after it was found to be in local use.

Portland Township ON In 1998 this township became part of South Frontenac, Frontenac County. It was named in 1798 after William Henry Cavendish Bentinck, 3rd Duke of Portland (1738–1809), British secretary of the home department and for the colonies, 1794–1801.

Port Lambton ON In 2001 this community became part of the township of St. Clair, Lambton County. Located northwest of Wallaceburg, this place was first called *Lambton Village*. It was renamed Port Lambton in 1871, when the post office opened.

Port La Tour NS This harbour, southwest of Shelburne, was named after Charles de Saint-Étienne de la Tour (1593–1666), governor of Acadia, 1651–66. A post office opened in 1855 in the community of **Port La Tour**.

Port Maitland NS The post office of this place north of Yarmouth was first called *Maitland* in 1851 after Sir Peregrine Maitland (1777–1854), lieutenant-governor of Nova Scotia, 1828–34. It was given its present name in 1884.

Port Maitland ON At the mouth of the Grand River and in the town of Dunnville, Haldimand-Norfolk Region, it was named in 1846 after Lt.-Gov. Sir Peregrine Maitland (1777–1854), who once visited the site in the 1820s.

Port McNeill BC This town (1984) on the northeastern coast of Vancouver Island was named after **McNeill Bay**. The bay was named by the Hudson's Bay Company in 1837 after Capt. William Henry McNeill (1803–75), who served with the HBC from 1832 to 1863. He was chief factor at the company's Fort Rupert, now in the district municipality of Port Hardy.

Port Moody BC At the head of Burrard Inlet, east of Vancouver, this city (1913) was named in 1879 after the adjacent bay, when it was projected it would become the western terminus of the Canadian Pacific Railway. The bay was named **Port Moody** in 1860 by Capt. George Richards (1820–96) after Lt. Col. Richard Clement Moody (1813–87), who served as commissioner of lands and works in the new colony of British Columbia, 1858–63.

Port Morien NS On **Morien Bay**, southwest of Glace Bay, this place's post office was called *Cow Bay* in 1855. In 1894 it was given its present name, which may derive from the Portuguese designation for the nearby cape, now called Northern Head. The French called it *Cap de Mordienne* and the bay was described as *Baye de Mordienne*.

Port Mouton NS Southwest of Liverpool, this community's post office opened in 1855. It was named after the bay, described as **Port Mouton** by Pierre Du Gua de Monts (c.1550–1628) in 1604, when a sheep (*mouton*) jumped overboard and drowned but was recovered for its meat. Sir William Alexander (c.1567–1640) called it *St. Luke's Bay* in 1623, and map-maker Joseph Frederic Wallet DesBarres (1722–1824) assigned the name *Gambier Harbour* to it in 1776, but the original designation prevailed.

Portneuf QC In the regional county of **Portneuf**, this community was created as a municipal parish in 1863, which became a village in 1914 and a town in 1961. Its post office opened in 1817. The name has its roots in a seigneury granted in 1647 to Jacques Leneuf (later Portneuf) de La Poterie (c.1606–85), which was located at the mouth of a river called about 1641 *port neuf* ('new port'). The regional county was created in 1982.

Port Perry ON In the township of Scugog, Durham Region, this urban centre was named in 1852 after Peter Perry (1792–1851), a Whitby merchant who laid out lots here in 1848. He was the member for Lennox and Addington in the House of Assembly of Upper Canada, 1825–36.

Port Rexton NL Situated on the northwest side of Trinity Bay and southwest of Bonavista, this municipal community (1969) was formerly called *Ship Cove* and *Robin Hood*. The name was chosen in 1910, because the first male child born here was a son of John Rex, a native of Longham, Dorset, England, who settled here in the 1790s.

Port Robinson ON In the city of Thorold, regional municipality of Niagara, this community was called *Port Beverley* in 1829, when the Welland Canal was built south to the Welland River. It was named after Sir John Beverley Robinson (1791–1863), chief justice of Upper Canada, 1829–1862, and a director of the canal company. In 1834 it was renamed Port Robinson.

Port Ryerse ON This community in the city of Nanticoke, Haldimand-Norfolk Region, south of Simcoe, was named in 1854 after Col. Samuel Ryerse (1752–1812), who received a large grant of land in 1795 and subsequently held a number of public offices. Ryerse's name was really Ryerson, but it was misspelled when he received his militia commission, and he decided to keep the new spelling. It also distinguished him from a rebel branch of the family.

Port Saunders NL Situated on Ingornachoix Bay, southeast of Port au Choix, this town (1956) was called after the port, named in 1767 by Capt. James Cook (1728–79) after Adm. Sir Charles Saunders (c.1715–75). From July to October 1752 Saunders served as the commodore for the protection of Newfoundland's fishery. He commanded the British naval forces in the capture of Quebec City in 1759.

Port Stanley ON This village (1874) in Elgin County, south of London, was named about 1824, when Edward George Geoffrey Smith Stanley, 14th Earl of Derby (1799–1869) visited Col. Thomas Talbot (1771–1853) at his home at Port Talbot, and the post office opened five years later. Lord Stanley was later prime minister of Great Britain for three terms and was the father of Frederick Arthur Stanley, 16th Earl of Derby (1841–1908), Canada's governor general from 1888 to 1893.

Portugal Cove-St. Philip's NL On the east side of Conception Bay and northwest of St. John's, this town was established in 1992 by amalgamating the town (1977) of Portugal Cove and the town (1977) of *St. Phillips*. Portugal Cove was named after the adjacent cove, noted in 1675 by map-maker Henry Southwood. *St. Phillips* was first called *Broad Cove*. It was renamed in 1905 by Canon Smith, rector of St. Philip's Catholic Church in Portugal Cove, 1886–1921.

Portugal Cove South NL East of Trepassey, this municipal community (1963) was officially given this name in 1913 to distinguish it from Portugal Cove in Conception Bay. It was identified in 1610 as *B of Portingal* and in 1625 as *B Portugall*. It may have been named as early as 1500 by Gaspar Corte-Real (c.1450–1502). Both names reveal the extensive Portuguese connection with the fishery around Newfoundland.

Port Union NL South of Catalina and on the northwest side of Trinity Bay, this town (1961) was founded in 1914 by Sir William Ford Coaker (1871–1938). He established the headquarters of the Fishermen's Protective Union and the Fishermen's Union Trading Company here in 1916, and the place was named that year.

Port Williams NS Located west of Wolfville, this village (1951) was named in 1856 after Sir William Fenwick Williams (1800–83), a native of the province who endured the siege of Kars, in present-day Turkey, in 1855, and was the lieutenant-governor of Nova Scotia, 1865–7. Its post office opened in 1858.

Postville NL On the Labrador coast and on the northwest side of Kaipokok Bay, this municipal community (1975) was founded by the Reverend William Gillett (1574–1641), a Pentecostal pastor, in 1641. It was named after a post established here in 1830 by D.R. Stewart and was taken over by the Hudson's Bay Company in 1837. Although the HBC moved its post nearer to the mouth of the bay in 1879, the original site continued to be called 'the Post'.

Potton QC This township municipality in the regional county of Memphrémagog, west of Lac Memphrémagog, was established in 1845, taking its name from **Potton Township**, proclaimed in 1797. Shown on a map two years earlier, it was named after a village in Bedfordshire, north of London, England.

Pouce Coupe BC The post office in this village (1932) on the Pouce Coupé River, southeast of Dawson Creek, was named in 1912 after the river. The river is reported to be named after a Sekani trapper who was nicknamed Pouce Coupé ('cut thumb') by French-speaking voyageurs, because he lost his thumb in a gun accident. Explorer Simon Fraser made a reference to him in 1806. Locally it is believed the real origin was a Beaver chief whose name was Pooscapee in his language, with voyageurs rendering it with the homonym Pouce Coupé. Although the village's name is pronounced 'poos-KOO-pay', it does not have an 'é' accent.

Pouch Cove NL On the southeast side of Cape St. Francis, and north of St. John's, this town (1970) was first noted in 1805 and was recorded by Joseph B. Jukes in 1840 as *Pouche Cove*. Pronounced like 'pooch', the name may derive from a French family name, although locally there is no accepted explanation for it.

Powassan ON This town (1904) in Parry Sound District, south of North Bay, was named in 1891 after the Ojibwa for 'bend in the river', because there are some sharp bends in the South River, just west of the town.

Powell River BC This district municipality (1955) on the mainland coast and at the west end of Malaspina Strait, was named after the river, which drains **Powell Lake**. The river and lake were named in 1881 by Lt. Cmdr. V.B. Orlebar after Dr. Israel Wood Powell (1836–1915), when they made a tour of the coast. Powell was a superintendent of education and a superintendent of Indian affairs in the province.

Powerview MB This village (1951) on the Winnipeg River, northeast of Winnipeg, was created in 1925 as a residential community outside the Manitoba Pulp and Paper Company's planned community of Pine Falls. Its post office opened in 1963.

Pownal PE On Pownal Bay, southeast of Charlottetown, this place's post office was established as Lot 49 about 1854, renamed *Pownall* in 1871, and given its present form in 1940. The bay was named *Pownall Bay* in 1765 by Samuel Holland (1728–1801) after John Pownall, secretary of the board of trade and plantations, 1758–61. In 1779 map-maker Joseph Frederic Wallet DesBarres (1722–1824) spelled it **Pownal Bay**, and this ultimately became the preferred form.

Prairies, Rivière des QC Separating the Île de Montréal and the Île Jésus, it was known to Samuel de Champlain (1567–1635) in 1610. In both his writings, and in the Jesuit *Relation* of 1637, there is a reference to a courageous young man from Saint-Malo called 'des Prairies'. According to the Jesuit *Relation*, it was named after him.

Preeceville SK North of Canora, this town (1946) was named in 1912 by the Canadian Northern Railway after Louise Preece and her son Fred, who homesteaded its site in 1904. Louise fed the men who laid the track. The post office was also opened in 1912.

Prelate SK Just east of the town of Leader and northwest of Swift Current, the site of this village (1913) was established by the Canadian Pacific Railway in 1913. Its post office opened in 1914, 5 km south of the village centre. A 'prelate' is a bishop or an abbot in the Anglican and Catholic churches.

Premier Range BC Located in the Cariboo Mountains, west of Valemount, this range's peaks exceeding 3048 m were reserved in 1927 to honour Canadian prime ministers not previously commemorated. Peaks were then named after prime ministers Sir John Thompson, Sir John Abbott, and Sir Mackenzie Bowell. The names of Richard Bennett, Arthur Meighen, and Mackenzie King followed in 1962, Louis St-Laurent was added in 1964, and Lester Pearson in 1972. Also in the group are mountains named for British prime minister Stanley Baldwin (1927), British Columbia premier John Oliver (1927), and pre-Confederation co-premier of Canada Sir Allan MacNab (1974). Eight peaks over 3048 m remain unnamed officially.

Prescott ON The county was named in 1798 after Maj. Gen. Robert Prescott (1725–1815), governor-in-chief of Canada, Nova Scotia, and New Brunswick, 1797–99, although retaining the official title until 1807. It became part of the united counties of Prescott and Russell in 1822.

Prescott ON This separated town (1868) in the united counties of Leeds and Grenville since 1849 was laid out in 1810 by Maj. Edward Jessop. It was named in 1817 for Maj. Gen. Robert Prescott (1725–1815), governor-in-chief of Canada, Nova Scotia, and New Brunswick, 1797–9.

President Range BC In Yoho National Park, north of Field, these mountains were named in 1907 by the Alpine Club of Canada after the senior officials of the Canadian Pacific Railway. As their surnames had already been used elsewhere, the highest peaks were called The President (3138 m) and The Vice President (3066 m).

Preston NS Located east of Dartmouth, this place was named in 1886 after Preston Township, established in 1784. The latter may have been named after Preston, Lancashire, England, or after Maj. Charles Preston, who served with Sir Guy Carleton (1724–1808) in the 1770s in the defence of British North America. Descendants of slaves expelled from Jamaica settled in Preston in 1796, but migrated four years later to Sierre Leone in Africa. In 1816 the British brought 924 African-American slaves to Halifax, and they were located in Preston and **North Preston**.

Prévost QC This municipality in the regional county of La Rivière-du-Nord, north of Saint-Jérôme, was created in 1977 through the amalgamation of the villages of Shawbridge (1909) and Prévost (1927). Shawbridge post office opened in 1860 and became Prévost in 1981, after having been a summer office since 1823. Its name may derive from Wilfrid Prévost (1832–98), member for Deux-Montagnes in the House of Commons, or for his son, Jean-Benoît-Berchmans Prévost (1870–1815), or his nephew, Jules-Édouard Prévost (1871–1943), the latter were both elected.

Price QC The post office in this village in the regional county of La Mitis, east of Mont-Joli, opened in 1891. The village was incorporated as *Priceville* in 1926, but because of confusion with Princeville, near Victoriaville, it was renamed Price in 1945. It was named after prominent lumberman William Evan Price (1827–80), who served in both the House of Commons, 1872–4, and the Legislative Assembly, 1875–80.

Primrose Lake AB, SK On the Alberta–Saskatchewan boundary and north of Cold Lake, this lake was named by boundary surveyors on 19 April 1909 on the anniversary of Primrose Day, and in commemoration of Benjamin Disraeli, Earl of Beaconsfield (1804–81) who died on that day in 1881.

Prince PE This county was named in 1765 by Samuel Holland (1728–1801) after George Augustus Frederick, Prince of Wales (1762–1830), who became George IV in 1820.

Prince Albert SK In 1866 the Reverend James Nisbet (1823–74) established a Presbyterian mission on the North Saskatchewan River and named it after the consort of Queen Victoria. Prince Albert died five years earlier. A post office was established in the city (1904) in 1879. **Prince Albert National Park** (3875 km²), northwest of the city, was created in 1927.

Prince Albert, Mount BC In the Royal Group, east of Invermere, this mountain (3209 m) was named in 1913 after Prince Albert (1895–1952), who was crowned George VI in 1936.

Prince Albert Peninsula NT In northwestern Victoria Island, this peninsula was first called *Prince Albert Land*, possibly by explorer Richard Collinson (1811–83) in 1852 after the consort of Queen Victoria. It was redesignated in 1905. **Prince Albert Sound**, which extends into Victoria Island between Wollaston and Diamond Jenness peninsulas, was named by Collinson in 1852.

Prince Charles Island NU In northern Foxe Basin, this island (9521 km²) was discovered in 1948 by a Royal Canadian Air Force aerial survey. It was officially named the following year, after Prince Charles, who was born 14 November 1948. It was the second last major Canadian island to be identified, the last being Stefansson Island, in the western Arctic, in 1952. *See also* Air Force Island.

Prince Edward ON In 1998 all of the towns, villages, and townships in this county became parts of the municipality of Prince Edward County. The county was named in 1792 after Prince Edward Augustus, Duke of Kent (1767–1820), fourth son of George III, and father of Queen Victoria. When he was commander-in-chief of the British forces in North America, he took a tour from Quebec to Niagara Falls and visited the county named after him on his return.

Prince Edward Island The province was named in 1798 by the Legislative Assembly after Prince Edward, Duke of Kent (1767–1820), who then commanded the troops in Halifax. It was confirmed 5 February 1799 by George III. After 1759 it was called *St. John's Island*, a translation of *Isle de Saint Jean*, given by French explorers and recorded by Samuel de Champlain (1567–1635) in 1604. **Prince Edward Island National Park** (18 km²), on the north shore of the province, was established in 1937.

Prince Edward Island, Mount YT In the Centennial Range of the St. Elias Mountains, this mountain (3737 m) was named in 1967 after the province.

Prince Edward, Mount BC In the Royal Group, east of Invermere, this mountain (3200 m) was named in 1913 after

Prince Edward (1894–1972), who was crowned Edward VIII in 1936. On abdicating the throne that year, he was appointed the Duke of Windsor.

Prince George BC This city (1915), located at the confluence of the Nechako and Fraser Rivers, was established in 1807 as Fort George by Simon Fraser (1716–1862) of the North West Company, who named the place after George III. The fort was closed by the Hudson's Bay Company in 1915. With the Grand Trunk Pacific Railway's planned arrival from Edmonton after 1910, it chose a site north of Fort George and called it Prince George after the Duke of Kent (1902–42), a younger brother of George VI (whose forename was Albert). During the first civic elections in 1915, the ratepayers indicated a preference for Prince George over Fort George by a vote of 153 to 13. **Mount Prince George** (2880 m) in the Royal Group, east of Invermere, was named in 1913 after the same prince.

Prince Gustav Adolf Sea NU Surrounded by Ellef Ringnes, King Christian, Lougheed, Mackenzie King, and Borden Islands, this body of water was named by Otto Sverdrup (1854–92) during his 1898–1902 expedition after the crown prince of Sweden.

Prince Henry, Mount BC In the Royal Group, east of Invermere, this mountain (3227 m) was named in 1913 after Prince Henry, the Duke of Gloucester (1900–74), a brother of Edward VIII and George VI.

Prince John, Mount BC In the Royal Group, east of Invermere, this mountain (3236 m) was named in 1913 after Prince John (1905–19), a brother of Edward VIII and George VI.

Prince of Wales Island NU Between Victoria and Somerset Islands, this island (33,339 km²) was named in 1851, possibly by explorers Erasmus Ommanney (1814–1904), Sherard Osborn (1822–75), and William Browne after Albert Edward, Prince of Wales (1841–1910). As Edward VII he was the king from 1901 to 1910. **Prince of Wales Strait**, between Melville and Banks Islands, was named by Robert McClure (1807–73) in 1852 after the same prince.

Prince Patrick Island NT One of the Parry Islands of the Queen Elizabeth Islands, this island (15,848 km²) was named about 1852 after Arthur William Patrick Albert, Duke of Connaught and Strathearn (1850–1942), third son of Queen Victoria. He served as governor general of Canada, 1911–16.

Prince Regent Inlet NU Between Somerset Island and Boothia Peninsula on the west, and Brodeur Peninsula on the east, this 300-km inlet was named in 1819 by Sir William Parry (1790–1855) on the anniversary of the birth of George

Augustus Frederick (1762–1830), eldest son of George III. He was appointed Prince Regent in 1811 and became George IV in 1820.

Prince Rupert BC A seaport just north of the mouth of the Skeena River, this city (1910) was founded by the Grand Trunk Pacific Railway as the western terminus for its intercontinental line. In 1906 the GTP decided to offer a prize of $250 for the best name with no more than 10 letters and three syllables. From 5000 entries the suggestion from Eleanor MacDonald of Winnipeg to name it after the first governor of the Hudson's Bay Company was accepted. Since her proposal had 12 letters, the GTP gave two additional first prizes for the name Port Rupert.

Princess Mary Lake NU Located west of Baker Lake, the name of this lake (471 km²) was proposed in 1958 by the Royal Canadian Corps of Signals after Princess Mary, the Princess Royal (1897–1965), eldest daughter of Queen Victoria.

Princess Mary, Mount BC In the Royal Group, east of Invermere, this mountain (3084 m) was named in 1913 after Princess Mary, the Princess Royal (1897–1965), eldest daughter of Queen Victoria.

Princess Mountain BC In the Coast Mountains, southeast of Bella Coola, this mountain (2941 m) was named in 1955 by a member of the Alpine Club of Canada, who observed that the glaciers surrounding it reminded him of a princess's white gown radiating from its summit.

Princess Royal Island BC The largest of the islands along the province's Inside Passage, this island (2251 km²) was named in 1788 by Capt. Charles Duncan after his trading ship, *Princess Royal*.

Princeton BC This town (1978) at the junction of the Tulameen and Similkameen Rivers, midway between Hope and Penticton, was named in 1860 by Gov. James Douglas (1803–77) after Prince Albert Edward, the Prince of Wales (1841–1910), who visited eastern North America that year. It was earlier called *Vermilion Forks* and *Red Earth Forks* (after a local red ochre source valued by Aboriginals), *Similkameen* (after the river), and *Allison's* (after pioneer rancher and miner John Fall Allison).

Princeville QC This town (1964) located northeast of Victoriaville, was created a village in 1857. The adjacent parish municipality of **Princeville** was named in 1969, having been called *Saint-Eusèbe-de-Stanfold* in 1855. *Stanfold* post office opened here in 1849 and was changed to Princeville in 1914. The name was given in honour of an early settler, Pierre Prince.

Prince William NB Located on the south side of Saint John River, 33 km west of Fredericton, this community's post office was named in 1845 after **Prince William Parish**. The parish, established in 1786, was created as a township in 1783 and named by Edward Winslow (c.1746–1815) and Daniel Murray (1777–1814) after Prince William, third son of George III, and the future William IV. He was the patron of the King's American Dragoons, which received land grants in the parish.

Prior Peak AB, BC Located on the continental divide, southwest of Howse Pass, this mountain (3270 m) was named in 1924 after Edward Gawler Prior (1853–1920), lieutenant-governor of British Columbia, 1919–20.

Pritchard BC Located on the south bank of the South Thompson River, east of Kamloops, this place's post office was named in 1911 after farmer Walter Pritchard, who settled here in 1904. Earlier it was called *Pemberton Spur* after sawmill owner Arthur G. Pemberton.

Procter BC Located on the south side of the West Arm of Kootenay Lake, east of Nelson, this place was named in 1906 after Nelson real estate speculator and first postmaster Thomas Gregg Proctor, who was the manager of the Kootenay Valley Company.

Prophet River BC Rising in the Muskwa Ranges of the Rocky Mountains, this river flows east and then north into the Muskwa River, south of the town of Fort Nelson. It was likely named for a prophet of the Beaver nation, such as a recent one called Notseta or an earlier one known as Decutla.

Prospect NS Located on the Atlantic coast, southwest of Halifax, this place's name may have originated from the Mi'kmaq *nospadakun* ('herb mixed with tobacco'). Between 1672 and 1744 it appeared in various forms, including *Passepec*, *Paspek*, *Paspee*, and *Prospec*, before occurring as Prospect in 1754. Its post office opened in 1852.

Proton ON In 2000 this township became part of the township of Southgate, Grey County. It was named in 1827, likely by Lt.-Gov. Sir Peregrine Maitland (1777–1854) after the Greek word for 'the first'.

Provost AB This town (1952) near the Saskatchewan border and southeast of Wainwright was named in 1907 by the Canadian Pacific Railway after the equivalent of a chief magistrate of a Scottish burgh. Its post office opened the following year.

Prud'homme SK A village (1922) northeast of Saskatoon, its post office was named in 1923 after Mgr. Joseph H. Prud'homme (1882–1952), bishop of Prince Albert and Saskatoon. It was called *Lily* when the Canadian Northern

Railway was built through it in 1904, and from 1906 to 1923 its post office was known as *Howell*.

Ptolemy, Mount BC, AB Located on the continental divide, south of Crowsnest Pass, this mountain (2813 m) was named in 1915 by surveyor Arthur O. Wheeler (1860–1945) because it resembled the head and chest of a man lying prone and gazing upwards, reminding him of Ptolemy, an astronomer and geographer of the second century.

Pubnico NS At the head of **Pubnico Harbour**, southeast of Yarmouth, this place's name derives from the Mi'kmaq *pogomkook* ('dry sandy place'). Its post office was called *Pubnico Harbour* in 1850, *Pubnico Head* in 1900, and its present form in 1918. On each side of the 15-km harbour are several communities, with each incorporating the name Pubnico. Their postal opening dates are as follows: **East Pubnico** (1860), **Lower East Pubnico** (1873), **Lower West Pubnico** (1873), **West Pubnico** (1874), **Middle East Pubnico** (1899), **Middle West Pubnico** (about 1899), **Upper West Pubnico** (1923), and **Centre East Pubnico** (1925).

Pugwash NS At the mouth of **Pugwash River** and on the Northumberland Strait, east of Amherst, the first post office in this village (1948) was called *Waterford* in 1825. It was renamed after the river in 1828. The name of the river derives from the Mi'kmaq *pagweak* ('shallow water' or 'shoal'). In 1957 Pugwash native, American industrialist, and philanthropist Cyrus Eaton (1883–1979) convened the first of his Pugwash Conferences here. In 1995 the promotion of peace and understanding by the Pugwash Movement among the world's nations was rewarded with a Nobel Peace Prize in 1995.

Pukaskwa River ON Rising west of Wawa, this river flows west into Lake Superior. Adopted in 1922, the name follows the spelling on a 1918 department of interior map, although its pronunciation, 'PUK-a-saw', suggests a name more like *Pukoso River*, shown on an 1878 Canadian chart of the lake. The name may have been taken from Ojibwa *Pagisowinakak* ('bathing place'). **Pukaskwa National Park**, established in 1971, has an area of 1878 km².

Punkeydoodles Corners ON In the regional municipality of Waterloo, midway between Kitchener and Stratford, this locality has one of the province's most amusing names. It is said that busy, prosperous farmers of German descent resented a lazy farmer among them, who grew only pumpkins, earning the nickname 'Punkeydoodle'. The name is also said to be a garbled rendition of the song 'Yankee Doodle'. For the record, Punkeydoodles Corners had a post office for six hours on 26 June 1982.

Punnichy SK Northeast of Regina, this village (1909) was named in 1908 by the Grand Trunk Pacific Railway as part of its alphabetical order of names, with Quinton and Raymore following to the west. Its post office opened in 1909. It is said that its name was a Saulteaux nickname given to pioneer settler Wolfe Armstrong Heuback, because his bald head fringed by a ring of hair reminded them of a chicken without feathers.

Purcell Mountains BC These mountains, part of the Columbia Mountains, extend north from the Idaho–Montana border to a point north of Golden, and from the upper valleys of the Columbia and the Kootenay Rivers on the east to Kootenay Lake, and Duncan and Beaver Rivers on the west. They were named in 1859 by Dr. Sir James Hector (1834–1907) after Dr. Goodwin Purcell (1817–76), who had taught Hector therapeutics and medical jurisdiction in Edinburgh.

Puslinch ON A township in Wellington County, it was named in 1835 after the Devon, England birthplace of Elizabeth Yonge (1790–1872), the wife of Sir John Colborne (1778–1863), lieutenant-governor of Upper Canada, 1828–36.

Puvirnituq QC The present spelling of the name of this northern village, located on the east shore of Hudson Bay and at the mouth of the **Rivière de Povungnituk**, was adopted in 1995. The place was erected as the northern village of Povungnituk in 1989. It took its name from the Inuit community, first identified on maps about 1945. In Inuktitut the name means 'it smells of rotting meat'.

Quaco Head NB Extending into the Bay of Fundy at St. Martins, this point was named after the Mi'kmaq *goolwahgahweek* ('place of the hooded seal'). Map-maker Jean-Baptiste-Louis Franquelin (c.1653–1712) noted it as *Ariquaki* in 1686. **Quaco Bay**, behind the head, was identified on a 1762 map.

Quadra Island BC Located at the north end of the Strait of Georgia and just north of Campbell River, this island was named in 1903 by the Geographic Board of Canada after Nootka governor Juan Francisco de la Bodega y Quadra (1744–94). He negotiated with Capt. George Vancouver (1757–98) a friendly transfer of the area of Vancouver Island in 1792 to the British Crown. Capt. Vancouver called the island *Quadra and Vancouver's Island*, but the addition of Quadra's name fell into disuse. The present Quadra, Maurelle, and Sonora Islands were formerly believed to be part of a single island called *Valdes Island*.

Qualicum Beach BC This town (1983) is located on the east coast of Vancouver Island, northwest of Nanaimo. Its post office was named in 1913 after the **Qualicum River**, whose name in the Nanaimo language means 'place of the dog (or chum) salmon'.

Qu'Appelle SK The post office in this town (1904) east of Regina and 25 km south of Fort Qu'Appelle was founded as *Troy* in 1882 on the Canadian Pacific Railway. It was renamed *Qu'Appelle Station* two years later, changed to *South Qu'Appelle* in 1902, and finally became Qu'Appelle in 1911. It took its name from the **Qu'Appelle River**, which rises northwest of Moose Jaw, and flows east to join the Assiniboine at St. Lazare, MB. The name is said to be from a legend of a Cree warrior travelling far from home, and hearing his lover's voice, asked 'who calls?' On returning home he found she had died, with her last words calling for him. This legend may have come from a poem by Métis poet Pauline Johnson. Among the Cree there is a legend of an old woman travelling upriver with four dogs, but when one would not go on, she beat it to death. Every summer after that the dog could be heard calling. The lakes at Fort Qu'Appelle are called Calling Lakes, with one known as Katepwa Lake, *katepwa* meaning 'calling' in Cree. *See also* Fort Qu'Appelle.

Quaqtaq QC This northern village on the northwest shore of Ungava Bay was called *Koartak* in 1950, *Notre-Dame-de-Koartac* in 1961, and *Koartac* in 1965. In Inuktitut

the name means 'intestinal worms', making the name *Notre-Dame-de-Koartac* a rather weird designation during the francization of northern Quebec place names in the early 1960s.

Quatsino Sound BC Located on the northwest coast of Vancouver Island, this inlet was identified on an Admiralty chart of 1849 as *Quatsinough Sound*, and the present form was adopted in 1920. It was called after the Koskimo, a Kwakiutl tribe, whose name may mean 'people of the north country' in the Kwakwala language. The post office in Quatsino, a community at the head of the sound, was named in 1896.

Quebec After the 1763 Treaty of Paris, the name Quebec was adapted to describe the former territory of New France, roughly centred on the St. Lawrence River, extending north to Lake Nipissing and south to the forty-fifth parallel. In 1774 it was extended north to the limits of the watershed of the St. Lawrence, west beyond the Great Lakes to the lands between the Ohio and Mississippi Rivers, and east to include the north shore of the Gulf of St. Lawrence and the present area of Labrador. In 1791 the territorial name of Quebec was replaced by Lower Canada and Upper Canada. The two were united as the Province of Canada in 1841, with each division being called Canada East and Canada West, although Upper and Lower Canada continued in both popular and official use. With the passing of the British North America Act in 1867, the name Quebec was restored as the name of the province centred on the lower St. Lawrence, with its northern limits following the heads of rivers flowing into the river and the gulf. These limits were extended north to the central part of the present province in 1898, and all of the land area of the territory of Ungava was added in 1912. Its area was reduced by the Imperial Privy Council in 1927 by awarding the area of present Labrador to Newfoundland.

Quebec QC Arguably North America's prettiest city, Quebec occupies a significant place in the hearts not only of its residents, but among Québécois wherever they live. In 1985 it was added to the list of world heritage sites by UNESCO. When Jacques Cartier (1491–1667) arrived at the site in 1535, the local Iroquoian-speaking people called it *Stadacone*. In 1601 its site was identified as *Quebecq*, the description in Algonquin and Abenaki of the narrow, relatively obstructed channel of the St. Lawrence between the city and the south shore. Samuel de Champlain (1567–

1635) founded the city in 1608, and built his 'Abitation' here, making it the focus of the vast French political and commercial empire based on the St. Lawrence and the Great Lakes.

Quebec, Mount YT This mountain (3749 m), in the Centennial Range of the St. Elias Mountains, was named in 1967 after the province.

Queen Bess, Mount BC In the Coast Mountains, southeast of Mount Waddington, this mountain (3290 m) was named in 1935 after Queen Elizabeth I in commemoration of the signing of the international law of the freedom of the seas, initiated by the Queen on the return to England of Sir Francis Drake (c. 1540–95) in 1580.

Queen Charlotte Islands BC These islands were named in 1787 by Capt. George Dixon (c.1755–1800) after one of his two ships, the *Queen Charlotte*. The ship was named after the consort of George III. The community of **Queen Charlotte**, at the south end of Graham Island, was called **Queen Charlotte City** in the 1800s, and this remains a second official name. **Queen Charlotte Sound**, now designating that part of the Pacific Ocean between Vancouver Island and the Queen Charlotte Islands, was given to the wide entrance between Vancouver Island and the mainland in 1786 by S. Wedgborough after the consort of George III. This entrance is now called **Queen Charlotte Strait**, which originally designated the channel uniting Johnstone Strait to Queen Charlotte Sound.

Queen Elizabeth Foreland NU On the north side of the entrance to Frobisher Bay, this point was named in 1576 by Sir Martin Frobisher (c.1535–94) after Queen Elizabeth I.

Queen Elizabeth Islands NT, NU All the islands in the Arctic Archipelago, north of Parry Channel, were named Queen Elizabeth Islands in 1954 after Queen Elizabeth II.

Queen Elizabeth Ranges AB Surrounding Maligne Lake, southeast of Jasper, these mountain ranges were named in 1953 by the Geographic Board of Alberta in honour of the coronation of Elizabeth II.

Queen Mary, Mount BC In the Royal Group, east of Invermere, this mountain (3245 m) was named in 1913 after Queen Mary (1867–1953), the consort of George V and the mother of Edward VIII and George VI.

Queen Mary, Mount YT Located in the Icefield Ranges of the St. Elias Mountains, this mountain (3886 m) was named in 1935 by American climber Bradford Washburn (1910–2007) in honour of the silver jubilee of George V and Queen Mary.

Queen Maud Gulf NU Located southeast of Victoria Island and southwest of King William Island, this gulf was named in

1904 by Roald Amundsen (1872–1928) after Queen Maud of Norway, the third daughter of Edward VII.

Queens NB Located to the west of Kings County, this county was named in 1785, likely as an expression of loyalty to George III and Queen Charlotte (1744–1818).

Queens NS Created as a county in 1762, and named after Queen Charlotte (1744–1818), the consort of George III, Queens became the region municipality of Queens on 1 April 1996.

Queens PE This county was named in 1765 by Samuel Holland (1728–1801) after Queen Charlotte (1744–1818), the consort of George III.

Queenston ON Located on the west bank of the Niagara River and in the town of Niagara-on-the-Lake, it was founded in 1789 by Robert Hamilton (1787–1851) and named about 1810. Possibly it was named after either Queen Charlotte, the wife of George III, or John Graves Simcoe's regiment, the Queen's Rangers.

Quesnel BC This city (1928) south of Prince George, and at the junction of the Quesnel and Fraser Rivers, was named in the early 1860s after the river. **Quesnel River** (203 km) was named in 1808 by explorer Simon Fraser (1776–1862) after his North West Company clerk Jules-Maurice Quesnel (1786–1842), who remained in New Caledonia for three more years. The river drains the 90-km-long **Quesnel Lake**.

Quetico Provincial Park ON Set aside as a forest reserve in 1909, this area became a provincial park in 1950. The meaning of Quetico is uncertain. The name may derive from the Ojibwa *Windego osestguan* ('cannibal head'), relating to a legendary giant knocking off the head of another giant, with the head appearing as an island the following spring.

Quidi Vidi Harbour NL On the northeast side of St. John's, this harbour was identified in 1669 as *Kitty-vitty* by Devon surgeon James Yonge (c.1646–1721). Between then and the late 1800s, another two dozen spellings were used for the name, but none reveal its meaning. In 1971 writer Edgar R. Seary (1908–84) suggested the name may derive from a French or Channel Islands family name, such as Quédville, Quidville, Quiédville, or Quetteville, or from Quetteville, near Honfleur, France.

Quill Lake SK The post office in this village (1906) located east of Humboldt and north of **Big Quill** and **Little Quill** lakes was named by first postmaster Robert (Dick) Gordon in 1904. When the Canadian Northern Railway arrived in the area the next year, it named its station *Lally* after a company official, but agreed to use Quill Lake when the post office was moved 3 km to its line. The Aboriginals collected pelican feathers at the lakes for their arrows.

Quincy Adams, Mount BC In the St. Elias Mountains, 4 km east of Fairweather Mountain, this mountain (4133 m) was named in 1923 after John Quincy Adams (1767–1848), president of the United States, 1825–9. As secretary of state in 1825, he negotiated the first treaty with Russia, which subsequently led to the establishment of the northwestern boundary between American and Canadian territory.

Quinte, Bay of ON The name of this long channel separating Prince Edward County from the mainland likely has Mohawk roots, possibly after *Yo-ya-da-do-konthe,* the sanctuary home of the Thunderbird. It is also possible that it is taken from *kenta* or *kenhenta* ('meadow', 'prairie', or 'stopping place').

Quinte West ON In 1998 the city of Trenton, the village of Frankford, and the townships of Sidney and Murray became parts of the city of Quinte West, Hastings County.

Quinton SK North of Regina, this village (1910) was named in 1908 by the Grand Trunk Pacific Railway after one of its engineers. It was assigned between Punnichy and Raymore as part of its alphabetical list of names. Its post office opened in 1909.

Quirpon NL At the northeast end of the Northern Peninsula, this place (pronounced 'kar-POON') was named after **Quirpon Harbour** and **Quirpon Island**, offshore in the entrance to the Strait of Belle Isle. Jacques Cartier (1491–1667) was forced to spend two weeks in 1534 in the harbour of *Le Karpont*. It may have been named after Havre Le Kerpont, between Saint-Malo and the Île de Bréhat in Bretagne, France.

Quispamsis NB This town (1982), northeast of Saint John, was named in 1857 by the European and North American Railway after the Maliseet *Quispem Sis* ('little lake'), in reference to Ritchie Lake. Its post office served the area from 1883 to 1931.

Quyon QC In the municipality of Pontiac since 1975, and at the point where **Rivière Quyon** flows into the Ottawa River, this community was incorporated as a municipality in 1875. Before then the name was spelled both *Quio* and *Couillon*. The current spelling was recommended by etymologist Edward Van Cortlandt (1805–75) of Ottawa, as best preserving its sound. The name likely means 'river with a sandy bottom' in Algonquin. The suggestion that it derives from a lacrosse-type game called *des couillons* has the marks of a folk tale evolving from the similar pronunciations of two words.

Raanes Peninsula NU On the west side of Ellesmere Island, this 90-km peninsula was named before 1910 after Oluf Raanes, a member of the Sverdrup (1854–1930) expedition, 1898–1902. He and Ivar Fosheim explored the west side of the island in 1901.

Rabbit Lake SK The postmaster of this village (1928) northeast of North Battleford was Ransford Rounds; Rounds worked there from 1910 to 1921, when he died. His wife Minerva was the postmaster until 1927. She wanted to change the name to *Round Stone* but the residents preferred keeping Rabbit Lake.

Race, Cape NL This most southeasterly point of Newfoundland was identified on early maps of the 1500s as *capo raso* ('flat cape'), a Portuguese description of the flat cliffs here. It may also have been named after Cabo Raso at the mouth of the River Tagus, the last point seen after sailing from Lisbon.

Radcliffe ON In 2001 this township became part of the township of Madawaska Valley, Renfrew County. It was named in 1859 after Thomas Radcliff (1794–1841), who fought with the Duke of Wellington during the Peninsular War in Spain. Radcliffe settled in Middlesex County in 1832 and was appointed to the Legislative Council of Upper Canada in 1839.

Radisson SK The first post office of this town (1913) southeast of North Battleford was called *Great Bend* in 1903 after the sharp left-angled turn of the North Saskatchewan River, while the growing community was known as *Goodrich* after homesteader J.S. Goodrich. In 1905 the Canadian Northern Railway named its station after French explorer Pierre-Esprit Radisson (1636–1710), and its post office name was also changed that year.

Radisson QC Located adjacent to the Barrage LG-Deux, à dam at the point where La Grande Rivière continues its course to James Bay, this community was named in 1973 by the Société de développement de la Baie James. The name was chosen to honour Pierre-Esprit Radisson (1636–1710), the noted explorer and fur trader, who was one of the founders of the Hudson's Bay Company in 1670.

Radium Hot Springs BC In the upper Columbia River valley, north of Windermere, this village (1990) was first called *Sinclair Hot Springs*. It took its name from adjacent Sinclair Canyon, given after trader James Sinclair (1806–56), who brought an Oregon-bound party of emigrants through the canyon in 1841. The place was renamed Radium Hot Springs in 1915 after the high radioactivity in the springs.

Radville SK Southwest of Weyburn, this town (1913) was founded by the Canadian Northern Railway in 1910, at a point where Conrad Paquin had settled. After reviewing various suggestions for the station's name, such as Conradville, the last syllable of Paquin's first name was fused with 'ville' to form Radville. *Wallindale* post office was opened nearby in 1909 with Erik Wallin as the postmaster, but two years later he moved into Radville and accepted the change.

Radway AB The post office in this community northeast of Edmonton was named in 1910 after merchant and postmaster Orland S. Radway, who settled here the year before, and first proposed calling it Radway Centre. His father, Frankford O. Radway, homesteaded in the area in 1897. It was an incorporated as a village from 1943 to 1996, when it became a hamlet.

Rae-Edzo NT At the head of the North Arm of Great Slave Lake and northwest of Yellowknife, this hamlet (1971) is divided into two distinct communities that are 24 km apart. Rae is the site of Fort Rae, established here in 1904 by the Hudson's Bay Company; it had been located 8 km to the southeast by Dr John Rae (1813–93) in 1852. Edzo was created in 1965 as a site with better drainage, but most of the Dogrib continued to live at the older location. The name Edzo recalls a Dogrib chief who worked out a peace settlement with the Yellowknife, a Chipewyan tribe, in the early nineteenth century. *See also* Behchokǫ̀.

Rae Isthmus NU A 75-km isthmus at the southwest end of Melville Peninsula, it was named after Dr. John Rae (1813–93), who explored the area of the isthmus in 1846-7.

Rae Lakes NT On an isthmus between Faber Lake and **Rae Lake**, northwest of Yellowknife, this settlement was named in 1978. Rae Lake and Rae Lakes were named after Dr. John Rae (1813–93), who established the Hudson's Bay Company's post of Fort Rae, northwest of Yellowknife, in 1852.

Raglan ON In 1999 this township became a part of the township of Brudenelll, Lyndoch and Raglan, Renfrew

County. It was named in 1857 after Fitzroy James Henry Somerset, 1st Baron Raglan (1788–1855), who commanded the British forces during the Crimean War and died here of cholera. **Raglan White Lake** is in the centre of the township. **Raglan Street** is the main street in the town of Renfrew.

Ragueneau QC Located in the regional county of Manicouagan, southwest of Baie-Comeau, this parish municipality was created in 1951, although some sources indicate it had been incorporated in 1933, 13 years after the township of **Ragueneau** was proclaimed. The township was named after Jesuit Fr. Paul Ragueneau (1608–80), who served as a missionary in New France from 1636 to 1662.

Rainbow Lake AB This town (1966) in the northwestern part of the province was named after an enlargement of Hay River, 23 km to the southeast. The name is a translation of the Dene description of its crescent shape. The post office opened in 1967.

Rainville QC This municipality in the regional county of Brome-Missisquoi, northwest of Cowansville, was known as the township municipality of *Farnham-Partie-Ouest* from 1855 to 1962. It was renamed after Théophile Rainville, the first francophone mayor, who served for several terms between 1887 and 1905.

Rainy Lake; Rainy River ON The boundary between Ontario and Minnesota goes through Rainy Lake and Rainy River, and the latter flows west into the Lake of the Woods. The French forms *Lac à la Pluie* and *Rivière à la Pluie* appear in records only after 1759. By 1800 they were being rendered as Rainy Lake and Rainy River. The names may be rooted in the Ojibwa expression *tekamammaouen* ('it rains all the time'), referring to the spray of the falls at Fort Frances. Explorer Pierre Gaulthier de la Vérendrye (1685–1749) wrote *Lac Tekemamihouenne* in 1738. **Rainy River** post office opened in 1886. However, the site of the town (1904) was called *Beaver Mills* in 1898, and was only changed to Rainy River in 1903. **Rainy River District** was separated from Thunder Bay District in 1914.

Raleigh NL Near the northern end of the Northern Peninsula and north of St. Anthony, this municipal community (1973) was first known as *Ha Ha* and *Ha Ha Bay* after the adjacent bay whose name refers to a narrow isthmus that separates it from Pistolet Bay. It was renamed in 1914 in honour of Sir Walter Raleigh (c.1552–1618), who supported Humphrey Gilbert, his half-brother, in his colonizing and fishing plans in Newfoundland. *See also* Ha! Ha!, Baie des, *and* Saint-Louis-du-Ha! Ha!

Raleigh ON In 1998 this township became part of the municipality of Chatham-Kent, Kent County. It was named in 1794 after the town of Rayleigh in Essex, England, east of London.

Raleigh, Mount BC In the Coast Mountains, east of Bute Inlet, this mountain (3131 m) was named in 1933 by George G. Aitken, provincial member of the Geographic Board of Canada, after Sir Walter Raleigh (c.1552–1618). Raleigh supported an expedition of his half-brother, Sir Humphrey Gilbert, who planned a voyage in the late 1500s to trade on the west coast of North America, but died at sea near Newfoundland. *See also* Gilbert, Mount.

Ralston AB Northwest of Medicine Hat and on the Suffield Experimental Station, this community was named in 1949 after Col. James Layton Ralston (1881–1948), minister of national defence, 1940–4.

Ramara ON In 1994 Rama and Mara townships were united to become the municipal township of Ramara in the reorganized Simcoe County. Rama Township was named in 1820, possibly after the Spanish word for 'branch' or after a town in the Holy Land, north of Jerusalem. Mara Township was also named in 1820, possibly after the Spanish word for 'tide' or the biblical Marah, where Moses sweetened the bitter water.

Ramea NL This town (1951) is on Northwest Island, one of the **Ramea Islands**, located off the southwestern coast of Newfoundland. The islands may have been named after the French *rameau* ('branch'), in reference to the narrow channels among the islands; after *ramée* ('leafy bushs'), perhaps alluding to the fact that they had vegetation when most of the islands along the coast were devoid of plants; or after Le Ramée on Guernsey, the largest of the Channel Islands.

Ramore ON The post office in this community located in Cochrane District, 40 km northwest of Kirkland Lake, was first called *Claybelt* in 1909. It was renamed in 1915 after a prospector, who was the first white man to die in the area.

Ramsay ON In 1998 this township became part of the town of Mississippi Mills, Lanark County. It was named in 1823 after Gen. George Ramsay, Earl of Dalhousie (1770–1838), governor-in-chief of British North America, 1820–8.

Rankin Inlet NU At the head of **Rankin Inlet**, on the west coast of Hudson Bay, this hamlet (1975) was established as a nickel-mining settlement in 1955. The inlet was named after Lt. John Rankin, who served in 1741–2 on HMS *Furnace*, which under the command of Christopher Middleton (d.1770), explored the west coast of Hudson Bay.

Rapid City MB Situated on the Little Saskatchewan River, north of Brandon, this town (1883) was almost called Saskatchewan City, but the name was deemed too lengthy. As the river was also called *Rapid River* (an English equivalent of Saskatchewan) in the 1800s, the name Rapid City was approved unanimously at a public meeting in 1877, and the post office opened two years later. Earlier the place was called *Ralstons Colony* after John Ralston, who had come from Burritts Rapids, ON, south of Ottawa, and brought many settlers with him.

Rapides-des-Joachims QC This municipality on the north shore of the Ottawa River, northwest of Pembroke, was erected in 1955, taking its name from its post office, opened in 1853. The office was named after rapids in the Ottawa River, which were submerged by a hydroelectric dam in 1951. The first reference to the rapids was as *Rapides des Joachims de l'Estang* in 1686. Subsequent references referred to *Portages des Deux Joachims*, but it is uncertain who the two Joachims might have been. There may have been a connection with Chevalier de Troyes (d.1688), who undertook a difficult trip in 1686 up the Ottawa and overland to Hudson Bay. He married Marie Petit de L'Estang five years earlier. In English the place's name is pronounced 'duh-SWISH-uh'. In newspapers one may find 'Swisha'.

Ratcliff, Mount BC Located in the Coast Mountains, southeast of Bella Coola, this mountain (3033 m) was named in 1948 by surveyor Maj. F.V. Longstaff after Walter E. Ratcliff, a pioneer settler in the area.

Rathwell MB Southwest of Portage la Prairie, this place's Canadian Pacific Railway station was named in 1887 after early settler John Rathwell. He arrived here five years before from Innisville, ON, near Perth. The post office was called *Brunton* in 1888 after a place in Yorkshire, England, and was renamed Rathwell in 1890.

Rawdon ON This township in Hastings County was named in 1798 after Francis Rawdon-Hastings, 1st Marquess of Hastings and 2nd Earl of Moira (1754–1826), Governor General of Bengal, 1812–23.

Rawdon QC This village (1919) in the regional county of Matawinie, west of Joliette, is surrounded by the township municipality of **Rawdon**, which was created in 1845, taking its name from the township, identified on a 1795 map, and proclaimed in 1799. It may have been named after Francis Rawdon-Hastings, 1st Marquess of Hastings and 2nd Earl of Moira (1754–1826), a noted military leader and a capable administrator. He became Baron Rawdon in 1783. There is a Rawdon in West Yorkshire, northwest of Leeds.

Ray, Cape NL This most southwesterly point of Newfoundland was named by the Portuguese *Cabo do Rei* ('king's point'). The Basques rendered this in the late 1500s as *Cap d'Array* and *Cadarrai*. In 1767 Capt. James Cook (1767–79) identified the cape's name as Cape Ray, and the nearby river as Grand Codroy River.

Raymond AB Southeast of Lethbridge, this town (1903) was named in 1902 by Jesse W. Knight after his eldest son Raymond. Knight (1872–1947) planned the town as the centre of a 10,522 ha (26,000 a) farm devoted to sugar beet production for the North Western Coal and Navigation Company Limited.

Raymond, Mount NB Southeast of Mount Carleton, this mountain was named in 1903 by naturalist William F. Ganong (1864–1941) after historian William Odber Raymond (1853–1923).

Raymore SK Located north of Regina, this town (1963) was named by the Grand Trunk Pacific Railway in 1908; the name follows the alphabetical arrangement favoured by the company, with Quinton to the east and Semans to the west. Its post office was also opened that year.

Rayside-Balfour ON In 2001 this town became part of the city of Greater Sudbury, Sudbury Region. It was created in 1973 by amalgamating Rayside Township with a part of Balfour Township. James Rayside and William Douglas Balfour were Liberal members in the Legislative Assembly of Ontario, 1882–94.

Razorback Mountain BC In the Coast Mountains, northeast of Mount Waddington, this mountain (3180 m) was named in 1924–5 by geologist Victor Dolmage after its long serrated crest.

R.C.A.F. Peak BC In the Coast Mountains, northwest of Pemberton, this mountain (2880 m) was named in the 1950s after the Royal Canadian Air Force.

Rear of Leeds and Lansdowne ON In 2001 this township became part of the township of Leeds and the Thousand Islands, united counties of Leeds and Grenville. It was created in 1850 from the interior portions of the townships of Leeds and Lansdowne. They were named in 1788, one for Francis Osborne, 5th Duke of Leeds (1751–99), secretary of state for foreign affairs, 1783–91, and the other for William Petty Fitzmaurice, 2nd Earl of Shelburne and Marquess of Lansdowne (1737–1805), prime minister of Great Britain, 1782–3. *See also* Leeds *and* Lansdowne.

Rear of Yonge and Escott ON In 2001 this township became part of the township of Athens, united counties of Leeds and Grenville. It was created in 1854 from the interior portions of the townships of Yonge and Escott. The former was named after George Yonge (1732–1812), British secretary of war, 1782–94, and the latter after the Yonge family estate near Honiton in Devon, England.

Red Bay NL On the north side of the Strait of Belle Isle, this bay was the site of Basque whaling stations in the last half of the

1500s. Its name derives from the red cliffs bordering the harbour. It was called *Havre des Buttes* by the French. This municipal community (1973) of **Red Bay** is on the east side of the bay.

Redcliff AB On the west side of Medicine Hat, the post office in this town (1912) was named in 1910 after the red shale cliffs along the banks of the South Saskatchewan River, south and east of the townsite.

Red Deer AB This city (1913) on the **Red Deer River**, midway between Calgary and Edmonton, was first known as *Red Deer Crossing* on the Calgary-Edmonton Trail, with Red Deer post office opening in 1884. When the Canadian Pacific's Calgary and Edmonton Railway crossed the river in 1891, 7 km downstream, the settlement was relocated. The river, which joins the South Saskatchewan just east of the Alberta–Saskatchewan border, was known in Cree as *Waskasioo* ('elk'), which Scottish fur traders confused with the 'red deer' in their homeland.

Red Indian Lake NL In the central part of Newfoundland, this lake was the area where the last of the Beothuk were found. By 1829 disease and slaughter had annihilated them. Because they extensively used powdered hematite to paint their bodies, canoes, and other items, they were given the nickname 'Red Indians'. As they were the first North American Aboriginals encountered by Europeans, the nickname was ultimately assigned to all North American Aboriginals.

Red Lake ON In northwestern Ontario, north of the city of Kenora, the lake was known to the Ojibwa as *Miskwa Sagaigon* ('blood-red lake'). Legendary hunters are said to have killed a great animal suspected to be *Matchee Manitou* ('evil spirit'), leaving the lake dyed blood-red. Gold was first discovered in 1897, and after rich deposits were found in 1925, a gold rush ensued. Red Lake post office opened the following year, and the place became a municipal township of **Red Lake** in 1960.

Red River MB This river is known as the Red River of the North south of the forty-ninth parallel, where it forms the boundary between Minnesota and North Dakota, and flows north through Winnipeg to Lake Winnipeg. In Ojibwa it was called *Miskwagama Sipi* ('red water river'), likely after the red-brown silt it carries. In 1738–9 explorer Pierre Gaultier de La Vérendrye (1685–1749) called it **Rivière Rouge**, which remains one of its official names.

Red Rock ON A municipal township at the mouth of Nipigon River in Thunder Bay District, south of the community of Nipigon, it was founded in 1915, and named after the dark red outcroppings in the area. There was a Hudson's Bay Company fort called Red Rock House at Nipigon in 1821.

Redvers SK Northeast of Estevan, this town (1960) was founded in 1900 by the Canadian Pacific Railway and named

after Gen. Sir Redvers Buller (1839–1908). He had taken part in an expedition to the Red River in 1870, and had commanded the British forces during the South African War, 1899–1900. The post office opened in 1902.

Redwater AB The post office in this town (1950) northeast of Edmonton and on the south side of the **Redwater River** opened in 1909. The river is identified on geographer David Thompson's map of 1814 as *Vermilion River*, but was renamed because of the frequent occurrence of that name in Western Canada.

Regina SK As the Canadian Pacific Railway surveyed its route in 1881 across the southern prairies, it reached Wascana on the Pile of Bones Creek, south of the Qu'Appelle River. As the proposed site of the capital of the North-West Territories, Princess Louise (1848–1939), the wife of the Marquess of Lorne (1845–1914), wondered if it could be called Wascana, Assiniboia, or Leopold (after the youngest son of Queen Victoria). They then proposed calling it *Victoria* after her mother. To avoid duplication, however, they chose the Latin equivalent of queen, used in her title. The post office opened on the first day of 1882. In 1883 the capital was moved from North Battleford. The town (1980) of **Regina Beach** is located to the northwest, on the southwest shore of Last Mountain Lake.

Reidville NL Located northeast of the town of Deer Lake, this municipal community (1975) was founded in the early 1930s by Thomas Reid—a native of Norris Point—on Bonne Bay, adjacent to the northwestern coast of Newfoundland.

Reliance NT At the east end of Great Slave Lake, this settlement is at the site of the Hudson's Bay Company's Fort Reliance, built in 1833 as winter quarters for Lt. Sir George Back (1796–1876). He named it as an expression of trust in the Creator.

Reliance Mountain BC Located in the Coast Mountains, east of Mount Waddington, this mountain (3140 m) was named in 1863 by Alfred Waddington (1801–72). He projected the route of a railway through the valley of the Homathko River, on the west side of the mountain, and possibly relied on its summit as a reference point.

Remillard Peak BC Located in the Selkirk Mountains, north of Revelstoke, this mountain (3051 m) was named in 1939 after Louis Norbert Remillard, who had prospected for gold from 1910 to 1930 near the head of Goldstream River.

Remote Mountain BC Located in the Coast Mountains, northwest of Mount Waddington, this mountain (3033 m) was named in 1933 by Walter Alfred (Don) Munday (1890–1950) after the apparent difficulty of reaching this location.

Rencontre East NL Located on the north side of Fortune Bay and northeast of Belleoram, this municipal community (1972) was named after **Rencontre Island**, the largest of the islands in front of its harbour. The island's name means 'meeting place', because French migratory fishermen met here in the eighteenth century. There is another place called **Rencontre West**, which is located on the southwest coast, southwest of the town of St. Alban's.

Renews-Cappahayden NL This municipal community (1967) is located on the east coast of the Avalon Peninsula. The name **Renews** may be traced to the early sixteenth-century description of **Renews Harbour** by the Portuguese as *ronhoso* ('scabby'), in reference to rocks being covered with shells and seaweed. **Cappahayden**, 8 km south of Renews Harbour, was first named *Broad Cove*. It was renamed in 1913, possibly by the Most Reverend Michael Howley (1843–1914), after the townland of Cappahayden, County Kilkenny, Ireland.

Renforth NB This village (1966) northeast of Saint John was named in 1903 by the Intercolonial Railway after James Renforth (1842–71), the stroke of the Tyne crew of Newcastle upon Tyne, England, who died 23 August 1871, after a race in Kennebecasis Bay against the Paris crew of Saint John. Its post office, named *Chalet* in 1911 after a Young Men's Christian Association building, was renamed Renforth in 1922.

Renfrew ON The county was named in 1845 after Renfrewshire, Scotland, southwest of Glasgow, and as in Scotland, is located beside Lanark County. The town (1895) of **Renfrew**, first called *Second Chute* after rapids on the Bonnechere River, was named in 1848, when the post office opened here. It was briefly known as *Renfrewville* in the 1840s.

Renous NB On the west bank of the Southwest Miramichi River and at the mouth of the Renous River, this place's post office was named *Renous Bridge* in 1856 and renamed Renous in 1911. The river was called after Mi'kmaq chief Sock Renou, whose family name may have been Renaud.

Repentigny QC This city (1956) is located in the regional county of L'Assomption at the point where the rivières de l'Assomption and Mille-Îles join the St. Lawrence. The name may be traced back to the parish municipality of *Notre-Dame-de-l'Assomption-de-Repentigny*, created in 1855, which was the name of the religious parish founded in 1699. The name was given for Pierre Legardeur de Repentigny (c.1608–48), who was granted a seigneury here in 1647.

Repulse Bay NU Located at the south end of Melville Peninsula and at the northwest side of Hudson Bay, this hamlet (1978) was established in the early 1960s. It was named after the bay, which was given its name in 1741 by explorer Christopher Middleton (c.1690–1770), who was disappointed in not finding the Northwest Passage.

Reserve Mines NS Between Sydney and Glace Bay, this community was named in 1873. It reflected the decision of the General Mining Association to hold the coal seams here in 'reserve' while mining continued elsewhere in the area.

Resolute NU Located on the south coast of Cornwallis Island, this settlement was established in 1947 as the site of a joint American/Canadian High Arctic weather station. The bay was named after HMS *Resolute*, which may have wintered here in 1850–1. It is commonly called Resolute Bay.

Resolution Island NU Located southeast of Baffin Island and at the entrance to Hudson Strait, this island (1015 km²) was named in 1612 by explorer Thomas Button (c.1601–34) after his ship *Resolution*.

Resplendent, Mount BC South of Mount Robson, this mountain (3426 m) was named in 1910 by British climber Norman Collie (1859–1942) after observing its brilliant colours in the first rays of the sun.

Restigouche River NB, QC Formed at the confluence of the Kedgwick and Little Main Restigouche Rivers, this river flows northeast into Chaleur Bay and forms the boundary with Quebec, below the mouth of the Patapedia River. Its name derives from the Mi'kmaq *lustagooch* (probably 'good river for canoeing', a similar meaning to that given for *Aroostook*) and for *Woolastook*, the Maliseet name for the Saint John River above tide. Map-maker Jean-Baptiste-Louis Franquelin (c.1653–1712) recorded it in 1686 as **Ristigouche**, which continues to be the official form in Quebec.

Reston MB Southwest of Virden, this community's first school was named in 1886 after Reston in Berwickshire, Scotland, northwest of Berwick-upon-Tweed. Subsequently the post office (1890) and the Canadian Pacific Railway station (1900) were named Reston, with the school being renamed Lanark.

Revelstoke BC The site of this city (1899) on the Columbia River was first called *The Eddy*, after a swirling current that had eroded the west bank of the river, and *Second Crossing* by Canadian Pacific Railway surveyors. The site on the east bank of the river was laid out by surveyor Arthur Stanley Farwell (1841–1908) in 1880 and named *Farwell*. When the CPR arrived, it avoided Farwell's exorbitant price for his land by locating its station on higher land to the west and naming it after Edward Charles Baring, 1st Lord Revelstoke (1828–97). His Baring Brothers banking house in London bought a $15 million CPR bond to prevent a financial disaster in the final months of building the CPR's line through the province. *Farwell* post office, opened in February 1886, was renamed Revelstoke in June 1886. There is access by road to the top of **Mount Revelstoke** (2027 m), which rises above the city in **Mount Revelstoke National Park** (263 km²), established in 1914.

Reversing Falls NB At the mouth of the Saint John River and within the city of Saint John, this rough water in the river has its flow reversed every 13 hours, when the tide rises in the Bay of Fundy. Its name was suggested by poet Sir Charles G.D. Roberts (1860–1943) in 1882, when he wrote about its reversible character.

Rexton NB On the south side of the Richibucto River, opposite the town of Richibucto, this village (1966) was named *Kingston* in 1850 by shipbuilders Holderness and Chelton after Kingston upon Hull, England. To reduce confusion with other places called Kingston, Dr. J.W. Doherty proposed the name Rexton in 1901, using the Latin for 'king'.

Rhein SK The post office at this village (1913) northeast of Yorkton was named in 1911 by hardware merchant Emil Meugersing after the German river on which his hometown of Köln (Cologne) was located. The area was settled by Germans, who had immigrated from the area of the Volga River in Russia.

Rhodes, Mount BC In the Clemenceau Icefield of the Rocky Mountains, southeast of Athabasca Pass, this mountain (3063 m) was named in 1927 by alpinist James Monroe (Roy) Thorington (1895–1989) after Sir Cecil Rhodes (1853–1902), who made a fortune developing the diamond mines at Kimberley, South Africa and gave most of it to fund scholarships.

Rice Lake ON A long lake separating Northumberland and Peterborough counties, it was known to the Mississauga as *Pamadusgodayong* ('lake of plains'), because the Mohawk had earlier cleared the land for corn. In the 1830s settler John Langton wrote about the wild rice beds giving the lake the appearance of being a large grass plot.

Richard Bennett, Mount BC In the Premier Range, west of Valemount, this mountain (3190 m) was named in 1962 after Viscount Richard Bedford Bennett (1870–1947), prime minister of Canada, 1930–5.

Richards Island NT In the Mackenzie Delta, this island (2165 km²) was named in 1826 by Sir John Richardson (1787–1865) after a governor of the Bank of England.

Richardson Mountains NT, YT Located between Fort MacPherson, NT, and Old Crow, YT, these mountains were named in 1825 by Sir John Franklin (1786–1847) after Sir John Richardson (1787–1865), a surgeon and natural historian

on Franklin's expeditions in 1819–20 and 1825–7. In 1848 he commanded an expedition in search of Franklin, who had disappeared three years earlier.

Richelieu QC On the east side of the Rivière Richelieu, opposite Chambly, this town (1968) was part of the parish municipality of *Notre-Dame-de-Bon-Secours* until 1869, when it became the village of Richelieu. The river was named after Fort Richelieu, built at its mouth in 1642. The fort's name was given in honour of Armand-Jean du Plessis, Cardinal de Richelieu (1585–1642), chief minister of Louis XIII. He created the Compagnie des Cent-Associés in 1627 to manage the development of New France during its early years.

Richer MB Northeast of Steinbach, this place was named in 1900 after H.I. Richer, who was the reeve of the rural municipality of Ste. Anne for many years.

Richibucto NB This town (1985) on the north bank of the **Richibucto River** was named *Liverpool* in 1826, when it was chosen as the shire town of Kent County. It was renamed Richibucto in 1832, and this was chosen as its postal designation the following year. The source of the name was the Mi'kmaq *elsedabooktook*, which may mean 'runs back bay place', in reference to **Richibucto Harbour**. Ten km east of the town is the community of **Richibucto-Village**, whose post office opened in 1872.

Richmond BC This city (1990) embracing Lulu and Sea Islands, south of Vancouver, was incorporated as a district municipality in 1979 and a township 100 years earlier. Australian Hugh McRoberts established Richmond View Farm here in 1862, with a daughter suggesting its name after a favourite place in Australia, possibly the town of Richmond near Sydney.

Richmond NS This county, on southwestern Cape Breton Island, and including Isle Madame and adjacent islands, was named in 1835 after *Richmond Island*—the name given by Samuel Holland (1728–1801) in 1767 to Isle Madame. Holland named it after Charles Lennox, 3rd Duke of Richmond (1734–1806), who held many official positions, including British ambassador to France.

Richmond ON In 1998 this township became a part of the town of Greater Napanee, Lennox and Addington County. It was named in 1786 after Charles Lennox, 3rd Duke of Richmond (1734–1806), who held many official positions, including ambassador to France. His nephew, Charles Gordon Lennox, 4th Duke of Richmond, was governor-in-chief of British North America, 1818–9.

Richmond ON In 2001 this community, 28 km southwest of the centre of Ottawa, became a part of the city of Ottawa. It was named in 1818 for Charles Gordon Lennox, 4th Duke of Richmond and Lennox (1764–1819), who was appointed governor-in-chief of British North America that year. While on a tour of settlements in Lower and Upper Canada the following summer, he was bitten by a pet fox in *William Henry* (now Sorel, QC), and after visiting Richmond, he became afflicted with rabies and died on 28 August 1819 in a barn 5 km to the north.

Richmond ON In 1998 this community became part of the municipality of Bayham, Elgin County. Located 10 km east of Aylmer, it was named after Charles Gordon Lennox, 4th Duke of Richmond (1764–1819), governor-in-chief of British North America, 1818–9. Its post office from 1829 to 1971 was *Bayham*.

Richmond PE This municipal community (1979) northwest of Summerside was named after **Richmond Bay**, the name given in 1765 by Samuel Holland (1728–1801) to the whole of Malpeque Bay, but in later years applied to the west side of the bay. He named the bay after Charles Lennox, 3rd Duke of Richmond (1734–1806).

Richmond QC The post office in this town (1882), situated midway between Sherbrooke and Drummondville, opened in 1820 and was named after Charles Gordon Lennox, 4th Duke of Richmond (1764–1819), governor-in-chief of British North America, 1818–9. It was erected as a village in 1863.

Richmond Hill ON This town (1957) in York Region was first called *Miles Hill* and *Mount Pleasant*. Although legend has the 4th Duke of Richmond stopping here in 1819 for a rest, it is more likely it was named in 1836 by schoolteacher Benjamin Barnard after Richmond Hill, Surrey, England.

Richmound SK West of Swift Current and near the Alberta border, this village (1947) was established by the Canadian Pacific Railway in 1924–5. Its post office opened in 1912, 5 km west of the village's site, and was named by Mrs Charlie Wilde after the area's rich earth and the rolling terrain.

Rideau ON In 2001 this municipal township became part of the city of Ottawa. It was formed in 1974 by amalgamating the municipal townships of North Gower and Marlborough with Long Island, formerly split between the municipal townships of Gloucester and Osgoode. The **Rideau River** forms its southern and eastern boundary.

Rideau River; Rideau Canal ON In 1613 Samuel de Champlain (1567–1635) observed the beauty of the 13-m **Rideau Falls**, noting that they looked like a curtain (*rideau*) behind which Aboriginals passed without getting wet. *Rivière du Rideau* only appeared on maps after 1694, and the English form appeared a century later. Among the well-known **Rideau Lakes**, southwest of the town Perth, are **Big Rideau**, **Lower**

Rideau, and **Upper Rideau** lakes. In 1998 the township of **Rideau Lakes** was created from the village of Newboro' and the townships of Bastard and South Burgess, North Crosby, South Crosby, and South Elmsley. The **Rideau Canal**, with 45 sets of locks, was built between 1827 and 1832 under the direction of Lt. Col John By (1781–1836).

Ridgetown ON Situated on a ridge separating the waters draining west into the Thames River and east into Lake Erie, this town became part of the municipality of Chatham-Kent, Kent County. Ridgetown was first settled in the 1820s; a post office opened in 1853 and it became a town in 1881.

Ridgeville ON Located in the town of Pelham, Niagara Region, this community was named in 1865 by Jonas Steele, the first postmaster, and John B. Crow after its location on a southern ridge of the Short Hills.

Ridgeway ON This community is located in the town of Fort Erie, west of the town centre. Its post office was named in 1873 from its location on Ridge Road, which divides the drainage flowing northeast to the Niagara River and south to Lake Erie.

Riding Mountain National Park MB Occupying rugged terrain between Neepawa and Dauphin, this 2973-km^2 park was created in 1929. The name relates to the trails followed by Aboriginals on horseback when crossing the densely treed landscape. The 750-m mountain west of McCreary was first noted as *Riding or Dauphin Mountain* on an 1858 Crown lands map. **Riding Mountain** post office opened south of McCreary in 1892.

Rigaud QC In the regional county of Vaudreuil-Soulanges, this town (1911) was incorporated as a village in 1880. Its post office opened in 1835. It owes its name to the grant of a seigneury in 1732 to Pierre de Rigaud de Vaudreuil de Cavagnial (1698–1778), governor of New France, 1755–60, and to François-Pierre de Rigaud de Vaudreuil (1703–79), governor of Trois-Rivières, 1749. It was in honour of the latter that the place was named.

Rigolet NL On the north side of Hamilton Inlet and northeast of Happy Valley-Goose Bay, this municipal community (1977) took its name from the French *rigolet* ('small stream'), describing the narrows of the inlet there. A trading post was established here in 1788 by Pierre Marcoux, a native of Quebec City.

Rimbey AB The post office in this town (1948) northwest of Red Deer was named in 1903 after postmaster James Rimbey and his two brothers, Sam and Ben. In 1901 Sam Rimbey (1868–1952) led a group of 200 pioneers from Kansas to the Blindman River valley.

Rimouski QC This city—the largest in the province east of Quebec City—is located on the south shore of the St. Lawrence, at the mouth of the **Rivière Rimouski**. Incorporated in 1869 as the town of *Saint-Germain-de-Rimouski*, it adopted its current name in 1920, taking its postal name in 1832. The river was noted as early as 1688, when the seigneury of Rimouski was granted to Augustin Rouer de Villeray et de La Cardonnière. The village of **Rimouski-Est** was erected in 1939. The regional county of **Rimouski-Neigette** was created in 1982, succeeding the former county of Rimouski. The name derives from the Mi'kmaq *animouski* ('place of the dog').

Riondel BC Located on the eastern shore of Kootenay Lake, northeast of Nelson, this place was named in 1907 after Comte Édouard Riondel, president of the French-owned Canadian Metal Company, which bought the Bluebell Mine here in 1905.

Ripley ON The post office in this community in Bruce County, west of Walkerton, was named in 1857 after Ripley, Derbyshire, England, north of the city of Derby. Postmaster Paul McInnes persuaded the postal authorities in 1873 to call it *Dingwall* after a place in Scotland, northwest of Inverness. However, its railway station was called Ripley that year, and six years later Ripley was restored as the postal name. It was annexed in 1994 by the municipal township of Huron. In 1999 the community became part of the township of Huron-Kinross.

Ripon QC This village in the regional county of Papineau, northeast of Buckingham, was separated in 1923 from the parish municipality of **Ripon**, which had been erected in 1855. The township was identified on a map in 1795, but was not proclaimed until 1855. The name recalls a town in West Yorkshire, England, north of Leeds.

Ripples NB Located 35 km northeast of Fredericton, this community's post office was called *Little River* from 1856 to 1903, when it was renamed for the rapids in Little River.

Riske Creek BC This place, 47 km southwest of the city of Williams Lake, took its name from **Riske Creek**, where a Polish gentleman called L.W. Riskie established a farm some time before 1872. Its post office opened in 1912.

River Bourgeois NS On Cape Breton Island, southwest of St. Peters, this community's name derives from the time of French occupation before 1758. Its post office opened in 1838.

River Denys NS Located northeast of Port Hawkesbury, this community's post office was named *River Dennis Station* in 1892, *River Denys Station* in 1926, and its current name in 1967. **River Denys** flows into **Denys Basin**, part of

Bras d'Or Lake. It may have been named after an Aboriginal chief who lived at its mouth, having adopted the surname of Nicolas Denys (c.1598–1688), governor of Acadia, 1653–87, and author of two books on the history and geography of the North American coasts. On his 1672 map he named Sydney Harbour *R. de Denys*.

Riverhead NL At the head of St. Mary's Harbour, and northwest of Trepassey, this municipal community (1966) was first noted in 1836. There is another **Riverhead** at the head of Harbour Grace, first recorded in the census of 1901.

River Hebert NS The post office in this village (1950) 20 km southwest of Amherst and on the **River Hébert** was named in 1851. The river was perhaps named after Louis Hébert (c.1575–1627), an apothecary who accompanied Pierre Du Gua de Monts (c.1558–1628) to Port Royal in 1604. The small community of **Lower River Hebert** is 4 km north of River Hebert.

Riverhurst SK Located near the southeastern bank of Lake Diefenbaker, northwest of Moose Jaw, the post office at this village (1916) was named in 1914, a year before the Grand Trunk Pacific Railway arrived. Its name combined those of former post offices *Riverside* (1907–1910) and *Boldenhurst* (1909–16).

River John NS East of Tatamagouche and at the mouth of the **River John** (where the river flows into Amet Sound), this community first received postal service in 1838. The river's name derives from the French *Rivière Jaune* ('yellow river'). Map-maker Joseph Frederic Wallet DesBarres (1722–1824) introduced the name River John in the 1770s. **Cape John** is on the east side of the entrance to Amet Sound.

River of Ponds NL Located on the northwestern coast of the Northern Peninsula and south of Port au Choix, this municipal community (1970) was settled about 1870 and named after the river, which drains several ponds. The river was perhaps named by Capt. James Cook (1728–79) in 1770. Earlier during that century French migratory fishermen knew it as the *Rivière des Roches* ('rocky river').

Rivers MB Located on the Little Saskatchewan River, northwest of Brandon, this town (1910) was established in 1907–8 by the Grand Trunk Pacific Railway and named after the chairman of its board of directors, Sir Charles Rivers Wilson (1831–1916).

Riverside-Albert NB In Albert County, south of Moncton, this village united the separate communities of Albert and Riverside in 1966. *Hopewell Corner* post office, named after the Hopewell Parish, opened on the north side of Shepody River in 1854 and was called *Albert* in 1882 after Albert County. On the south side of the river, *River Side* post office opened in 1867 and was renamed Riverside in 1932.

Rivers Inlet BC Located on the mainland coast, north of Vancouver Island, this 50-km fiord was named in 1792 by Capt. George Vancouver (1757–98) after George Pitt, 1st Baron Rivers (1721–1803), a British writer and politician.

Riverton MB Located north of Gimli, this village (1951) was first known as *Icelandic River* after the river that rises west of Arborg. It was changed to Riverton in 1914, when the Canadian Pacific Railway made it the northern terminus of a line on the western shore of Lake Winnipeg.

Riverton NS Located on the East River of Pictou and south of the town of Stellarton, this community was first called *Fish Pools*. The residents had it changed to Riverton in 1877.

Riverview NB This town on the Petitcodiac River, opposite Moncton, took its name from Riverview Heights, a postal designation in the central part of the town from 1949 to 1957 and a village from 1966 to 1973. In 1973 the villages of Riverview Heights, Gunningsville, and Bridgedale were united with adjacent parts of Coverdale Parish to form the town of *Coverdale*, which was changed to Riverview the following year. The parish, established in 1828, was named after *Coverdale River*, given before 1788 to present Little River. The river's original name was possibly for Bible translator Miles Coverdale (c.1488–1569).

Rivière-Beaudette QC This municipality is in the regional county of Vaudreuil-Soulanges, at the mouth of **Rivière Beaudette** (which rises north of Cornwall, ON). The name has its roots in the seventeenth-century discovery of a wire-frame bed (*baudet*) in a burned shack on nearby **Pointe Beaudette**. The present municipality was created in 1990 through the amalgamation of the parish municipality of Rivière-Beaudette (1887) and the village of Rivière-Beaudette (1978).

Rivière-Bleue QC Situated in the regional county of Témiscouata, southeast of Rivière-du-Loup and on the border with Maine, this municipality was created in 1975 through the merger of the village (1914) and the parish municipality (1920) of *Saint-Joseph-de-la-Rivière-Bleue*. Its post office opened in 1910 and was named after a river rising west of Cabano, on the western shore of Lac Témiscouata, and flowing southwest into the Rivière Saint-François.

Rivière-du-Gouffre QC In the regional municipality of Charlevoix, near Baie-Saint-Paul, this municipality was erected in 1921. The river was noted by Samuel de Champlain (1567–1635) in 1608. Among the explanations of the name, the one favoured relates to landslides, with the river becoming turbulent (*engouffrant*) when a clay bank collapses into it.

Rivière-du-Loup QC The name of this city on the south shore of the St. Lawrence was noted as early as 1673 in reference to the grant of a seigneury to Charles Aubert de La Chesnaye (1632–1702). The *Rivière-du-Loup-en-Bas* post office opened in 1828, but when the place was incorporated as a village in 1850 it was called *Fraserville*, which continued as the name of the town until 1874. The village was named after Alexander Fraser (1763–1837), who bought the seigneury in 1802. The name was changed to Rivière-du-Loup in 1919. There are three possible origins for the name: harbour seals, called *loups marins* by Jacques Cartier (1491–1557); an Aboriginal nation called the Loups or Mahicans; and a vessel called *Le Loup* ('the wolf'), which may have wintered here about 1660. The regional county of **Rivière-du-Loup** was erected in 1982, succeeding the former county of Rivière-du-Loup.

Rivière-Malbaie QC This municipality north of La Malbaie in the regional county of Charlevoix-Est was named after the **Rivière Malbaie**. The river was named in 1608 by Samuel de Champlain (1567–1635), because the bay at its mouth was too difficult (*mal*) for safe anchorage.

Rivière-Ouelle QC Situated in the regional county of Kamouraska, east of La Pocatière, this place was known as the parish municipality of *Notre-Dame-de-Liesse-de-la-Rivière-Ouelle* in 1855. The name was shortened to its present form in 1983. Noted on a 1641 map as *R. Hoel*, and mentioned in the 1672 grant of a seigneury as *rivière Houelle*, the river may have been named after Louis Houel (or Ouel, sometimes written Houël), who performed several duties in New France and was a friend of Samuel de Champlain (1567–1635).

Rivière-Verte NB The post office in this village (1966) southeast of Edmundston was called *Bellefleur* from 1884 to 1906 and *Green River Station* from 1906 to 1935, when it became Rivière-Verte. *Green River* post office opened in 1863, became *Lynch* in 1906, and Prime in 1910. The river is officially called both **Green River** and **Rivière Verte**.

Robert-Cliche QC This regional county centred on Beauceville, south of Quebec City, was named in 1982 after Robert Cliche (1921–78), a native of Saint-Joseph-de-Beauce and a distinguished writer, teacher, judge, and politician.

Robert's Arm NL This town (1954) on the south side of Notre Dame Bay was first known as *Rabbits Arm*. By 1911 it was called Robert's Arm, possibly after local resident John Roberts.

Roberts Creek BC On the mainland shore of the Strait of Georgia, northwest of Gibsons, this community was named in 1904 after Thomas Roberts, who had built a cabin at the mouth of the creek in 1889. The first postmaster was J.F.

Roberts, followed by F.J. Roberts in 1908 and L.H. Roberts from 1910 to 1930.

Robert Service, Mount YT Located at the head of the North Klondike River, east of Dawson, this mountain was named in 1968 by geologist Dirk Tempelman-Kluit after Robert William Service (1874–1958), the 'poet of the Yukon' and author of several collections of poems, including *Songs of a Sourdough*, *Ballads of a Cheechako*, and *Rhymes of a Rolling Stone*.

Robertsonville QC This village in the regional county of L'Amiante, just east of Thetford Mines, was erected in 1909, taking its name from the railway station that opened in 1883. It was named after Joseph Gibb Robertson (1820–99), first president of the Quebec Central Railway, who also served as treasurer of the province and postmaster of Sherbrooke.

Robertville NB Located northwest of Bathurst, this place was established as a free-grant settlement in 1879. Its post office opened as *Dumfries* in 1884 and was renamed in 1890 after Fr. François-Antoine Robert (1820–88), parish priest at Petit-Rocher, 1866–88.

Roberval QC This town (1903) on the western shore of Lac Saint-Jean was established as a village in 1884. The post office opened in 1862 and a year later the township of **Roberval** was proclaimed. The name was given after Jean-François de La Rocque de Roberval (c.1500–60), lieutenant-general of New France, 1541–3.

Robichaud NB The post office in this community east of Shediac opened in 1878. The name derives from Hippolite Robichaud, its postmaster until 1899.

Roblin MB Located west of Dauphin and near the Saskatchewan border, this town (1962) was first called *Goose Lake* after a small lake south of the town. It was renamed by the Canadian Northern Railway in 1904 after Sir Rodmond Palen Roblin (1853–1937), premier of Manitoba, 1900–15.

Robson BC On the north side of the Columbia River, opposite Castlegar, this place was first called *Sproat's Landing* after the local gold commissioner Gilbert Sproat. It became *East Robson* in 1890, with Robson post office opening two years later. **Robson West** is on the south bank and in the west end of present-day Castlegar. Both were named after John Robson (1824–92), premier of British Columbia, 1889–92.

Robson, Mount BC North of the Yellowhead Pass, this highest mountain (3954 m) in the Canadian Rockies was likely named after Colin Robertson (1783–1842). An officer of the Hudson's Bay Company, he led an expedition of 10 canoes, 10 officers, and 100 voyageurs to the Peace River country, 1819–20. It may have been named about 1820 by Ignace Giasson, an HBC party

leader, after Robertson sent him and a party of fur traders to explore the west side of the Yellowhead Pass.

Rocanville SK The post office in this town (1967) north of Moosomin was named in 1884 after Auguste Henry Rocan Bastien, who was born in 1842 in Saint-Vincent-de-Paul, QC, (now Laval) and baptised Honoré Rocan. The office was located 5 km to the northeast, and was moved to the line of the Canadian Pacific Railway in 1903.

Roche Percee SK Located between Estevan and the North Dakota border, this village (1909) received its name from a long sandstone rock with a large hole through it. Its post office opened in 1905, having been the name of the post office at *Coalfields*, 5 km to the northeast, 1896–7.

Roches Point ON Situated on the east shore of Cook's Bay, Lake Simcoe, and in the town of Georgina, York Region, north of Newmarket, this place was the first location of Keswick post office in 1836. It was renamed *Roach's Point* after settler James Roche in 1870 and changed to *Roche's Point* in 1906. The present form was adopted in 1950.

Rochester ON In 1999 this township became part of the town of Lakeshore, Essex County. It was named in 1792 after the town of Rochester in Kent, England.

Rockcliffe Park ON In 2001 this village (1925) became part of the city of Ottawa. The village was laid out by engineer Thomas Coltrin Keefer (1821–1915) in 1864. He named it after Rockcliff House, built by Duncan MacNab (d.1837) and acquired by Keefer in 1864 for his mother-in-law, Anne McKay. Her late husband Thomas McKay (1792–1855) built Rideau Hall, the official residence of governors general since 1868.

Rock Forest QC In 2002 this city (1983) became part of the city of Sherbrooke. It was established as a municipality in 1921. Its post office was named in 1872, two years after Parker Nagle called the place Rock Forest after a residence he had owned in his native Ireland. Before 1872 the place had been called *Drop Off*.

Rockglen SK South of Moose Jaw and near the Montana border, this town (1957) was named after a valley surrounded by rocky hills. Its post office was named by William Dennison in 1926, when the Canadian Pacific Railway was built south from Assiniboia.

Rockingham NS In Halifax and on the west side of Bedford Basin, this place was named *Rockingham Station* in 1886 after the Rockingham Club established by Sir John Wentworth (1737–1820) when he was lieutenant-governor of Nova Scotia, 1792–1808. He named the club after his patron Charles

Watson-Wentworth, Marquess of Rockingham (1730–82), British statesman and prime minister, 1765–6 and 1782.

Rock Island QC Located on the Vermont border, south of Magog, this town (1957) was known as *Kilborn's Mills* at the beginning of the nineteenth century. Col. Charles Kilborn constructed a canal across one of the bends of the Tomifobia River and created a small rocky island. Rock Island post office opened in 1863. In 1995 Rock Island became part of the town of Stanstead.

Rockland ON In 1998 this town (1908) became part of the city of Rockland-Clarence, united counties of Prescott and Russell. It was named in 1869 by postmaster William Cameron Edwards (1844–1921). He built a sawmill in 1868, after acquiring timber limits in the Gatineau Valley.

Rockwood ON This community 12 km northeast of Guelph became part of the township of Guelph/Eramosa, Wellington County in 1999. It was called *Strange's Mills* and *Brotherstown* before William Wetherald (1820–98), founder of Rockwood Academy, changed it to Rockwood in 1853 for its rocky and well-treed area.

Rockyford AB Located northeast of Calgary, this village (1919) was named in 1914 by the Canadian Northern Railway's chief surveyor Beaumont after a narrow crossing of Serviceberry Creek, just south of the village site. The 'rocky ford' was well known to Aboriginals, ranchers, and surveyors.

Rocky Harbour NL The shoreline of this municipal community (1966), on the western coast of Newfoundland and at the mouth of Bonne Bay, is comprised of rocky ledges. The harbour was occupied by fishermen in the early 1800s.

Rocky Mountain House AB The post office in this town (1939) west of Red Deer was named in 1912. The North West Company established Rocky Mountain House here in 1799, and the outpost continued to be operated intermittently by the Hudson's Bay Company from 1821 to 1875.

Rocky Mountains AB, BC Within Canada this division of the Cordilleran Region's eastern system extends 1375 km northwest from the United States border to the Liard River, west of Fort Nelson. The system is approximately 100 km wide, with the **Rocky Mountain Trench** to the west and the **Rocky Mountain Foothills** to the east. The mountains were called *Shining Mountains* by Hudson's Bay Company governor James Knight (1640–1719) in 1716 and *Montagnes de Roches* by explorer Jacques Legardeur de Saint-Pierre (1701–55) in 1752, although he had not seen them. Anthony Henday, a fur trader for the Hudson's Bay Company, saw the Rocky Mountains two years later; he was the first European to see the mountains, although he did not mention them in his journal.

Roddickton NL At the head of Canada Bay and on the east coast of the Northern Peninsula, this town (1953) was named in 1906 in honour of surgeon Sir Thomas George Roddick (1846–1923), a native of Harbour Grace. He was the dean of medicine at McGill University, 1901–08, and a member of Parliament, 1896–1904. The site of the town was earlier known as *Easter Brook.*

Rodney ON In 1998 this place became part of the municipality of West Elgin, Elgin County. Located southwest of St. Thomas, this urban centre was first known as *Stewart's Mills* and *Centreville* before it was renamed after Sir George Brydges Rodney (1718–92) in 1865. Local resident Lachlan MacDougall had proposed the name several years before to honour the English admiral's distinguished naval career. Created a village in 1907, Rodney was annexed by the municipal township of Aldborough in 1994.

Roes Welcome Sound NU This 300-km channel between Southampton Island and the mainland was named *Roe's Welcome* in 1631 by Luke Foxe (c.1586–1635) after Sir Thomas Roe (1580–1644), a diplomat who supported Foxe's voyage of discovery. Several eighteenth- and nineteenth-century maps identified it as *Sir Thomas Roe's Welcome*, but the Geographic Board in 1902 named it Roes Welcome Sound.

Rogers Pass BC This route through the Selkirk Mountains was discovered in 1882 by Maj. Albert Bowman Rogers (1829–89) for the transcontinental route of the Canadian Pacific Railway, and was named after a promise made by CPR director James J. Hill (1838–1916) to name a useful pass after him. He framed the $5000 cheque given to him by the CPR's William Van Horne (1843–1915). **Mount Rogers**, a three-peaked mountain north of the pass, was named in 1890 by climber Carl Sulzer.

Rogersville NB The post office in this village (1966) in the city of Miramichi, southeast of Newcastle, was called *Forest Station* in 1876 and renamed the following year to *Carleton Station* after Carleton Parish. It was renamed in 1884 after Mgr. James Rogers (1826–1903), Catholic bishop of Chatham, 1860–1902.

Roland MB Founded in 1889 on the Canadian Northern Railway line from Morris to Somerset, this place was named by the company after lumber dealer Roland MacDonald, who provided room and board for its surveyors. Its post office was called *Lowestoft* in 1884 and was changed to Roland in 1890.

Rollo Bay PE West of Souris, this place's post office was named about 1854 after the nearby bay. The bay was named in 1765 by Samuel Holland (1728–1801) after Andrew Rollo, 5th Lord Rollo (1700–65). He accepted the surrender of the island (then called *Isle de Saint Jean*) by the French in 1759.

Romney ON In 1998 this township became part of the municipality of Chatham-Kent, Kent County. It was named in 1794 after an ancient port in Kent, England, on the Strait of Dover.

Roosevelt, Mount BC Located in the Muskwa Ranges of the Rocky Mountains, this mountain (2972 m) was named in 1944 by provincial minister of lands E.T. Kenny after President Franklin Delano Roosevelt (1882–1945). It was given to honour Allied leaders of the Second World War.

Root, Mount BC In the St. Elias Mountains, 9 km northeast of Fairweather Mountain, this mountain (3901 m) was named in 1908 after Elihu Root (1845–1937), the secretary of state in President Theodore Roosevelt's administration.

Rosalind AB The post office in this village (1966) southeast of Camrose was named in 1905, drawing upon the two local school district names, Montrose and East Lynne. The former perhaps derives from Montrose, Angusshire, Scotland, northeast of Dundee. East Lynne came from the title of a book read by an early settler.

Rose Blanche-Harbour Le Cou NL This town (1983) is situated on the southwestern coast of Newfoundland and east of Channel-Port aux Basques. **Rose Blanche**'s name derives from the French description of the rosy white granite here. **Harbour Le Cou** has a harbour shaped like a figure eight, with the narrow part named after the French *le cou* ('the neck').

Rosemary AB Northeast of Brooks, this village (1951) was named in 1914 by the Canadian Pacific Railway after Rosemary Millicent (1893–1930), the wife of the 3rd Earl of Dudley (1894–1969) and daughter of the 4th Duke of Sutherland (1851–1913). The duke acquired extensive lands in the Brooks area.

Rosemère QC Situated on the north shore of Rivère des Mille-Îles, north of Montreal, this town (1958) was created a parish municipality in 1947. The Canadian Pacific Railway station was named Rosemere in 1880 after the abundance of wild roses and the old English word for a lake. The post office here was open from 1901 to 1960. The parallel French form, Rosemère, was adopted in 1940.

Rosemont ON The post office in this community on the boundary of Dufferin and Simcoe counties was named in 1861, possibly after wild roses blooming on the nearby hills. In providing its spelling, the post office department may have been influenced by Rosemont, a present-day neighbourhood in east-central Montreal.

Roseneath ON In 2001 this place became part of Trent Hills, Northumberland County. Its post office was named in 1858 after Rosneath, Dunbartonshire, Scotland. This place northwest of Glasgow was the birthplace of Mr. and Mrs. James Campbell, who had settled on the east side of nearby Rice Lake 20 years earlier.

Rosenfeld MB Located southwest of Morris, this community was founded by Mennonites and named in 1882 when the Canadian Pacific Railway arrived. In German the name means 'rose field'.

Rosetown SK Southeast of Saskatoon, this town (1911) was settled in 1904–5 and its post office opened in 1907. The name derives from pioneer settler James Rose. The lines of the Canadian Pacific and Canadian Northern Railways crossed here in 1908.

Rose Valley SK Between Tisdale and Wadena, this town (1962) was named about 1915, when Martin Nelson proposed it at a meeting of grain growers. The post office opened 1 January 1916 and the Canadian Pacific Railway station was established here in 1924.

Ross ON In 2001 this township became part of the township of Whitewater Region, Renfrew County. It was established in 1830, and was possibly named by its surveyor and settlement agent John McNaughton after Ross-shire, part of the Scottish Highlands county of Ross and Cromarty. The name possibly honours Adm. Sir James Clark Ross (1800–62), who joined his uncle Sir John Ross (1777–1856) on six Arctic voyages.

Rossburn MB Southwest of Riding Mountain National Park, this village (1913) was named in 1880 after R.R. Ross (d.1904), who had arrived here in 1879 from Molesworth, ON, northwest of Listowel. The Rural Municipality of Rossburn was created in 1933.

Rosseau, Lake ON Jean Baptiste Rousseau (1758–1812), a fur trader who lived near the mouth of the Humber River, acted as an interpreter during discussions, agreements, and treaties with the Ojibwa in Lake Simcoe and the Muskoka Lakes. In 1835 Lt. John Carthew of the Royal Navy, who took part in an exploration from the Severn River to Lake Nipissing, reported *Rousseau's Lake* was a large lake studded with beautiful islands. Geologist Alexander Murray (1810–84) called it *Lake Rousseau* in 1853, and surveyor Vernon Wadsworth referred to it as Lake Rosseau in 1860. The community of **Rosseau**, on the north shore of the lake, was named in 1866. It was an incorporated village from 1926 to 1971, when it merged with the municipal township of Muskoka Lakes.

Rossignol, Lake NS The largest lake in the southwestern part of the province, this lake was named after Jean Rossignol, whose ship and furs were confiscated in 1604 in present-day

Liverpool Harbour by Pierre Du Gua de Monts (c.1558–1628). Four years later Rossignol proved he was legally trading on the coast and recovered his ship and compensation for the seized furs.

Rossland BC Ross Thompson founded this city (1897) west of Trail and called it *Thompson*. Likely because of possible confusion with Thompson's Landing on Lower Arrow Lake, the post office department established its post office as Rossland in 1894.

Ross River YT Located at the junction of the **Ross River** and Pelly River, this place was named about 1903 by store-keeper Tom Smith. Hudson's Bay Company trader Robert Campbell (1808–94) named the river in 1843 after HBC chief factor Donald Ross (c.1797–1852).

Rosthern SK Midway between Saskatoon and Prince Albert, this town (1903) emerged about 1890 when the line of the Qu'Appelle, Long Lake and Saskatchewan Railway and Steamboat Company was built from Regina to Prince Albert. The line became part of the Canadian Northern Railway in 1906. The place was possibly named after a man called Ross, who drowned in the creek flowing through the townsite. The post office opened in 1893.

Rothesay NB This town (1956) northeast of Saint John was named in 1860 by Robert Thompson after the Prince of Wales, Duke of Saxony, Cornwall, and Rothesay and the future King Edward VII (1841–1910). He visited New Brunswick that year and sailed to Fredericton from a wharf nearby. Rothesay was first used as a European and North American Railway station. The post office was named *Kennebecasis Bay* in 1853, but became Rothesay in 1866.

Rougemont QC Located in the regional county of Rouville, between Chambly and Granby, this village was separated from the parish municipality of *Saint-Michel-de-Rougemont* in 1914. Its post office opened 1852, taking its name from the adjacent 390-m **Mont Rougemont**, which has bright red leaves in the autumn day.

Rouleau SK Southwest of Regina, this town (1907) was established by the Canadian Pacific Railway in 1893 and named after Charles-Borromée Rouleau (1840–1901). He was appointed a stipendiary judge of the North-West Territories in 1883, serving until 1887, when he became a judge in the district of Alberta. The post office opened in 1895.

Rouville QC This regional county between Chambly and Granby was named in 1982 after the former county of Rouville. The former county was named after Jean-Baptiste Hertel de Rouville (1668–1722), a military officer who was granted the seigneury of Rouville in 1694.

Rouyn-Noranda QC The origins of Rouyn-Noranda—both a regional county (1981) and a city (1986)—are in the discovery of gold and copper on the shore of Lac Osisko in 1911, and a gold rush a decade later. **Noranda** (a contraction of 'north' and 'Canada') became a company mining village and was incorporated as a town in 1926. **Rouyn** was named after **Rouyn Township** (1916). It was developed in the early 1920s on the south side of Noranda and was erected as a town in 1927. The township was named after Jean-Baptiste Rouyn, a captain who served with the Royal-Roussillon Regiment in 1759–60.

Rowley Island NU At the north end of Foxe Basin, this island (1090 km^2) was named in 1941 after Graham M. Rowley (1912–2003) the first non-Aboriginal person to explore the area. Rowley was subsequently the secretary coordinator of the Advisory Committee on Northern Development in the department of northern development and natural resources.

Roxboro QC In 2002 this town (1914) became part of the city of Montreal and a sector of Montreal in 2006. It is located on the south shore of the Rivière des Prairies.

Roxborough ON In 1998 this township became part of the township of North Stormont, united counties of Stormont, Dundas and Glengarry. It was named in 1798 after John Ker, the 3rd Duke of Roxburghe (1740–1804), a close friend of George III. The title of Lord Roxburghe was granted in 1600 by James VI of Scotland to Robert Ker, and was given after the Scottish border county of Roxburghshire.

Roxton Falls QC Located in the municipal county of Acton, midway between Drummondville and Granby, this village was created in 1863, when it was separated from the township municipality of **Roxton**. The latter was established in 1855, taking its name from the township of **Roxton**, noted on a 1795 map and proclaimed in 1803. The township was named after a village in Bedfordshire, England, west of Cambridge. **Roxton Pond**, a postal name since 1864, became a village in 1886 and a parish municipality in 1985, succeeding *Sainte-Pudentienne*.

Royal Geographical Society Islands NU Located between Victoria and King William Islands, this group of islands was named in 1905 by Roald Amundsen (1872–1928) after the Royal Geographical Society of London, England.

Royal Road BC This body of water, between Victoria on the east and Albert Head on the west, was named *Royal Bay* in 1846 by Capt. Henry Kellett (1806–75), possibly because of the two royal names on each side honouring the Queen and her consort. As a good location to anchor ships, it became known as Royal Roads, the name in general use on marine charts by the first half of the twentieth century.

Royston BC On the east coast of Vancouver Island, southeast of Courtenay, this place was named in 1910 by William Roy, who had settled here in 1890, and by land developer Frederick B. Warren, who had come from Royston, Cambridgeshire, England.

Rundle, Mount AB A landmark in Banff, this mountain (2949 m) was named in 1885 by Dr. Sir James Hector (1834–1907) after Methodist missionary Robert Terrill Rundle (1811–96). Rundle joined the Hudson's Bay Company in 1839 and was sent to its Saskatchewan district. He travelled through the West extensively and would have seen the mountain named after him in either 1844 or 1847. He returned to England in 1847.

Rupert, Rivière QC Draining Lac Mistassini in northwestern Quebec, this river flows west for 483 km, emptying into the southeast corner of James Bay. It was named in 1668 after Prince Rupert (1619–82), a son-in-law of Charles I and a first cousin of Charles II. He was appointed the first governor of the Hudson's Bay Company. The trading post at its mouth was first called Fort Charles after Charles II, and then called Rupert House in 1670. The Cree village was known as *Fort Rupert* until 1978, when it was changed to Waskaganish.

Rusagonis NB Located on **Rusagonis Stream**, south of Fredericton, this place's post office was called *Rusagornis* (following local pronunciation) from 1853 to 1930, when it became Rusagonis until 1936. A nearby community's post office was known as *Rusagornis Station* from 1871 to 1930, when it became **Rusagonis Station** until 1945. The stream's name derives from the Maliseet *tesegwanik* (possibly 'meeting with the main stream' or 'flat branch').

Rushoon NL Located on the western shore of Placentia Bay, and northeast of Marystown, this municipal community (1966) was noted in French records during the 1700s as *Rashoon*. Its name possibly derives from *roches jaunes* ('yellow rocks'), a description of the rocky shore.

Russell MB The post office in this town (1913) west of Riding Mountain National Park was called *Shell River* in 1880. It was renamed in 1889 by Col. Charles Arkoll Boulton (1841–99) after Gen. Lord Alexander George Russell (1821–1907), commander of the Canadian forces, 1883–8.

Russell ON The county and the township in the united counties of Prescott and Russell were named in 1798 after Peter Russell (1733–1808). He was the administrator of Upper Canada from the departure of Lt.-Gov. John Graves Simcoe (1752–1806) in 1796, until the appointment of Peter Hunter (1746–1805) as lieutenant-governor in 1799. Russell post office was named in 1848, with developer William Duncan as the postmaster. His son John, the next postmaster, renamed the community *Duncanville* four years later, but the postal name did not change. Russell was restored when it became a police village in 1898.

Russell Island NU North of Prince of Wales Island, this island (940 km²) was named in 1819 by Sir William Parry (1790–1855) after John Russell, 1st Earl Russell (1792–1878).

Rustico Bay PE René Rassicot (c.1705–1760), a native of Normandy, settled on the north side of the island in 1724. By 1752 Joseph de la Roque referred to the bay as *Grand Racico*. In 1765 Samuel Holland (1728–1801) called it *Harris Bay*, with *Grand Rastico* as a secondary name, but the name Rustico Bay soon took precedence. The bay is enclosed by **Rustico Island**, which had also been known as *Gotteville Island*, *Peters Island*, *McAuslin Island*, and *Robinsons Island*. *See also* North Rustico.

Ruthven ON In Essex County, west of Leamington, this place was first called *Inkermanville* after the 1854 battle in the Crimea. Its post office opened in 1860, with Hugh Ruthven as the first postmaster.

Rycroft AB This village (1944) north of Grande Prairie was near the first site of Spirit River. In 1920 the Spirit River post office was moved 8 km to the west, with the original site named *Roycroft* after Robert Henry Rycroft, an early settler and justice of the peace. It was corrected to Rycroft in 1931. Three other residents—W.S.O. English, 'Doc' Calkin, and George Garnett—wanted their names chosen, but Rycroft's was picked from a hat.

Ryley AB The post office in this village (1910) southwest of Vegreville was named in 1908 after George Urquhart Ryley, land commissioner of the Grand Trunk Pacific Railway. A train station was established here in 1909.

Saanich BC This district municipality (1906) is immediately north of Victoria and at the base of the **Saanich Peninsula**. Its name derives from the Saanich tribe, whose name in Straits Salish means 'elevated' in reference to Mount Newton (307 m), which looks like a raised rump. The deep 23-km bay on the west side of the peninsula is called **Saanich Inlet**. *See also* Central Saanich *and* North Saanich.

Sabine Peninsula NT, NU The peninsula in this northern extension of Melville Island was named in 1820 by Sir William Parry (1790–1855) after Sir Edward Sabine (1788–1883), the astronomer on Parry's expedition in search of the Northwest Passage.

Sable Island NS Located in the Atlantic Ocean, 300 km southeast of Halifax, this island was named on a mid-1500s map of eastern North America as *Isola dell rena*. A map by Guillaume Levasseur in 1601 has *Y sable*, and Samuel de Champlain's 1613 map has *isle de sable*.

Sachs Harbour NT On the west coast of Banks Island, this hamlet (1986) was established in 1953 and named two years later when a meteorological station and post office opened. The harbour was named in 1947 after the schooner *Mary Sachs*, which was beached here in 1914 while carrying provisions for an expedition.

Sackville NB The post office in this town (1903) on the Tantramar River was named in 1837. The name derives from **Sackville Parish**, created in 1786 and established earlier in 1772 as Sackville Township. The township was called after George Sackville-Germain (1716–85), who became 1st Viscount Sackville in 1782.

Sackville NS North of the centre of Halifax, this suburban area unites a number of residential communities. It takes its name from Fort Sackville, constructed at the head of Bedford Basin in 1749. The fort was named after George Sackville-Germain (1716–85), who became 1st Viscount Sackville in 1782. In 1745 he distinguished himself at the Battle of Fontenoy in France. Postal service was established in 1884 at **Lower Sackville**, **Middle Sackville**, and **Upper Sackville**.

Sacré-Coeur QC This municipality (1973) northwest of Tadoussac became the parish municipality of *Sacré-Coeur-de-Jésus* in 1915. A village of the same name was incorporated in 1937, and the two were merged as Sacré-Coeur in 1973. Its post office was called *Dolbeau* in 1884 and was renamed Sacré-Coeur-Saguenay in 1927.

Saguenay QC This city formed in 2002 by merging the cities of Chicoutimi, Jonquière, and La Baie, which subsequently became the three boroughs of Saguenay. Chicoutimi encompasses Laterrière and the township of Tremblay. Jonquière has Arvida, Kénogami, Lac Kénogami, and Lac Shipshaw. La Baie has Grand Baie, Port Alfred, and Bagotville.

Saguenay, Rivière QC Draining a basin of 88,000 km², this river (160 km long, but 698 km to the head of Rivière Péribonka) enters the St. Lawrence at Tadoussac. In his *Relation* of 1535–6, Jacques Cartier (1491–1557) drew attention to the river, the royal road, and the land of the Saguenay. The name, referring to the territory and not to the river, means 'place where the water flows out', likely from Montagnais or Algonquin.

Saint-Adolphe-d'Howard QC This municipality, northwest of Saint-Jérôme, was created in 1939, having been called the township municipality of *Howard* in 1883. The township of Howard was named in 1883 after Sir Frederick Howard, colonial commissioner at the end of the eighteenth century. The name of the municipality honours Fr. Adolphe Jodoin (1836–91), who served a mission here, 1878–82.

Saint-Agapit QC This municipality in the regional county of Lotbinière, southwest of Quebec City, was formed in 1979 through the merger of the parish municipality of *Saint-Agapit-de-Beaurivage* (1867) and the village of *Saint-Agapitville* (1911). The name recalls St. Agapetus (d.536), the 57th Pope, 535–6.

St. Agatha ON The post office of this community in the regional municipality of Waterloo, west of the city of Waterloo, was named in 1852 after St. Agatha parish and church, dedicated in the 1830s. St. Agatha was a third-century Sicilian martyr.

St. Alban's NL On the west side of Bay d'Espoir and near the southwestern coast of Newfoundland, this town (1953) was named in 1915 by Fr. Stanislaus St. Croix after the third-century English martyr St. Alban. St. Albans, Hertfordshire, England, northwest of London, is also named after him. St. Alban's was formerly called *Ship Cove*.

St. Albert AB This city (1976) on the northwest side of Edmonton was named in 1861 by Mgr. Alexandre Taché (1823–94) after Fr. Albert Lacombe (1827–1916). He was a missionary among the Aboriginal and Métis communities in the present area of Alberta from 1852.

Saint-Albert-de-Warwick QC This parish municipality in the regional county of Arthabaska, southwest of Victoriaville, was erected in 1864. Its mission, established three years earlier, was named in honour of St. Albertus Magnus (c.1200–80), a scholar and theologian.

Saint-Alexandre QC Located southeast of Saint-Jean-sur-Richelieu, this community was established in 1988 through the merger of the village and the parish municipality of *Saint-Alexandre*. The parish was organized in 1850, taking its name from a fourth-century bishop of Alexandria, Egypt.

Saint-Alexandre QC In the regional county of Kamouraska, southwest of Rivière-du-Loup, this parish municipality was founded in 1851. It took its name from Mgr. Alexandre-Antonin Taché (1823–94), who was born nearby and became archbishop of Saint-Boniface in Manitoba in 1853, and from local settler Alexandre Thériault. Its post office, Saint-Alexandre-de-Kamouraska, opened in 1854.

Saint-Alexis-des-Monts QC In the regional municipality of Maskinongé, northwest of Louiseville, this parish municipality was created in 1984 through the amalgamation of the municipality of *Belleau* (1973) and the parish municipality of *Saint-Alexis* (1877). Saint-Alexis-des-Monts post office opened in 1876 and was named after pioneer settler Alexis Bélanger.

Saint-Alphonse QC This parish municipality southwest of Granby was named in 1875 after the parish erected six years earlier. The parish honoured the founder of the Redemptorists, St. Alphonso Maria de' Liguori (1696–1787). He was the patron saint of Fr. Joseph-Alphonse Gravel (1843–1901), secretary of the diocese of Saint-Hyacinthe, 1875–86.

Saint-Alphonse-Rodriguez QC This municipality northwest of Joliette was erected in 1991 and had been called *Bienheureux-Alphonse-de-Rodriguez* since 1855. Alfonso de Rodríguez (1531–1617), a Spanish brother of the Company of Jesus, was canonized in 1888.

Saint-Amable QC Located northeast of Longueuil, this municipality (1984) was a parish municipality from 1921. The religious parish was erected in 1913 and named after Fr. Amable Prévost (1757–1820), who had served in the area of Chambly and Beloeil, 1807–20.

Saint-Ambroise QC This municipality northwest of the city of Saguenay received its current status in 1982. It was created

a village in 1971 by merging the village (1917) and the municipality (1902) of the same name. The religious parish, founded in 1883, was named after a parish in the borough of Jonquière, which was named after Fr. Ambroise-Martial Fafard (1840–99), pastor of the cathedral in the borough of Chicoutimi, 1880–9.

Saint-Ambroise-de-Kildare QC Located northwest of the city of Saguenay, this parish municipality was created in 1855, taking its name from the religious parish established in 1839. It was named after St. Ambrosius (c.340–97), bishop of Milan and a noted doctor of the church. The township of Kildare was erected in 1803, taking its name from the town and county southwest of Dublin, Ireland.

Saint-André NB The first post office in this village (1967) north of Grand Falls was called *Chambord* in 1884 after Henry V, Comte de Chambord (1820–83). It was renamed St-André-de-Madawaska in 1912.

Saint-André-Avellin QC This village in the regional county of Papineau, northeast of Buckingham, was named in 1911 when it was severed from the parish municipality of **Saint-André–Avellin**. The parish municipality and the post office were both established in 1855. The religious parish was created in 1851, taking its name from André Trudeau, who surveyed lots in the area in 1832, and from St. Andrea Avellino (1521–1608), who was canonized in 1712.

Saint-André-d'Acton QC This parish municipality, southwest of **Acton Vale**, was erected in 1864. It was named after St. Andrew, the younger brother of Simon Peter. The township of **Acton** was named after a suburb of London, England, west of the city centre.

Saint-André-Est QC Located south of Lachute, the village of *St. Andrews* was created in 1958, and the present name was adopted 20 years later. The Anglican parish of St. Andrews was established here in 1822, three years after the *St. Andrews East* post office opened. The parish municipality of **Saint-André-d'Argenteuil** was erected in 1855.

St. Andrews NB Located in Charlotte County and at the mouth of the St. Croix River, this town (1903) was named after **St. Andrews Parish**, created in 1786. A post office opened here in 1817. William Fitz-William Owen (1774–1857) identified *St. Andrews Point* on his 1770 chart. The point was perhaps named after a priest called St-André or by a priest that celebrated mass here on the day of St. Andrew. The town is commonly known as St. Andrews by the Sea.

Saint-Anicet QC Located on the south shore of Lake St. Francis, southwest of Salaberry-de-Valleyfield, this parish municipality was established in 1885. The post office opened in 1851, taking its name from the mission created in 1810. St. Anicetus was the Pope from about 155 to 166.

Saint-Anselme QC This village in the regional county of Bellechasse, southeast of Lévis, was erected in 1920, when it was severed from the parish municipality of **Saint-Anselme**. It was named after the parish that was established in 1827. St. Anselm (1033–1109), a scholar and theologian, was an archbishop of Canterbury.

St. Anthony NL This town (1945) on the northeastern coast of the Northern Peninsula was the site of a French fishing harbour in the 1700s and became an English-speaking settlement in the mid-1800s. The harbour was perhaps named by Jacques Cartier (1491–1557) in the spring of 1534. On 13 June 1534 he named *H. de St. Antoine*, on the north shore of the estuary of the St. Lawrence River, between Havre Saint-Pierre and Sept-Îles.

Saint-Antoine NB This village north of Moncton was incorporated in 1966 as *St. Anthony* and changed to its present name in 1969. Its post office was called *St. Anthony* from 1873 to 1928, when it was changed to St-Antoine-de-Kent. It was perhaps named after a French mission located on the Richibucto River about 1700, which was possibly given after the French seminary of St-Antoine-de-Padoue, where Fr. Chrestien LeClercq (1641–95) was ordained about 1668.

Saint-Antoine QC Located just south of Saint-Jérôme, this town was incorporated in 1967, and had been the village (1956) and the parish (1940) of *Saint-Antoine-des-Laurentides*. The village was named after Fr. Antoine Labelle (1833–91), parish priest of Saint-Jérôme, 1868–91, who actively promoted the settlement of the lands to the north.

Saint-Antoine-de-Lavaltrie QC This parish municipality south of Joliette was created in 1855. The name was given in honour of St. Anthony of Padua (1195–1231), a native of Portugal who is claimed as a patron saint by Padua, Italy.

Saint-Antoine-de-Richelieu QC Situated on the west bank of the Richelieu, downriver from Beloeil, the parish municipality was created in 1890. It was named after the parish founded in 1741 in honour of St. Anthony of Padua (1195–1231), a doctor of the church. The current municipality was erected in 1982.

Saint-Antonin QC Located southeast of Rivière-du-Loup, this parish municipality was created in 1856 and named after Louis-Antonin (or Antoine) Proulx (1810–96), the first parish priest, 1840–54.

Saint-Apollinaire QC This municipality in the regional county of Lotbinière, southwest of Quebec City, was created

in 1974 when the parish municipality of **Saint-Apollinaire** (1855) merged with the village of *Francoeur* (1919). The post office here was named in 1858. St. Apollonaris (d.c.200) was a bishop and martyr who lived at Ravenna, Italy.

Saint-Athanase QC Situated south of Iberville and across the Richelieu from Saint-Jean-sur-Richelieu, this parish municipality was named in 1845. The religious parish was named in 1828, likely after St. Athanasius (c.295–373), bishop of Alexandria, Egypt, 328–73.

Saint-Augustin-de-Desmaures QC In 2002 this municipality became part of Quebec City but regained its status as a municipality in 2006. It was erected in 1845, taking its name from the parish founded in 1679. The name recalls Augustin de Saffray de Mézy, governor of New France, 1663–5, and Jean Juchereau de Maure, a grantee of the seigneury of de Maure (or Saint-Augustin) about 1681.

Saint-Basile NB On the Saint John River, southeast of Edmundston, this village was incorporated in 1966. Its post office was called *Upper St. Bazil* from 1852 to 1910, when it was renamed *Upper St. Basil*. It was *St. Bazil* from 1911 to 1938, when it was changed to the present name. **Saint-Basile Parish** was created in 1850, taking its name from St. Basil the Great (c.330–79), noted for organizing Greek monasticism.

Saint-Basile-le-Grand QC This town on the west bank of the Richelieu, east of Montreal, was erected as a town in 1969. The religious parish was created in 1870, followed by the parish municipality the next year. It was named after local farmer Basile Daigneault (1830–1901), whose name recalls the celebrated St. Basil the Great (c.330–79), who organized monastic life in Greece.

Saint-Bernard QC This municipality on the west side of the Rivière Chaudière, north of Sainte-Marie, was created in 1987 through the amalgamation of the village (1959) and the parish municipality (1845) of Saint-Bernard. The religious parish was named in 1821 after St. Bernard (1090–1153), the abbot of Clairvaux, France, and a doctor of the church.

St. Bernard's NL Located on the eastern shore of Fortune Bay and northeast of Marystown, this municipal community (1967) was named in 1915 after the local Catholic church, built here about 1890. It was formerly called *Fox Cove*.

Saint-Boniface-de-Shawinigan QC This village southwest of Shawinigan was erected in 1918, and the parish municipality of *Saint-Boniface-de-Shawinigan* (1956) was annexed to it in 1961. St. Boniface (c.673–754), a native of Devon, England, evangelized Germany.

St. Brendan's NL Situated on Cottel Island in Bonavista Bay, this municipal community (1953) was first called *Cottel Island*. It was renamed in the early 1900s after the Irish saint who undertook a legendary voyage in a leather boat across the Atlantic in search of the 'promised land of the saints' around 500 BCE.

St. Bride, Mount AB This mountain (3315 m) northeast of Lake Louise, and directly south of Mount Douglas, was named in 1898 after the patron saint of the Douglas family.

St. Bride's NL Situated on the southeastern shore of Placentia Bay, this municipal community (1972) was called *Distress* as early as the 1830s, likely after the difficulty of finding a safe haven on the Cape Shore during rough seas. It was renamed about 1870 after St. Brigid (453–523), a patron saint of Ireland.

St. Brieux SK Southwest of Melfort, this village (1913) was established in 1904 by Fr. Paul Le Flock, who brought Breton settlers from Saint-Brieuc, Bretagne, France, west of Saint-Malo. A post office opened here in 1905.

Saint-Bruno QC This municipality in the regional county of Lac-Saint-Jean-Est, south of Alma, was created in 1886 and annexed the village of Saint-Bruno (1910) in 1975. The religious parish of Saint-Bruno was erected in 1884 and named after Fr. Bruno-Élisée Leclerc (1838–1907), who was then pastor of Notre-Dame-d'Hébertville. The name also recalls St. Bruno (c.1030–1101), the founder of the Carthusian order.

Saint-Bruno-de-Montarville QC Located on the south side of **Mont Bruno**, east of Montreal, this city was erected in 1958, 110 years after its post office opened. The religious parish of Saint-Bruno was founded in 1842, its name adapted from François-Pierre Bruneau, the seigneur of Montarville. The seigneury was granted to Pierre Boucher de Boucherville the younger (1653–1740), with its name constructed from the words *montagne* and *Boucherville*. First called *Colline de Montarville*, Mont Bruno came into general use for the mountain after 1842.

Saint-Calixte QC In the regional county of Montcalm, northeast of Saint-Jérôme, this municipality was named in 1954, and had been the township municipality of Kilkenny since 1855. Its post office was called *Saint-Calixte-de-Kilkenny* in 1877. St. Calixtus was the 16th Pope, 217–22. The township of Kilkenny was proclaimed in 1832 after the county and town of Kilkenny, southwest of Dublin.

St. Catharines ON This city (1876) in Niagara Region was named about 1796 by Queenston merchant Robert Hamilton for his wife Catharine Askin Robertson, who died that year.

It is often misspelled because of the Catholic diocesan cathedral of St. Catherine's on Catherine Street, and because the post office was *St. Catherines* from 1817 to 1849, when it was respelled after the name of the town (1845). In the early years it was called *The Twelve* after Twelve Mile Creek and *Shipman's Corners* after tavern keeper Paul Shipman.

Saint-Célestin QC This village in the regional county of Nicolet-Yamaska, southeast of Trois-Rivières, replaced *Annaville* in 1991. *Annaville* was named in 1896 after a relic of St. Ann brought from Rome by the founder of the parish of Saint-Célestin, Mgr. Calixte Marquis. The parish was named after St. Celestine V (d.1296), the Pope in 1294.

Saint-Césaire QC This town was erected in 1962 in the regional county of Rouville, midway between Chambly and Granby, and had been a village since 1859. Its post office opened in 1832. The municipal parish was established in 1857 and the religious parish was founded in 1822. St. Caesarius (c.470–542) was a bishop of Arles and primate of Gaul and Spain.

Saint-Charles QC This village in the regional county of Bellechasse, southeast of Quebec City, was created in 1915 from the parish municipality of Saint-Charles-Borromée, established in 1855. St. Charles Borromeo (1538–84) was a sixteenth-century archbishop of Milan and the principal author of the 1566 Roman catechism.

Saint-Charles-Borromée QC This municipality, located in the regional county of Joliette and north of the city of Joliette, was created in 1986, and had been a parish municipality from 1855. St. Charles Borromeo was the founder in 1578 of the Oblates of the Blessed Virgin and St. Ambrose, which preceded the familiar Oblates of Mary Immaculate, established in 1816.

Saint-Charles-de-Drummond QC Located on the east side of Drummondville, this municipality was established in 1988, and its post office had opened in 1950. The parish was erected in 1868 and named after St. Charles Borromeo (1538–84), who was an energetic reformer of the church during the time of the Council of Trent.

Saint-Charles-de-Mandeville QC Located north of Joliette, this municipality was established in 1905, two years after the religious parish was created. The parish was named after either Fr. Charles-Olivier Gingras or Fr. Charles Turgeon. In 1905 Mandeville post office opened here, taking its name from Maximillien Mandeville, who settled on the north shore of Lac Maskinongé about 1824.

Saint-Christophe-d'Arthabaska QC This parish municipality, southeast of Victoriaville, was named in 1845 after the religious parish created in 1846. The parish was named after

Jean-Chrysostome (also known as Christophe and Christo) Marcoux, who hunted in the area before 1830. It also recalls the name of St. Christopher, the patron saint of travellers, especially drivers.

Saint-Chrysostome QC This village encircled by the parish municipality of Saint-Jean-Chrysostome, south of Montreal, was established in 1902, 20 years after its post office opened. St. John Chrysostom (c.347–407) was a patiarch of Constantinople and a scripture scholar.

St. Clair, Lake ON Between Lake Huron and Lake Erie, this body of water was named by René-Robert Cavelier de La Salle (1643–87) and Fr. Louis Hennepin (c.1626–1705) on 12 August 1679, the feast day of St. Clair of Assisi. The St. Clair River comprised the first part of the *Rivière du Détroit* during the French regime and was later called *Huron River*, before being named St. Clair River in the nineteenth century. The village of **St. Clair Beach**, east of Windsor, was incorporated in 1914. In 1999 this village became a part of the town of Tecumseh.

St. Claude MB Southwest of Winnipeg, this village (1963) was named in 1891 by the Order of Canons Régulaires, based at nearby Notre Dame des Lourdes. They named it after a town in France, near the Swiss border, northeast of Lyon. The first settlers were French and Swiss.

Saint-Colomban QC This parish municipality west of Saint-Jérôme was created in 1845, taking its name from the religious parish established in 1835–6. The parish was named after St. Colomban (543–615), an Irish missionary who revived the monastic life in France, Switzerland, and Italy.

Saint-Constant QC Located south of Montreal, adjacent to the Kahnawake Reserve, this town (1973) was established as a parish municipality in 1855; its post office opened a year earlier. There is some uncertainty about the origin of the name, but it is possibly connected to Constant Le Marchand de Lignery (or Ligneris) (c.1663–1731), whose son, Jacques Le Marchand de Lignery, was the pastor at Laprairie from 1731 to 1775 and served the mission of Saint-Constant for a few years.

St. Croix River NB Forming part of the boundary between Maine and New Brunswick, this river was named *Rivière saincte Croix* by Pierre du Gua de Monts (c.1558–1628) in 1604. The St. Croix, Oak Bay, and Waweig Rivers portray the shape of a cross. By the late 1700s, the estuary retained the name St. Croix, but the river above tide and rising in Maine was called the *Scoodic*, with the river on the boundary above Grand Falls Flowage called the *Chiputneticook*. By 1885 the St. Croix was recognized as the boundary river rising in the Chiputneticook Lakes and flowing into Passamaquoddy Bay.

Saint-Cyrille-de-Wendover QC This municipality northeast of Drummondville was erected in 1982 and had been the village of *Saint-Cyrille* from 1905. The Saint-Cyrille-de-Wendover post office opened in 1875. It was named after first settler, Cyrille Brassard, whose name recalls St. Cyril (c.313–86), a bishop of Jerusalem and a doctor of the church. The township of **Wendover** was proclaimed in 1805, taking its name from a village in Buckinghamshire, England, northwest of London.

Saint-Damase QC This village south of the city of Saint-Hyacinthe was separated in 1952 from the parish municipality of **Saint-Damase**. The latter was erected in 1845 taking its name from the religious parish that organized in 1823. The post office opened in 1837. The name was chosen by Mgr. Joseph-Octave Plessis (1763–1825) after St. Damasus (c.305–84), the Pope from 366 to 384.

Saint-Damien-de-Buckland QC This parish municipality was erected in 1891 in the regional county of Bellechasse, southeast of Quebec City. The parish of **Saint-Damien** was created in 1848, taking its name from St. Damian, a celebrated physician in Asia Minor who was beheaded about 303. The township of **Buckland** was proclaimed in 1806 and was named after a place in England, possibly Buckland in Buckinghamshire.

Saint-David-de-Falardeau QC Located north of the city of Saguenay, this municipality was established in 1948 and named after the religious parish created in 1937. The parish was named after Fr. David Roussel (1835–98), pastor of Sainte-Anne-de-Chicoutimi after 1870. The township of **Falardeau** was proclaimed in 1920 and named after noted painter Antoine-Sébastien Falardeau (1822–89).

Saint-Denis-de-Brompton QC Created in 1935, this parish municipality northwest of Sherbrooke was named after its founder, Fr. Joseph-Denis Bellemare, who was a local parish priest. The township of **Brompton** was named in 1795 and proclaimed in 1801, possibly after a town in North Yorkshire, England, north of Northallerton.

Saint-Dominique QC Located east of Saint-Hyacinthe, this municipality was created in 1969 through the amalgamation of the village (1914) and the parish municipality of **Saint-Dominique** (1845). The parish was established in 1833. The post office, called Saint-Dominique in 1853, was renamed Saint-Dominique-de-Bagot in 1876. The third seigneur of Saint-Hyacinthe, Hyacinthe-Marie Delorme (1777–1814), may have chosen the name in memory of his brother-in-law, Pierre-Dominique Debartzch (1782–1846), or after Debartzch's son of the same name, who acquired part of the seigneury in 1811.

Saint-Donat QC Located east of Mont Tremblant, this municipality was established in 1953. It was the parish municipality of **Saint-Donat-de-Montcalm** from 1874, the same name as the post office that opened five years later. It was possibly named after Fr. Donat Coutu, the first pastor here in 1874, although recent evidence indicates Fr. Alexis-Henri Coutu was the first pastor and Fr. Donat Coutu never served in the parish.

Sainte-Adèle QC Created a town in 1973, this popular all-season resort north of Saint-Jérôme was previously a parish municipality (1855), which annexed the village of **Sainte-Adèle** (1922) in 1955. The religious parish was created in 1852 and named after Adèle Raymond, the wife of Augustin-Norbert Morin, who donated land for the church.

Sainte-Agathe QC This village in the regional county of Lotbinière, southwest of Quebec City, was named in 1914 after the parish municipality of **Sainte-Agathe** (1857). The Sainte-Agathe post office opened in 1858. St. Agatha was martyred in 251 CE.

Sainte-Agathe-des-Monts QC The town in this popular tourist destination in the mountains north of Saint-Jérôme was incorporated in 1915, and had been erected as a village in 1896. The adjacent village of **Sainte-Agathe-Sud** was named in 1964. The municipality of **Sainte-Agathe-Nord** was created in 1991, succeeding the parish municipality of **Sainte-Agathe** (1863). Their names recall a third-century Sicilian martyr.

Ste. Anne MB The name of this village (1963) north of Steinbach was given in 1864 by Fr. Jean-Marie Le Floc'h, a native of France's Bretagne, where there was a special devotion to the mother of the Virgin Mary. The village was earlier known as *Pointe des Chênes* and *Grande Pointe des Chênes*, and the village's post office was called *Ste. Anne des Chênes*. The oaks (*chênes*) have long disappeared from the banks of the Seine River, which flows into the Red River in Winnipeg.

Sainte-Anne-de-Beaupré QC This town northeast of Quebec City was formed in 1973 through the merger of the village (1906) and the parish municipality of **Sainte-Anne-de-Beaupré** (1920). The name has its roots in the early seventeenth-century phrase *le beau pré* ('the pretty meadow'), and occurs in such names as the town of **Beaupré** and the regional county of **La Côte-de-Beaupré**.

Sainte-Anne-de-Bellevue QC This city became part of the city of Montreal in 2002, but recovered its status as a city in 2006. Located at the extreme west end of the Île de Montréal, the town was established in 1895, having been incorporated as a village in 1878, a year before the *Sainte-Anne-de-Bout-de-l'Île* post office (1835) was changed to agree with Sainte-Anne-de-Bellevue. The beautiful views over both Lac Saint-Louis and Lac des Deux Montagnes account for the ultimate part of the name.

Sainte-Anne-de-la-Pérade QC On the north shore of the St. Lawrence, northeast of Trois-Rivières, this municipality was created in 1989 when the parish municipality of **Sainte-Anne-de-la-Pérade** (1845) and the village of *La Pérade* (1912) were merged together.

Sainte-Anne-de-Madawaska NB Southeast of Edmundston, this village (1966) was first known as *André Settlement*. Its first post office was *Quisibus* in 1879, named after the Rivière Quisibis. It was renamed Ste-Anne-de-Madawaska in 1897. The church dedicated to St. Ann was built in 1872, and **Sainte-Anne Parish** was created five years later.

Sainte-Anne-des-Monts QC This town (1968) at the mouth of the Rivière Sainte-Anne, on the south shore of the St. Lawrence and in the shadow of the Monts Chic-Chocs, is noted as early as 1709 on a map. The religious parish originated in 1815, with the post office following in 1853 and the municipality two years later. Fr. Jean-Baptiste Sasseville arrived here at the beginning of the nineteenth century and may have dedicated the parish to his native Sainte-Anne-de-la-Pocatière.

Sainte-Anne-de-Sorel QC Located on the east side of the city of Sorel, the parish municipality was established in 1877, a year after the religious parish was set up. The post office opened in 1879.

Sainte-Anne-des-Plaines QC Situated in the regional county of Thérèse-De Blainville, northeast of Blainville, this town was created as a parish municipality in 1845. The municipality was named after the religious parish of **Sainte-Anne-des-Plaines** (1816), which was created as Sainte-Anne-de-Mascouche in 1787. The name 'Plaines' has its roots in the seigneury of Belle Plaine, granted to Louis Lepage de Sainte-Claire (1656–1718) in 1731, and in the Algonquin meaning of *Mascouche* ('level plain').

Sainte-Anne, Mont QC A well known all-season leisure destination, just north of Sainte-Anne-de-Beaupré, this 820-m mountain was named in the early 1800s after the parish of **Sainte-Anne**. The parish was named in the mid-1600s after the mother of the Virgin Mary.

Sainte-Brigitte-de-Laval QC Located north of Quebec City, this municipality has its roots in the religious parish, established in 1863. It was part of the seigneury granted to Mgr. François de Laval (1623–1708), the first bishop of Quebec, 1674–88. The land was settled after 1830 by Irish immigrants who identified their community with St. Brigid (c.455–528), a patron saint of Ireland.

Sainte-Catherine QC This town (1973) on the south side of the St. Lawrence, directly south of Montreal, was created the parish municipality of *Sainte-Catherine-d'Alexandrie-de-Laprairie* in 1937, a year after the religious parish of **Sainte–Catherine** was erected. St. Catherine of Alexandria was considered a fourth-century martyr, but her name is now omitted from the official calendar of saints.

Sainte-Catherine-de-la-Jacques-Cartier QC Located on the Rivière Jacques-Cartier, and in the regional county of La Jacques Cartier, west of Quebec City, this municipality was named in 1984. It was erected as the parish municipality of *Sainte-Catherine* in 1855, taking its name from the religious parish of Sainte-Catherine-de-Fossambault, erected in 1824.

Sainte-Claire QC This municipality in the regional county of Bellechasse, southeast of Quebec City, was erected in 1855. It was established 10 years earlier as *Sainte-Claire-de-Joliette* but abolished in 1847. In 1977 it annexed the municipality of *Louis-Joliette* (1926). The land embraced the seigneury of Jolliet, granted to explorer Louis Jolliet (1645–1700) in 1697. His wife was Claire-Françoise Byssot, perhaps the source of the name Sainte-Claire. St. Clare of Assisi (1194–1253) was the founder of the order of the Poor Nuns.

Sainte-Croix QC A village in the regional county of Lotbinière, southeast of Quebec City, it was severed from the parish municipality of **Sainte–Croix** in 1921. The latter, established in 1845, had its roots in the seigneury of Sainte-Croix, reserved in 1637 for the education of girls by the religious orders in Quebec City and taken over by the Ursulines in 1647. A mission and a parish were established in the early 1700s, and Samuel de Champlain (1567–1635) referred to the place in 1613, noting it was originally further upriver at the present Pointe Platon.

Sainte-Félicité QC This village east of Matane was separated from the parish municipality of **Sainte–Félicité**, created in 1868, four years after the post office opened. The site was called Pointe-au-Massacre, likely because many shipwrecks happened here, but was renamed in 1860 by Mgr. Baillargeon. St. Felicity was a second-century Roman martyr.

Sainte-Foy QC In 2002 this city became part of Quebec City and then a borough in Quebec City, joined with the city of Sillery, in 2006. Sainte-Foy was created a parish municipality in 1845, became a town in 1949, and annexed the parish municipality of L'Ancienne-Lorette in 1971. The name has its roots in the seigneury of Sainte-Foy, granted in 1637 to Pierre Puiseaux, and possibly took its name from a French village.

Sainte-Geneviève QC This town became a part of the city of Montreal in 2002 and a sector in the city of Montreal in 2006. Located on the south shore of the Rivière des Prairies, it was

erected in 1959. It was created in 1935 as the village of *Sainte-Geneviève-de-Pierrefonds*, and before that, the village of *Sainte-Geneviève* in 1860. *See also* Pierrefonds.

Sainte-Hélène-de-Breakeyville QC Situated south of Quebec City, this parish municipality was created in 1909. The name recalls lumberman John Breakey (1846–1911) and his wife, Helen Henderson. The post office is called **Breakeyville**.

Sainte-Hélène, Île QC The principal site of Man and His World (Expo '67), this island was called *Saincte Elaine* in 1611 by Samuel de Champlain (1567–1635). Although he did not say so, the island was likely named after Hélène Bouillé (1598–1654), whom he married the previous year.

Sainte-Jeanne-d'Arc QC Located north of Lac Saint-Jean and east of Mistassini, this village was erected in 1922, two years after a mission was established here. St. Joan of Arc (c.1412–31) was canonized on 16 May 1920.

Sainte-Julie QC Located midway between the St. Lawrence and the Richelieu, east of Montreal, this city was erected in 1971 and had been created a parish municipality in 1855. The religious parish was established in 1850 in honour of St. Julia, a fifth-century martyr, and Julie Gauthier *dit* Saint-Germain, whose husband donated land in 1849 for the chapel.

Sainte-Justine QC This municipality in the regional county of Les Etchemins was erected in 1993 and had been a parish municipality from 1891 and the township municipality of *Langevin* from 1869. The name was given after Marie-Justine Têtu (1833–82), wife of Sir Hector-Louis Langevin (1826–1906), a Father of Confederation and minister of public works in the government of Canada, 1879–91. The township of Langevin was proclaimed in 1862.

St. Elias, Mount YT This mountain (5489 m) is on the Yukon–Alaska border at the point where the Alaska panhandle begins its long, sinuous boundary with Canada south to the 54°40' parallel. Cape St. Elias, on the tip of Kayak Island in Alaska, was named on 16 July 1741 by Vitus Bering in honour of the saint's day. Bering, a Dane, was sailing on behalf of the Russian government. It appears that Bering did not name the mountain himself, but that it was named by eighteenth-century map-makers. The **St. Elias Mountains** extend for 500 km from Alaska through the southwestern corner of the Yukon and across the most northwesterly part of British Columbia. They were called the *St. Elias Range* and the *St. Elias Alps* in the late 1800s, with the present name confirmed in 1918.

Saint-Élie-d'Orford QC This municipality in the regional county of Sherbrooke, west of the city of Sherbrooke, was established in 1992 and had been created a parish municipality

SAINTE-MADELEINE

in 1899. The parish was created in 1889, six years after Fr. Alfred-Élie Dufresne (1826–91) opened a mission here. The post office was called *Glen Iver* in 1885 and was changed to the present name in 1931.

Sainte-Madeleine QC This village midway between Mont-Saint-Hilaire and Saint-Hyacinthe was established in 1919 and its post office opened in 1876. The parish of Sainte-Marie-Madeleine was created in 1870, taking its name from St. Mary Magdalen, the repentant sinner and follower of Jesus Christ.

Sainte-Madeleine-de-Rigaud QC Located on the Quebec–Ontario border, and surrounding the town of Rigaud, this parish municipality was erected in 1855, with its mission set up about 1802. As well as honouring St. Mary Magdalen, it was also named after Louise-Madeleine Chaussegros de Léry (1726–1809), the wife of Michel Chartier de Lotbinière (1723–98), who had acquired the seigneury of Rigaud in 1763.

Saint-Malachie QC Located southeast of Lévis, this parish municipality was named in 1948. It was established in 1874 as *Saint-Malachie-de-Frampton*, named after a mission opened here in 1841. It was settled by Irish, who likely suggested the name after St. Malachy (1094–1148), archbishop of Armagh, the primatial seat of Ireland. The township of Frampton, shown on a 1795 map and proclaimed in 1806, may have been named after a place near Boston in Lincolnshire, England.

Saint-Malachie-d'Ormstown QC Located adjacent to the town of Ormstown south of Salaberry-de-Valleyfield, this parish municipality was named in 1855 after St. Malachy (1094–1148), archbishop of Armagh, who reformed the church in Ireland.

Sainte-Marie QC The present limits of this town on both banks of the Rivière Chaudière, midway between the cities of Quebec and Saint-Georges, were established in 1978 when the town (1958) of Sainte-Marie (erected a village in 1913) and the parish municipality (1845) *Sainte-Marie* were merged. Its name was given for Marie-Claire de Fleury de La Gorgendière (1708–97), whose mother married Thomas-Jacques Taschereau (1680–1749) in 1728, the seigneury of Sainte-Marie from 1736.

Sainte-Marie-de-Monnoir QC This parish municipality between Chambly and Granby was established in 1845, taking its name from the religious parish created in 1801. Claude de Ramezay (1659–1724) was granted the seigneury of Monnoir in 1708, naming it after a fief he owned in France. *See also* Marieville.

Sainte-Marie-Saint-Raphaël NB Located on Île Lamèque, northeast of Shippagan, this village (1986) was established by amalgamating the communities of *Sainte-Marie-sur-Mer* and *Saint-Raphaël-sur-Mer*. The former was a postal name from 1947 to 1970. The latter's post office was first called *Hachi* in 1915. It was renamed Saint-Raphaël-sur-Mer in 1946. Raphael Chiasson had a land grant here.

Sainte-Marthe-du-Cap-de-la-Madeleine QC This municipality was created in 1916, when it was separated from the parish municipality of *Sainte-Marie-Madeleine-du-Cap-de-la-Madeleine*. It was named after St. Martha of the Gospels.

Sainte-Marthe-sur-le-Lac QC Located on the north shore of the Lac des Deux Montagnes, this town was erected in 1973. It became a municipality in 1960, when the parish (1956) was separated from the town of Saint-Eustache. The parish was named after St. Martha of the Gospels.

Sainte-Martine QC This municipality in the regional county of Beauharnois-Salaberry was created in 1991 and had been a parish municipality from 1855. The religious parish was established in 1829 and named after St. Martina, a third-century Roman martyr.

Sainte-Mélanie QC Located in the regional county of Joliette, north of the city of Joliette, this municipality was established in 1845. *Daillebout* was its post office from 1836 to 1881, when Sainte-Mélanie was adopted. It was named after Charlotte-Mélanie Panet (1794–1872), the wife of Marc-Antoine-Louis Lévesque (1782–1833), who donated land to erect a chapel in 1830. The name also recalls St. Melanie the Younger (383–439) of Rome, who became a nun in Jerusalem.

Saint-Émile QC In 2002 this town became part of Quebec City. In 2006 it became a sector of Quebec City, located 13 km north of the city centre. This town (1993) was incorporated as a village in 1956 and as a municipality in 1929. The parish was erected in 1925, but the post office had been called Saint-Émile-de-Quebec in 1904. The parish was named after Fr. Joseph-Nazaire-Émile Bédard, the pastor here from 1925 to 1940.

Sainte-Pétronille QC Located at the southwestern end of Île d'Orleans, this village was erected in 1980. It was called *Beaulieu* in 1874, the name of its post office that opened three years earlier and continued until 1991. The religious parish was established in 1879. St. Petronilla was a first-century martyr. *Beaulieu* was given for Jacques Gourdeau de Beaulieu (1622–63), who in 1652 married the widow of the first seigneur, Eléonore de Grandmaison (1619–92).

Sainte-Rosalie QC Located on the east side of the city of Saint-Hyacinthe, this village was incorporated in 1949. It was detached from the parish municipality of **Sainte-Rosalie**, erected in 1845, abolished two years later, and re-established

254

in 1855. The original parish was created in 1832 and named in honour of St. Rosalia (d.1160), the patron saint of Palermo, Sicily. Noted Quebec women with this name include the Louis-Joseph Papineau's mother, Rosalie Cherrier, and his sister, Marie-Rosalie. The latter was the wife of Jean Dessaulles, who was the proprietor of the seigneuries of Dessaulles and Saint-Hyacinthe when the parish was established.

Ste. Rose du Lac MB The post office of this village (1920) east of Dauphin and south of Dauphin Lake was named in 1894 by Fr. Eugène Le Coq.

Sainte-Thècle QC This municipality in the regional county of Mékinac, northeast of Shawinigan, was created in 1989 through the amalgamation of the village (1909) and the parish municipality (1874) of the same name. The religious parish was erected in 1873 and the post office opened six years later. The name recalls the first-century martyr St. Thecla, who studied with St. Paul.

Sainte-Thérèse QC This city in the regional county of Thérèse-De Blainville, north of Montreal, achieved its present status in 1916, after being incorporated as the village of *Sainte-Thérèse-de-Blainville* in 1849. The religious parish was created in 1825 and was named in honour of Marie-Thérèse Dugué de Boisbriand (1671–1744), the daughter of Michel-Sidrac Dugué de Boisbriand (1638–88), who was granted the seigneuries of Mille-Îles and Blainville in 1683.

Saint-Étienne-de-Lauzon QC This municipality southwest of Quebec City was erected in 1982 and had been simply *Saint-Étienne* since 1957. The religious parish of Saint-Étienne-de-Lauzon, in the original seigneury of Lauzon, was established in 1860 and named after Fr. Étienne-Baillargeon (1807–70), pastor of Saint-Nicolas, 1838–70. Its post office was called *Baillargeon* from 1862 to 1937, when the current name was adopted.

Saint-Eustache QC This city in the regional county of Deux-Montagnes, northwest of Montreal, was established with its present area in 1972 by annexing the parish municipality of *Saint-Eustache-sur-le-Lac* (1912). The religious parish was founded in 1768 and named after Eustache-Lambert Dumont (1767–1835), who was granted an extension of the seigneury of Mille-Îles in 1749. He built a flour mill here in 1762. His son Eustache-Louis, who developed the seigneury, is considered the real founder of the place.

Sainte-Véronique QC This village east of Mont-Laurier was named in 1984 and had been the township municipality of *Turgeon* in 1904. The religious parish of **Sainte-Véronique** was established in 1894 and named after St. Veronica, who had a special devotion to the Holy Face of Christ because she had wiped his brow when he was taken to the cross on Golgotha.

The township was proclaimed in 1900 and named after Fr. Adrien Turgeon (1846–1917), rector of Collège Sainte-Marie in Montreal.

Sainte-Victoire-de-Sorel QC Situated south of Sorel, this parish municipality was erected in 1845, abolished two years later, and re-established in 1855, two years after its post office opened. The religious parish was created in 1842 and named in honour of Queen Victoria, who ascended the throne in 1837.

Saint-Fabien QC Located southwest of Rimouski, this parish municipality was erected in 1855. The religious parish was established in 1828 and the post office opened in 1856. The name recalls St. Fabian, who was the Pope from 236 to 250 CE.

Saint-Félicien QC This town northwest of Lac Saint-Jean took on its present form in 1976 with the merger of the town (1946) and the municipality (1882) of Saint-Félicien. The post office was named in 1875 after St. Felicianus, a martyr who was beheaded at the beginning of the fourth century by Roman Emperor Maximian.

St. Felix PE On the south side of Tignish, this municipal community (1977) was established as a school district in 1846. The origin of the name is not recorded in the official records.

Saint-Félix-de-Valois QC This village north of Joliette was erected in 1926 from the township municipality of **Saint-Félix-de-Valois**, established in 1845, abolished two years later, and re-established in 1855. The religious parish was organized in 1840, taking its name from St. Felix of Valois (c.1127–1212), a founder of the Order of Trinitarians in 1197.

Saint-Flavien QC Located southwest of Quebec City, adjacent to Laurier-Station, this village was established in 1912 when it was detached from the parish municipality of **Saint-Flavien-de-Sainte-Croix**, created in 1855. The religious parish was set up in 1834 and named after Mgr. Pierre-Flavien Turgeon (1787–1867), 14th bishop of Quebec, 1850–67.

St. Francis, Cape NL North of St. John's, this peninsula was called *C de S francisco* by the Portuguese in the early 1500s. Explorer Gaspar Corte-Real (c.1450–1502) may have named it after St. Francis of Assisi.

St. Francis, Lake ON; **Lac Saint-François** QC This enlargement of the St. Lawrence River, below Cornwall, was named in 1656 in honour of St. Francis Xavier (1506–52), who was canonized in 1602. It was perhaps given more directly after François de Lauson, a seigneur near Montreal, or after Fr. François Le Mercier, the superior of the New France missions who took some Jesuit missionaries to Huronia in 1656.

St. Francis River NB; **Rivière Saint-François** QC Rising in **Lac Saint-François**, 20 km southeast of the city of Rivière-du-Loup, this river flows south through Lac Pohénégamook. From the lake's outlet it forms the international boundary, with Maine on the west and Quebec and New Brunswick on the east. About 1687 Mgr. Jean-Baptiste de Saint-Vallier (1653–1727) called it *Petite rivière St-François*.

Saint-François-de-Madawaska NB Southwest of Edmundston, this village (1966) is located on the Saint John River. Its first post office was *Webster's Creek*, opened in 1847, with Augustin Webster as the first postmaster. In 1874 it was called *Winding Ledges* after rapids in the Saint John River. It was given its present name in 1901 after **Saint-François Parish**, created in 1877 and named after the nearby river.

Saint-François-du-Lac QC This village in the regional county of Nicolet-Yamaska, near the mouth of the **Rivière Saint-François**, was separated in 1917 from the parish municipality of **Saint-François-du-Lac**. The latter was created in 1855, having been called *Saint-François-du-Lac-Saint-Pierre* ten years earlier. The religious parish dates from 1714, a few years after the Jesuits established a mission among the Abenaki on Lac Saint-Pierre. They had a mission called *Saint-François-de-Sales* at the mouth of the Chaudière, near Quebec City.

Saint-François, Rivière QC This major river in the south-eastern part of the province flows through Sherbrooke and Drummondville before emptying into Lac Saint-Pierre. Often called the St. Francis River in English, it was named in the mid-1600s after François de Lauson (d.1661), who mentioned *Rivière Saint-François des Prés* in granting the seigneury of Saint-François to Pierre Boucher de Grosbois (1622–1717) in 1662.

Saint-Fulgence QC This municipality on the north side of the Rivière de Saguenay, northeast of the city of Saguenay, was created in 1973 through the merger of the village (1947) and the parish municipality (1873) of *Saint-Fulgence*. A mission was established here in 1843 and named after St. Fulgentius (c.467–533), appointed bishop of Ruspe in North Africa, 507 CE.

Saint-Gabriel QC Located north of Joliette, this town was erected in 1967, having been the village of *Saint-Gabriel-de-Brandon* since 1892. The village was separated from the parish municipality of *Saint-Gabriel-de-Brandon*, which was erected in 1855. The religious parish was called Saint-Gabriel-du-Lac-Maskinongé in 1837, but was changed three years later to Saint-Gabriel-de-Brandon. The Angel Gabriel announced the births of John the Baptist and Jesus. The township of Brandon, noted on a map in 1795 and proclaimed in 1827, was named after the town of Brandon, in Suffolk, England, northeast of Cambridge.

Saint-Gabriel-de-Valcartier QC Adjacent to Canadian Forces Base Valcartier, northwest of Quebec City, this municipality was created in 1862, having been called a parish municipality in 1855. Ten years before it was called the municipality of *Valcartier*, contracted from 'vallée de la rivière Jacques-Cartier'. The seigneury of Saint-Gabriel was granted to Robert Giffard in 1647.

Saint-Gédéon QC A village midway between Lac-Mégantic and Saint-Georges, it was erected in 1950 when it was separated from the parish municipality of **Saint-Gédéon** (1912). The religious parish of Saint-Gédéon-de-Beauce was established in 1910, having been a mission since 1889. St. Gideon was a judge who delivered Israel from the desert hordes in the eleventh and twelfth centuries BCE.

St. George NB Near the mouth of the Magaguadavic River, this town (1904) was surveyed in 1786 and called *Magaguadavic*. Its post office was called St. George in 1829, taking its name from **Saint George Parish**, established in 1786.

St. George ON In 1999 this community became part of Brant County. It was named in 1835 after the first postmaster, George Stanton. The post office was called *St. George Brant* until it closed in 1970.

St. Georges MB This community on the Winnipeg River, northeast of Winnipeg, was named St. George in 1902 after the patron saint of England, and was subsequently given a perceived (but improperly spelled) name in French. It is a residential community upriver from the Manitoba Pulp and Paper Company's planned community of Pine Falls, created in 1925.

St. George's NL Located on the southeast side of **St. George's Bay**, this town (1965) was first called *South Side* and *Little Bay*. It was renamed St. George's in 1904, when Mgr. Neil McNeil moved the seat of the area's diocese to *South Side*. The bay was named as early as 1534, when Jacques Cartier sailed across it. **Cape St. George**, the southwesterly point of the Port au Port Peninsula, was possibly named at the same time.

Saint-Georges QC In 1990 the towns of Saint-Georges (1948) and *Saint-Georges-Ouest* (1943) were united to form the city of Saint-Georges, the most populous municipality in the Beauce valley. The religious parish was created in 1835 and named in honour of merchant Johann Georg Pfozer (1752–1848), who acquired the seigneury of Aubert-Gayon in 1808 and recruited 189 German settlers to immigrate to Saint-Georges.

Saint-Georges QC The name of this village in the Saint-Maurice valley, opposite Grand-Mère, was adopted in 1919, two years after the religious parish was founded. From 1927 to

1951 its post office was *Saint-Georges-de-Champlain*. St. George, the patron saint of England, was a fourth-century warrior and martyr, reputed to have rescued a maiden from a dragon in Palestine.

St. Georges Bay NS Northeast of Antigonish, this 35 km² bay was named in the 1770s by map-maker Joseph Frederic Wallet DesBarres (1722–1824) after the patron saint of England. It was renamed *George Bay* in 1902 by the Geographic Board, but the original name was restored in 1967.

Saint-Gérard QC This village midway between Sherbrooke and Thetford Mines was named in 1924 after the religious parish of **Saint-Gérard-Majella**, established in 1905 by Bishop Paul Larocque (1846–1926) of Sherbrooke, who assisted at the canonization of St. Gerard Majella (1726–55) in Rome the previous year. From 1886 to 1924 the village was called *Lac-Weedon*, while the post office was known as *Lake Weedon* from 1869 to 1911, when it was changed to Saint-Gérard. The township of Weedon, shown on a 1795 map and proclaimed in 1822, was named after Weedon, Buckinghamshire, England.

Saint-Gérard-Majella QC This parish municipality south of Joliette was adopted in 1982, having been created as *Saint-Gérard-Magella* in 1906. St. Gerard Majella (1726–55) was canonized in 1904 in Rome.

Saint-Germain-de-Grantham QC This village west of Drummondville was separated from the parish municipality of **Saint-Germain-de-Grantham** in 1946. The religious parish of Saint-Germain was created in 1858, with the **Saint-Germain-de-Grantham** post office opening in 1867, followed by the parish municipality in 1871. The parish was named after early settler Germain Sylvestre, whose name recalls the sixth-century Paris bishop. The township of **Grantham**, shown on a 1795 map, was proclaimed in 1800 and named after a town in Lincolnshire, England.

Saint-Grégoire-de-Greenlay QC North of Sherbrooke and across the Rivière Saint- François from Windsor, this village was erected in 1947. *Greenlay* was the post office from 1903 to 1973, named after Louisa Stevens Greenlay (d.1895). She was the widow of Lazenby Greenlay, a native of East Yorkshire, England, and the first European to settle in the township of Brompton. The mission of Saint-Grégoire was established in 1931 and named after Pope Gregory VII (1015–85).

Saint-Grégoire-le-Grand QC This parish municipality east of Saint-Jean-sur-Richelieu was erected in 1855. It was named after Grégoire Bourque, who donated land in 1805 for a church site, as well as in honour of Pope Gregory I (c.540–604), known as Gregory the Great, who was the pontiff from 590 to 604.

Saint-Guillaume QC Located directly west of Drummondville, this village was named in 1902, when it was separated from the parish municipality of **Saint-Guillaume**. The religious parish of Saint-Guillaume was erected in 1833, and named in honour of Charles William (the English for Guillaume) Grant, Baron de Longueuil (1782–1848), proprietor of the township of **Upton**, 1806–48. The post office was named *Saint-Grégoire-d'Upton* in 1862. The township of Upton was proclaimed in 1800 and possibly named after Upton near Grantham (the name of an adjoining township) in Lincolnshire, England.

Saint-Guillaume-de-Granada QC This municipality, just south of the city of Rouyn-Noranda, was created in 1978, having been established as a religious parish in 1935. It was named after St. William the Great (c.755–812), a prominent political and military figure during the time of Charlemagne. **Granada**, its post office since 1936, recalls the Granada Gold Mines, which started developing the site in 1927. The company's name also recalls the rich lead mines of the Spanish province of Granada.

Saint-Henri QC Situated south of the city of Lévis, the present municipality was established in 1976 through the annexation of the municipality of *Rivière-Boyer*. The municipality of Saint-Henri had been erected the previous year by merging the village (1913) and the parish municipality of *Saint-Henri* (1855). The name recalls the sixth bishop of Quebec, Mgr. Henri-Marie Dubreuil de Pontbriand (1708–60).

Saint-Hilaire NB Southwest of Edmundston, this village (1967) is located on the Saint John River. Its post office was called *Baker's Creek* in 1848, renamed *St. Hilaire* in 1873, closed in 1947, and reopened as Saint-Hilaire in 1968 for two years. **Saint-Hilaire Parish** was named in 1877 after the church consecrated in 1868 by Mgr. James Rogers (1826–1903), who named it after the former bishop of Tours in France. Albertine was the railway station and a second post office (1893–1968) in Saint-Hilaire.

Saint-Hippolyte QC This parish municipality north of Saint-Jérôme was created in 1951, having been called the township municipality of *Abercrombie-Est* in 1855. The post office opened as Saint-Hippolyte-de-Kilkenny in 1870. St. Hippolytus (c.165–235), was a Roman theologian and martyr. The township of Kilkenny was proclaimed in 1832, and named after the Irish city and county. The township of Abercrombie, established in 1842, recalls Gen. James Abercromby (1706–81), whose corps was defeated in 1758 by Montcalm's French forces at Fort Carillon, near present-day Ticonderoga, NY.

Saint-Honoré QC This municipality north of the city of Saguenay was created in 1973 through the amalgamation of the village (1953) and the parish municipality (1914) of *Saint-Honoré*. The religious parish was organized in 1911 and named in honour of Honoré Petit (1847–1922), member for Chicoutimi in the House of Commons, 1892–7.

Saint-Hubert QC This city east of Montreal was incorporated in 1958 and the following year annexed the city of *Laflèche*, which had been called the town of *Mackayville* in 1947. Saint-Hubert was erected as a parish municipality in 1860, taking its name from St. Hubert (d.727), a Belgian bishop and patron saint of hunters.

Saint-Hyacinthe QC Situated on the Rivière Yamaska, east of Montreal, this city attained its present area in 1976 through the amalgamation of the towns of Saint-Hyacinthe (1850) and *La Providence* (1965), and the villages of *Saint-Joseph* (1898) and *Douville* (1947). It owes its name to Jacques-Hyacinthe-Simon Delorme *dit* Lapointe (c.1718–78), who acquired the seigneury of Maska in 1753. The religious parish of Saint-Hyacinthe-le-Confesseur was created in 1757; its name recalls the founder of the Dominican Order in Poland in the thirteenth century.

Saint-Isidore NB This village (1991) northwest of Tracadie was established about 1867 as a free-grant settlement, and its post office opened in 1878. The name was perhaps given after the patron saint of farmers.

St. Isidore ON In 1998 this village became part of the Nation Municipality, united counties of Prescott and Russell. Southwest of Hawkesbury, its post office was first called *Kerry* in 1863. It was renamed St. Isidore in 1882, three years after a church dedicated to St. Isidore, a noted theologian of the early Catholic church, was erected. The post office name was altered to *St. Isidore de Prescott* in 1930. When the village was incorporated in 1989, the modifier was dropped.

Saint-Isidore QC Located south of Lévis, this municipality was established in 1962 and had been the parish muncipality of *Saint-Isidore-de-Lauzon* from 1855. The religious parish was erected in 1829 and named after St. Isidore (c.560–636), a distinguished theologian and primate of Spain, 610–36 CE.

Saint-Isidore QC Located south of Montreal and south of the Kahnawake Indian Reserve, this parish municipality was erected in 1842, taking its name from the religious parish set up in 1833 and named for St. Isidore (c.560–636), the patron saint of farmers. The post office, called *Saint-Isidore-de-Laprairie* in 1853, is now Saint-Isidore-de-La Prairie.

Saint-Jacques NB A village (1966) northwest of Edmundston, its post office was first called *Silverstream* in 1870. It was renamed St-Jacques in 1902 after **Saint-Jacques Parish**, created in 1877. The church was named after the French trans-

lation of the forename of Mgr. James Rogers (1826–1903), bishop of Chatham.

Saint-Jacques QC This village southeast of Joliette was detached from the parish municipality of *Saint-Jacques-de-l'Achigan* in 1912, which became Saint-Jacques in 1920. The religious parish of Saint-Jacques-de-l'Achigan was created in 1831 and Saint-Jacques post office opened four years later. The parish was named after Fr. Jacques Degeay (1717–74), long-time pastor of L'Assomption, who took a special interest in the plight of the Acadians. The Algonquin word *achigan*, as reflected in the nearby Rivière de l'Achigan, means 'bass'.

St. Jean Baptiste MB On the west bank of the Red River, south of Morris, this community was named in 1876. Also that year the parish church was built and named after the patron saint of French-speaking Canadians.

Saint-Jean-Baptiste QC This parish municipality southeast of Mont-Saint-Hilaire was named in 1855 after the religious parish of **Saint-Jean–Baptiste-de-Rouville**, founded in 1797. The seigneury of Rouville was granted in 1694 to Jean-Baptiste Hertel de Rouville (1668–1722).

Saint-Jean-Baptiste-de-Nicolet QC Located in the regional county of Nicolet-Yamaska, east of the town of Nicolet, this parish municipality was erected in 1845, abolished two years later, and re-established in 1855. The religious parish of Saint-Jean-Baptiste-de-Nicolet was created in 1831 and named after Jean-Baptiste Poulin de Courval (1657–1727), an important Trois-Rivières merchant who facilitated the setting up of the parish.

Saint-Jean-Chrysostome QC This town south of Quebec City and near the mouth of the Rivière Etchemin was established in 1965. The parish municipality was created in 1845, abolished two years later, and re-established in 1855. The religious parish was created in 1828. Although identified with St. John Chrysostom, the patriarch of Constantinople, 398–407 CE, it also honoured Sir John Caldwell (1775–1842), a prominent politician and industrialist, who managed the seigneury of Lauzon.

Saint-Jean-de-Dieu QC Located south of Trois-Pistoles and northeast of Rivière-de-Loup, this municipality was erected in 1947 and its post office opened in 1881, taking its name from the religious parish established in 1873. A patron of hospitals and the sick, St. John of God (1495–1550) founded his first hospital in 1537 in Granada, Spain.

Saint-Jean-de-Matha QC Situated northwest of Joliette, this municipality was established in 1993 and had been a parish municipality since 1855. The religious parish was set up three years earlier and named after St. John of Matha (c.1160–1213), a co-founder with St. Felix of Valois of the Order of Trinitarians in 1197.

Saint-Jean, Lac QC Covering an area of over 1000 km², this well-known lake at the head of the Rivière Saguenay was named in 1652 by Fr. Jean de Quen (c.1603–59) in honour of his patron saint. In his *Relation* of 1647 he had called it *Lac Piouagamik*, meaning 'shallow lake' in Montagnais. In 1603 Samuel de Champlain (1567–1635) had described it as *Mer du Nord*, and in 1544 navigator Jean Fonteneau *dit* Alfonse (1484–1544) referred to it as *Mer du Saguenay*.

Saint-Jean-Port-Joli QC Situated on the south shore of the St. Lawrence, midway between Montmagny and La Pocatière, this municipality was established in 1857, having been created a parish municipality two years earlier. The religious parish was created in 1721 in the seigneury of Port-Joly and was dedicated to St. John the Baptist. The seigneury at the mouth of **Rivière Port Joli** was granted to Noël Langlois-Traversy (1651–93) in 1677. The river's name describes the fine harbour at its mouth.

Saint-Jean-sur-Richelieu QC Located on the west bank of the Richelieu, the present name of this city was adopted in 1978, having been incorporated as the town of *Saint-Jean* in 1856. In 1665 Jean-Frédéric Phélypeaux (1701–81) erected a fort here, and called it Fort Saint-Jean. The religious parish was established 1667 and called Saint-Jean-l'Évangeliste, which became a parish municipality in 1855 and was united with the city in 1970. It was also officially known as *St. Johns*, but this name was dropped in 1962.

Saint-Jérôme QC This city northwest of Montreal was erected in 1881, having been incorporated as a village in 1856. The religious parish of Saint-Jérôme-de-la-Rivière-du-Nord was founded in 1832 and was named after St. Jerome (c.347–420), noted for his translations of scripture and commentaries.

Saint John NB This city was named and incorporated in 1785, making it the oldest incorporated city in the country. It was named after the river, identified as *Rivière saincte-Jean* by Pierre du Gua de Monts (c.1558–1628) on 24 June 1604, the day dedicated to St. John the Baptist. In 1783 the central part of the city was called *Parr Town* after John Parr (1725–91), governor of Nova Scotia, 1782–91. The west part was called *Carleton* after Sir Guy Carleton, Lord Dorchester (1724–1808), governor-in-chief of British North America, 1786–96. In 1889 the city annexed the city of *Portland* (1883), and in 1966 it annexed the city and the parish of *Lancaster* and part of the parish of Simonds. Although the 'saint' in the city's name is officially spelled in full, most people living in the province outside the city prefer to spell the river's name as St. John River. But the names authorities, having decreed that names

of common origin should be spelled the same, made **Saint John River** official.

St. John's NL **St. John's Harbour** is supposed to have been entered on 24 June 1497, perhaps by explorer John Cabot (c.1455–98), who sailed on behalf of the Bristol merchants that year. A Portuguese map of 1519–20 described it as *R de Sam johan*, and a letter of 1527 written by British seaman John Rut called it *Haven of St. John*. In the mid-1500s the French called the harbour *baie de Saincte Jehan*. By 1689 the *English Pilot* used the present form of the harbour's name. St. John's became the seat of the government of Newfoundland in 1832 and its first incorporated city in 1888.

Saint-Joseph NB The post office in this village (1966) on the Memramcook River, northwest of Sackville, was named in 1869. It is a common name in New Brunswick—**Saint-Joseph** and a **Saint-Joseph-de-Kent** are both in Kent County, and **Saint-Joseph-de-Madawaska** is north of Edmundston.

Saint-Joseph-de-Beauce QC Situated on the east bank of the Chaudière, northwest of Saint-Georges, this town was erected in 1965, having been incorporated as a village in 1889. The religious parish of *Saint-Joseph-de-la-Nouvelle-Beauce* was set up in 1835, became the parish municipality of *Saint-Joseph* in 1855, and was amended to Saint-Joseph-de-Beauce in 1957. In 1747 Joseph de Fleury de La Gorgendière (1676–1755) acquired a seigneury in the Beauce valley that was given his name. He had recruited the settlers in 1738 and built the first chapel the following year.

Saint-Joseph-de-la-Rive QC In the regional county of Charlevoix, east of Baie-Saint-Paul, this village was erected in 1931, and its name replaced *Les Éboulements-en-Bas* as its postal designation the next year. The religious parish was called Saint-Joseph in 1931 either after church architect Joseph Archer or after Saint-Joseph, Christ's father, who sailors prayed to in order to arrive safely ashore. *Rive* means 'shore' in French.

Saint-Joseph-de-la-Sorel QC This town on the west bank of the Richelieu opposite the city of Sorel was erected in 1942, 35 years after the village was detached from the parish municipality of **Saint-Joseph-de-la-Sorel**. The religious parish was established in 1875, taking its name from Mgr. Joseph La Rocque (Laroque) (1808–87), bishop of Saint-Hyacinthe. Pierre de Saurel (1628–82) was granted the seigneury of Saurel (Sorel) in 1672.

Saint-Joseph-du-Lac QC This parish municipality in the regional county of Deux-Montagnes is located west of Saint-Eustache and inland from Pointe-Calumet. The religious parish of *Saint-Joseph* was created in 1853 and became the parish municipality of Saint-Joseph-du-Lac three years later when the post office opened. In the late 1700s the name Saint-Joseph described a hillside (*côte*) in the area of the present municipality.

Saint-Jovite QC A popular tourist destination south of Mont Tremblant, this town was incorporated in 1986, having been erected as a village in 1917. The parish municipality of **Saint-Jovite**, established in 1960, had been set up as the united townships of *De Salaberry-et-Grandison* in 1881. Charles-Michel d'Irumberry de Salaberry (1778–1829) successfully blocked an American invasion in 1813. Sir Charles Grandison was a hero in a 1753 novel by British writer Samuel Richardson.

Saint-Lambert QC In 2002 this city in the regional county of Champlain became part of the city of Longueuil. Four years later it recovered its status as a city. Located on the east side of the St. Lawrence opposite Montreal, it was established in its present area in 1969 when it annexed the town of *Préville*, erected in 1948. Established as a Protestant parish in 1855 and a municipality in 1857, it became a village in 1892 and a town six years later, with its post office opening in 1904. In the seventeenth century the shoreline was known as **Côte-Saint-Lambert**, likely named after Raphaël-Lambert Closse (c.1618–62), commander of Ville-Marie (Montreal), 1655–7. The Protestant parish was perhaps named in honour of reformer Francis Lambert (1486–1530).

Saint-Lambert-de-Lauzon QC This parish municipality on the east bank of the Rivière Chaudière, south of Quebec City, was established in 1855, taking its name from the religious parish erected in 1851. The name recalls surveyor Pierre Lambert, who laid out plans for the seigneury of Lauzon (1828) and the city centre of Lévis (1849). Jean de Lauson (1584–1666) was granted the seigneury of Lauzon (Lauson, Loson) in 1636.

St. Laurent MB On the southeastern shore of Lake Manitoba, this community's mission was named in 1862 by Fr. Joseph Charles Camper (1842–1916) after the third-century martyr, St. Lawrence, who was put to death by Emperor Valerian. Its post office was named in 1883.

St. Lawrence NL Located on the southeastern end of the Burin Peninsula, this town (1949) was named after **Great St. Lawrence Harbour**. The harbour was perhaps named by Richard Clarke (1541–96) during Sir Humphrey Gilbert's 1583 voyage, because he found salmon as plentiful there as in the St. Lawrence River. Or it may have been called after a parish in Jersey in the late 1500s by fishermen from the Channel Islands.

St. Lawrence River ON, QC On 10 August 1535 Jacques Cartier (1491–1557) named a small bay, on the north shore of the **Gulf of St. Lawrence**, after St. Lawrence, whose feast day was on that date. Both Cartier and Samuel de Champlain (1567–1635) referred to the river and its mighty estuary as *Rivière du Canada*, but ultimately the bay's name was extended to both the gulf and the river. **St. Lawrence Islands National Park** (4 km²) was created in 1904, comprising 18 islands, several islets, and a small part of the mainland in the area of the Thousand Islands, east of Kingston, ON.

St. Lazare MB On the east bank of the Assiniboine River, opposite the mouth of the Qu'Appelle River, this village (1949) had been established as an Oblate mission in 1880. When the Oblates decided to abandon the mission in 1894, Archbishop Alexandre Taché (1823–94) ordered them to keep it open. Its resurrection prompted its naming after Lazarus, who was raised from the dead. The post office here opened in 1895.

Saint-Lazare QC This parish municipality in the regional county of Vaudreuil-Soulanges, just west of the towns of Vaudreuil and Dorion, was established in 1875, and its post office was called *Saint-Lazare-Vaudreuil* three years later. Located beside the parish of Sainte-Marthe, its religious parish was named after Lazarus, the brother of Martha and Mary, who was miraculously raised from the dead.

Saint-Léolin NB The first post office in this village (1978) west of Caraquet was called *Saint-Joseph* in 1888. It was renamed *Pépère* in 1903 and became Saint-Léolin the following year.

Saint-Léonard NB The first post office in this town (1920) on the Saint John River, northwest of Grand Falls was named *Grand River* in 1847 after a nearby river. It was called *St. Leonard Station* in 1883 and was changed to *St-Léonard* in 1925. The place was named after Leonard Reed Coombs, who settled here about 1840.

Saint-Léonard QC In 2002 this city became part of Montreal. Four years later it became a borough in Montreal. It was created in 1962, after being established as the town (1915) and the parish municipality (1886) of *Saint-Léonard-de-Port-Maurice*. The religious parish was erected in 1885, taking its name from **Côte-Saint-Léonard**, which described a hillside in 1706. That name was perhaps given after St. Leonard of Port Maurice (1676–1751), who was canonized in 1867, or after Sulpician missionary Léonard Chaigneau (1663–1711), who persuaded several pioneers to settle at Côte-Saint-Léonard.

Saint-Léonard-d'Aston QC This village in the regional county of Nicolet-Yamaska, north of Drummondville, was separated in 1912 from the municipality of **Saint-Léonard-d'Aston**. The religious parish was established in 1857 and named after the sixth-century founder of the Saint-Léonard-de-Noblat monastery near Limoges, France.

Saint-Liboire QC Situated east of Saint-Hyacinthe, this village was created in 1919 when it was detached from the parish municipality of **Saint-Liboire**, established in 1860, the same year the religious parish was set up and the post office opened. The name was given for Fr. Liboire-Henri Girouard (1798–1876), who participated actively in the founding of the parish.

Saint-Lin QC This municipality in the regional county of Montcalm northeast of Saint-Jérôme was established in 1855, having been erected as a parish municipality in 1845 but abolished two years later. Its post office opened in 1847. The name recalls St. Linus, successor to St. Peter as the pontiff of the church, 67–76 CE.

St. Louis PE Northwest of Alberton, this municipal community (1883) had been incorporated as a village in 1964. The school district was called St. Louis about 1890, having been previously called *Smith Road* and *Union Road*. The post office, opened as *Kildare Station* in 1882, was renamed **St. Louis** in 1896.

St. Louis SK On the south bank of the South Saskatchewan, south of Prince Albert, this village (1959) was founded as *Boucher Settlement* in 1882. Its post office was called *Boucher* in 1893 after Jean Baptiste Boucher, a native of St. Boniface, MB. It was changed to St. Louis in 1897, in honour of Louis Schmidt (1844–1935), the first settler who had arrived here about 1880.

Saint-Louis-de-France QC Located north of Trois-Rivières, this town was erected in 1993, taking its name from the religious parish, established in 1903. The name was perhaps given in honour of Mgr. Louis-François Laflèche (1818–98), bishop of Trois-Rivières from 1870. It was also possibly adapted from the name of the national French church in Rome, Saint-Louis-des-Français.

Saint-Louis-de-Kent NB The first post office in this village (1966) northwest of Richibucto was called *Palmerston* in 1859, taking its name from the parish. The parish was renamed Saint-Louis in 1866, and the postal designation was changed in 1879.

Saint-Louis-du-Ha! Ha! QC This parish municipality southeast of Rivière-du-Loup was named in 1874, with its mission having been established in 1860. The first part of its name was perhaps given after pioneer Louis Marquis, or after either Fr. Louis-Antoine Proulx (1810–96) of Rivière-du-Loup or Fr. Louis-Nicolas Bernier (1833–1914), pastor at Notre-Dame-du-Lac when the parish was named. The last part of the name has nothing to do with laughter, but is an old French word for an unexpected barrier or dead end. The dead end is 8 km east in Lac Témiscouata, where canoeists were forced to portage by land to Notre-Dame-de-Portage, 80 km to the west. *See also* Ha! Ha!, Baie des.

Saint-Louis, Lac QC The name of this place west of Montreal and at the point where the Ottawa River joins the St. Lawrence first appeared in the Jesuit *Relations* of 1656. Samuel de Champlain (1567–1635) had previously named the rapids at present Lachine *Le Grand Sault St. Louis* after a young man in the service of Pierre Du Gua de Monts (c.1558–1628) called Louis, who drowned in the rapids.

Saint-Luc QC Located north of Saint-Jean-sur-Richelieu, this town was erected in 1963, having been incorporated as the municipality of Saint-Luc in 1855. The name was chosen in 1799 by Mgr. Pierre Denaut (1743–1806), who wanted to assure that each of the authors of the four Gospels had a parish south of Montreal.

St. Lunaire-Griquet NL On the northeastern coast of the Northern Peninsula, this municipal community (1958) is comprised of two separate places. Both were developed fishing stations when Jacques Cartier visited them in 1534. **St. Lunaire** is known locally as St. Leonard's. **Griquet** may have been named after the French word *grecqué* ('sawtooth'), because the surrounding hills look like the teeth of a saw.

St. Malo MB Located midway between Emerson and Steinbach, this place's post office was named in 1890 after settler Louis Malo, who was living in nearby St. Pierre. He was teased about leaving Saint Malo from the French port where Jacques Cartier (1491–1557) sailed in 1534.

Saint-Marc-des-Carrières QC This village in the regional county of Portneuf, southwest of Quebec City, was incorporated in 1918. Its post office was named seven years before, after being called *Poiré* (1863) and *Châteauvert* (1901). The religious parish was set up in 1901, taking its name from St. Mark's Basilica in Rome and the local limestone quarries.

St. Margarets Bay NS West of Halifax, this bay was identified on a 1615 map as *B de s margarita* and on a 1640 map as *B S Marguerite*. It was anglicized in the mid-1700s. Joseph Frederic Wallet DesBarres (1722–1824) portrayed it on a chart of the 1770s as *Charlotte Bay alias Margarets*, but his effort to name the bay after Queen Charlotte was ignored. **Head of St. Margarets Bay** was given postal service in 1860.

Saint-Martin QC Located south of Saint-Georges and near the head of the Beauce valley, this parish municipality was founded in 1912, taking its name from the religious parish of **Saint-Martin-de-Tours**, also known as **Saint-Martin-de-la-Beauce**. St. Martin of Tours (c.316–97) is venerated by the valley's francophone residents. Its post office has been called *Bolduc* since 1882. It was named after Joseph Bolduc (1847–1924), member for Beauce in the House of Commons, 1876–84, and then a senator until 1922.

St. Martins NB Located on the Bay of Fundy east of Saint John, this village (1966) was named in 1844 after **Saint Martins Parish**. The parish was named in 1786, possibly after St. Martins in Maryland or after Martin Head, 33 km to the northeast. In the 1800s the place was commonly called *Quaco*, after Quaco Bay and nearby Quaco Head.

St. Mary's NL This municipal community (1966) on **St. Mary's Harbour**, on the east side of **St. Mary's Bay**, was named before 1836. In the mid-1550s the bay was identified on maps as *Sa Maria* and *B St. marie*. It was likely named after **Cape St. Mary's** at the southern side of Placentia Bay, shown on a map of 1536 as *Cabo de Sancta Maria*.

St. Marys ON This separated town (1864) in Perth County was named in 1844 for Elizabeth Mary Jones, wife of Thomas Mercer Jones (1795–1868), commissioner of the Canada Company, and daughter of Bishop John Strachan (1778–1867). She donated £10 for the new stone school then being constructed.

St. Marys Bay NS Separating the Nova Scotia mainland from Digby Neck, and Long and Brier Islands, it was called *Baye Ste Marie* by Pierre Du Gua de Monts (c.1558–1628) in 1604.

St. Marys River ON Joining Lake Superior to Lake Huron at Sault Ste. Marie, this river was named soon after 1641 by Jesuit missionaries, who dedicated their mission to the Virgin Mary and named the place and the falls on the St. Marys River *Sainte Marie du Saut*.

Saint-Mathias-de-Richelieu QC This parish municipality on the east side of the Richelieu, opposite Chambly, was given this name in 1988, having been the municipality of **Saint-Mathias** since 1855. The religious parish, called Saint-Olivier in 1772 after Mgr. Jean-Olivier Briand (1715–94), then bishop of Quebec, was renamed in 1828 by Mgr. Joseph-Octave Plessis (1763–1825) after the apostle who replaced Judas after the Ascension of Christ.

Saint-Mathieu-de-Beloeil QC Located between Beloeil and Sainte-Julie, this municipality was established in 1992, having been a parish municipality from 1855. The religious parish was founded in 1772 and named after Mathieu Camin LaTaille (1725–82), its first parish priest.

Saint-Maurice, Rivière QC Draining almost 43,000 km², this river rises in Réservoir Gouin and flows some 300 km south to the St. Lawrence at Trois-Rivières. It was identified on Guillaume Levasseur's 1601 map as *3 Rivieres*, a description of the river's mouth. During the early 1700s, it was renamed after Maurice Poulin de La Fontaine (c.1620–76), the seigneur and king's attorney of Trois-Rivières in the late 1600s. The parish

municipality of **Saint-Maurice**, northeast of Trois-Rivières, was founded in 1855, three years after its post office opened. *See also* Trois-Rivières.

St. Maur, Mount BC In the Purcell Mountains, east of Kootenay Lake, this mountain (2863 m) was named in 1953 after Lady Susan St. Maur, Duchess of Somerset (d.1936).

Saint-Michel QC This parish municipality in the regional county of Les Jardins-de-Napierville, south of Montreal, was erected in 1855, two years after the religious parish was organized, taking its name from the Archangel Michael. Its post office has been called Saint-Michel-de-Napierville since 1880.

Saint-Michel-des-Saints QC Located north of Joliette, and northeast of Mont Tremblant, this municipality was incorporated in 1979, when the parish municipality of *Saint-Michel-des-Saints* was amalgamated with the united townships of *Masson-et-Laviolette*. The mission was established in 1863, taking its name from the Spanish Trinitarian St. Michael of the Saints (1591–1625).

Saint-Narcisse QC This parish municipality east of Shawinigan was established in 1859, with the religious parish having been organized in 1851. It took its name from St. Narcissus (c.106–212), the third bishop of Jerusalem.

Saint-Nazaire QC Located in the regional county of Lac-Saint-Jean-Est, northeast of Alma, this municipality was named in 1988, having been the township municipality of *Taché* since 1906. The religious parish was organized in 1890, named in honour of Mgr. Louis-Nazaire Bégin (1840–1925), second bishop of Chicoutimi, 1888–91, archbishop of Quebec, 1898–1925, and a cardinal from 1914. The post office was called *Saint-Louis-Nazaire* from 1908 to 1927, when it was renamed Saint-Nazaire-de-Chicoutimi. The township of Taché was proclaimed in 1883, taking its name from Pascal (baptized Paschal-Jacques) Taché (1757–1830), proprietor of part of the seigneury of Kamouraska after 1790.

Saint-Nicéphore QC This municipality southeast of Drummondville was created in 1944. The religious parish was set up in 1916, and named after Fr. Nicéphore Lessard (1879–1951), who was then the vicar of Saint-Frédéric-de-Drummondville. St. Nicephorus (c.758–829) was a patriarch of Constantinople.

St. Nicholas PE The name of this municipal community (1991), west of Summerside, was first noted in 1845 in the *Journal of the House of Assembly*. Postal service was provided by Muddy Creek from 1870 to 1917.

Saint-Nicolas QC Situated on the south shore of the St. Lawrence southwest of Quebec City, this town was incorporated in 1962, having been a parish municipality since 1845. The creation of a religious parish dates from 1660, with the name Saint-Nicolas being assigned to it in 1694. The name was given in honour of the parish of Saint-Nicolas-de-la-Ferté in the diocese of Chartres, Normandie, France. St. Nicholas was a celebrated fourth-century bishop, possibly in Asia Minor, who became the patron saint of schoolchildren and sailors and the progenitor of Santa Claus.

Saint-Noël QC This village in the regional county of La Matapédia, southwest of Matane, was named in 1945, having been the village of *Saint-Moïse* since 1906. The religious parish of Saint-Noël was organized in 1951, taking its name from Fr. Noël Chabanel (1613–49), one of the Canadian martyrs who was canonized in 1930.

St. Norbert MB Founded in 1857, this neighbourhood on the south side of Winnipeg west of the Red River was named after Mgr. Joseph-Norbert Provencher (1787–1853), bishop of the North-West, 1847–53.

Saint-Ours QC Located on the east bank of the Richelieu south of Sorel, this community became a town in 1866, having been created a village in 1847, and a municipality two years earlier. The name derives from the seigneury of Saint-Ours, which Pierre de Saint-Ours (1640–1724) had acquired through marriage in 1668. He was a captain in the Carignan-Salières Regiment, who arrived to Canada in 1665 and encouraged the settlement of the seigneury.

Saint-Pacôme QC This municipality in the regional county of Kamouraska, east of La Pocatière, was established in its present territory in 1980 through the merger of the village (1926) and the parish municipality (1855) of Saint-Pacôme. It recalls the monastic life of an Egyptian abbot of the fourth century.

Saint-Pamphile QC Located on the Maine border, due east of Montmagny, this place became a village in 1889 and an incorporated town in 1963. The religious parish was founded about 1870 and was named after Pamphile-Gaspard Verrault (1832–1906), member for L'Islet in the Legislative Assembly, 1867–78. He had been named after St. Pamphilus (c.240–309), a doctor of the church, teacher, and translator.

Saint-Pascal QC This town in the regional county of Kamouraska, northeast of La Pocatière, was erected in 1966, having been made a village in 1939. It was established as the parish municipality of *Saint-Paschal-de-Kamouraska* in 1855, with its post office called *Saint-Paschal* from 1851 to 1916, when it was changed to Saint-Pascal. The religious parish was named in 1827 in honour of Paschal-Jacques Taché (1786–

1833), who became the seigneur of Kamouraska in 1830 on the death of his father.

Saint-Patrice-de-la-Rivière-du-Loup QC This parish municipality, incorporated in 1855, was founded as a mission at Rivière-du-Loup in 1683, and its first chapel was built in 1792. The name honours the patron saint of Ireland, St. Patrick (c.385–461).

Saint-Patrice-de-Sherrington QC This parish municipality in the regional county of Les Jardins-de-Napierville was erected in 1855. The religious parish was set up in 1848, and named after St. Patrick (c.385–461), who converted Ireland to Christianity in the fifth century. **Sherrington** was proclaimed as a township in 1809 and named after the village of Sherington, in Buckinghamshire, England, northwest of London.

St. Paul AB North of the North Saskatchewan River and northeast of Edmonton, this town (1936) was the site of the mission of *St. Paul des Cris* in 1866, but it was abandoned eight years later. In 1896 Fr. Albert Lacombe (1827–1916) and Fr. Adéodat Therien (1862–1936) reopened the mission. *St. Paul des Cris* post office was established in 1899 and its name was shortened in 1929.

Saint-Paul QC Located south of the city of Joliette, this municipality was given its name in 1954, having been called *La Conversion-de-Saint-Paul* in 1855 (four accounts of the conversion of Paul appear in the New Testament). That was the name of the religious parish set up in 1716, which was later called *Saint-Paul-de-Lavaltrie*. In 1851 its post office was called *Saint-Paul-d'Industrie*, *Industrie* having been an early name for Joliette.

Saint-Paul-d'Abbotsford QC Located in the regional county of Rouville northwest of Granby, this parish municipality was established in 1855. The St. Paul Episcopal Church was constructed here in 1822, and the Catholic parish of Saint-Paul-d'Abbotsford was set up in 1855. The post office was called *Yamaska Mountain* in 1825, and renamed *Abbotsford* four years later after Joseph Abbott (1790–1862) and his wife, Harriet Bradford, the parents of Canada's fourth prime minister, Sir Joseph J.C. Abbott (1821–93).

St. Paul Island NS This island is located north of Cape Breton Island and in Cabot Strait. In the 1500s the tip of the Cape Breton Island was called St. Paul. In the 1600s the tip became Cape North, with the island north of Cape North becoming *I S Pol* and *I S Paul*. In 1829 the humorist Thomas C. Haliburton called the island as 'a barren and rocky isle with precipitous shores of which have been the unseen grave of thousands'. In 1837 there were two lighthouses erected on the island.

St. Pauls NL At the south side of a bar separating **St. Pauls Inlet** from **St. Pauls Bay**, and surrounded by Gros Morne National Park, this municipal community (1968) was settled after 1870. The origin of its name is not recorded in official records.

St. Peters NS Located on a narrow isthmus of Cape Breton Island, separating the Atlantic Ocean from Bras d'Or Lake, this village (1940) was founded as a Portuguese fishing station in 1521 and called *San Pedro*. From 1650 to 1713 it was known as *Saint-Pierre*, where Gov. Nicolas Denys (c.1598–1688) had his headquarters until 1669. The French renamed it *Port Toulouze* in 1713 after Comte de Toulouse, a son of Louis XIV. Postal service was established at St. Peters in 1844. **St. Peters Canal** has connected the ocean to the lake since 1869.

St. Peters Bay PE Northwest of Souris and at the head of **St. Peters Bay**, this municipal community (1883) was incorporated as the village of *St. Peters* in 1953. The bay was named *havre St. Pierre* in 1721 by Louis Denys de la Ronde (1675–1741) after Comte de Saint-Pierre, equerry to the Duchesse d'Orléans at the French court.

Saint-Philippe QC Located east of Candiac and southeast of Montreal, this parish municipality was erected in 1855. It was set up as a mission in 1750 and became a religious parish in 1841. The parish was named after the Apostle Philip. Its post office, called Saint-Philippe in 1852, was renamed *Saint-Philippe-de-La Prairie* in 1876.

Saint-Pie QC This village southeast of Saint-Hyacinthe was incorporated in 1904 when it was detached from the parish municipality of **Saint-Pie**, which was created in 1855. The religious parish was set up in 1828 and was likely named after St. Pius V (1504–72), who introduced several reforms in church practices. When the parish was named, Pius VIII (1761–1830) was the Pope. The place was named *Village-Bistodeau* about 1817, after merchant Joseph Bistodeau (1768–1856). In 1837 its post office was called Saint-Pie-de-Bagot. The former county of Bagot was named after Sir Charles Bagot (1781–1843), governor of the Province of Canada, 1841–3.

Saint-Pierre QC In 2002 this town became a part of the city of Montreal. In 2006, it became a sector of Montreal. The town was adjacent to Montréal-Ouest and Lachine. It was incorporated in 1908, having been called the village of *Saint-Pierre-aux-Liens* in 1894, during the time when the religious parish was organized. The name recalls an event in the life of St. Peter, when he was miraculously released from the chains of King Herod.

Saint-Pierre QC A village on the west side of the regional county of Joliette, it was erected in 1922 as *Saint-Pierre-de-Joliette* and was modified to its present form seven years later.

It is usually referred to as Village Saint-Pierre to distinguish it from other places called Saint-Pierre.

St. Pierre-Jolys MB Located west of Steinbach, this village (1947) was named after the parish established in 1872. Fr. J.M. Jolys was the first parish priest. The post office was first called *Joly* in 1883, then *Laurier* in July 1897 and *St. Pierre* in October 1897, which was changed to St. Pierre-Jolys in 1922.

Saint-Pierre, Lac QC This enlargement of the St. Lawrence, extending for 35 km downriver from Sorel, was probably named by Samuel de Champlain (1567–1635) on 29 June 1603, the feast day of St. Peter, although he made no reference to it by name until six years later. It may have been named *Lac d'Angoulême* by Jacques Cartier (1491–1557) from 1535 to 1540, as the name appeared on several maps during the rest of that century. Angoulême, northeast of Bordeaux, is the chief town of the French department of Charente. It had been the ancient capital of the county of Angoulême.

Saint-Polycarpe QC This municipality in the regional county of Vaudreuil-Soulanges, northwest of Salaberry-de-Valleyfield, was created in 1988 through the merger of the village (1887) and the parish municipality of *Saint-Polycarpe*. The religious parish was founded in 1818 and named after St. Polycarp (c.69–167), bishop of Smyrna in Asia Minor and a martyr.

Saint-Prime QC This municipality west of Lac Saint-Jean and between Roberval and Saint-Félicien was established in its present area in 1968 through the amalgamation of the village (1923) and the municipality (1873) of Saint-Prime. The religious parish was founded in 1863 and the post office opened in 1872, named by Fr. Prime Girard (1829–76), its first pastor, after St. Primus, a third-century martyr.

Saint-Prosper QC This municipality in the regional county of Les Etchemins and east of Saint-Georges was established in 1929, having been called the township municipality of *Watford-Ouest* in 1886. Its post office was called *Saint-Prosper-de-Dorchester* in 1882, as it was then in the county of *Dorchester*. It was named after Fr. Prosper-Marcel Meunier, who built a chapel here in 1882. The township of Watford was shown on a map of 1795, but not proclaimed until 1864, taking its name from a town in Hertfordshire, England, northwest of London.

Saint-Quentin NB Midway between Grand Falls and Campbellton, the first post office in this village (1966) was called *Anderson Siding* in 1912. It was renamed in 1919 after an Allied victory in early October 1918 at St-Quentin, France, near the Belgian border.

Saint-Raphaël QC This village in the regional county of Bellechasse east of Quebec City was severed from the parish municipality (1855) of **Saint–Raphaël** in 1921. The religious parish was organized in 1851 and named after Fr. François-Raphaël Paquet (1762–1836), first pastor of the mission.

Saint-Raphaël-de-l'Île-Bizard QC In 2002 this parish municipality became a borough in the city of Montreal. Embracing the whole of Île Bizard, it was established in 1855, taking its name from the religious parish set up in 1839. Saint-Raphaël was proposed by Denis-Benjamin Viger (1774–1861) after a college in the old manor house of Vaudreuil where he studied. The island was named after Jacques Bizard (1642–92), its first seigneur in 1678.

Saint-Raymond QC In the regional county of Portneuf west of Quebec City, this town was created 1957, having been detached from the parish municipality of Saint-Raymond as a village in 1898. The municipality was created in 1845, abolished two years later, and re-established in 1855. Its religious parish was organized in 1842 as Saint-Raymond-Nonnat in honour of St. Raymond (1203–40), a Catalan cardinal noted for freeing Christian slaves.

Saint-Rédempteur QC This town (1981) near the mouth of the Rivière Chaudière, south of Quebec City, was established as a village in 1919. It took its name from the religious parish, created then as *Très-Saint-Rédempteur* ('most holy redeemer'), one of the loftiest titles given to Jesus Christ.

Saint-Rémi QC Located in the regional county of Les Jardins-de-Napierville south of Montreal, this town was established in 1949 and absorbed the village of Saint-Rémi (1859) in 1975. The municipality of Saint-Rémi was created in 1855, and the post office opened in 1831, taking its name from the religious parish of Saint-Rémi-de-Lasalle (La Salle) in 1828. The name was given in honour of Daniel de Rémy de Courcelle (Corcelles) (1626–98), governor of New France, 1665–72. He had a special devotion for St. Remi (c.437–533), who was bishop of Reims from 459.

Saint-Roch-de-l'Achigan QC Located midway between Saint-Jérôme and Joliette and on the Rivière de l'Achigan, this parish municipality acquired its current name in 1957, having been erected as the municipality of *Saint-Roch* in 1855. Ten years earlier it had been organized as the parish municipality of Saint-Roch-de-l'Achigan (abolished in 1847), taking its name from the religious parish, founded in 1787. The name was given after Paul-Roch de Saint-Ours de l'Eschaillon (1747–1814), seigneur of L'Assomption from 1781, who donated land for the church. In Algonquin, *achigan* means 'bass'.

Saint-Romuald QC This town (1982) on the south shore of the St. Lawrence, opposite Quebec City, was incorporated as the town of *Saint-Romuald-d'Etchemin* in 1963, and attained city status in 1965 when it annexed the municipality of Saint-

Télesphore. The religious parish was organized in 1853 and named after St. Romuald (952–1027), the founder of the monastic order of Camaldolese Benedictines in 1012.

Saint-Sauveur-des-Monts QC This village in the popular resort destination in the mountains north of Saint-Jérôme was severed from the parish municipality of Saint-Sauveur in 1926. The religious parish of Saint-Sauveur was officially erected in 1853 and two years later became the municipality of Saint-Sauveur ('holy saviour', a title of Jesus Christ).

St. Sepulchre, Mount BC In the Tower of London Range of the Muskwa Ranges of the Rocky Mountains, this mountain (2819 m) was named in 1960 by Capt. M.F.R. Jones after the regimental chapel of the Royal Fusiliers in London.

St. Shott's NL This most southerly place in Newfoundland took its name from the old French word *chinchette* ('small harbour with shoals'). On a 1544 map the adjacent cape was called *cap de chincete*. In 1775 Capt. James Cook (1728–79) and Michael Lane (d.1795) referred to the place as *St. Shot or Chink Hole*. In 1849 Joseph B. Jukes (1811–69) used its present form in his journal.

Saint-Siméon QC This village on the north shore of the St. Lawrence, opposite Rivière-du-Loup, was established in 1911 when it was detached from the parish municipality of Saint-Siméon. The municipality the religious parish were created in 1869, taking their names from St. Simeon, bishop of Jerusalem in the first century and a close relative of Jesus Christ.

St. Stephen NB This town (1871) on the St. Croix River was first called *Morris Town* in 1784 by Charles Morris Jr. (1731–1802) and Moses Gerrish (1820–93) after Charles Morris Sr. (1711–81), surveyor general of Nova Scotia, 1759–81. It was later called *Dover Hill*, resulting in Calais being built across the river in Maine. It was also known as *Scoodic* after part of the St. Croix. The post office was named in 1825 after **Saint Stephen Parish**. The parish was created in 1786 and named after surveyor Stephen Pendleton, with its name complementing the other local 'saint' names for parishes, including Saint Andrews and Saint George. The town was known as *St. Stephen-Milltown* for a few months in 1973 when the two towns were amalgamated, but Milltown was soon dropped as part of the official name.

St. Thomas ON This city (1881) in Elgin County was named in 1825 after Col. Thomas Talbot (1771–1853). 'Saint' was added to Thomas out of respect for Talbot, who organized the settlement of thousands of acres south of London during the first half of the nineteenth century.

Saint-Thomas QC This municipality on the east side of the city of Joliette attained its current status in 1993, having been established as a parish municipality in 1855. The religious parish was founded about 1840, and named in honour of Fr. Thomas-Léandre Brassard (1805–91), the pastor of an adjoining parish. In 1845 it was incorporated as the municipality of *Saint-Thomas-de-North-Jersey*, which described a concession road here. The place was also known as *Saint-Thomas-de-Voligny* after an officer who had donated land for the church, presbytery, and cemetery.

Saint-Thomas-d'Aquin QC This parish municipality northwest of Saint-Hyacinthe was created in 1893, two years after its post office opened. Served by a Dominican mission between 1889 and 1891, it was named after St. Thomas Aquinas (1225–74), a celebrated theologian of the thirteenth century.

Saint-Timothée QC Located east of Salaberry-de-Valleyfield, this municipality was created in 1990 through the amalgamation of the village (1919) and the parish municipality (1855) of Saint-Timothée (originally erected in 1845, and abolished two years later). The religious parish of Saint-Timothée-de-Beauharnois was organized in 1820 and named after St. Timothy, a disciple of St. Paul during the first century.

Saint-Tite QC This town northeast of Shawinigan was severed from the parish municipality of **Saint-Tite** in 1910. The latter was erected in 1863, taking its name from the religious parish established four years earlier, the same year the post office opened. St. Titus was a companion of St. Paul during the first century.

Saint-Tite-des-Caps QC Located in the regional county of La Côte-de-Beaupré, northeast of Sainte-Anne-de-Beaupré, this municipality was established in 1872. Serving as a mission since 1853, the religious parish was organized in 1876, ten years after the post office opened. At the time that it was named, Pope Pius IX had entered the name of St. Titus, St. Paul's disciple, into the Roman calendar.

Saint-Ubalde QC Located in the regional county of Portneuf, northeast of Trois-Rivières, this municipality was established in 1973 through the union of the village of Saint-Ubalde (1920) and the parish municipality of *Saint-Ubald*. The form of the name without the final 'e' was adopted for the post office (1874) in 1930. The religious parish of Saint-Ubald was organized in 1866, and named after Ubald (Ubalde) Gingras (1824–74), brother-in-law of Mgr. Charles-François Baillargeon, archbishop of Quebec, 1867–70, who was the first sacristan of Saint-Ubald.

Saint-Vallier QC Located in the regional county of Bellechasse, between Lévis and Montmagny, this municipality was established in 1993, having been incorporated as a village in 1958. The religious parish of Saint-Vallier was organized in

1714 and named after Jean-Baptiste de la Croix de Chevrières de Saint-Vallier (1653–1727), second bishop of Quebec.

Saint-Victor QC Located west of Saint-Georges, this village was created in 1955, when it was detached from the municipality of **Saint-Victor-de-Tring**. The municipality was established in 1870, taking its name from the religious parish organized in 1848 and itself named after St. Victor, the fourteenth Pope, 186–197 CE. Prior to that it was part of the township municipality of Tring. The post office was called Tring from 1852 to 1865, then *Saint-Victor-de-Tring* until 1937, when it became Saint-Victor-de-Beauce. The township of Tring was identified on a 1795 map and proclaimed in 1804.

St. Vincent ON In 2001 this township became part of the town of Georgian Highlands, Grey County. It was named in 1840 after John Jervis, Earl of St. Vincent (1735–1823), who achieved a great naval victory in 1797 over a larger Spanish fleet off Portugal's Cabo de São Vincente.

St. Vincent's-St. Stephen's-Peter's River NL On the east side of St. Mary's Bay, this improvement district was created in 1971. **St. Vincent's** was known as *Holyrood* as early as the 1830s and later as *Holyrood South*, but it was renamed in 1910 to avoid confusion with Holyrood on Conception Bay. **St. Stephens** was called *Middle Gut* until 1945, when it was renamed after Fr. Stephen O'Driscoll (c.1854–1936) of St. Mary's. The origin of the name **Peters River** is not recorded in the official records.

St. Walburg SK The post office in this town (1953) northeast of Lloydminster, was named in 1910 after Walburga Musch, a woman widely respected for her charitable work in the community. Her name was given in honour of St. Walburga, an eighth-century English missionary who served in Germany at the time of St. Boniface. The post office moved 4 km north in 1920 to the site of *Clansman*, with the Canadian Northern Railway arriving here the following year.

Saint-Wenceslas QC This village in the regional county of Nicolet-Yamaska was separated from the municipality of **Saint-Wenceslas** in 1922. The municipality was established in 1864, and named after the religious parish erected in 1857. The parish was named after St. Wenceslas (c.907–35), a duke of Bohemia and a pious man who was murdered by his brother.

St. Williams ON This community in the township of Delhi, Haldimand-Norfolk Region was first known as *Walsingham* after the original township. Later it became *Cope's Landing* after settler William Cope, and after that *Neal's Corners* after the Reverend George Neal, who owned a farm here. It was renamed in 1869 after William Gillaspey, an early settler much admired for his upright Christian principles.

Saint-Zacharie QC Near the Maine border and in the regional county of Les Etchemins, east of Saint-Georges, this municipality was created in 1990 by amalgamating the village (1961) and the parish municipality (1932) of Saint-Zacharie. The latter was formerly the township municipality of *Metgermette-Nord*, organized in 1886. The religious parish was set up in 1873, and named after Fr. Zacharie Lacasse (1845–1921), who had promoted the settlement of the area. The township, proclaimed in 1885, was named after a river and a lake whose names in Abenaki express the ideas of 'disaster' or 'misfortune'.

Saint-Zotique QC This village in the regional county of Vaudreuil-Soulanges and on the north shore of Lake St. Francis was created in 1913 and annexed the parish municipality (1855) of Saint-Zotique in 1967. Mgr. Ignace Bourget (1799–1885) obtained a relic of the martyr St. Zoticus during a European journey in 1849.

Salaberry-de-Valleyfield QC This city at the east end of Lake St. Francis was created in 1874. The first part of the name honours Lt. Col. Charles-Michel d'Irumberry de Salaberry (1778–1829), who defeated the superior American forces at Châteauguay in 1813. The second recalls The Valleyfield Paper Mills, established here by Thomas F. Miller in 1854, the same year the Valleyfield post office opened.

Salisbury NB Located west of Moncton, this village (1966) was named in 1846 after **Salisbury Parish**, created in 1787. The parish may have been called after *Salisbury Cove*, a name given about 1777 by map-maker Joseph Frederic Wallet DesBarres (1722–1824) to present Rocher Bay in the Bay of Fundy. The cove was perhaps named in honour of John Salisbury, who accompanied Gov. Edward Cornwallis (1713–76) in Nova Scotia.

Salluit QC Located near the southern coast of Hudson Strait, this northern village was given its present spelling in 1979, having been earlier spelled *Saglouc* (1962), *Notre-Dame-de-Sugluc* (1961), and *Sugluk* (1947). The meaning of the name is uncertain, although it possibly derives from the Inukititut word for 'sparse'.

Salmo BC This village (1946) south of Nelson was named in 1897 after the **Salmo River**, which rises east of Nelson and flows south to join the Pend d'Oreille River southeast of Trail. The river was called the *Salmon River* as early as 1859. *Salmo* is Latin for 'salmon'.

Salmon Arm BC This district municipality (1970) east of Kamloops and on the **Salmon Arm** of Shuswap Lake had been incorporated as a city in 1912. Its post office was named in 1890. It had its beginnings when a projected route for

an intercontinental railway was surveyed in 1871 by Walter Moberly (1832–1915).

Salmon Cove NL Northeast of Carbonear, this town (1974) was referred to by this name in the 1680s. *The English Pilot* of 1689 stated that 'a River in the said Cove runs up, in which are a store of salmon'.

Saltcoats SK Southeast of Yorktown, this town (1910) was first called *Stirling* in 1886 by the Manitoba and North Western Railway after the hometown of the Allan brothers of the Allan Steamship Lines. When that name was found to be in use elsewhere, it was renamed by Sir Hugh Allan (1810–82) and his brother James Allan (1808–80) after Saltcoats in North Ayrshire, Scotland, southwest of Glasgow. A post office opened here in 1888.

Saltspring Island BC The largest (180 km²) of the Gulf Islands, north of Victoria, it was named *Salt Spring Island* by the Hudson's Bay Company in the early 1800s. In 1859 Capt. George Richards (1820–96) substituted *Admiral Island* after RAdm. Robert L. Baynes (d.1869), commander of the Pacific station, 1857–60, but it did not supplant the earlier name. In 1910 the Geographic Board of Canada adopted the current name, fusing the words 'salt' and 'spring', a practice the board preferred for multiple-word specifics of geographical names.

Salvage NL The name of this fishing community on the outer end of Eastport Peninsula may refer to a marine incident or tragedy. It was visited by migratory fishermen from England as early as 1676.

Sampson, Mount YT This mountain (3353 m) in the St. Elias Mountains, was named in 1970 by the Alpine Club of Canada after Herbert E. Sampson (1871–1962), president of the club, 1930–2.

Sandringham NL On the Eastport Peninsula and east of Glovertown, this municipal community (1968) was founded in 1939 for the resettlement of many nearby communities. It was likely named after the summer residence of the Royal family in northwestern Norfolk, England.

Sandwich South ON In 1999 this township became part of the town of Tecumseh, Essex County. It was named in 1792 for the English borough of Sandwich in Kent. The town of *Sandwich* was formed in 1858, but Windsor annexed it in 1935. The municipal townships of *Sandwich East*, Sandwich South, and *Sandwich West* were created in 1854, but only Sandwich South was able to keep its separate municipality until 1999.

Sanford MB Situated on the La Salle River southwest of Winnipeg, this community's post office was called *Mandan* in 1900, but was renamed in 1906 after Senator W.E. Sanford

(1838–99) who drowned in Lake Windemere, district of Muskoka.

Sango Bay NL On the inner side of Davis Inlet, this area was chosen in 1996 as a relocation site for the Innu community of Davis Inlet on an adjoining island. In the language of the Innu the name means 'sandy plateau'. It is pronounced 'shango'.

Sangudo AB The post office in this village (1937) northwest of Edmonton was named in 1912, created as an acronym from the names of settlers and other local names: Sutton or Sides, Albers, Nanton (where Mrs Albers formerly lived), Gaskell, United, Deep Creek (the first proposal), and Orangeville (the school district name).

Sanikiluaq NU Located at the north end of Flaherty Island, one of the Belcher Islands, this hamlet (1976) was established in 1970 and named after the first Inuk to hunt seals here. Before Sanikiluaq was founded, the Inuit of the Belcher Islands had previously lived at two separate places called *North Camp* and *South Camp*.

Sarawak ON In 2001 this township became part of the township of Georgian Bluffs, Grey County. It was named in 1855 after the state of Sarawak (now part of Malaysia) by Viscount Bury (1832–94), superintendent of Indian affairs in Canada. In 1841 the rajah of Sarawak ceded the state to English soldier and explorer Sir James Brooke (1803–68), a relative of the viscount.

Sarnia ON This township was named in 1829 by Sir John Colborne (1778–1863) after the Roman name for Guernsey in the Channel Islands, where Colborne had been lieutenant-governor, 1821–8. In 1836 a growing community on the St. Clair River was named *Port Sarnia*. In 1860 'Port' was dropped from the postal name to conform with the name of the town, incorporated three years earlier. The township became the town of *Clearwater* in 1988. It was annexed by the city (1914) of Sarnia on 1 January 1991, which existed as the city of *Sarnia-Clearwater* for one year before reverting to Sarnia.

Saskatchewan The district of Saskatchewan was established in the North-West Territories in 1882. The limits of the present province were decided in 1905. The name was taken from a Cree term for *kisiskaciwanisipi*. In the present years Cree speakers refer to the province as *kisiskaciwan* or *saskaciwanihk*.

Saskatchewan, Mount YT Located in the Centennial Range of the St. Elias Mountains, this mountain (3472 m) was named in 1967 after the province.

Saskatchewan River MB, SK Rising as the **North Saskatchewan River** in the Rocky Mountains, and as the **South Saskatchewan River** east of Lethbridge, AB,

it officially becomes Saskatchewan River 45 km east of Prince Albert, SK. It derives from the Cree *Kisiskatchewan* ('swift current'). Geographer David Thompson (1770–1857) established the present spelling 1813, extending the river to the mouth of the Nelson River.

Saskatoon SK John Neilson Lake founded a temperance colony on the South Saskatchewan River in 1882, and planned to call it Minnetonka (Siouan for 'big water'), possibly after a western suburb of Minneapolis, MN. When a branch of reddish purple berries was brought to him, he was told the Cree called the berries *misaskwatomina* ('fruit of the much wood'). It sounded like Saskatoon to him and he pronounced it the name of the new colony. It became a town in 1903 and a city in 1906.

Saturna Island BC The most southeasterly of the Gulf Islands, this island was named in 1791 by José Maria Narvaez (1768–1840) after his Spanish ship *Saturnina*. As early as 1862 the name was rendered to Saturna.

Saugeen ON In 1999 this township became part of the town of Saugeen Shores, Bruce County. It was named in 1850 after the **Saugeen River**. *Saugeen* is an Ojibwa word meaning 'river mouth'. Admiralty surveyor Henry W. Bayfield (1795–1885) spelled the river's name *Sauggink* in 1822, but by the late 1840s it was spelled Saugeen. The river rises north of Dundalk in Grey County, and has numerous tributaries, including the **South Saugeen**, the **North Saugeen**, the **Rocky Saugeen**, the **Beatty Saugeen**, and the Teeswater Rivers. Based on the knowledge of Chief Newash at Owen Sound, surveyor Charles Rankin (1797–1886) encountered the *Saugin* in 1837 at the site of Mount Forest. John McDonald resurveyed the Rankin route to Owen Sound in 1841 and changed the name of the Saugeen at Mount Forest to the Maitland, deeming it to be that river's headwaters. In 1844 a survey party led by Sir Casimir Gzowski (1813–98) explored downriver from Mount Forest to Hanover, finding that it was clearly the Saugeen.

Saugstad, Mount BC Located in the Coast Mountains, southeast of Bella Coola, this mountain (2905 m) was named in 1948 by surveyor Maj. F.V. Longstaff after the Reverend Saugstad. He and Thorwald Jacobsen brought Norwegian settlers to the area about 1892.

Sault-au-Mouton QC The post office in this village (1947) located on the north shore of the St. Lawrence across from Rimouski opened in 1906. The name, which occurred as *Saut a mouton* on Jean Guérard's 1631 map, describes the foaming froth that looks like the white wool of sheep ('*mouton*') at the foot of the falls near the mouth of the **Rivière du Sault au Mouton**.

Sault Ste. Marie ON The site of the city (1912) was called *Pawating* ('turbulent waters') by the Ojibwa. Étienne Brûlé (1592–1633) named it *Saut de Gaston* in the early 1600s after Louis XIII's brother. In 1641 Jesuit missionaries dedicated their mission to the Virgin Mary and called the place *Sainte Marie du Sault*. The North West Company opened a trading post here in 1783 and retained the French name for the post. When the post office was established in 1846 the historic French name was maintained. In the seventeenth and eighteenth centuries, the French word '*sault*' was used as an equivalent for 'falls' and 'rapids', but was gradually replaced in everyday language and place names by '*chute*'.

Savona BC On the south shore of Kamloops Lake, west of Kamloops, this place was originally founded on the north shore by François Saveneux, a native of Corsica who became known as Francis Savona (d.1862). In 1859 he established a ferry across the Thompson River, where the river flows out of the lake. When the Canadian Pacific Railway passed along the south shore in 1882, its station here was called *Port Van Horne* after Sir William Van Horne (1843–1915), but it was soon superseded by Savona. In 1881 the post office was called *Savona's Ferry*, and was changed to Savona in 1896.

Sawyerville QC Located east of Sherbrooke, this village was established in 1892 and its post office had opened in 1853. Josias Sawyer (d.1837) crossed the border from Vermont about 1792 to inspect the site and subsequently built sawmills on the Rivière Eaton. He donated land for a school in 1822.

Sayabec QC Situated west of Lac Matapédia and southwest of Matane, this municipality was erected in 1982 by merging the parish municipality of *Sainte-Marie-de-Sayabec* (1894) and the village of Sayabec (1951), incorporated as *Saindon* in 1917. The latter was the railway station name, given after Fr. Joseph-Cléophas Saindon (1866–1941), who was appointed the pastor here in 1896. The post office was named Sayabec in 1900 after the **Rivière Sayabec**, which means 'obstructed river' in Mi'kmaq.

Sayward BC Located on the northeastern coast of Vancouver Island, northwest of Campbell River, this village (1968) was named in 1911 after lumberman William Parsons Sayward (1818–1905), who moved to Victoria from California in 1858. Its post office had been called *Port Kusam* in 1899.

Scarborough ON In 1998 this city became part of the city of Toronto. Its area was first called *Glasgow Township* in 1791. Two years later, after Elizabeth (Gwillim) Simcoe (1762–1850) noted how the impressive bluffs reminded her of the magnificent cliffs of Scarborough in North Yorkshire in England, Lt.-Gov. John Graves Simcoe (1752–1806) renamed it. The township became a borough in 1967 and a city in 1983.

Scatarie Island NS The name of this island off the east coast of Cape Breton derives from the Basque *Escatari* ('steep coast' or 'line of cliffs'). The island had postal service from 1884 to 1957.

Sceptre SK Northwest of Swift Current and south of the South Saskatchewan River, this village (1913) was named in 1913 by the Canadian Pacific Railway, possibly after the staff carried by a prelate (the village to the west was named Prelate). A post office also opened here in 1913.

Schefferville QC This town (1955) north of Labrador City was a centre of iron ore mining from 1953 to 1982, when its population tumbled from 5000 to a little over 100. Although the town was officially dissolved in 1986, its status was restored four years later as market centre for nearby Montagnais and Naskapi communities. It was named after Mgr. Lionel Scheffer (1903–66), first apostolic vicar of Labrador, 1946–66.

Schomberg ON In York Region, west of Newmarket, this community was first called *Brownsville*, after Thomas Brown had built a mill here in 1836. Because of possible confusion with similar names, the post office department declined to accept the name Brownsville in 1861. Thomas R. Ferguson, a member of the Legislative Assembly and a staunch Orangeman, proposed Schomberg in 1862 after the Duke of Schomberg (1615–90), commander-in-chief of the British forces at the Battle of the Boyne in Ireland, where he was killed.

Schreiber ON When the Canadian Pacific Railway arrived at this site on the north shore of Lake Superior in 1885, its station was named after Collingwood Schreiber (1831–1918), who became the CPR's chief engineer in 1880. He was appointed the deputy minister of the federal department of railways and canals in 1892 and was knighted in 1916.

Schumacher ON Located east of the city centre in Timmins, this community was named in 1912 after Fred Schumacher, who was a wealthy manufacturer of patent medicines in Ohio. He had come to the Porcupine area that year, invested wisely in property, and made a fortune when his lots were sold for gold exploration.

Scotch Village NS Located near the mouth of the Kennetcook River and east of Windsor, this place was named after pioneer settler John Smith who came from Scotland. A post office opened here in 1858.

Scotland ON This community in Brant County, southwest of Brantford, was first known as *Malcolm's Mills* after Loyalist Finlay Malcolm, whose ancestors were Scottish. It was renamed in 1852 by Janet Graham when the post office opened.

Scots Bay NS North of Wolfville and east of Cape Split, this place is located on the shore of **Scots Bay**. The bay was first called *Scotch Bay* after some Scottish immigrants were driven ashore and stayed here for the winter before proceeding to their destination. When its post office opened in 1855, it was called *Scotts Bay*, and *Scotts Bay Road* post office opened to the south in 1877.

Scotsburn NS Southwest of Pictou, this place's post office was called *Rogers Hill* in 1845 after John Roger, who settled here in the late 1700s. It was renamed in 1874 after the birthplace of Hugh Ross in Ross and Cromarty, north of Inverness, Scotland.

Scotstown QC A town (1892) located between Sherbrooke and Lac-Mégantic, its post office opened in 1873. It was named after John Scott, director of the Glasgow Canadian Land and Trust Company, established in Scotland in 1873. He acquired land in the area of Scotstown and built a sawmill to serve the settlers, but he was dismissed in 1875. The company ceased operations 21 years later.

Scott ON Part of the municipal township of Uxbridge, Durham Region since 1974, Scott Township was named in 1820 after Thomas Scott (1746–1824), chief justice of Upper Canada, 1806–16.

Scott QC This village (1978) in the regional county of La Nouvelle-Beauce, north of Sainte-Marie, replaced the parish municipality of *Saint-Maxime* (1895). Its station was called *Scott-Jonction*, established when the Lévis and Kennebec Railway was built in the Beauce valley between 1868 and 1875. It was named after Charles Armstrong Scott (d.1893), a contractor who built the first section of tracks.

Scott SK This town (1910) southwest of Battleford was named in 1908 after Frank Scott, the treasurer of the Grand Trunk Pacific Railway. Postal service also arrived here that year. With a population of 118 in 1991, it tied Fleming as the province's smallest town.

Scott, Cape BC This most northwesterly point of Vancouver Island may have been named in 1786 by trader James Strange after David Scott, a member of a Bombay (now Mumbai), India syndicate who financially supported Strange's expedition to trade on the northwestern coast of North America.

Scott, Mount AB, BC On the continental divide and northeast of Athabasca Pass, this mountain (3300 m) was named in 1913 by climbers Arnold L. Mumm and Edward Howard after British naval officer and explorer Robert Falcon Scott (1868–1912). Scott reached the South Pole in 1912, but died returning to his base camp.

Scugog ON Named as a municipal township in 1851, this community was united with the village of Port Perry and the municipal townships of Cartwright and Reach in 1974 to form an enlarged municipal township of Scugog in Durham Region. Its name probably derives from the Mississauga *sigaog* ('waves leap over a canoe'). This may refer to the flooding of the **Scugog River** valley in 1834, when William Purdy built a dam at Lindsay, which created both **Lake Scugog** and **Scugog Island**.

Seabright NS On the east side of St. Margarets Bay and west of Halifax, this place's post office was called *Hubley Settlement* in 1896. It was renamed six years later after the Seabright Hotel.

Seaforth ON In 2001 this town (1874) became part of municipality of Huron East, Huron County. Located 27 km southeast of Goderich, it was named in 1855 by Barrie lawyer and developer James Patton, possibly after the Seaforth Highlanders, a Scottish regiment raised by Francis H. Mackenzie, Baron Seaforth and Mackenzie (1754–1815). The title may have been taken from Loch Seaforth, on the east side of Lewis in the Outer Hebrides.

Seal Cove NB At the south end of Grand Manan Island, this urban community was an incorporated village from 1966 to 1995, when it became part of the village of Grand Manan. Its post office was named in 1875. Both the hooded seal and the harp seal have played significant roles as sources of food and clothing in the economic development of the Atlantic coast.

Seal Cove NL This municipal community (1972) on the northwest side of Fortune Bay, and west of Harbour Breton, was settled about 1837. The town (1958) of **Seal Cove**, on the eastern shore of White Bay and west of Baie Verte, was occupied about 1840. A third place called **Seal Cove**, in the town of Conception Bay South and on the southeastern shore of Conception Bay, was settled in the early 1800s.

Searletown PE North of Borden-Carleton, this place was settled by James Searle in 1767. It was called *Searle Town* as early as 1843. Searle's grandson, James Searle Mann, a native of Philadelphia, moved here in 1854 and arranged to open the Searletown post office the next year.

Seattle, Mount YT In the St. Elias Mountains, this mountain (3069 m) was named in 1890 by explorer and geologist Israel C. Russell (1852–1906) after Seattle, WA.

Sebringville ON In 1998 this place became part of Perth East, Perth County. Northwest of Stratford, it was named in 1852 after miller and first postmaster P.A. Sebring. John Sebring, a native of Vermont, built a sawmill here in 1834 and a store a few years later.

Sechelt BC This district municipality (1986) on the **Sechelt Peninsula**, northwest of Vancouver, was named after the community of **Sechelt**, whose post office opened in 1896. The community, on a narrow isthmus separating **Sechelt Inlet** from the Strait of Georgia, was known as *Se-shalt* by the Seechelt tribe of the Coast Salish. The tribe's name may derive from *chatelech* ('climb over'), in reference to a tree that had to be climbed over to get to the beach. The Indian government district of **Sechelt** was created in 1988.

Sedgewick AB The post office in this town (1966) southeast of Camrose was named in 1907 after Robert Sedgewick (1848–1906), deputy minister of justice, 1888–93, and justice of the Supreme Court of Canada from 1893. A native of Scotland, Sedgewick practised law in Halifax from 1873 to 1888.

Sedley SK Located southeast of Regina, the post office at this village (1907) was named in 1904 by Dr. R.J. Blanchard after his brother Sedley Blanchard, a Winnipeg lawyer who died of typhoid in 1886.

Seeleys Bay ON In 2001 this community became part of the township of Leeds and the Thousand Islands, united counties of Leeds and Grenville. Located northeast of Kingston, it was settled in 1825 by trader Justus Seeley (d.1828), and later by his son John. It was first called *Coleman's Corners*, and William Coleman became the first postmaster of *Seely's Bay* in 1851. The name was changed to Seeleys Bay in 1950.

Seldom-Little Seldom NL On the south side of Fogo Island, the two names of this town (1972) may relate to the fishing schooners that were seldom willing to negotiate the treacherous Stag Harbour Run to the west, resulting in the only access to its harbour being from the east. Seldom was formerly called *Seldom Come By*.

Selkirk MB Located on the west bank of the Red River, north of Winnipeg, the post office in this town (1882) was named in 1876 after Thomas Douglas, 5th Earl of Selkirk (1771–1820), who established the Red River Colony in 1812.

Selkirk, Mount BC Located in the Rocky Mountains, northeast of Invermere, this mountain (2938 m) was named about 1886 by geologist George M. Dawson (1849–1901) after Thomas Douglas, 5th Earl of Selkirk (1771–1820), who founded the Red River Colony in present-day Manitoba in 1811.

Selkirk Mountains BC Extending from the Washington state border on the south to the Big Bend of the Columbia River on the north, and between the Columbia River on the west, and Kootenay Lake and Duncan and Beaver Rivers on the east, these mountains were first called *Nelson's Mountains* about 1811 by geographer David Thompson (1770–1857) after Adm.

Lord Horatio Nelson (1758–1805). In 1821 the Hudson's Bay Company named them after Thomas Douglas, 5th Earl of Selkirk (1771–1820).

Selwyn Lake NT, SK Located along the sixtieth parallel, this lake (593 km^2) was named before 1910 after Alfred Richard Cecil Selwyn (1824–1902), director of the Geological Survey of Canada, 1869–95.

Selwyn, Mount BC In the Selkirk Mountains, south of Rogers Pass, this mountain (3360 m) was named in 1901 after Alfred Richard Cecil Selwyn (1824–1902), director of the Geological Survey of Canada, 1869–95.

Selwyn Mountains YT These mountains, a division of the Mackenzie Mountains, extend for 650 km along the west side of the territorial boundary with the Northwest Territories. They were named in 1901 by geologist Joseph Keele (1862–1923) after Alfred Richard Cecil Selwyn (1824–1902), director of the Geological Survey of Canada, 1869–95.

Semans SK North of Regina, this village (1908) was named in 1908 by the Grand Trunk Pacific Railway after the birth name of the wife of one of its officials. The post office was also opened the same year.

Senneterre QC Located northeast of Val-d'Or, this town (1956) was incorporated as a village in 1948, the same year the post office was opened. The township of Senneterre was surveyed between 1911 and 1913 and proclaimed in 1916. It is possible that the town and the township were named after Henri de Senneterre, an officer of the Languedoc Regiment in Montcalm's army, who fought at the Battle of Sainte-Foy in 1760.

Senneville QC In 2002 this village (1895) became a part of the city of Montreal. In 2006 it restored its status as a village. Located north of Sainte-Anne-de-Bellevue, it was named after Jacques Le Ber de Saint-Paul de Senneville (1633–1706), who shared the rear fief of Boisbriand after 1679 and built a fort, store, and mill. He was born at Senneville-sur-Fécamp, Seine-Maritime, France. *See also* Val-Senneville.

Sept-Îles QC The metropolis of the north shore of the St. Lawrence, this city is situated on a natural harbour with seven islands sited in front of its entrance. It was incorporated in 1951, and since 1981 has been the principal urban centre of the regional county of Sept-Rivières. The post office was called *Seven Islands* in 1886 and was renamed Sept-Îles in 1931. In 1535 Jacques Cartier referred to the bay by the name of *Sept Ysles*.

Sept-Rivières QC This regional county on the north shore of the Gulf of St. Lawrence was named in 1981 after its seven rivers: Trinité, Penticôte, aux Rochers, Sainte-Marguerite, Moisie, Pigou, and Manitou.

Serra Peaks BC Located in the Coast Mountains, northeast of Mount Waddington, these peaks (3642 m) were named in 1933 by climber Walter Alfred (Don) Munday (1890–1950), because the peaks had a sharp serrated edge along their crest.

Seul, Lac ON A large lake between Lake Nipigon and Lake of the Woods, it was called in Ojibwa *Opasiccocan* ('white pine at the narrows') but which French traders interpreted as *Lac Seulment*, possibly because of disappointment in not finding that it led to the Western Sea. It was then shortened to *Lac Seul*, the form adopted by English fur trader Edward Umfreville (c.1755–89) in his 1784 diary.

Severn ON This municipal township in Simcoe County was created in 1994 by merging the village of Coldwater, the municipal townships of Orillia and Matchedash, and parts of the municipal townships of Medonte and Tay. It was named after the **Severn River**, which drains Lake Couchiching into Georgian Bay and forms the western part of the Trent-Severn Waterway. The river was possibly named by Admiralty surveyor Henry W. Bayfield (1795–1885) in the 1820s.

Severn River ON This main river of northwestern Ontario flows northeast for 575 km to Hudson Bay. In 1631 it was named the *New Severn River* by explorer Thomas James (c.1593–1635) after England's River Severn.

Sexsmith AB The original post office in this town (1979) 20 km north of Grande Prairie was located 5 km farther south, and named after David Sexsmith, a trapper who arrived here in 1898, moved to Edmonton in 1901, and returned in 1912. The townsite, first known as *Benville*, after John Bernard 'Benny' Foster, was surveyed in 1915. It was named Sexsmith the next year by the Edmonton, Dunvegan and British Columbia Railway, and the post office was transferred here.

Seymour ON In 2001 this township became a part of the Trent Hills, Northumberland County. The township was named in 1798 after Lady Elizabeth Seymour (later Baroness Percy), the widow of the Duke of Northumberland.

Seymour, Mount BC Located in the district municipality of North Vancouver, this mountain (1455 m) was named in 1951 after Frederick Seymour (1820–69), governor of the colony of British Columbia, 1864–9. **Seymour River** flows south, on the west side of the mountain, into Burrard Inlet. **Seymour Inlet**, on the mainland coast, opposite the north end of Vancouver Island, was also named after him. **Seymour Narrows** in Discovery Passage, northwest of Campbell River, was named in 1846 by Cdr. George T. Gordon (d.1887) after

RAdm. Sir George Francis Seymour (1787–1870), commander of the Pacific station, 1844–8.

Shackleton, Mount BC In the Clemenceau Icefield and west of Howse Pass, this mountain (3330 m) was named in 1923 by surveyor Arthur O. Wheeler (1860–1945) after Sir Ernest Shackleton (1874–1922), who led British Antarctic expeditions in 1907–9 and 1914–6.

Shakespeare ON In 1998 this community became a part of the township of Perth East, Perth County. Located 11 km east of Stratford, this community was settled by David Bell in 1832 and its post office was named *Bell's Corners* in 1848. Four years later, it was named after William Shakespeare (1564–1616) by either first postmaster Alexander Mitchell or Stratford notary John James Edmonstoune Linton.

Shallow Lake ON In 1998 this village (1911) became part of the township of Keppel, Grey County. Northwest of Owen Sound, it was first known as *Stoney Creek*. In 1891 Shallow Pond was proposed after a nearby shallow water body, where marl was being excavated for the production of cement. Because Shallow Pond sounded too dull, it was named Shallow Lake.

Shanadithit Brook NL This brook, which flows into the northwest side of Red Indian Lake, was named in 1956 after Shawnadithit, a Beothuk woman who was captured in 1823, but died nine years later in St. John's. She may have been the last survivor of her people.

Shand, Mount BC Located in the Coast Mountains, northeast of Mount Waddington, this mountain (3095 m) was named in 1947 by mountaineer Fred W. Beckey after climber William Shand Jr. (1818–46), who had been killed in a car accident. Shand had climbed in the St. Elias Mountains in the early 1940s.

Shannon QC The post office in this municipality (1947) northwest of Quebec City served the area from 1905 to 1968. It was settled early by Irish immigrants, suggesting it might have been named after Ireland's River Shannon, but it would appear the name has its roots in a family name, because local church registers of the 1830s noted the deaths of Richard and Simon Shannon.

Shannonville ON This community in Hastings County, east of Belleville, was named in 1833, after the *Shannon River* (now the Salmon River). It had been named after Ireland's River Shannon, from where several Tyendinaga Township families originated.

Sharbot Lake ON In 1998 this community became part of the township of North Frontenac, Frontenac County. Located

69 km north of Kingston, it was settled in 1827 by Francis Sharbot (1822–97), a Mohawk, and its post office was named in 1877. The lake, divided into two equal sections, was first called *Crooked Lake* and was identified as *Chabot Lake* in 1856.

Sharon ON This community is located in York Region, north of Newmarket. The name was given by Children of Peace community founder David Willson (1778–1866) in 1841, in reference to the rose of Sharon in the Bible's Song of Solomon. It was earlier called *Hope* and *Davidtown*.

Shaughnessy, Mount BC In Glacier National Park, north of Rogers Pass, this mountain (2807 m) was named in 1900 after Thomas George Shaughnessy, 1st Baron Shaughnessy (1853–1923), president of the Canadian Pacific Railway, 1899–1918.

Shaunavon SK This town (1914) southwest of Swift Current was named by the Canadian Pacific Railway in 1913 on the suggestion of Thomas George Shaughnessy, 1st Baron Shaughnessy, president of the CPR, 1899–1918. He proposed the name after 'an area in the old country', although he was a native of Milwaukee, WI. Its post office opened the same year.

Shawinigan QC This city (1958) in the Saint-Maurice valley, north of Trois-Rivières, was incorporated as the village of *Shawinigan Falls* in 1901 and became a town the following year. The name had many spellings until the formation of the Shawinigan Water and Power Company in 1898. Its origin points to the idea of 'portage', perhaps 'portage over a pointed crest' in Abenaki. The town of **Shawinigan-Sud** (1961) on the east side of the river became a village in 1953. Before that it was called *Almaville*, derived from *Alma Mater*, refering to the Virgin Mary and meaning 'generous mother'.

Shawnigan Lake BC Located at the north end of **Shawnigan Lake**, southeast of Duncan, this community's post office was named in 1894. The lake may have been named in the 1850s by blending the surnames 'Shaw' and 'Finnegan'.

Shawville QC This village in the regional county of Pontiac was named in 1874 after James Shaw (1818–77), who had settled in the township of Clarendon in 1843. In 1856 he became the postmaster of *Clarendon Centre*, which had been established in 1852. The first name proposed for the village was Daggville, after the pioneer Dagg family, but Shaw's gift of almost a hectare of land to the village ensured the perpetuation of his name.

Shedden ON In 1998 this community became a part of the municipality of West Elgin, Elgin County. Southwest of St. Thomas, its Canada Southern Railway station was named in 1872 after railway contractor and Toronto and Nipissing Railway president John Shedden (1825–73). He was accidentally killed the following year at Cannington in Victoria County.

Its post office was named *Corseley* in 1875, but was renamed Shedden in 1883. There is also a municipal township in Algoma District, west of Espanola, named after John Shedden.

Shediac NB The post office in this town (1903) northeast of Moncton opened about 1829. It took its name from the **Shediac River**, which flows east into **Shediac Bay**, north of the town. The river's name derives from the Mi'kmaq *Esedeiik* ('running far back'), possibly referring to the indentation formed by the bay as part of Northumberland Strait, or to the portage route to the Petitcodiac River. Map-maker Pierre Jumeau called it *R. Chedaik* in 1685. In 1832 Surveyor General Thomas Baillie (1796–1863) wrote 'Shediac river by the Acadians Gidaic'.

Sheet Harbour NS This place is on the Eastern Shore and at the head of Sheet Harbour. The harbour was first known as *Port North*, likely given in the 1770s by map-maker Joseph Frederic Wallet DesBarres (1722–1824) after Lord Frederick North (1732–92), prime minister of Great Britain, 1770–82. The present name came into use about 1818, taking its name from a prominent white cliff at the harbour's entrance, which appeared to look like a white sheet spread out to dry. The place was first called *Campbelltown*, likely after Lord William Campbell (c.1730–78), governor of Nova Scotia, 1766–73. It was also known as *Manchester*, before Sheet Harbour post office opened in 1852.

Sheffield ON In 1998 this township became a part of the township of Stone Mills, Lennox and Addington County. It was named in 1798 after John Baker Holroyd, Lord Sheffield (1734–1821), who served in many British government ministries.

Sheho SK Located northwest of Yorkton, this village (1905) was named in 1892, after **Sheho Lake**, 3 km to the north. The lake was named by pioneer settler George Hill after the Nakota word '*sio*' ('prairie chicken').

Shelburne NS Located on the South Shore and at the head of **Shelburne Harbour**, this town (1907) was called *Port Razoir* during the French regime, because the V-shaped harbour had the appearance of a partly opened razor. It was called *Port Roseway* by New Englanders; Roseway River remains the name for the river rising 45 km to the north in Roseway Lake. In 1783 Gov. John Parr (1725–91) named it after William Petty Fitzmaurice, 1st Marquess of Lansdowne and Earl of Shelburne, 1737–1805, prime minister of Great Britain, 1782–3.

Shelburne ON This town (1976) in Dufferin County was first called *Jelly's Corners*. William Jelly wanted to call it Tandragee, after a town in County Armagh, Ireland, where his ancestors had lived. However, at a session of the Legislative

Assembly in Quebec City in 1865, it was named after Henry Petty-Fitzmaurice, 3rd Marquess of Lansdowne and Earl of Shelburne (1780–1863), who had served in several government ministries.

Shellbrook SK The post office in this town (1948) just south of a stream called **Shell Brook**, west of Prince Albert, was named *Shell Brook* in 1894 and was changed to Shellbrook in 1948.

Shell Lake SK Located west of Prince Albert, the post office at the village (1940) and the rural municipality were both named in 1913 after a lake to the southwest. The Canadian Northern Railway arrived here in 1927.

Sherbrooke NS Located on St. Marys River, this community was the site of Fort Sainte-Marie that was built in the 1650s by the French and also provided the name for the river. Postal service was established in 1829, when the office was named after Sir John Coape Sherbrooke (1764–1830), lieutenant-governor of Nova Scotia, 1811–6, and governor-in-chief of British North America, 1816–8.

Sherbrooke PE The school district in this municipal community (1983) northeast of Summerside was named in 1905, possibly after Sherbrooke, NS. Its post office was called *Grangemount* from 1909 to 1912.

Sherbrooke QC This city acquired its present status in the mid-1800s, having been incorporated as a village in 1823. Its post office opened in 1819, taking its name from Sir John Coape Sherbrooke (1764–1830), governor-in-chief of British North America, 1816–8. His father, William Coape (1790–1863), annexed Sherbrooke to his name on his marriage to Sarah Sherbrooke. The Abenaki knew the place as *Shacewanteku* ('place where vapour rises'). The French first called it *Grandes-Fourches*, in reference to the forks of the Saint-François and the Magog.

Sherridon MB Located northeast of Flin Flon and on the east side of Kississing Lake, this place was first called *Kississing*, a Cree word meaning 'cold'. Carl Sherritt had staked copper and zinc near the lake in 1925. John Gordon, an engineer, put an option on the property that year. In 1929 the Sherritt Gordon Mining Company opened the zinc and copper mines here. Its population rose to 2000, but declined after 1951 when the operations were moved to Lynn Lake, and less than 120 people are now living here.

Sherwood Park AB Urban service area in Strathcona County, east of Edmonton, it was named in 1957 after the Sherwood Forest in Nottinghamshire, England. The name was likely chosen to elicit a sense of woodsy surroundings in a rural landscape.

Sheshatsheits NL On the west side of the mouth of the Naskaupi River and northeast of Happy Valley-Goose Bay, this place was founded by the Innu (Naskapi and Montagnais) in the 1950s, and separated from North West River in 1979. The name means 'narrow place', a description of the narrows between Grand Lake, a widening of the river, and Lake Melville.

Shilo MB The rural municipality of Shilo is the site of a Canadian Forces Base, which had been opened in 1934. The Canadian Northern Railway station arrived here in 1905. It was named after a Jewish pedlar who had come from the biblical Shiloh, now in the state of Jordan.

Shippagan NB The post office in this town (1958) on **Baie de Shippegan**, east of Caraquet, was called *Shippegan* in 1850–2, 1862–1900, and 1955–83, and *Shippigan* in 1852–62, and 1900–55. The Acadians' preference for the town's current spelling was acknowledged in 1980, but most of the associated names, such as Baie de Shippegan, **Shippegan Gully**, and **Shippegan Channel** retain the older spelling. The bay's name derives from the Mi'kmaq *Sepaguncheech* ('duck passage') and was called *Cibaguen* on a 1656 map. Shippegan Gully connects the bay to the Gulf of St. Lawrence.

Shipshaw QC This municipality (1930) became part of the city of Saguenay. Its present area was established in 1977, when it absorbed the village of *Saint-Jean-Vianney* (1952), which had been wiped out by a landslide six years earlier. Shipshaw post office opened in 1904. The name in Montagnais means 'blocked river', probably in reference to an earlier landslide into the Rivière Shipshaw. The religious parish of Saint-Jean-Vianney was named in 1928 after St. Jean Baptiste Marie Vianney (1786–1859), the famed Curé d'Ars, who was said to have many curative powers and was canonized in 1925.

Shipton QC This township municipality in the regional county of Asbestos and surrounding the towns of Asbestos and Danville, was erected in 1845. It took its name from the **Shipton Township**, shown on a 1795 map and proclaimed in 1801. The name possibly came from a place in Buckinghamshire, England, northwest of London.

Shoal Lake MB Located northwest of Minnedosa, this village (1909) was named after the rural municipality of Shoal Lake (1881), which was named after a shallow lake to the south. There was a North West Mounted Police station at the south end of the lake as early as 1876. When the Manitoba and North Western Railway was built in 1909, the village was moved to the north end of the lake.

Shubenacadie NS Situated on the **Shubenacadie River** and between Halifax and Truro, this place's post office was named in 1836. The river's name derives from the Mi'kmaq *Segubunakade* ('place where ground nuts grow').

Shulaps Peak BC In the Shulaps Range of the Coast Mountains, northwest of Lillooet, this mountain (2772 m) was named in 1913 after the Lillooet word for 'ram' of the bighorn sheep.

Shuniah ON In 1873 the Ontario government united several townships to create the municipal township of Shuniah at the head of Lake Superior. Although it only comprises the townships of McGregor and McTavish now, it extends for 50 km northeast of the city of Thunder Bay. The name may derive from the Ojibwa *joniiag* ('silver'), possibly in reference to Silver Islet at the south end of the Sibley Peninsula.

Shuswap Lake BC This lake with its four long arms, north of Salmon Arm, was named after the Shuswap, an Interior Salish tribe. The meaning of the tribal name is obscure. The **Shuswap River** (185 km) rises just south of Revelstoke, but takes a convoluted route south, then north, before entering the lake at Sicamous.

Sibbald, Mount YT In the St. Elias Mountains, this mountain (3063 m) was named in 1970 by the Alpine Club of Canada after Andrew S. Sibbald (1888–1945), president of the club, 1934–8.

Sibley Peninsula ON This prominent peninsula shelters Thunder Bay from the open waters of Lake Superior. It comprises the township of **Sibley**, named in 1873 after Maj. Alexander Sibley (d.1878) of Detroit, who bought the silver mine at Silver Islet in 1869. *Sibley Provincial Park* became Sleeping Giant Provincial Park in 1992. As seen from the city of Thunder Bay, the peninsula portrays the profile of The Sleeping Giant, with The Head, The Adam's Apple, and The Chest as distinctive features.

Sicamous BC The post office in this district municipality (1989) northeast of Salmon Arm was named in 1887. In Shuswap the name means 'narrow' or 'squeezed in the middle', in reference to the delta of Eagle River having created Mara Lake, rather than leaving it as an arm of Shuswap Lake.

Sidney BC This town (1967) near the north end of the Saanich Peninsula, 29 km north of Victoria, was named in 1892 after **Sidney Island**, offshore in Haro Strait. The island, called *Sallas Island* about 1850 by the Hudson's Bay Company, was renamed in 1859 by Capt. George Richards (1820–96), likely in 1891 for Frederick W. Sidney, who was also a surveyor with the British Navy. The origin of the name *Sallas Island* is not known.

Sidney MB Midway between Portage la Prairie and Brandon, this place was named in 1881 by the Marquess of Lorne (1845–1914) after Sidney Austin, a correspondent for the London *Graphic* who followed the progress of the Canadian Pacific Railway to the West. For Sidney there are three other names revealed: one for Sidney Smith, a friend of Prince of Wales (1841–1910) on a trip in 1860 in Canada and the United States; the second for Sydney Hall in England; and the third for Sydney, Australia, as the next CPR station is named Melbourne.

Sidney ON In 1998 this township became part of the city of Quinte West, Hastings County. It was named in 1787 after Thomas Townshend, 1st Viscount Sydney (1732–1800), British home secretary, 1782–9, lord of the Admiralty, 1790–3, and lord of the treasury, 1793–1800.

Sifton MB North of Dauphin, this place was founded in 1898 by the Canadian Northern Railway and named after William M. Sifton, a railway contractor and a resident of Minitonas. He was an uncle of Sir Clifford Sifton (1861–1929), who aggressively promoted the settlement of Western Canada. Sir Clifford objected to the name, so the townsite was registered as *Lemberg*, the capital of Galicia (now L'viv in Ukraine). However, Sifton was not supplanted.

Signal Hill NL This distinctive landmark (153 m) at the entrance of St. John's Harbour had a signal cannon placed on it in the late 1500s. Subsequently, flags were flown to warn ships about hazards and bad weather. Guglielmo Marconi (1874–1937) received the first transatlantic radio signals from Cornwall, England on this hill in 1901.

Sikanni Chief River BC Rising in the Muskwa Ranges of the Rocky Mountains, this river flows northeast into the Fort Nelson River, east of the town of Fort Nelson. It was named after Makenunatane, a Beaver prophet who was also known as the Sikanni Chief.

Sillery QC In 2002 this town became part of Quebec City. In 2006 Sillery became a sector of Quebec City. It recalls the name of Noël Brulart de Sillery (1577–1640), a French nobleman whose name was given to the first mission here in 1637, because he financially supported its establishment on the St. Lawrence shore.

Silverton BC This village (1930) on the eastern shore of Slocan Lake was laid out in 1893 and named *Four Mile City* after a nearby creek. Its post office was named in 1894 after Silverton, CO. The latter is in San Juan County, in the southwestern part of the state.

Silverwood NB Located in the west end of the city of Fredericton and on the south bank of the Saint John River, this community was established as a residential area in 1961. Incorporated as the village of *Springhill* in 1968, it was changed to Silverwood in 1969 and annexed by Fredericton in 1973. Springhill post office was named in 1859 after a residence established by Chief Justice George D. Ludlow (1734–1808) in 1786, which he named after the residence of New York Gov. Cadwallader Colden (1769–1834).

Simcoe ON The county was named in 1798 for John Graves Simcoe (1752–1806), Upper Canada's first lieutenant-governor. Simcoe was appointed in September 1791 and arrived at the capital Newark (now Niagara-on-the-Lake) the following spring. He left the province in 1796 and resigned two years later. **Lake Simcoe** was named in 1793 after the lieutenant-governor's father Capt. John Simcoe, who died in 1759 on his way up the St. Lawrence River to take part in the capture of Quebec City.

Simcoe ON The site of this town (1878) in Haldimand-Norfolk Region was visited in 1795 by Lt.-Gov. John Graves Simcoe (1752–1806). Some merchants at the north end of the place wanted to call its post office Wellington in 1829 after the victor at the Battle of Waterloo. However, the proposal by Aaron Culver, who was granted land here, to honour Simcoe was adopted.

Similkameen River BC Rising in Manning Provincial Park, near the Washington state border, this river (84 km in British Columbia) flows north through Princeton, and then passes southeast through Keremeos. It crosses the border west of Osoyoos and joins the Okanogan River in the state of Washington, just south of the border. It was named after a designation of several Okanagan bands, which came from the extinct language of the Nicola-Similkameen.

Simpson SK South of Watrous, this village (1911) was named in 1910 by the Canadian Pacific Railway after Sir George Simpson (1792–1860), governor of the Hudson's Bay Company, 1821–60. The post office opened in 1911.

Simpson Pass AB This pass (2107 m) west of Banff, was named in 1859 by Sir James Hector (1834–1907) for Sir George Simpson (1792–1860), the long-serving governor of the Hudson's Bay Company. **Simpson River** drains the area of the pass into the Vermilion River in British Columbia and is adjacent to **Simpson Ridge**.

Sintaluta SK On the main line of the Canadian Pacific Railway, east of Regina, this town (1907) was first called *Carson* in 1885. Its post office was renamed Sintaluta three years later, after the Lakota word for 'at the end of the fox's tail'. The area was then known as *Red Fox Valley*.

Sioux Lookout ON This town (1912) in Kenora District, northeast of Dryden, was first called *Knowlton* when the Grand Trunk Pacific Railway arrived here in 1909. It was renamed *Graham* in 1911 after George P. Graham, minister of railways and canals. Two years later it was changed to Sioux Lookout in memory of a defeat of the Sioux by the Ojibwa in the late 1700s or early 1800s.

Sioux Narrows ON This municipal township in Kenora District, southeast of Kenora, is centered on a narrow passage separating Regina Bay from Whitefish Bay. Named in 1938, it commemorates a victory by the Ojibwa over the Sioux.

Sir Alexander, Mount BC In the Rocky Mountains, east of Prince George, this mountain (3270 m) was named in 1914 by alpinist Samuel Prescott Fay (1778–1856) after Sir Alexander Mackenzie (1764–1820), who had completed the first crossing of North America, north of Mexico, in 1793.

Sir Donald, Mount BC In the **Sir Donald Range** of the Selkirk Mountains, south of Rogers Pass, this peak (3297 m) was originally called *Syndicate Mountain* after the financiers who ensured that the Canadian Pacific Railway's bonds were covered during the building of the CPR through the mountains. By Order-in-Council in 1887, it was renamed after Sir Donald Alexander Smith (1820–1914), who was elevated to the peerage as 1st Baron Strathcona and Mount Royal in 1897.

Sir Douglas, Mount AB, BC Located at the southeastern end of Banff National Park, this mountain (3406 m) was named in 1916 by the Alberta–British Columbia Boundary Commission after Gen. Sir Douglas Haig (1861–1928), commander of the British Expeditionary force in France, 1915–9.

Sir Francis Drake, Mount BC On the east side of Bute Inlet, northeast of Campbell River, this mountain (2695 m) was named in 1939 by surveyor R.P. Bishop after Sir Francis Drake (1540–95), who had navigated up the west coast of North America in 1579, possibly as far as Vancouver Island.

Sir John Abbott, Mount BC Located in the Premier Range, west of Valemount, this mountain (3411 m) was named in 1927 after Sir John Joseph Caldwell Abbott (1821–93), prime minister of Canada, 1891–2.

Sir John Thompson, Mount BC This mountain (3250 m) in the Premier Range, west of Valemount, was named in 1927 after Sir John Sparrow Thompson (1844–94), prime minister of Canada, 1892–4.

Sir Mackenzie Bowell, Mount BC West of Valemount in the Premier Range, this mountain (3280 m) was named in 1927 after Sir Mackenzie Bowell (1823–1917), prime minister of Canada, 1894–6.

Sir Robert, Mount BC In the Coast Mountains, northeast of Terrace, this mountain (2407 m) was named in 1916 after Sir Robert Laird Borden (1854–1937), prime minister of Canada, 1911–20.

Sir Sandford, Mount BC In the **Sir Sandford Range** of the Selkirk Mountains and south of Rogers Pass, this mountain (3530 m) was named in 1902 by surveyor Arthur O. Wheeler (1860–1945) after Sir Sandford Fleming (1827–1915), engineer-in-chief of the Canadian Pacific Railway. He supervised the surveys for an intercontinental rail line through both the Kicking Horse and Yellowhead passes.

Sir Wilfrid Laurier, Mount BC The highest peak in the Premier Range, west of Valemount, this mountain (3520 m) was named in 1927 after Sir Wilfrid Laurier (1841–1919), prime minister of Canada, 1896–1911.

Siva Mountain BC Located in the Pantheon Range of the Coast Mountains, northeast of Mount Waddington, this mountain (2981 m) was named in 1964 after the third diety of the Hindu triad. Powers of reproduction and dissolution are attributed to him.

Skeena River BC Rising in the Skeena Mountains, north of Hazelton, this river (579 km) was identified as *Ayton's River* in 1788 by Capt. Charles Duncan. It was also known as *Simpson's River* after Capt. Aemilius Simpson, and *Babine River* after a tributary of the Skeena. The river's name derives from the Tsimshian for 'water out of the clouds'.

Skidegate BC Located on Skidegate Indian Reserve and on the southeastern coast of Graham Island (one of the Queen Charlotte Islands), this place was noted as early as 1805 by Samuel Patterson as *Skittagates*. In the 1790s a principal chief of the Haida was called Skiteiget, whose name meant 'red paint stone'. The bay to the southwest is called **Skidegate Inlet** and **Skidegate Channel** separates Graham Island from Moresby Island.

Skihist Mountain BC Located in the Coast Mountains, south of Lillooet, this mountain (2972 m) was named about 1895 after the Thompson Salish word *sk-haest* ('split rock').

Skinners Pond PE Northwest of Alberton, this place's post office opened in 1856. It took its name from the sea-level pond, which was perhaps named after a Capt. Skinner who was shipwrecked here or derived from *Étang des Peaux* ('skin pond').

Skookumchuck BC Located in the Kootenay River valley, north of Cranbrook, this place's post office opened in 1915. In Chinook Jargon the name means 'swift water'.

Skookum Jim, Mount YT This mountain, in the Ogilvie Mountains, north of Dawson, was named in 1973 on the seventy-fifth anniversary of the discovery of gold on Bonanza Creek by Skookum Jim Mason (d.1916), George Carmack (1860–1922), and Tagish (later Dawson) Charlie (d.1908).

Slade, Mount BC In the Purcell Mountains, west of Invermere, this mountain (3218 m) was named *Slade Mountain* in 1914 after a prospector associated with the Parradice mine. Three years earlier climber E.W. Harnden had called it *Boulder Peak*. It was renamed Mount Slade in 1960.

Slaggard, Mount YT In the St. Elias Mountains, this mountain (4663 m) was named in 1958 after Joseph R. Slaggard, a prospector who discovered copper on the nearby White River.

Slave Lake AB At the point where Lesser Slave River drains from the eastern end of Lesser Slave Lake, the post office at this town (1965) was called *Sawridge* until 1922, when it was changed to Slave Lake.

Slave River AB, NT This river (415 km), part of the Mackenzie River system, drains Lake Athabasca north to Great Slave Lake. It was named after the Slavey, a Dene tribe, which has several communities around the lake and in the valleys of the Slave, Mackenzie, Hay, and Liard Rivers.

Slocan BC At the south end of **Slocan Lake**, this village (1958) was an incorporated city from 1901 to 1958. Its post office opened as *Slocan City* in 1896, but it was changed that year to Slocan. The Canadian Pacific Railway continued to use Slocan City after 1958. **South Slocan** is at the mouth of the **Slocan River**, where it flows into the Kootenay River, northeast of Castlegar. The community of **Slocan Park** is 10 km upriver from the mouth. In Okanagan *slocan* means 'pierce in the head', in reference to the practice of spearing salmon.

Smallwood Reservoir NL Described as the third largest man-made lake (6527 km²) in the world, it was created in 1965 after the Churchill River was dammed at Churchill Falls, and several other rivers were diked. It was named after Joseph Roberts Smallwood (1900–91), the first premier of the province of Newfoundland, 1949–72, whose vision led to the construction of the huge Churchill Falls hydroelectric power project in Labrador.

Smeaton SK Northwest of Nipawin, this village (1944) was named in 1930 by the Canadian Pacific Railway after Senator R. Smeaton White (1865–1936). A post office opened here in 1931. Earlier it was called *Dorrit*, from *Little Dorrit* the novel of Charles Dickens.

Smith ON In 1998 this township became part of the township of Smith-Ennismore, which became part of township of Smith-Ennismore-Lakefield, Peterborough County, in 2001. Smith Township was named in 1821, likely for Samuel Smith (1756–1826), a member of the Executive Council from 1813 and administrator of Upper Canada during brief periods in 1817 and 1820. It is less likely that it was named for Sir David William Smith (Smyth) (1764–1837), surveyor general of Upper Canada until 1802, who returned to England in 1805.

Smithers BC This town (1967) on the Bulkley River, northeast of Prince Rupert was founded in 1913 by the Grand Trunk Pacific Railway and named after Sir Alfred Waldron Smithers (1850–1924), chairman of the railway's board of directors.

Smiths Cove NS East of Digby, this place was first called *Lower Clements*. It was named Smiths Cove in 1856 after Loyalist Jeremiah Smith.

Smiths Falls ON Loyalist Thomas Smyth (1768–1832) received large grants in the upper Rideau Valley after the American Revolution. He built a sawmill at *Smyth's Falls* in 1823, but neither he nor any member of his family ever lived here. He lost his land in 1825 through a foreclosure. The growing community was briefly called *Wardsville* after miller Abel Russell Ward (1796–1882). Rideau Canal plans in 1827 had Smiths Falls, and this spelling without an apostrophe was subsequently adopted locally. It became a separated town in 1902.

Smith Sound NU Located at the north end of Baffin Bay and between Ellesmere Island and Kalaallit Nunaat (Greenland), this water body was named in 1616 by William Baffin (1584–1622) and Robert Bylot (d.1622) after Sir Thomas Smith (1558–1625). A London merchant, Sir Thomas was the first governor of the Company of Adventurers for the Discovery of the North-West Passage.

Smokey, Cape NS A dominating elevation on the east side of Cape Breton Island and just south of Ingonish, this feature was identified as *Cap Enfumé* on maps of 1600 and 1602, and on Samuel de Champlain's 1632 map. The name was anglicized in the late 1700s.

Smoky Lake AB The post office in this town (1962) northeast of Edmonton opened in 1909, taking its name from a nearby lake. Known in Cree as *Kaskapite Sakigan* ('smoky lake'), because vapours often obscure the opposite shore, the lake was identified in 1810 by Alexander Henry (d.1814) the younger as *Lac qui Fume*.

Smoky River AB Rising east of Mount Robson, this river (380 km) flows northeast to join the Peace at the town of Peace River. Known as *Kaskapite Sipi* ('smoky river'), it received its name from smouldering coal beds on its banks in the Grande Cache area.

Smooth Rock Falls ON This town (1929) in Cochrane District, southeast of Kapuskasing, was founded in 1917 and named after a large rock in the Mattagami River, which was washed smooth after a dam had been constucted here in 1915.

Snafu Creek YT A tributary of Lubbock River between Jakes Corner and Atlin, BC, this creek was named in 1949–50 by Canadian Army engineers after the Second World War phrase 'situation normal, all fouled up'. *See also* Tarfu Creek.

Snag YT This locality, southwest of Dawson and on **Snag Creek**, a tributary of the White River, was named in 1942 when a landing strip and a weather station were located here. The creek had been named in 1899 by geologist Alfred Brooks and topographer William Peters of the United States Geological Survey. Canada's coldest temperature, −81°F (−62.8°C) was recorded here on 3 February 1947.

Snelgrove ON Located in the city of Brampton, Peel Region, north of the city centre, this community was first called *Edmonton* in 1851 after the district in north central London, England. To avoid confusion with the new settlement that would become the capital of Alberta, it was renamed in 1859 after J.C. Snell, who won a contest by getting the most mail during a certain period.

Snowbird Lake NT Near the sixtieth parallel and southeast of Great Slave Lake, this lake (490 km²) was possibly named in 1894 by geologist Joseph Burr Tyrrell (1858–1957). Tyrrell explored the rivers and lakes from the Saskatchewan River northeast to near present-day Arviat on the Hudson Bay coast.

Snow Dome AB, BC On the continental divide and at the centre of the Columbia Icefield, this summit (c.3520 m) was first named *Dome* by British climber Norman Collie (1859–1942) in 1899. In 1819 the Alberta–British Columbia Boundary Commission determined it was the hydrographic apex of North America, with waters draining from it to the Pacific, Arctic, and Atlantic Oceans.

Snow Lake MB Located east of Flin Flon, this town (1976) was founded in 1945 by Howe Sound Exploration Company Ltd to develop the gold deposits that were discovered by Lew Parres (d.2004) in 1927 at **Snow Lake**. He named the lake because he found its water as soft as melted snow.

Sointula BC Located on Malcolm Island and on the northeastern side of Vancouver Island, this place was founded by the Kalevan Kansa Colonization Company in 1901. It was designed as a Finnish co-operative community, with its name in Finnish meaning 'harmony'. Within four years the venture failed, because of poor business practices, but the place remained occupied.

Sombra ON In 2001 this township became part of the township of St. Clair, Lambton County. It was named in 1822 by Lt.-Gov. Sir Peregrine Maitland (1777–1854) after the Spanish word for 'shade', because he found the area heavily wooded. Sombra post office opened in 1851.

Somerset MB This village (1962) northwest of Morden was named in 1881 by settlers from Somerset, England. There is a tall story that the name really came from an incident where a Mr. Stevenson was somersaulted into a creek from his democrat, a double-seated carriage. The creek was then called *Somersault Creek*, which eventually became **Somerset Creek**.

Somerset Island NU North of Boothia Peninsula and between Prince of Wales Island and Brodeur Peninsula of Baffin Island, this island (24,786 km²) was named *North Somerset* in 1820 by Sir William Parry (1790–1855) after his native county in England. The Geographic Board amended it to its present name in 1905.

Somervell, Mount BC In the Clemenceau Icefield of the Rocky Mountains, southeast of Athabasca Pass, this mountain (3120 m) was named in 1927 by alpinist Alfred J. Ostheimer III after Dr. Theodore Howard Somervell (1890–1975), who was a British climber in the Himalayas as well as a physiologist.

Sonora Island BC Between Vancouver Island and the mainland, north of Campbell River, this island was named in 1903 by Capt. John Walbran (1848–1913) after the Spanish schooner *Sonora*, which was under the command in 1775 of Juan Francisco de la Bodega y Quadra (1743–94), who undertook an exploratory voyage along the northwestern coast. Until 1903 the island was considered part of *Valdes Island*, but it was then divided among Sonora, Maurelle, and Quadra Islands.

Sooke BC On **Sooke Inlet**, southwest of Victoria, this community's post office was named in 1864. It took its name from the Sooke tribe of the Coast Salish, which was almost annihilated in 1848 by neighbouring tribes. The meaning of the name is not available in published records.

Sophiasburgh ON In 1998 this township became part of the municipality of Prince Edward County. It was named in 1788 for Princess Sophia (1777–1848), fifth daughter and twelfth child of George III.

Sorcerer Mountain BC In the Selkirk Mountains, northwest of Rogers Pass, this mountain (3166 m) was named in 1907 by surveyor Percy Carson. In 1900 botanist Charles Shaw called it

The Hub of the Big Bend. Carson did not explain what possessed him to give the name.

Sorel QC Situated at the junction of the Richelieu with the St. Lawrence, this city's site was called Fort Richelieu in 1642. In 1792, Gov. Frederick Haldimand (1718–91) issued the municipal charter for *William Henry* after buying the ancient seigneury of Saurel (Sorel). Five years earlier Prince William (who became William IV in 1830) had visited the province. In 1814 the post office was called *William Henry*, which became the town's name in 1848. The town was renamed Sorel in 1860, and its post office adopted this name two years later. The seigneury was granted in 1672 to Pierre de Saurel (1628–82), an officer with the Carignan-Salières Regiment. Within a few years the spelling Sorel superseded the original form.

Sorrento BC Located on Shuswap Lake, northwest of Salmon Arm, this place was established in the early 1880s by J.R. Kinghorn, an eastern businessman, in anticipation of the arrival of the Canadian Pacific Railway. The view over the lake reminded him of the view of the Isle of Capri from Sorrento, Italy, where Kinghorn had gone for his honeymoon. The railway bypassed it, but the post office was called Sorrento when it opened in 1913.

Souris MB The post office in this town (1903) at the junction of Plum Creek and **Souris River**, southwest of Brandon, was called *Plum Creek* before 1882, when it was renamed after the river. Alexander Henry (d.1814) the younger recorded it as *Rivière à la Souris* in 1799, and geographer David Thompson (1770–1857) noted it as *Mouse Rivulet* in 1814. In North Dakota it is commonly called Mouse River. *Souris* means 'mouse' in French.

Souris PE The post office in this town (1910) near the east end of the province opened about 1830. It was called *Souris East* from 1867 to 1967, when the original form was restored. Although it was claimed as early as 1816 that the adjacent **Souris Harbour** and **Souris River** were named after plagues of mice ('*souris*'), and French maps of the mid-1700s called the harbour *Havre à la Souris*, it might be more likely that the harbour may have been called *Havre de l'Échourie* ('barred harbour'), an apt description of the harbour. During the French regime, present South Lake, east of Souris, was identified as *Havre de l'Échourie*. The municipal community of **Souris West**, on the west side of the mouth of the Souris River, was established in 1972.

Southampton ON In 1999 this town (1904) became part of the town of Saugeen Shores, Bruce County. Southampton is located at the mouth of the Saugeen River and was first called *Saugeen* in 1851. Later that year, James Hervey Price (1797–1882), commissioner of Crown lands (1848–51), named it after the seaport city on England's south coast.

Southampton Island NU At the north end of Hudson Bay, this island (41,214 km²) was named in 1631 by explorer Luke Foxe (c.1586–1635) after Henry Wriothesley, 3rd Earl of Southampton (1573–1624), a politician and soldier.

South Brook NL This town (1965) at the head of Halls Bay, a southwesterly extension of Notre Dame Bay, is located at the outlet of **South Brook**, which rises just north of Millertown Junction. Between 1945 and 1965, South Brook and Springdale had been incorporated as a rural district.

South Bruce Peninsula ON This town was created in 1999. The town of Wiarton, the village of Hepworth, and the communities of Colpoy's Bay, Sauble Beach, and Cape Croker became parts of the town of South Bruce Peninsula.

South Burgess ON In 1998 this township became part of the township of Rideau Lakes, united counties of Leeds and Grenville. Burgess Township was named in 1798, possibly for James B. Burgess, a British member of Parliament who voted for the Canada Bill in 1791. In 1841 that part of the township south of Big Rideau Lake was united with Bastard Township in the united counties of Leeds and Grenville. *See also* North Burgess.

South Buxton ON This place became part of the municipality of Chatham-Kent, Kent County. This community was founded in 1849 as a settlement of black Americans and named *Elgin Settlement* after Lord Elgin, the governor of the Province of Canada. It was renamed in 1874 after Sir Thomas Fowell Buxton (1837–1915), a British member of Parliament who promoted the passing of the 1833 Emancipation Act. *See also* North Buxton.

South Cayuga ON Since 1974 this township was part of the town of Haldimand, Haldimand-Norfolk Region. The township was named in 1835, after the Cayuga tribe of the Six Nations confederacy. The name has many interpretations, including 'place where the canoes are drawn out', 'mountain rising from the water', and 'advising nation'. *See also* North Cayuga.

South Crosby ON Crosby Township was created in 1798, and probably named after Brass Crosby (1725–93), Lord Mayor of London, member of Parliament, and a friend of Lt.-Gov. John Graves Simcoe (1752–1806). South Crosby was separated from North Crosby in 1806, with both remaining in the united counties of Leeds and Grenville.

South Dorchester ON In 1998 this township became part of the township of Malahide, Elgin County. Dorchester Township, created in 1798 in Middlesex County, was named after Sir Guy Carleton, Baron Dorchester (1724–1808), governor of Quebec, 1768–78, commander-in-chief of forces in North America, 1782–6, and governor-in-chief of British North America, 1786–96. It was divided in 1851, with North Dorchester remaining in Middlesex County and South Dorchester transferring to Elgin County.

South Dumfries ON In 1999 this township was transferred into the County of Brant, Brant County, the south half of Dumfries Township. This township was named in 1816 by Niagara merchant William Dickson after his birthplace of Dumfries in Dumfriesshire, Scotland. *See also* North Dumfries.

South Easthope ON In 1998 this township became part of the township of Perth East, Perth County. Easthope Township was named in 1830 for Sir John Easthope (1784–1865), a director of the Canada Company. This British company was established in 1826 to develop the Huron Tract, a large area of what is now Southwestern Ontario. It was divided into North Easthope and South Easthope townships in 1843. North Easthope is in the regional municipality of Waterloo.

South Elmsley ON In 2001 this township became part of the township of Rideau Lakes, united counties of Leeds and Grenville. Elmsley Township was named in 1798 after Upper Canada's chief justice John Elmsley (1762–1805). In 1841 that part of the township south of the Rideau River was attached to the united counties of Leeds and Grenville, and North Elmsley Township was transferred to Lanark County.

Southern Harbour NL Located on the northeastern shore of Placentia Bay and south of Arnold's Cove, the bay at this town (1968) was identified in 1770 by hydrographer Michael Lane as **Southern Harbour**.

Southesk, Mount AB This mountain (3120 m) in Jasper National Park, east of Maligne Lake, was named in 1859 after James Carnegie, 9th Earl of Southesk (1827–1905). He travelled through the Rocky Mountains at the time that the Palliser expedition was undertaking its extensive surveys in Western Canada.

Southey SK North of Regina, this town (1980) was named for the poet laureate Robert Southey (1774–1843). His two-volume *The Life of Nelson* remains a classic of historical writing. The town's main street is called Keats, with other streets honouring Burns, Byron, Cowper, Emerson, and Browning. The Canadian Pacific Railway arrived in 1907.

South Fredericksburgh ON Fredericksburgh Township was named in 1784, likely after Prince Augustus Frederick (1773–1843), sixth son of George III. Ernestown Township, to the east, was called after his next older brother, and Adolphustown Township, to the west, was named in honour of his next younger brother. As Prince Frederick had been commemorated in Osnabruck Township, and the townships named after the 12 royal children were given in chronological order, his second name was used in naming Fredericksburgh Township.

It was divided in 1858 into North Fredericksburgh and South Fredericksburgh townships in Lennox and Addington County.

South Gower ON Gower Township was created in 1798 in Grenville County and was divided in 1850, with South Gower Township becoming part of the united counties of Leeds of Grenville. The original township was named after John Levenson Gower (1740–1792), lord of the Admiralty from 1783 to 1789. *See also* North Gower.

South Henik Lake NU West of Arviat, this lake (512 km²) was named on an eight-mile map sheet produced in 1942. That year anthropologist Diamond Jenness (1886–1969) proposed *Henik*, a contraction of the Inuktitut *Henningyouyouak* ('the large lake that lies over to one side'). The Hydrographic and Map Service of the department of mines and resources perceived there were two lakes, calling them South and **North Henik** lakes. The Geographic Board approved the two names in 1945.

South Marysburgh ON In 1998 this township became part of the municipality of Prince Edward County. It was named in 1786 for Princess Mary (1776–1857), fourth daughter of George III, and the wife of the Duke of Gloucester, her first cousin. South Marysburgh was separated from North Marysburgh in 1871.

South Monaghan ON In 1998 this township became part of the township of **Otonabee–South Monaghan**, Peterborough County. It was originally part of Monaghan Township, named in 1820 after County Monaghan in north central Ireland. *See also* North Monaghan.

South Nahanni River NT Rising in the Mackenzie Mountains, this river (563 km) flows southeast into the Liard River, 150 km upriver from Fort Simpson. It was named after the Nahanni, an Athapascan tribe, whose name means 'people of the west'. **Nahanni National Park** (4,766 km²) was established in 1972. It extends for 210 km on both sides of the river.

South Nation River ON Rising near Brockville, this river flows northwest to the Ottawa River. Known as the *Rivière de la Petite Nation* during the French regime, it was called *Petite Nation River* and *Nation River* during the 1800s. In 1908 it was called South Nation River to distinguish it from the Rivière de la Petite Nation, which flows south into the Ottawa River, opposite the mouth of the South Nation.

South Ohio NS North of Yarmouth, this place's post office was named in 1873. It and two other communities called **Ohio** in the province owe their names to the movement in the 1820s to the Ohio Territory, west of the Allegheny Mountains. As migration to the territory took place, there were simultaneous moves into the back country of the province, where their new lands were called Ohio.

South Plantagenet ON In 1998 this township became part of the Nation Township, united counties of Prescott and Russell. The original Plantagenet Township was named in 1798 after the royal family surname from 1154 to 1485. This municipal township was separated from the municipal township of North Plantagenet in 1850, and both remained in the united counties of Prescott and Russell.

Southport PE In the town of Stratford, across the Hillsborough River from Charlottetown, its post office served the area from 1860 to 1967. Created as a municipal community in 1983, it was united with Bunbury, Cross Roads, and Keppoch-Kinlock to form the town of Stratford in 1995.

South River NL This town (1966) at the head of Bay de Grave and on the west side of Conception Bay is located at the outlet of **South River**. It was known as *Southern Gut* until the beginning of the twentieth century.

South River ON The post office in this village (1882) in Parry Sound District was named in 1882 after the South River, which flows north into the South Bay of Lake Nipissing.

South Saskatchewan River AB, SK The Bow and Oldman Rivers unite 70 km west of Medicine Hat and become the South Saskatchewan. The river flows generally east through Diefenbaker Lake, and north through Saskatoon to unite with the North Saskatchewan to form the **Saskatchewan River**. In 1814 geographer David Thompson (1770–1857) labelled the entire South Saskatchewan as Bow River. *See also* Saskatchewan River *and* North Saskatchewan River.

South-West Oxford ON This township in Oxford County was created in 1975 by amalgamating the village of Beachville and the municipal townships of West Oxford and Dereham.

Spalding SK This village (1924) is located south of Melfort. James and Paddy Hutchison arrived here in 1905. The next year the post office was named for Paddy who was born in Spalding, Lincolnshire, England. She died in 1920, leaving 11 children with her husband. When the Canadian Pacific Railway was extended north from Watson in 1921, the post office was moved 3 km southwest to the rail line.

Spallumcheen BC This district municipality (1892) north of Vernon, surrounding the city of Armstrong, was named after the *Spallumcheen River*, a former name of the Shuswap River. The name derives from the Okanagan *spalmtsin* ('flat area along the edge'). In the form of Spillamacheen, the name was transferred east to the area of the Purcell Mountains, where it identifies **Spallumcheen River**, **Spallumcheen Mountain**, **Spallumcheen Range**, and **Spallumcheen Glacier**.

Spaniards Bay NL Located at the head of **Spaniard's Bay** and on the western side of Conception Bay, this town (1965) was named after the bay, noted by pioneer settler John Guy who came in 1610. He died in 1629. The name may have been given by English fishermen, who sometimes identified Portuguese and Basque fishermen as Spaniards.

Spanish ON In Algoma District, west of Espanola, this place's post office was first called *Spanish River Station* in 1887. The river had been named in the 1820s by Admiralty surveyor Henry W. Bayfield (1795–1885). There are many legends about the origin of the name, most involving the Ojibwa capturing of a Spaniard near the Gulf of Mexico, resulting in the Espaniel family being given the river as its hunting grounds. *See also* Espanola *and* The Spanish River.

Spanish Bank BC Located on the northwestern side of Vancouver and at the outer limits of Burrard Inlet, it was here on 22 June 1792 that Capt. George Vancouver (1757–98) met the Spanish sea captains Dionisio Alcalá Galiano (1760–1805) and Cayetano Valdés (1767–1835). *See also* English Bay.

Sparwood BC In the valley of the Elk River and extending up Michel Creek toward the Alberta border, this district municipality was established in 1966 by amalgamating Sparwood, Natal, *Michel*, and *Middletown*. Sparwood's post office opened in 1903, taking its name from the good quality of spars obtained from the trees here for the construction of the Crows Nest Pass Railway.

Spear, Cape NL This most easterly point of Canada extends into the Atlantic east of St. John's. It was named in Portuguese *Cauo de la spera* ('place of waiting'). Identified on a 1505–8 map, it may have been the point where Portuguese vessels waited for the lost expeditions of Gaspar and Miguel Corte-Real. It became an important rendezvous point in the sixteenth century for explorers and fishermen on the Grand Banks.

Spences Bridge BC Located on the Thompson River, northeast of Lytton, this place was first called *Cook's Ferry* after Mortimer Cook, who started the ferry here in 1862. Three years later a toll bridge was built by Thomas Spence. The *Spence's Bridge* colonial post office opened in 1868, followed by a Canadian office in 1872. The apostrophe was dropped in the 1950s.

Spirit River AB The post office in this town (1951) north of Grande Prairie was named in 1920, near the present site of Rycroft on the Spirit River, 7 km to the east. It was moved to its current location in 1920 when the Edmonton, Dunvegan and British Columbia Railway was built. The river was known in Cree as *Chepe Sipi* ('ghost river'), and *Ghost River* appeared on some early maps of the Peace River country.

Spiritwood SK The post office in this town (1965) west of Prince Albert was named in 1923 by postmaster Rupert Dumond, after his hometown east of Jamestown, ND.

Split, Cape NS Extending into the Minas Channel, this cape was called *Cap Fendu* ('split cape') during the French regime. Its original name may have been the source of the name 'Fundy' for the Bay of Fundy.

Springdale NL This town (1965) on the western side of Halls Bay, a southwesterly extension of Notre Dame Bay, was settled in the 1870s. It was first known as *Little Wolf Cove* and *Island Rock Cove*, and the two places became Springdale in 1898, when the post office opened.

Springfield ON In 1998 this village (1877) became part of the township of Malahide, Elgin County. East of St. Thomas, it was named in 1863 after the many springs in the fields near the head of Catfish Creek.

Springhill NS Southeast of Amherst, this town (1889) was first settled in the 1820s. Its post office opened in 1852 and named after the springs on its hillside. Coal had been discovered here in 1834, but mining was not undertaken in a large scale until 1873.

Spring-Rice, Mount AB, BC Located on the continental divide and south of the Columbia Icefield, this mountain (3275 m) was named in 1918 by the Alberta–British Columbia Boundary Commission after Sir Cecil Arthur Spring-Rice (1859–1918), British ambassador to Washington, 1913–18.

Springside SK Located northwest of Yorkton, the post office in this town (1985) was named in 1904 after the good quality of spring water in the area.

Springwater ON This municipal township in Simcoe County was created in 1994 by merging the village of Elmvale and the municipal townships of Flos and Vespra. A contest had been held to choose a suitable name, with Springwater being accepted because no one objected to it. *See also* Elmvale.

Spruce Grove AB The post office in this city (1986) west of Edmonton, was named in 1894 after a nearby grove of spruce trees. Its Grand Trunk Pacific Railway station was established in 1910, slightly to the west.

Spy Hill SK The post office in this village (1910) east of Esterhazy was named in 1888 after a nearby hill used by the Cree to keep watch on enemies approaching from various directions. Legend has it that a spying Dakota (Sioux) was discovered and killed on the hill, and his body was left there for the birds and animals to devour, resulting in the name *Kappa Gammaho* ('spy hill').

Squamish BC The post office in this district municipality (1972) at the mouth of **Squamish River**, which flows south into Howe Sound, was named in 1892. The office was renamed *Newport Beach* in 1912 to provide the place with a more suitable name. When the change was not accepted, the Pacific Great Eastern Railway held a contest in 1914 to select a better name. The winning name was Squamish. The river's name derives from the Squohomish, a Coast Salish tribe, whose name possibly means 'strong wind'.

Stafford ON In 2000 this township became part of the township of Laurentian Valley, Renfrew County. It was named in 1843 after Staffordshire in England, the home county of Sir Charles Bagot (1781–1843), governor of the Province of Canada, 1841–3. *See also* Admaston-Bromley.

Standard AB This village (1922) east of Calgary was named in 1911 by the Canadian Pacific Railway, possibly after the Danish flag, the oldest European 'standard', dating from the thirteenth century. A Danish settlement had been established here two years earlier. Its post office opened in 1912.

Stand Off AB Located on the Blood Indian Reserve, southwest of Lethbridge, it was named *Fort Stand Off* in 1871 by American whisky traders, who claimed they could not be pursued and charged by a United States marshal. The name was retained in 1882 by the North-West Mounted Police. Its post office opened in 1896.

Stanhope PE North of Charlottetown, and adjacent to Prince Edward Island National Park, this place's post office was called Stanhope by the Sea in 1961. It took its name from *Stanhope Cove*, the name given in 1765 to present Covehead Bay by Samuel Holland (1728–1801). Holland had named it after William Stanhope, Viscount Petersham, 1719–79.

Stanley NB This village (1966) northwest of Fredericton was named in 1834 by the New Brunswick and Nova Scotia Land Company after Edward George Geoffrey Smith Stanley, 14th Earl of Derby (1799–1869). One of the organizers of the company, he was prime minister of Great Britain three times. A post office opened here in 1847.

Stanley ON In 2001 this township became part of the municipality of Bluewater, Huron County. It was named in 1835 after Edward Geoffrey Smith Stanley, 14th Earl of Derby (1799–1869), then a joint secretary of state for the colonies. Lord Derby had three brief terms as prime minister. His son, Lord Stanley of Preston, was governor general of Canada, 1888–93. *See also* Port Stanley.

Stanley Baldwin, Mount BC Located in the Premier Range, west of Valemount, this mountain (3249 m) was named in 1927 by Dr. John D. MacLean, acting premier of the province, after Stanley Baldwin, 1st Earl Baldwin of Bewdley (1867–1947). Prime minister of Great Britain during three terms between 1924 and 1937, he toured British Columbia in 1927.

Stanley, Mount BC Located in the Clemenceau Icefield of the Rocky Mountains, southeast of Athabasca Pass, this mountain (3090 m) was named in 1927 by alpinist James Monroe Thorington (1895–1989) after Henry Morton Stanley (1841–1904), an American newspaper reporter who found explorer David Livingstone (1813–73) in Africa in 1871. *See also* Livingstone, Mount.

Stanstead Plain QC This village on the Vermont border and adjacent to the villages of Rock Island and Beebe Plain was separated in 1857 from the township municipality of **Stanstead**. Stanstead post office was opened here in 1817. The township municipality was incorporated in 1845, taking its name from the township, shown on a 1795 map, and proclaimed in 1800.

Starbuck MB On the La Salle River, west of Winnipeg, this community was named by a Canadian Northern Railway contractor in 1885 after Starbuck, MN, northwest of Minneapolis.

Star City SK The post office in this town (1921) midway between Melfort and Tisdale was named in 1902 after postmaster Walter Starkey (1854–1923), who left Brighton, Sussex, England, and homesteaded in 1900 near the site of Star City.

Stavely AB Located fetween Nanton and Claresholm, south of Calgary, this town was first called *Oxley* after the Oxley Ranching Company, established here in 1882 by Alexander Staveley Hill, judge advocate of the British fleet. The company was named after Oxley Manor, Wolverhampton, West Midlands, England. When the town was incorporated in 1912, the second 'e' was dropped. Its post office had been opened in 1903.

Stayner ON The post office in this urban area in Simcoe County, southeast of Collingwood, was called *Nottawasaga Station* in 1855, and it was incorporated as the village of *Dingwall* two years later. Both were renamed in 1864 after Thomas Stayner (1788–1868), deputy postmaster general, 1848–9, who donated land for a church. His son, Sutherland Stayner, purchased land in the area. Stayner was a town from 1888 to 1994, when it was united with the village of Creemore and the municipal townships of Nottawasaga and Sunnidale to form the municipal township of Clearview.

Steele, Mount YT In the St. Elias Mountains, this mountain (5072 m) was named in 1909 by surveyor James J. McArthur

283

(1856–1925) after Maj. Gen Samuel (later Sir Samuel) Benfield Steele (1849–1919). Steele began his career with the North West Mounted Police in 1874 and commanded the NWMP posts in the territory during the Klondike Gold Rush.

Steeves, Mount NB South of the Nepisiguit River, this mountain was named in 1964 by Arthur F. Wightman (1905–88), then the provincial names authority, for William Henry Steeves (1814–73). Steeves was a Father of Confederation and one of the original 12 senators from New Brunswick.

Stefansson Island NU Located on the northeast side of Victoria Island, this island (4463 km²) was recognized in 1947 by a Royal Canadian Air Force aerial survey as being separated from Victoria Island by Goldsmith Channel. It was named in 1952 after explorer Vilhjalmur Stefansson (1879–1962), who had investigated Victoria Island in 1910–1 in search of Inuit settlements. It was the last island to be named in the Arctic Ocean.

Steinbach MB This city town (1946) southeast of Winnipeg was founded by Mennonite immigrants in 1874 and named after their former home in Ukraine. In German the name means 'stone brook'.

Stellarton NS The postal way office in this town (1889), south of New Glasgow, was called *Albion Mines* in 1842 after coal mining had that started here in 1827. It was renamed Stellarton on 1 February 1870 after the top quality Stellar coal was mined here.

Stephen ON In 2001 this township became part of the municipality of South Huron, Huron County. It was named in 1835 after James Stephen Jr., who was then British under-secretary of state for the colonies.

Stephen, Mount BC In Yoho National Park, southeast of Field, this mountain (3199 m) was named in 1886 after George Stephen (1829–1921), president of the Canadian Pacific Railway, 1880–8. Created a baronet in 1886, he was promoted to the peerage in 1891, when he took the title of Baron Mount Stephen.

Stephenville NL This town (1952) is located on the north side of St. George's Bay, and on the west coast of Newfoundland. The town was named in the early 1870s after St. Stephen's Catholic Church, given by Catholic missionary Fr. Thomas Sears; the first child baptized here was Stephen Le Blanc (also called White). It was earlier called *Indian Head*. The town (1958) of **Stephenville Crossing** is located to the east, where the former railway crossed the mouth of the St. George's River.

Stettler AB The post office in this town (1906) east of Red Deer was named *Blumenau* in 1905, as it was the centre of a German-Swiss colony. Later that year, the Canadian Pacific Railway was built through the colony. The post office was moved 5 km east to the townsite, and renamed in 1906 after Carl Stettler (1861–1919), who had homesteaded here three years earlier.

Stewart BC This district municipality (1976) at the head of Portland Canal and beside the state of Alaska was settled in 1902 by brothers John and Robert Stewart. Robert was appointed the first postmaster in 1905.

Stewart, Mount AB This mountain (3312 m) east of the Columbia Icefield, was named in 1902 after Louis B. Stewart (1861–1937), a professor of surveying and geodesy at the University of Toronto, who surveyed the boundaries of Banff National Park. His father, George A. Stewart (1830–1917), was also a surveyor and was the first superintendent of the park.

Stewart River YT Rising in the Selwyn Mountains, this river (644 km) flows west to join the Yukon River, 80 km upstream from Dawson. It was named in 1849 by Hudson's Bay Company trader Robert Campbell (1808–94) after James G. Stewart, his assistant.

Stewiacke NS The name of this town (1906) derives from the **Stewiacke River**, which flows into the Shubenacadie River here. The river's name in Mi'kmaq is *Esiktaweak* ('oozing slowly from still water'). Its post office was called *Lower Stewiacke* in 1836 and was only changed to Stewiacke in 1913.

Stikine River BC Rising in the Cassiar Mountains, southwest of Fort Nelson, this river (539 km) flows west, and then south-west, crossing the Alaska border northwest of Stewart, BC. In Tlingit the name means 'the river', in the sense of being a big river.

Stirling AB This village (1901) southeast of Lethbridge was named in 1899 after John A. Stirling, managing director of the London-based Trusts, Executors and Securities Corporation, a large shareholder in the Alberta Railway and Coal Company.

Stirling ON The post office in this village (1858) in Hastings County, northwest of Belleville, was called *Rawdon* from 1832 to 1852 after the township of Rawdon. It was then changed to Stirling, because its site recalled the countryside of Stirlingshire in Scotland.

Stittsville ON In 2001 this community became part of the city of Ottawa. The community was named in 1854 after first postmaster Jackson Stitt, who had arrived here in 1818.

Stockholm SK West of Esterhazy, the Canadian Pacific Railway station was erected at this village (1905) in 1903 and its post office was named by first postmaster Alex Stenberg the following year. The area was settled by Swedes in the 1880s.

Stoneham-et-Tewkesbury QC Located north of Quebec City, the municipality of these two united townships was erected in 1845, abolished two years later, and re-established in 1855. The township of Stoneham was founded in the late 1700s by the Reverend Philip Toosey, an Anglican priest from Stoneham, Suffolk, England, and was proclaimed in 1800. The township of Tewkesbury was also proclaimed in 1800, and named after the hometown of its first settler, Kenelm Chandler, in Gloucestershire, England.

Stonewall MB Northwest of Winnipeg, the post office in this town (1908) was named in 1878. The first postmaster, O.P. Jackson, named it after his brother, the Hon. S.J. Jackson, who had donated the land for the post office. The latter was nicknamed 'Stonewall' after the famed Confederate general, Thomas 'Stonewall' Jackson (1824–63), because he walked with an erect military bearing during his political campaigns.

Stoney Creek ON In 2001 this city (1984) became part of the city of Hamilton. It was likely named after **Stoney Creek**, which flows north into Lake Ontario. There are claims it was named after trapper Jim Stoney or after Anglican priest Edmund Stoney. Its post office was called *Stony Creek* in 1827, but it was changed to Stoney Creek about 1832 to be identified with the War of 1812 battle that took place here and became a well-known turning point for the British forces.

Stoney Point ON In 1999 this community became part of the town of Lakeshore, Essex County. It was named after the nearby point, called *Pointe aux Roches* during the French regime. Stoney Point post office was named in 1865, but it was changed to Pointe-aux-Roches in 1950. However, Stoney Point continued as the police village's name. In 1996 the municipal township of Tilbury requested equal recognition of both names for the post office and the community.

Stony Mountain MB Situated between Winnipeg and Stonewall, its post office was named in 1880, having been called *Rockwood* in 1873. The nearby mountain was identified on Henry Y. Hind's map of 1858.

Stony Plain AB A town (1908) west of Edmonton, its post office was named in 1893 after the surrounding land. The plain may have been originally called after the Stoney (Aboriginals), a variant name of the Assiniboine, but Dr. Sir Hector (1834–1907) observed in 1858 that it 'well deserves the name from being covered with boulders which are rather rare in general in this district or country'.

Stony Rapids SK On the Fond du Lac River, east of Lake Athabasca, this northern hamlet (1992) was named after the boulder-strewn fast water of the river. It was settled by trappers in the 1920s and its post office opened in 1937.

Storkerson Peninsula NU The northeastern extension of Victoria Island, this 260-km peninsula was named in 1961 by geologist Raymond Thorsteinsson after Storker Storkerson (1883–1940), who investigated the north coast of Victoria Island in 1915 and 1917. A member of the Leffingwell-Mikkelson Arctic expedition of 1906–7, Storkerson was a Norwegian sailor who had remained in Alaska to study the geography of the North.

Stormont ON The county was named in 1792 after David Murray, 7th Viscount Stormont and 2nd Earl of Mansfield (1727–1796), who held many official posts, including justice general of Scotland. The title was taken in 1621 from Stormont Loch in Perthshire, Scotland. In 1852 it became part of the united counties of Stormont, Dundas, and Glengarry.

Storrington ON In 1998 this township became part of the township of South Frontenac, Frontenac County. It was named in 1845 after the English village where Sir Henry Smith (1812–68), speaker of the Legislative Assembly of Canada, 1856–60, was born. Storrington is in West Sussex, England, northwest of Brighton.

Stouffville ON In York Region, east of Aurora, this community was named in 1832 after miller Abraham Stouffer (1776–1851), who settled here in 1804. In 1971 it was united with Whitchurch Township to form the town of **Whitchurch-Stouffville**.

Stoughton SK This town (1960) east of Weyburn was founded by the Canadian Pacific Railway in 1904 and named after John Stoughton Dennis (1820–85), the son of Joseph Dennis and Mary Stoughton. He was Canada's first surveyor general, 1871–8, and deputy minister of the interior, 1878–1881. Its post office was also opened in 1904.

Strasbourg SK The post office in this town (1907) north of Regina was named *Strassburg* in 1886 after the chief city of Alsace, then part of Germany. It was called *Strassburg Station* in 1905. After Alsace was restored to France following World War I, the Canadian town's post office was renamed *Strasbourg Station* in 1919 and was shortened to Strasbourg in 1956.

Stratford ON The post office in this city (1885) in Perth County was named in 1835. Possibly the London, England-based Canada Company instructed its Canadian co-commissioner Thomas Mercer Jones (1795–1868) to call it that. Or it may have been inspired by a sign portraying William

Shakespeare that Jones gave to William Sargint to hang outside his inn, which he had built in 1832.

Stratford PE This town (1995) south of Charlottetown was created through the amalgamation of the municipal communities of Southport, Bunbury, Cross Roads, and Keppoch-Kinlock. During the previous December the local residents voted to call it Waterview, but widespread dislike of it led to a second ballot, which endorsed the second choice, Stratford. It was named after the main road in Southport and Cross Roads, which had been the name of a school district, founded in Southport in 1858.

Strathclair MB Located northeast of Minnedosa, this place was the location of a Hudson's Bay Company trading post, taking its name from the Gaelic word *strath* ('valley') and the last syllable of surveyor Duncan Sinclair's name. Its post office opened in 1880.

Strathmore AB This town (1911) east of Calgary was named by the Canadian Pacific Railway in 1884 after Claude Bowes-Lyon, 13th Earl of Strathmore (1824–1904).

Strathroy ON In 2001 this town (1870) became part of the township of Strathroy-Caradoc, Middlesex County. Located 28 km west of London, it was named in 1832, likely after Straughroy (also called Strathroy), County Tyrone, Ireland. A post office opened here in 1851.

Strickland, Mount YT This mountain (4212 m) in the St. Elias Mountains was named about 1918 after North West Mounted Police inspector D'Arcy Strickland (d.1908), who commanded the White Pass detachment in 1898.

Strome AB The first post office in this village (1910) southeast of Camrose was called *Knollton* after postmaster Mac Knoll. It was renamed in 1906 after Stromeferry on Loch Carron, east of the Isle of Skye, and in the county of Ross and Cromarty, Scotland.

Stroud ON In the town of Innisfil, Simcoe County, southeast of Barrie, this place was named in 1873 by Member of Parliament William C. Little after a town near his birthplace in Gloucestershire, England.

Stuart Lake BC Northwest of Prince George, this lake was known to Simon Fraser (1776–83) in 1806 as *Sturgeon Lake*. It was soon named after John Stuart (1780–1847), who spent the winter of 1806–7 at McLeod Lake, to the northeast, as a clerk of the North West Company. He became a partner of the NWC in 1813, and after the merger with the Hudson's Bay Company in 1821, he served as a chief factor in New Caledonia (the northern part of British Columbia) for three years.

Stukely-Sud QC This village midway between Granby and Magog was detached in 1935 from the municipality of **Stukely-Sud**, which had been created in 1855. Ten years earlier the latter had been erected as the township municipality of **Stukely-Sud**. Well known as Stukely South, the name derives from the township of Stukely, proclaimed in 1800, and named after Stewkley in Buckinghamshire, England, northwest of London.

Stupendous Mountain BC In the Coast Mountains, southeast of Bella Coola, this mountain (2728 m) was named in 1793 by Sir Alexander Mackenzie (c.1764–1820). On descending from the Interior Plateau into the Bella Coola River valley, he was much impressed with this mountain, whose summit disappeared into the clouds.

Sturgeon Falls ON This town (1895) in Nipissing District, west of North Bay, is located on the **Sturgeon River**. After the transcontinental Canadian Pacific Railway arrived in 1882, the Sturgeon Falls post office opened.

Sturgeon Point ON In 2001 this village became part of the city of Kawartha Lakes, Victoria County. Located 16 km north of Lindsay, it is on a peninsula where **Sturgeon Lake** divides into two large arms. Incorporated in 1899, it was Ontario's smallest village with 103 permanent residents in 1996. It is no longer a village.

Sturgis SK North of Canora, the post office of this town (1951) was named in 1908 by postmaster Fred Brooks (1874–1944) after his hometown northwest of Rapid City, SD.

Stutfield Peak AB On the northwest side of the Columbia Icefield, this mountain (3459 m) was named in 1899 after climber Hugh Edward Millington Stutfield (1858–1929), who made several ascents in the area of the icefield.

Sudbury ON The site of the city (1930) was named in 1883 by the Canadian Pacific Railway superintendent of construction James Worthington. It was given in honour of his wife's birthplace in Suffolk, England, west of Ipswich. Sudbury District was created from Nipissing District in 1894. In 1973 the regional municipality of **Sudbury** was severed from the district and divided into the city of Sudbury and the towns of Capreol, Nickel Centre, Valley East, Rayside-Balfour, Onaping Falls, and Walden. **Greater Sudbury** was created in 2001 by amalgamating the cities and towns of the former regional municipality. The official name in French is **Grand-Sudbury**. *See also* Greater Sudbury.

Suffield AB Northwest of Medicine Hat, this place was named in 1883 by the Canadian Pacific Railway after Charles Harbord, 5th Baron Suffield (1830–1914). He was a brother-in-law of Lord Revelstoke, a major financier of the

CPR's construction in British Columbia. The nearby Suffield Experimental Station is a military training ground, where biological warfare studies are undertaken for the Canadian Defence Research Board. During the Second World War the British troops were trained here for chemical warfare.

Sullivan ON In 2000 this township became part of the township of Chatsworth, Grey County. It was named in 1840 after Robert Baldwin Sullivan (1802–53), then the commissioner of Crown lands in Upper Canada.

Sullivan QC Situated north of Val-d'Or, this municipality was named in 1972 after its post office, Sullivan Mines, which opened in 1935. The place was called *Carrièreville* ('quarry town') from 1937 to 1967, when the mine closed. Jos Sullivan discovered gold here in 1911, and mining began in 1934.

Sulphur Mountain AB This mountain (2451 m), overlooking Banff, was named in 1916 after the distinctive odour of the hot springs at its base.

Summerford NL This municipal community (1971) on New World Island was first called *Farmer's Arm*. It was renamed before 1911 to avoid confusion with *Farmer's Arm* near Twillingate, now called Gillesport.

Summerland BC This district municipality (1906) on the west side of Okanagan Lake and north of Penticton was founded in 1902 by developer John Moore Robinson (1855–1934). It was named after the pleasant sunny climate of the Okanagan Valley.

Summerside PE This city (1995) was first incorporated as a town in 1877. In creating the city, Summerside annexed the neighbouring municipal communities of St. Eleanors and Wilmot, and part of Sherbrooke. It was named in 1852 after Summerside House, established by Joseph Green in 1840. The name of the inn was suggested by Maj. Harry Compton, because he described the site as the 'sunny side' of the island.

Sunbury NB Southeast of Fredericton, this county was created in 1765 to cover most of the western part of present New Brunswick. Twenty years later it was confined to the present area, centred on Oromocto. It was named after George Montagu Dunk, 2nd Earl Halifax, Viscount Sunbury (1716–71). He held several positions in the British government, including president of the board of trade and lord privy seal.

Sunbury ON In 1998 this place became part of the township of South Frontenac, Frontenac County. Northeast of Kingston, its post office was named in 1864, probably by Member of Parliament Sir Henry Smith after a district in Greater London, England, west of London's city centre.

Sunderland ON In Durham Region, west of Lindsay, this community's post office was called *Brock*, after the township of Brock, from 1836 to 1868, when it was renamed after Sunderland, on the North Sea coast of County Durham, southeast of Newcastle upon Tyne.

Sundre AB This town (1956), northwest of Calgary, was named in 1909 after the birthplace in Norway of first postmaster Nels T. Hagen, who had arrived here three years earlier, and bought a store.

Sundridge ON The post office in this village (1889) in Parry Sound District, north of Huntsville, was named in 1879. First postmaster John Paget had suggested *Sunridge*, a description of the place's setting at the north end of Lake Bernard. The postal authorities may have been inspired by Sundridge in Kent, England, southeast of London.

Sunnyside NL Located at the north end of the Avalon Isthmus, and at the head of Bull Arm, an extension of Trinity Bay, it was formerly called *Bay Bulls Arm*. It was renamed in 1930, presumably because it was on the northern (sunny) side of the arm.

Sunwapta Peak AB This mountain (3315 m) southeast of Jasper was named in 1892 by climber Arthur P. Coleman (1852–1939) after the Stoney words for 'turbulent water'. The **Sunwapta River** rises on the north flank of Mount Athabasca and flows northwest into the Athabasca River.

Superior, Lake ON Called *Grand Lac* by Samuel de Champlain (1567–1635) in 1632, this lake was identified on later maps as *Lac de Tracy ou Svperievr* in honour of Alexandre de Prouville, Marquis de Tracy (c.1602–70), commander-in-chief of French forces in America, 1665–7. The lake's name describes its position as the most elevated of the Great Lakes.

Surrey BC On the south side of the Fraser River, southeast of Vancouver, this city (1993) was created a district municipality in 1879. It was named that year after the English county of Surrey. Its location south of New Westminster likely inspired the name, as Surrey in England is south of the city of Westminster in Greater London.

Sussex NB This town (1904) in the Kennebecasis River valley was founded in the early 1800s. It was named after **Sussex Parish**, established in 1786, and possibly after Sussex, NJ. Its post office was named *Sussex Vale* about 1810, and was changed to Sussex in 1898. The post office of the adjacent village (1966) of **Sussex Corner** was named in 1860.

Sutton ON In the town of Georgina, York Region, northeast of Newmarket, this urban centre was first known as *Bourchier's Mills*, after miller James O'Brien Bourchier (1797–1872).

Bourchier was appointed the first postmaster of *Georgina* in 1831. The post office was renamed Sutton West in 1885, possibly after Sutton on Hull, a suburb of Kingston upon Hull in East Yorkshire, but the place is usually called just Sutton.

Sutton QC This town (1962) in the regional county of Brome-Missisquoi and on the west flank of the Monts Sutton, southeast of Cowansville, was incorporated as a village in 1896. The township municipality of **Sutton** was organized in 1845, abolished two years later, and re-established in 1855. The post office opened in 1837 and named after the township of **Sutton**, shown on a 1795 map and proclaimed in 1802. It may have been named after Sutton, Bedfordshire, England (adjacent to Potton, the name of the township east of Sutton in Quebec), and reinforced by places called Sutton in four of the New England states.

Sverdrup Islands NU In the Queen Eizabeth Islands, the group comprising Axel Heiberg, Amund Ringnes, Ellef Ringnes, Cornwall, King Christian, and Meighen Islands was named before 1910 after Norwegian Capt. Otto Neumann Sverdrup (1855–1930). From 1898 to 1902 Sverdrup led an expedition to southern Ellesmere Island and the islands west of it.

Swan Hills AB This town (1967) in the **Swan Hills**, north of Whitecourt, was named in 1960 after an oil field had been developed here. The hills are said to be have been named after huge swans, which make thunderous noises when they flap their wings.

Swan Lake MB Northwest of Morden, this place's post office was named in 1881 after a lake 7 km to the southwest. White swans had a habitat at the lake, which is an enlargement of the Pembina River.

Swannell Ranges BC Located west of Williston Lake, these ranges were named in 1950 after Frank Cyril Swannell (1879–1969), who performed several land surveys throughout the province. **Mount Swannell**, south of the Nechako Reservoir, was named after him in 1947.

Swan River MB Located on the Swan River, which rises west of the Porcupine Hills in Saskatchewan, this town (1908) took its name from *Swan River House*, a fur trading post founded in the late 1700s. During 1875 it was the legislative capital of the North-West Territories.

Swastika ON In the town of Kirkland Lake, Timiskaming District, this place was named in 1911, five years after brothers Bill and Jim Dusty found gold at a nearby lake and named the mine after a visitor's good luck charm. Because of the symbol's later association with Adolph Hitler, the Ontario government tried to rename the place *Winston* after Winston Churchill

during the Second World War, but local residents protested the desecration of their name.

Swift Current NL At the mouth of **Swift Current**, which flows into the north part of Placentia Bay, this place formerly called *Piper's Hole* was renamed about 1920. There is a legend attached to Piper's Hole that ghosts could be seen in the area, accompanied by the mournful sound of bagpipes.

Swift Current SK The post office in this city (1914) on the main line of the Canadian Pacific Railway was named in 1883. Its name is a translation of the Cree name for **Swift Current Creek**, *Kisiskatchewan*, also the Cree name for the Saskatchewan River.

Sydenham ON In 2001 this township became part of the town of Georgian Highlands, Grey County. It was named in 1842 after Charles Edward Poulett Thomson, Baron Sydenham (1799–1841), governor-in-chief of British North America, 1839–41. Sydenham River rises south of Owen Sound, and flows north into Georgian Bay, which is part of Lake Huron.

Sydenham ON In 1998 this community became part of the township of South Frontenac, Frontenac County. North of Kingston, it was first named Loughborough in 1836 after the township of Loughborough, but it was changed in 1839 to honour Lord Sydenham, governor-in-chief of British North America, 1839–41.

Sydenham River ON This river rises north of the city of London and flows southwest, parallel to the Thames River, to enter Lake St. Clair and ultimately into St. Clair River. The river passes the cities of Windsor and Detroit to flow into Lake Erie. It was named for Lord Sydenham, governor-in-chief of British North America, 1839–41.

Sydney NS This metropolitan area in the regional municipality of Cape Breton since 1 August 1995 was incorporated as a town in 1886 and as a city in 1904. It was named after **Sydney Harbour**, which had been named in 1784–5 by Joseph Frederic Wallet DesBarres (1722–1824), then governor of Cape Breton, after Thomas Townshend, 1st Viscount Sydney (1733–1800), British home secretary, 1782–9, lord of the Admiralty, 1790–3, and lord of the treasury, 1793–1800. The harbour had been called *Dartmouth Harbour* in 1767 by Samuel Holland (1728–1801), replacing *Spanish Bay*. The latter had been named *Riviere aux Espagnols* in the late 1600s, perhaps reflecting not only Spanish fisherman coming ashore here, but Portuguese and Basque as well. The community of **Sydney River**, southwest of Sydney, was named in 1892. **Sydney Forks**, also southwest of Sydney, and at the confluence of **Sydney River** and Meadows Brook, was named in 1874.

Sydney Mines NS Located on the north side of **Sydney Harbour**, this urban community has been in the regional municipality of Cape Breton since 1 August 1995. It had been incorporated as a town in 1889.

Sylvan Lake AB Located on the south shore of **Sylvan Lake**, west of Red Deer, the post office in this town (1946) was named in 1907. The lake was once called *Snake Lake*. Geographer David Thompson (1770–1857) recorded it as *Methy Lake* in 1814. The present name is from the Latin *silvanus* ('forested').

Taber AB The station in this town east of Lethbridge was named in 1894 by the Canadian Pacific Railway. Its post office was called *Tabor* in 1904 after Mount Tabor in the Holy Land. The townsite was first registered as *Tabor*, but was changed to Taber when the town was incorporated in 1907. Although claims had been made that the name derives from the first part of 'tabernacle', Judge J.A. Jackson of Lethbridge reported in 1928 that this was not true. Horace Tabor (1830–99), an appointed United States senator for Colorado in the 1880s, may have visited the place, leading to the erroneous conclusion that it was named after him.

Tabusintac NB At the mouth of the **Tabusintac River**, southwest of Tracadie, this place's post office was named *Tabisintac* in 1840, changed to *Tabucintac* in 1857, and given its present spelling in 1931. The river's name in Mi'kmaq may mean 'two entrances', referring to the main river and the entrance to French Cove. Map-maker Pierre Jumeau called it *R. tabochemkek* in 1685.

Tadoussac QC Situated on the north side of the mouth of the Rivière Saguenay, this village has one of the prettiest settings in Quebec. Its name in Montagnais, *Totouskak*, means 'breasts', in reference to two rounded sandy hills to the west of the village. In 1535 Jacques Cartier (1491–1557) visited the site, which became a major trading centre during the next two centuries. Its post office opened in 1851. The village was erected in 1899 and the parish municipality was established in 1937. The latter was dissolved 12 years later because its population had declined below 500.

Tagish Charlie, Mount YT Located in the Ogilvie Mountains, in northern Yukon, this mountain was named in 1973 on the 75th anniversary of the discovery of gold on Bonanza Creek, a tributary of the Yukon River, by Tagish (later Dawson) Charlie (d.1908), George Carmack (1860–1922), and Skookum Jim Mason (c.1855–1916). A Tagish, he lived at Carcross and died here after a fall from a railway bridge.

Tagish Lake BC, YT This lake, southeast of Whitehorse, extends south from Tagish, YT, for 100 km and connects with Atlin Lake, BC, through Taku Arm. It was named in 1887 by geologist George M. Dawson (1848–1901) after the Tagish tribe. Four years earlier American Army Lt. Frederick Schwatka (1849–92) had called it *Lake Bove* after Lt. Bove of the Italian Navy, but Dawson restored the Aboriginal designation. The Tagish, who originally spoke an Athapaskan dialect, now speak the language and follow the customs of the coastal Tlingit.

Tahsis BC This village (1979) is located at the head of **Tahsis Inlet**, an arm of Nootka Sound, and west of Campbell River. A post office was established here in 1938. The name of the inlet is a Nootka word meaning 'trail at beach', referring to the practice of coming up the inlet by boat, and then proceeding by a trail to the head of the north-flowing Nimpkish River, leading to the east side of Vancouver Island.

Takakkaw Falls BC On the Yoho River and in Yoho National Park, this set of falls (380 m) is the second highest in Canada, after Della Falls on Vancouver Island. It was named in 1897 by Sir William Van Horne (1843–1915). In Cree *takakkaw* means 'it is magnificent'.

Takla Lake BC Located east of Hazelton and north of Babine Lake, this lake was named in 1914. It was previously called *Tacla Lake* after the Carrier word for 'lower end of the lake', in reference to the original site of Bulkley House.

Talbotville Royal ON In Elgin County, northwest of St. Thomas, it was first called *Five Stakes* in 1811, after five survey stakes marking the junction of five roads in Southwold Township. First postmaster and innkeeper John Allworth named it in 1853 after Col. Thomas Talbot (1771–1853). Talbot, who was born at Malahide Castle, north of Dublin, was the private secretary to Lt.-Gov. John Graves Simcoe, 1792–4. In 1801 he was granted 2023 ha (5000 a) of land south of London, and eventually quadrupled his land holdings, while promoting British immigration to the area.

Talchako Mountain BC Located in the Coast Mountains, southeast of Bella Coola, this mountain (3063 m) was named about 1933 by climber Walter Alfred (Don) Munday (1890–1950) after the **Talchako River**, named in 1922 by the Geographic Board. The name may be a reference to the devil in either the Carrier or the Bella Coola language.

Taloyoak NU Located on the west side of the south end of Boothia Peninsula, this hamlet (1981) had been called *Spence Bay* in 1964. The Inuit name, in use for many generations, was adopted in 1992. In Inuktitut the name means 'caribou blind', in reference to a pair of stone piles along a path where hunters speared caribou. The bay was named in 1831 by Sir John Ross (1777–1856) after a relative.

Tancook Island NS This placei s located on Big Tancook Island, in the entrance to Mahone Bay. A post office opened here in 1866. The island's name derives from the Mi'kmaq *Uktankook* ('facing the open sea'). **Little Tancook Island** is located on its east side.

Tanquary Fiord NU Extending north from Greely Fiord, in central Ellesmere Island, this fiord was named in 1915 by geologist W. Elmer Ekblaw (1882–1949) after Maurice Cole Tanquary (1881–1954), zoologist with the United States' Crocker Land Expedition, 1913–16.

Tantallon SK On the north bank of the Qu'Appelle River, southeast of Esterhazy, this village (1904) was founded in 1893 by the Reverend James Moffat Douglas (d.1920). Its post office opened in 1897. Douglas called it Tantallon after his ranch, which had been named after Tantallon Castle, east of Edinburgh. His ancestors built it as a stronghold, but it was destroyed in 1651.

Tantalus, Mount BC Located in the **Tantalus Range** of the Coast Mountains, northwest of Squamish, this mountain (2606 m) and the range were named about 1953 by climber Dr. Neal M. Carter after the unnamed mountains to the east, in the area of Mount Garibaldi, that tantalized early climbers. This recalled to him the Greek legend of King Tantalus, which described food and drink that was just beyond the king's grasp.

Tantramar River NB Rising east of Moncton, this river flows south through the **Tantamar Marshes**, and empties into Cumberland Basin, south of the town of Sackville. The name derives from the French *tintemarre* ('thundering noise') in reference either to the flocks of geese or to the rushing tide. Map-maker Dugald Campbell referred to it in 1799 as *Tantaramar*, and it was not until 1901 that the current spelling was confirmed.

Tara ON In 1999 this village (1880) became part of the municipality of Arran-Elderslie, Bruce County. Located southwest of Owen Sound, it was called *Eblana* in 1862 after an ancient name of Dublin, Ireland, but was changed to Tara two years later after the site of the ancient royal palaces northwest of Dublin.

Tarfu Creek YT A tributary of Lubbock River between Jakes Corner and Atlin, BC, this creek was named in 1949–50 by Canadian Army engineers after a variation of the Second World War phrase, which provided the name Snafu Creek. Tarfu means 'things are really fouled up'.

Taschereau QC This village in the regional county of Abitibi-Ouest, midway between Amos and La Sarre, was detached in 1980 from the municipality of **Taschereau**, which had been erected in 1926. The village was named after Louis-Alexandre Taschereau (1867–1952), premier of Quebec, 1920–36. Until then it had been called the township municipality of *Privat*, established in 1919 and named after the township proclaimed three years earlier. The township was named after Marc-Antoine de Privat, an officer in the Languedoc Regiment, who was wounded at the Battle of the Plains of Abraham, 1759.

Taseko Mountain BC Located in the Coast Mountains, northwest of Pemberton, this mountain (3062 m) was named about 1923 after the **Taseko River** and the **Taseko Lakes**, both named in 1911. In Chilcotin *taseko* means 'mosquito river'.

Tasiujaq QC This northern village near the mouth of the Rivière aux Feuilles, northwest of Kuujjuaq, was incorporated in 1980. The name in Inuktitut means 'it looks like a lake'.

Tatamagouche NS The name of this village (1950) situated on the south side of **Tatamagouche Bay** and west of Pictou, derives from the Mi'kmaq *Takamegoochk* ('barred across the entrance by sand'). Postal service was provided in 1738. An effort by early Scottish settler Wellwood Waugh to have it renamed *Southampton* failed.

Tathlina Lake NT Located southwest of Hay River, this lake (573 km²) was officially named in 1923. In 1875 Fr. Émile Petitot (1838–1916) made a reference to the lake, stating its meaning (possibly in Slavey) was 'river flowing out of a corner of a lake', in reference to its location, where Kakisa River flows north from the lake.

Tatlow, Mount BC Located in the Coast Mountains, east of Mount Waddington, this mountain (3062 m) was named in 1911 after Robert Garnett Tatlow (d.1910), provincial minister of finance, who was accidentally killed when his horse bolted, throwing him from his carriage.

Tatshenshini River BC, YT A tributary of the Alsek River, this river rises near Chilkat Pass and flows north into Yukon, where it turns south to cut its way through the St. Elias Mountains. It was officially approved by the Geographic Board in 1898, but its meaning is not provided in the names records. In 1993 the British Columbia government reserved this northwestern part of the province as **Tatshenshini-Alsek Wilderness Park**.

Tavistock ON In Oxford County, southeast of Stratford, this urban centre was first called *Freiburg* after a city in Baden, Germany and then *Inkerman* after a Crimean War battle. In 1857 postal authorities renamed it after the town of Tavistock, Devon, England, on the west edge of Dartmoor. In 1975 it was joined with East Zorra Township to form the municipal township of **East Zorra-Tavistock**.

Tay ON A township in Simcoe County, it was named in 1822 after a pet dog of Lady Sarah Maitland (1792–1873), the wife of Lt.-Gov. Sir Peregrine Maitland (1777–1854). In 1994, it annexed the villages of Victoria Harbour and Port McNicholl. *See also* Tiny.

Taylor BC This district municipality (1989) on the Peace River, southeast of Fort St. John, was named in 1906 after homesteader D.H. (Herbie) Taylor, a former Hudson's Bay Company trader.

Tecumseh ON In 1999 this town (1921) became part of the town of Tecumseh, with the village of St.Clair Beach and the township of Sandwich South, Essex County. East of Windsor, it was named *Ryegate* in 1870. Six years later it was renamed after Tecumseh Road, the old route from Windsor to Chatham named after the famous Shawnee chief Tecumseh, who fought on the British side during the War of 1812, dying near present-day Thamesville in 1813.

Tecumseth ON Established as a township in Simcoe County in 1822, this community was named after the great Shawnee chief Tecumseh, who was killed in 1813 at the Battle of Moraviantown. The spelling followed that of a vessel called *Tecumseth*, sunk in 1819 at Penetanguishene. In 1991 it was united with the town of Alliston and the villages of Tottenham and Beeton to form the town of **New Tecumseth**.

Teepee Mountain BC Located in the Rocky Mountains, northeast of Cranbrook, this mountain (3118 m) was named in 1933 by climber Katie Gardiner after the shape of its summit. She and Lillian Gest made its first ascent that year.

Teeswater ON This village (1874) on the **Teeswater River** and in Bruce County, southwest of Walkerton, was named in 1856. The river had been named four years earlier after the River Tees in England, which forms the boundary between Yorkshire and County Durham. In 1998 the village and the township of Culross became the township of Teeswater-Culross Mildmay-Carrick. In 1999, the township became part of the municipality of South Bruce, Bruce County.

Telegraph Creek BC On the Stikine River, where **Telegraph Creek** flows into it from the north, this place's post office was named in 1899. The creek was named in 1866, when the projected Collins Overland Telegraph, designed to connect the United States with Russia, was surveyed up the creek. It was abandoned when the trans-atlantic cable was successfully laid that year, but several names, including Telegraph Creek, remain as evidence of the project.

Telkwa BC Located in the Bulkley River valley, south of Smithers, this village (1952) is located at the mouth of the

Telkwa River. Its post office opened in 1910. In Carrier the name possibly means 'frog'.

Temagami ON This municipal township in Nipissing District, north of North Bay, is located at the east end of the Northeast Arm of **Lake Temagami**. The Hudson's Bay Company's Temagamang Post was located at the lake in 1834. The site was named *Timagami* in 1903, when the Temiskaming and Northern Ontario Railway was built through it. The lake's name was spelled *Timagami* until 1968, when the Ontario names authority was persuaded to accept the preferred spelling, but the postal name was not changed to Temagami until 1974. The name means 'deep lake' in Ojibwa.

Témiscaming QC Located on the east bank of the Ottawa River, northeast of North Bay, this town was created in 1920 as *Kipawa*, which had annexed *South Temiscaming* and *Lumsen's Mill*. The next year, however, it was renamed Témiscaming, after the municipality of **Témiscaming**, erected in 1888. Its name derives from the nearby Lac Témiscamingue.

Témiscamingue QC This regional county in north-western Quebec was established in 1981. It took its name from the former county, which had been named after **Lac Témiscamingue**, taken from Algonquin *Timi-s-timing* ('there is deep and shallow water'). In the lower 80 km of its 122-km length, the lake is narrow and quite deep, but the north part is much wider and relatively shallow. In Ontario the official spelling is Timiskaming.

Témiscouata QC This regional county southeast of Rivière-du-Loup was named in 1992 after the former county, which was called after the 40-km-long **Lac Témiscouata**. Noted in 1683 as *Cecemiscouata* and in 1746 as *Temisquata*, the name in Mi'kmaq means 'deep lake'.

Temple, Mount AB Northwest of Banff, this mountain (3543 m) was named in 1884 by geologist George M. Dawson (1849–1901) after Sir Richard Temple (1826–1902), who led an expedition to the Rockies that year.

Terence Bay NS Located on the Atlantic Ocean, 33 km southwest of Halifax, this place was early known by a variety of names, including *Terrants Bay*, *Turns Bay*, *Turner Bay*, and *Twins Bay*. Postal service was provided at *Turns Bay* in 1856, but it was renamed Terence Bay that year.

Terrace BC This city (1987) on the Skeena River, east of Prince Rupert, was established as a village in 1927 and a district municipality in 1960. It was settled in 1905 by George Little, who laid out a townsite in 1911 and called it *Littleton*. The post office department declined to accept the name because of similar names elsewhere in Canada. Little then proposed Terrace after a series of four benches on the north side of the Skeena, and the post office opened on 1 January 1912.

Terrace Bay ON This municipal township on the north shore of Lake Superior and in Thunder Bay District, east of Schreiber, was founded in 1947 and named after a series of flat terraces separated by escarpments and cliffs. They had developed after the last ice age, as the water level of Lake Superior receded.

Terra Nova River NL Rising in the east central part of Newfoundland, this river flows into Bonavista Bay at Glovertown. It took its name from the Latin rendering of the island's name, used by Girolamo da Verrazzano (c.1485–1528) in 1529. **Terra Nova National Park** (397 km²) was established in 1957.

Terrebonne QC Situated on the north shore of the Rivière des Mille-Îles, north of Montreal, the town of Terrebonne was established in 1860, having being erected as a village seven years earlier and a parish municipality in 1855. The seigneury of Terrebonne (Terbonne) was granted to André Daulier Des Landes in 1673. It was named because the fertility of the land ('*terre*') was equally good ('*bonne*') in every concession.

Terrenceville NL Located at the northeastern head of Placentia Bay, this town (1972) was first known as *Head of Fortune Bay* and *Fortune Bay Bottom*. It was renamed in 1905, likely after Sir John Terence Nicholls O'Brien (1830–1903), governor of Newfoundland, 1889–95.

Terry Fox, Mount BC Located in Mount Robson Provincial Park, south of Yellowhead Pass, this mountain (2651 m) was named in 1981 after Terrance Stanley (Terry) Fox (1958–81), who set out from St. John's, NL, in 1980 to run across the country to raise funds for cancer research. Running with one artificial leg, his Marathon of Hope came to an end at Thunder Bay, ON, when the renewed cancer forced him to curtail the heroic run.

Teslin YT This village, located on the eastern shore of Teslin Lake, became the site of Tom Smith's trading post in 1903, and its post office opened 10 years later. The lake extends south for 125 km from Johnsons Crossing, YT, into British Columbia. The **Teslin River** (393 km) rises in British Columbia and drains the lake north to the Yukon River, downriver from Lake Laberge. The Tagish called it *Nasathane* ('no salmon'). In 1881 Michael Byrne, of the Western Union Telegraph Company, was told it was called *Hootalinkwa*. American Army Lt. Frederick Schwatka (1849–92) called it *Newberry River* after an American professor, but it was ignored. In the Athapaskan language spoken here in the 1800s, possibly Tagish or Nahane, *Teslintoo* meant 'long, narrow water'.

Tête Jaune Cache BC This community is located at the west end of the Yellowhead Pass and on the Fraser River, northwest of Valemount. The name means 'yellow head's hiding place', which recalls Pierre Bostonais (d.1827) who was part Iroquois. This yellow-headed trader, who worked with both the North West Company and the Hudson's Bay Company, also provided the name Yellowhead Pass.

Texada Island BC Located in the Strait of Georgia, south of Powell River, this island (351 km²) was named *Isla de Texada* in 1791 by Spanish Capt. José Maria Narvaez (1768–1840) after Spanish RAdm. Felix de Tejada (or Texada).

Thamesford ON On the **Middle Thames River** and in Oxford County, west of Woodstock, this place was named when the post office opened in 1851.

Thames River ON Rising near Tavistock, Oxford County, this river flows southwest through Woodstock, London, and Chatham to Lake St. Clair. During the French regime it was called *Rivière à la Tranche* ('cutting river'), possibly because at its mouth it appeared to be cutting through tall trees. It was renamed in 1792 after England's River Thames by Lt.-Gov. John Graves Simcoe (1752–1806). Its main branches, the **North Thames** and the **Middle Thames Rivers**, rise near Stratford.

Thamesville ON This village (1873) in Kent County, northeast of Chatham, was named in 1832 when the post office opened, and village lots were laid out 20 years later on the southeast side of the Thames River. Lots were also laid out on the northwest side and named *Tecumseh* after the great Shawnee chief who died nearby in 1813. When a railway was built through *Tecumseh* in 1854, its station was called Thamesville after the post office was transferred here.

Thedford ON The post office in this village (1877) in Lambton County, northeast of Sarnia, was named in 1867 by Nelson Southworth, a native of Thetford, VT. He had donated a site in 1859 for a railway station, which was then called *Widder* after a nearby place. A misinterpretation of handwriting resulted in the spelling error. The village of Thedford in central Nebraska was named after the Ontario village.

Thelon River NT, NU Rising in Whitefish Lake, east of Great Slave Lake, this river (904 km) flows northeast to Baker Lake and Chesterfield Inlet. In Chipewyan the name means 'whitefish'. In Inuktitut the river is called *Arkinlinik* ('wooded river').

Theodora SK This village (1907) northwest of Yorkton was named in 1893 after Theodora Seeman, the wife of Richard Seeman, a wealthy landowner from London, England. He bought 80,000 acres along the Manitoba and North Western Railway.

The Pas MB Located at the point where the Pasquia River flows into the Saskatchewan River, the site of this town (1912) has a long history relating to exploration, fur trading, and resource development. Its name has its roots in the Cree *opasquaow* ('narrows between wooded banks'). During the period of French exploration, the name was rendered as *Le Pas*, coincidentally part of the family name of the wife of explorer Pierre Gaultier de La Vérendrye (1685–1755).

Thérèse-De Blainville QC This regional county, north of Rivière des Mille-Îles, comprises part of the former county of Terrebonne. Its name, given in 1982, united the names of Marie-Thérèse Dugué de Boisbriand (1671–1744) and her son-in-law, Louis-Jean-Baptiste Céleron de Blainville (1696–1756), inheritors of parts of the seigneury of Mille-Îles.

The Spanish River ON This municipal township in Sudbury District extends 80 km from Espanola on the east to the mouth of the Spanish River on the west. It was created in 1975 by amalgamating the townships of Salter, May, Harrow, Victoria, and Hallam.

Thessalon ON The post office in this town (1892) at the mouth of the **Thessalon River**, Algoma District, southeast of Sault Ste. Marie, was named *Thessalon River* in 1874 and shortened to Thessalon in 1881. The river was described by explorer René de Bréhant de Galinée (1645–78) in 1669 as *R de Tessalon*. The name derives from the Ojibwa *Neyashewan* ('point of land') referring to the 2-km-long **Thessalon Point**.

Thetford Mines QC Known as the city of white gold and the world capital of asbestos, this city was established in 1905. Its name had been chosen for the post office in 1881 after the township of Thetford, proclaimed in 1802, and named after Thetford, Norfolk, England. In 1892 the area of the present city had been incorporated as the village of *Kingsville*, named after William King (d.1892), a wealthy owner of the mines.

Thicket Portage MB Located on the Hudson Bay Railway, south of Thompson, this place is on a narrow isthmus separating Landing and Wintering lakes. In Cree it is called *Sagaskawskow Uniga* ('heavily wooded crossing place').

Thlewiaza River NU Draining Nueltin Lake east into Hudson Bay, this river's name in Chipewyan means 'small fish' or 'whitefish'.

Thompson MB This city (1970) was created in 1956 and named after International Nickel Company president Dr. John F. Thompson. In 1956 large deposits of nickel had been discovered in the area, and smelting, concentrating, and refining of nickel, copper, cobalt, and precious metals were undertaken five years later. Thompson is the third largest city of the province, with a population of 14,000.

Thompson River BC This river (489 km to the head of the North Thompson River) was named on 20 June 1808 by Simon Fraser (1776–83) after geographer David Thompson (1770–1857), who explored the West extensively but is not known to have seen the river. Five years later, Thompson named the Fraser River after Simon Fraser.

Thorhild AB The post office in this village (1949) northeast of Edmonton opened in 1914, 7 km east of its present location. When the Alberta and Great Waterways Railway was built in 1914 to Lac La Biche, the post office was moved to the line. It is said that first postmaster M.G. Jardy was inspired by lightning and thunder on a nearby hill, and created the name from the hill and the Norse god Thor.

Thornbury ON In 1998 this town (1887) became part of the town of Blue Mountains, Grey County. Located on Georgian Bay and 46 km east of Owen Sound, its post office was named in 1853 by surveyor William Gifford after Thornbury, Gloucestershire, England, north of Bristol.

Thorndale ON In 2001 this community became part of the municipality of Thames Centre, Middlesex County. Northeast of London, its post office was named in 1859 after the Irish residence of settler Lt. Col. James Shanly, a native of County Meath, Ireland.

Thornhill ON Divided down the middle between the city of Vaughan and the town of Markham in York Region, this urban centre's post office was named in 1829 after miller Benjamin Thorne (1794–1848), who settled here in 1820. Thorne, a prosperous importer and exporter, became one of two presidents of the Bank of Montreal in 1842. He was bankrupted after the repeal of Britain's Corn Laws in 1846.

Thornloe ON The post office in this village (1916) in Timiskaming District, northwest of New Liskeard was named in 1909 after the Right Reverend George Thorneloe (1896–1926), the Anglican bishop of Algoma.

Thorold ON This city (1975) in Niagara Region embraces part of the area of the township of Thorold, named in 1798 in Lincoln County after Sir John Thorold (1734–1815), who represented Lincolnshire in the British House of Commons. Thorold post office was named in 1826.

Thorsby AB The post office in this village (1949) southwest of Edmonton was named in 1908 after the Norse god Thor and the Norse word *by* ('village').

Thousand Islands ON Located in the St. Lawrence River, between Kingston and Brockville, these islands were described as *Mille Isles* in 1721 by French historian Pierre-François-Xavier Charlevoix (1682–1761), although he concluded that there were only about 500 islands. Various counts have ranged from 1149 to 1800. Checking large-scale navigation charts, a methodical count in 1985 revealed 1149 islands and islets, 665 on the Canadian side and 484 on the American side. There are only 367 islands with official names, with 241 of these on the Canadian side of the border.

Three Hills AB The post office in this town (1929) northeast of Calgary was established in 1904. There are three small hills running in a line from southeast to northwest.

Three Mile Plains NS This place is located three miles (5 km) southeast of Windsor and in a flat physiographic area. Its post office opened in 1865, closed in 1873, and reopened in 1900. An effort to name the place Mapleton in 1901 failed.

Thrums BC This community northeast of Castlegar was named in 1906 after a 'Scottish village', described by Sir James Barrie in *A Window in Thrums* (1889). Perhaps he had Thrumster in mind, 7 km southwest of Wick, Caithness, or another village to which he attached this fictitious name.

Thunder Bay ON This city on **Thunder Bay**, at the head of Lake Superior, was created in 1970 through the amalgamation of Fort William, Port Arthur, and parts of the municipal townships of Neebing and Shuniah. Only three names were on the ballot, with Thunder Bay receiving 15,821 votes; Lakehead, 15,302; and The Lakehead, 8477. Although the majority of voters preferred a form of 'Lakehead', the ballot was skewed against it. However, Thunder Bay was soon fully accepted. **Thunder Bay District** was created in 1871.

Thurlow ON In 1998 this township became part of the city of Belleville, Hastings County. It was named in 1787 after Edward Thurlow, 1st Baron Thurlow (1732–1806), who held many British ministerial posts, including solicitor general, attorney general, and lord chancellor.

Thurlow Islands BC Located between Vancouver Island and the mainland, north of Campbell River, these islands were named in 1792 by Capt. George Vancouver (1757–98) after Edward Thurlow, 1st Baron Thurlow, who had been appointed British chancellor of the exchequer in 1778. The two islands are officially known as **East Thurlow Island** and **West Thurlow Island**.

Thurso QC This town in the regional county of Papineau, east of Buckingham, was created in 1963, having been organized as a village in 1886. The post office was named in 1853 after the town of Thurso, in the north of Scotland, from where some pioneer settlers emigrated to western Quebec in 1807.

Tide Head NB The post office in this village (1966) west of Campbellton was named *Head of Tide* in 1873 after the head

of the tide of the Restigouche River. The post office was renamed Tide Head in 1920.

Tidnish NS On the shore of Northumberland Strait, and near the New Brunswick border, this place's post office was named in 1861 after the **Tidnish River**. The name of the river derives from the Mi'kmaq *tedeneche* ('straight across') in reference to a straight entrance into the river. *See also* Tignish.

Tiedemann, Mount BC In the Coast Mountains, directly east of Mount Waddington, this mountain (3848 m) was named in 1926 by climber Walter Alfred (Don) Munday (1890–1950) after surveyor Hermann Otto Tiedeman (1821–91). In 1862 he surveyed a railway route for Alfred Waddington to connect Vancouver Island with the rest of Canada. In 1875 Canadian Pacific Railway surveyors named **Tiedemann Glacier**, which extends southeast from the mountain.

Tignish PE Located near the northwestern end of the province, this municipal community (1983) had been incorporated as a village in 1952. It was named after the **Tignish River**, whose name may derive from the Mi'kmaq *Tedeneche* ('straight across') referring to the direct entrance to the harbour through **Tignish Run**. *See also* Tidnish.

Tilbury ON In 1999 Tilbury North Township and Tilbury West Township became parts of the town of Lakeshore, Essex County. Tilbury and Tilbury East Township became parts of the municipality of **Chatham-Kent**, Kent County. Tilbury and Tilbury East were named in 1794, both after the town of Tilbury in Essex, England. Tilbury North Township in Essex County was taken from Tilbury West in 1891. The town (1910) of Tilbury in Kent County had been incorporated as the village of *Tilbury Centre* in 1887, and was shortened to Tilbury in 1896.

Tilley AB This village (1940) southeast of Brooks was named in 1894 by the Canadian Pacific Railway after Sir Samuel Leonard Tilley (1818–96), a Father of Confederation, minister of customs and of finance in Ottawa, and lieutenant-governor of New Brunswick. His brother, Sir Malcolm Tilley, was a CPR director.

Tilley Ridge NB South of the Nepisiguit River, this ridge was named in 1964 by Arthur F. Wightman (1905–88), the provincial names authority, after Sir Samuel Leonard Tilley (1818–96), a Father of Confederation and lieutenant-governor of New Brunswick, 1873–8 and 1885–93.

Tillsonburg ON The post office in this town in Oxford County was named in 1836 after George Tillson, a native of Massachusetts who settled here in 1825 and built a sawmill and a forge. It was incorporated as the town of *Tilsonburg* in 1872, with the spelling being corrected by an act of the Ontario Legislature in 1902.

Tilting NL Located on Fogo Island and southeast of Joe Batt's Arm, this municipal community (1975) had been known as *Tilton Harbour* after the tilts (shacks) built here for migratory fishermen. In 1906 the present name was adopted to distinguish the place from Tilton on the west side of Conception Bay

Tilton NL Located on the northwestern side of Spaniard's Bay and southwest of Harbour Grace, this local improvement district (1979) was formerly called *Tilts* in reference to the temporary huts used by early fishermen. Soon after 1900, the Reverend Dr. William Pilot (1841–1913), the superintendent of Church of England and Salvation Army schools, proposed renaming it Tilton.

Timberlea NS West of Halifax, this place was first known as *Nine Mile River*. Its post office opened as *Bowser Station* in 1905, named for hotel keeper Angus Bowser. It was renamed Timberlea in 1917 after the meadows and an active lumbering and sawmilling industry in the area from the mid-1800s.

Timiskaming ON Created as a district in 1902, this town was named after Lake Timiskaming. The lake received its name from Algonquin *Timi-s-timing* ('there is deep and shallow water'). In the lower 80 km of its 122-km length, it is narrow and quite deep, but the north part is much wider and relatively shallow. In Quebec, the official spelling is Témiscamingue for the lake and the regional county, and Témiscaming for the town.

Timmins ON This city is now the second city in its area (3000 km²) in Canada, with the city of Greater Sudbury having the area of 3300 km2. It was founded in 1911 by Noah and Henry Timmins, former Mattawa storekeepers. They made a fortune in silver mining at Cobalt. Noah Timmins (1867–1936) became the president of Hollinger Consolidated Gold Mines Ltd.

Tiny ON This township in Simcoe County was named in 1822 after a pet dog of Lady Sarah Maitland (1792–1873), the wife of Lt.-Gov. Sir Peregrine Maitland (1777–1854). *See also* Tay.

Tisdale SK This town (1920) east of Melfort was named in 1904 by the Canadian Northern Railway after Frederick W. Tisdale, an agent of the Canadian Northern. Its post office opened the same year. It was earlier called *Doghide*, after the river flowing south through the town. The postmaster asked the chief geographer of Canada in 1905 whether Doghide River could be renamed, as 'you would confer a great favour on me and also all the people of Tisdale and community', but it was never changed. Tisdale's motto is 'The Land of Rape and Honey'.

Tiverton NS Located on the northeast end of Long Island, and southwest of Digby, the first post office at this village (1969) was called *Petite Passage* in 1862 after the narrow Petit Passage, separating the island from Digby Neck. It was renamed Tiverton in 1883 after the birthplace of teacher Thomas Mildon in Tiverton, Devon, England.

Tiverton ON In 1999 this village (1878) became part of the municipality of Kincardine, Bruce County. It is located northeast of Kincardine. The post office was named in 1860 after a town in England's Devon, north of Exeter.

Tobermory ON In 1999 this community became part of the municipality of Northern Bruce Peninsula, Bruce County. It was first known as *St. Edmunds* after the township and *Bury* after Viscount Bury (1832–94), the superintendent of Indian affairs in the 1850s who organized the purchase of the peninsula from the Ojibwa. It was renamed in 1882 after Tobermory, Island of Mull, Scotland.

Tobique River NB Rising in the west central part of the province, this river flows southwest to enter the Saint John River at Perth-Andover. It was named after a Maliseet chief, possibly Noel Toubic (c.1706–67), who once lived at the mouth but died at Kingsclear, west of the centre of Fredericton. In Maliseet it was called *Naygoot* or *Naygootcook*, probably meaning 'flat banks beside it'. Some early maps combined both names, such as *R. Tobed Nigaurlegoh* on Charles Morris's map of 1765. Dugald Campbell called it *Tobique's River* on his 1784 map.

Toby, Mount BC Located in the Purcell Mountains and on the east side of Kootenay Lake, this mountain (3222 m) was named in 1888 after Dr. Levi Toby, a physician and prospector who had settled nearby in 1864.

Tofield AB This town (1909) southeast of Edmonton was named in 1908 by the Grand Trank Pacific Railway after the local school district. It had been named after Dr. James Henry Tofield (1849–1918), who settled briefly at the site of the town in 1896, before moving to near Fort Saskatchewan and then returning to Tofield in 1903. The name fits the alphabetical arrangement used by the Grand Trunk Pacific Railway, with Ryley and Shonts to the southeast.

Tofino BC This district municipality (1984) on the east side of Clayoquot Sound and on the west coast of Vancouver Island was named after **Tofino Inlet**, an easterly arm of the sound. The inlet was named in 1792 by Dionisio Alcalá Galiano (1760–1805) and Cayetano Valdés (1767–1834) after Spanish hydrographer Vincente Tofiño de San Miguel (1732–95).

Togo SK Located on the Manitoba border, southeast of Canora, this village (1906) was founded in 1904 by the

Canadian Northern Railway and named after VAdm. Heihachiro Togo (1848–1934), whose Japanese Navy had defeated the Russian forces during the Russo-Japanese War, 1904–5. The post office opened in 1905.

Toledo ON In 2001 this community became part of the township of Elizabethtown-Kitley, united counties of Leeds and Grenville. Located 20 km south of Smiths Falls, it was first known as *Koyl's Bridge*, *Kitley Corners*, and *Chamberlain's Corners*. *Kitley* post office, opened in 1832, was renamed Toledo in 1856 after either the city in Spain or the city in Ohio.

Tombstone Mountain YT Northeast of Dawson, at the head of **Tombstone River**, this mountain (2499 m) was named *Mount Campbell* in 1896 by surveyor William Ogilvie (1849–1912) after Hudson's Bay Company trader Robert Campbell (1808–94). Unaware of that name, miners called it after a great shaft of black rock, which rises 1600 m above the surrounding terrain.

Tompkins SK On the main Canadian Pacific Railway line, southwest of Swift Current, this village (1910) was named in 1883 after railway contractor Thomas Tompkins. Its post office was named in 1904.

Toodoggone River BC Rising northwest of Williston Lake, this river is a tributary of the Finlay River. It was earlier called *Two Brothers Creek* and was known to the Sekani as *Thudegade*. In Sekani the word *toodoggone* may mean 'water's arms' or 'eagle nest'. **Toodoggone Peak** (2350 m) is situated on the north side of the river.

Topley BC Located in the Bulkley River valley, east of Houston, this place's post office opened in 1921 and named after pioneer settler William J. Topley (1845–1930).

Torbay NL This town (1972), north of St. John's, is located on **Tor Bay**. In 1612 pioneer settler John Guy (d.1629) referred to it as *Torrebay*. It would appear that the bay may have been named by English fishermen, because of its resemblance to Tor Bay, adjacent to Devon, England.

Tornado Mountain AB, BC On the continental divide, north of the Crowsnest Pass, this mountain (3099 m) was named about 1917 by Richard W. Cautley (1873–1953) of the Alberta–British Columbia Boundary Commission because it seemed to be the centre of thunderstorm activity. It was originally called *Gould Dome* in 1858 by surveyor Lt. Thomas Blakiston (1832–91). Gould Dome was then transferred 4 km to the southeast to a lower peak (2894 m).

Torngat Mountains QC, NL The Torngat Mountains extend north between Ungava Bay and Labrador Sea. In Inuktitut the name suggests a terrifying spirit which controls all the spirits

of the land, sea, sky, wind, and clouds. Mont d'Iberville, QC, and Mount Caubvick, NL, comprise the adjoining summits of the same mountain (15 m apart), the highest in the Torngats.

Toronto ON The capital of the province and Canada's largest city, its name derives from the Mohawk *tkaronto* ('trees standing in the water'), referring to ancient fish weirs in The Narrows between Lakes Simcoe and Couchiching. The oft-quoted 'place of meeting' is erroneous. The name was transferred (1680–1759) through *Lac de Taronto* (Lake Simcoe), *Passage de Taronto* (Holland River to the mouth of the Humber), *Rivière Taronto* (Humber River), and Fort Rouillé, also called Fort Toronto. Its site was known as Toronto until 1793, when Lt.-Gov. John Graves Simcoe (1752–1806) renamed it York after the Duke of York's victory in Flanders. It was renamed Toronto when it was incorporated as a city in 1834. Most of the area of the present city of Mississauga was named *Toronto Township* in 1805. Toronto Gore Township, named in 1819, was merged with the city of Brampton in 1974. On 1 January 1998 the cities of Etobicoke, North York, Scarborough, and the borough of East York became parts of the city of Toronto.

Torquay SK A village (1923) west of Estevan, it was named in 1913, when the Canadian Pacific Railway built a line west to Minton. A railway official is reported to have said that its well water reminded him of Torquay on the Devon coast, east of Plymouth, England. It received its post office in 1914.

Torrington AB In 1997 this village (1964) became a hamlet. Located southeast of Red Deer, it was named in 1930 by the Canadian Pacific Railway. It may have been named after Torrington, Devon, England.

Tosorontio ON Part of the municipal township of **Adjala-Tosorontio** in Simcoe County since 1994, this township was named in 1822. It is believed to have been named after a famous Mohawk chief, possibly John Deserontyon, also known as Odeserundiye (c.1740–1811), who led the Mohawk to the Bay of Quinte in 1784. *See also* Adjala-Tosorontio *and* Deseronto.

Tottenham ON In the town of New Tecumseth, Simcoe County, this urban centre was named in 1858 after the first postmaster Alexander Totten (1816–98). It also replicates the name of the well-known district of London, England.

Tracadie NS Located on the south side of St. Georges Bay and east of Antigonish, this place received postal service in 1834. The name derives from the Tracadie River, whose name derives from the Mi'kmaq *tulakadik* ('camping ground'). *See also* Grand Tracadie *and* Tracadie-Sheila.

Tracadie-Sheila NB This town (1992) in the northeastern part of the province is comprised of the former town (1966) of

Tracadie and the former village (1978) of Sheila. Its post office was called *Tracady* in 1845. It was renamed Tracadie six years later, after the **Big Tracadie River**. The river's name derives from the Mi'kmaq *Tulakadik* ('camping ground'). Samuel de Champlain (1567–1635) referred to it as *Tregate* in 1604, and map-maker Pierre Jumeau called it *R. tracadi* in 1685. In 1880 Surveyor General Thomas Loggie (1854–1931) identified it with its present name, but in 1948 the Canadian Board on Geographical Names authorized *Tracadie River*. The locally used name was endorsed in 1968. The post office in Sheila was named in 1898 after Sheila Foster, whose husband established the Tracadie Mills here in the 1890s.

Tracy NB the post office in this village (1966) south of Fredericton was called *Tracey Station* in 1871 and was renamed Tracy in 1925. Jeremiah Tracy (1744–1812), a native of Maine, was the first settler here. His son Jeremiah Tracy Jr. built a mill on Yoho Stream, and the latter's son Jeremiah ('Boss') Tracy became a well-known lumberman.

Tracy QC The town of Tracy is located on the west side of the mouth of the Richelieu opposite Sorel. It was created in 1954 when it was separated from the parish municipality of *Saint-Joseph-de-Sorel*. It was named after Alexandre de Prouville de Tracy (c.1596–1670), who built Fort Richelieu at the mouth of the river in 1665.

Trail BC The post office in this city (1901) on the Columbia River was named *Trail Creek* by Eugene S. Topping in 1891 and it was shortened to Trail in 1897. The creek was the Columbia River end of the Dewdney Trail, which was cut through from Hope by Edgar Dewdney (1835–1916) in 1860.

Tranquille BC On the north side of the Thompson River and at the west end of the city of Kamloops, the post office was named in 1916 after the **Tranquille River**. The river was named after a chief who had died in 1841. He was known to the French traders as being quiet ('*tranquille*') and patient.

Transcona MB This urban community in the eastern part of the city of Winnipeg had been an incorporated city before 1972. In 1910 its site had been chosen by the Grand Trunk Pacific Railway for its repair shops, with the name (chosen through a contest) being a blend of Transcontinental Railway and Strathcona. Lord Strathcona (1820–1914) drove the last spike of the first transcontinental line, the Canadian Pacific Railway, at Craigellachie, BC, in 1885.

Traytown NL On the north side of Terra Nova National Park and east of Glovertown, this municipal community (1978) was originally called Troytown. This name may derive from Troytown in Dorset, England, where the name is often equated with disorder or maze. Perhaps the maze of passages and channels in Bonavista Bay suggested the name. *See also* Triton.

Treherne MB Located southwest of Portage la Prairie, the post office in this village (1948) was named in 1880 after pioneer settler George Treherne. Six years later the Canadian Pacific Railway built a line from Winnipeg to Souris, and the site of the present village was relocated to the line.

Trenton NS This town (1911) on the north side of New Glasgow, was named in 1882 by Harvey Graham after Trenton, NJ. A noted manufacturing centre, it became the site of a steel plant that year, and glass, paint, railway cars, and woodworking operations were built here later.

Trenton ON In 1998 this city became part of the city of Quinte West, Hastings County. Located at the mouth of the **Trent River**, it was first known as *River Trent, Port Trent, Trent Port,* and *Trentown,* before the village was incorporated as Trenton in 1853. The river, named after the River Trent in central England, rises in Rice Lake, although its watershed drains the Kawartha Lakes north of Peterborough. The **Trent Canal** permitted navigation from Lake Ontario to Lake Simcoe in 1918, and the **Trent–Severn Waterway** was completed to Georgian Bay two years later.

Trepassey NL Located at the head of **Trepassey Bay** and near the southeastern end of the Avalon Peninsula, this town (1967) was named after the bay. The bay was shown on a map as *trepasse* about 1555, with the present form coming into use by the early 1600s. Edgar R. Seary (1908–84), author of *Place Names of the Avalon Peninsula* (1971), concluded that it was likely a transfer name from Baie des Trépassés, north of Pointe du Raz, on the southwestern side of Bretagne, France.

Trinity Bay NL Separating the north side of the Avalon Peninsula from the rest of the island of Newfoundland, this bay was called *Baia de s ciria* in the early 1500s after an obscure seventh-century saint of Portugal, and may have been given about 1500 by explorer Gaspar Corte-Real (c.1450–1502). It was only in the early 1600s that it acquired its present name. The municipal community (1969) of **Trinity** on the west side of the bay was called 'the best and largest harbour in all the land' by the 1689 *English Pilot. See also* Centreville-Wareham-Trinity.

Triton NL This town (1980) on the east side of **Triton Island**, which is in the western side of Notre Dame Bay, was formerly the rural district (1961) of *Triton-Jim's Cove-Card's Harbour*. The island may have been named after the expression 'troytown', used in the West Country (Devon) of England to describe a maze, perhaps in reference to the narrow tickles and difficult harbour entrances around the island. The island was settled by 1840 and Triton occurred in the census of 1845.

Trochu AB This town (1962) southeast of Red Deer was first known as *Trochu Valley* after Armand Trochu (1857–1930), who led a group of French Army officers to Alberta in 1905, and established the St. Ann Ranch Trading Company. When the place became a village in 1911, its name was shortened to Trochu. Most of the officers returned to France when the First World War broke out, and Armand Trochu himself returned in 1917.

Trois-Pistoles QC On the south shore of the St. Lawrence and southwest of Rimouski, this town was established in 1916. It took its name from the **Rivière des Trois Pistoles**, which appeared on the 1631 map by Jean Guérard. The real story about the naming of the river has been lost in the mists of time. Perhaps it might relate to a tale of a sailor losing a silver goblet, valued at three *pistoles* (gold coins), while dipping for fresh water, or it may refer to three firearms.

Trois-Rivières QC Located at the mouth of the Rivière Saint-Maurice, where the islands of La Poterie and Saint-Quentin separate the three outlets of the river, this city has had a long and vibrant history. The parish of Immaculée-Conception-des-Trois-Rivières was set up in 1615, and was formally erected in 1678. The post office was called *Three Rivers* from 1763 to 1906, when it was changed to its present form. The city was incorporated as both Trois-Rivières and *Three Rivers* until 1937, when the English form was abolished. *Three Rivers* remained in popular use among English-language speakers and the media until about 1980. Since then the English-language media (radio, television, newspapers, magazines) have used Trois-Rivières.

Trout Creek ON This town (1913) in Parry Sound District and on a tributary of the South River, south of North Bay was first known as *Little Bend of the South River*, *Melbourne*, and *Barkerton*, before it was named Trout Creek in 1890.

Trout River NL This municipal community (1966) on the west coast of Newfoundland and southwest of Gros Morne National Park was settled about 1830. It was noted in the census of 1857. The river rises in the Long Range Mountains and flows through the Upper Trout River Pond to the Gulf of St. Lawrence.

Truro NS This town (1875) was named in 1759, after Truro, Cornwall, England. Its post office opened in 1812. During the French regime, the Acadian settlement was called *Cobequid* after the nearby Cobequid Bay.

Trutch, Mount AB, BC This mountain (3210 m), southwest of Howse Pass, was named in 1920 after Sir Joseph Trutch (1826–1904), lieutenant-governor of British Columbia, 1871–6.

Tryon River PE Flowing into the Northumberland Strait, southeast of Borden-Carleton, this river was named in 1765 after William Tryon (1725–88), a former governor of New York, who later became lieutenant-governor of South Carolina. Samuel Holland (1728–1801) served under Tryon during the American Revolution. *Tryon River* post office opened in 1827 and became **Tryon** about 1864. Another post office opened at **North Tryon** in 1872

Tsar Mountain BC Located in the Clemenceau Icefield and south of Athabasca Pass, this mountain (3424 m) was named in 1920 by surveyor Arthur O. Wheeler (1860–1945) because he was struck by its majestic domination of its surroundings.

Tsiigehtchic NT The name of this charter community (1993) at the confluence of the Arctic Red River with the Mackenzie River name replaced *Arctic Red River* in 1994. The name in Gwich'in means 'mouth of the iron river', in reference to the reddish colour of the Arctic Red River.

Tuckersmith ON In 2001 this township became part of the municipality of Huron East, Huron County. It was named in 1830 after Martin Tucker Smith (1803–80), a director of the Canada Company, a British company established in 1826 to develop the Huron Tract, a large area of what is now Southwestern Ontario.

Tugaske SK This village (1908) northwest of Moose Jaw was founded by the Canadian Pacific Railway in 1907 and named after the Cree word for 'flat land' or 'good land'. Its post office opened the following year.

Tuktoyaktuk NT On the shore of Beaufort Sea and northeast of Inuvik, this hamlet (1970) was known as *Tuktuyaktok* from 1928 to 1936, when the Hudson's Bay Company opened its Port Brabant post there and named it after HBC chief factor Angus Brabant. *Port Brabant* post office opened in 1948, but was renamed Tuktoyaktuk in 1950. In Inuvialuktun the word *tuktuujaartuq* means 'rock caribou place'. There is a legend that a shaman went looking for food for the hungry Inuvialuit. He turned to find two caribou, escaping into the sea and into protruding rocks. The hamlet is commonly called both Tuk and Tuktuk.

Tuktut Nogait National Park NT Located on the south shore of Amundsen Gulf, east of Inuvik, this national park (28,000 km²) was established in 1996. In Inuvialuktun the name means 'calving ground of the young caribou'.

Tulita NT Located at the confluence of the Great Bear and Mackenzie Rivers, this hamlet (1984) was formerly known as *Fort Norman*. It was renamed Tulita on 1 January 1996 after the Slavey word for 'where the waters meet'. Named by the Hudson's Bay Company in 1810, after either Alexander Norman McLeod or Archibald Norman McLeod. *Fort Norman* had been created a hamlet in 1984.

Tumbler Ridge BC This district municipality was created in 1981 to provide for community facilities for coal miners and their families in the Rocky Mountain Foothills, 112 km southwest of Dawson Creek. Its town centre was developed in the following three years. The ridge, on the east side of the town centre, rises some 375 m above the site of the municipality's town centre.

Tupper, Mount BC This mountain (2816 m) in the Selkirk Mountains, north of Rogers Pass, was first known as *Hermit Mountain*. It was renamed in 1895, after Sir Charles Tupper (1821–1915), prime minister of Canada from 1 May 1896 to 8 July 1896.

Turnberry ON In 2001 this township became part of the municipality of **Morris–Turnberry**, Huron County. It was named in 1850 after Turnberry Castle, southwest of Ayr, Scotland, and at the mouth of the Firth of Clyde. The castle had long associations with the ancestors of James Bruce, 8th Earl of Elgin, governor of the Province of Canada, 1847–54.

Turner Valley AB The post office in this town (1930) south of Calgary was named in 1926 after Robert and James Turner, who had homesteaded in the Sheep River valley in 1886.

Turtle Mountain MB Situated south of Boissevain and on the North Dakota border, this range of hills exhibits the outline of a turtle. Alexander Henry the younger (d.1814) mentioned it in 1806, and the maps of David Thompson (1770–1857) in 1814 and Peter Fidler (1769–1822) identified it. Robert Douglas, in his *Place-Names of Manitoba* (1933), claimed the turtle was the dove or pigeon, not the tortoise, but North Dakota state historian Dana Wright, in Penny Ham's *Place Names of Manitoba* (1980), asserted that it was the tortoise.

Turtleford SK Northwest of North Battleford, the post office at this town (1983) was opened in 1913. It was named after a convenient crossing of the Turtlelake River, where the Canadian Northern Railway crossed it in 1914.

Tuscarora ON This township in Brant County was named in 1840 after the Tuscarora nation, which migrated in 1722 from North Carolina to New York to become the sixth of the Six Nations confederacy. The name means 'shirt wearer'.

Tusk Peak BC In the Clemenceau Icefield, northeast of Revelstoke, this peak (3360 m) was named in 1920 by the Alberta–British Columbia Boundary Commission after its 'sharp cone of rock'.

Tuzo, Mount AB, BC This mountain (3245 m) on the continental divide, south of Lake Louise, was named in 1906 by Henrietta Tuzo (1880–1955) who was the first to ascend it. She married Canadian geophysicist Dr. John A. Wilson (who used 'Tuzo' for his nickname).

Tweed ON In 1998 this village (1891) became part of the municipality of Tweed, Hastings County. Located 30 km north of Belleville, its post office was named in 1852 by miller James Jamison after the River Tweed, which forms part of the boundary between England and Scotland.

Tweedsmuir Provincial Park BC In the Coast Mountains, northeast of Bella Coola, this park was named in 1936 after John Buchan, 1st Lord Tweedsmuir (1875–1940), governor general of Canada, 1935–40.

Twillingate NL Situated on the west side of **South Twillingate Island**, this town (1962) was named after the two Twillingate islands. They took their name from Pointe de Toulinguet at the entrance to the harbour of Brest, Bretagne, France. In 1992 the town annexed Durrell, which had been incorporated as a town in 1971 when it had joined together the settlements of Durrell's Arm, Hart's Cove, Jenkin's Cove, Gillesport, and Blow-Me-Down. Durrell's Arm was likely named after an early fishing family. Twillingate also annexed the municipal community (1986) of Bayview, which had been an amalgamation of Manuel's Cove and Gillard's Cove.

Two Hills AB The post office in this town (1955) northeast of Vegreville was named in 1913 after two distinctive hills southwest of the town. Alexander Henry (d.1814) the younger commented in 1808 on *les Deux Grosses Buttes*, where he rested for an hour.

Tyendinaga ON This township in Hastings County was named in 1800 after Joseph Brant (1742–1809), whose Mohawk name was Thayendanegea. After the American Revolution, he led many Mohawk to the area of the Bay of Quinte, and later to the Brantford area on the Grand River.

Tyne Valley PE The post office in this municipal community (1983) northwest of Summerside opened in 1872. The name had been proposed by James Rogers for a school district, likely after the River Tyne in Northumberland, England.

Tyrrell, Mount YT Southwest of Dawson, this mountain (1447 m) was named in 1906 on a Geological Survey map after geologist Joseph Burr Tyrrell (1858–1957), who extensively explored the Yukon and the Northwest Territories.

U

Ucluelet BC Located on the northwest side of Barkley Sound and on the west coast of Vancouver Island, this village (1952) was named in 1894 after the Nootka word meaning 'people of the sheltered bay', in reference to a protected landing place for canoes.

Ulukhaktok NT This hamlet (2006) is located on the southwestern shore of Diamond Jenness Peninsula, on Victoria Island, replacing Holman. Holman was a hamlet (1984) at the site in 1960 by the Hudson's Bay Company. It was previously called Holman Island after the island 8 km to the south. The island may have been named after John R. Holman, who was the surgeon general in 1853 and 1854 on the voyages of Edward Inglefield.

Ulu Mountain YT In the St. Elias Mountains, southeast of Mount Kennedy, this mountain (3097 m) was named in 1970 after the Inuit woman's knife, which was used that year as the symbol of the Arctic Winter Games held in Whitehorse.

Umingmaktok NU This settlement, on *Baychimo Harbour*, became the site in 1964 of the Hudson's Bay Company's Bathurst Inlet trading post. The post was called *Baychimo Harbour*, but confusion with Fort Chimo (now Kuujuak) in Quebec persuaded the HBC to call it Bathurst Inlet. As the former site at the mouth of Burnside River, 95 km to the south, was still called Bathurst Inlet, a new name was needed for the HBC trading post. Umingmaktok, named in 1975, took its name from an Inuktitut word meaning 'musk-ox place'. *See also* Bathurst Inlet.

Umiujaq QC This northern village on the eastern shore of Hudson Bay was founded in the mid-1980s by Inuit from Kuujjuarapik, who chose to move away from the busier centre, 160 km to the south, in order to be nearer to natural surroundings and wildlife. In Inuktitut, the name means 'it has the form of a loaf of bread', 'looks like a turned over ship', or 'it seems like a beard', all in reference to rounded grassy hills on the bar separating the bay from Lac Guillaume-Delisle.

Ungava Bay NU Administratively part of Nunavut Territory, this 250-km bay is surrounded on the east, south, and west by the province of Quebec. The bay has a width of 275 km at its mouth, from Cap Hopes Advance, QC, on the west to Killiniq Island, NL, NU, on the east side. Of uncertain meaning in Inuktitut,

Ungava may mean 'toward the open water', 'far away', 'unknown land', 'place to the south', or 'place visited by white whales'. The vast peninsula to the west of the bay, with a base of 520 km between Inukjuaq and the mouth of Rivière aux Feuilles, is called **Péninsule d'Ungava**. In 1879 the area of present-day Quebec north of the St. Lawrence River watershed was conveyed by the British government to Canada. The government of Canada called the area the provisional district of Ungava. It transferred Ungava to Quebec in 1912.

Unity SK The Grand Trunk Pacific Railway station in this town (1919) southwest of Battleford was named in 1909 after Unity, WI, southeast of Wausau. Its post office opened the following year.

Unwin, Mount AB This mountain (3268 m), on the west side of Maligne Lake, was named in 1908 by climber Mary Schäffer after guide Sidney Unwin, who climbed the mountain. He died in 1917 in France during the First World War.

Upper Arrow Lake BC The upper of the two Arrow lakes, this narrow 65-km-long widening of the Columbia River was named in the early 1800s after Arrow Rock. The rock was, before the flooding of the lake behind the Keenleyside Dam, a steep cliff on the east side of the Lower Arrow Lake where the arrows of Aboriginal warriors were lodged. Arrows that remained lodged in the rock were believed to bring good luck to the brave.

Upper Island Cove NL This town (1965) on the north side of Spaniard's Bay and on the west side of Conception Bay, was referred to as *Haylinscove* in 1697 and *Island Cove* in 1773. The cove is on the north side of Big Island, which is almost joined to the shore.

Upper Mazinaw Lake ON Located ear the head of the Mississippi River system, north of Kaladar, this lake was considered part of Mazinaw Lake until 1981, when it was divided at The Narrows into Lower and Upper Mazinaw lakes. *Mazinaw* is an Algonquin word meaning 'picture', referring to pictographs on the face of **Mazinaw Rock**, on the east shore of the lake.

Upsalquitch River NB Rising in its Northwest and Southeast branches, north of Mount Carleton, this river flows north into the Restigouche River, southwest of

Campbellton. Its name derives from the Mi'kmaq *Apsetkwechk* ('little river') in reference to its small size compared to the Restigouche. Shown on a map in 1786 as *Upsatquitch*, a map of 1803 by William Vondenvelden and Louis Chartrand did not have the 't' crossed, resulting in its current spelling.

Usborne ON In 2001 this township became part of the municipality of South Huron, Huron County. It was named in 1830 after Henry Usborne (c.1780–1840), a director of the Canada Company. This British company was established in 1826 to develop the Huron Tract, a large area of what is now Southwestern Ontario.

Utopia, Lake NB Northeast of St. George, this lake was named in 1784 by either Capt. Peter Clinch (1792–1846) or Lt.-Gov. Thomas Carleton (1736–1817), when it was discovered that a plan of land grants extended under the lake. Accessing the underwater regions would have been as impossible as achieving the ideal of Sir Thomas More's *Utopia* (1515–16). A second plan in 1829 stated that it was a 'Reserve to make good the deficiency caused by the Lake Eutopia'.

Uxbridge ON This municipal township in Durham Region was created in 1974 through the merging of the town of Uxbridge and the municipal townships of Scott and Uxbridge. The original township was named in 1798 after Uxbridge in Greater London, England, west of the city centre. The post office in the urban centre of **Uxbridge** was named in 1832.

Val-Bélair QC In 2002 this town became part of Quebec City. In 2006 it became a sector of Quebec. Located northwest of the centre of Quebec City, it was erected in 1973 through the merger of the town of *Bélair* (1965) and the municipality of *Val-Saint-Michel* (1933). Bélair was an informal name as early as 1733 of the seigneury of Guillaume-Bonhomme (1682), in the area of the present town, and the name of another seigneury (also called Pointe-aux-Écureuils) to the southwest near Portneuf.

Val Caron ON Located in 1969 this town became part of the town of Valley East, Sudbury Region. In 2001 Valley East with Val Caron became part of the city of Greater Sudbury. Val Caron was named in 1944 after Fr. Hormidas Caron, the first Jesuit missionary in the region, who founded the parish of Blezard Valley in 1901.

Val-Côté ON Located in Cochrane District, southeast of Hearst, this place was named *Côté Siding* in 1927 after first postmaster G. Côté. It was changed to Val-Côté about 1935. It became part of the municipal township of **Mattice-Val-Côté** in 1983.

Valcourt QC Situated northwest of Sherbrooke, this town was established in 1974, having been erected as a village in 1929. It is surrounded by the township municipality of Valcourt, organized in 1965, which was the municipal township of *Ély* since 1855. Valcourt post office opened in 1864, taking its name from a perceived short valley (*val court*) here. The township of Ely was identified on a 1795 map, and proclaimed in 1802, probably acquiring its name from the village of Ely, northeast of Cambridge, England.

Val-David QC North of Saint-Jérôme and adjacent to Sainte-Anne-des-Monts, this village was established 1921. It was named after Louis-Athanase David (1882–1953), secretary of the province of Quebec, 1919–36, and his father, Laurent-Olivier David (1840–1926), member for Berthier in the House of Commons, 1887–99, and a prolific writer on the careers of noted Québécois.

Valdes Island BC Located in the Gulf Islands, between Gabriola and Galiano Islands, this island was named in 1859 by Capt. George Richards (1820–96) after Spanish Cdr. Cayetano Valdés (1767–1834), who explored the shores of the Gulf of Georgia with Cdr. Dionisio Alcalá Galiano (1760–1805) in 1792. The present Quadra, Maurelle, and

Sonora Islands had been jointly known as *Valdes Island* until 1903.

Val-des-Monts QC Located in the regional county of Papineau, north of the city of Gatineau, this municipality dates from 1975 when Wakefield-Partie-Ouest (1893), Portland-Partie-Ouest (1907), Portland-Ouest (1953), and Perkins (1960) were amalgamated. Embracing 455 km², its landscape is marked by numerous lakes, streams, valleys, and hills.

Val-d'Or QC Located in the regional county of **Vallée-de-l'Or** (1981), the area of this city was established in 1968 through the amalgamation of the towns of Val-d'Or (1937) and Bourlamaque (1934) with the municipality of *Lac-Lemoine* (1958). Val-d'Or had been incorporated as a village in 1935, following a gold rush comparable to the Yukon's Klondike. Bourlamaque took its name from the township, noted on a 1911 map, and proclaimed in 1920. It was named after a noted officer of the French regime, François-Charles de Bourlamaque (1716–64), who wrote *Mémoire sur le Canada* (1762). *Lac-Lemoine*, the first post office in 1935, was named after missionary Georges Lemoine (1860–1912), author of a French/Montagnais dictionary.

Valemount BC The post office in this village (1962) in the Rocky Mountain Trench and near the watershed of the drainage basins of the Fraser and Columbia Rivers was named *Cranberry Lake* in 1913. It was renamed *Swift Creek* five years later, and then was called Valemount in 1927. Its location, at 900 m, is framed by mountains rising over 2600 m on the east and west.

Valhalla Ranges BC Between Lower Arrow and Slocan lakes, these ranges in the Selkirk Mountains were named *Valhalla Mountains* in 1875 by geologist Reginald W. Brock (1874–1935) after the hall of the immortal souls of Norse heroes. The Geographic Board substituted the word 'ranges'.

Vallée-Jonction QC Located in the Beauce valley at an important Canadian Pacific Railway junction, with lines leading west to Thetford Mines and south to Saint-Georges, this municipality was formed in 1989 through the fusion of the village of Vallée-Jonction (1949) and the parish municipality of *L'Enfant-Jésus* (1900). Its post office was first called *Beauce-Jonction* in 1883, and was changed to Vallée-Jonction in 1922.

Valley East ON In 2001 this town (1973) became part of the city of Greater Sudbury. It was created a municipal township in 1969 by amalgamating the municipal township of Blezard with the municipal township of Capreol and Hanmer. On the creation of Sudbury Region four years later, parts of three adjoining townships were added to it. The name decribes the agricultural valley in the heart of the region.

Valleyfield NL This neighbourhood (1996) in the town of New-Wes-Valley was first called *North West Arm*. It became known as Valleyfield by 1891.

Valleyfield PE This municipal community (1974), west of Montague, embraces the localities of Head of Montague, Kilmuir, Commercial Cross, and Brooklyn. Valleyfield was named about 1864 by the Reverend Alexander Munro (c.1851–1935) and its post office opened in 1871.

Valleyview AB The post office in this town (1957) east of Grande Prairie was named in 1929 for the view of the Little Smoky River valley and the valleys of the river's tributaries, the Red Willow and Sturgeon creeks.

Val Marie SK South of Swift Current and near the Montana border, this village (1926) was founded in 1910 and named by Fr. Claude Passaplan after its location in the valley of the Frenchman River and after the Virgin Mary. The post office opened two years later and the Canadian Pacific Railway arrived in 1924.

Valparaiso SK Midway between the towns of Tisdale and Star City, this village (1924) was named in 1904–70 by postmaster George E. Green, after the city of Valparaiso recalling the seaport city in Chile. Green had first proposed Beaver Forks, but that was rejected because it was too similar to other names in Canada.

Val Rita ON This city in Cochrane District, northwest of Kapuskasing, was first named in 1925 after the parish church, dedicated to St. Rita. Since 1983, it has been part of the municipal township of **Val Rita-Harty**.

Val-Senneville QC Northeast of Val-d'Or, this municipality was created in 1980. A post office first opened here in 1945. The names were taken from a lake and a river named Senneville, with both of them recalling the township of Senneville, proclaimed in 1916, and named after a lieutenant in the Languedoc Regiment of Montcalm's army. From 1940 to 1973 the place had been named the mining village of *Pascalis* after the adjacent township (1916) and called after a captain in the La Reine Regiment in 1760. *See also* Senneville.

Vancouver BC The first settlement at the site of Vancouver was made in the 1860s, with the names *New Brighton, Hastings,*

and *Gastown* being attached to developing urban centres. In 1870 *Granville* was selected by residents in honour of George Leveson-Gower, 2nd Earl of Granville (1815–91), British secretary for the colonies, 1868–70, and foreign secretary, 1880–5. In 1882 pioneers John Morton and Sam Brighouse, anticipating the arrival of the Canadian Pacific Railway, laid out a street plan in present downtown Vancouver and called the proposed development the city of *Liverpool*. After the CPR chose Coal Harbour in Burrard Inlet as its West Coast terminus in 1884, another townsite was surveyed by the CPR's L.A. Hamilton. He asked Sir William Van Horne (1843–1915) what the new seaport should be called. Van Horne replied that 'this eventually is destined to be a great city in Canada. We must see that it has a name that will designate its place on the map of Canada. Vancouver it shall be, if I have the ultimate decision'. No doubt he was guided by the knowledge that both he and Capt. Vancouver (1757–98) had Dutch roots. In the spring of 1886 Vancouver was incorporated as a city, and *Granville* post office was renamed Vancouver.

Vancouver Island BC This island (31,285 km²) was named the *island of Quadra and Vancouver* in 1792 by Capt. George Vancouver (1757–98), after he and Spain's Nootka Gov. Juan Francisco de la Bodega y Quadra (1743–94) agreed at the head of Tahsis Inlet that an appropriate feature should be named jointly after them. Subsequent marine charts had *Quadra and Vancouver's Island*, but Hudson's Bay Company traders soon shortened the name to *Vancouver's Island*. By the mid-1800s it was called simply Vancouver Island.

Vancouver, Mount YT On the Yukon–Alaska boundary and in the St. Elias Mountains, this mountain (4785 m) was named in 1874 by William H. Dall (1845–1927), of the Western Union Telegraph Company, after Capt. George Vancouver (1757–98).

Vanderhoof BC This district municipality (1982) west of Prince George was named in 1914 by the Grand Trunk Pacific Railway after Chicago publicity agent Herbert Vanderhoof. In 1908 the GTP had joined the Canadian government, the Canadian Pacific Railway, and the Canadian Northern Railway to encourage Americans to migrate north of the forty-ninth parallel.

Vanguard SK This village (1912) southeast of Swift Current was named in 1912 by the Canadian Pacific Railway after the HMS *Vanguard*, commissioned in 1909. Its post office was Burradon (1910–1912), after a village in Northumberland, England, before opening Vanguard in 1912.

Van Horne Range BC Located in Yoho National Park, northwest of Kicking Horse Pass, this range of mountains was named in 1884 after Sir William Cornelius Van Horne (1814–1915), who managed the construction of the Canadian

Pacific Railway in the West, 1882–5, and was the president of the CPR, 1888–99.

Vanier ON In 2001 this city became part of the city of Ottawa. In 1908 it was the village of *Eastview*, taking its name from its view of the Parliament Buildings, from its eastern limits of Ottawa. It became a town in 1912 and a city in 1950. In 1969 it was renamed after Georges Philias Vanier (1888–1967), governor general of Canada, 1959–67.

Vanier QC In 2002 this town became part of Quebec City. Four years later it became a sector of Quebec City. It was on the north side of the Rivière Saint-Charles, then surrounded by Quebec City. It was established in 1966 on the occasion of the fiftieth anniversary of the founding of the town of *Quebec-Ouest*, and named in honour of Georges Vanier, a native of Montreal and governor general of Canada, 1959–67.

Vanier, Île NU West of Bathurst Island and between Massey and Cameron Islands, this island (1126 km^2) was named in 1961 after Georges Vanier, governor general of Canada, 1959–67. In 1963 a small island between Massey and Vanier Islands was named Île Pauline, after the governor general's wife. **Mount Vanier** in northern Ellesmere Island was named in 1969 by glaciologist Geoffrey Hattersley-Smith.

Vanier, Mount YT Located 50 km west of Whitehorse, this mountain (1845 m) was named in 1967 by the Whitehorse Lions Club after Georges Vanier, governor general of Canada, 1959–67.

Vankleek Hill ON In 1998 this town (1897) became part of the township of Champlain, united counties of Prescott and Russell. Located 12 km south of Hawkesbury, it was first settled about 1798 by Loyalist Simon Vankleek (1743–1827). Its post office was named in 1831 after him, his son Simon (1767–1865), and his grandsons Peter and Barnabus.

Vanscoy SK Southwest of Saskatoon, the post office in this village (1919) was named in 1908 by the Canadian Northern Railway after pioneer settler Clinton Verne Vanscoy. The post office opened the following year.

Varennes QC Located on the eastern shore of the St. Lawrence River, northeast of Montreal, this town was created in 1972 through the amalgamation of the village of Varennes (1848) and the parish municipality of *Sainte-Anne-de-Varennes* (1855). The parish of Sainte-Anne-de-Varennes had its first pastor in 1692, taking its name from the seigneury of Varennes, granted in 1672 to René Gaultier de Varennes (c.1635–89), who was then governor of Trois-Rivières.

Vaudreuil QC Located in the regional county of **Vaudreuil-Soulanges** (1982), this town was created in 1963 through the merging of the village of Vaudreuil (1850) and the parish municipality of *Saint-Michel-de-Vaudreuil* (1855). The seigneury of Vaudreuil was established in 1702 and granted to Philippe de Rigaud de Vaudreuil, Marquis de Vaudreuil (c.1643–1725), governor of New France, 1703–25.

Vaughan ON This city in York Region was created a township in 1792 and named after Benjamin Vaughan, a British negotiator in 1783 of the treaty of peace with the United States. It became a town in 1971 and a city in 1991.

Vauxhall AB This town (1961) north of Taber was founded in 1910 by the Canada Land and Irrigation Company. Its post office was named in 1920 after Vauxhall, a district between Lambeth and Battersea in London, England, on the south side of the River Thames. Presumably the name was chosen to inspire English investment in the company's lands.

Vaux, Mount BC Located in Yoho National Park, south of Field, this mountain (3319 m) was named in 1858 by Dr. Sir James Hector (1834–1907) after William Sandys Wright Vaux (1818–85), an antiquarian and numismatist at the British Museum.

Vavenby BC Located on the North Thompson River, northeast of Kamloops, this place's post office opened in 1910. Its name was suggested by settler Daubney Pridgeon after his birthplace of Navenby, south of the city of Lincoln in Lincolnshire, England. The post office department misread his handwriting.

Vegreville AB East of Edmonton, this town (1906) was named in 1895 by French-speaking settlers from Kansas after Fr. Valentin Végréville (1829–1903), a missionary in Western Canada after 1852. He became an accomplished linguist in Cree, Chipewyan, and Assiniboine, and was a director of the Collège Saint-Boniface in present-day Winnipeg.

Verchères QC On the southeast shore of the St. Lawrence and northeast of Montreal, this municipality dates from 1971 when the village of Verchères (1913) and the parish municipality of *Saint-François-Xavier-de-Verchères* (1855) were united. Its post office had been opened in 1827. The name has its roots in the seigneury of Verchères, granted in 1672 to François Jarret de Verchères (1641–1700), an officer with the Carignan-Salières Regiment.

Verdun QC In 2002 this city became a part of the city of Montreal. In 2006 its status was a borough of Montreal. Verdun was established in 1907, having been incorporated in 1875 as the village of *Rivière-Saint-Pierre*, a name in use as early as 1830. Verdun is not named after the city in eastern France, made famous during the First World War, but after the small village of Saverdun, south of Toulouse in southern

France. Zacharie Dupuy (c.1608–76), a native of Saverdun, was granted some land in 1662 along the shore of the St. Lawrence and called it Verdun.

Veregin SK This village (1912), located between Canora and Kamsack, was named by the Canadian Northern Railway in 1904 after Peter Veregin (1859–1924), who led about 8000 pacifist Doukhobors from Russia to Canada in 1899. Its post office opened as Verigin in 1906. The Doukhobors held pacifist views, but the federal government wanted them to swear an oath of allegiance to get their homesteads. Peter Veregin took two thirds of his people to the area of Grand Forks, BC.

Verendrye, Mount BC On the western border of Kootenay National Park, this mountain (3086 m) was named in 1984 by George M. Dawson (1849–1901) after Pierre Gaultier de Varennes de La Vérendrye (1685–1749), who explored the West, but may have only got as far as the Black Hills of South Dakota.

Vermilion AB This town (1906) between Vegreville and Lloydminster was named by the Canadian Northern Railway in 1906 after the **Vermilion River**, which rises south of Vegreville and flows into the North Saskatchewan, northeast of the town. Its post office from 1905 to 1906 was called *Breage*, after a location in southwestern Cornwall, England.

Vermilion Pass AB, BC This mountain pass (1651 m), west of Banff, was named by Dr. Sir James Hector (1834–1907) in 1858, after the red, yellow, and orange ochre beds in the mineral springs adjacent to **Vermilion River**, 9 km south of the pass. The river is one of the headwaters of the Kootenay River.

Verner ON Located in Nipissing District, northwest of Sturgeon Falls, this community's post office was named about 1883 after the family name of the wife of Archer Baker, general superintendent of the Canadian Pacific Railway.

Vernon BC This city (1892), located near the north end of the Okanagan Valley, was first known as *Priest's Valley* after Fr. Paul Durieu, who had built a cabin here. In 1887 it was renamed after Forbes George Vernon, who with his brother Charles, bought the nearby Coldstream Ranch in 1869. He was elected to the provincial legislature and served as chief commissioner of lands and works.

Verona ON In 1998 this place became part of South Frontenac, Frontenac County. Located 28 km north of Kingston, this community was first known as *Buzztown*, because it was a boisterous place. Called Verona in 1858 after the city in Italy, the name may have been inspired by a local Italian hotel keeper.

Verret NB Located on the southwest side of Edmundston, the post office in this village (1978) was opened in 1908 and closed in 1948. The first postmaster was Joseph Verret.

Verulam ON In 2001 this township became part of the city of Kawartha Lakes, Victoria County. It was named in 1823 after James Walter Grimston, Earl of Verulam (1775–1845), a brother-in-law of the prime minister Lord Liverpool (1770–1828).

Veteran AB This village (1914) east of Stettler was named in 1911 by the Canadian Pacific Railway. It was named during the year of the coronation of George V, reflecting the King's long service during the reign of his mother, Queen Victoria. Its post office was called *Wheat Belt* from 1910 to 1913.

Vibank SK Southeast of Regina, the post office at this village (1911) was named *Elsas* in 1908, but it lasted only a month, when it was renamed *Ubank*. After another two months, it was called Vibank. There are two meanings of Vibank: a German phrase of *vieh bank* ('cattle market') and Andrew Jameson's report that the name was from his daughter Violet and the Bank of Ireland.

Victoria BC This city (1862), at the southeast end of Vancouver Island, was founded in 1843 by James Douglas (1803–77) as the site of a Hudson's Bay Company depot. Chief trader Charles Ross (1794–1844) built the fort, which he believed was to be named after Prince Albert (1819–61). However, the HBC's northern department decided on 10 June of that year that it was to be called Fort Victoria and a terse message from London confirmed it. The townsite was laid out in 1851–2 and in 1868 it was chosen as the capital of the colony of British Columbia. In Canada there are over 300 populated places and physical features that have been named after Queen Victoria.

Victoria NB This county, in the area of Grand Falls, was named in 1844 after Queen Victoria (1819–1901).

Victoria NL This town (1971) north of Carbonear was founded in the early 1800s as a place to cut wood in the winter. It was first named *Victoria Village* about 1860 after Queen Victoria (1819–1901).

Victoria NS This county on Cape Breton Island was named in 1851 after Queen Victoria (1819–1901).

Victoria ON The county was named in 1851 after Queen Victoria (1819–1901).

Victoria PE On **Victoria Harbour**, southwest of Borden-Carleton, this municipal community (1983) was incorporated as a village in 1952. Its post office was named in 1870 after Queen Victoria (1819–1901). **Victoria Cross**, west of Montague and **Victoria West** on Egmont Bay, west of Tyne Valley, were also named after her.

Victoria, Grand lac QC Located near the head of the Ottawa River, southeast of Val-d'Or, this lake has an area of 108 km². It was named in the 1860s after Queen Victoria (1819–1901).

Victoria Harbour ON In Tay Township, Simcoe County, east of Midland, this community's post office was named in 1872 after Queen Victoria (1819–1901). It was first known as *Hogg's Bay* after the bay named for early settler John Hogg.

Victoria Island NT, NU Canada's second largest island (217,291 km²), Victoria Island was named in 1838 by Hudson's Bay company trader Thomas Simpson (1808–40) after the Queen (1819–1901), who was crowned the year before.

Victoria Lake NL Southwest of Red Indian Lake, this lake was likely named after Queen Victoria (1819–1901). The lake is drained northeast into Red Indian Lake by **Victoria River**.

Victoria, Mount AB, BC This mountain (3464 m) on the continental divide, and west of Lake Louise, was named in 1886 by surveyor James J. McArthur (1856–1925) after Queen Victoria (1819–1901).

Victoria Peak Located on Vancouver Island, west of Campbell River, this mountain (2163 m) was originally called *Mount Victoria* after Queen Victoria (1819–1901), but was designated a peak in 1887 by George M. Dawson (1849–1901).

Victoriaville QC Located in the regional county of Arthabaska, almost midway between Montreal and Quebec, this community was created a village in 1860 and named after Queen Victoria (1819–1901). In 1890 it was reorganized as a town. It became the city of *Victoriaville-Arthabaska* in the fall of 1993 by amalgamating the towns of Victoriaville and Arthabaska and the parish municipality of *Sainte-Victoire-d'Arthabaska*. The following summer the city's name was abbreviated to Victoriaville.

View Royal BC This town (1988) west of Victoria was named in the 1950s after its fine view of Royal Roads, the wide bay as part of the Juan de Fuca Strait.

Viking AB The post office in this town (1952) southeast of Edmonton was named in 1904 by Norwegian settlers after their Norse ancestors. When the Grand Trunk Pacific Railway passed between Viking and Harland in 1909, it planned to call its station Meighen, as part of its alphabetical arrangement of names. The settlers disliked a name that sounded like 'mean', and persuaded the GTP to accept Viking. At that time Arthur Meighen (1874–1960), who later became the prime minister

of Canada, was solicitor general in Sir Robert Borden's cabinet.

Ville-Marie QC Located in the regional county of Témiscamingue, this town was erected in 1962, having been incorporated as a village in 1897. In 1863 its name was given to the mission of the Oblates of Mary Immaculate after their patron, the Virgin Mary. Its post office was called *Baie-des-Pères* in 1891, after the Oblate fathers, but was renamed Ville-Marie in 1898.

Vilna AB North of the North Saskatchewan River and midway between Edmonton and Cold Lake, this village (1923) was named by the Canadian Northern Railway in 1919 after Vilna, then in Poland, but now known as Vilnius, the capital of Lithuania. The first post office was 3 km to the east, and was called *Villett*. It was moved to Vilna in 1919 and renamed after the station. Polish homesteaders arrived here in 1918–9.

Virden MB Located west of Brandon, near the Saskatchewan border, this town (1904) was first known as *Gopher Creek*, but was named *Manchester* in 1882 by the Canadian Pacific Railway, after the 8th Duke of Manchester. Because there were other places called Manchester in Canada, it was renamed Virden the following year. It may have been named after the duke's country residence in England, which may have been called after a place in Germany, the home of the duke's wife.

Virgin Arm NL On New World Island and south of Twillingate, this community may have been named because the land around its narrow arm was not settled until the 1870s, while most of the island had been occupied much earlier.

Virginia Falls NT On the South Nahanni River, this waterfall (90 m) was named in 1928 by American explorer Fenley Hunter after his new-born daughter, VA.

Viscount SK In anticipation of the arrival of the Canadian Pacific Railway's tracks in 1909, this village was named in January 1908 after William Conyngham Plunket, 1st Baron Plunket (1764–1854), a noted Irish lawyer and judge, and a spokesman for Irish rights. When he was appointed lord chancellor of Ireland in 1830, he became Baron Plunket of Newton, and was thereafter called Viscount Plunket. The next station to the east was called Plunkett.

Viscount Melville Sound NT, NU Part of Parry Channel, and between Victoria and Melville Islands, this water body was named in 1819 by Sir William Parry (1790–1855) after Robert Dundas, 2nd Viscount Melville (1771–1851), then first lord of the Admiralty.

Voisey Bay NL The site of intensive mineral exploration in 1995–6, this bay on the Labrador coast, 35 km south of Nain, was named after Amos Voisey (d.1887). A native of Plymouth, England, he settled on the bay about 1850. The former settlement of *Voisey's Bay* was first recorded in the census in 1921, but by the 1950s most residents had relocated to Nain and Postville.

Vonda SK This town (1907) northeast of Saskatoon was named in 1905 by the Canadian Northern Railway after Vonda Warman, the daughter of American journalist Cy Warman, who followed the progress of the railway from Winnipeg to Edmonton. The post office opened as *Vaunder* the following year, but was quickly corrected. *See also* Warman.

Vulcan AB Midway between Calgary and Lethbridge, this town (1921) was named by the Canadian Pacific Railway in 1910 after the Roman god of fire and metalworking. Postal service was provided the same year.

Vuntut National Park YT Located in north central Yukon, north of Old Crow, this national park (4345 km²) was created in 1994 to protect valuable wetlands and fossils, as well as the habitat of the Porcupine caribou herd and other wildlife. Its name in Gwitch'in means 'crow flats'.

Wabamun AB The post office in this village (1980) on the north shore of **Wabumun Lake**, west of Edmonton, was named in 1903. Identified as *White Lake* on the Palliser expedition map of 1865, the lake's present name derives from the Cree word for 'mirror'.

Wabana NL This town (1950) on Bell Island and in Conception Bay was named in 1895 by Thomas Cantley (1857–1945) of the Nova Scotia Steel and Coal Company, devising it from the Mi'kmaq words *wâbun* ('dawn' or 'east land') and *aki* ('place'). He chose the name because the mine was the most easterly in North America.

Wabasca-Desmarais AB North of Lesser Slave Lake, this hamlet was named in 1882 by amalgamating the hamlets of **Wabasca** and **Desmarais**. The post office at Wabasca was named in 1908 after the **Wabasca River**, whose name in Cree means 'grassy narrows'. The post office at Desmarais was named in 1927 after Fr. Alphonse Desmarais (1850–1940), the first Catholic missionary at Wabasca in 1891.

Wabush NL Southeast of Labrador City and on **Wabush Lake**, this town (1967) was named after the lake. It was developed in the 1950s when iron ore was being mined by Wabush Mines Ltd., and the original townsite was inform-ally called 'city of Wabush' in the mid-1960s. The lake's name derives from the Montagnais *waboz* ('rabbit').

W.A.C. Bennett Dam BC This 180-m-high dam on the Peace River above Hudson's Hope was completed in 1967 and officially opened by William Andrew Cecil Bennett (1900–79), premier of British Columbia, 1952–72.

Waddington, Mount BC This mountain—the highest (4016 m) in the Coast Mountains, northwest of Bute Inlet—was named in 1928 after Alfred Penderell Waddington (1801–72). A Victoria businessman from 1858, Waddington set out three years later to create a railway route to the Cariboo gold fields, which would follow the shoreline of Bute Inlet, and then follow the Homathko and Chilco Rivers to Alexandria on the Fraser. After 19 of his workers were murdered in 1864 by Chilcotin men, he abandoned the project. From 1867 until his death he promoted a transcontinental railway scheme, which would have followed the Bute Inlet route. **Waddington Peak** (2630 m), in the Rocky Mountains south of the

Yellowhead Pass, was named *Mount Waddington* in 1918 by surveyor Arthur O. Wheeler (1860–1945) after Alfred Waddington, and was given its present name in 1951.

Wadena SK This town (1912) southwest of Humboldt, was named in 1905 by the Canadian Northern Railway on the suggestion of the Tolen family, which had come from Wadena, MN, in the north central part of the state. Wadena in that state was from Ojibwa meaning 'village'. The post office was also opened in 1905.

Wager Bay NU · On the northwestern coast of Hudson Bay, this bay was named in 1742 by explorer Christopher Middleton (d.1770), after Sir Charles Wager (1666–1743). Middleton was seeking an outlet to the 'Western Sea'.

Wainwright AB This town (1910) southwest of Lloydminster was named in 1908 by the Grand Trunk Pacific Railway after William Wainwright (1840–1914), who was then second vice-president of both the Grand Trunk and the Grand Trunk Pacific railways. The post office had been called *Demwood* from 1907 to 1908. Demwood became the post office of the Wainwright Regional Training Area of the department of national defence in 1961.

Wakaw SK South of Prince Albert and at the west end of **Wakaw Lake**, the post office in this town (1953) was named in 1905 after the Cree name of the lake, *Wakawkomah*. Meaning 'crooked lake', it is an apt descrip-tion of the crescent-shaped lake.

Wakefield QC This community on the west bank of the Rivière Gatineau and in the municipality of La Pêche was an incorporated village from 1917 to 1975. Also in 1975 the township municipality of **Wakefield** (1845) was merged with La Pêche. The township was identified on a 1795 map, but it was not proclaimed until 1843. It was named after Wakefield in West Yorkshire, England, south of Leeds.

Waldeck SK The post office in this village (1913) east of Swift Current was named in 1906 by the Reverend Klaas Peters, who had joined a group of Mennonites four years earlier when they emigrated from Westphalia in Germany. It was named after Pierre-Marie-René Waldeck-Rousseau (1846–1904), president of France, 1899–1902, who promoted the right of religious freedom and association.

Walden ON In 2001 this town became a part of the city of Greater Sudbury, Sudbury Region. It was created in 1973 when the following communitites were amalgamated: the town of Lively; the townships of Denison, Dieppe, Drury, Graham, Louise, Lorne, and Waters; and parts of the townships of Dowling and Balfour. The name was blended from letters in the names Waters, Lively, and Denison, replicating the name of the pond in Massachusetts where writer Henry Thoreau lived in the mid-1800s.

Waldheim SK North of Saskatoon, this town (1967) was settled by German immigrants in the 1880s, and its post office was named in 1900. In German the name means 'forest home'. There is a town called Waldheim in Saxony, Germany, between Leipzig and Dresden.

Wales Island NU In Committee Bay, between Melville and Simpson peninsulas, this island (1137 km²) was first called *Prince of Wales Island*, possibly by Dr. John Rae (1813–93) in 1854 after Albert Edward, Prince of Wales (1841–1910). It was renamed in 1926 to avoid confusion with the larger Prince of Wales Island to the northwest, named in 1851.

Walker, Mount AB This mountain (3303 m), located at the head of the North Saskatchewan River, was named in 1897 by British climber Norman Collie (1859–1942) after Horace Walker (1838–1908), president of the Alpine Club of England in 1890.

Walkerton ON In 1999 this town (1871) became part of the municipality of Brockton, Bruce County. It was named *Brant* after the Brant Township in 1852. It was renamed five years later after miller Joseph Walker (1801–73) and his son William, who laid out the place in village lots. Joseph Walker died on Manitoulin Island in 1873, having moved there in 1871.

Walkerville ON The post office in this neighbourhood on the east side of the city of Windsor first opened in 1869, 10 years after Hiram Walker (1816–99) established a distillery here. Incorporated as a town in 1890, it was amalgamated with Windsor in 1935.

Wallace NS At the mouth of the Wallace River, east of Amherst, this place was first called *Ramsheg*, after a Mi'kmaq designation. It was renamed in 1810 after Michael Wallace (c.1744–1831), then treasurer and deputy surveyor general of the king's woods in Nova Scotia, and its postal service was established in 1828. Other post offices opened in the area include **Wallace River** (1848), **Head of Wallace Bay** (1851), **Head of Wallace Bay North** (1856), **Wallace Bridge** (1864), **Wallace Ridge** (1864), **Wallace Grant** (1884), **Wallace Station** (1892), and **Wallace Highlands** (1903).

Wallace ON In 1998 this township became part of the town of North Perth, Perth County. It was named in 1849 after Baron Thomas Wallace (1768–1844), a promoter of free trade who served in the government of Viscount Goderich (1827–33), 1827–8.

Wallaceburg ON In 1998 this town (1896) became part of the municipality of Chatham-Kent, Kent County. It was named in 1837 by first postmaster Hugh McCallum in honour of the great Scottish hero Sir William Wallace (1270–1305), who was hanged by the English in London.

Walsh, Mount YT On the Yukon–Alaska boundary and in the St. Elias Mountains, this mountain (4505 m) was named in 1900 by surveyor James J. McArthur (1856–1925) after James Morrow Walsh (1840–1905), commissioner and superintendent of the North West Mounted Police in the territory from the fall of 1897 to the spring of 1898.

Waltham QC This community in the regional county of Pontiac takes its name from the township of **Waltham**, identified on a 1795 map, but not proclaimed until 1849. Its post office has been called Waltham Station since 1898, although the Canadian Pacific Railway ceased serving the place in 1959. The township was named after a village in England, possibly Waltham in Kent.

Walton NS Located on the south shore of Minas Basin and northeast of Windsor, this place was named in 1837 after Halifax lawyer and Baptist newspaper editor James Walton Nutting (c.1787–1870). Born nearby at Cheverie and a major land owner in the area, he was the son of Mary Walton Nutting.

Wanham AB This village (1958) northeast of Grande Prairie was likely named in 1916 by engineer J.B. Prest of the Edmonton, Dunvegan, and British Columbia Railway after Wonham Manor in Surrey, England. The post office opened in 1918. Its site may have had a name in Cree meaning 'warm winds'.

Wapella SK The post office in this town (1903) located on the main line of the Canadian Pacific Railway, midway between Moosomin and Whitewood, was named in 1883 after the Cree word for 'water under ground', in reference to the ease of drilling for water. There is another meaning from the Dakota Sioux of 'white snow'.

Wapusk National Park MB Located on the shore of Hudson Bay, southeast of Churchill, this national park (11,475 km²) was established in 1996 to protect the denning areas of polar bears and the habitat of other wildlife. In Cree the name means 'white bear'.

Warburg AB The post office in this village (1953) southeast of Edmonton was named in 1916 after an ancient castle in Varberg, Sweden, south of Göteborg. The first settlers were from Sweden.

Warden QC Located east of Granby and just north of Waterloo, this community was organized in 1916, taking its name after the post office, which replaced *Knowlton* in 1860. It was named after settler Jack Warden. Knowlton had been given in 1851 after *Knowlton Falls*, and the flour mill operated here by Col. Paul Knowlton (1787–1863) at the beginning of the 1800s. *See also* Knowlton.

Ward Hunt Island NU On the northwestern side of Ellesmere Island, this island was named in 1875 by explorer Sir George Nares (1831–1915) after George Ward Hunt (1825–77), then the first lord of the Admiralty.

Wardsville ON In 2001 this village (1867) located southwest of London became part of the municipality of Southwest Middlesex, Middlesex County. The post office was named *Mosa* after Mosa Township in 1832. It was renamed Wardsville in 1856 after George Ward, who settled here in 1810.

Warfield BC This village (1952) on the west side of Trail was founded in 1939 and named after an associate of F.A. Heinze, who constructed the first smelter at Trail.

Warkworth ON In 2001 this community became part of the municipality of Trent Hills, Northumberland County. It was named Warkworth in 1857 by postmaster Israel Humphries after Warkworth in Northumberland, England, north of Newcastle upon Tyne.

Warman SK In 1905 the Winnipeg-Edmonton line of the Canadian Northern Railway was built north of Saskatoon, crossing a railway constructed from Regina to Prince Albert in 1890. First called *Diamond*, after the crossing, it was renamed by the Canadian Northern Railway after American journalist Cy Warman (1855–1914), who was following the progress of the railway. *See also* Vonda.

Warner AB This village (1908) southeast of Lethbridge was named in 1906, after American land agent A.L. Warner, who, with his partner, O.W. Kerr, encouraged settlers to take up land from Lethbridge to Coutts, along the line of the Alberta Railway and Irrigation Company.

Warren Grove PE This municipal community (1983) northwest of Charlottetown was named after the former school district of *Warrens Grove*, established before 1880.

Warren, Mount AB This mountain (3300 m) southeast of Maligne Lake was named in 1911 by climber Mary Schäffer

after William Warren (1885–1943), her head packer and guide, and after 1915, her second husband.

Warsaw ON In 1998 this Dummer Township became part of the township of Douro-Dummer, Peterborough County. Northeast of Peterborough, this community was first called *Dummer's Mills* and *Choate's Mills* after Thomas George Choate (1809–1900). In 1839, Choate named the post office after Warsaw, NY, where he had taken the trade of millright. Warsaw, NY, is near Buffalo and directly south of Warsaw, ON.

Warwick ON 1998 this township (with the village of Watford) became part of the township of Warwick, Lambton County. It was named in 1834 by Lt.-Gov. Sir John Colborne (1778–1863) after the 3rd Earl of Warwick (1779–1853), who was instrumental in obtaining a military commission for Colborne.

Warwick QC Situated south of Victoriaville, this town was founded in 1956, having been created a village in 1866 when it had been separated from the township municipality of **Warwick**. The latter was established in 1864, taking its name from the township (1804) and likely named after Warwick, the principal town of Warwickshire near Coventry, England.

Wasa BC North of Cranbrook, this community was named in 1902 by Nils Hanson after Vaasa, on the west coast of Finland. **Wasa Lake**, to the north, was formerly called *Hanson Lake*.

Wasaga Beach ON The post office in this town (1974) in Simcoe County and at the mouth of the Nottawasaga River was named in 1923. It is one of Ontario's most popular summer resorts, and its beach, part of **Wasaga Beach Provincial Park**, during some years is one of the longest and widest on the continent, depending on the water level of Georgian Bay.

Wascana Creek SK Rising 100 km southeast of Regina, this creek flows through the capital city and into the Qu'Appelle River at Lumsden. In Cree *wascana* means 'pile of bones', in reference to the bleached buffalo bones found at the site of Regina in the 1880s.

Waseca SK Southeast of Lloydminster, this village (1911) was named by the Canadian Northern Railway in 1905. It is possible that the village's name came from the Cree for 'hill of the swan', referring to a hill to the south of the village. Its post office opened in 1907. There is a Waseca County, with a town of Waseca, in Minnesota, with the meaning in Dakota 'place of abundance'.

Washademoak Lake NB This lake extends for 37 km from the mouth of the Canaan River southwest to the Saint John River. The lake was named after the Maliseet word *wasetemoik*, whose meaning is unknown. In 1685 map-maker Pierre Rameau identified it as *Quaigesmock*. The present form occurred in the *Land Journal* of 1785.

Washago ON Located in Ramara Township, Simcoe County, north of Orillia and at the outlet of Lake Couchiching, this community was named in 1868 by Ojibwa chief Joseph Big Win at the request of miller Henri St. George. He created the name from *washagomin* ('green and sparkling waters') referring to the clear water of the Severn River, before the Black River joins it to the north.

Washburn, Mount BC Located in the Rocky Mountains, west of Sparwood, this mountain (3039 m) was named in 1964 after FO Dean J. Washburn of Fernie, who was killed in action in Europe on 24 December 1944.

Waskada MB In the southwestern part of the province, this village (1948) was created by the Canadian Pacific Railway in 1883. The name may be from Sioux *wastadaow* ('better further on') because the Sioux wanted homesteaders to move beyond Turtle Mountain and leave them alone. The postmaster in 1905 stated that the post office was named in 1884 by the post office department, and that he was told it meant 'the best of everything'.

Waskaganish QC Situated at the mouth of the Rivière Rupert, this Cree village was reconstructed in 1987. Nine years earlier, when it had been incorporated, it was officially called *Waskaghegaganish* in Cree, *Fort Rupert* in French, and *Rupert House* in English. The English and French forms were given in 1670 after Prince Rupert, the first governor of the Hudson's Bay Company. In Cree, Waskaganish means 'little house', referring to the fort.

Waskatenau AB The post office in this village (1932) northeast of Edmonton was named in 1919 after **Waskatenau Creek**. In Cree *waskatenau* means 'opening in the banks', referring to a cut in a ridge through which the creek flows to the North Saskatchewan River.

Waskesiu SK The post office in this popular tourist destination on the southeastern end of **Waskesiu Lake** in Prince Albert National Park was named *Waskesiu Lake* in 1929. In Cree *wawaskesiu* means 'red deer'.

Waswanipi QC Located at the outlet of **Lac Waswanipi**, west of Chibougamau, this Cree village was named in 1978, two years after it was constructed. The name translates as 'fishing by torch water'.

Waterdown ON In 2001 this community became part of the city of Hamilton. Its post office was named in 1840 after the plunging of Grindstone Creek over Great Falls at the Niagara Escarpment.

Waterford ON In the city of Nanticoke, Haldimand-Norfolk Region, north of Simcoe, this community was first known as *Averill's* (or *Avery's*) *Mills*, *Sovereign's Mills*, and *Loderville*, before it was named in 1826 after Waterford on the Hudson River, north of Albany, NY.

Waterloo ON The township was named in 1817 after the British-led victory in 1815 at Waterloo, Belgium. The county was created in 1849 and was reorganized in 1972 as the regional municipality of **Waterloo**, with three cities and four townships. In 1973 the township was divided among the cities of Cambridge, Kitchener, and **Waterloo**, and the municipal township of Woolwich. The city of Waterloo was named in 1831 when its post office opened, and it became a village in 1857, a town in 1876, and a city in 1948.

Waterloo QC Situated between Granby and Magog, this town was established in 1890, having been incorporated as a village in 1867. The place had been named in 1815 in honour of Wellington's victory in Belgium, and its post office opened in 1836.

Waterton Lakes AB These lakes, which include **Upper**, **Middle**, and **Lower Waterton** lakes, were named in 1858 by surveyor Thomas Blakiston (1832–91) after Charles Waterton (1782–1865), a noted English naturalist, who had visited the northwest of the United States. **Waterton Lakes National Park** (526 km²) was named in 1895. It became part of the first international peace park in 1932, when it was joined with Glacier National Park in Montana.

Waterville QC Erected as a town in 1965, and having been created a village in 1876, this place south of Sherbrooke was named in 1852 when its post office opened. An excellent mill site on the Rivière Coaticook, it was earlier called *Pennoyer's Mills*, *Hollister's Mills*, and *Ball's Mills*.

Watford ON In 1998 this village (1873) became part of the township of Warwick, Lambton County. Its post office was named in 1854 after the city of Watford in Hertfordshire, England, northwest of London.

Watrous SK Southeast of Saskatoon, this town (1909) was named by the Grand Trunk Pacific Railway in 1908. The name was given in honour of Frank Watrous Morse, vice-president and general manager of the company. Its choice followed the Grand Trunk Pacific Railway practice of naming its stations in alphabetical order, with Venn to the east and Xena to the west.

Watson SK East of Humboldt, this town (1908) was founded by the Canadian Northern Railway in 1905 and named after

Senator Robert Watson (1853–1929) of Portage la Prairie, MB, who owned the site of the station. *Vossen* post office opened in the area in 1904, but was changed to Watson in 1906. Frank Joseph Vossen Jr. was the postmaster of *Vossen*.

Watson Lake YT This town was established in 1942, on the building of the Alaska Highway through the southern part of the territory, and the construction of an airport with two 1524-m (5000-ft) runways. It took its name from the lake, 5 km to the east, that Francis (Frank) Watson (1883–1938) travelled from California with his father when he was 14 years old. He stayed here, with his father returning to California in 1900. The Kaska had named the lake as *Fish Lake*.

Waubaushene ON Located in Tay Township, Simcoe County, east of Midland, this community was variously named *Baushene*, *Wabashene*, and *Wabaushene*, before the present spelling was introduced in the late 1860s. It derives from an Ojibwa word meaning 'place of the meeting of the rocks' after two rocks that once obstructed navigation in the entrance to the harbour.

Wawa ON Located in Michipicoten Township, Algoma District, north of Sault Ste. Marie, this community's post office was first called *Wa-Wa* in 1899, but it was closed in 1908. It was opened again as Wawa in 1933 after the Algoma Central and Hudson Bay Railway arrived from Sault Ste. Marie. In Ojibwa, the name means 'wild goose', referring to **Wawa Lake**, where wild geese congregate in the spring and fall. It was renamed *Jamestown* in 1951 after Algoma Steel president Sir James Dunn (1874–1956). Wawa was restored in 1960.

Wawanesa MB The post office in this village (1908), southeast of Brandon, was first proposed in 1890 as *Sipweske*, after a Cree word, but objections were raised by the temperance movement. It was then named after *Wawonaissa*, which had been a post office from 1882–3, 3 km to the southwest. That name was taken from Wawonaissa, the whippoorwill in Henry Wadsworth Longfellow's *Hiawatha*.

Wawota SK The post office in this town (1975) southwest of Moosomin was named in 1884. In Nakota the name means 'lots of snow' or 'deep snow'.

Webbwood ON The post office in this town (1906) in Sudbury District, west of Espanola, was named in 1889 after Andrew Webb, its first settler, who arrived in 1884.

Webequie ON Located on Winisk Lake, Kenora District, northeast of Thunder Bay, Webequie post office operated here from 1941 to 1944, reopened in 1964 as *Webekwei*, and became Webequie again in 1966. In Cree, it means 'place of many ducks'.

Webster, Mount NB South of the Nepisiguit River, this mountain was named in 1969 by director of surveys Willis F. Roberts after John Clarence Webster (1863–1950), a historian and antiquarian.

Weedon Centre QC This village northeast of Sherbrooke was established in 1887, when it was separated from the township municipality of **Weedon**, which had been erected in 1855. The township, identified on a 1795 map but not proclaimed until 1822, took its name from Weedon, Buckinghamshire, England, northwest of London.

Weldon SK Northwest of Melfort, the post office at this village (1914) was named on 1 October 1895 after Weldon Ellis, who came to this area in 1888. He was the son of postmaster George Ellis, who had settled here in 1883. The post office actually opened in the winter of 1896, a few months before Weldon died.

Welland ON The county was created in 1851, taking its name from the **Welland River**. In 1970 it was united with Lincoln County to form the regional municipality of Niagara. The river had been named in 1792 by Lt.-Gov. John Graves Simcoe (1752–1806) after the Welland River in Lincolnshire, England. *Chippawa Creek*, its previous name, still has strong local usage more than 200 years later. The **Welland Canal**, first opened in 1829 and named after the river, has never been connected to it. The second canal was opened in 1845, the third in 1887, and the current route in 1932. In 1849 the site of the present city (1917) was named *Merrittsville* after William Hamilton Merritt (1793–1862), and was changed to Welland in 1858. *See also* Merritton.

Wellesley ON This township in the regional municipality of Waterloo was named in 1840 after Richard Wellesley, 2nd Earl of Mornington and Baron Wellesley (1760–1842), eldest brother of the Duke of Wellington and governor general of India, 1798–1805. The post office in the community of **Wellesley** was named in 1851.

Wellington ON The county was named in 1851 after Arthur Wellesley, Duke of Wellington (1769–1852), who won major battles in Spain during the Peninsular War and at Waterloo, Belgium. He was prime minister of Great Britain, 1828–30.

Wellington ON In 1998 this village (1862) became part of the Prince Edward County. The village was first called *Smokeville* after Daniel Reynolds, nicknamed Old Smoke by Aboriginals. In 1830 it was renamed after the Duke of Wellington (1769–1852), then the British prime minister, 1828–30.

Wellington PE This municipal community (1983) northwest of Summerside was incorporated as a village in 1959. Its post office was named *Wellington Station* about 1875 after the Duke of Wellington (1769–1852). About 1855 its school district was called *Quagmire* after the Long Swamp, which extends east for about 7 km toward Miscouche. **Wellington Centre**, 4 km to the north, was the area of *Wellington* school district about 1864. *Quagmire* post office opened here about 1853, but was changed to *Wellington* in 1871 and was closed in 1913.

Wells Gray Park BC In the east central part of the province, this park was established in 1939 and named after Arthur Wellesley (Wells) Gray, provincial minister of lands, 1933–41. The lake embraces the headwaters of the Clearwater River and Mahood, Murtle, Azure, Hobson, and Angus Horne lakes.

Welwyn SK The post office (1884) at this village (1907) on the Manitoba border, northeast of Moosomin, was named in 1902 by James Wake after Welwyn in Hertfordshire, England, north of London. Welwyn Garden City in Hertfordshire was designed as a model of ideal urban planning in 1920.

Wembley AB The station and post office in this town (1980) west of Grande Prairie were named in 1924 by the Lake Saskatoon Board of Trade after the British Empire Exhibition, held in 1924–5 in Wembley, England, in the northwestern part of Greater London.

Wemindji QC Located on the eastern shore of James Bay, this Cree village was erected in 1978, having been called *Paint Hills* and *Nouveau-Comptoir*. In Cree, the name means 'ochre mountain'.

Wentworth ON In 2001 this county became part of the city of Hamilton. It was named in 1816 after Sir John Wentworth (1737–1820), lieutenant-governor of Nova Scotia, 1792–1808, and the brother of Annabella Wentworth Gore (wife of Lt.-Gov. Francis Gore). In 1974 the county was reorganized as the regional municipality of Hamilton-Wentworth. *See also* Hamilton.

Wentworth Valley NS Northwest of Truro, this valley provides the route for the Trans-Canada Highway through the Cobequid Mountains. It was named after Sir John Wentworth (1737–1820), lieutenant-governor of Nova Scotia, 1792–1808.

Wesleyville NL This neighbourhood (1996) in the town of New-Wes-Valley was first known as *Coal Harbour*. It was renamed in 1884 after John Wesley (1703–91), the founder of Methodism. Incorporated as a town in 1945, it had become part of the town of Badger's Quay-Valleyfield-Pool's Island-Wesleyville-Newtown in 1992.

Westbank BC On the west bank of Okanagan Lake, opposite Kelowna, this community's post office was named in 1902 on the suggestion of John Davidson, ships carpenter from Glasgow Scotland who settled here in 1892.

West Carleton ON In 2001 this municipal township became part of the city of Ottawa. It was created in 1974 when the three municipal townships of Huntley, Fitzroy, and Torbolton, in the western part of Carleton County, were amalgamated.

Westchester Station NS Located northwest of Truro, this community's post office was called *Greenville* in 1870. It was changed in 1895 after a name given to the area in the 1780s by Loyalists from Westchester, NY, northeast of New York City.

Westcock NB South of Sackville, this place was named in 1854 after the Mi'kmaq word *oakshaak*, whose meaning is unknown. It was spelled several ways in the 1700s, including *Worshcock*, *Westqua*, and *West Coup*, before the present form appeared on a plan in 1792.

Western Bay NL On the west side of Conception Bay, northeast of Carbonear, this place is located on a small inlet, with the point called **Western Bay Head** on its south side. The two names originated during a hydrographic survey by Michael Lane in 1774. Before then they were called *Green Bay* and *Point Prime*, the latter because it was the first point seen by mariners on rounding Cape St. Francis, on the east side of Conception Bay.

Westfield NB The post office in this village (1966) northwest of Saint John opened as *Mouth of Neripis* in 1846, renamed *Westfield Station* in 1876, changed back to *Mouth of Neripis* in 1879, and finally called Westfield in 1895. It took its name from **Westfield Parish**, created in 1786, which was possibly named after Westfield, MA, or Westfield, NJ, or for its location on the west side of the Saint John River.

West Garafraxa ON This township in Wellington County was separated from East Garafraxa Township in 1869, and the latter was added to Dufferin County in 1874. There are many guesses as to the meaning of Garafraxa, with none of them more convincing than any other.

West Hawkesbury ON In 1998 this municipal township became part of the township of Champlain, united counties of Prescott and Russell. It was separated in 1884 from Hawkesbury Township. The latter was named in 1798, either for Charles Jenkinson (1727–1808), Baron Hawkesbury and Lord Liverpool, or for his son, Robert Banks Jenkinson (1770–1828), made Baron Hawkesbury in 1796. The son, who became Lord Liverpool in 1808, was prime minister of Great Britain, 1812–27. *See also* East Hawkesbury *and* Hawkesbury.

West Lincoln ON This municipal township in Niagara Region was created in 1970 by amalgamating the municipal townships of Caistor, Gainsborough, and South Grimsby, all formerly in Lincoln County.

Westlock AB The original location of this town (1947) northwest of Edmonton was 7 km to the west. The town was first named *Edison* after early settler Jack Edgson, who had arrived here in 1902. When it was moved to its present site in 1912, it occupied the homesteads of two settlers, Westgate and Lockhart. The postal name was devised from their surnames.

West Lorne ON In 1998 this village became a part of the municipality of West Elgin, Elgin County. In 1872 the Canada Southern Railway named a station in Elgin County's Aldborough Township after the German chancellor, Prince Otto von Bismarck (1815–98). The next year the post office was called West Lorne after Archibald McKillop's Lorne Mills, named after the Marquess of Lorne (1845–1914), who married Queen Victoria's daughter Princess Louise (1848–1939) in 1871 and became the governor general in 1878. The station was renamed West Lorne in 1907 after one of McKillop's shipments was left at Bismarck in Lincoln County by mistake. That year the village was incorporated as well.

West Luther ON Luther Township, named in 1831 after Protestant reformer Martin Luther (1483–1546), was divided in 1879, with East Luther transferring to Dufferin County in 1883. West Luther remained in Wellington County.

Westmeath ON In 2001 this township became part of the township of Whitewater Region, Renfrew County. It was named in 1830 after the east central county in Ireland. *Bellowston* post office opened on the Ottawa River in 1832 and named after first postmaster Caleb Strong Bellows. It was changed to Westmeath in 1837, when it was moved downriver to *Goddard's Corners*, which also adopted the name **Westmeath**.

Westmorland NB Located in southeastern New Brunswick, this county was named in 1785. It was located northwest of Cumberland County, NS, named in 1759. In the northwest of England there were Westmorland County and Cumberland County. In 1974 Westmorland County and Cumberland County became the county of Cumbria in England.

Westmount QC In 2002 this city became part of the city of Montreal. In 2006 Westmount had recovered its status of a city. With an area of only 3.96 km², it is one of the smallest municipalities in the province.

West Nissouri ON Nissouri Township was named in 1818 and attached to Oxford County in 1821. West Nissouri Township was separated from it in 1852 and transferred to Middlesex County. There is speculation that the name Nissouri is similar to Missouri ('gurgling' or 'struggling waters').

Westport NL On the east side of White Bay and southwest of Baie Verte, this municipal community (1967) is comprised of the former settlements of *Western Cove*, *Pound Cove*, and *Wiseman's Cove*. The name was adopted in the early 1900s.

Westport NS On Brier Island, southeast of Digby, postal service was established in this village (1946) in 1835. It was named for its location on the west side of Grand Passage, opposite Freeport, with which it is connected by ferry.

Westport ON This village (1904) in the united counties of Leeds and Grenville, southwest of Perth, was named in 1841 after its location at the west end of the Upper Rideau Lake and on the Rideau Canal system.

West Redonda Island BC Located between Vancouver Island and the mainland, northeast of Campbell River, this island was considered by Spanish explorers Dionisio Alcalá Galiano (1760–1805) and Cayetano Valdés y Bazan (1767–1835) in 1792 to be part of *Isla Redonda*, which included present West Redonda Island. The two names were endorsed in 1950. In Spanish *redonda* means 'round'.

West River PE One of the three rivers flowing into Charlottetown Harbour, this river was known during the French regime as *Rivière de l'Ouest*. In 1765 Samuel Holland (1728–1801) called it *Elliot River* after Edward Eliot, 1st Baron Elliot (1727–1804), Lord commissioner of trade and plantations in 1760. Both names competed for acceptance, until West River was endorsed in 1970. *See also* Eliot River.

West Road (Blackwater) River BC Rising in the Chilcotin, this river (227 km) flows east to join the Fraser between Prince George and Quesnel. It was named *West Road River* in 1793 by Sir Alexander Mackenzie (c.1764–1820) because he had followed its route to reach the Pacific Ocean, near Bella Coola. Known locally as the Blackwater River, its official designation is West Road (Blackwater) River.

West St. Modeste NL Located on the north side of the Strait of Belle Isle and on the west side of Pinware Bay, the name of this municipal community (1975) may have been given by French explorers, because the name of the eighth-century abbess sounded like *Semadet*, a Basque name given in the 1500s and still used informally across Pinware Bay at the unoccupied site of *East St. Modeste*.

West Vancouver BC This district municipality was separated from the district municipality of North Vancouver in 1912, although the name had already come into general use. It embraces an area of 990 km².

Westville NS This town (1894) on the west side of Stellarton was first called *Acadia Village* after the Acadian Coal Company, which started mining operations here in 1866. It was renamed Westville on 25 February 1868, likely because it was west of the other Pictou County coal mining towns.

West Wawanosh ON Wawanosh Township was named in 1840 for Chief Joshua Wawanosh (c.1786–1879) of the Chippewas on the Sarnia Reserve, who was among chiefs who transferred a large area of Southwestern Ontario to the British Crown in 1827. It was divided in 1867 into the municipal townships of East Wawanosh and West Wawanosh, with both remaining in Huron County.

West Williams ON Williams Township, created in Middlesex County in 1830, was named after William Williams, a deputy governor of the Canada Company (British company established in 1826 to develop the Huron Tract, a large area of what is now Southwestern Ontario). It was divided into the municipal townships of East Williams and West Williams in 1860.

West Zorra ON Zorra Township was divided into the municipal townships of East Zorra and West Zorra in 1850. On the restructuring of Oxford County in 1975, West Zorra became the municipal township of Zorra, and East Zorra became the municipal township of East Zorra–Tavistock.

Wetaskiwin AB This city (1906) south of Edmonton was named by the Calgary and Edmonton Railway about 1891 after the Cree *Witaskiwinik* ('place of peace') referring to the nearby Peace Hills, where the Cree and Blackfoot made peace about 1867.

Weyburn SK This city (1913) was named in 1893 by Sir William Whyte of the Canadian Pacific Railway, after either a construction contractor who laid the steel or his brother-in-law, J.W. Churchman. Its post office opened in 1895.

Weymouth NS Located on the Sissiboo River, southwest of Digby, this village (1924) was settled by fishermen in the 1760s from Weymouth, MA. Its post office was called *Weymouth Bridge* in 1865 and became Weymouth in 1907. It was earlier called *Sissiboo*, but it was discarded because it was considered uncouth. The first Weymouth post office opened in 1833 nearer the river's mouth, but it became **Weymouth North** in 1907.

Whalley BC The principal centre of the city of Surrey, it was founded in 1925 by Arthur Whalley (1886–1952). Whalley post office opened in 1948, changed to *North Surrey* in 1966, and renamed Surrey three years later.

Whapmagoostui QC Located at the mouth of the Grande rivière de la Baleine, this Cree village shares its site with the northern (Inuit) village of Kuujjuarapik. In Cree, the name means 'river of the white whale'. *See also* Baleine, Grande rivière de la *and* Kuujjuarapik.

Whati NT Northwest of Yellowknife and on Lac la Martre, this community previously known as *Lac la Martre*, was renamed on 1 January 1996. Its name in Slavey and French means 'marten lake'. *See also* Martre, Lac la.

Wheatley ON In 1998 this village (1914) became part of the municipality of Chatham-Kent, Kent County. Northeast of Leamington, it was named in 1864 after Richard Wheatley, the father-in-law of first postmaster William Buchanan. Wheatley had settled here in 1832 and died shortly thereafter.

Wheeler, Mount BC In the Selkirk Mountains, south of Rogers Pass, this mountain (3386 m) was named in 1904 after Arthur Oliver Wheeler (1860–1945), who had surveyed in the area of Glacier National Park, 1900–2. He was the British Columbia representative on the Alberta–British Columbia Boundary Commission, 1913–25.

Whistler BC This resort municipality (1975) 120 km north of Vancouver was named after **Whistler Mountain** (2182 m). The mountain was named in 1965 after the whistling marmots on its slopes. Major ski magazines have noted that it is one of the best skiing destinations in North America. Its population is almost 10,000. It had been called *London Mountain* by the British Royal Navy in the 1860s.

Whitbourne NL Southwest of St. John's, this town (1968) was the site of the Grange estate of Sir Richard Bond (1857–1927), prime minister of Newfoundland, 1900–9. He proposed the name in 1889 after Sir Richard Whitbourne (1579–1628), who was involved in the fishery off Newfoundland as early as 1579, and governed a colony at Aquaforte for Sir William Vaughan (1575–1641), 1618–20. The place was earlier called *Harbour Grace Junction*, after a rail line constructed north to Harbour Grace in the 1880s, and *Davenport Junction*, after Daniel Davenport, who contracted to build the line.

Whitby ON Whitby Township was named in 1792 after the seaside town of Whitby in England's North Yorkshire. The centre of the town was first known as *Hamer's Corners* and *Perry's Corners*, with the port on Lake Ontario called *Windsor*. The two areas were united as the town of Whitby in 1854. In 1974 on the creation of Durham Region, the municipal township of Whitby was merged with the town of Whitby.

Whitchurch-Stouffville ON Whitchurch Township was named in 1798, probably after one of the several places with that name in England and Wales. When York Region was created in 1971, most of the township, part of the municipal township of Markham, and the village of Stouffville became the town of Whitchurch-Stouffville.

White City SK East of Regina, this village (1967) was established in 1960 as a residential community. John Kadannek, with a new store in the village, proposed White City, after the White City district in London, England.

Whitecourt AB This town (1971) on the south bank of the Athabasca River, northwest of Edmonton, was named in 1909 after the first postmaster, Walter White, who previously carried the mail from his former home in Greencourt, 33 km to the southeast.

White Fox SK The post office in this village (1941) on the **White Fox River**, north of Nipawin, was named in 1920, 10 years before the Canadian Pacific Railway was extended west toward Prince Albert.

Whitehorn Mountain BC Located northwest of Mount Robson, this mountain (3395 m) was named in 1911 by surveyor Arthur O. Wheeler (1860–1945) after its sharp, snow-covered peak.

Whitehorse YT The capital and only city in the territory, Whitehorse was established in 1900 at the head of navigation on the Yukon River. It was named after the **Whitehorse Rapids**, which likely received its name from the first miners in 1880–1, who perceived the manes of horses in its white waters. The first townsite was laid out in 1899 on the east side of the river, but it developed the following year on the west side, when the White Pass and Yukon Railway was completed from Skagway. The place was first called *Closeleigh* after the Close brothers, of London, England, who financed the construction of the railway. But by 21 April 1900 the railway officials renamed it Whitehorse because it had become well known around the world. The post office and town were called *White Horse*, which was changed to the one-word form in 1957.

White Lake ON Located on the east shore of **White Lake** and in Renfrew County, southwest of Arnprior, this place was named in 1848. The lake was shown on some early maps as *Wabalac*, a blend of Algonquin for 'white' and French for 'lake'.

Whitemantle Mountain BC Located in the Coast Mountains, south of Mount Waddington, this mountain (2969 m) was named about 1927 by climber Walter Alfred (Don) Munday (1890–1950) because there was a glacier near its summit.

Whitemouth MB Located on the **Whitemouth River**, which flows into the Winnipeg River, 18 km downriver from the community on the main line of the Canadian Pacific Railway, this place's post office was named in 1877. The river was identified on the Palliser expedition map of 1865. It had other names in the late1800s: *Rivière Blanche*, *Mud River*, and *Whitemud River*.

White Pass BC A pass (889 m) on the British Columbia–Alaska boundary, it is the summit of the famous route from

Skagway to the Klondike. It was named in 1887 by surveyor William Ogilvie (1849–1912) after Thomas White (1830–88), minister of the interior, 1885–8.

White River ON In Algoma District, midway between Sault Ste. Marie and Thunder Bay, this municipal township is where the Canadian Pacific Railway and the Trans-Canada Highway cross **White River**, which flows west into Lake Superior. Called *Snowbank* by the CPR in the mid-1880s, the station was renamed White River in 1887.

White River YT Rising west of the Yukon–Alaska boundary and in the St. Elias Mountains, this river (265 km) was named in 1850 by Hudson's Bay Company trader Robert Campbell (1808–94) after its colour, caused by suspended volcanic ash. Volcanic eruptions had occurred about 1000 CE, and ash was deposited to the depth of 30 m in some places.

White Rock BC This city (1957) just north of the forty-ninth parallel and southeast of Vancouver was named after a large rock on the beach, painted white to guide mariners. There is an Aboriginal legend that a chief hurled the rock across the Strait of Georgia and agreed to live with the girl he loved where it landed.

Whitesaddle Mountain BC In the Coast Mountains, northeast of Mount Waddington, this mountain (2972 m) was named in 1933 by mountaineer Henry S. Hall Jr. of Cambridge, MA. A glacier flowing down its face reminded him of a saddle, which he deemed appropriate for this cattle ranching country.

White Tower, The BC In the Tower of London Range of the Muskwa Ranges of the Rocky Mountains, this mountain (2819 m) was named in 1960 by Capt. M.F.R. Jones after one of the towers of the Tower of London. A party of British and Canadian fusiliers climbed it.

Whiteway NL Located on the southeast side of Trinity Bay, this municipal community (1975) was first known as *Witler's Bay* and *Witless Bay*. It was renamed in 1912 after Sir William Vallance Whiteway (1828–1908), who served three terms as prime minister of Newfoundland between 1878 and 1897.

Whitewood SK This town (1892) on the main line of the Canadian Pacific Railway, east of Regina, was founded in 1882. Its post office was called *Whitewood Station* from 1883 to 1894, when it was shortened to Whitewood. A bluff (grove) of white poplars inspired the name.

Wholdaia Lake NT Southeast of Great Slave Lake, this lake (608 km²) was identified on Samuel Hearne's map of 1772. In Chipewyan the name means 'icefish'.

Whonnock BC On the north shore of the Fraser River and in the district municipality of Maple Ridge, this community's post office was called *Whonock* in 1885. It was renamed Whonnock in 1969 after a local petition. In Halkomelem the name means 'place where there are (always) humpback salmon'.

Whycocomagh NS Located at the head of St. Patricks Channel of Bras d'Or Lake, its name derives from the Mi'kmaq *Wakogumaak* ('beside the sea' or 'end of the bay'). Postal service was established here in 1834.

Wiarton ON In 1999 this town (1894) became part of the town of South Bruce Peninsula, Bruce County. Located 30 km northwest of Owen Sound, its post office was named in 1868 after Wiarton Place, the birthplace near Maidstone, Kent, England of Sir Edmund Walker Head (1805–68), governor of the Province of Canada, 1854–61.

Wickham QC South of Drummondville, this municipality was created in 1957, having been incorporated as the village of *Wickham-Ouest* in 1922. In 1867 it had been erected as the municipality *Wickham-Ouest*, although the post office from 1874 to 1954 was called *Wickham West*. The township of Wickham was shown on a map in 1795, and was proclaimed in 1802, taking its name from a place in England, possibly Wickham in Berkshire, west of London.

Wikwemikong ON Located on Manitoulin Island, southeast of Little Current, this community was founded about 1825 by the Ottawa on their return from exile on the west side of Lake Michigan. The post office opened in 1890. The name in Ottawa means 'beaver bay'.

Wilberforce ON This township became part of the township of **North Algona-Wilberforce**, Renfrew County. It was named in 1851 after William Wilberforce (1759–1833), a distinguished British statesman, who strongly opposed slavery.

Wilberforce Falls NU On the Hood River and west of Bathurst Inlet, this waterfall (49 m) was named in 1821 by Sir John Franklin (1786–1847) after William Wilberforce (1759–1833), the noted philanthropist.

Wilcox SK Directly south of Regina, this village (1907) was founded by the Canadian Pacific Railway in 1902. Prior to that year new settlers had to haul their possessions from Milestone, 14 km to the southeast. The settlers agreed to name a station after CPR official Albert Wilcox (1865–1937) if the CPR would provide a regular stop. Wilcox came west in 1883. It is the location of the Athol Murray College of Notre Dame, founded in 1927 by Fr. Athol Murray (1892–1975).

Wilkie SK This town (1910) southeast of Battleford was first known in 1906 as *Glen Logan* after Charles John Logan (1873–1954), its only postmaster. The Canadian Pacific Railway was built through in 1908, with plans to locate its Wilkie station 8 km east of Unity, and the present site was to be called Adanac (Canada spelled backward). When water was not found at Wilkie, the CPR switched the two names. Wilkie was named after Daniel Robert Wilkie (1846–1914), president of the Imperial Bank of Canada and a promoter of the CPR. Imperial is the main street in Wilkie.

Williamsburgh ON In 1998 this township became part of the township of South Dundas, united counties of Stormont, Dundas, and Glengarry. It was named in 1787 after Prince William Henry (1765–1837), the third son of George III. In 1830 Prince William succeeded his brother George IV and served as William IV until his death. The post office in the community of **Williamsburg** (without an 'h') in the township was named *Williamsburg North* in 1841, changed the following year to *North Williamsburg*, and to Williamsburg in 1907.

Williams Lake BC This city (1981) in the Cariboo Regional District was named as a colonial post office in 1861 after the **Williams Lake** to its southeast. The lake was named after Chief William of the Shuswap's Sugarcane band. When the Chilcotin Region killed 19 whites in 1864 during Alfred Waddington's railway survey, Chief William dissuaded other Aboriginals from taking part in the massacre.

Williamstown ON In 1998 this community became part of the township of South Glengarry, united counties of Stormont, Dundas, and Glengarry. Located northeast of Cornwall, it was founded in 1790 by Sir John Johnson (1742–1830), who named it after his father, Sir William Johnson (c.1715–74), superintendent of the northern Indians in New York state.

Willingdon AB This village (1928) northeast of Edmonton was named in 1928 by the Canadian Pacific Railway after Freeman Freeman-Thomas, 1st Marquess of Willingdon (1866–1941), governor general of Canada, 1926–31. Its post office was also named in 1928. **Mount Willingdon** (3373 m), north of Lake Louise, was named for the 1st Marquess of Willingdon (1866–1941) in 1927.

Williston Lake At the head of the Peace River, this reservoir (1660 km²) was created in 1968. It was named after Ray Gillis Williston (1914–2006), the provincial minister of lands and forests in W.A.C. Bennett's Social Credit government. The reservoir is impounded by the W.A.C. Bennett Dam.

Willow Bunch SK Almost due south of Moose Jaw, this town (1960) was first settled by Métis from Manitoba about 1865. They found a coulee filled with red willows, which they called *Talle de Harre Rouge* ('bunch of red willow'). When the North West Mounted Police arrived in 1877, the name was translated as *Red Willow Bunch* and was shortened to Willow Bunch in 1895 when the post office opened.

Willowdale ON In 1998 this urban centre became part of the city of Toronto. Its first name was called *Lansing*. Willowdale had been in the city of North York. Its post office was named in 1855 by David Gibson (1804–64), who had migrated from Scotland in 1829. He named the post office after the many willow trees in the area of Yonge Street and Sheppard Avenue.

Wilmot NS In the Annapolis Valley, between Middleton and Kingston, this community's postal way office was named in 1837 after Wilmot Township. The township was named in the 1760s after Montagu Wilmot (d.1766), lieutenant-governor of Nova Scotia, 1763–4, and governor, 1764–6.

Wilmot ON This township in the Regional Municipality of Waterloo was named in 1825, likely after Sir Robert John Wilmot Horton (1784–1841). Horton was the under-secretary for war and the colonies in Lord Liverpool's administration and was also involved in the Canada Company, which developed the Huron Tract. He assumed the additional name of Horton when he married Anna Beatrix Horton in 1823. The township may also have been named after surveyor Samuel Street Wilmot (1774–1856), who was a government inspector of Crown and clergy lands.

Wilmot PE Part of the city of Summerside, Wilmot was incorporated as a village in 1965 and became a municipal community in 1983. Called *Wilmot District* before 1880, it took its name from the **Wilmot River**. The river had been named *Wilmot Cove* in 1765 by Samuel Holland (1728–1801) after Montague Wilmot (d.1766), governor of Nova Scotia, 1764–6.

Wilno ON In 2001 this place became part of the township of Madawaska Valley, Renfrew County. Located 10 km east of Barry's Bay, it was settled by Polish immigrants in 1864, and named in 1885 after the birthplace of Fr. Ludwick Dembski, which is now Vilnius, the capital of Lithuania.

Wilson, Mount AB This mountain (3260 m), east of the Columbia Icefield, was named in 1898 by British climber Norman Collie (1859–1942) after Thomas (Tom) Edmonds Wilson (1859–1933), a Banff packer and guide.

Winchester ON In 1998 this township became part of the township of North Dundas, united counties of Stormont, Dundas, and Glengarry. It was named in 1798 after the English city of Winchester, Hampshire. The village (1887) of **Winchester** was first called *Bates Corners*. Its post office opened as *West Winchester* in 1855, because Chesterville's post office was called Winchester from 1845 to 1876. In the mid-1880s the station at *West Winchester* was called Winchester, leading to its post office dropping 'West'.

Windermere BC On the eastern shore of **Windermere Lake**, and in the upper Columbia River valley, this place was founded in 1887. In the early 1800s the lake was called *Kootenae Lake* and *Lower Columbia Lake* before it was named in 1883 by G.M. Sproat, because it resembled Lake Windermere in England's Lake District.

Windsor NS This town (1878) on the Avon River was named in 1784 after Windsor Township, created 20 years before and named after Windsor in England. The site was earlier called *Pisiquid (Pesiquid)* by the Acadians from the Mi'kmaq for 'place where the tidal flow forks'.

Windsor ON This city (1892) in Essex County was named in 1835 after the town in Berkshire, England, the site of the famous Windsor Castle. One hundred years later it annexed the towns of Sandwich, East Windsor, Walkerville, and Ojibway, and in 1966, the separate town of Riverside.

Windsor QC Located north of Sherbrooke, this town (1914) was incorporated as the town of *Windsor Mills* in 1899, which had been erected as a village in 1876. The township of Windsor was shown on a 1795 map and proclaimed in 1802, taking its name from the town of Windsor in Berkshire, England, west of London.

Windthorst SK South of Grenfell, this village (1907) was founded in 1907 by the Canadian Pacific Railway, and named after German parliamentarian Count Ludwig Windthorst (1812–91), who vigorously debated many policies of Prince Otto von Bismarck (1815–98). The post office was also opened in 1907.

Winfield BC On the north side of Kelowna, this place was first called *Alvaston*, likely after a suburb of Derby, England. It was renamed in 1948 after Winfield Lodge, the residence of rancher Thomas Wood.

Wingham ON In 2001 this town (1879) became part of the township of North Huron, Huron County. Located northeast of Goderich, the post office here was named in 1862 after Wingham in Kent, England, east of Canterbury.

Winisk ON A Hudson's Bay Company post called Fort Weenisk was opened in 1820 at the mouth of the **Winisk River**. The post office was called *Weenusk* in 1945 and renamed Winisk two years later. Destroyed by a flood in 1986, it was relocated upriver and named Peawanuck. In Cree, *winisk* means 'woodchuck'.

Winkler MB In 1892 the Canadian Pacific Railway wanted to name its station at this town (1954) after landowner Isaac Wiens, but he declined because such practice went against his Mennonite faith. Morden lumber merchant and legislator

Valentine Winkler (1864–1920) exchanged a quarter section at the station site with Wiens, and the CPR named it after him. Winkler built an elevator, flour mill, and hotel here.

Winnipeg MB This name for the city first appeared on the front page of the *Nor' Wester* of 24 February 1866, with the previous issue of the newspaper being headed by 'Red River Settlement, Assiniboia'. References to the town of Winnipeg occurred in 1870. The first post office opened that year as *Fort Garry*, but it was changed to Winnipeg in 1873, the year the city was incorporated. The *Red River Colony* was established here by Thomas Douglas, 5th Lord Selkirk (1771–1820) in 1812, and the Hudson's Bay Company's Fort Garry was erected 1821–2. The **Winnipeg River** drains the Lake of the Woods and several other lakes in northwestern Ontario and flows across the Manitoba border to **Lake Winnipeg**. In Cree and Ojibwa, the name of the lake means 'murky water', in reference to the cloudiness of the water where the river flows into the lake.

Winnipeg Beach MB On the shore of Lake Winnipeg and south of Gimli, this town (1914) was incorporated as a village in 1909, seven years after the Canadian Pacific Railway was built north along the shore of Lake Winnipeg. Its post office opened in 1904.

Winnipegosis MB This village (1915) on the southwestern shore of Lake Winnipegosis and north of Dauphin was first called *Mossy Point*. Winnipegosis post office opened in 1898 and the Canadian Northern Railway arrived a year later. A map of 1720 identified the lake as *Ouenpigouchib* ('little Winnipeg' or 'little murky lake').

Winona ON In 2001 the city of Stoney Creek became part of the city of Hamilton. This place was called *Ontario* in 1851. No one objected to calling it 'Ontario, Ontario' after Confederation in 1867, but it was changed to Winona, after the legendary first-born daughter of the Sioux.

Winston Churchill Range AB Embracing an area of 325 km² in the Rocky Mountains, north of the Columbia Icefield, this range of mountains was named in 1965 for Sir Winston Leonard Spencer Churchill (1874–1965). He is remembered, among many accomplishments, for his perseverence as prime minister of the United Kingdom in preventing the Nazis from overrunning Great Britain during the Second World War.

Winstone, Mount BC In the Coast Mountains, northwest of Pemberton, this mountain (3124 m) was named in 1962 by Alpine Club of Canada climbers after Harry P. Winstone (1926–59). Winstone was killed while climbing Mount Argus in Strathcona Provincial Park, BC. He was born Heinrich Weinstein in Vienna, Austria. In 1938 he escaped to London,

England. Ten years later he changed his name and soon after migrated to Canada.

Winterton NL This town (1964) on the eastern shore of Trinity Bay, northwest of Carbonear, was called *Sille Cove* in 1675, and *Sillee Cove* and *Scilly Cove* in later records. In 1912 it was renamed after Sir James Spearman Winter (1845–1911), prime minister of Newfoundland, 1897–1900.

Wishart SK Northeast of Yorkton, the post office at this village (1937) was named in 1884 after homesteader Robert Wishart (1885–1910), who failed at farming here and went to Dauphin, MB, in 1891–2, where he prospered. In 1928 the Canadian Pacific Railway built a line to this location from Foam Lake.

Witless Bay NL South of St. John's, this municipal community (1986) is located at the head of **Witless Bay**, whose name has engendered much speculation over the years. The present spelling was in use in the mid-1600s, but spellings such as *Whittles*, *Whitley's*, and *Whitles* during the latter part of the 1600s suggest the possibility of it being a personal name. Because the bay is quite open to the sea, its name might suggest a seaman would have to be deranged to consider trying to enter it during a heavy storm.

Wolfe Island ON Named *Grande Isle* by the French, it was renamed in 1760 after Maj. Gen. James Wolfe (1727–59), who died while his British forces won the Battle of the Plains of Abraham. It became a township in 1792, and **Wolfe Island** post office opened in Marysville in 1845.

Wolford ON This township became a part of the village of Merrickville-Wolford, united counties of Leeds-Grenville. It was created in 1797 and named after Wolford Lodge, John Graves and Elizabeth Simcoe's family home, in Devon, England.

Wolfville NS In the Annapolis Valley and on the Cornwallis River, this town (1893) was named in 1829 after Judge Elisha De Wolf (1756–1837). De Wolf was the postmaster of *Horton*, opened in 1786 and named after Horton Township. The site was also known as *Upper Horton* and *Mud Creek*.

Wollaston Lake SK With an area of 2681 km², this lake in northeastern Saskatchewan was named in 1821 by explorer Sir John Franklin (c.1653–1712) after George Hyde Wollaston (1766–1828), a member of the governor's committee of the Hudson's Bay Company.

Wolseley SK This town (1898) on the main line of the Canadian Pacific Railway, east of Regina, was named in 1882 after Col. (later 1st Viscount) Garnet Wolseley (1833–1913), leader of the Red River Expedition in 1870 to put down the first North-West Rebellion, and commander-in-chief of the British Army, 1895–1900. A post office opened here in 1887.

Wolstenholme, Cap QC The most northerly point of the province, this location was named in 1610 by Henry Hudson (c.1611) after Sir John Wolstenholme (1562–1639), who supported Hudson's search for the Northwest Passage. In 1744 map-maker Jacques Nicolas Bellin (1703–72) identified it as *Cap Saint-Louis*, and this name was still being shown on maps as recently as 1980, although Cap Wolstenholme had been endorsed as the sole official name in 1968.

Wood Buffalo National Park AB Canada's largest national park embraces an area of 27,840 km² in northern Alberta and in the Northwest Territories, south of Great Slave Lake. It was established in 1922 as a preserve for the wood bison, with plains bison being moved here between 1925 and 1927. On 1 April 1995 the city (now an urban service centre) of Fort McMurray and the Improvement District No. 143 were amalgamated to form the regional municipality of **Wood Buffalo**.

Woodbridge ON In the city of Vaughan, York Region, this urban centre was first called *Burwick* about 1837 after miller Rowland Burr. When a post office application was made that year, *Burwick* was not accepted, because of possible confusion with Berwick in Eastern Ontario. It was then called *Vaughan* until 1855, when it was renamed after Woodbridge in Suffolk, England, northeast of Ipswich.

Wood Island PE At the southeastern side of the province, this place is the terminus of a ferry to Caribou, NS. Its post offices were called *Wood Islands North* in 1889 and *Wood Islands West* in 1905. The two original islands, called *Isles à bois* during the French regime, were greatly altered after 1868, when the harbour facilities were developed.

Wood, Mount YT In the St. Elias Mountains, this mountain (4842 m) was named in 1900 by surveyor James J. McArthur (1856–1925) after Zachary Taylor Wood (d.1915), a North West Mounted Police inspector in Dawson during the Klondike Gold Rush. He was later the commissioner of the NWMP.

Woodridge MB Located southeast of Steinbach, this place was named in 1899 by the Canadian Pacific Railway after it crossed a ridge and built its station at the edge of woods. Its post office opened in 1902.

Woods Harbour NS On the South Shore and southwest of Shelburne, this narrow harbour was named after the Reverend Samuel Wood, who settled here shortly after 1772. Post offices were located at **Upper Woods Harbour** (1872), **Lower Woods Harbour** (1872), and **Central Woods Harbour** (1897).

Woods, Lake of the MB, ON First called *Lac aux Iles, lac des Assiniboines*, and *lac des Gens de la Pierre-Noire*, this lake was called *Lac des Bois* in 1730 by explorer Pierre Gaultier de La Vérendrye (1685–1755). This name was subsequently translated as the Lake of the Woods.

Woodstock NB The post office in this town (1856) on the west bank of the Saint John River opened in 1830. It was named after **Woodstock Parish**, established in 1786. The parish may have been named after William Henry Cavendish Bentinck, 3rd Duke of Portland and Viscount Woodstock (1738–1809), who was briefly the prime minister of Great Britain in 1783, or it may have been after Woodstock, in Oxfordshire, England.

Woodstock ON This city (1901) in Oxford County was founded in 1832 by Capt. Andrew Drew. He and RAdm. Henry Vansittart, who arrived two years later, chose the name Woodstock in 1835 after the village of Woodstock in Oxfordshire, England, northwest of the city of Oxford.

Woodville ON In 2001 this village (1884) became part of the city of Kawartha Lakes, Victoria County. Located northwest of Lindsay, the village was named in 1853 by postmaster and later village clerk John Calder Gilchrist. As it could be confused with other names, a plebiscite in 1877 resulted in Otago, a region of New Zealand's South Island, outpolling Woodville by one vote (46 to 45), but the change was not made.

Wooler ON In 2001 this community became part of Trent Hills, Northumberland County. Northwest of Trenton, this place's post office was named in 1857 after Wooler in Northumberland, England, south of Berwick-upon-Tweed.

Woolley, Mount AB This mountain (3405 m), in the Winston Churchill Range north of the Columbia Icefield, was named in 1898 by British climber Norman Collie (1859–1942) after British alpinist and publisher Herman Woolley (1846–1920).

Woolwich ON This municipal township in the regional municipality of Waterloo was named in 1822 after Woolwich, Kent, England, beside Greenwich. In 1974, Woolwich annexed the town of Elmira and part of the municipal township of Waterloo.

Wotton QC This municipality north of Sherbrooke was organized in 1993 when it annexed the village (1919) of *Wottonville*. It had been established as the township municipality of Wotton in 1855, taking its name from the township, shown on a 1795 map but not proclaimed until 1849. The township was named after a village in Surrey, England, southwest of London.

Wrigley NT On the east bank of the Mackenzie River, 190 km northwest of Fort Simpson, this settlement was named in 1915. It took its name from Fort Wrigley, a Hudson's Bay Company post founded in 1880 on the west bank, and named after its chief commissioner, Joseph Wrigley. Efforts in 1974 to rename the place Fort Wrigley were rejected, as it is not the site of the original fort.

Wunnummin Lake ON Located on **Wunnummin Lake** in Kenora District, north of Thunder Bay, this community's post office was named in 1964. The lake's name is from the Cree word for 'red paint'.

Wycliffe BC Midway between Cranbrook and Kimberley, this place was named in 1906 after John Wycliffe (c.1330–84), a church reformer and translator of the Bible.

Wyebridge ON In Simcoe County, south of Midland, this community's post office was named in 1861 after a bridge over the Wye River. Its twisting course reminded its namer of the crooked channel of the River Wye in western England.

Wyevale ON A community in Simcoe County, south of Midland, its station, where the North Simcoe Railway crossed the Wye River, was named in 1871. A post office opened here in 1880.

Wynndel BC North of Creston and in the Kootenay River valley, this community was named in 1910 after an early fruit grower in the valley.

Wynyard SK On the Canadian Pacific Railway, and south of the Quill Lakes, this town (1911) was named in 1909 by the wife of railway agent W.H. McNalley, after Wynyard, County Durham, England.

Wyoming ON In 2001 this village (1873) became part of the town of Plympton-Wyoming, Lambton County. Located east of Sarnia, its post office was named in 1858 by the Great Western Railway after Wyoming County, northwest of Scranton, PA. That name was from the Delaware *maughwauame* ('large meadows'). The Wyoming Territory in the American West was named 10 years later.

Yamachiche QC This municipality southwest of Trois-Rivières was established in 1987 when the village of Yamachiche (1887) and the parish municipality of *Sainte-Anne-d'Yamachiche* (1855) were united. The **Rivière Yamachiche** flows south into Lac Saint-Pierre. Its name in Abenaki means 'little whitefish'.

Yamaska QC Located near the mouth of the **Rivière Yamaska**, east of Sorel, this village was incorporated in 1968, having been erected as the village of *Saint-Michel* in 1867. Yamaska post office opened in 1826. The village of **Yamaska-Est** was established in 1955. In Abenaki *yamaska* means 'there are rushes all around' at the mouth of the river.

Yarmouth NS This town (1890), in southwestern Nova Scotia, was named as early as 1759 by New England planters and fishermen from Yarmouth, MA. Samuel de Champlain (1567–1635) had named the harbour *Port Fourchu* ('forked harbour') in 1604. That name is reflected in Cape Forchu, at the western entrance to the harbour.

Yarmouth ON In 1998 this township became part of the municipality of Central Elgin, Elgin County. It was named in 1792 after the town of Great Yarmouth, on the North Sea coast of Norfolk, England.

Yathkyed Lake NU Southwest of Baker Lake, this lake (1334 km²) was visited in 1894 by geologist Joseph Burr Tyrrell (1858–1957). In Chipewyan, the name means 'snow'.

Yellow Grass SK Northwest of Weyburn, this town (1906) was presumably named by Canadian Pacific Railway surveyors in 1885, when they observed high grass waving in the setting sun, giving it a yellowish glow. The CPR station was named in 1893, but the post office did not open until 1896.

Yellowhead Pass AB, BC West of Jasper and south of Mount Robson, this pass (1131 m) on the continental divide was named in the early 1800s after the mixed-blood, yellow-haired Iroquois Pierre Bostonais (d.1827). He was a trader for both the North West and Hudson's Bay companies. *See also* Tête Jaune Cache.

Yellowknife NT On the east side of the North Arm of Great Slave Lake, and at the mouth of **Yellowknife River**, this city (1970) was established in the 1930s, when a gold rush resulted in a boom town by 1940. The river was named after a Chipewyan band, whose name implied they made knives from copper. The band remained a distinct group at the beginning of the twentieth century, but by the 1960s it was blended with the neighbouring Dogrib and Chipewyan bands.

Yoho National Park BC This national park (1313 km²) on both sides of Kicking Horse River, and embracing some of the most rugged alpine landscape in the Rocky Mountains, was named in 1886 after the **Yoho River**. In Cree, *yoho* is a cry of astonishment.

York NB Established in 1785, this county was named after Prince Frederick, the Duke of York and Albany (1763–1827), second son of George III. He was made the Duke of York in 1784.

York ON The county was named in 1792 by Lt.-Gov. John Graves Simcoe (1752–1806) after Yorkshire, in east central England. The township, embracing the area of the city of Toronto, earlier called *Dublin Township*, was also named in 1792. The county, less the city of Toronto, became the regional municipality of **York** in 1979. The township of **York** with the town of Weston became the borough of **York** in 1970 and a city in 1983. In 1998 the city of York became an urban centre of the city of Toronto. *See also* East York *and* North York.

York PE This municipal community (1986), northeast of Charlottetown, was first known as *Little York* in the 1830s, and Little York has been its post office since 1872. Emigrants from Yorkshire, England settled here.

York Factory MB Located at the mouth of the Hayes River, this place was established as the site of a Hudson's Bay Company fort, built in 1684 by Pierre Radisson (1636–1710) and Médard Chouart Des Groseilliers (1618–96). It was named after James, Duke of York (1633–1701), third governor of the company, who became James II in 1685.

Yorkton SK In 1882 *York City* was established some 4 km northeast of the present site of the city (1928) by the York Farmers Colonization Company. The company had been formed in York County, ON, to help prospective settlers move to the North-West Territories. Its post office was named Yorkton in 1884 and was moved to the Manitoba and North Western Railway line in 1889.

Young SK Southeast of Saskatoon, this village (1910) was founded by the Grand Trunk Pacific Railway in 1908 and named after real estate agent Fred George Young. The name maintained the alphabetical arrangement of the GTP stations, with Xena to the east and Zelma to the west.

Youngstown AB The post office in this village (1936) southeast of Hanna was named in 1912 after pioneer settler Joseph Victor Young (d.1952).

Yukon Yukon was established as a district in the North-West Territories in 1894. Four years later it was upgraded as a separate territory. It took its name from the **Yukon River**, which the Gwitch'in call *Yukunah* ('great river'). The fifth longest river on the North American continent; its length, from the head of the Nisutlin River to the mouth in Alaska, is 3185 km. **Mount Yukon** (3231 m), in the Centennial Range of the St. Elias Mountains, was named in 1967 after the territory.

Zealandia SK Southwest of Saskatoon, this town (1911) was first called *Brock* by the Canadian Northern Railway in 1908, but the local settlers objected. (Brock was later given to another station between Rosetown and Kindersley.) When choosing a post office for the area two years earlier, the settlers put forward several suggestions, and Thomas Englebrecht's proposal of Zealandia was chosen. He had immigrated a few months before from New Zealand on the S.S. *Zealandia*.

Zeballos BC At the head of **Zeballos Inlet**, west of Campbell River, this village (1952) was named in 1937 after the inlet. The latter was named in 1791 by Capt. Alexandro Malaspina (1754–1810) after Lt. Ciriaco Cevallos, one of his Spanish officers.

Zenon Park SK Northeast of Tisdale, the post office in this village (1941) was named in 1916 after first postmaster Zénon Chamberland (1873–1938). He had a small recreation ground on his property for local settlers to gather on Sundays and holidays.

Zone ON In 1998 this township became part of the municipality of Chatham-Kent, Kent County. It was named in 1821 after the Moravian Indian Reserve on the Thames River, which was then known as the 'Indian Zone'.

Zorra ON The original Zorra Township was named in 1819 by Lt.-Gov. Sir Peregrine Maitland (1777–1854) after the Spanish word *zorra* ('female fox') and divided into the municipal townships of **East Zorra** and **West Zorra** in 1845. A new municipal township of **Zorra** in Oxford County was created in 1975 by amalgamating the municipal townships of East Nissouri, West Zorra, and North Oxford. *See also* East Zorra *and* West Zorra.

Zurich ON In 2001 this village (1960) became part the municipality of Bluewater, Huron County. Located 18 km northwest of Exeter, it was founded in 1854 by Frederick K. Knell, who named it after the city of Zurich in his native Switzerland. Two years later, Knell was appointed its first postmaster.

Index

The select index includes place names that are embedded within main entries that may otherwise be difficult to locate in the book.